Medieval Women: Texts and Contexts in Late Medieval Britain

MEDIEVAL WOMEN: TEXTS AND CONTEXTS

3

MEDIEVAL WOMEN: TEXTS AND CONTEXTS

EDITORIAL BOARD UNDER THE AUSPICES OF THE

CENTRE FOR MEDIEVAL STUDIES
UNIVERSITY OF HULL

Medieval Women:
Texts and Contexts in Late
Medieval Britain

Essays for Felicity Riddy

Edited by

Jocelyn Wogan-Browne, Rosalynn Voaden, Arlyn Diamond,

Ann Hutchison, Carol M. Meale, Lesley Johnson

MEDIEVAL WOMEN: TEXTS AND CONTEXTS

3

BREPOLS

British Library Cataloguing in Publication Data

Medieval women : texts and contexts in late Medieval Britain :
essays for Felicity Riddy
1.Women in literature 2.Women – History – Middle Ages,
500-1500 3.English literature – Middle English, 1100-
1500 – History and criticism
I.Wogan-Browne, Jocelyn
820.9'352'042'0902

ISBN 2503509797

© 2000, Brepols n.v., Turnhout, Belgium
Printed in the European Union on acid-free paper.
D/2000/0095/67
ISBN 2-503-50979-7

Contents

PREFACE AND ACKNOWLEDGEMENTS ix

LIST OF FIGURES AND ILLUSTRATIONS xi

LIST OF ABBREVIATIONS xiii

INTRODUCTION: 'THE MIXED LIFE'

    The Present Volume 1
        ARLYN DIAMOND

    Felicity Riddy 4
        ROSALYNN VOADEN

A BIBLIOGRAPHY OF FELICITY RIDDY 11
        COMPILED BY ROSALYNN VOADEN WITH THE
           ASSISTANCE OF JOHN RIDDY

I. READING MATTERS

    'My bright buke': Women and their Books in Medieval and
    Renaissance Scotland 17
        PRISCILLA BAWCUTT

    'Many grete myraclys... in divers contreys of the eest': The
    Reading and Circulation of the Middle English Prose *Three
    Kings of Cologne* 35
        JULIA BOFFEY

'This is a deed bok, the tother a quick': Theatre and the Drama of Salvation in the *Book* of Margery Kempe 49
    CAROL M. MEALE

'Lete me suffre': Reading the Torture of St Margaret of Antioch in Late Medieval England 69
    KATHERINE J. LEWIS

'Almighty and al merciable Queene': Marian Titles and Marian Lyrics 83
    HELEN PHILLIPS

The 'Querelle des femmes': A Continuing Tradition in Welsh Women's Literature 101
    CERIDWEN LLOYD-MORGAN

Reading Constructed Narratives: An Orphaned Medieval Heiress and the Legal Case as Literature 115
    NOËL JAMES MENUGE

The Origins of Criseyde 131
    SALLY MAPSTONE

II. MATTERS OF CONDUCT

Chaucer and the French Tradition Revisited: Philippe de Mézières and the Good Wife 151
    CAROLYN P. COLLETTE

Fashioning the Puritan Gentry-Woman: Devotion and Dissent in *Book to a Mother* 169
    NICHOLAS WATSON

Bodily Walls, Windows, and Doors: The Politics of Gesture in Late Fifteenth-Century English Books for Women 185
    KIM M. PHILLIPS

Chaucer's Criseyde and Feminine Fear 199
    ALASTAIR MINNIS AND ERIC J. JOHNSON

How Margaret Blackburn Taught Her Daughters: Reading Devotional Instruction in a Book of Hours 217
    PATRICIA CULLUM AND JEREMY GOLDBERG

CONTENTS vii

'A Fulle Wyse Gentyl-Woman of Fraunce': *The Epistle of
Othea* and Later Medieval English Literary Culture 237
    DOUGLAS GRAY

Elizabeth Clere: Friend of the Pastons 251
    COLIN RICHMOND

III. HOUSEHOLD MATTERS: FAMILY, SOCIETY, PLACE, AND
    SPACE

In Bed with Joan of Kent: The King's Mother and the Peasants'
Revolt 277
    W. M. ORMROD

Heroic Subjects: Women and the Alliterative *Morte Arthure* 293
    ARLYN DIAMOND

Houses and Households in Late Medieval England: An
Archaeological Perspective 309
    JANE GRENVILLE

Unnatural Mothers and Monstrous Children in *The King of Tars*
and *Sir Gowther* 329
    JANE GILBERT

Clothing Paternal Incest in *The Clerk's Tale*, *Émaré*, and the
Life of St Dympna 345
    ANNE SAVAGE

The Earliest Heretical Englishwomen 363
    PETER BILLER

'A peler of Holy Cherch': Margery Kempe and the Bishops 377
    SARAH REES JONES

Outdoing the Daughters of Syon? Edith of Wilton and the
Representation of Female Community in Fifteenth-Century
England 393
    JOCELYN WOGAN-BROWNE

LIST OF CONTRIBUTORS 411

INDEX 413

TABULA GRATULATORIA 435

Felicity Riddy

Preface and Acknowledgements

This volume honours Felicity Riddy's scholarship and contribution to medieval research but it must be said at the outset that the 'Riddy effect' is produced by a notable partnership. The first acknowledgement the editors would like to make is of John Riddy, for all that he has done to encourage Felicity's career and to foster the warm hospitality and stimulating environment of the Riddy household. His vigorous, shrewd, and supportive participation in the instigation of research and discussion has left the academic community in his debt: like his wife, he commands unbounded respect and affection.

The editors would like to thank our contributors and also all those who wished to contribute, but who graciously accepted the limitations of time and space for this volume. Scholars in the United Kingdom owe particularly great debts to Felicity Riddy for the value of her personal example over several demanding and difficult decades for British universities, and the contributors to this volume consist of scholars in personal contact with its honorand, rather than a proportionate representation of the wider community of those who admire and are stimulated by Felicity Riddy's work.

We are very grateful to Louise Harrison, Amanda Lillie, Alastair Minnis, and Mark Ormrod at the Centre for Medieval Studies, University of York, for support and help over this volume and the colloquium marking the occasion of its presentation. We thank Louise Harrison, in addition, for all her work on the Tabula Gratulatoria. For their constructive and thoughtful work on the volume, we thank our two external readers for the Board of Brepols' Medieval Women Texts and Contexts Series, and Dr Bridget Morris as Board liaison for the volume

and Dr Simon Forde of Brepols. We are grateful to our copy-editor
Elizabeth Wall, for her patience and skill and we thank Christina Francis,
research assistant to Rosalynn Voaden, for her bibliographical and
indexing work. The other editors would like to thank Rosalynn Voaden
for her generosity in sharing her research assistance.

The other editors wish especially to thank Jocelyn Wogan-Browne,
without whose dedication, energy, and generous labours this volume
would not have been possible.

The photograph of National Library of Wales, Peniarth MS 99 on p.
106 is reproduced by kind permission of the National Library of Wales.
The photographs of York Minster Library, Add. MS 2 on pp. 226 and 229
are reproduced by kind permission of the Dean and Chapter of York. The
cover photograph of Liverpool Cathedral of Christ, MS 6, the Hours of
the Guardian Angel, is reproduced with the kind permission of Dr
Maureen Watry, Head of Special Collections and Archives, Sydney Jones
Library, University of Liverpool. For the photograph of Felicity Riddy we
thank Rosalynn Voaden.

List of Figures and Illustrations

Frontispiece: Felicity Riddy

Ceridwen Lloyd-Morgan

Figure 1. Aberystwyth, National Library of Wales, Peniarth MS 99, p. 121 106

Patricia Cullum and Jeremy Goldberg

Figure 1. Margaret Blackburn kneeling in devotion before St Sitha. York Minster Library MS Add. 2, fol. 40^v 226

Figure 2. St Anne instructing the Virgin with the Holy Spirit above. To the right Mary Cleophas and Mary Salome. York Minster Library MS Add. 2, fol. 35 229

Colin Richmond

Figure 1. Family tree of Elizabeth Clere 256

Jane Grenville

Figure 1. Bowes Morrell House 318

Figure 2. Access analysis diagram, Bowes Morrell House 319

Figure 3. 7 Shambles House 322

Figure 4. The timber frame at 7 Shambles 323

Figure 5. Access analysis diagram, 7 Shambles 324

List of Abbreviations

AB	*Analecta Bollandiana*
Add.	Additional
BIHR	Borthwick Institute of Historical Research
BL	British Library, London
BN	Bibliothèque Nationale, Paris
c.	*circa*
c.	contra (in lawsuits)
Cal. Anc. Deeds	*Calendar of Ancient Deeds*
CCR	*Calendar of Close Rolls*
CIPM	*Calendar of the Inquisitions Post Mortem*
ClT	'The Clerk's Tale', Chaucer, *The Canterbury Tales*
col.	colophon
CPR	*Calendar of Patent Rolls*
d.	died
da.	daughter
EETS	Early English Text Society
ES	extra series
OS	original series
SS	supplementary series
EHR	*English Historical Review*
ELH	*English Literary History*
EUL	Edinburgh University Library
fol./fols	folio/folios
FMLS	*Forum for Modern Language Studies*
HMSO	Her/His Majesty's Stationery Office

IMEV	Carleton Brown and Rossell Hope Robbins, *The Index of Middle English Verse* (New York: Medieval Academy, 1943). See also SIMEV.
IR	*Innes Review*
JMH	*Journal of Medieval History*
MED	*Middle English Dictionary*, ed. by Hans Kurath, Sherman Kuhn and Robert E. Lewis (Ann Arbor: University of Michigan Press, 1952–).
MLN	*Modern Language Notes*
MP	*Modern Philology*
MS/MSS	Manuscript/Manuscripts
NLS	National Library of Scotland
NRO, NCC	Norwich Record Office, Norwich County Council
OED	*Oxford English Dictionary*
ParsT	'The Parson's Tale', Chaucer, *The Canterbury Tales*
pers. comm.	personal communication
PL	*Patrologiae Cursus Completus...Series Latina*, ed. by J.-P. Migne (Paris, various years).
PMLA	*Publications of the Modern Language Association*
PRO	Public Record Office, London
RES, NS	*Review of English Studies*, new series
SAC	*Studies in the Age of Chaucer: The Yearbook of the New Chaucer Society*
SATF	Société des anciens textes français
SCH	Studies in Church History
SHR	*Scottish Historical Review*
SIMEV	Rossell Hope Robbins and John L. Cutler, *Supplement to the Index of Middle English Verse* (Lexington: Kentucky University Press, 1965). See also IMEV.
SNP	The Second Nun's Prologue, Chaucer, *The Canterbury Tales*
SRO	Scottish Record Office
STC	*A Short-Title Catalogue of Books Printed in England, Scotland, and Ireland, 1475–1640*, first compiled by A. W. Pollard and G. R. Redgrave, 2nd edn begun by W. A. Jackson and F. S. Ferguson, and completed by Katharine F. Pantzer,

	3 vols (London: Bibliographical Society, 1976, 1986, 1991).
STS	Scottish Text Society
VCH	*The Victoria County History of England*
YES	*Yearbook of English Studies*
Yorks., N.R.	Yorkshire, North Riding

Introduction: 'The Mixed Life'

ARLYN DIAMOND AND ROSALYNN VOADEN

Part 1: The Present Volume

BY ARLYN DIAMOND

Our introduction is necessarily an afterword, an attempt to map a convoluted terrain bounded by two contested concepts: 'women' and 'medieval'. These essays were inspired by the model of Felicity Riddy's own work, with its insistence on taking nothing for granted and bringing together different disciplines and methodologies, in the hopes that the result would reveal the deeper contours of women's presence in medieval life. Thus the studies assembled here move from legal cases to actual buildings to conduct books to romances and saints' lives to the medieval unconscious and back again. We have grouped them in three main categories which reflect both the kinds of work Felicity Riddy has done and the contributors' own interests. Our subdivisions into matters of reading, conduct, and place are, however, an initial reading suggestion: many approaches and materials could with profit be read under more than one of these categories.

Beyond these groupings we saw the essays initiating some unexpected conversations, and as we read, we had a sense of the book as a whole forming a dense network of possibilities for future work—gaps to be filled in, knots to be unravelled, debates to be continued. For example, our contributors take very different approaches to the concepts of household and family. Jane Grenville looks at physical structures from

the perspective of an archaeologist using social theory; Jane Gilbert, a
literary critic, looks at the symbolic structures of families, bringing
together Lacan and Aristotle in a reading of fictions of fatherhood; Anne
Savage, from the perspective of contemporary feminist thinking, looks at
what seems deliberately invisible in much medieval narrative—incest as
real trauma. In one way or another all these essays can be seen as re-
readings generated by serious attention to women as idea and reality in
medieval life and thought. Noël James Menuge, Peter Biller, and Colin
Richmond do their reading in the archives, reconstructing women's lives
from documentary hints, making available to the rest of us unfamiliar
materials which test our assumptions about women in the Middle Ages.
Richmond's biography of Elizabeth Clere reveals the role of a landowner
and householder in the 'production and reproduction of daily life' and in
the maintenance of female friendships. Menuge and Biller both show us
women who refused to accept the dominant structures of their world.
Menuge's 'heroine' is a clever and determined woman who was able to
resist the laws governing women's status in marriage, using the legal
system on her own behalf. Biller's protagonists are much more
mysterious and provocative figures—the forerunners of the later and
better known women in England who defied religious orthodoxy at the
risk of their own lives.

Such women also resist (and perhaps provoke) what many texts
exhibit—a deep concern with women's behaviour, explicitly or implicitly
linking their virtue with the larger social order. Such a function of course
charges the literary representation of women with peculiar power. As
Sally Mapstone's essay on Criseyde shows, female models provide
copious and sometimes surprising literary matter for authors, while Helen
Phillips's analysis of Marian praise poetry explores the unresolved
contradictions of ascribing hyperbolic power to a human, female figure.
Alastair Minnis and Eric Johnson investigate medieval discourses of
psychology in scholasticism and Christine de Pisan's writings in order to
position Criseyde's fear outside C. S. Lewis's influential modern
regulation of female conduct as romance heroinism. The various guides to
behaviour discussed by Nicholas Watson, Kim Phillips, Patricia Cullum
and Jeremy Goldberg show in how many ways medieval texts formed
what Kim Phillips calls a 'modelling and policing' function for women,
while Carolyn Collette's essay on Chaucer and marriage handbooks
redraws the boundary lines between matters of conduct and political
matters.

Inscribed female audiences, whether Kim Phillips's women romance readers, a male author's mother (Watson), or a female owner of a book of hours and her daughters (Cullum and Goldberg), could not, of course, be guaranteed to learn the right lesson. Women created textual meanings in many ways. Some, as Priscilla Bawcutt's pioneering study of women's books in Scotland and Julia Boffey's tracing of reading circles and modes in late medieval London demonstrate, acquired manuscripts and books on the basis of their own interests. Others, as writers or readers, incorporated, adapted, or rewrote what their culture offered them. Ceridwen Lloyd-Morgan shows how Welsh women were able to re-invigorate the rather tired tradition of the *querelle des femmes*, continuing to make it relevant to their own writing. Douglas Gray looks at Christine de Pisan, the most self-conscious and productive of the women writers here considered, from the point of view of her medieval reception. De Pisan is revealed as deeply embedded in her own culture, rather than as a kind of feminist phoenix. The essays by Carol Meale and Sarah Rees Jones on Margery Kempe add still further ways of seeing women in relation to their historical context: Meale shows how Kempe both uses and suppresses her own experience of dramatic and other kinds of performance, in an astute reading of what is and is not culturally authoritative. Rees Jones challenges separatist readings of women and their representation by arguing that Kempe's book shows episcopal use of the newly-prestigious model of the holy woman for the control of lower clergy. In one way or another, the work on women assembled here reintegrates them into medieval society and thought, rather than isolating them.

Above all, it seems from reading these essays, which are of course infinitely richer than the brief characterizations given here, that women are never really just women. They appear almost inevitably to carry a cultural meaning, a figurative capacity which seems at times a terrible burden and, on occasion, an opportunity. If women's refusal of ordinariness is occluded in the records scrutinized by Peter Biller, it becomes, in Katherine Lewis's study of the semi-legendary Margaret of Antioch, martyrdom of a spectacular and culturally resonant kind. In the historical and much reinvented Edith of Wilton, as Jocelyn Wogan-Browne argues, the figurative capacity of women to represent the sacred serves Lancastrian ideology and also voices the prerogatives of female community. Violence and suffering, rather than being denied as in incest tales, become explicitly valued in biographies of exemplary virgins, the most extreme form of conduct books.

In secular texts, too, as Mark Ormrod's and Arlyn Diamond's essays show, being real or fictional doesn't seem radically to distinguish women's textual treatment. Both Joan of Kent, in the chronicles, and Guenevere, in Arthurian romance, seem primarily important as symbolic representations of aristocratic social structures, validating hierarchy in their very weaknesses. In these essays by a historian and a literary critic, the example of Felicity Riddy, as so often in this volume and elsewhere, provokes scholars and critics of different kinds and disciplines to value and use each other's questions and concerns.

In such work, the study of medieval women is confidently and freshly mainstream: non-separatist; prompting the exploration both of new source materials and the rereading of established sources from whose conceptualization women have been excluded; able to consider the broadest implications for the study of medieval culture without risk of re-containing or rendering women once more invisible; profiting from the development of newly flexible models of gender, literacy, the political, the social, the domestic. Felicity Riddy's responsible, infinitely curious and creative version of historical enquiry makes the definitions and relations of text and context continuingly vital matters.

Part 2. Felicity Riddy

BY ROSALYNN VOADEN

As scholars from many parts of the world can attest, to enjoy the hospitality of the Riddy household is to be caught up in a heady atmosphere, where one can delight in thoughtful conversation and witty exchange, and experience conviviality in the fullest sense of the word. Toward the end of just such an evening, my conversation with Felicity turned to writing, and how we write out of who and where we are in our lives. And, as is so often the case with Felicity, mistress of the probing question and the interrogative pause, I ended up discovering that I don't write for the reasons I thought I did, and gained a wholly different perspective on the relationship between my work and my life. On this occasion, however, she too reflected on how her academic interests have reflected the various stages of her life. When she lived in Scotland, teaching at the University of Stirling, she worked on medieval Scottish texts; when she moved to the walled city of York, she became interested in urban culture. Her academic career developed while she and her husband John raised three children; now that her own parents had died, and her youngest child was in the process of leaving home, she had become interested in the nature and function of the household in the Middle Ages.

A reflective and frank acknowledgement that research is done in a specific context is one of the strengths of Felicity's work, whether in her changing interests or in the many abiding attachments that also mark her research—to Arthurian literature, to women's writing and to gentry culture, among others. The range of her scholarly interests is very broad: from language and dialect in medieval Scotland, to the implications of the use of Anglo-Norman, to the social theories of Jürgen Habermas. This variety of interests, fermented in her agile mind, has resulted in a rich vintage, a body of work which transcends disciplinary boundaries with aplomb and conviction, and which transforms the perspective of those who encounter it.

Amanda Lillie, a lifetime family friend, and a colleague at the University of York, believes that this openness to new experiences and perspectives developed when she was young.

> Felicity's sense of household was no doubt formed in her childhood. The Maidment household was where we went for witty soirées and erudition, for affectionate and energetic engagement with any problem, personal or political. It was a family life that began in Oxford, that led to America and New Zealand and then back again to Oxford, and which carried with it a sense of openness and of new possibilities. Both Felicity's parents passed their love of learning, their sense of fun and their robust dismissal of nonsense, pedantry, and pretension on to their four children.

Felicity has always been committed to the idea of the scholarly community, to the belief that new ideas and perspectives germinate in conversation rather than in isolation. When she became Director of the Centre for Medieval Studies at the University of York, it was rumoured that whenever she saw two or more people speaking together she would say, 'You should form a Research Group'. Lesley Johnson, one of the editors of this volume, writes:

> I first met Felicity when she was invited to Leeds to give an undergraduate lecture on a feminist/medieval topic, and I was struck not only by her intellectual rigour and robust practices of thinking but also by her approachability and genuine interest in the views of all other members of the academic community, no matter how officially junior or senior they might be. She is such an important catalyst for the work of others: co-operative research and fruitful academic exchange flourish in her presence.

The informal day meetings that she and I set up on such themes as 'The Use of French in Medieval England' (and that she and Colin Richmond and others set up between York and Leeds on 'Gentry Culture', on 'Hagiography' and other topics) represented a gesture in the direction of co-operation rather than competition. There are no conference proceedings in print to commemorate the meetings, but a great deal of the material that was under discussion did appear later in published form in a variety of venues.

Felicity's latest enterprise represents perhaps the ultimate in co-operative, interdisciplinary scholarship in the humanities. The Household Project, funded by a prestigious grant from the Humanities Research Board, consists of a consortium of scholars working on various aspects of the household in late medieval England. The volumes which result will represent an experiment not only in joint research, but in joint authorship. They will consist not of separate papers written by individual scholars on a common theme, as is usually the case; instead each volume will be written/composed in concert by the entire group. One can imagine the commitment of time and energy needed for the meetings, and the endless debate required to co-ordinate findings and to agree on formulations, but one can also imagine the stimulation and productivity which results. The style of the project perhaps mirrors its content, in as much as a household consists of a group of individuals, each of whom has her or his own requirements and aspirations but who is at the same time united by shared goals and needs which can only be achieved by the co-operation of the group as a whole.

What drives this encouragement of co-operative scholarship intellectually is Felicity's rigorous intelligence, intense curiosity, and impatience with formulaic boundaries and specious theorizing. Arlyn Diamond speaks for many on both sides of the Atlantic when she writes of the rewards of engaging with her on any topic, anywhere:

It is, as all her friends know, an exhilarating experience to share an idea with Felicity—the formidable energy and erudition she applies to it, the fiercely penetrating questions which reveal great gaps in one's reading, and yet the enthusiastic encouragement which makes it a matter of pleasure and honour to keep working.

Awe of Felicity's erudition and intense focus was expressed time after time by the contributors to this volume. All were challenged to rise to her standards and intimidated by the thought of what they might have missed that she would instantly home in on.

These contributions to the scholarship of others include much editorial work, as James Carley testifies:

> Felicity has often called me a demon editor, but the term can more accurately be applied to her: she is formidably learned, *au courant* with the latest trends, has great energy and an eye for detail. Richard Barber assured me that being edited by Felicity was a more penetrating process than he remembered undergoing even in his undergraduate days. When I offered a piece to the journal, I too discovered just how lucky I was to have such a generous and engagé editor: errors were dealt with, improvements suggested but there was never any sense of one-upmanship in the process. Every contributor to whom I have spoken has shared this response to Felicity: respect for her erudition and gratitude for her guidance. Felicity was adept at introducing new material and methodologies and making these fit together with the more old-fashioned approaches: indeed, one of her gifts was to turn disparate articles into a coherent narrative by means of placement, subtle cross-referencing and so forth. The journal never set out to be thematic issue by issue, but inevitably each volume did turn out to be a coherent whole.

In addition to her qualities as scholar and editor, Felicity is a remarkable teacher. It is in this role that her influence is perhaps the most significant, as Hermione Lee, a long-time colleague at the University of York, attests:

> Felicity Riddy is modest and ironical and doesn't stand for pretension, and I can hear her snorts of self-deprecating laughter in my ear as I am writing this. But without exaggeration, it's true to say that she became a professional role-model and heroine for me. It's for others to speak about her distinguished scholarship, her pioneering and inspirational leadership at the Centre for Medieval Studies, and her indefatigable resilience, integrity and authority as a University administrator. My knowledge of her is as a teacher, a colleague, and a friend, and (though she might be surprised to hear this) as an advisor. I can't count the number of students I knew at York who spoke of Felicity Riddy as of no other teacher, because she gave them space in which to feel their way and develop their ideas, as well as teaching them how to think, how to structure their thoughts, and how to do scholarly research at a very early stage. I imitated everything Felicity told me she was doing in her classes, and learned a great deal from her about how non-authoritarian, collaborative methods of teaching could be productive rather than time-wasting.

As a colleague, Hermione Lee adds,

> what I most admire in Felicity Riddy is her refusal, ever, to toe the line, and her admirable pragmatic rages. She is a good fighter, and she will

never give up or shut up when she thinks injustice or stupidity is afoot. But none of this is ever petty or spiteful; she is a benign force, and is also known for great generosity, patience, and humaneness.

Unfailingly encouraging to women colleagues, Felicity Riddy has often (perhaps without knowing it) taught me what to do and how to behave. I would trust her with my life. On the other hand, she's not a person who invites garrulous blabbering, and she has a quality of fine steely reserve which can stop one getting too close. She is frank, candid, and direct, but not easily intimate. Strength, professionalism, and integrity are the key words. And, so that I don't seem to be constructing a monument of virtue, I should add that she can also be funny, scathing, and wicked.

Felicity's support of her colleagues is not restricted to academics. She has always insisted on acknowledging the indispensable contribution clerical staff make to the functioning of the university. Louise Harrison, secretary of the Centre for Medieval Studies, writes of the formidable energy brought by Felicity to administrative tasks in their teamwork at the Centre for Medieval Studies:

Under Felicity's leadership the Centre for Medieval Studies blossomed and grew: in part this was made possible because of new accommodation, but her energy and zest had much to do with it. Felicity is extremely persuasive, convincing you to do things that you probably didn't think you could. As a boss, she is demanding and has high expectations, but she drives herself harder than anybody else, working through the night, rushing between the two York campuses, usually late (the traffic of course), typically whirling into the office issuing greetings, requests, and instructions all in one breath before rushing out again. She will tell you firmly if you are wrong, but the nice thing is that you can tell her if she is wrong, too-although you must have pretty good grounds for doing so. All this is made possible by her personal charm: when she is talking to you she is interested in everything-not just academic things, but what your children are up to, or the knotty problem of whether or not to wear a hat to a wedding. She is always generous with praise and in acknowledging assistance. Working for Felicity has been something I would not have missed for the world. Life is always interesting and lively when she is around. And to know that there is somebody who will support you in the most positive way in everything you try to do, and who will back you to the hilt, is just marvellous.

Why assemble a Festschrift for Felicity now? She is not retiring, although she is moving on to a new phase in her career to become Pro-Vice-Chancellor of the University of York. While this volume does celebrate her birthday, she has not reached the kind of advanced age which is usually the occasion for a Festschrift. The answer is that we wanted to pay tribute to the enormous influence Felicity has had, and continues to have, on medieval studies and on each of our lives, and to celebrate the career of one of the foremost medievalists and women scholars in Britain while that career is in full blossom. We wanted to create a new model for marking exceptional academic achievement, a feminine Festschrift if you will, one which celebrates the process as well as the product of Felicity's life as a scholar.

We also wanted the process of creating this volume to embody her values of co-operative, innovative scholarship, of inclusivity, of pushing the boundaries, while acknowledging that all of us have lives outside of academia, lives which affect our work for good or ill. The editors have supported each other during various personal or professional crises; senior editors have given junior scholars extra time and attention with their papers, while benefiting from the new theories and insights which younger colleagues offered. In all, the experience of editing this volume has been revelatory, demanding, and stimulating—like Felicity herself. And, while we may have missed her incisive mind as part of the editorial team, she has been an inspiration and a guiding presence throughout.

A Bibliography of Felicity Riddy

COMPILED BY ROSALYNN VOADEN
WITH THE ASSISTANCE OF JOHN RIDDY

Felicity Riddy began her academic and teaching career at the University of Auckland, New Zealand. After further study at Oxford in the UK, she then taught at Ahmadu Bello University in Northern Nigeria for two years before moving to Scotland. After a year spent teaching at Glasgow, she went to the University of Stirling, where she spent twenty years. In 1988, she joined the University of York as reader, then professor, in English studies. For three years she was the Director of the Centre for Medieval Studies. In August 2000 she will become a Pro-Vice-Chancellor of the University of York.

BOOKS

Felicity Riddy, ed., *Prestige, Authority and Power in Medieval Manuscripts* (York: York Medieval Press, forthcoming, 2000).

———, Claire Cross and Sarah Rees Jones, eds, *Learning and Literacy in the Middle Ages* (York: York Medieval Press, forthcoming, 2001).

——— and Jeremy Goldberg, eds, *Youth in the Middle Ages* (York: York Medieval Press, forthcoming, 2001).

——— and James P. Carley, eds, Arthurian Literature XII–XVI (Cambridge: D. S. Brewer, 1993–98). Five annual volumes of essays.

——— and Priscilla Bawcutt, eds, *Selected Poems of Henryson and Dunbar* (Edinburgh: Scottish Academic Press, 1992).

————, ed., *Regionalism in Late Medieval Manuscripts and Texts: Essays Celebrating the Publication of 'An Atlas of Late Mediaeval English'* (Cambridge: D. S. Brewer, 1991).

———— and Michael J. Alexander, eds, *Macmillan Literary Anthologies: vol. I, Old and Middle English Literature* (Basingstoke: Macmillan, 1989).

————, *Sir Thomas Malory* (Leiden: Brill, 1987).

———— and Priscilla Bawcutt, eds, *Longer Scottish Poems, 1375–1650* (Edinburgh: Scottish Academic Press, 1987).

———— and R. J. Lyall, eds, *Proceedings of the Third International Conferences on Scottish Literature, Medieval and Renaissance* (Stirling and Glasgow: Glasgow University Press, 1981).

ARTICLES

'Julian of Norwich', in *The Cambridge Companion to Women's Writing* (Cambridge: Cambridge University Press, 1999).

'Margery Kempe', in *The New Dictionary of National Biography* (Oxford: Oxford University Press, forthcoming).

'Chivalric Nationalism and the Holy Grail in Harding's *Chronicle*', in *The Holy Grail*, ed. by Dhira Mahoney (New York: Garland, 1999), pp. 397–414.

'Interiority in Family and Household', in *Weltflucht und Selbsterfahrung: Gesellschaftliche, psychologische und religiöse Aspecte von Interiorität in Lebenswelt und Literatur des Spätmittelalters* (Munster: forthcoming 2000).

'Middle English Romance: Family, Marriage, Intimacy', in *The Cambridge Companion to Medieval Romance*, ed. by Roberta Krueger (Cambridge: Cambridge University Press, forthcoming 2000).

'Giving and Receiving: Exchange in the *Roman van Walewein* and *Sir Gawain and the Green Knight*', *Tijdschrift voor Nederlandse taal- en letterkunde*, 112 (1996), 18–20. Reprinted in *Arthurian Literature* XVII, *Originality and Tradition in the Middle Dutch Roman* Roman van Walewein, ed. by Bart Bescamusca and Erik Kooper, Gen. ed. Keith Busby (Cambridge: D. S. Brewer, 1999), pp. 101–14.

'Julian of Norwich and Self-Textualization', in *Editing Women*, ed. by Ann M. Hutchison (Toronto: University of Toronto Press, 1998), pp. 101–24.

'"Abject Odious": Masculine and Feminine in Henryson's *Testament of Cresseid*', in *The Long Fifteenth Century*, ed. by Helen Cooper and Sally Mapstone (Oxford: Clarendon Press, 1997), pp. 229–48. Reprinted in *Medieval English Literature: A Reader*, ed. by Derek Pearsall (Oxford: Blackwell, 1999).

'Jewels in *Pearl*', in *A Companion to the Gawain-Poet*, ed. by D. Brewer and J. Gibson (Cambridge: D. S. Brewer, 1997), pp. 143–55.

'Empire and Civil War: Contexts for *Le Morte Darthur*', in *A Companion to Malory*, ed. by A. S. G. Edwards and Elizabeth Archibald (Woodbridge: Boydell and Brewer, 1996), pp. 55–73.

'Mother Knows Best: Reading Social Change in a Courtesy Text', *Speculum*, 71 (1996), 66–86.

'Nature, Culture and Gender in *Sir Gawain and the Green Knight*', in *Arthurian Romance and Gender*, ed. by F. Wolfzettel (Amsterdam: Rodopi, 1995), pp. 215–25.

'The Speaking Knight: Sir Gawain and Other Animals', in *Culture and the King: The Social Implications of the Arthurian Legend*, ed. by James P. Carley and Martin B. Shichtman (Albany: State University of New York Press, 1994), pp. 149–62.

'Engendering Pity in "The Franklin's Tale"', in *Feminist Readings in Middle English Literature: The Wife of Bath and All Her Sect*, ed. by Ruth Evans and Lesley Johnson (London: Routledge, 1994), pp. 54–71.

'Hardyng's *Chronicle* and the Wars of the Roses', in *Arthurian Literature XII*, ed. by James P. Carley and Felicity Riddy (Cambridge: D. S. Brewer, 1993), pp. 91–108.

'"Women Talking About the Things of God": a Late Medieval Subculture' in *Women and Literature in Britain, c. 1100–1500*, ed. by Carol M. Meale (Cambridge: Cambridge University Press, 1993, 2nd edn 1996), pp. 104–27.

Introduction, facsimile edition of *Brogyntyn Manuscript No. 8* (Middle English Prose *Brut*) (Moreton-in-Marsh: Porkington Press, 1991).

'John Hardyng in Pursuit of the Grail' in *Arturus Rex: Koning Artur en de Nederlanden: la matière de Bretagne et les anciens Pays-Bas*, ed. by W. Van Hoecke, G. Tournoy, and W. Verbeke, II (Leuven: Leuven University Press, 1991), pp. 419–29.

'Glastonbury, Joseph of Arimathea and the Grail in John Hardyng's Chronicle', in *The Archaeology and History of Glastonbury Abbey*, ed. by Leslie Abrams and James P. Carley (Woodbridge: Boydell Press, 1991), pp. 316–31. To be reprinted in a collection of essays on

Glastonbury Abbey, ed. by James P. Carly (Woodbridge: Boydell and Brewer, forthcoming 2000).

'Reading for England: Arthurian Literature and National Consciousness', *Bibliographical Bulletin of the International Arthurian Society*, XLIII (1991), 314–32.

'The Alliterative Revival', in *A History of Scottish Literature* I, ed. by R. D. S. Jack (Aberdeen: Aberdeen University Press, 1988), pp. 39–54.

'Dating *The Buke of the Howlat*', *Review of English Studies*, NS 37 (1986), 1–10.

'The Revival of Chivalry in Late Medieval Scotland', in *Actes du 2e Colloque de Langue et de Littérature Ecossaises*, no ed. (Strasbourg: Institut d'études anglaises de Strasbourg et l'Association des médiévistes anglicistes de l'enseignement supérieur, [1979?]), pp. 54–62.

'Structure and Meaning in "The Fair Maid of Astolat"', *FMLS*, 21 (1976), 54–66.

'The Uses of the Past in *Sir Orfeo*', *Yearbook of English Studies*, 6 (1976), 5–15.

'Robin Hyde and New Zealand', in *The Commonwealth Writer Overseas: Themes of Exile and Expatriation*, ed. by A. Niven (Brussels: Didier, 1976), pp. 185–94.

'*Squyer Meldrum* and the Romance of Chivalry', *Yearbook of English Studies*, 4 (1974), 25–36.

'The Provenance of *Quia Amore Langueo*', *Review of English Studies*, NS 18 (1967), 429–33.

'Language as Theme in *No Longer at Ease*', *Journal of Commonwealth Literature*, 9 (1970), 38–47. Reprinted in *Critical Perspectives on Chinua Achebe*, ed. by C. L. Innes and B. Lindfors (London: Heinemann, 1979), pp. 150–59.

I. Reading Matters

'My bright buke': Women and their Books in Medieval and Renaissance Scotland

PRISCILLA BAWCUTT

A striking image of one Scotswoman and her book occurs in Dunbar's *Tua Mariit Wemen and the Wedo*:

> Quhen that I go to the kirk cled in cair weid,
> As foxe in a lambis fleise fenye I my cheir.
> Than lay I furth my bright buke on breid on my kne,
> With mony lusty letter ellummynit with gold,
> And drawis my clok forthwart our my face quhit,
> That I may spy unaspyit a space me beside.
> Full oft I blenk by my buke and blynis of devotion
>
> . . . .
>
> So keik I throw my clokis and castis kynd lukis
> To knychtis and to cleirkis and cortly personis. (ll. 422 ff.[1])

(When I go to church dressed in mourning, I assume a false appearance, like a fox in a lambskin. Then I display my bright book wide open on my knee, with many a fine letter illuminated in gold, and draw my cloak over my pale face, so that I may observe all around without being observed myself. I often glance away from my book and cease from devotion . . . so I peep through my cloaks and bestow affectionate looks on knights and clerks and courtiers.)

I owe an immense debt, in gathering material for this article, to Miss Elspeth Yeo, formerly of the Department of Manuscripts at the National Library of Scotland.

[1] Cited from William Dunbar, *Selected Poems*, ed. by P. Bawcutt (London: Longman, 1996).

This vivid scene fleetingly recalls the pious female owners, often depicted in books of hours.[2] But Dunbar's purpose is satiric. He deftly implies the Widow's status and wealth, not only in possessing such a fine book, but in the fact that she places it on her knee, and is therefore sitting in the church rather than standing or kneeling. The Widow's particular interest in the gold-illuminated letters perhaps hints that her literacy is elementary. Her 'bright buke', although ostensibly an aid to 'devotion', is chiefly an adjunct to flirtation. Such coquettish 'keking and bakluking' in church were singled out for condemnation in treatises on women's conduct.[3]

Dunbar's Widow, of course, is a humorous fiction. How much is known about actual women and their books in medieval and Renaissance Scotland? Book-ownership in this period is a topic that has excited growing interest in recent years, and many studies exist of individual collectors, ranging from William Elphinstone, the late medieval bishop of Aberdeen, to William Drummond of Hawthornden, the Renaissance poet and polymath.[4] The pioneering work in this field is John Durkan and Anthony Ross's *Early Scottish Libraries* (Glasgow: J. S. Burns, 1961); although largely confined to learned books, owned chiefly by ecclesiastics and printed before 1560, it is remarkably wide-ranging, and 'an indispensable work of reference'.[5] Yet no more than two women figure in *Early Scottish Libraries*, and only a few individuals, notably the exceptional figure of Mary Queen of Scots, have received attention, despite the enormous growth of interest in women's cultural activities outside Scotland.[6] This brief article is a first attempt to assemble what evidence

---

[2]   See the depiction of Mary of Burgundy reproduced in S. Penketh, 'Women and Books of Hours', in *Women and the Book: Assessing the Visual Evidence*, ed. by L. Smith and J. H. M. Taylor (London: British Library, 1996), pp. 266–81.

[3]   Cf. *Documenta Matris ad Filiam*, 207–08, in *Ratis Raving*, ed. by R. Girvan (Edinburgh: STS, 1939).

[4]   See L. J. Macfarlane, 'William Elphinstone's Library Revisited', in *The Renaissance in Scotland: Studies in Literature, Religion, History and Culture*, ed. by A. A. MacDonald, M. Lynch and I. B. Cowan (Leiden: Brill, 1994), pp. 66–81; and *The Library of Drummond of Hawthornden*, ed. R. H. MacDonald (Edinburgh: Edinburgh University Press, 1971).

[5]   Cf. B. Hillyard, '"Durkan and Ross", and Beyond', in *The Renaissance in Scotland*, pp. 367–84.

[6]   See Julian Sharman, *The Library of Mary, Queen of Scots* (London: E. Stock, 1889); and J. Durkan, 'The Library of Mary, Queen of Scots', in *Mary Stewart: Queen in Three Kingdoms*, ed. by M. Lynch (Oxford: Blackwell, 1988), pp. 71–104. On the wider background, cf. S. G. Bell, 'Medieval Women Book Owners: Arbiters of Lay Piety and

exists concerning Scotswomen and their books, both manuscript and printed, up to the early seventeenth century.

The evidence, unfortunately, is both scattered and scanty, although more survives than is often realised.[7] Scotland was not a wealthy country and had a small population; what is more, the Reformation entailed a massive destruction of archives, manuscripts, and printed books.[8] For this reason I have cast my net widely, and interpreted 'Scotswomen' rather freely. I include women born in Scotland who went abroad, such as the daughters of James I and Joan Beaufort: Margaret (d. 1445), Isabella (d. *c.* 1495), and Eleanor (d. 1480), who married, respectively, the French dauphin (later to reign as Louis XI), the duke of Brittany, and the duke of Austria-Tyrol. I also include incomers from other countries, who spent much of their lives in Scotland, such as Margaret Tudor, who married James IV, Mary of Guise, who married James V, and Esther Inglis (*c.* 1571–1624), a distinguished calligrapher, who was the daughter of Huguenot refugees.

Space does not permit a full account of the varied historical contexts in which these women lived. Many, but not all, were queens, princesses, or of noble birth: wealthy and privileged, they were likely to enjoy a better education and to have more leisure than other women. A particular problem arises, however, with royal book-owners, who have sometimes been wrongly credited with the ownership of books, whether from honest mistake or with fraudulent intent. The most notorious instance is probably Mary Queen of Scots, whose possession of a book is clearly likely to raise

---

Ambassadors of Culture', *Signs* 7 (1981–82), 742–68; and C. M. Meale, '... "Alle the Bokes that I Haue of Latyn, Englisch, and Frensch": Laywomen and their Books in Late Medieval England', in *Women and Literature in Britain 1150–1500*, ed. by C. M. Meale (Cambridge: Cambridge University Press, 1993), pp. 128–58.

[7] It is striking how many of the young James VI's books came from women donors; see G. F. Warner, 'The Library of James VI', *Miscellany of the Scottish History Society*, 1 (1893), xi–lxxv.

[8] Cf. R. J. Lyall, 'Books and Book Owners in Fifteenth-Century Scotland', in *Book Production and Publishing in Britain 1375–1475*, ed. by J. Griffiths and D. Pearsall (Cambridge: Cambridge University Press, 1989), pp. 239–56; also D. McRoberts, 'Material Destruction Caused by the Scottish Reformation', in *Essays on the Scottish Reformation 1513–1625*, ed. by D. McRoberts (Glasgow: Burns and Sons, 1962), pp. 457–59. On the wider historical background, see R. Nicholson, *Scotland: the Later Middle Ages* (Edinburgh: Mercat Press, 1989), and G. Donaldson, *Scotland: James V to James VII* (Edinburgh: Oliver and Boyd, 1971).

its value in the sale room. Forgers have sometimes tampered with the bindings of sixteenth-century books, adding marian gold-tooled stamps, so that they appear to have come from her library.[9]

Margaret Tudor (1489–1541), queen of James IV and dowager queen during the reign of her son, James V, well illustrates some of these problems of provenance. Margaret was the focus for poetic activity at the Scottish court, particularly in her youth: she was commended in verse by Dunbar, Sir David Lindsay, and William Stewart. It has also been asserted that Stewart's metrical translation of Hector Boece's *History of Scotland* was commissioned by her in 1535 for the instruction of her son. This is mistaken, and results from misinterpretation of a feminine pronoun in the prologue to that work.[10] Little is known of Margaret's education at the English court in the 1490s, but it seems unlikely to have been neglected. She was the favourite grandchild and also the goddaughter of the learned and pious Lady Margaret Beaufort. Margaret brought at least one book with her from England in 1503; another book, equally unspecified, was purchased by her in Scotland in 1512.[11]

At least five manuscripts are said to have been in Margaret Tudor's possession. One, a fifteenth-century book of hours (Paris, Bibliothèque Nationale, MS lat. 1390) contains a note (fol. 2) that it belonged to 'Marie [sic] d'Ecosse, grandmère de Marie Stuart'.[12] There is no other evidence, however, for Margaret's ownership, which seems somewhat

[9] Cf. Durkan, 'Library of Mary, Queen of Scots', p. 74; and P. Robinson, 'John Leslie's *Libri Duo*: Manuscripts Belonging to Mary Queen of Scots?', in *Order and Connexion: Studies in Bibliography and Book History*, ed. by R. C. Alston (Cambridge: D. S. Brewer, 1997), pp. 63–75.

[10] Cf. Dunbar, *Selected Poems*, nos 10, 41, 60 and 61; Lindsay, *Testament of the Papyngo*, 542–48 (*Works*, ed. by D. Hamer, STS, 1931–36); a carol by Stewart, in *The Early English Carols*, ed. by R. L. Greene (Oxford; Clarendon Press, 1977), no. 121. 2. See also A. A. MacDonald, 'William Stewart and the Court Poetry of the Reign of James V', in *Stewart Style 1513–1542: Essays on the Court of James V*, ed. by Janet Hadley Williams (East Linton: Tuckwell Press, 1996), pp. 179–200.

[11] See Michael K. Jones and M. G. Underwood, *The King's Mother: Lady Margaret Beaufort, Countess of Richmond and Derby* (Cambridge: Cambridge University Press, 1992), pp. 148–49; J. Bain, *Calendar of Documents Relating to Scotland* (Edinburgh: H. M. General Register House, 1888), IV, 346 (26 June 1503); and *Treasurer's Accounts*, IV, 339: 'ane buk to the Quenis Grace'.

[12] See V. Leroquais, *Les Livres d'heures manuscrits de la Bibliothèque Nationale*, I (Paris: [n.p.], 1927), 216–17 (no. 103); and D. McRoberts, *Catalogue of Scottish Medieval Liturgical Books and Fragments* (Glasgow: Burns and Sons, 1953), no. 117.

dubious. The manuscript more probably belonged to Mary of Guise, mother (not grandmother) of Mary Queen of Scots. Another book of hours, in the collection of the Duke of Northumberland (Alnwick, MS 498), has also been associated with Margaret. The heraldry, however, shows that it was made for Lady Margaret Beaufort; nothing definitely connects it with her granddaughter.[13] A devotional manuscript, known as 'Le Chappelet de Jhesus et de la Vierge Marie' (London, British Library, MS Additional 25693) is said to have been first executed for Anna of Hungary, wife of Ferdinand, king of the Romans, but to have 'afterwards come into the possession of Margaret Tudor'.[14] The evidence for this, however, seems flimsy: the letters of the name 'Marguerite' are found on the Tudor roses that form the bosses of the binding. Margaret predeceased Anna, and I am not aware of a personal link between them. Another book of hours, in the Library at Chatsworth, is more securely attached to Margaret's name. This was apparently given to her by her father, and bears the inscription: 'Remember your kind and loving father in your good prayers. Henry' (fol. 14; cf. also 32^v).[15] The manuscript that is associated most certainly with Margaret is also the finest, and a very 'bright buke' indeed. This is a book of hours now in the Austrian National Library (MS lat. 1897). It has portraits of James IV and Margaret, and is beautifully illuminated, containing IM monograms tied with love knots, and intertwined emblematic thistles and marguerites. This manuscript was 'almost certainly a gift to Margaret Tudor on the occasion of her marriage', commissioned either by James IV or Henry VII.[16] At some later date she presented it, either to her sister Mary or her

---

[13] For a reproduction from this manuscript, see frontispiece to P. H. Buchanan, *Margaret Tudor, Queen of Scots* (Edinburgh: Scottish Academic Press, 1985). I am indebted to the advice of Miss Janet Backhouse; see also her 'Illuminated Manuscripts Associated with Henry VII and Members of his Immediate Family', *Harlaxton Medieval Studies*, 5 (1995), 175–87 (186–87).

[14] See *Catalogue of Additions to the Manuscripts in the British Museum* (1854–75), p. 223.

[15] See *Catalogue of the Library at Chatsworth*, vol. IV (1879), p. 323: 'Henry Seventh's Missal'; also *Medieval and Early Renaissance Treasures in the North West* (Manchester: Whitworth Art Gallery, University of Manchester, 1976), part 1, no. 55 (p. 31).

[16] L. Macfarlane, 'The Book of Hours of James IV and Margaret Tudor', *IR*, 11 (1960), 3–21 (p. 3). See *Das Gebetbuch Jakobs IV von Schottland und seiner Gemahlin Margaret* [facsimile], ed. by Franz Unterkircher (Graz: Akademische Druk-u. Verlagsanstalt, 1987). This manuscript is confused with Alnwick, MS 498 by L. O. Fradenburg, 'Sovereign

sister-in-law Catherine of Aragon; an inscription reads: 'Madame I pray
your grace Remember on me when ye loke upon thys boke. Your lofing
syster Margaret'.

A few manuscripts survive that may have belonged to Scottish nuns.
Two are associated with the Augustinian house of Iona: these are the late
twelfth-century Iona Psalter (Edinburgh, National Library of Scotland,
MS 10,000), written in England, possibly for Beatrix, its first prioress;
and a fifteenth-century book of hours, said to have been at Iona in the
middle of the sixteenth century (NLS, MS 16,499).[17] A leaf from a
fifteenth-century Cistercian breviary, found in Haddington (SRO,
Haddington Burgh Records 223 / 1) may have belonged to the Cistercian
priory there, founded in the twelfth century by Ada, Countess of
Northumberland (d. 1178).[18] One of the last nunneries to be established in
Scotland (1517), on land to the south of Edinburgh, was a Dominican
foundation, the Sisters of the order of St Catherine of Siena, commonly
known as 'the Sciennes'. This was a community that attracted well-off
and pious widows, such as Lady Seton, one of its founders, and Elizabeth
Auchinleck, sister-in-law of Gavin Douglas.[19] Two works associated with
this nunnery survive: a sixteenth-century Gospel Book written for the
community (Edinburgh University Library, MS 150);[20] and a printed
psalter, dated 1552, which belonged to a nun: 'this buk pertenis to sister

---

Love: the Wedding of Margaret Tudor and James IV of Scotland', in *Women and Sovereignty*, ed. by L. O. Fradenburg (Edinburgh: Edinburgh University Press, 1992), pp. 78–100 (p. 84 and n. 16).

[17] Information about Scottish nunneries is scanty: see I. B. Cowan and D. E. Easson, *Medieval Religious Houses: Scotland*, 2nd edn (London: Longman, 1976), pp. 143–56. See the descriptions of these manuscripts in National Library of Scotland, *Catalogue of Manuscripts Acquired since 1925*. On the Iona Psalter, cf. Nigel Morgan, *Early Gothic Manuscripts I: 1190–1250* (Oxford: Clarendon Press, 1982), no. 29.

[18] Cf. Walter Bower, *Scotichronicon*, ed. by D. E. R. Watt and others (Edinburgh: Mercat Press, 1987–98), VIII. 25; also B. Chandler, 'Ada de Warenne, Queen Mother of Scotland c. 1123–1178', *SHR* 60 (1981), 119–39.

[19] On the Sciennes, see Cowan and Easson, *Medieval Religious Houses: Scotland*, pp. 152–53. On Lady Seton, see Sir Richard Maitland, *History of the House of Seytoun* (Glasgow: Maitland Club, 1829), p. 40.

[20] See McRoberts, *Catalogue*, no. 80; C. R. Borland, *A Descriptive Catalogue of the Western Medieval Manuscripts in Edinburgh University Library* (Edinburgh: Edinburgh University Library, 1916), no. 150; and *Liber Conventus S. Katherine Senensis prope Edinburgum*, [ed. by James Maidment] (Edinburgh: Abbotsford Club, no. 21, 1841).

Marione Crafurde in the place of the Senis besyde Edinburgh' (NLS, H.8.f.17).[21]

It comes as no surprise that most of the books now extant, even those that belonged to laywomen, are largely pious and devotional. The earliest in date is the gospel lectionary (Oxford, Bodleian, MS Lat. liturg. f.5) that belonged to Queen Margaret of Scotland (*c.* 1046–1093), the daughter of Edward Aetheling, who became the wife of Malcolm III. This small volume 'combines the elements of a gospel book, a liturgical reading book, and a private prayer book'.[22] Another manuscript in the Bodleian (Fairfax 5), containing theological treatises by St Jerome and others, is inscribed with the name of Lady Dervorguilla Balliol (d. 1290), and was presented by her to Sweetheart Abbey, which she founded in 1273.[23]

Books of hours, however, comprise the single largest category. Isabella, duchess of Brittany, possessed at least three, of which the most magnificent is now in the Fitzwilliam Museum, Cambridge (MS 62); two others are in the Bibliothèque Nationale (BN, MS lat. 1369; MS lat. N. A. 588).[24] One late fifteenth-century book of hours that bears the signature 'Marie R' (fol. 1) belonged to Mary of Guise, queen of James V; it might possibly have been the 'buke of the quenis' for which two gold clasps were made in 1539.[25] Only the names are recorded of the socially less

---

[21] See *Early Scottish Libraries*, p. 86; McRoberts, *Catalogue*, no. 140.

[22] Cf. S. Mapstone, *Scots and their Books in the Middle Ages and the Renaissance* (Oxford: Bodleian Library, 1996), no. 1; and Richard Gameson, 'The Gospels of Margaret of Scotland', in *Women and the Book* (n. 2), pp. 148–71. On Matilda, Margaret's daughter, see also L. L. Huneycutt, '"Proclaiming her Dignity Abroad": the Literary and Artistic Network of Matilda of Scotland, Queen of England 1100–1118', in *The Cultural Patronage of Medieval Women*, ed. by J. H. McCash (Athens: University of Georgia Press, 1996), pp. 155–74.

[23] See *A Summary Catalogue of Western Manuscripts in the Bodleian Library at Oxford*, vol. II, part II, no. 3885. On Dervorguilla, see G. Stell, 'The Balliol Family and the Great Cause of 1291–2', in *Essays on the Nobility of Medieval Scotland*, ed. by K. J. Stringer (Edinburgh: John Donald, 1985), pp. 150–65 (155–57).

[24] For a fuller account of Isabella, see P. Bawcutt and B. A. Henisch, 'Scots Abroad in the Fifteenth Century: the Princesses Margaret, Isabella and Eleanor', in *Women in Scotland c.1100–c.1750*, ed. by E. Ewan and M. Meikle (East Linton: Tuckwell Press, 1999), pp. 45–55; and M. R. Toynbee, 'The Portraiture of Isabella Stuart, Duchess of Brittany', *Burlington Magazine*, 88 (1946), 300–306.

[25] On this manuscript (Fort Augustus Abbey; NLS, Acc. 11218/7), see N. Ker, *Medieval Manuscripts in British Libraries [MMBL]*, 4 vols (Oxford: Clarendon Press, 1969–), II (1977), 850–51; Mark Dilworth, 'The Book of Hours of Mary of Guise', *IR*, 19 (1968), 77–80; also *Treasurer's Accounts*, VII, 197 (21 May 1539).

exalted owners of two other books of hours: Marion Scott and Mary Gray.[26] More, however, is known of Jane Chisholm, the illegitimate daughter of William Chisholm, bishop of Dunblane in the mid-sixteenth century. Termed by one recent historian, 'a managing woman', she married Sir James Stirling of Keir, and owned an *Heures a lusaige de Rome*, printed at Paris in 1549 (NLS, Bdg.S.53). This has a fine binding, with IANE L. K. [Lady Keir] stamped on the front cover, and CHISHOLME L. K. on the back.[27] Elizabeth Danielstoun, wife of Patrick Cockburn of Clerkington, recorded her ownership of a book of hours with an inscription on the first leaf: 'This buik pertenis to ye honorable Elizabeth Danielstoun, ladie of Clarkingtone 1577'. This fifteenth-century manuscript (BL, MS Add. 39,761) was made in France, but apparently designed for a Scottish owner, since it includes saints such as Andrew and Margaret of Scotland (depicted wearing a cloak with the lion rampant).[28]

Books of hours, associated more conjecturally with Scottish women owners, include a manuscript sometimes known as 'Andrew Lundy's Primer' (Blairs College; NLS, Dep. 221/5), which Neil Ker considered 'perhaps for female use';[29] and the 'Murthly Hours' (NLS, MS 21,000), made in England in the fourteenth century for a woman who was either English or Scottish. This was in Scotland by 1421 at the latest, and owned by the Stewarts, Lords of Lorne.[30] One particularly fine manuscript, the

---

[26] On the first (Blairs College; NLS, Dep. 221/1), see Ker, *MMBL*, II, 113–118. McRoberts, *Catalogue*. nos 77 and 88 both refer to this manuscript. The second (Blairs College, H.14.10) is said by McRoberts, no. 96, to have been printed at Paris *c.* 1510. It has not so far been traced in the NLS.

[27] See M. B. Sanderson, *Scottish Rural Society in the Sixteenth Century* (Edinburgh: John Donald, 1982), pp. 90 and 179–80; also J. Durkan and J. Russell, 'Additions to J. Durkan and A. Ross, *Early Scottish Libraries*, at the National Library of Scotland', *Bibliotheck*, 11 (1982), no. 2, 29–37 (p. 33).

[28] Elizabeth Danielstoun had died by 21 April 1590; see Register of Edinburgh Testaments (SRO, cc. 8/8/21, fols 196^v–197^v). I have not seen E. S. Dewick, 'On a MS Book of Hours written in France for the Use of a Scottish Lady', *Transactions of St Paul's Ecclesiological Society* VII (1911–15), 109–20; cf. McRoberts, *Catalogue*, no. 58; and *Angels, Nobles and Unicorns: Patronage in Medieval Scotland* (Edinburgh: National Museum of Antiquities of Scotland, 1982), p. 85.

[29] See Ker, *MMBL*, II, 122–4; McRoberts, *Catalogue*, no. 49; and W. J. Anderson, 'Andrew Lundy's Primer', *IR*, 11 (1960), 39–51.

[30] See McRoberts, *Catalogue*, no. 23; and E. D. Yeo, 'The Murthly Hours', *National Art Collections Fund Review* (1987), 97–98.

Taymouth Hours (BL, Yates Thompson, MS 13), owes its name to an eighteenth-century owner, the Earl of Breadalbane, of Taymouth Castle, Perthshire, and is said to have been in Scotland since at least the sixteenth century. It was made in the fourteenth century for a royal lady, who has not been certainly identified; 'a strong candidate' is Joan, daughter of Edward II, who in 1328 was married to David II of Scotland.[31] Joan's interest in finely illuminated manuscripts is implied by the loan to her in 1362 of the Abingdon Apocalypse (BL, MS Add. 42555) by the abbot and community of Abingdon priory.[32]

By the middle of the sixteenth century devout Scotswomen were increasingly attracted to the Reformed faith. One of these was Marjorie Roger, the wife of Adam Fullarton, a merchant and leading Protestant in Edinburgh. She predeceased her husband, and her testament (recorded in the Register of Edinburgh Testaments, January 1584) is unusual in that it itemizes her books, revealing an impressive collection of English works by Tyndale, Cranmer, Jewel, Becon, Foxe and Hooper.[33] Another to whom books were important was Alison Sandilands (d. 1586), the wife of John Cockburn of Ormiston, a prominent Reformer and a friend of John Knox. She possessed a treatise by John Bradford, the English martyr, which she lent to James, Earl of Morton, shortly before his execution in 1581. She was instrumental in preserving from destruction the manuscript of *The Confession of Faith* (*STC*, 1340), a theological work by the Reformer Henry Balnaves. Thomas Vautrollier, who printed this work in 1584, wrote a dedicatory epistle to Alison Sandilands, in which he gives a vivid account of the episode.[34] Esther Inglis's staunch adherence to Protestantism is evident in the contents of her fine calligraphic manuscripts.

---

[31] See M. R. James, *A Descriptive Catalogue of the Second Series of Fifty Manuscripts (Nos. 51–100) in the Collection of Henry Yates Thompson* (Cambridge: Cambridge University Press, 1902), no. 57; John Harthan, *Books of Hours and their Owners* (London: Thames and Hudson, 1977), pp. 48–49; McRoberts, *Catalogue*, no. 31.

[32] Cf. Janet Backhouse, 'Sir Robert Cotton's Record of a Royal Bookshelf', *British Library Journal*, 18 (1992), 44–51 (pp. 47–48).

[33] See Michael Lynch, *Edinburgh and the Reformation* (Edinburgh: John Donald, 1981), pp. 84–85.

[34] For fuller information, see Sir Robert Cockburn and H. A. Cockburn, *The Records of the Cockburn Family* (London: Foulis, 1913), pp. 119–20; G. Hewitt, *Scotland under Morton 1572–80* (Edinburgh: John Donald, 1982), p. 201; Charles Rogers, *Three Scottish Reformers* (London, 1875), p. 20; and Jasper Ridley, *John Knox* (Oxford: Clarendon Press, 1968), p. 487. On the literary interests of the Cockburns, see S. Mapstone, 'The Thre Prestis of Peblis in the Sixteenth Century', in *A Day Estivall*, ed. by A. Gardner-Medwin and J. H. Williams (Aberdeen: Aberdeen University Press, 1990), pp. 124–42.

Over fifty survive, written in a variety of hands, often illuminated, and
some containing a self-portrait.[35] In 1598 a collection of prayers and
poetry, called *A Spirituall Propine*, was published by the minister James
Melvill (d. 1614). The BL copy, which has intelligent textual
emendations and is inscribed 'Eupham Melvill with mien hand' (p. 52),
seems to have been owned by his granddaughter.[36]

A particularly interesting figure is Marie, Countess of Mar (*c.* 1573–
1644); she was the daughter of Esmé Stewart of Aubigny, the favourite of
the young James VI, who created him Duke of Lennox. After the death of
her parents, Marie was brought from France to Scotland by James, and in
1592 married to John Erskine, seventh Earl of Mar. Despite her Catholic
upbringing, she became a Protestant and in later life an ardent supporter
of the Covenanting cause. Her 'Compte Book' (Account book) of 1638
records various book-purchases, such as a book 'callit David Lyndesay',
and payment for binding 'ye buik of the Martyres of England's Lives',
presumably Foxe's *Book of Martyrs*.[37] One of her books is now in the
Huntington Library, and bears her half-erased signature, 'Marie contes. of
Mar', together with verses from psalm 71. The work is a copy of *Hymnes
or Sacred Songs* (1599) by the Protestant poet Alexander Hume. Marie
seems to have been a close friend of Hume, and is mentioned in his
testament (August 1609), along with Elizabeth Melville, Lady Comrie, to
both of whom he leaves his Christian affection and blessing.[38] Hume
dedicated *Hymnes or Sacred Songs* to Elizabeth Melville, traditionally
believed to be the poet of *Ane Godly Dreame* (1603); both she and Marie
clearly belonged to that circle of 'godly and elect ladies in this our age'
whom he praised in this dedication.

Few secular works possessed by Scotswomen are now extant. Three
manuscripts of vernacular poetry, however, survive, compiled in the
fourteenth, fifteenth, and sixteenth centuries. Written respectively in
French, English, and Scots, they have a kind of emblematic significance,
illustrating the varied strands in Scottish literary culture.

---

[35] See A. H. Scott-Elliott and E. D. Yeo, 'Calligraphic Manuscripts of Esther Inglis
(1571–1624): a Catalogue', *The Papers of the Bibliographical Society of America*, 84
(1990), 11–86.

[36] Cf. *The Autobiography and Diary of Mr James Melvill*, ed. R. Pitcairn (Edinburgh,
1842), p. xxxv.

[37] See *Scots Peerage*, V, 621; *Miscellany of the Scottish History Society*, 1 (1893), 78–80;
and *Extracts from the Household Book of Lady Marie Stewart, Daughter of Esmé, Duke of
Lennox, and Countess of Mar*, [ed. by Charles K. Sharpe] (Edinburgh, 1815), pp. 38 and 30.

[38] *The Poems of Alexander Hume*, ed. by Alexander Lawson, STS, 1902, pp. 212–13.

The first is a copy of *Le Roman de la Rose*, commissioned by Christian de Lindsay (?1266–1335). Christian, a wealthy heiress, was the daughter of Ada, sister of John Balliol (and granddaughter of Lady Dervorguilla), and William de Lindsay, Lord of Lamberton, who owned large estates both in Scotland and England. She married Enguerrand de Guines (in what is now Pas de Calais), who later became Sire de Coucy. The manuscript, copiously illustrated with miniatures, was completed for Christian on 30 April 1323, shortly after she had been widowed:

> Mil et IIIe et XXIII ce fu en bone estrengne
> Fist faire cest roumans la bonne Crestienne,
> Ditte de Monmyrel, et dame de Coucy,
> En a[vr]il fu parfais le derrier samedi ...[39]

(In 1323 in a good time (*or* as a gift) the worthy Christian of Montmirail, Lady of Coucy, had this romance made, finished on the last Saturday of April . . .)

The second is Lydgate's *Siege of Thebes*, a popular work, which survives in several copies. One (Boston Public Library, MS f. Med. 94), dating from the 1430s, was towards the end of the fifteenth century in the possession of Marion, daughter of the second Lord Lyle, and wife of Peter Houston in Renfrewshire. An inscription (fol. 75^v) records that Robert Lyle, probably her brother, borrowed another unspecified 'buk' from her.[40] By 1592 this manuscript of *The Siege of Thebes* had joined the small collection of romances formed by Sir Duncan Campbell, seventh laird of Glenorchy. Duncan's mother, who belonged to a family that owned an early manuscript of Gavin Douglas's *Eneados*, herself possessed a copy of Sleidan's *Chronicle* (London, 1560): 'this buke pertenis to Catherine Ruthven lady of Glenurquhay'.[41]

---

[39] The manuscript, owned by the Earl of Crawford and Balcarres, is 'the earliest book known to have belonged to the family' (*Handlist of Personal Papers from the Muniments of the Earl of Crawford and Balcarres Deposited in the John Rylands Library of Manchester*, 1976, p. 6). I am indebted to Professor Meradith McMunn for information about this work. On Christian's life, see *Scots Peerage*, III, 5–6; Lord Lindsay, *Lives of the Lindsays*, 3 vols (Wigan, 1840), I, 28–32; and G. W. S. Barrow, *Robert Bruce and the Community of the Realm of Scotland* (Edinburgh: Edinburgh University Press, 1988), pp. 12–13.

[40] For fuller information, see *Scots Peerage*, V, 549–58.Cf. William Lyle, *De Insula, or the Lyles of Renfrewshire* (Glasgow, 1936), esp. pp. 91 and 94; Lyall, 'Books and Book Owners' (n. 8), p. 240.

[41] Sir Duncan owned copies of *Florimund*, and Sir Gilbert Hay's *Buik of King Alexander the Conquerour*. On Catherine, see the preface (by Cosmo Innes) to *The Black Book of*

   The third manuscript is the Maitland Quarto (Cambridge, Magdalene College, Pepys Library, MS 1408), a poetic miscellany, somewhat over-shadowed by larger and more famous literary anthologies, such as the Maitland Folio and the Bannatyne Manuscript. The Maitland Quarto is inscribed 'Marie Maitland 1586', and was owned by the youngest daughter of Sir Richard Maitland of Lethington (1496–1586); the Maitland Folio, compiled about the same time, may have belonged to her older sister, Helen. The Quarto is written in a mixture of secretary and italic hands, possibly by Marie herself.[42] Whether this is so or not, the compilation reflects her tastes and interests. It is, in the first place, a monument to her father, containing his own poems and verse tributes to him. But it is also very much a woman's book: among its contents are a 'Contrapoysoun [antidote] to the ballat falslie intitulit the properties of gud wemen' (no. xxxv); and an 'Elagie' on an unhappy marriage, voiced by the wife, which is a free re-handling of a poem by Clément Marot (no. lxvi). Several poems are eulogies of Marie herself, and one, which compares her to Sappho and 'Olimpia ... lampe of Latine land', urges her to write more poetry (no. lxxxv). Another celebrates the superior quality of female love: 'Thair is mair constancie in our sex' (no. xlix).[43] A few pieces in the Quarto recall the allegoric tradition of the *Roman de la Rose*, but the collection as a whole looks forward to the seventeenth century, when miscellanies of music and verse, including one containing poems by Alexander Montgomerie, were compiled by the daughters and wives of the Scottish gentry.[44]

   It is often impossible to tell how or when a book came into the pos-session of a specific person. A few, however, carry precious information on this point. Some manuscripts, we know, were specially commissioned by their owners. This is the case with Christian de Lindsay's copy of the

---

Taymouth (Edinburgh, 1855), p. vi; and R. Marshall, *Virgins and Viragos* (London: Collins, 1983), p. 135.

[42] On the literary activities of the Maitland family, see Bawcutt, 'The Earliest Texts of Dunbar', in *Regionalism in Late Medieval Manuscripts and Texts*, ed. by F. Riddy (Cambridge: D. S. Brewer, 1991), pp. 183–98, esp. 190–93. See also *The Maitland Quarto Manuscript*, ed. by W. A. Craigie, STS, 1920.

[43] Cf. J. Farnsworth, 'Voicing Female Desire in "Poem XLIX"', *Studies in English Literature 1500–1900*, 36 (1996), 57–62.

[44] The Montgomerie manuscript (EUL, De.3.70) bears the name of an as yet unidentified 'Margaret Ker'. See also Bawcutt, 'Manuscript Miscellanies in Scotland from the Fifteenth to the Seventeenth Century' (forthcoming).

Roman de la Rose. So too with the *Livre des Vices et des Vertus*, or *Somme le Roi*, which belonged to Isabella of Brittany, and is inscribed:

> Isabeau, aisnee fille du roy d'Escoce, duchesse de Bretaigne, contesse de Montfort et de Richemont, fist faire ce livre—qui le trouvera le luy rende—et le fist escripre, a sa devotion, de la main de Jehan Hubert, en l'an mil quatre cens soisante quatre.[45]

> (Isabella, eldest daughter of the king of Scotland, duchess of Brittany, countess of Montfort and Richmond, ordered this book to be made— whoever finds it should return it—and had it written with great care, by the hand of Jean Hubert, in the year 1464.)

Many books of hours are thought to have been wedding gifts. Others were family bequests, or tokens of friendship.

A gift of an unusual and intriguing kind was made to Lady Arabella Stuart (1575–1615) by the Scottish poet William Fowler (?1560–1612). Arabella's tragic story is well-known: the daughter of Charles, Earl of Lennox, she was a cousin of James VI, and through her descent from Margaret Tudor (who was her great-grandmother), she had a title to the English throne. She was regarded with suspicion by both Elizabeth and James (when he became James I of England), and after a clandestine marriage to William Seymour in 1612 was imprisoned in the Tower, where she died in 1615.[46] William Fowler, who was secretary to Queen Anne, first met Arabella in 1603. He sent her letters and sonnets, and wrote admiringly to the Earl of Shrewsbury: 'I can not forbeare from geving you advertisment of my great and goode fortune in obteaning the acquentance of my lady Arbella'.[47]

Arabella was an intelligent, well educated woman, who spoke several languages. Fowler seems to have felt for her a genuine friendship and respect. He himself was a translator of Petrarch and Machiavelli, and it was presumably awareness of her linguistic abilities that led him to present her with an *horologion* (BL, MS Harley 5642), a devotional

---

[45] BN, MS fr. 958, fol. 122ᵛ; see F. Avril and N. Reynaud, *Les Manuscrits à peintures en France 1440–1520* (Paris: Flammarion, 1993), no. 95; also Toynbee, 'Isabella Stuart' (n. 24), 305.

[46] There are numerous biographies, of which the fullest is E. T. Bradley, *Arabella Stuart*, 2 vols (London, 1889).

[47] The best account of Fowler is in vol. III of his *Works*, ed. by H. W. Meikle, J. Craigie and J. Purves, 3 vols, STS, 1914–1940. For the letter, see III, xxxii; the sonnets are printed in I, 261–62.

manuscript in Church Slavonic, which is similar in structure and purpose to a book of hours. In an inscription, dated 1 March 1607/8, Fowler says that he had found the book *in Pomona Orcadum insula*, i.e. the chief island of the Orkneys, and presented it: *castissimae et sine labe virgini celsissimaeque dominae D. Arbellae Stuardae ob incredibilem omnium scientiarum cognitionem [et] linguarum peritiam* [to the most chaste and spotless maiden and most lofty lady, lady Arabella Stuart, on account of her incredible learning and skill in languages].[48] How the Russian manuscript came to be in the Orkneys is unknown, and prompts speculation as to whether it was acquired by a seaman or merchant. It is less surprising that Fowler, who had travelled widely, had visited the Orkneys. His own poems confirm his travels there. One, which begins: 'Vpon the vtmost corners of the warld', is entitled 'a Sonet in Orknay'; another, beginning 'I have the Orcades seen', is addressed to Arabella.[49]

In 1473 the humanist Heinrich Steinhöwel dedicated his translation of Boccaccio's *De claris mulieribus* to Eleanor, daughter of James I and duchess of Austria-Tyrol. Such dedications to women, usually of royal or noble birth, steadily increased in the sixteenth century. Franklin B. Williams, however, is sceptical about the motives of many authors, stressing the 'fortuitous' element in dedications: 'for the most part no especial appropriateness governed the choice, unless perhaps a known piety in sponsors of religious treatises'.[50] Yet Steinhöwel's choice of Eleanor was far from a matter of chance; she was an educated woman, who possessed other books, and has long been credited with the translation of *Pontus and Sidonia* into German (1483).[51] There is nothing 'fortuitous' either about the dedication of the fiercely anti-English

---

[48] A brief description is found in Ralph Cleminson, *A Union Catalogue of Cyrillic Manuscripts in British and Irish Collections* (London: School of Slavonic and East European Studies, 1988). The absence of water damage 'suggests it was not from a shipwreck'.

[49] *Works*, I, 221; and I, 317–18.

[50] See 'The Literary Patronesses of Renaissance England', *Notes and Queries*, 207 (1962), 364–66; also his *Index of Dedications in British Books before 1641* (London: Bibliographical Society, 1962).

[51] See Bawcutt and Henisch (n. 24), pp. 50–53; and A. M. Stewart, 'The Austrian Connection c. 1450–1483: Eleonora and the Intertextuality of *Pontus und Sidonia*', in *Bryght Lanternis: Essays on the Language and Literature of Medieval and Renaissance Scotland*, ed. by J. D. McClure and M. R. G. Spiller (Aberdeen: Aberdeen University Press, 1989), pp. 129–49.

Complaynt of Scotland (Paris, ?1550) to Mary of Guise.[52] Some dedications have a value in that they reveal literary contacts otherwise unsuspected; one such, to Lady Jean Fleming (d. 1609), wife of Sir John Maitland of Thirlestane, is prefixed to her copy of Fowler's translation of Petrarch's *Trionfi* (1587).[53]

Marie, Countess of Mar, was the recipient of several dedications. Most of the books, which are religious and devotional, reflect her 'known piety', and do not necessarily prove intimate acquaintance with their authors.[54] One, however, was written by a clergyman certainly known to her, and the dedication is by her physician. It has a title arresting in its intertextuality: *The Countesse of Marres Arcadia, or Sanctuarie, Containing Morning and Evening Meditations . . . by M. Ia. Caldwell, Sometimes Preacher of Gods Word, at Fawkirke ...* (Edinburgh, 1625).[55] This clearly alludes to *The Countess of Pembroke's Arcadia*, still an immensely popular work, and recently issued in a new edition (1621), with a Supplement by the Scottish poet William Alexander. The Epistle Dedicatorie confirms this:

> Sir Philip Sidneys Arcadia hath manie faire and recreatiue discourses for ladies; a faire Field indeede to feede on, for young and fond Lovers . . . But this is a spirituall Arcadia: it is your Honours litle Arcadia. For heere is a Spiritual foode for wearied soules: heere are Pasturages for the Flock of Christ . . . the Countesse of Pembrokes Arcadia is for the bodie; but the Countesse of Marre her Arcadia is for the soule.

A much earlier and little discussed dedication is that of *The Buke of the Howlat*, a major alliterative poem of the fifteenth century. The last stanza constitutes a brief envoi, in which the poet voices customary modesty about his skills, tells us his name, and where and for whom he wrote the poem:

> Thus for ane dow of Dunbar drew I this dyte,
> Dowit with ane Douglas - and boith war thai dowis -
> In the forest forsaid, frely parfyte,

---

[52] *The Complaynt of Scotland*, ed. by A. M. Stewart, STS, 1979. For other dedications to Mary, see *STC*, 5458 and 15066, and Jean Le Feron, *Le Simbol Armorial des Armoiries de France, d'Escoce et de Lorraine* (Paris, 1555).

[53] EUL, De./10/1; Fowler, Works, I, 15–17. See N. Mann, 'Petrarch Manuscripts in the British Isles', in Italia Medioevale e Umanistica, 18 (1975), 187–89.

[54] STC, 5937, 5943, 12478.

[55] STC, 4366.

Of Terneway, tender and tryde, quhoso trast trowis.

. . . . . .

In mirthfull moneth of May,
In myddis of Murraye,
Thus on a tyme by Ternway
    Happinit Holland.
        (989–1001)[56]

(Thus I composed this poem for a dove of Dunbar, married to a Douglas -
they were both doves, completely perfect, tender and trustworthy - in the
forest of Darnaway mentioned earlier, whoever knows the truth . . . In the
joyous month of May, once upon a time, in the heart of Moray, this is what
happened to Holland.)

Richard Holland was a priest, notary, and secretary to Archibald, Earl of
Moray (d. 1455). He composed the poem, in or near Darnaway Castle in
Morayshire, for Archibald's wife, Elizabeth Dunbar, probably some time
between 1445 and 1452. With ingenious puns on *dow*, 'dove', *dowit*,
'endowed', and *Douglas*, Holland pays tribute to the innocence and constancy of Elizabeth, and also compliments the family of her husband:
'boith war thai dowis'. The central section of *The Howlat* is largely
devoted to the Douglases, praising their courage, and loyalty to the cause
of Robert Bruce. Yet it should be noted that in this earlier, highly
heraldic, section Holland incorporates Elizabeth's coat of arms (586–91).
(Technically, the Douglas arms are quartered with those of Moray.)
Holland also embeds the name of Elizabeth within the poem, by a reference to her patron saint, mother of John the Baptist (731–32).

By May 1455 the growing strife between the over-powerful Douglas
family and James II culminated in the battle of Arkinholme, in which
Archibald was killed. Shortly afterwards an indenture of marriage was
drawn up between the earl's widow and one of his former enemies,
George Gordon, Master of Huntly. Holland was not only a witness, but a
party to this contract, as one of Elizabeth's 'men', or retainers. Huntly
stated that he would obtain 'full and hale remissione to the said ladyis
men'; as Marion Stewart notes, 'the document is concerned with the
safety of these men, as much as with the matrimonial arrangements of
Elizabeth Dunbar'.[57] In fact the contract was annulled, and both parties

---

[56] Cited from *Longer Scottish Poems I: 1375–1650*, ed. by P. Bawcutt and F. Riddy
(Edinburgh: Scottish Academic Press, 1987).

[57] Cf. M. Stewart, 'Holland of the *Howlat*', *IR*, 23 (1972), 3–15 (10). On Elizabeth, see
Scots Peerage, VI, 306.

made other marriages. Elizabeth died in 1486; Holland was so identified with the Douglas cause that he fled to England, where he is last recorded in 1482.

The Howlat is often regarded as a eulogy of the Douglases, and Felicity Riddy suggests that, 'with its singular blend of learning, earnestness, wit and sycophancy', it may have been intended to ingratiate the poet with Archibald, and secure him the post of secretary.[58] But we should not overlook the dedication to Elizabeth. The feminine audience envisaged by Holland has implications for other fifteenth-century Scottish poems, such as *Lancelot of the Laik*. In the Prologue to this work the poet speaks of being an unsuccessful lover, whom the God of Love advises to commend himself to his mistress, by composing not trite love epistles ('sedulis and billis') but rather some narrative

> Of love, ore armys, or of sum othir thing,
> That may hir one to thi remembryng brynge.
> (147–48)[59]

This passage may well seem conventional, yet is not necessarily a fiction. Arthurian stories, and those concerning Lancelot in particular, seem to have been popular with women.[60] Pushing speculation further, I would suggest that the most famous Scottish anthology of the fifteenth century (Bodleian, MS Arch. Selden. B. 24) must surely have had female readers. This contains many of Chaucer's poems, and the unique text of *The Kingis Quair*. It was compiled in the first place for Henry, Lord Sinclair (d. 1513), but is likely to have been read by Margaret Hepburn, his wife, and by their daughters, Elizabeth and Jean, whose names are found in the manuscript.[61]

It is unknown whether Elizabeth Dunbar read *The Howlat* herself, or listened—as Dunbar's fictional Widow listened to love 'ballatis'—to it being read aloud, either by the poet or another member of her household. The extent of female literacy is as problematic in medieval Scotland as

---

[58] See 'Dating *The Buke of the Howlat*', RES, NS 37 (1986), 1–10 (10).

[59] *Lancelot of the Laik*, ed. by M. M. Gray, STS, 1912.

[60] Cf. Meale, 'Alle the Bokes' (n. 7), p. 139.

[61] See *The Works of Geoffrey Chaucer and The Kingis Quair: a Facsimile of Bodleian Library, Oxford, MS Arch. Selden. B. 24*, ed. by J. Boffey and A. S. G. Edwards (Cambridge: D. S. Brewer, 1997), pp. 18–22; fols 231 and 231ᵛ. Margaret Hepburn, at her death in June 1542, owned 'duos libros': *Notices from the Local Records of Dysart*, ed. W. Muir (Glasgow: Maitland Club, 73, 1853), pp. 8–9.

elsewhere. Literacy is, of course, not a simple concept, and may refer to a wide range of skills. We hear of girls being taught by nuns at Aberdour and Elcho, with 'perhaps some reading'; and schools run by women, probably of the 'little school type', are mentioned in the Edinburgh Records for 1499.[62] Many women must have had some competency in reading the vernacular, but reading Latin was a different matter. If the learned Lady Margaret Beaufort could regret her insufficiency in Latin,[63] we must wonder how closely other women followed the sense of their books of hours. By the second half of the sixteenth century the position was different. Many women associated with the Reforming cause seem to take literacy, in the vernacular at least, for granted. It was his wife, not a minister, whom on his death bed John Knox asked to read aloud the seventeenth chapter of St John's Gospel.[64] It was his elder sister Isobel (d. 1574), not a brother, who read to the young James Melvill passages from the poetry of Sir David Lindsay.[65] *The Countess of Marres Arcadia* perhaps symbolizes the change: designed chiefly for pious women, as were many books of hours, this small book is densely packed with words, and has not a single illustration.

The purpose of this article has been to explore a neglected area of Scottish history. A surprising amount of evidence survives concerning Scotswomen and their books in the Middle Ages and the Renaissance, but it is far from easy to interpret the precise significance of such scattered data, spread over many centuries. Some conclusions, however, are obvious: the largely pious character of these women's reading; the strong literary bent of certain prominent Scottish families, such as the Cockburns and Maitlands, in which the female members participated; and the closeness of Scotland's cultural links with both France and England.

---

[62] See J. Durkan, 'Education in the Century of the Reformation', in *Essays on the Scottish Reformation* (n. 8), pp. 155 and 156.

[63] *The King's Mother* (n. 11), p. 184.

[64] Cf. J. Ridley, *John Knox*, pp. 24 and 517.

[65] See *The Autobiography and Diary of Mr James Melvill* (n. 36), pp. 18–19.

'Many grete myraclys . . . in divers contreys of the eest': The Reading and Circulation of the Middle English Prose *Three Kings of Cologne*

JULIA BOFFEY

Scholarly studies of the reading tastes and habits of medieval women are making ever clearer the permeability and fluidity of what have been conceived of as specifically female textual communities, while at the same time illuminating in a more gradual way the significance of such communities and sub-cultures in the transmission and availability of particular works.[1] Felicity Riddy's own researches have led her from 'Women talking about the things of God' to the more heterogeneous concerns of reading in family and household contexts, where considerations of devoutness may be assimilated into textual environments of a less obviously pious kind.[2] The following discussion explores within this frame of reference the late medieval circulation and readership of a narrative

---

[1] The following abbreviations are used: IMEV and SIMEV, for Carleton Brown and Rossell Hope Robbins, *The Index of Middle English Verse* (New York: Medieval Academy, 1943), and Rossell Hope Robbins and John L. Cutler, *Supplement to the Index of Middle English Verse* (Lexington: Kentucky University Press, 1965); STC, for *A Short-Title Catalogue of Books Printed in England, Scotland, and Ireland, 1475–1640*, first compiled by A. W. Pollard and G. R. Redgrave, 2nd edn begun by W. A. Jackson and F. S. Ferguson, and completed by Katharine F. Pantzer, 3 vols (London: Bibliographical Society, 1976, 1986, 1991). The orthography of all quotations from Middle English has been lightly modernized.

[2] '"Women talking about the things of God": a late medieval sub-culture', in *Women and Literature in Britain, 1150–1500*, ed. by Carol M. Meale, 2nd edn (Cambridge: Cambridge University Press, 1996), pp. 104–27; '"Mother Knows Best": Reading Social Change in a Courtesy Text', *Speculum*, 71 (1996), 66–86.

whose subject matter and general features advertise no great applicability
to the concerns of female communities, yet which seems for a number of
reasons to have come the way of women readers of various kinds: the
Middle English prose *Three Kings of Cologne.*

Medieval narratives of the three kings were based on the account in
Matthew's Gospel (2. 1) where the triumvirate are described simply as
'magi ab oriente' ('wise men from the east').[3] Details of various kinds
about their origins, their journey, and the significance of their gifts accu-
mulated in biblical commentaries and found their way into Latin texts,
one of which was the influential *Historia SS. Trium Regum*, compiled by
John of Hildesheim, a Carmelite friar who died in 1375. This account told
of the visit made by the three kings at the nativity, and it covered among
other things their knowledge of prophecies of a star in the east, the
significance of the gifts they took to Bethlehem, their outwitting of
Herod, and the posthumous fate of their bodies, which, having been
brought by St Helena to Constantinople from their own lands, were translated from there to Milan, and finally to Cologne in 1164. John of
Hildesheim's interest was stimulated by a local cult which began at this
time when three fingers of the relics were given to the cathedral in his
own home town. His Latin text survives in different versions in numerous
copies—many originating in Germany, but others also from different
countries of Europe.[4] Over time it made its way into a number of vernacular expositions. Of the various more or less abridged English versions
of his work, the most widely circulated was produced in the early fifteenth century and published in a modern edition for the Early English
Text Society, from two of its several variant forms, by Carl Horstmann in
1886.[5]

---

[3] On the development of the legend see Hans Hofmann, *Die heiligen drei Könige zur
Heiligenverehrung im kirchichen, gesellschaftlichen und politischen Leben des Mittel-
alters* (Bonn: Ludwig Röhrscheid, 1975); Geoffrey Grigson, 'The Three Kings of
Cologne', *History Today*, 4 (1954), 793–801; Sylvia Harris, 'The "Historia Trium Regum"
and the medieval legend of the magi in Germany', *Medium Aevum*, 28 (1959), 23–30;
Bernard Hamilton, 'Prester John and the Three Kings of Cologne', *Studies in Medieval
History Presented to R. H. C. Davis*, ed. by Henry Mayr-Harting and R. I. Moore
(London: Hambledon Press, 1985), pp. 177–91.

[4] For a list of the Latin manuscripts, see Hofmann, *Die heiligen drei Könige*, pp. 13–17.

[5] *The Three Kings of Cologne: An Early English Translation of the "Historia Trium
Regum" by John of Hildesheim*, ed. by C. Horstmann, EETS, OS 85 (London: N. Trübner
& Co., 1886). Horstmann edits the versions in Cambridge University Library MS Ee. 4. 32
and London, British Library MS Royal 18 A. x, with 'various readings' from the other

One of the features of John of Hildesheim's account, and hence of this English abridgement, is its authorization of many of the accretions to the story by means of reference to 'dyuerse bokes' in which the ancestry of the kings, and the courses of their lives after the nativity, were supposedly enshrined.[6] But it offers in addition to this ostensibly factual information much detail about the topography and customs of the kings' native lands, 'grete waters and wildirnesses ful of wilde and perlous beestis and horribil serpentys' (p. 40).

This serves to offer tasters of the marvels of the east, small opportunities to make imaginative travels outside the boundaries of quotidian experience into different and sometimes exotic worlds.[7] Such possibilities are occasionally intensified through the provision of detail about the splendour of the kings' own persons and life-styles, inviting the exploration of worlds unfamiliar because of social, rather than geographical distance. On their arrival at Bethlehem, for example, the kings

> light doune of her hors and chaunged all her arraye and clothed hem in the beest and richest aray that they hadde, and as kyngis scholde be, arayed hem (p. 66).

At the same time as appearing to insist upon areas of social, geographical and cultural difference, though, the text also invites its readers to establish points of identification or familiarity in its story. This is achieved in part through quotation from the Scriptures and reference to episodes familiar through biblical accounts—the nativity, for example, is narrated following Luke's gospel, quoted in part in Latin, and then trans-

---

manuscripts known to him in an appendix, and, for comparison, the Latin text of the former Brandenburg MS I, 1. 176, now Berlin, Staatsbibliothek Preussischer Kulturbesitz MS cod. theol. lat. 565. An edition of the English translation in London, Lambeth Palace MS 491 is being prepared by Dr Frank Schaer, who is also undertaking a study of the complex relationships between the different English versions.

[6] Horstmann, *Three Kings*, p. 2. Subsequent page references will be supplied after quotations from this text.

[7] On some of the significances of the exotic for medieval readers, see Mary B. Campbell, *The Witness and the Other World. Exotic European Travel Writing, 400–1600* (Ithaca, NY: Cornell University Press, 1988); John M. Fyler, 'Domesticating the Exotic in The Squire's Tale', *ELH*, 55 (1988), 1–26; Susan Schibanoff, 'Worlds Apart: Orientalism, Antifeminism and Heresy in Chaucer's Man of Law's Tale', *Exemplaria*, 8 (1996), 59–96; Kathryn L. Lynch, 'East Meets West in Chaucer's Squire's and Franklin's Tales', *Speculum*, 70 (1995), 530–51; Iain Macleod Higgins, *Writing East: The "Travels" of Sir John Mandeville* (Philadelphia: University of Pennsylvania Press, 1997).

lated into English. Elsewhere, when telling physical details authenticate the biblical or pseudo-biblical stories, they often supply practical or domestic information, or physical description of a notably 'homely' kind:

> that same day that thes iij. kyngis soughten god and worscheppud hym with gifftes in bethleem, oure lord jhesu crist was that tyme in his manhede a litil childe of xiij. dayes age, and he was sumdele [i.e. a little] fatte; and he laye wrapped in poure clothis and in his modir lappe. [Also oure lady, seynt Marye, hys moder] . . . sche was in persone flesshy and sumdele broune . . . (p. 70).

Where it is possible for readers to assume familiarity, either through prior knowledge of biblical stories, or through access to common experience, the text seems to capitalize on the opportunity.[8]

Domestication of the three kings' story of course took place in other ways. Just as the homely details of the narrative countered the assumed strangeness of their physical features and their lifestyles, so the frequency with which they appeared in art and in narrative conferred a certain familiarity.[9] Over time they assumed a growing importance in the liturgy with the development of different versions of an *Officium Stellae*—an Epiphany play representing their visit to Bethlehem, with an opportunity to meet the returning shepherds, whose visit seems to have been less easy to dramatize in the already packed liturgy of Christmas Day. These liturgical accretions were reflected in the incorporation into civic play cycles of episodes dramatizing the kings' visit and their interviews with Herod.[10] English compilations for pastoral use like Mirk's *Festial* and the

---

[8]   Cf. the remarks of Douglas Gray, 'Popular Religion and Late Medieval English Literature', in *Religion in the Poetry and Drama of the Late Middle Ages. The J. A. W. Bennett Memorial Lectures, Perugia, 1988*, ed. by Piero Boitani and Anna Torti (Cambridge: D. S. Brewer, 1990), pp. 1–28. Similar opportunities are offered in Nicholas Love's translation of the pseudo-Bonaventuran *Mediationes vitae Christi*, on which see most recently Richard Beadle, '"Devoute ymaginacioun" and the Dramatic Sense in Love's *Mirror* and the N-Town Plays', in *Nicholas Love at Waseda: Proceedings of the International Conference 20–22 July 1995*, ed. by Shoichi Oguro, Richard Beadle, Michael G. Sargent (D. S. Brewer: Cambridge , 1997), pp. 1–17.

[9]   For recent discussion of their representation in art, see Olga Pujmanová, 'Portraits of Kings depicted as Magi in Bohemian Painting', in *The Regal Image of Richard II and the Wilton Diptych*, ed. by Dillian Gordon, Lisa Monnas, and Caroline Elam (London: Harvey Miller, 1997), pp. 247–66.

[10]   Glynne Wickham, *The Medieval Theatre*, 3rd edn (Cambridge: Cambridge University Press, 1987), pp. 44, 68 etc. See also the extensive commentary in R. M. Lumiansky and David Mills, ed., *The Chester Mystery Cycle*, EETS, SS 3 and 9 (London: Oxford

Speculum Sacerdotale, and collections like *The Northern Homily Cycle* and *The Golden Legend* made parts of their stories available in the context of discussion of the feast of Epiphany,[11] and the kings were frequently invoked for protection or intercession, as for example in the Latin prayers which Richard Duke of York had inserted into a book of Hours made for him in the Low Countries.[12] Epiphany carols of different kinds feature in almost all the major manuscript repertories, including those which preserve the lyrics of John Audelay and the Franciscan James Ryman.[13] Over time the kings' names alone acquired a spurious power, and were sometimes used, completely out of any Epiphany context, in charms and recipes:

> Take the blode of the litill fynger of hym that is seke and wryte thir thre names in his forhed of the iij kynges of Colayn, that is to say: Jasper fert aurum [gold], thus [frankincense] Melchior, Attro pamirram [myrrh]. he that beris thir names of thir iij kyngis with hym, he sall be lesid thurgh the petee of God of the falland evyll [falling sickness]. Or write tham with the sam blode & hynge tham abowt his nek in a writ.[14]

The Yorkshire manuscript-compiler Robert Thornton, who copied this recipe into the collection which survives as Lincoln Cathedral MS 91, had in its sister-volume (London, British Library Additional MS 31042) a verse account of the Three Kings' stories;[15] his contemporary Robert

---

University Press, 1974, 1986), ii, 124–44; the visit of the Magi to Herod, and their offering, appear in all the major English cycles.

[11] See *A Manual of Writings in Middle English*, general eds. J. Burke Severs and Albert E. Hartung (New Haven: Connecticut Academy of Arts and Sciences, 1967–), ii, 630 for bibliography. References to the three kings surface frequently in other contexts, as for instance in connection with advice on offerings at Mass in the *Layfolks' Mass Book* , ed. by Thomas Frederick Simmons, EETS, os 71 (London: Oxford University Press, 1879) pp. 22–23, lines 247–40. I am grateful to Annette Kern for alerting me to this.

[12] Eamon Duffy, *The Stripping of the Altars: Traditional Religion in England 1400–1580* (New Haven: Yale University Press, 1992), p. 216; Anne F. Sutton and Livia Visser-Fuchs, *Richard III's Books: Ideals and Reality in the Life and Library of a Medieval Prince* (Stroud: Sutton, 1997), pp. 21–22, 58.

[13] R. L. Greene, *The Early English Carols*, 2nd edn (Oxford: Clarendon Press, 1977), pp. 122–30 (Epiphany carols).

[14] *The 'Liber de Diversis Medicinis' in the Thornton Manuscript (MS Lincoln Cathedral A. 5. 2)*, ed. by M. S. Ogden, EETS, os 207 (London: Oxford University Press, 1938), p. 42 (see further pp. 42–43, and p. 99).

[15] Fols 111ʳ–119ᵛ; see H. N. MacCracken, 'Lydgatiana III. The Three Kings of Cologne', *Archiv*, 129 (1912), 50–68.

Reynes, of Acle in Norfolk, names them in two charms in his common-place book.[16]

The most widely circulated of the English prose abridgements of John of Hildesheim's *Trium Regum* survives in numbers which suggest some considerable popularity: twenty-one manuscripts, and at least four early printed editions, all the work of Wynkyn de Worde.[17] Statistics such as these prompt speculation about what precisely may have determined the text's appeal, and about the nature of its readership. One factor may have been simply the general growing interest in vernacular hagiography and extra-biblical or extra-liturgical material—a taste which was clearly identified by Caxton, who produced translations to cater for it, and was to be further nurtured by the printers who succeeded him.[18] The collocation of a version of the prose *Three Kings* together with *The Golden Legend* in London, Lambeth Palace MS 72, may be testimony to this aspect of its appeal.[19]

Other collocations are not without interest. Some manuscripts preserve the *Three Kings* on its own (Oxford, Bodleian Library MSS Douce 301, Laud misc. 658 and Laud misc. 749; Cambridge University Library Add. MS 43, for example). In CUL Kk. 1. 3 it is a separate part of what may have been a fascicular collection, alongside large-scale best-sellers such as Hoccleve's *Regiment of Princes* and Lydgate's *Life of Our Lady* (a role

[16] *The Commonplace Book of Robert Reynes of Acle: An Edition of Tanner MS 407*, ed. by Cameron Louis (New York: Garland, 1980), items 28, fol. 15 (p. 169) and 91, fol. 48[v] (p. 288).

[17] Cambridge University Library MSS Ee. 4.32, Kk. 1. 3 (section XII), and Add. 43; Magdalene College, MS Pepys 2006; Trinity College MS R. 5.43; Durham Cathedral Library MS Hunter 15; London, BL MSS Add. 36983, Harley 1704, Royal 18. A. x, Stowe 951, Cotton Titus A. xxv, Cotton Vespasian E. xvi; Lambeth Palace MS 72; Oxford, Bodleian Library MSS Ashmole 59, Douce 301, Laud misc. 658, Laud misc. 749, Eng. th. c. 58; Stonyhurst College MS B. xxiii; Cambridge, MA, Harvard University, Houghton Library MS Eng. 530; STC 5572 [1496?], 5573 [after July 1499], 5574 (1511), 5575 (1526).

[18] One factor here suggesting to de Worde the probable commercial success of a printed *Three Kings* may have been the availability of printed French versions of similar material: J-C. Brunet, *Manuel du libraire et d'amateur de livres*, 5th edn, 6 vols (Paris: Librairie de Firmin Didot Frères, Fils et Cie., 1860–1888), v, 1205, lists a work called *La Vie des troys roys, Jaspar, Melchior et Balthazar, translate de latin en francois*, printed by Jean Trepperel in 1498: earlier lost editions may have been in circulation.

[19] M. R. James, *A Descriptive Catalogue of the Manuscripts in the Library of Lambeth Palace: The Medieval Manuscripts* (Cambridge: Cambridge University Press, 1932), pp. 116–17.

preserved in a later printed *sammelband*).[20] Elsewhere in anthologies it tends to appear with other very well-known or popular texts: with the prose *Brut* in Cambridge, Trinity College MS R. 5. 43, CUL Ee. 4. 32, and Cambridge, MA, Harvard Eng. 530; with *The Canterbury Tales,* whole or in part, in Cambridge, Magdalene College, Pepys 2006, BL Harley 1704, and Stonyhurst MS B. 23.[21]

One clue to the text's appeal is suggested by the nature of the illustrations which sometimes accompany it in manuscript and printed form. None of these indicate any special interest in what the narrative relates about the geography or topography of the lands of the east: it does not appear to have been considered as a Mandeville analogue, or to have attracted any illustration along Mandeville lines.[22] Only one of the manuscripts (Bodl. Laud misc. 658) includes a miniature, and this represents simply the kings themselves, in an Adoration scene.[23] This emphasis on the kings' role in the nativity story seems to have been retained in de Worde's printed editions, of which the second, dating from some time after 1499, has Adoration and Crucifixion woodcuts,[24] and the third and fourth offer two further Adoration scenes.[25] The other uses of all the woodcuts in de Worde's printed editions might offer clues about the kind of text *The Three Kings* was thought to be. All appear elsewhere in works

---

[20] M. C. Seymour, 'The manuscripts of Hoccleve's *Regiment of Princes*', *Transactions of the Edinburgh Bibliographical Society*, 4 (1974), 253–97 (p. 282). A copy of one of the printed editions is preserved in a *sammelband* together with a number of other early printed texts: see William Beattie, introduction, *The Taill of Rauf Coilyear, printed by Robert Lekpreuik at St Andrews in 1572. A Facsimile of the Only Known Copy* (Edinburgh: John G. Eccles, 1966).

[21] In Durham Cathedral Library MS Hunter 15 the *Three Kings* is preserved in the part of the manuscript which includes prose tracts on diet and the seven deadly sins, and a sermon by Thomas Wimbledon.

[22] Malcolm Letts, *Sir John Mandeville: The Man and his Book* (London: Batchworth Press, 1949); Josephine Walters Bennett, *The Rediscovery of Sir John Mandeville* (New York: Modern Language Association, 1954).

[23] On the connections of the artist, see Kathleen L. Scott, *Later Gothic Manuscripts 1390–1490*, 2 vols (London: Harvey Miller, 1996), ii, 340.

[24] Edward Hodnett, *English Woodcuts, 1480–1535* (Oxford: Oxford University Press, 1973), numbers 317, 374. STC 5572, the earliest edition, lacks a title-page (where a woodcut might be located) in its surviving copy: see E. Gordon Duff, *Fifteenth Century English Books* (Oxford: Bibliographical Society, 1917), p. 110.

[25] Hodnett, *English Woodcuts,* nos 78, 795.

read for purposes of devotion or spiritual edification: the Adoration scenes in printed books of hours, in *The Golden Legend* and successive editions of the English *Meditationes vitae Christi*; the Crucifixion woodcut in the *Meditationes* and the *Legend*; the *15 Oes*, de Worde's small reduction of Margery Kempe, Mirk's *Festial*, treatises by Bishop John Alcock, and *The Abbey of the Holy Ghost*.[26]

This last (which perhaps significantly is also a part of the printed *sammelband* in which a copy of *The Three Kings* figures)[27] constitutes an illuminating analogy to *The Three Kings* in both its nature and its forms of circulation; it is another shortish text which seems to have appealed to a wide audience, and over time an increasingly secular one. It survives in over twenty-five manuscripts, and like the *Three Kings*, it was printed and reprinted several times at the end of the fifteenth century and the beginning of the sixteenth by Wynkyn de Worde.[28] Its formulation in a number of the surviving texts suggests that it was often addressed to lay readers (or perhaps to those of quasi-religious status, such as vowesses), and that its audiences were assumed to include both men and women:

> My dere brother and sister, I se weel that many wolde ben in religioun but they mowe nowt [may not] for poverte or for awe or for drede of her kyn [relatives] or for bond of maryage. Therfore I make here a book of relygyoun of the herte, that is of the Abbey of the Holy Goost, that all tho that mow nout been in bodylyche relygyon mow been in gostly.[29]

Its appeal in family or household contexts is suggested by its inclusion by Robert Thornton in Lincoln Cathedral MS 91.[30] It offers a practicable programme for the cultivation of piety outside the context of a religious institution, and yet has the attraction of depending on an allegory which elaborates precisely the corporateness of a religious house—the construction of a spiritual edifice representing Conscience, which takes the form

[26] See Hodnett, *English Woodcuts*.

[27] See n. 19 above.

[28] Edited from Bodl. MS Laud misc. 210 by N. F. Blake, *Middle English Religious Prose* (London: Edward Arnold, 1972), pp. 88–102. For listings of the manuscripts, and other editions, see *Manual*, vii, 2545–47 and R. E. Lewis, N. F. Blake, and A. S. G. Edwards, *Index of Printed Middle English Prose* (New York: Garland, 1985), p. 16 (entry 39). The printed editions are STC 13608.7 [1496?], 13609 [1497?], and 13610 [1500?].

[29] Blake, *Religious Prose*, p. 89.

[30] *Yorkshire Writers*, ed. by C. Horstmann, 2 vols (London: Swan Sonnenschein, 1895), i, 321–37, and G. G. Perry, *Religious Pieces in Prose and Verse*, EETS, os 26 (London: Oxford University Press, 1914), pp. 48–58.

of an abbey building staffed with the personnel necessary for its efficient and proper working, and its defence against assault.[31] As the narrative of *The Three Kings* draws the reader from exotic description to the homelier detail of the nativity at its heart, so the architectural metaphor of the *Abbey* very cleverly turns to inward and individual devotional purposes the features of an external, material, and notably collective institution.

While the *Abbey*'s model of spirituality is clearly workable for and directed to lay people of both sexes, it may have held some special invitingness for female readers, since its concern with the construction of a spiritual edifice in the individual conscience is realized through an elaborate allegory involving female personnel: Charity is abbess, Honesty in charge of the nuns who inhabit the abbey. Some copies of the various French versions (of which the English *Abbey* translates one) were produced specifically for women readers: Bodl. MS Douce 365, for example, was made by David Aubert for Margaret of Burgundy;[32] and it seems likely too that some manuscripts of the English text were directed at female audiences. There is, for instance, a copy in Bodl. MS Eng. poet. a. 1, the Vernon manuscript.[33]

In the light of the *Abbey*'s appropriateness for female audiences or female readers, the contents of the manuscripts in which it occurs together with the *Three Kings* take on a particular interest. Some of these have the air of anthologies with a pronounced interest in women's conduct and their piety; others seem to be collections directed at the devotional needs of a mixed secular audience such as a family or household. In BL Harley 1704, for example (a composite manuscript), the two texts occur in a group of paper gatherings in which one scribe has copied a verse paraphrase of the seven penitential psalms; material mainly in prose on the commandments, the virtues, and the life of Adam;

---

[31] See further Jill Mann, 'Allegorical Buildings in Medieval Literature', *Medium Aevum*, 63 (1994), 191–210; Christiania Whitehead, 'Making a Cloister of the Soul in Medieval Religious Treatises', *Medium Aevum*, 67 (1998), 1–29.

[32] K. Chesney, 'Notes on Some Treatises of Devotion Intended for Margaret of York (MS Douce 365)', *Medium Aevum,* 20 (1951), 11–39. Hope Emily Allen, *Writings Ascribed to Richard Rolle Hermit of Hampole and Materials for his Biography* (New York: D. C. Heath, 1927), p. 337, notes that the *Abbey* 'must have been originally written for women, since the personages are all women, and the original French text was perhaps composed for lay women of high position', and discusses some female readers of the French version.

[33] On the possible audience(s) of the Vernon MS, see most recently *Studies in the Vernon Manuscript*, ed. by Derek Pearsall (Cambridge: D. S. Brewer, 1990).

Chaucer's Prioress's Tale, and a moral lyric. The refrain of this ('In thy most welth wysely be ware') is introduced as a text copied on 'a fayre gold ring' offered to the narrator by a lady, and interestingly invokes one of the pronouncements of Chaucer's Wife of Bath in the form of a cancelled heading which reads 'Alas that euer loue was synne' (cf. The Wife of Bath's Prologue, line 614).[34] In a rather similar collocation the Stonyhurst manuscript (a good quality parchment manuscript, with ornamentation in red, blue, and gold) sets between *The Three Kings* and the *Abbey* Chaucer's Tale of Melibee, and then concludes with the short poem known from its refrain as 'Parce michi domine' (otherwise, 'The Bird with Four Feathers').[35]

BL Add. 36983, the largest of these anthologies, and perhaps the most likely to have served mixed household needs, is an extensive compilation, seemingly produced by several scribes working in association. Together with the *Three Kings* and the *Abbey* it offers an expanded version of *Cursor Mundi*; and a number of texts which combine diversion with advice on conduct or devotion: lives of St Erasmus, St Michael (from the *South English Legendary*), and St Dorothy; *Ipotis* and *The ABC of Aristotle*; the couplet version of *Titus and Vespasian*; William Lychfield's *Dialogue*; the *Speculum Guidonis*, and *The Mirror of Mankind*. Its shorter pieces include Chaucer's 'Truth' and his *ABC*—a devotional address to the virgin, organized according to an alphabetical acrostic, whose evocation of the elements of literacy encapsulates the flavour of instruction which seems to pervade this collection.[36]

The appeal of the *Three Kings* to female readers seems though to have been rather more than a simple consequence of its codicological association with *The Abbey of the Holy Ghost*, and there is evidence of other kinds suggesting that copies were owned and presumably read by women. Horstmann noted in his edition a German translation of 1389 addressed to

---

[34] Described by J. M. Manly and Edith Rickert, *The Text of the Canterbury Tales*, 8 vols (Chicago: University of Chicago Press, 1940), i , 238–40. The portion of the manuscript copied by this one scribe occupies fols 13^r–75^v; it is preceded by twelve parchment leaves on which another, apparently earlier, hand has copied 'leges edwardi & wil*lelmi* regum anglie', and followed by post-medieval material. The anonymous verse contents are respectively IMEV 1591, 3533, 345 (fols 19^r–22^v, part of the treatise, are wanting but have been supplied by a later hand).

[35] Described by Manly and Rickert, *Canterbury Tales*, i, 519–21.

[36] Gisela Guddat-Figge, *A Catalogue of Manuscripts Containing Middle English Romances* (Munich: Fink, 1976), pp. 166–68.

'Frau Elsbeth von Katzenellenbogen, Herrin von Erlbach' (Basle University Library MS 58),[37] and Sir Edmund Rede of Boarstall in Buckinghamshire left in his will a bequest to his wife of 'vnum librum de Gower cum tractatu trium Regum de Coleyn coopertum cum coreo albeo'.[38] The involvement of women readers furthermore seems to be suggested by the form of the English text in BL MS Royal 18 A. x—an anthology of religious works,[39] whose text of the *Three Kings* has been slightly modified so that the initial letters to all the chapters, read in sequence, produce the names of 'Margareta Moningtown' and 'Maud Stranslea'.

Horstmann's edition of the English *Three Kings* noted the inclusion of this device, and supplied the text from MS Royal 18 A. x, with the observation that the same acrostic was to be found in BL MS Cotton Vespasian E. xvi. Horstmann could not identify either of the women named, however, and since the appearance of his edition the origins and transmission of this personalized version of the text have not been much pursued. A plausible candidate for one of the women named is however the 'Margaret Monyngtoun' who was, at least in the 1440s, abbess of the prestigious house of Franciscan nuns at Aldgate in London.[40] MS Royal 18 A. x would certainly have been an appropriate book for someone of this standing: It is made of parchment, with initials worked in red, blue, and silver, and with some ornamentation and rubrication, and its contents (in English or simple Latin) cater with some specificity for women's spiritual concerns.[41] The vestigial form of the acrostic preserved in BL MS Cotton Vespasian E. xvi suggests that the scribe of this text of the *Three Kings* was unaware of it, or ignorant of its significance; the prove-

---

[37] *Three Kings of Cologne*, p. 10.

[38] *The Boarstall Cartulary,* ed. by H. E. Salter, Oxford Historical Society, 88 (1930), 286–95.

[39] Described by G. Warner and J. Gilson, *A Catalogue of Western Manuscripts in the Old Royal and Kings' Collections, in the British Museum*, 4 vols (London: British Museum, 1921), ii, 265–67.

[40] For fuller discussion of this identification, see Julia Boffey, 'Some London Women Readers and a Text of *The Three Kings of Cologne*', *The Ricardian*, 10: 132 (1996), 387–96.

[41] Many of the contents are indexed in Peter Revell, *Fifteenth-Century English Prayers and Meditations* (New York and London: Garland, 1975); and P. G. Jolliffe, *A Check-List of Middle English Prose Writings of Spiritual Guidance* (Toronto: Pontifical Institute of Mediaeval Studies, 1974).

nance and readership of this manuscript in other respects does not advance an argument for the text's appeal to female audiences.[42] But one further copy in BL MS Stowe 951, unknown to Horstmann, preserves the acrostic in a context of some interest, amalgamated with William of Nassington's *Speculum Vitae*, and accompanied by the unique surviving copy of Quixley's translation of Gower's *Traitie pour essampler les amantz mariets*.[43] The very deliberate address to a mixed lay audience here is nicely underlined by the fact that the contents of this volume suggest that it has some claim to be the 'librum de Gower cum tractatu trium Regum de Coleyn' which Sir Edmund Rede left to his wife.

It is tempting to explain the acrostic refiguring of the *Three Kings*, and its circulation with material which draws attention in other ways to the letters of the alphabet, as in some way related to its appeal for audiences concerned with the elementary stages of reading: women notably, or those in their care or supervision. Other reasons might also be advanced to explain the significance of alphabetical patterns in some of the copies.[44] The totemic power of the kings' own names, widely repeated in charms and prayers of the kind mentioned earlier here, may have prompted a fascination, in anything concerning them, with written letters and their signification. Whatever the derivation of these refigured texts, they would seem to demonstrate that certain copies of *The Three Kings* were aiming themselves at private readers whose contact was to be with written letters in a manuscript rather than with something read aloud, since acrostics, unless of the most obvious, are generally lost on a listening audience. De Worde's successive reprintings confirm the enduring appeal of the work well into what was presumably the era of private reading.

For English readers, part of the long-lasting appeal of *The Three Kings of Cologne* may have been the curious mixture of the exotic and the more

---

[42] The contents of the relevant part of the manuscript—*Titus and Vespasian*, and scientific treatises in Latin prose—are described in H. L. D. Ward, *Catalogue of Romances in the Department of Manuscripts in the British Museum*, 3 vols (London: British Museum, 1883–1910), i, 185–86, and in Guddat-Figge, *Catalogue*, pp. 178–79. See also Ralph Hanna III, 'Contextualizing *The Siege of Jerusalem*', *Yearbook of Langland Studies*, 6 (1992), 109–21.

[43] Described by Henry Noble MacCracken, 'Quixley's Ballades Royales (?1402)', *Yorkshire Archaeological Journal*, 20 (1908), 35–50.

[44] The copy made by the London scribe John Shirley in Bodl. MS Ashmole 59 presents an alphabetical acrostic running across the opening letters of chapters 10 to 33; see *Secreta Secretorum: Nine English Versions*, ed. by M. A. Manzalaoui, EETS, os 276 (Oxford: Oxford University Press, 1977), pp. xxxiii–xxxvi.

familiar which their legend distilled. On the one hand they embodied the
mysteries of the east, the unknown, and the foreign—aspects signified in
the supposed potency of their strange names. On the other hand they were
intensely familiar: present in nativity scenes and narratives, in carols, and
other celebrations of Epiphany. Perhaps too we should consider the comparative accessibility of their relics to pilgrims and travellers. Caxton
after all was only one of many English people who resided in Cologne.
The journey related by Margery Kempe which took her from Danzig to
Aachen could have taken in the city and its relics. Robert Langton's early
sixteenth-century guide for pilgrims, printed by Copland, mentions 'the iij
kynges in ecclesia maiori' first in a long list of things to venerate in
Cologne.[45] Middle English readers of the three kings' legend may have
viewed the exotica of the narrative as simply one aspect of a spiritual
journey designed to lead inwards, from features of the external, material
world to the responsibilities of the inner self; and a notable number of
these readers seem to have been women.

---

[45] *The Pilgrimage of Robert Langton,* transcribed with an introduction and notes by E. M.
Blackie (Cambridge, MA: Harvard University Press, 1924), pp. 35–36, and see also the
facsimile introduced by Robert Brian Tate and Thorlac Turville-Petre, *Two Pilgrim
Itineraries of the Later Middle Ages* (Santiago: Xunta de Galicia, 1995).

'This is a deed bok, the tother a quick': Theatre and the Drama of Salvation in the *Book* of Margery Kempe

CAROL M. MEALE

sithen it is leveful [permissable] to han the miraclis of God peintid, why is it not as wel leveful to han the miraclis of God pleyed, sithen men mowen [since men can] bettere reden the wille of God and his mervelous werkis in the pleyinge of hem than in the peintinge? And betere they ben holden in mennes minde and oftere rehersid by the pleyinge of hem than by the peintinge, for this is a deed bok, the tother a quick. (*A Tretise of Miraclis Pleyinge*)[1]

Whilst the 'performative' aspects of the narrative recounted in Margery Kempe's *Book* have been acknowledged by critics, they have, in the main, been examined in the context of the influences offered in the spiritual guides and biographies, many of them about, if not authored by, women, which appear to have constituted the primary form of instruction relayed to Kempe by her religious counsellors.[2] The specifically gendered nature

---

[1] *A Tretise of Miraclis Pleyinge*, ed. by Clifford Davidson, Early Drama, Art, and Music Monograph Series, 19 (Kalamazoo: Medieval Institute Publications, Western Michigan University, 1993), p. 98. All subsequent quotations are taken from this edition.

[2] See, e.g., Gail McMurray Gibson, *The Theater of Devotion: East Anglian Drama and Society in the Late Middle Ages* (Chicago and London: University of Chicago Press, 1989), Chapter Three; Ralph Hanna III, 'Some Norfolk Women and Their Books, ca. 1390–1440', in *The Cultural Patronage of Medieval Women*, ed. by June Hall McCash (Athens and London: University of Georgia Press, 1996), pp. 288–305; Carolyne Larrington, 'The Candlemas Vision and Marie d'Oignies's Role in its Dissemination', in *New Trends in Feminine Spirituality: The Holy Women of Liège and Their Impact*, ed. by Juliette Dor, Lesley Johnson, and Jocelyn Wogan-Browne, Medieval Women: Texts and Contexts, 2 (Turnhout: Brepols, 1999), pp. 195–214.

of 'participatory' visions—that is, those in which the subject becomes
actively involved with the protagonists of biblical history—has been
stressed in recent studies, and a subtle, yet clear, differentiation drawn
between these and superficially similar accounts of ecstatic meditation
given by male mystics.[3] Thus, crucially, a female lineage for Kempe's
particular manifestation of affective piety has been painstakingly, and
convincingly, established.[4] The battle for the authorization of female
spirituality is not, however, the only politically contested issue inscribed
within Kempe's text.[5] It is my suggestion in this essay that, without
diverting attention from Kempe's literary debt to her continental predecessors, it is possible to add another dimension to an understanding of her
diversity of religious experience and its recording: that of popular drama,
and the questions both of the constraints surrounding its accessibility to
medieval women, and of the status accorded it within contemporary
culture.[6]

---

[3]   Larrington, 'The Candlemas Vision'.

[4]   As so often, Hope Emily Allen set the lead for all subsequent work in this area in her
Introductory Note and Notes to *The Book of Margery Kempe*, ed. by Sanford Brown
Meech and Hope Emily Allen, EETS, os 212 (London: Oxford University Press, 1940 for
1939). All citations in this paper are from this edition, by book, chapter, line, and page
number. Runic letters have been silently transliterated. Recent publications stressing the
debt to foreign antecedents include: Susan Dickman, 'Margery Kempe and the Continental
Tradition of the Pious Woman', in *The Medieval Mystical Tradition in England: Exeter
Symposium III*, ed. by Marion Glasscoe (Cambridge: D. S. Brewer, 1984), pp. 150–68;
Karma Lochrie, *Margery Kempe and Translations of the Flesh* (Philadelphia: University
of Pennsylvania Press, 1991); Lynn Staley, *Margery Kempe's Dissenting Fictions*
(University Park: Pennsylvania State University Press, 1994); and Janette Dillon, 'Holy
Women and Their Confessors or Confessors and Their Holy Women? Margery Kempe and
Continental Tradition', in *Prophets Abroad: The Reception of Continental Holy Women in
Late-Medieval England*, ed. by Rosalynn Voaden (Cambridge: D. S. Brewer, 1996),
pp. 115–40.

[5]   In this essay I follow the practice of distinguishing between 'Kempe' the author/agent
of authorship, and 'Margery', her fictional persona, as established by Staley, *Margery
Kempe's Dissenting Fictions*.

[6]   For debate over women's access and control regarding the stage see Meg Twycross,
'"Transvestism" in the Mystery Plays', *Medieval English Theatre*, 5: 2 (1983), 123–80;
Richard Rastall, 'Female Roles in All-Male Casts', *Medieval English Theatre*, 7: 1 (1985),
25–50; whilst Peter Meredith envisages a female actor for the Virgin ('Performance, Verse
and Occasion in the N-Town *Mary Play*', in *Individuality and Achievement in Middle
English Poetry*, ed. by O. S. Pickering (Cambridge: D. S. Brewer, 1997), pp. 205–21, p.
206 n. 1).

The potential of theatrical display and discourse to spark controversy by entering into political debate remains as true today as it was in the Middle Ages[7] and, given the heavily politicized nature of religion throughout the medieval period—particularly, perhaps, in England during Kempe's lifetime[8]—it is hardly surprising that both the established Church and its outlawed offshoots attempted to intervene in the production and reception of religious plays. When, for instance, the author of *A Tretise of Miraclis Pleyinge* inveighed against the dramatic enactment of events taken from biblical and religious history, he informed his rhetorically-structured rebuttal of such 'gamen and play' (p. 98) as a legitimate means of stimulating popular devotion by a comparison with painting—'a deed bok'—which, he evidently believed, had a lesser impact on the imagination than did performance—characterized by him as 'quick', or living (p. 49 above). It was this very quality of vitality which incurred his censure. 'Miracle' plays, he stated unequivocally, were empty signifiers ('singnis ... withoute dedis') which encouraged worldly distraction and temptation, diverting both attention and money away from the life of active charity (pp. 99–101). Yet, written at some point in the final decades of the fourteenth century, or in the early years of that following, this so-far anonymous Lollard writer's critique of the medieval theatre affords us, as has long been recognized, some of the earliest textual evidence of the possibilities plays offered for promoting affective piety. He was not alone in this perception amongst those with Lollard persuasions. Lines from the contemporary alliterative poem, *Pierce the Ploughman's Creed*, likewise attest to the emotive power of 'miracles', but this author elaborates his distaste for the genre by making the pointedly gendered remark concerning the effect upon *women* of apocryphal representations such as the presence of the midwives at the nativity.[9] This latter is a proposition which, as I shall go on to emphasize, holds an especial relevance for discussion of the materials which were available for Kempe to draw on in the narrative fashioning of Margery's visions.

---

[7]   See, e.g., with reference to York, Sarah Beckwith, 'Ritual, Theater, and Social Space in the York Corpus Christi Cycle', in *Bodies and Disciplines: Intersections of Literature and History in Fifteenth-Century England*, ed. by Barbara A. Hanawalt and David Wallace, Medieval Cultures, 9 (Minneapolis and London: University of Minnesota Press, 1996), pp. 63–86. Cf. n. 36 below.

[8]   See the essay by Sarah Rees Jones in this volume.

[9]   *The Piers Plowman Tradition*, ed. by Helen Barr (London: Dent, 1993), p. 64/77–78.

The composition of these works during the period coincident with the childhood and early womanhood of Margery Kempe leads me to argue that the nature of Kempe's devotion and, indeed, elements of her *Book*'s structure and expression, manifest the effectiveness of the dynamics of performance upon an individual consciousness, occluded though this influence undoubtedly is in the process of translating and mediating the experiential into the authority of the written word. I shall additionally suggest that the possible reasoning underlying this occlusion offers, of itself, an additional insight into Kempe's understanding of her religious project, as it was finally realized in the pages of her *Book*.

The theory that Kempe was acquainted with sacred drama from a young age is an attractive, although hypothetical one. In the Chamberlains' accounts for Bishop's Lynn for 1384/5, for example, one of the five occasions of the mayoralty of John Brunham, Kempe's father,[10] there is a record of 3s 4d being paid 'ludentibus inter*ludium* die Corp*or*is Xpi'', but there is no indication of the play's audience or evidence that this constituted more than a 'one-off' performance. Given John Brunham's standing, however, Kempe, as a girl of about twelve years old, may well have seen it.[11]

Greater certainty exists about Kempe's witnessing of one of the great municipal cycles. Whilst a detailed chronology of Kempe's life and spiritual development is hindered by the absence of narrative sequentiality within the *Book*, one of the key moments in her text may be pinpointed with accuracy. This is the account of her journey from York to Bridlington one 'Fryday on Mydsomer Evyn', during the course of which Kempe/Margery negotiated with her husband to take a vow of chastity within marriage (I, 11). Supplementary archival sources and biographical

---

[10] *Book of Margery Kempe*, ed. Meech and Allen, Appendix III, pp. 359–62; Anthony Goodman, 'The Piety of John Brunham's Daughter, of Lynn', in *Medieval Women*, ed. by Derek Baker, Studies in Church History, Subsidia, 1 (Oxford: Blackwell, 1978), pp. 347–58, esp. pp. 351–52 for Brunham's urban patriciate standing.

[11] *Records of Plays and Players in Norfolk and Suffolk 1330–1642*, ed. by David Galloway and John Wasson, Malone Society Collections XI (Oxford: Oxford University Press for the Malone Society, 1980/1), p. 38. It is possible that Norwich, as a major regional centre, mounted a cycle of plays, which Kempe could have seen, but only early-sixteenth-century fragments remain, and the situation is therefore ambiguous: see Alan H. Nelson, 'On Recovering the Lost Norwich Corpus Christi Cycle', *Comparative Drama*, 4 (1970/71), 241–52; and Joanna Dutka, 'Mystery Plays at Norwich: Their Formation and Development', *Leeds Studies in English*, 10 (1978), 107–20 and 'The Lost Dramatic Cycle of Norwich and the Grocers' Play of the Fall of Man', *Review of English Studies*, NS 35 (1984), 1–13. Cf. n. 20, below.

information concerning some of the individuals whom she mentions in connection with this incident identify the year as 1413.[12] The previous day, Thursday 22 June, was the feast of Corpus Christi (on only one other occasion in the fifteenth century did this celebration precede Midsummer Eve),[13] and surviving documents from York strongly suggest that the civic play-cycle, as opposed to any other religious play—the Creed play or the *Pater Noster* play, or the ecclesiastically-promoted procession alone— was mounted on 22 June that year.[14] Allowing for this circumstantial detail, the textual evidence of the climactic set-piece meditation on the Crucifixion in Book I (80), in which both the imaging of the scene and the language deployed have strong echoes of what has now come to be known as the York Crucifixion Pageant (XXXV), takes on an especial significance.[15]

I shall confine my discussion here to the salient correspondences, which transcend the inevitable generic stylistic differences. Margery's observation that

> sche sey the Iewys wyth gret violens rendyn of owr Lordys precyows body a cloth of sylke, the which was cleuen & hardyd so sadly & streitly to owr Lordys body wyth hys precyows blood that it drow a-wey al the hyde & al the skyn of hys blissyd body & renewyd hys preciows wowndys & mad the blod to renne down al a-bowtyn on euery syde (pp.191–92/35–36, 1–5),

---

[12] *Book of Margery Kempe*, ed. Meech and Allen, pp. 269, 23/9n. (Book I/11); 333, note to 187/19ff. (Book I/79).

[13] This was in 1424: see *Handbook of Dates for Students of English History*, ed. by C. R. Cheney, corrected edn (London: Royal Historical Society, 1991), p. 149, Table 33.

[14] See Margaret Dorrell, 'Two Studies of the York Corpus Christi Play', *Leeds Studies in English*, 6 (1972), 63–111; and Alexandra F. Johnston, 'The Plays of the Religious Guilds of York: The Creed Play and the Pater Noster Play, *Speculum*, 50 (1975), 55–88 and 'The Guild of Corpus Christi and the Procession of Corpus Christi in York', *Mediaeval Studies*, 38 (1976), 372–84; also R. B. Dobson, 'Craft Guilds and City: The Historical Origins of the York Mystery Plays Reassessed', in *The Stage as Mirror: Civic Theatre in Late Medieval Europe*, ed. by Alan E. Knight (Cambridge: D. S. Brewer, 1997), pp. 91–105.

[15] All quotations taken from *The York Plays*, ed. by Richard Beadle (London: Edward Arnold, 1982). Although this pageant, in the York *Ordo Paginarum* of 1415, was noted as two originally separate episodes played by the Painters and the Latteners, their amalgamation into one, *c.* 1422, which was placed under the control of the Pinners, does not seem to have entailed any rewriting by the so-called 'York Realist', which lends weight to textual comparison: see J. W. Robinson, 'The Art of the York Realist', *Modern Philology*, 60 (1963), 241–51 and Clifford Davidson, 'The Realism of the York Realist and the York Passion', *Speculum*, 50 (1975), 270–83, esp. p. 275. The comparison was first pointed out by Allen, *Book of Margery Kempe*, p. 335, n. to 192ff., but was not developed.

acts as a commentary on the words of the three soldiers in the Shearman's
pageant (York Plays, XXXIV/p. 314/311–21), in which the first dis-
passionately states that Christ shall 'naked as a stone be stedde', and he
and one of his fellows then discuss the fact that Christ's 'clothis', due to
the 'bloode that he has bledde' 'tille his sidis … clyng'. The third soldier
dismisses these practicalities in his words 'Whedyr thei clynge or cleue /
Naked he schalle be ledde'. Even more striking than this concentration on
the particular, however, are the technical details of the crucifixion. To
begin with, there is the similarity of Christ's mounting upon the cross.
Nicholas Love (whose early-fifteenth-century translation of the pseudo-
Bonaventuran *Meditationes Vitae Christi* was almost certainly known to
Kempe)[16] offered alternative methods of execution for his audience to
meditate upon, allowing each member to choose which he or she individually found to be most effective in their imaginative identification with
Christ's suffering: the first simply involves Christ mounting the cross by
means of upright ladders (pp. 176–77/32–43/24).[17] Not only is this
method less dramatically shocking than the alternative, by which Christ is
tied and nailed to the prostrate instrument of his death, which is then
raised by ropes and dropped into the waiting mortise, but it would also
have been technically impossible to stage with any conviction, and would
consequently have carried little emotive weight. The workmanlike
approach to their task adopted by the soldiers in the York Pinners'
Crucifixion Play (XXXV), in which they assemble their 'hammeres and
nayles large and lange' (p. 316/30), comment on the misplaced bore holes
previously drilled to accommodate Christ's nailed hands and feet, and, to
stretch His limbs into position, use a 'roope' or 'corde' to 'tugge hym to,
by toppe and taile' (p. 318/131/113–14), bears direct comparison with
Margery's account of how she saw

---

[16] All quotations from Nicholas Love's *Mirror of the Blessed Life of Jesus Christ*, ed. by
Michael G. Sargent (New York and London: Garland, 1992). Allen, again, initially
pointed out analogies with Love in the notes to *Book of Margery Kempe*; for the most
recent discussion of Kempe's reading see Hanna, 'Some Norfolk Women and Their
Books', esp. pp. 295, 296–97.

[17] Important textual comparisons must also be noted here between the *York* Crucifixion
and the contemporary metrical *Northern Passion*: see the edition by Frances Foster, 3 vols,
EETS, os 145, 147, 183 (London: Kegan Paul, Trench, Trübner; and Oxford University
Press, 1913, 1916, 1930), pp. 190–93; and cf. *The Cambridge Companion to Medieval
English Theatre*, ed. by Richard Beadle (Cambridge: Cambridge University Press, 1994),
pp. 104, 150 and 162 n. 16. There is no evidence to suggest, however, that Kempe would
have had any knowledge of the poem.

> wyth hyr gostly eye [spiritual sight] ... the Iewys festenyd ropis on the other hand, for the senwys & veynys wer so schrynkyn wyth peyne that it myth not come to the hole that thei had morkyn therfor, & drowyn theron to makyn it mete wyth the hole (p. 192/17–21).

Emphasis is placed in both texts on the physical pains endured by Christ: Margery saw 'how hys precyows body schrynkyd & drow to-gedyr wyth alle senwys & veynys in that precyows body for peyne that it suffyrd & felt' (p. 192/13–16), whilst in the pageant the second soldier comments 'Yaa, assoundir are bothe synnous and veynis / On ilke a side, so haue we soughte' (p. 319/147–48). The jolting and shuddering of the cross as it is dropped into the mortise and Christ's body is further distorted by pain is, again, horrifically conveyed through the media both of dramatic action and its accompanying dialogue, and prose. In the York Plays, as he issues instructions for the cross to be lowered from the height to which it has been raised, the fourth soldier comments laconically that all Christ's 'bones / Are asoundre nowe on sides seere. / This fallyng was more felle / Than all the harmes he hadde' (p. 321/223–26). Margery, for her part, paints a verbal picture of the event:

> a-non sche sey hem takyn vp the Crosse wyth owr Lordys body hangyng ther-on & madyn gret noyse & gret crye & lyftyd it vp fro the erthe a certeyn distawnce & sithyn letyn the Crosse fallyn down in-to the morteys. & than owr Lordys body schakyd & schoderyd, & alle the joyntys of that blisful body brostyn & wentyn a-sundyr (p. 192/33–38).

Although Nicholas Love's *Mirror of the Blessed Life of Jesu Christ* has in general been credited with helping to shape Margery's meditations, and giving them a pseudo-'dramatic' form,[18] there are sufficient essential differences between his handling of the Crucifixion and that employed by the playwrights to arouse some scepticism. As orthodox and influential as Love's work unquestionably was for the purposes of arousing meditative compassion,[19] it is also briefer, more distanced and intellectualized, missing the felt and witnessed immediacy of Christ's pain in the narratives of both the Plays and Margery's *Book*:

---

[18] Gibson, *Theater of Devotion*, esp. pp. 49–53, regards Love as the defining influence upon Kempe's 'performative' narrative strategy.

[19] The text was licensed for publication and circulation by Thomas Arundel, archbishop of Canterbury, in 1410: see the Latin authorization in Sargent, *Mirror*, p. 7. Margery, of course, had a personal interview with Arundel (I/14/pp. 34–35/26–36, 1–15).

... first liggyng the crosse on the gronde'. Thei nailede him there vpon, &
after with him so hangyng thei liften vp the crosse & festen it done in the
erthe.

   And if it were done in this manere', than maist thou se, howe vileynsly
thei taken him as a ribaude & kasten him done vpon the crosse, & than as
wode thefes drowen on bothe sides first hees handes & after hees feete, &
so nailede him fast to the crosse, & after with alle hir [their] miht liften vp
the crosse with him hangyng als hye as thei miht & than lete it falle done
into the morteise.

   In the which falle as thou may vndurstande, alle the senewes to-breken,
to His souereyn peyne (*Mirror*, p. 177/26–37).[20]

Comparing all three versions, Margery's seems to function as reportage
of action she has seen and absorbed into her meditative consciousness.

   I would add to the circumstantial evidence that she had been in York
whilst the plays were being staged the fact that the whole of the city was
given over to the performances, which lasted approximately sixteen
hours.[21] The cumulative evidence would therefore seem to suggest that
Margery was one of the many 'strangers' who witnessed the cycle and
that it created an indelible memory which she was later able to draw upon
in her meditations. Women may have been excluded from determining the
nature of dramatic structure, from acting itself, and in some cases,
perhaps, from viewing plays at all,[22] but their access to the great
municipal performances must be a given: the author of the *Tretise of
Miraclis Pleyinge* concedes as much (p. 102). Margery may even have
been attracted to the city in the first place by the cycle's widespread
fame: she was, for example, sufficiently acquainted with some of the

[20] For discussion and bibliography concerning Love's probable influence on the composition of the N-Town Plays see Sargent, *Mirror*, pp. lxvi–lxix. Although it is conceivable
that Margery saw performances of some of the individual pageants before their incorporation into the existing cycle (the surviving manuscript, London, British Library MS Cotton
Vespasian D. viii, contains only one date, that of 1468, at the end of the Purification play: see
the facsimile, *The N-Town Plays*, with introduction by Peter Meredith and Stanley J.
Kahrl, Leeds Texts and Monographs, Medieval Drama Facsimiles, IV (Leeds: University
of Leeds, School of English, 1977), p. xiii and fol. 100ᵛ), this is not capable of proof. See
Peter Meredith's reconstruction of the Passion sequence in his edition, *The Passion Play
From the N.Town Manuscript* (London and New York: Longman, 1990), for the text.

[21] See the discussion and bibliography in Richard Beadle, 'The York Cycle', in Beadle,
The Cambridge Companion to Medieval English Theatre, pp. 85–108.

[22] For the possible exclusion of women from an extant morality play, see John Marshall,
'O 3e souereyns that sytte and 3e brothern þat stonde ryght wppe': Addressing the
Audience of *Mankind*, in *European Medieval Drama*, 1, 189–202.

lesser-known manifestations of popular piety to seek out the confessor of the late St John of Bridlington (I/11;52/p.125/34–37);[23] whilst on her later expedition to York in 1417, when questioned by the ecclesiastical authorities, she answered that her purpose in being there was to 'come on pilgrimage to offyr her at Sent William' (I/51/12–13), the late archbishop of the city (d. 1154), whose commemorative window in the Minster may well have been under construction, or planning, at this time.[24]

Other, less clear-cut references in the *Book* may have arisen through Margery's experience of drama. On several occasions, for instance, she refers to the 'so swet & delectable' 'melodye' in Paradise, which formed part of her ecstatic state from the time of her conversion onwards (I/3/35/79). The mental and spiritual inspiration for these auditory manifestations could, it must be acknowledged, have come rather from a variety of other sources: liturgical song; her attested knowledge of Rolle's *Incendium Amoris*, in which the idea of heavenly 'canor' is elaborated upon;[25] Hilton's *Of Angels' Song* (five of the six surviving manuscripts of which also contained his *Scale of Perfection*, with which she was acquainted);[26] or common iconographic representations such as those of the famous carved angels holding musical instruments at Lincoln Cathedral and Beverley Minster. (For visits to the latter places see I/14/54.)[27] The fact, however, that in her extended meditation on the Passion in I/79, Christ comforts his mother by prophesying her Assumption, mentioning 'al [the] maner of musyk, melody, & joy' (p. 188/29) that will accompany her reception, might argue for a more specific

---

[23] On this saint see Jennifer R. Bray, 'Concepts of Sainthood in Fourteenth-Century England', *Bulletin of the John Rylands Library*, 66 (1984), 40–77, (pp. 43–46).

[24] David Hugh Farmer, *The Oxford Dictionary of Saints*, 2nd edn (Oxford: Oxford University Press, 1987), p. 439, describes the 'strong local cult' which surrounded this saint.

[25] *Incendium Amoris*, ed. by Margaret Deansley (Manchester: Manchester University Press, 1915): see Nicholas Watson, *Richard Rolle and the Invention of Authority*, Cambridge Studies in Medieval Literature (Cambridge: Cambridge University Press, 1991), pp. 113–41.

[26] *Two Minor Works of Walter Hilton: Eight Chapters on Perfection and Of Angels' Song*, ed. by Toshiyuki Takamiya (Tokyo: privately printed, 1980); see pp. 3–8 for manuscript descriptions. I am most grateful to Professor Takamiya for sending me a copy of his edition.

[27] See Arthur Gardner, *Lincoln Angels*, Lincoln Minster Pamphlets (First Series), 6 and K. A. Macmahon, *Beverley Minster* (London: Pitkin Pictorials, 1970), p. 19. The possible influence of iconography on Kempe's thinking and feeling cannot be ruled out, though it forms a separate study from the one undertaken here; cf. n. 30 below.

attribution of the influence of contemporary plays, since the idea that 'alle hefne makyth melody' at the Assumption, as well as at other moments of angelic intervention, is now documented as a well-established aspect of medieval theatrical practice.[28]

On a broader scale, the techniques of dramatic production whereby ordinary citizens of towns or inhabitants of particular villages adopted the roles of biblical 'characters' may be paralleled stylistically within the *Book* by Margery's envisioning of herself as an active participant within biblical history, both by engaging in dialogue—in a manner which may, with no distortion, be described as dramatic—with the principal protagonists of the Christian story; and by direct impersonation. In Book I/6, for instance, she prays to St Anne 'to be hir mayden & ... seruawnt', acts as midwife at the Virgin's birth and nurtures her until the Conception and, in a somewhat strange reversal of sanctioned authority, herself tells Mary that she will 'be the Modyr of God', eliciting from her the famous response that she 'wold' that she 'wer worthy to be the handmayden of hir that xuld conseive the Sone of God' (p. 18/16–17,21–24).[29] Margery then proceeds to accompany Mary on her visit to Elizabeth, begs the latter to intercede with Mary so that she might continue to serve her, then performs the role of midwife at the Nativity, all the while begging for lodgings, swaddling clothes, and food. It can scarcely be coincidental in this female-centred text that Zacharias and Joseph—both present during some or all of these scenes in the great municipal play cycles—are absent in this scenario.[30] Later, in Book 1/28, during her first vision of the

---

[28] The quotation is from the Assumption pageant in *The N-Town Play*, ed. by Stephen Spector, 2 vols, EETS, SS 11, 12 (Oxford: Oxford University Press, 1991), 1, p. 407/494–95. For discussion and bibliography see Richard Rastall, *The Heaven Singing: Music in Early English Religious Drama*, 1 (Cambridge: D. S. Brewer, 1996). It should be noted that in the *Middle English Dictionary* 'melodie', 2 (a), is defined as 'Vocal or instrumental music'.

[29] For a comparable, though not identical, appropriation of authority by a female visionary see the *Revelations* of St Elizabeth of Hungary (or more probably Toess) in *Women's Writing in Middle English*, ed. by Alexandra Barratt (London and New York: Longman, 1992), p. 79/141–43.

[30] The N-Town and Chester cycles include the traditional two midwives (one of them sceptical as to the nature of Christ as Son of God) in their Nativity scenes, but it is Joseph who is instrumental in fetching them to aid Mary. As observed in n. 27 above, visual iconography may have suggested this form of vision to Kempe: she must certainly have been familiar with Giotto's magnificent representation of the scene (in which, too, Joseph is present) in the lower Basilica of St Francis at Assisi, where she saw 'owyr Ladys kerche' in August 1414: I/31/p. 79/8–28. She may also have been familiar with stained glass and

Passion during her pilgrimage to Jerusalem, Kempe's account of her response to her contemplation of the Crucifixion in which 'sche fel down & cryed wyth lowde voys, wondyrfully turnyng & wrestyng hir body on euery syde, spredyng hir armys a-brode as yyf sche xuld a deyd' (p. 70/17–20), is not, I would suggest, her own form of Imitatio[31] but, rather, her adoption of the role of Mary Magdalene, a saint (and, like Margery herself, a one-time sinner) with whom, from frequent references to her within the text, she especially identified.[32]

In these examples, as in others, Margery goes far beyond the contemplative bounds advocated by contemporary, or near-contemporary, male spiritual advisers. Nicholas Love, for instance, whilst frequently enjoining members of his audience to 'beholde' the events of the lives of Mary and Christ, positions each one as spectator rather than actor, encouraging 'sorrouful compassion' for Christ's death (p. 181/18), at the same time highlighting the theological lessons to be drawn from each meditation. Equally, although Love exhorts his readers/listeners to use

---

alabaster images, though their destruction has, in the main, left no trace. One midwife is shown about to swaddle Christ in the Nativity in the East window of the church of St Peter Mancroft in Norwich, but the re-glazing of this window is dated *c.* 1440–60, and there is no evidence of the iconography of the glass which it replaced: see Christopher Woodforde, *The Norwich School of Glass Painting in the Fifteenth Century* (London: Oxford University Press, 1950), frontispiece and pp. 16, 25. Francis Cheetham, *English Medieval Alabasters* (Oxford: Phaidon. Christie's, 1984), reproduces one Nativity image which includes the midwives (Cat. no. 106, p. 179), but there is no evidence as to provenance. A study of the European tradition which is of relevance is Henrik Cornell, *The Iconography of the Nativity of Christ* (Uppsala: A.-B. Lundequistska Bokhandeln, 1924). It is striking that it is only in women mystics' visions of the Nativity that Joseph is absent. See, e.g., *The Liber Celestis of St Bridget of Sweden*, 1, ed. by Roger Ellis, EETS, OS 291 (Oxford: Oxford University Press, 1987), Book VII, Chapter XXII, p. 486/4, in which Joseph 'wente ... furthe, for [Mary] was nere time of deliuering' (unlike Margery, however, Bridget does not engage in dialogue with the Virgin).

[31] *Contra* Sarah Beckwith, *Christ's Body: Identity, Culture and Society in Late Medieval Writings* (London and New York: Routledge, 1993), pp. 81–82.

[32] According to the scribe, the rewriting of the extant copy of the *Book* began 'on the day next aftyr Mary Maudelyn' (Proheme to Book I/p. 6/22–23). Susan Eberly's article, 'Margery Kempe, St Mary Magdalene, and Patterns of Contemplation', *Downside Review*, 368 (1989), 209–33, is suggestive; Suzanne Craymer's, 'Margery Kempe's Imitation of Mary Magdalene and the "Digby Plays"', *Mystics Quarterly*, 19 (1993), 173–81, less so, due to the ahistorical comparisons drawn with these later-fifteenth-century plays. Gibson, *Theater of Devotion*, pp. 64–65, proposes an identification on Kempe/Margery's part with St Margaret.

their 'deuoute ymaginacion', instructing them to 'confort oure lady' and
Christ's friends, following His death, by 'praiyng hem to ete sumwhat, for
yit thei ben fastyng, & after to slepe' (p. 190/15–18), and invoking the
notion of Holy service which so appealed to Margery, active participation
in meditative scenes of the kind Margery was evidently inclined to would,
I suspect, have been viewed by him as of a kind with the 'grete foly &
gostly perile', the seeking '*curiously* in ymaginacion' (my italics), which
he so condemns in his supplementary text to the *Mirror*, *De Sacramento*
(p. 229/31–32).[33]

The comparison with Love and the noting of the difference in his
methodology whereby he endorses techniques of meditative identification
within strictly-defined limits proves useful in regard to another of the
features of Kempe's text which continues to resist interpretation. By
analogy with Love's didactic approach, it is through stylistic and linguistic analysis of Margery's own contemplations that is possible to
detect an awareness—though whether that of Kempe, or her clerical
scribe remains a matter for debate[34]—of the suspicion on the part of
religious conformists to which her text may have been subject. In the
deployment of such phrases as Christ's answering 'to hir mend' (I/35/p.
88/35), or the speaking of various saints 'to the vndirstondyng of hir
sowle' (I/87/p. 215/15–16) the audience becomes aware of the reins that
are periodically tightened upon her imagination. Such phrases appear to
constitute an attempt to defuse possible misunderstandings or misreadings
of her form of spirituality, serving the function of being salutary reminders to Margery's readers and/or listeners to retain the decorum of
distance: that is, reducing the immediacy of her experiences, whilst
simultaneously authorizing their validity.

One additional facet of Margery's engagement with dramatic, or semi-
dramatic, spectacle I would wish to explore, but which is too complex an

---

[33] Love sets out his definition of the limits which should be placed on the imagination in
his Proheme: 'so that it be not ayeyns the beleue or gude maneres'; the guarantors of
'the beleue' are the Church fathers, 'seynt Gregory & other doctours' (p. 11/4, 1–2).

[34] For contrasting opinions as to whether the scribe should be attributed with co-author-
ship, see, e.g., John C. Hirsch, 'Author and Scribe in the *Book of Margery Kempe*',
Medium Aevum, 44 (1975), 245–50; Robert C. Ross, 'Oral Life, Written Text: The
Genesis of The Book of Margery Kempe', *Yearbook of English Studies*, 22 (1992), 226–
37; and Sue Ellen Holbrook, '"About Her": Margery Kempe's Book of Feeling and
Working', in *The Idea of Medieval Literature: New Essays on Chaucer and Medieval
Culture in Honor of Donald R. Howard*, ed. by James M. Dean and Christian K. Zacher
(Newark: University of Delaware Press, 1992), pp. 265–84.

issue to develop within the confines of this essay, is that which Hans-Jürgen Diller has termed the 'liturgico-dramatic interface':[35] that is, church ritual. Kempe's recounting of her emotional responses to ecclesiastically-approved processions and certain liturgical celebrations, alike, offer a unique insight into their efficacy as a means of inciting devotion. It is now widely accepted, for example, that Corpus Christi processions were not as socially inclusive as was once thought,[36] and Margery's own behaviour as a participant highlights the potential these occasions held to promote civic disruption. When in Bristol in 1417, for instance, during the period prior to her embarkation for St James Compostella, she walked in the procession sponsored by the parish church of All Saints,[37] her 'holy thowtys & meditacyon, sor wepyng & boystows sobbyng' caused her to have to withdraw to a sympathizer's house after a gentle reproof from a 'good woman' (I/45/p. 107/29–30). But her treatment in Hull later in the year, when she walked in some unidentified 'processyon' and earned outright hostility ('a gret woman al-to-despysed hir, & ... [m]any other folke seyd that sche xulde be sett in preson', I/53/p. 129/7–9), indicates that civic order and individual composure were seen by some as commensurate with each other, and not to be infringed by emotionalism, whether politically or devotionally inspired.

In her native Lynn, on the other hand, where she was not a 'stranger' as in Bristol or Hull, her outbursts, whilst causing obvious embarrassment to many of her fellow townspeople, also endeared her to them 'at her [their] deyng' (I/72/p. 172/36): her uncontrollable sobbing, whether induced by the festival of Corpus Christi, or by witnessing the carriage of the Host to the sick and dying, presumably engendered belief in her powers as intercessors for their souls. The significance of her vizualizations of the Gospel which had their genesis in the liturgical services covering the

---

[35] Hans-Jürgen Diller, *The Middle English Mystery Play: A Study in Dramatic Speech and Form*, trans. by Frances Wessels (Cambridge: Cambridge University Press, 1992), p. 11.

[36] See Mervyn James, 'Ritual, Drama and Social Body in the Late Medieval English Town', *Past and Present*, 98 (1983), 3–29, and Benjamin R. McRee, 'Unity or Division? The Social Meaning of Guild Ceremony in Urban Communities', in *City and Spectacle in Medieval Europe*, ed. by Barbara A. Hanawalt and Kathryn L. Reyerson, Medieval Studies at Minnesota, 6 (Minneapolis and London: University of Minnesota Press, 1994), pp. 189–207, *contra* Charles Phythian-Adams, 'Ceremony and the Citizen: The Communal Year at Coventry', in *Crisis and Order in English Towns 1500–1700*, ed. by Peter Clark and Paul Slack (London: Routledge and Kegan Paul, 1972), pp. 57–85.

[37] Martha C. Skeeters, *Community and Clergy: Bristol and the Reformation c. 1530–c. 1570* (Oxford: Clarendon Press, 1993), pp. 28 and 217–18, nn. 96–98.

period from Palm Sunday until Easter morning, too, deserve more critical attention than they have received. Margery's own church of St Margaret's, unlike its rival chapel of St Nicholas, does not seem to have had an Easter Sepulchre as such,[38] and therefore is unlikely to have mounted mimetic practices recorded from elsewhere in the country (such as the guarding of the Tomb by the soldiers until the symbolic moment of the Resurrection). But her detailed reporting of the Easter liturgy is of no little interest when looked at from the point of view of the evolution of the non-institutionalized form of the 'Easter Play' as it developed within individual parishes during the later Middle Ages.[39] Whilst her account of the festival as celebrated in St Margaret's Church (I/78) leaps from a description of the congregation's procession around the 'chirch-yerd' on Palm Sunday to Easter morning, the proceedings conducted by the clergy at this latter time give a tantalizing glimpse into local practice:

> ... whan the preste toke the crosse-staf & smet on the chirche-dore & the dor openyd a-geyn hym, & than the prest entryd wyth the Sacrament & al the pepil folwyng in-to chirche, than thowt sche that owr Lord spak to the Deuyl & openyd Helle-yatys confowndyng hym & alle hys oste & what grace & goodnes he schewd to tho sowlys, delyueryng hem fro eyer-lestyng preson mawgre the Deuyl & alle hys ... Whan thei wer comyn in-to the cherch & sche beheld the preystys knelyng be-forn the Crucifixe, and, as thei songyn, the preyste whech executyd the seruyse that day drow up a cloth be-for the Crucyfixe thre tymys, euery tyme heyar than other, that the pepil xulde se the Crucifixe, than was hir mende al holy takyn owt of al erdly thyngys & set al in gostly thyngys... (pp. 186–7/35–36, 1–6, 10–16).

What is of additional interest here is the co-mingling of influences within Margery's mind. It is unclear whether the Crucifix which is gradually unveiled by the priest is that which would normally have been suspended from the rood-loft, or whether it was a duplicate brought into the church for the specific requirements of the mimetic re-enactment of the liturgical ceremony of the 'Elevatio'.[40] What *is* clear, however, is an element of the

---

[38] Pamela Sheingorn, *The Easter Sepulchre in England*, Early Drama, Art, and Music Reference Series, 5 (Kalamazoo: Medieval Institute Publications, Western Michigan University, 1987), and see p. 247 for the sepulchre at the chapel of St Nicholas.

[39] See Alexandra F. Johnston, 'The Emerging Pattern of the Easter Play in England', *Medieval English Theatre*, 20 (1998), 3–23.

[40] Karl Young, *The Drama of the Medieval Church*, 2 vols (Oxford: Clarendon Press, 1933), 1, Chapters IV and V, 'The Burial of Cross and Host' and 'The Harrowing of Hell'. On the 'Elevatio' see pp. 113–16.

performative. But this, by itself, does not satisfy Margery. In her recalling of the apocryphal scene of the Harrowing of Hell is she, in fact, remembering the play of that name from a cycle, perhaps that of York (XXXXVII)?

Another liturgical ritual which Margery mentions in relation to her devotions is that of 2 February, 'the Purificacyon Day er ellys Candilmesse Day' (I/82), during which she once more reaches an understanding of the divine essence which informs the everyday. Perhaps, again, she was recalling actual dramatic enactments of the Purification. (It is unlikely that she saw the elaborate costumed procession in Beverley, in which [silent] impersonation formed a vital ingredient, since her confinement and examination in that town seems to have taken place in the autumn of 1417, although it is possible that it was of such renown that she heard about it.)[41] The act of purification itself, together with the regular churching of women, constitutes a form of ceremonial with particular resonances for women. Once more, though, we are confronted with the problem of determining whether it was the female contemplative tradition, possibly originating with Marie d'Oignies, which inspired Margery, or recollection of plays on the theme.[42] Perhaps she was primarily influenced here by the biographies of Marie and St Bridget of Sweden, as Carolyne Larrington has suggested,[43] especially since it is by no means certain that the pageant on this theme in York (XVII), at least, was played annually during the early fifteenth century.[44] What is notable about Margery's experience here, though, is that she for once positions herself as an onlooker, rather than an active participant. But its personal impact on her should not be underestimated, given that she was the mother of fourteen children, and her own regular churchings, in

---

[41] *Book*, I/53. On Beverley see H. F. Westlake, *The Parish Gilds of Mediaeval England* (London: Society for Promoting Christian Knowledge, 1919), p. 233. Eamon Duffy, *The Stripping of the Altars: Traditional Religion in England 1400–1580* (New Haven, CT and London: Yale University Press, 1992), pp. 17–21, gives an extremely useful summary of parochial celebration of Candlemas, but he does not consider its specific relevance for women.

[42] Larrington, 'Representing the Presentation'; Gail McMurray Gibson, 'Blessing from Sun and Moon: Churching as Women's Theater', in Hanawalt and Wallace, *Bodies and Disciplines*, pp. 139–54.

[43] Larrington, 'Representing the Presentation'.

[44] Beadle, *York Plays*, pp. 27, 434–36.

addition to those of others which she observed (p. 198/24–25), reflect a form of dramatic ritual exclusive to women.

I should like to extend this argument for a female-orientated 'drama' through brief discussion of what may be called 'medieval women's street theatre'. Although not part of any official ecclesiastical culture, the experience of Margery and the women of Rome in witnessing the unveiling of an image of Christ carried on an ass by an unnamed woman accompanied by two friars minor, is conveyed as a spontaneous response to what was, in a strong sense, theatrical display deliberately designed to evoke female piety. It was in the laps of 'worshepful wyfys' that the woman placed the image, and they joined in the improvised 'drama' by clothing it in 'schirtys' and kissing it 'as thei it had be God hym-selfe' (I/30/p. 77/17–20, 30–34).[45]

Prominent within the text as this last example is, principally because of the support it lends to the Christological emphasis within the *Book*, the basis of my argument is that Margery's knowledge of, and reactions to, contemporary drama forms a hidden sub-text to her spiritual 'Life'; but one which is capable of recovery. Whilst the witnessing of plays, as I have attempted to show, was probably a formative religious experience for her, it was also one which was deliberately suppressed in the eventual composition of the *Book*. If, as is strongly implied, Margery saw herself as privileged among both the Christian faithful on earth and the saints in Heaven (see, e.g., I/78/84/88), her silence on this issue is hardly surprising. It is only one of many such silences, or gaps. The *Book* may be replete with references to 'authoritative' spiritual writings, and to preaching, but these serve the purpose of conveying an equal authority to Margery's individual beliefs, visions, and actions. If the ultimate aim of the *Book*'s publication in manuscript was the revelation of Margery's intercessory powers, then it may not be stretching credibility overmuch to suggest that the unwritten agenda on the part of Margery and/or her confessors was canonization, perhaps preceded by beatification. As Christ says to Margery: "'Dowtyr, thei that wil not beleuyn the goodnes & the grace that I schewe on-to the in this lyfe, I xal make hem to knowe the

---

[45] For Gibson, *Theater of Devotion*, p. 63, this incident rather 'provides suggestive evidence about the close connection in Margery's time between Christian piety and sympathetic magic'—that is, the emphasis in the placing of the image on women's laps 'suggests a ritual blessing of the womb to ensure fruitfulness and protection from the dangers of childbirth'. This view does not negate my points that the incident is essentially dramatic, and essentially female, in its improvisational nature.

trewth whan thei arn dede & owt of this world.'" (I/78/p. 186/3–6.) If this conjecture is tenable, then drama, as representative of an essentially oral, and popularly-based culture—open to members of all levels of society and not simply to a spiritual elite—though frequently welcomed, and undoubtedly in many cases written, by clerics, could not be taken to validate Margery's status. Just as the fact of her maternity is invoked only to emphasize her suffering in this life and her potential to bring about conversion in others (hence the narrative's concentration upon her way-ward son's spiritual development (II/1/2)), and is clearly stated early on in the *Book* to be subordinate in importance to both God and Margery (I/21/pp. 48–49/20–35, 1–34), so any other aspect of her life which would not strengthen her *extra*ordinary claim to sanctity was marginalized.[46]

This exploration of the *Book* as both a drama of salvation and a piece of metatheatre—in the sense in which the theatrical elements are para-doxically transcended by their very subsumption within a greater whole—has had, of necessity, to be selective. Other instances of dramatic role-playing have been noted: Mary Erler, for example, has singled out Margery's adoption of white clothing for attention, and in her donning of this colour—the signification of which was usually that of 'spiritual virginity and spiritual validation'—[47] Margery can be seen to be taking on the role of the justified sinner who has achieved salvation whilst on earth. Another link in the chain of formation of textual authority can be pin-pointed with reference to dramatic strategies. In the separation within the *Book* between the authorial and narrative personae, so helpfully formu-lated by Lynn Staley as, respectively, 'Kempe' and 'Margery',[48] a connection can be drawn with the theatrical technique whereby contem-porary dramatists either prefaced, or enclosed, their separate pageants or episodes by means of a presenter, variously identified by titles such as 'Expositer' or 'Contemplacio', whose primary function is explication and

---

[46] Cf. Wendy Harding, 'Medieval Women's Unwritten Discourse on Motherhood: A Reading of Two Fifteenth-Century Texts', *Women's Studies*, 21 (1992), 197–209. There is a similar absence of domestic biographical detail in the *Liber Celestis* of St Bridget; Ellis, in his edition, observes that the 'warmth and spontaneity' of Bridget, her 'lawhyng cher' as recalled to Margery by the saint's maidservant in Rome (*Book*, I/39/17–18) 'find almost no echo in the *Liber*' (p. xv).

[47] Mary C. Erler, 'Margery Kempe's White Clothes', *Medium Aevum*, 62 (1993), 78–83, (p. 81).

[48] See nn. 4 and 5, above.

control of audience response.[49] Thus, in the N-Town pageant of the *Conception of Mary*, Meg Twycross notes of the figure of Joachim that he 'is both the presenter of the character and the character himself' in his self-introduction as 'a man in godys substancyall', who is 'Ryghtful' in his partitioning of his goods into three; this self-characterization allows him to make the following didactic reminder to parish priests to behave in a similar fashion of righteous charity.[50] In just the same way, Kempe is able to control her audience's responses. The narrative—albeit one which lacks linearity in both time and space—is told, but it is interspersed throughout with Margery's performative and dramatic involvement with the players of the biblical story, interwoven with injunctions to her contemporaries and, presumably, members of her intended posthumous audience, to take example by her. As Christ says to her, 'I haue ordeyned the to be a merowr' to [your] fellows (I/78/13).

In this reading Kempe cannot be restricted to the category of a woman who embodied written texts, as Ralph Hanna has powerfully argued in relation to Kempe and Julian of Norwich, as well as to the Norfolk heretics Margery Baxter and Avis Mone.[51] Her *Book* is additionally, and vitally, I suggest, multi*vocal*: it is composed of interactive layers of different discourses, ranging from those of the sympathetic spirituality of Julian of Norwich (I/18) and the authoritarianism of the established Church, to those of the ordinary people with whom Margery came into contact at home and abroad. Intrinsic to this multivocalism is the language of the theatre. To recognize the contribution of dramatic 'voices' and techniques of presentation of both self, and the revelation of biblical truth, simultaneously reveals the complexities of thought and experience which went into the making of the text, and demonstrates the extent to which the drama was embedded within the late-medieval

---

[49] In the N-Town cycle, e.g., the episode entitled 'Passion Play II' by Meredith is introduced by a stage direction, the end part of which reads 'than come ther an exposytour in doctorys wede': this character is named as 'Contemplacio'; see Meredith, *Passion Play*, p. 89. Such examples could be multiplied.

[50] Meg Twycross, 'Books for the Unlearned', in *Themes in Drama*, 5: *Drama and Religion*, ed. by James Redmond (Cambridge: Cambridge University Press, 1983), pp. 65–110, p. 91. This article has been formative in my thinking. The play quotations come from Spector, *N-Town Play*, pp. 72–73/46–57.

[51] Hanna, 'Some Norfolk Women and Their Books', esp. pp. 294–6, 247, 301.

cultural consciousness. Above all, it attributes spiritual and authorial agency to the historical Margery Kempe.[52]

---

[52] My choice to write about Margery Kempe in tribute to Felicity Riddy stems in part from the sometimes difficult negotiations between domesticity and vocation which create a community between medieval and modern women; and in part from my happy experience in co-teaching an M.A. seminar on Kempe with Felicity when I visited York to give a guest lecture several years ago. I should like to thank my own M.A. students at Bristol for their generosity and forbearance as I developed the ideas within this paper in subsequent years.

'Lete me suffre': Reading the Torture of St Margaret of Antioch in Late Medieval England

KATHERINE J. LEWIS

> The Iuge [Judge] thanne vpon a galowe tre
> Lete hangen vp thus holy pure virgyne,
> Hir flesshe be rent in his cruelte
> Whos blode ran doun right [straight] as eny lyne.[1]

This description of the public torture of a beautiful young woman is taken from Lydgate's life of St Margaret. Such scenes of brutal violence are commonplace in the lives of virgin-martyr saints and have frequently been interpreted as 'pornographic' by modern scholars.[2] Factors that are cited in support of this interpretation are the sexual nature of the torture, its status as a displaced rape, the texts' inscription of misogyny and their reiteration and confirmation of patriarchal social values.[3]

The following analysis takes issue with this interpretation, as it does little justice to the many men and women who heard, read, and owned virgin-martyrs' lives in fifteenth-century England and who responded to them by displaying their devotion to favourite saints in wills and other

---

I would like to thank Sarah Salih, Bella Millett, Caroline Howlett, Robert Mills, and Mark Donnelly for some valuable insights on reading, torture, and representation.

[1] *The Minor Poems of John Lydgate*, part 1, ed. by Henry Noble MacCracken, EETS, os 107 (London: Oxford University Press, 1911), p. 181, ll. 225–29.

[2] Marina Warner, *Alone of All Her Sex: The Myth and Cult of the Virgin Mary* (London: Picador, 1990), p. 71.

[3] See, for example, Kathryn Gravdal, *Ravishing Maidens: Writing Rape in Medieval French Literature and Law* (Philadelphia: University of Pennsylvania Press, 1991).

documentary sources. To identify these texts as forms of pornography is reductive and simplistic.[4] On a very basic level it occludes the fact that 'pornography' itself is not a given entity, but a discursive construction around whose identification and definition rages a variety of intellectual, political, and legal debates.[5] The definition of whether a text or image is pornographic frequently resides in the eye of the beholder.[6] Indeed further justification for using the term to describe virgin-martyrs' lives usually rests on some discussion of the way in which the audience 'must' have read and understood them. Some argue that the scenes of torture are 'obviously' aimed at male readers, who are given a licit space in which to enjoy the spectacle.[7] For women, reading these texts can only be deleterious—necessitating the internalization of negative ideas about themselves and their bodies.[8] This sort of approach may tell us more about the reactions of the scholars than of the contemporary medieval audience as it elides the two without further argument. The 'audience'

---

[4]   Robert Mills is currently undertaking a much more detailed, and extremely lucid, analysis of the relationship between virgin-martyr narratives and pornography as part of a forthcoming Ph.D. thesis on late medieval punishment imagery (Department of Art History, University of Cambridge). I am very grateful to him for allowing me to read his work-in-progress.

[5]   For a useful introduction to the subject see Daniel Linz and Neil Malamuth, *Pornography* (London and New Delhi: Sage Publications, 1993). *Making Violence Sexy: Feminist Views on Pornography*, ed. by Diana E. H. Russell (New York and London: University of Columbia Press, 1993) exemplifies the feminist anti-pornography stance, whereas *Sex Exposed: Sexuality and the Pornography Debate*, ed. by Lynne Segal and Mary McIntosh (London: Virago Press, 1992) attempts to problematize that position, from what might be termed a liberal feminist standpoint.

[6]   Linz and Malamuth illustrate this point by defining three different viewer perceptions about sexually explicit material and applying them to *The Story of O*: see their *Pornography*, pp. 2–5.

[7]   For example, Gravdal, p. 24 argues that these texts were 'doubtless aimed at male readers', as part of a wider discussion of virgin-martyr lives as rape narratives. Similarly Simon Gaunt, *Gender and Genre in Medieval French Literature* (Cambridge: Cambridge University Press, 1995), p. 196 judges that such texts were written primarily in the interests of men, not women, because of the scenes of torture. He also draws a direct comparison between such descriptions and modern pornographic descriptions of bondage, p. 197. Karen A. Winstead, *Virgin Martyrs: Legends of Sainthood in Late Medieval England* (Ithaca and London: Cornell University Press, 1997), p. 12 argues that these texts could have provided the (implicitly) male reader with the means to enjoy fantasies of 'harmless' violence against women.

[8]   See Gaunt, pp. 194–98.

discussed in this sort of analysis has not usually been surmised from any surviving evidence about those who read or owned saints' lives and does not allow for the possibility of multiple or resistant readings.[9]

Rather than considering virgin-martyr lives as manifestations of a particular literary genre, the ensuing reading proceeds with an awareness of the forms that devotion towards them took and of the ways in which people appropriated them as patrons and exemplars in late-medieval England. The most popular virgin-martyr was St Katherine of Alexandria.[10] It is important to note that hers is by far the least gory of all the Middle English virgin-martyr lives. Versions of her life composed in fifteenth-century England afford far more space to her debate with the Philosophers and her mystical marriage than to her physical suffering. On the other hand, there is little evidence for a particularly flourishing late medieval English cult of St Agatha, who had her breasts cut off, and is therefore often used to support the sorts of readings outlined above.[11] It

---

[9] My own approach to the medieval audience of saints' lives has been influenced by Jocelyn Wogan-Browne's work on early medieval virgin-martyr hagiography: see for example 'The Virgin's Tale', in *Feminist Readings in Middle English Literature: The Wife of Bath and All Her Sect*, ed. by Ruth Evans and Lesley Johnson (London and New York: Routledge, 1994), pp. 165–94. Roberta L. Krueger, *Women Readers and the Ideology of Gender in Old French Verse Romance* (Cambridge: Cambridge University Press, 1993), provides a useful model for the consideration of medieval women as critical and resistant readers, while retaining an awareness of the advantages and problems entailed in such an approach.

[10] The relative popularity of the virgin-martyr saints can be gauged by a survey of extant documentary, literary, and visual sources, as the following examples demonstrate. For a catalogue of extant Middle English lives see Charlotte D'Evelyn, 'Saints' Legends', in *A Manual of the Writings in Middle English, 1050–1500*, ed. by J. Burke Severs, vol. 2 (Hamden, CT: Archon, 1970), pp. 561–635. For virgin-martyrs' relative popularity as patrons of gilds, according to the 1389 gild returns, see H. F. Westlake, *The Parish Gilds of Mediaeval England* (London: Society for Promoting Christian Knowledge, 1919), pp. 137–238, see also Virginia R. Bainbridge, *Gilds in the Medieval Countryside: Social and Religious Change in Cambridgeshire c. 1350–1558* (Woodbridge: Boydell and Brewer, 1996). For extant wall paintings of virgin-martyrs and their lives see E. W. Tristram, *English Medieval Wall Painting of the Fourteenth Century* (London: Routledge and Kegan Paul, 1955); A. Caiger-Smith, *English Medieval Mural Paintings* (Oxford: Clarendon Press, 1963).

[11] For example, Martha Easton, 'Saint Agatha and the Sanctification of Sexual Violence', *Studies in Iconography*, 16 (1994) 83–119. This issue will be discussed at greater length in my study of the cult of St Katherine of Alexandria in late medieval England (Woodbridge: Boydell and Brewer, 2000).

may be that the medieval audience was not as interested in the graphic torture of young women as its modern counterpart.

This article will consider four versions of the life of St Margaret of Antioch, the second most popular virgin-martyr in late medieval England.[12] Evidence of patronage, manuscript ownership and manuscript content indicate elite socio-economic groups of patrons and readers: aristocratic, gentry, and urban elite.[13] The manuscript contexts suggest social, cultural, and devotional nexuses which can inform our reading of the life of St Margaret in a more nuanced way than the pornography argument allows. The four versions of the life are as follows: the life contained in the early fourteenth-century Auchinleck MS (hereafter A); the life in the fifteenth-century Oxford, Bodleian Library MS, Ashmole 61 (AB); Lydgate's *Legende of Saynte Margarete,* commissioned from him by Anne Mortimer, Lady March, between 1415 and 1426 (L); and Osbern Bokenham's life of St Margaret, originally written in 1443 for his friend Thomas Burgh, who subsequently arranged for the compilation of Bokenham's female saints' lives (OB).[14] In addition to the manuscript

---

[12] Twenty-one gilds are listed as dedicated to St Katherine in 1389: of the virgin-martyr saints St Margaret is the next most popular with nine (Westlake, *Parish Gilds,* pp. 137–238).

[13] For discussion of reading habits and manuscript ownership within these groups see Julia Boffey and John J. Thompson, 'Anthologies and Miscellanies: Production and Choice of Texts', in *Book Production and Publishing in Britain: 1375–1475,* ed. by Jeremy Griffiths and Derek Pearsall (Cambridge: Cambridge University Press, 1989), pp. 279–315; Carol M. Meale, 'Patrons, Buyers and Owners: Book Production and Social Status', in ibid., pp. 208–38; Phillipa Hardman, 'A Medieval "Library *in parvo*"', *Medium Aevum,* 47 (1978), 262–73.

[14] See Derek Pearsall and I. C. Cunningham, *The Auchinleck Manuscript: National Library of Scotland Advocates MS 19.2.1* (London: Scolar Press, 1979). For the text of A see C. Horstmann, *Altenglische Legenden: Neue Folge* (Heilbronn: Henniger, 1881), pp. 225–35. For AB see ibid., pp. 236–41. An incomplete version is also to be found in the Brome Common Place Book; see *A Commonplace Book of the Fifteenth Century,* ed. by Lucy Toulmin Smith (London: Trübner, 1886), pp. 107–18. For L see MacCracken, pp. 173–92. The life survives in six fifteenth-century manuscripts. For a discussion of Lydgate's readership see A. S. G. Edwards, 'Lydgate Manuscripts: Some Directions for Future Research', in *Manuscripts and Readers in Fifteenth-Century England,* ed. by Derek Pearsall (Cambridge: D. S. Brewer, 1981), pp. 15–26 (pp. 22–23). For the most recent discussion of this life see Winstead, pp. 122–41. For OB see *Legendys of Hooly Wummen,* ed. by Mary S. Serjeantson, EETS, OS 206 (London: Oxford University Press, 1938; reprinted Woodbridge: Boydell and Brewer, 1997), pp. 7–38. For Bokenham and his patrons see A. S. G. Edwards, 'The Transmission and Audience of Osbern Bokenham's *Legendys of Hooly Wummen*', in *Late-Medieval Religious Texts and their Transmission:*

context and what it says of patronage and readership there are important text-internal ways of arguing for more nuanced readings.

The life of St Margaret is particularly useful for an attempt to posit contemporary readings, because the saint is given an awareness that her suffering and death will be read and potentially misread, not just by those who witness it within the text, but by those who will have access to written accounts of it. While there seems to have been a contemporary sense that all female saints' lives were particularly appropriate and valuable reading matter for women, St Margaret's status as patron of childbirth gives her a special link to their experiences. Thus her life is a particularly suitable vehicle for a consideration of possible female readings.[15]

This article does not seek to suggest a monolithic reading to replace those outlined above. It cannot be denied that some men may have been titillated and some women oppressed by reading the life of St Margaret. But this is only one possibility. These narratives were popular with women. They describe women engaged in active resistance to male authority.[16] Christine de Pisan considered saints' lives to be the most

---

Essays in Honour of A. I. Doyle, ed. by Alastair Minnis (Cambridge: D. S. Brewer, 1994), pp. 157–67. References to the lives will be made by line number within the body of the text.

[15] On reading matter for women see Edwards, 'Transmission and Audience', p. 164; Carol M. Meale, '"...alle the bokes that I haue of latyn, englisch, and frensch": Laywomen and their Books in Late Medieval England', in *Women and Literature in Britain: 1150–1500*, ed. by Carol M. Meale (Cambridge: Cambridge University Press, 1993), pp. 128–58 (pp. 137–38). On St Margaret and women see Jocelyn Wogan-Browne, 'The Apple's Message: Some Hagiographic Accounts of Textual Transmission', in Minnis, pp. 39–53 (pp. 46–48). Virgin-martyr lives were used to instil appropriate feminine values and conduct in young women: see Katherine J. Lewis, 'Model Girls? Virgin-martyrs and the Training of Young Women in Late-Medieval England', in *Young Medieval Women*, ed. by Kim M. Phillips, Noël James Menuge, and Katherine J. Lewis (Stroud: Sutton, 1999), pp. 25–46 and 'The Life of St Margaret of Antioch in Late-Medieval England: A Gendered Reading', *Studies in Church History*, 34 (1998), 129–42 for the ways in which women may have read and appropriated virgin-martyrs as models.

[16] For some alternative readings of virgin-martyr torture which discuss the body as a textual device and a site of multiple meanings see Margaret M. Miles, *Carnal Knowing: Female Nakedness and Religious Meaning in the Christian West* (Boston: Vintage Books, 1989), pp. 53–77; Sarah Salih, 'Performing Virginity: Sex and Violence in the Katherine Group', in *Constructions of Widowhood and Virginity in the Middle Ages*, ed. by Cindy Carlson and Angela Jane Weisl (St Martin's Press, forthcoming). See Jocelyn Wogan-Browne, 'Saints' Lives and the Female Reader', *Forum for Modern Language Studies*, 27 (1991), 314–32 for the argument that virgin saints provide women with models of resistance to male authority. See also Catherine Innes-Parker, 'Sexual Violence and the Female Reader: Symbolic "Rape" in the Saint's Lives of the Katherine Group', *Women's Studies*, 24 (1995), 205–17; Winstead, *Virgin Martyrs*, pp. 105–11.

fitting way to conclude her *Book of the City of Ladies*.[17] Thus we are forced to consider the ways in which women may have read these texts without lending complicity to the sadism directed against women, or colluding in the patriarchal norms which they produce.[18]

The first part of this analysis will look at the ways in which St Margaret's torture is described; the second part will consider her execution.[19] The status of Margaret as a publicly observed spectacle within the text is crucial for informing us as to possible readings of it. In order to establish some 'pornographic' criteria against which to measure representations of Margaret, it is useful to consider some of the terms used by Susanne Kappeler to define the 'woman-object' in pornographic texts:

> She is characterised by a lack of control even where she is, linguistically, the grammatical subject....
> Her fragmented body [is] beyond her control, its parts acting autonomously, and the only successful 'act' on her part being that of letting others do things to her.[20]

In essence, what Kappeler describes is the fundamental elision of the woman as subject. For this, passivity is the basic trope.[21]

---

[17] Christine de Pisan, *The Book of the City of Ladies*, trans. by Earl Jeffrey Rivers (New York: Persea Books, 1982), pp. 217–57. A lucid discussion of de Pisan's use of virgin-martyr hagiography is provided by Maureen Quilligan, *The Allegory of Female Authority: Christine de Pizan's* Cite des Dames (Ithaca and London: Cornell University Press, 1991), pp. 189–245.

[18] My reading thus aligns itself with recent scholarship on several other kinds of texts that were and are popular with female readers and which have been judged to trap the female reader into an immasculated subject position, e.g. gothic novels, modern romance novels. It has been argued that these texts do, in some instances, constitute an exploration of the meaning of patriarchy and address problems faced by women within apparently desirable social arrangements: see Carol Thurston, *The Romance Revolution: Erotic Novels for Women and the Quest for a New Sexual Identity* (Urbana and Chicago: University of Illinois Press, 1987); Anne Williams, *The Art of Darkness: A Poetics of Gothic* (Chicago and London: University of Chicago Press, 1995); Laura E. Tanner, *Intimate Violence: Reading Rape and Torture in Twentieth Century Fiction* (Bloomington and Indianapolis: Indiana University Press, 1994). For the application of this kind of approach to virgin-martyr hagiography see Wogan-Browne, 'Saints' Lives and the Female Reader', passim.

[19] Due to constraints of space the Dragon episode will not be considered within this analysis.

[20] Susanne Kappeler, *The Pornography of Representation* (Minneapolis: University of Minnesota Press, 1986), pp. 88–89.

[21] Brigitte Cazelles, *The Lady as Saint: A Collection of French Hagiographic Romances of the Thirteenth Century* (Philadelphia: University of Pennsylvania Press, 1991) identifies

St Margaret could be described as passive insofar as she does let others do things to her. But it is she who controls the sequence of events leading to her torture by refusing to renounce Christianity:

> Sytthe [since] Criste for me suffred peyne and dethe...
> So for his sake, of hole affeccyoun,
> Be assured that I haue no drede
> To deye for him, and al my blode to shed. (L, ll. 220–24).

Her public avowal of Christianity presents a challenge to Olibrius's authority, both temporal and spiritual, and he has no other option than to have her tortured, as she knows. Margaret suffers two sets of torture; first she is scourged, and on a second occasion she is burned with brands or oil and an attempt is made to drown and/or boil her in a vat of water.[22] On both occasions Margaret explicitly invites and instigates her own torture by provoking Olibrius.[23]

Thus Margaret arranges the spectacle of her tortured body for the benefit of Olibrius and the on-looking crowd. Her suffering is clearly informed by the debt which she owes to Christ: in one text she prays 'lete me suffre! for me thou suffredest more' (A, l. 156). [24] Her lacerated body is described in bloody detail:

> They rent her flesh on euery syde
> So dispetously [unmercifully], that than a ryuer
> Hyr blood to grounde swyftlyere ded glyde (OB, ll. 653–55).[25]

In order that the audience should be in no doubt as to the horrifying and disturbing nature of this spectacle, we are told that even Olibrius cannot bear to watch:

---

the virgin-martyr as a mute and passive victim (p. 44) trapped within 'the construct of an authoritative male discourse on the proper place of women' (p. 82).

[22] For the scourging: A, 125–28, 141–44; AB, 194–202, 224–31; L, 225–31; OB, 568–78, 652–55. For the burning: A, 289–92; AB, 456–59; L, 410–17; OB, 792–802. For the attempted drowning: A, 309–12; AB, 309–12; L, 419–20; OB, 803–05.

[23] This is not to imply that Margaret seeks her own torture and death in an unorthodox way. Margaret's voluntary assent to martyrdom was seen (by medieval standards) to be entirely different to suicide. See St Augustine's discussion of this issue in relation to the rape of Lucretia, *City of God*, trans. by Henry Bettenson (Harmondsworth: Penguin Books, 1984), pp. 28–32.

[24] For the debt to Christ motif see also A, 150–52, 154–56; AB, 155–61, 187–89; L, 218–24; OB, 561–67.

[25] For Margaret's blood: A, 126–28; AB, 200–02; L, 225–31.

> The vnpetous prefect his eyne [eyes] ded hyde
> Wyth his mantel, & myht not suffre to se
> Blood rennyng owt so gret plente (OB, ll. 656–58).[26]

Olibrius and the rest of the pagan crowd cannot comprehend why Margaret is voluntarily undergoing such torment, especially because she is so beautiful. Her beauty heightens both the horror and meaning of her sacrifice.[27] The crowd does not take voyeuristic pleasure in her suffering, but understands her torture as an act of destructive self-annihilation, addressing her thus:

> ...feyre meyden Mergarete,
> Thou that arte so feyre & suete,
> Turne to hym & be hys wyue...
> [we] wold that thou sauyd were (AB, ll. 236–41).[28]

This allows Margaret to enter into a debate with them in which she contests their reading of her suffering as a sexual assault inflicted by a man who desires her:

> After you, sche seyd, I wyll not do,
> Bot go your wey, sche seyd, me fro!
> Alle that fore me [for my sake] repente
> And se me haue this turment,
> As thei thinke both gode & euylle [as they think good or evil of it],
> They schall be quyte [rewarded] after ther wylle [as they desire]
>   (AB, ll. 242–47).[29]

She seems to indicate that for those who 'se me haue this turment' there is a right and a wrong way of perceiving it. The whole point of this memorable image of unexpected fortitude in the face of brutal torture is to demonstrate the veracity of Christian doctrine, and to introduce the intercessory power that is bestowed upon Margaret as a result of her

---

[26] Cf. L, 267–73. A and AB do not contain parallel descriptions.

[27] It should be noted that in none of these Middle English texts is Margaret stripped before her torture, nor is her body described in any detail at all, beyond the fact that it bleeds. The authors therefore do not act in keeping with Gravdal and Gaunt's assertion (see n. 7 above) that the producers of this brand of hagiography sought to provide the audience with the opportunity to enjoy the spectacle of naked female bodies.

[28] Cf. A, 146–48; AB, 232–41, 460–65; L, 232–52; OB, 579–88.

[29] Cf. A, 150–52; L, 253–59; OB, 589–630.

willingness to suffer for Christ. The torture does not stop Margaret from speaking. In fact it lends greater authority to her words; Bokenham, for example, gives her a sermon-like speech on the worthlessness of pagan deities and the salvific power of her God.[30] She will not be saved by avoiding torture, but by undergoing it, and she is able to effect the salvation of others by her sacrifice, provided that they understand that this is its essence and import. Bokenham has her addressing the onlookers thus:

> Wherfore, my counsel if ye whyl do,
> My soule for yours, ye shul saf be (OB, ll. 624–25).

For the audience of the text to read Margaret's torture as a sexual assault would be to align themselves with the pagans, above all Olibrius, who reads it in the 'wrong' way.[31] In order to emphasize this interpretation, the audience is given the example of a group of pagans, Margaret's converts, who do understand her sacrifice in the 'right' way. Olibrius attempts to drown or boil Margaret but God intervenes with thunder and, in some texts, an angel, and she is saved. Instantly,

> ...fyve thousand, for [because] God wolde hem save,
> Conuerted weren from there myscreaunce [their false belief],
> For Cristes sake heveded [beheaded] by venegeaunce (L, ll. 430–32).[32]

One basic message that emerges from this incident is that the truth of Christianity is something to which one must adhere and bear witness whatever the cost. Furthermore, Margaret's sacrifice should be understood as something in which the audience (both within and outside the text) can share. Readers would not be expected to do this by actually becoming martyrs themselves, but by using the sort of affective contemplative strategies that they would have learned from texts such as Love's 'Mirror of the Blessed Life of Jesus Christ', which taught them to read and understand each element of the torture inflicted upon Christ's body.[33] The idea of Margaret's suffering body as a text that can be read in

---

[30] OB, 591–625.

[31] An observation also made by Wogan-Browne, 'Saints' Lives and the Female Reader', p. 329 and Salih, 'Performing Virginity'.

[32] Cf. A, 325–28; AB, 479–85; OB, 813–14. This attribution to God does not remove Margaret's agency because of the double referential structure of the narrative; Wogan-Browne, 'The Virgin's Tale', pp. 179–80.

[33] See Elizabeth Salter, *Nicholas Love's 'Myrrour of the Blessed Lyf of Jesu Christ'* (Salzburg: Salzburg University Press, 1974), pp. 119–78.

order to understand the nature and precise terms of the beneficial contract that it represents bears similarities to the popular devotional poem 'The Charter of Christ'.[34] This text appears with the life of St Margaret in Oxford, Bodl., MS Ashmole 61. Such meditative techniques would allow audiences to 'Se how a mayde in al hir tormentrie / The feith of Crist coude magnifie' [L, 433–434]. The audience would also be trained to read and understand Margaret's torture, like Christ's, as part of a bargain which she is striking with God for the benefit of those who are moved by it to ask for her intercession.

Thus we can see that Margaret does not fit Kappeler's description of the 'woman-object', despite superficial similarities between the two. The torture is intended to eradicate her body and herself, but ironically it only serves to make her more and more visible. It is intended to silence her, but actually serves to construct an affective and authoritative platform from which to speak and preach. Olibrius seeks to harm and correct her, but she turns the punishment back upon him: her ability to withstand sustained and ferocious torture renders him and his people unable to watch, thus destabilizing him from his position as apparent author of the spectacle. Her exemplary suffering further undermines his position and authority by converting thousands of his people, who have read it as a confirmation of the truth of Christianity, as she intended, rather than as an exposition of its fallacy, the reading which Olibrius attempts to impose. This leaves Olibrius 'dredyng more peple wold turne hyr to / If she lengere lyuyd' [OB, 817–818]. Margaret, the putative 'passive' victim, becomes agent and campaigner, using her bleeding body and her un-wavering speech as weapons against Olibrius. Thus torture is presented in the texts not as something that is done to Margaret, but something that she allows to happen to herself. She appropriates it and directs its meaning: it becomes a self-representational act.

The climax of this act comes when Olibrius orders Margaret's execution. This happens after the conversion of the five thousand demonstrates the subversive power of her example. Margaret dies not just as an ultimate expression of gratitude for Christ's own sacrifice, but in order to make a bargain with God. This bargain has been written on her body through torture and will be signed by her decapitation. This links back to the contractual understanding of Christ's suffering and death

---

[34] For the text of the Charter, which survives in over forty manuscripts, see *The Minor Poems of the Vernon Manuscript*, part 2, ed. by F. J. Furnivall, EETS, os 117 (London: Kegan Paul, 1901), pp. 637–57.

articulated by 'The Charter of Christ'. Having received God's confirmation that her request will be granted, Margaret tells the executioner
that he may now dispatch her, remaining in control of the narrative, just
as she did during her torture.[35] This serves to establish her and her life as
a receptacle of intercessory power, which will be made available to her
devotees. It is a standard feature of martyrs' lives for the moment of death
to be represented in this way. But Margaret's demand is unusually
detailed. Bokenham tells us that she prays:

> For them specyally that my passyoun
> Othyr rede, or wryte, or other do teche [teach to others],
> Or cherche or chapel make if they moun [may],
> Or lyht or launpe fynde [provide] of [out of] deuocyoun
> To me-ward: lord, for thy gret grace,
> Hem repentaunce graunte er they hens pace [go hence]
>   (OB, ll. 835–40).[36]

Margaret is aware that her life will become a text; it will have the
power to help and save those who read, write, or teach it. The life in MS
Ashmole 61 also includes a plea on behalf of those who 'berythe on them
my lyffe' [AB, 563], those who 'carry' or perhaps even 'wear' her life.
Given Margaret's earlier concern to contest and control readings of
herself, there may be an implication that in order to reap the benefit of her
intercession, one must be sure to understand her life and passion in the
right way. Margaret is also aware that reading her life is only one part of
wider practices of devotion towards her, which are performed in response
to the promise for intercession that her sacrifice offers.[37] The specificity
with which Margaret lists the options open to people of varying levels of
wealth (from a church to a candle) undoubtedly contributed to her
popularity. Over 200 medieval English churches were dedicated to St
Margaret, more than any other female saint, and the evidence of extant
literary and visual lives, as well as gild dedications indicates her
continuing and increasing popularity throughout the fourteenth and
fifteenth centuries.[38] Late medieval wills give us an indication of the

---

[35] See A, 379–88; AB, 569–80; L, 481–87; OB, 855–59.

[36] Cf. A, 353–72; AB, 328–64; L, 449–76.

[37] For a discussion of the intercessory dimension of virgin-martyrs' cults see Eamon
Duffy, 'Holy Maydens, Holy Wyfes: The Cult of Women Saints in Fifteenth- and
Sixteenth-Century England', *Studies in Church History*, 23 (1990), 175–96.

[38] F. Arnold-Foster, *Studies in Church Dedications*, 3 vols (London: Skeffington, 1899),
still provides the most comprehensive guide. See also the works cited in n. 10.

eagerness with which people responded to Margaret's promises. One lavish example is provided by the 1523 will of Edward Stanley, Lord Monteagle, who left a hundred marks, or as much as was needed, to decorate the new chapel of St Margaret which he had built in Hornby, and in which he wished to be buried.[39] Lesser demonstrations of devotion are provided by Margaret Hansford who in 1447 left a gold rosary to the chapel of her namesake in Hull, and Alice Cook, whose will of 1488 left one kercher to the image of St Margaret in Hucking Church, Kent.[40] Margaret's final prayer stresses the importance of remembering her in some fashion. Margaret Bate (London) could have accomplished this through the ownership of a silver cup bearing the image of St Margaret, which she left to her son in 1467.[41] William Gunwarby, Bishop of Dunkeld, in 1457, left Agnes Barbour a gold ring with an enamel picture of St Margaret set in it.[42] The Paston letters tell us that John Paston I owned a similar ring, given to him by his wife (Margaret) which was evidently intended to serve not just as a remembrance of the saint, but of herself as well.[43] Thomas Rotherham, Archbishop of York, owned a gold statue of St Margaret, according to his will of 1500.[44]

Demonstrating devotion to St Margaret through these practices was one way of reaching her and attempting to gain her favour. There was another way of tapping into her power, through the medium of her body, which can be thought of less as a dead body than itself a sign, left behind as an indenture to the intercessory contract sealed by her death. The life in MS Ashmole 61 describes the creation of a shrine around her body in Antioch, which effects miraculous cures.[45] John, Lord Scrope of Upsal, possessed a jewel containing a bone of St Margaret, which he left to St

---

[39] *North Country Wills*, part 2, ed. by J. W. Clay, Surtees Society 116 (Durham: Andrews, 1908), p. 112.

[40] For Margaret Hansford's will: *Testamenta Eboracensia*, part 2, ed. by J. Raine, Surtees Society 30 (Durham: Andrews, 1855), p. 126; for Alice Cook's: *Testamenta Cantiana: East Kent*, ed. by Arthur Hussey (London: Mitchell, Hughes & Clarke, 1907), p. 173.

[41] *Bedfordshire Wills Proved in the Prerogative Court of Canterbury: 1383–1548*, ed. by Margaret McGregor, Bedfordshire Historical Record Society 58 (Bedford: Bedfordshire Historical Record Society Publications, 1979), p. 23.

[42] Ibid., p. 18.

[43] *Paston Letters and Papers of the Fifteenth Century*, part 1, ed. by Norman Davis (Oxford: Oxford University Press, 1971), p. 217.

[44] *Testamenta Eboracensia*, part 4, ed. by J. Raine, Surtees Society 53 (Durham: Andrews, 1868), p. 145.

[45] AB, 591–602.

Mary's York, in 1451.[46] Osbern Bokenham describes relics of St Margaret's foot and a miracle which it performed in his prologue to her life.[47]

Just as Margaret's body is semiotic (more than just matter) so texts of her life could become contact relics. This extends particularly to the other part of Margaret's pre-execution request, in which she specifically offers her protection and intercession to women in labour. To continue with Bokenham's version of the prayer (as quoted above on p. 79):

> Also if wummen in trauaylyng be
> Oppressyd wyth peyne & greuaunce,
> And for helpe deuoutly do preye to me,
> Graunth hem sone good deliueraunce (OB, ll. 841–45).[48]

Margaret's intercession for women in childbirth could be gained not only through simple prayer, but, as the formulation in Ashmole 61 quoted above suggests, through actually wearing her life in the form of amulets.[49] Thus Margaret knows not only that her life will become a popular text but that reading and responding to it in a range of ways will provide her devotees with access to her power. In ordering her death Olibrius hopes to obliterate her and the effects of her example, but in her final prayer Margaret demonstrates that death only serves to make her more powerful. Martyrdom is not a defeat, but a victory. The execution reifies her intercession, which is literally embodied in her relics and made tangible through the practices she lists. Like Kappeler's 'woman-object' Margaret's body is fragmented, but its parts do not act autonomously, they remain firmly under her control as vehicles of her intercession. She does indeed become other people's object as relic, as text, as patron, as example, but possession of her does not elide her subjectivity. Rather it is reiterated and strengthened, whenever a devotee who invokes her name and her intercession enacts that possession.

As a concluding point we should consider the possibility that these narratives were popular with a female readership because suffering was in some respects often represented as the definitive experience not just of virgin-martyrs but of all women. Christine de Pisan's use of virgin-martyr

---

[46] *Testamenta Vetusta*, vol. 1, ed. by N. H. Nichols (London: Nichols & Son, 1826), p. 271.

[47] Serjeantson, *Legendys of Hooly Wummen*, pp. 4–5, lines 135–70.

[48] Cf. A, 366–68; AB, 545–51; L, 463–73.

[49] Wogan-Browne, 'The Apple's Message', p. 48.

narratives indicates that she equates their torture with the suffering that
some women undergo at the hands of brutal husbands. She advises them
to attempt reform by example, but to bear all with patience. Through this
they will 'acquire great merit for their souls... and everyone will bless
them and support them'.[50] These observations on the varying treatment
which wives can expect at the hands of their husbands follows directly on
from de Pisan's description of the exploits of female martyrs. Thus the
wife's ordeal is made personally bearable and spiritually valuable because
it is interpreted as an inscription upon her own body and identity of the
physical and personal suffering of the virgin-martyrs, and through them,
of Christ.[51] This shared subject position was not only spiritually but also
politically valuable to Margery Kempe. She used public performance of
the role of examined and persecuted virgin-martyr to stage confrontations
with the male representatives of both secular and religious authority and
to challenge the various social and religious inscriptions which they
attempted to impose upon her body.[52]

It would seem reasonable to suggest that, to judge by their devotional
responses to her life, medieval people's dominant reading of the torture
and death of St Margaret would understand it (as Margaret herself is
represented as doing) in terms of voluntary self-sacrifice and the power
that can be bestowed and shared through suffering. This provides an
alternative that must at least be considered alongside the processes of
voyeurism and self-harm that are frequently taken to characterize the act
of reading a virgin-martyr's life.

---

[50] De Pisan, *Book of the City of Ladies*, p. 97.

[51] This formulation has been much influenced by Caroline Howlett's work on suffragette
accounts of forcible feeding, see her 'Writing on the Body? Representation and Resistance
in British Suffragette Accounts of Forcible Feeding', in *Bodies of Writing, Bodies in
Performance: Genders 23*, ed. by Thomas Foster, Carol Siegel, and Ellen E. Berry (New
York: New York University Press, 1996), pp. 3–41 (p. 35).

[52] *The Book of Margery Kempe*, ed. by Sanford Brown Meech and Hope Emily Allen,
EETS, OS 212 (Oxford: Oxford University Press, 1940), pp. 29–30 for Margery's imagination of the martyrdom which she would be able to undergo; pp. 121–28 for
representative interrogations of Margery, in York. For a discussion of Kempe's use of
hagiography as a form of social criticism see Lynn Staley, *Margery Kempe's Dissenting
Fictions* (University Park: Pennsylvania State University Press, 1994), pp. 39–82.

'Almighty and al merciable queene': Marian Titles and Marian Lyrics

HELEN PHILLIPS

Heyl! chast lyly decended from Iesse,
Heyl! cristall clere, Heyl! closet of clennesse,
Heyl! blessed burioun, Heyl! blome of all beaute. (anon., 15th century)[1]

Emprice of pris, imperatrice,
Bricht, polist, precious stane,
Victrice of vice, hie genetrice [...]

Imperiall wall, place palestrall
Of peirless pulcritude,
Triumphale hall, hie trone regall
Of Godis celsitude. (Dunbar)[2]

O! Deifere delicate and doghter dyuyne,
Mother of mercy and meyden melleffluus,
Devoide of dysseyte, dubbet in doctryne,
Trone of the trinite, triete thow for vs. (anon., 15th century)[3]

I am grateful to Ann Hutchison for her helpful editing.

[1] *Religious Lyrics of the Fifteenth Century*, ed. by Carleton Brown (Oxford: Clarendon Press, 1939), no. 30, p. 54. *Closet*: enclosed place, chamber, cell, chapel (translating 'castitatis cella', see Guido M. Dreves, *Ein Jahrtausend Lateinischer Hymnendichtung*, 2 vols (Leipzig: Reisland, 1909), II, p. 245; *burioun*: 'bud'; *genetrice*: female parent.

[2] William Dunbar, *The Poems of William Dunbar*, ed. by James Kinsley (Oxford, Clarendon Press, 1958), no. 30, p. 54. *Pulcritude*: beauty; *celsitude*: highness.

[3] Brown, *Fifteenth Century*, no. 38, ll. 49–52, p. 69. *Deifere delicate*: splendid god-bearer; *devoide*: empty; *dubbet*: adorned; *triete*: plead.

'Cristall clere', 'blome of all beaute', 'mother of mercy', 'imperiall wall' ...

Honorific titles, a mode of invocation undoubtedly as old as religion itself and with a long history in marian tradition, indebted to liturgy, Bible, and exegesis, become so common in late medieval lyric prayers to Mary as to constitute one of their distinctive characteristics.[4] They are used most frequently in lyrics celebrating Mary's heavenly elevation: her queenship, her Assumption into heaven, and her (theologically ambiguous) power to dispense mercy through supplication to her Son. This short study considers three lyrics which employ this style of praising and defining Mary, all of which offer the reader surprising and unconventional versions of the mode. They all exploit creatively the polysemy and instability that characterize the hyperbolic verbal structures used to praise the Queen of Heaven, a mystic concept centred on contradictions as a human woman is raised to quasi-divine status by virtue of female qualities (motherhood, obedience, supplication, and purity) which lack powerful agency.

Other strands in marian literature, such as affective devotion and the pseudo-Bonaventuran tradition, present Mary, at least occasionally, as a physical and quasi-historical woman, even a sentient subject. The miracles show her operating with power and individual wilfulness in the physical world, and in sympathy with human sinners far removed from her own matchless perfection. In contrast, honorific titles produce intricate abstractions and static, emblem-like images for the reader's veneration. There is a paradox here, since Mary is an object of Christian veneration who remains, unlike the persons of the Trinity, even in her queenly role, purely human. If there is physicality in this style, it tends to be that of non-human things with which Mary is identified metaphorically: flower, tower, gate, closet, ladder, sealed fountain, and so on. Two verbal modes remote from common vernacular usage and often associated with marian titles, aureation and macaronic verse (verse alternating

---

[4] Important studies of English marian lyrics include Felicity Riddy's unpublished B.Phil. thesis, 'A Textual and Literary Study of the Two Versions of *Quia Amore Langueo*', Oxford University, 1965; Theodor Wolpers, 'Geschichte der Englischen Marienlyrik im Mittelalter', *Anglia*, 69 (1950), 3–88; Rosemary Woolf, *The English Religious Lyric in the Middle Ages* (Oxford: Clarendon Press, 1968); and Douglas Gray, *Themes and Images in the Medieval English Religious Lyric* (London: Routledge and Kegan Paul, 1972). There are lists of marian titles in René Laurentin, *Maria Ecclesia Sacerdotium* (Paris: Nouvelles Editions Latines, 1952), pp. 214–18, and Dominico Casagrande, *Enchiridion Marianum Biblicum Patristicum* (Rome: Cor Unum, 1974), pp. 2003–13.

between different languages), help further to create a Mary severed from common experience. The aureate term *deifere*, above, for example, may appropriately convey one of her unique theological roles, a role unshared by other human women, but *genetrice* and *pulcritude* extend the same remoteness to motherhood and beauty.[5] Certain syntactic practices associated with marian titles increase this effect of distance and semantic difficulty: these include the listing of titles with limited further syntactic links within in the text, as in the extracts above, or the use of phrasal genitives: a 'mother of mercy' is not the same as a merciful mother nor is a 'blome of all beaute' a beautiful bloom, for the epithet becomes a universalized abstraction and the relation of the two noun-terms becomes mysteriously opaque. The phrasal genitives and noun phrases, sometimes translating Latin, frequently construct composite images which resist fully satisfactory realistic visualization, such as 'well of beautee', 'ros intact', 'buxom lanterne', 'gemme of chastite', or 'launtern of odour'. The mind's difficulties with encompassing what such titles denote make their referent seem exalted beyond common human comprehension or experience.[6] Combining familiar English with rare Latinate vocabulary, as in 'wife mundificate' or 'kynde curatrix', has a similar effect.[7] The allusive biblical or liturgical images, combined with lexical and syntactic devices like those just described, forge a lyric language which is manifestly not self-sufficient, requiring knowledge of other writings for interpretation and often having an air of being only half-way translated from another body of texts, Latin sources.[8]

The overall effect of such language is both to fragment the reader's sense of the figure or person of Mary and to create the impression of a diffused and displaced power: power refracted through a multitude of

---

[5]   Both recall and half translate Latin phrases that run through the Assumption liturgy: 'o pulcherrima inter mulieres', 'pulchra es' (from Song of Songs 1. 8, 15) and 'exaltata est sancta Dei Genitrix', 'Beata es, Virgo Maria, Dei Genitrix' (versicles).

[6]   Brown, *Fifteenth Century*, no. 13, ll. 4, 9–10, pp. 26–27; no. 26, l. 36, p. 48; no. 35, ll. 1–2, p. 61.

[7]   Brown, *Fifteenth Century*, no. 12, l. 3, p. 25; no. 28, l. 13, p. 50.

[8]   Woolf, p. 283, calls carols to the Virgin 'liturgical' because they resemble Latin hymns and sequences: 'in style and content they resemble no vernacular lyric genres, but recall the typological sequences of writers such as Adam of St Victor [...] [They] demand intelligence and learning in the hearer if they are to be fully understood' (p. 283). R. N. Swanson, *Religion and Devotion in Europe, c. 1215–c. 1515* (Cambridge: Cambridge University Press, 1995), pp. 77–78, observes that in biblical translations Latinisms were sometimes preferred as preserving the technical language of theology.

objects in the visible world. Marian titles shift the reader's attention onto
a host of other objects, many of them themselves slightly altered from
their normal appearance and associations by the characteristic stylistic
devices discussed above. Fragmentation also occurs in what Beverley
Boyd terms 'collage': the juxtaposition, common in liturgy and marian
lyrics, of disparate phrases, phrases divorced from their original context
and meaning in biblical source-texts.[9] Ricoeur's studies of metaphor
illuminate particularly aptly the effect of writing like this that relies
heavily on metaphoric titles. For Ricoeur metaphor is not just substitution
of one term for another and cannot be simply translated: it combines with
its referent to create a new, extended language and an enlarged
experience, while at the same time drawing attention to the fictionality of
its statement.[10] A metaphor and its referent are two objects for comprehension, not one, as in other signification. When Mary becomes 'emprice
of helle', a 'swete salue for al maner sare', or a sling with her son as the
stone, the realm of what is imaginatively conceivable expands and the
reader's sense of Mary's identity as a powerful being is dispersed and
fictionalized.[11]

It will already be clear that, like many aspects and tenets of the marian
cult, this style is only ambiguously feminist. While attributing hyperbolic
power to Mary it deflects attention onto other objects; the stylistic devices
associated with it make it hard to comprehend the precise nature of
Mary's power or to visualize completely satisfactorily even the symbolic
representations of its nature, literary effects which parallel the theological
ambiguities involved in the quasi-apotheosis of a human, and the celebration of a woman who is both mother and virgin. The result may be a
deeply mysterious, powerfully attractive, and reverent splendour, but the
verbal artifice, semantic alienations and dichotomies that play a part in
creating the particular type of jewelled and mentally dazzling hyperbole
to which writers of late medieval marian praise are so often drawn could

---

[9] 'Our Lady according to Geoffrey Chaucer: Translation and Collage', *Florilegium*,
Carleton University Papers on Late Antiquity and the Middle Ages, 9 (Ottawa: Carleton
University Press, 1987), pp. 147–54.

[10] Paul Ricoeur, *The Rule of Metaphor: Multi-disciplinary Studies of the Creation of
Meaning in Language*, trans. by Robert Czerny (Toronto: University of Toronto Press,
1977), pp. 143–57, 173–200, 247–56.

[11] Brown, *Fifteenth Century*, no. 15, l. 60, p. 31; no. 23, l. 11, p. 41; *Religious Lyrics of
the Fourteenth Century*, 2nd edn, rev. by G. V. Smithers (Oxford: Clarendon Press, 1957),
no. 32, l. 25, p. 47.

be seen also as expressions of unresolved contradictions in the elevation to so high a place in theology and devotion of a woman, in a society that gives women and female qualities in general little power or respect. Verbal creations like 'dulcis diamounde', 'tabernakyll of the trynyte', and 'cleir clarite Off Sapour sueit' may be new and original offerings to lay at the feet of the Mother of God but they evade any sense of affection, pregnancy, or purity, which is familiar or readily graspable by the reader's mind, not just because no other human has experienced virginal motherhood but because the words refer to this mystery through metaphors far removed from the organic, human body.[12]

Marian titles and typological images are sometimes employed in a syntactically unmediated form, remaining a lexicon rather than a language. We see examples above, or in this Latin *ABC* prayer:

> Arca deitatis,
> Aula summae majestatis,
> Fons totius bonitatis [...][13]

At other times writers embed them within flexible and dynamic syntax, forming islands of static, meditative liturgical evocation amid a variety of other discourses which may include action, emotion, and narrative. Alphabetic and acrostic structures combine so often and so successfully with the 'collage' style and with syntactically unmediated titles and images because they are also styles that fragment the figure of Mary.[14]

Marian titles, whether familiar or recondite, are necessarily intertextual and always to some extent a riddle, drawing on other texts and conveying

---

[12] 'Dear diamond', 'tabernacle of the Trinity', 'clear purity of sweet taste'; Brown, *Fifteenth Century*, no. 28, l. 49, p. 51; no. 23, l. 39, p. 42; no. 22, l. 75, p. 40.

[13] 'Ark of the deity, hall of the highest majesty, fountain of all goodness', *Analecta hymnica medii aevi*, ed. by Guido M. Dreves and Clemens Blume, 58 vols (Leipzig: Reisland, 1893) XV, p. 107.

[14] See *Lexikon der Marienkunde*, ed. by Konrad Algermissen et al. (Regensburg: Friedrich Pustet, 1967–), I, *Abecedarien*, pp. 17–19. Woolf, p. 284, saw in lyrics built on a sequence of marian types not fragmentation but a procession through human history: 'the value lies in the effect of a triumphant procession of types: the Virgin is praised by the amassing together of the people or objects in the Old Testament that prefigured her'. The *Psalter of Mary* is a long string of titles (*Hymni Latini medii aevi*, ed. by F. J. Mone, 3 vols (Freiburg: Herder, 1853–55), I, no. 504, pp. 233–60). On enumeration see Patrick S. Diehl, *The Medieval European Religious Lyric: an Ars Poetica* (Berkeley, Los Angeles, London: University of California Press, 1985), pp. 113–18.

mysteries whose full meaning lies elsewhere.[15] Given the riddle-element
intrinsic to the style, and given the fact that, in actuality, the riddles in
most marian titles were completely familiar and conventional, it is
interesting to explore here a few examples which are either puzzling or
unusual in themselves or used creatively by writers exploiting the
multiple sources, implications and themes often present in the small
compass of an honorific title.

My first example is a little-studied fifteenth-century lyric, 'Regina celi,
qwene of th[e] sowth'. It takes the collage style of disjointed, allusive
titles and, far from minimizing its potential for disconnectedness and
oddness, exploits it with powerful results.[16] Baffling shifts and juxtapositions, combined with wording which twists already mysterious
typological titles, offer a series of genuinely difficult verbal riddles which
yield, as they are unravelled by the reader, compact image clusters with
multiple theological references. The poem presents Mary simultaneously
as the Bride of the Lamb at the Last Judgement, the Bride called by Christ
to her own Assumption, as Wisdom drawn to God, as virginity which is
naturally drawn to the eternal realm, and as the Mother of Mercy
summoning sinners to salvation.

> Regina celi, qwene of th[e] sowth,
> A-fourmed by Salomon in his sapience,
> Ful swete or tho wordis come out of thy mowth,
> Thow blisful mayde, with grete prudence,
> Quo progredieris from youre presence?
> Most hiest in montibus, most salience,
> Maria Virgo assumpta est.
>
> Harvest is com, I com to shere,
> The myrrour of Immortalitee,
> Vox dilecta is in her eere,
> Thus she saide, transite ad me. (ll. 1–11)[17]

---

[15] See *The Myroure of our Ladye*, ed. by J. H. Blunt, EETS, ES 19 (London, 1873), pp.
49, 62–67, on the labour and concentration which should be involved in worship, spiritual
reading, and meditation.

[16] London, British Library, Harley MS 2250, fols 33–34. The original reads 'thy sowth'.
Printed by H. N. MacCracken in 'Lydgatiana V: Fourteen Short Religious Poems', *Archiv
für das Studium der Neueren Sprachen und Literatur,* 131 (1913), 40–59 (pp. 50–51).

[17] *A-fourmed*: created; *wordis*: the words spoken by Wisdom in Ecclesiasticus 24, specifically verses 11–12, a reading for the Assumption Vespers; *Quo progredieris*: 'Whither
are you going?' (*Virgo prudentissima, quo progredieris*, antiphon for Assumption
Vespers); *presence:* companions; *in montibus*: in the mountains; *salience*: skipping up,

The title 'qwene of the sowth' signals this multiplicity of roles. It denotes the Queen of Sheba. She was identified with the Bride of the Song of Songs (the key text for the doctrine of the Assumption) and therefore with Mary. Under this title 'queen of the south' she appears in Matthew 12. 42, where it is prophesied that she will 'rise up in the judgement'. She was also identified with the Sibyl and Wisdom, who seeks Solomon.[18] The subterranean unifying factor in the text's sequence of disparate references and contexts is the theme of humanity being drawn towards union with the divine.

The exegesis underlying the doctrine and liturgy of the Assumption had conflated many different texts which could be interpreted as prefigurations of the Virgin's union with the deity: the Song of Songs; the descriptions of Wisdom and her search for 'rest' (contemplation), in Wisdom 24 and Ecclesiasticus 24; the Queen of Sheba's journey to Solomon in I Kings 10; and Mary of Bethany's choice of the 'better part' (interpreted as virginity or contemplation), Luke 10. The Bride of the Lamb and woman clothed with the sun, in Revelation 12 and 19, were identified with Mary in her Assumption and at the Last Judgement, and also with Wisdom, created from eternity by God (Ecclesiasticus 24. 2–5, 9). That is why line 2 says she was created, 'A-fourmed ... in his sapience' by Solomon who, as the lover of Queen of the South, represents the eternal godhead to which the Virgin and Wisdom are drawn.[19] Line 42 of this lyric will call Mary 'a cypres in science', linking this identification with Wisdom (a theme prominent in the liturgy of the Assumption) to the imagery of the Crucifixion discussed below.[20]

---

prominent (Song of Songs 2. 8); *Vox dilecta*: the voice of the beloved (Song of Songs 1. 8), *transite ad me*: come to me [all you who love me] (Ecclesiasticus 24. 19); *Maria Virgo assumpta est*: the Virgin Mary has ascended, from antiphon for Assumption Vespers.

[18] Lines from the Song of Songs appear in the legend of Mary's death and Assumption: Jacobus de Voragine, *Golden Legend: Readings on the Saints*, trans. by William Granger Ryan, 2 vols (Princeton: Princeton University Press, 1934), II, pp. 79–83.

[19] William O'Shea, 'The History of the Feast of the Assumption', *The Thomist*, 14 (1951), 118–32; *Marienlexikon*, ed. by Remigius Bäumer and Leo Scheffczyk, 6 vols (St Ottilien: Erzabtei St Ottilien, 1988–), III, *Himmelfahrt Mariae*, pp. 199–208. Ecclesiasticus 24 yields the images of honey and comb, cedar and cypress, and of Wisdom/Mary seeking 'rest' (contemplation, Christ), and bidding the people come and feed from her; it also explains lines 2–3, since Wisdom says she was created from the mouth of the most high; see Marina Warner, *Alone of All her Sex: The Myth and the Cult of the Virgin Mary* (London: Wiedenfeld and Nicolson, 1976), pp. 192–205, on milk and Wisdom.

[20] Wisdom calls herself 'a cedar of Lebanon [...], a cypress on the slopes of Hermon', Ecclesiasticus 24. 13.

Stanza two continues to operate simultaneously in multiple contexts:
the Assumption, Last Judgement, and the tradition of Mary as immaterial
Wisdom which is in union with God. The marian title used in its second
line, 'myrrour of Immortalitee', comes from 'speculum sine macula Dei
maiestatis', Wisdom 7. 26, exegetically interpreted as a reference to
Mary's virginity.[21] Virginity lies at the heart of the dogma of the Assumption, giving Mary her affinity with eternity and making ordinary mortality
unsuitable for her (Mary did not die but ascended to heaven from her
deathbed). The first line of stanza two associates this, Mary's affinity
with the eternal, with Judgement, through the harvest imagery from
Revelation 14. 14–20, and Mary appears later at line 58 explicitly as the
woman crowned with stars, the Bride, from Revelation 12, 19.[22] There is
not space here to explore all the complexities of this lyric, but it is
relevant to note its disconcerting, highly original shifts in focalization:
sometimes a human voice speaks to Mary, sometimes she is described in
the third person, and sometimes she speaks. There is theological subtlety
in these shifts: they partly reflect the fact that Wisdom herself speaks in
Ecclesiasticus 24 (and line 3 prepares us for the first-person speech of
Mary as the incarnation of eternal wisdom), but they also dramatize her
role as Mother of Mercy to sinners. Thus stanza two forges a link
between Mary's own summons to heaven, 'Vox dilecta is in her eere',
voiced by the narrator, and her own power to draw humanity after her:
'transite ad me', voiced by Mary. She is both a human suppliant elevated
by God and a heavenly queen with power to dispense mercy. Mary's
identification with Wisdom in these two stanzas, epitomized in the two
titles that designate her as Queen of Sheba and immortal wisdom, lines 1
and 9, itself leads, in the exegetical subtext to the sequence of bizarre
juxtapositions, to her call to humanity in line 11, since Wisdom expresses
a desire to draw humanity to heaven in Wisdom 6. 13–9. 16. Mary's close
bond with her human companions is present already in stanza one: 'Quo
progredieris', line 5, was the cry of the apostles standing round Mary's
deathbed as she ascended, found in the *Legenda Aurea*'s Assumption
narrative and a Vespers antiphon for the Assumption. 'Youre presence'
means the apostles. This theme of Mary's help to sinners to rise to eternal
life comes to full prominence in the final stanzas: 'Sucurre nobis or we be
layde on beere' ('Help us before we are laid on the bier'), prays the

---

[21] 'Spotless mirror of the majesty of God'.

[22] Perhaps analogously, *Pearl*, lines 39–40, combines harvest imagery with August, the
month of the feast of the Assumption.

narrator in the last stanza, line 74, echoing the Hours of the Virgin anthem *Sancta Maria, sucurre.*

In stanzas four and six images of nurturing fruitfulness dominate. Mary announces herself as a cedar raised up in Lebanon and as fruit of the Godhead, titles bringing imagery of the Cross into the already multiple identity the lyric creates for her:

stanza 4
> With my mylke I drank the wyne,
>   Water and bloode my sustenaunce,
> The Rede appul of my gardyne,
> For mannes soule hath made fyaunce
> Thus she saith with grete Retenaunce... (ll. 24–28)

stanza 6
> As a Cedre I am haunced in libano,
>   Above al bankis I do sprede,
> And as a cypres in science also;
>   I am the fruyte of the hye godhede,
>   I bere the grapes Crist to feede,
> The clustris hang vpon my brest,
>   To mylke mankynd whan he hath nede.
> Maria Virgo assumpta est. (ll. 40–47)[23]

The Bridegroom's summons to the garden, Song of Songs 5. 1, and the metaphor of the Bride as a garden, Song of Songs 4. 12, texts signifying exegetically Mary and her Assumption, are integrated here with tree-imagery that combines Mary as suckling mother—to humanity—and the

---

[23] These images run through the readings for the Assumption: Wisdom speaks of herself as a cedar, cypress, and vine, from which humanity can feed and drink, Ecclesiasticus 24. 13–22; in Song of Songs 1. 1–4, the Bride's breasts are sweeter than wine; in John 2, a reading for the Vigil of the Assumption, 'Blessed are the breasts that gave thee suck'; the reading for Nocturns, a sermon by St John Damascene, refers to a paradise of the New Adam, in which is planted the tree of life; the Lauds hymn, 'O gloriosa virginum', refers to Mary suckling the Child and restoring what Eve lost; the Lauds antiphon says 'Blessed are you, daughter, by the Lord, because by you we receive the fruit of life. *Fyaunce*: promise, *retenaunce*: company (Mary's retinue of angels or apostles), *haunced*: raised up ('*Quasi cedrus exaltata sum in Libano, et sicut cypressus in monte Sion*', I am raised up like a cedar in Lebanon, a cypress in mount Sion), Response for Nocturns, Assumption. The 'rede appul', reversing the apple of Eden, as Mary reverses Eve (see 'Ave Maris Stella', Dreves, *Jahrtausend*, p. 238), but also, like 'grapes', an image of the Blood of Christ.

Cross on which the Redeemer hangs as humanity's life-giving 'Rede appul'.[24] The food images—milk, fruit, breasts, wine, and grapes—derive from the Song of Songs and Ecclesiasticus 24, key sources for the Assumption and its liturgy, but here used polysemically also for Mary's motherhood and the Nativity, Crucifixion, and Eucharist, as well as the Last Judgement where iconographical tradition often represented Mary showing her breasts in intercession while Christ showed his wounds.

The poet exploits Mary's dual role as celestial co-redemptrix and fellow human being. Wine and milk, line 24, derive from Wisdom 7. 24; here Mary drinks her own milk as well as eucharistic wine, and as well as the water and blood of the Atonement, a bewildering combination signifying her double position in heaven as both recipient and mediatrix of divine mercy. She defines herself, lines 43–44, as the 'fruyte' (offspring) of God as well as a bearer of the fruit, a tree (apple tree/cedar/cypress/vine). Mary's breasts and Christ's blood, as he hangs on the tree, the Cross, become one at the end of stanza six, the poet drawing on the medieval physiological theory that milk and blood had the same origins, as well as the display of breasts and wounds at the Last Judgement.[25]

In the last stanza Mary names herself not with one of the titles of the Queen of Heaven but as humanity's loving relative:

> Youre cousyn, youre kynde, so hye imprest:
> Loke up youre strength is in my toure. (ll. 60–61)

Wisdom 8. 17, 'immortalitas est in cognatione sapientiae' ('in kinship with wisdom there is immortality') underlies Mary's plea. Though their rhetorical simplicity is striking after the esoteric allusions of previous stanzas, these homely self-designations by Mary as 'Youre cousyn, youre kynde', and her call to the human family to aspire to join her in heaven, develop a theme typologically implicit in the double marian title of the

---

[24] See Guillaume de Deguileville, *Pélerinage de l'âme*, ed. by J. J. Stürzinger, Roxburghe Club (London: Nichols, 1895), ll. 5591–6702, pp. 185–220, for an extended allegory of Jesus as apple and Mary as apple tree.

[25] See Caroline Walker Bynum, *Holy Feast and Holy Fast: The Religious Significance of Food to Medieval Women* (Berkeley: University of California Press, 1987), pp. 205–222; see also the important discussion of this and the wider question of the implications of representations of sacred bodies in David Aers, 'The Humanity of Christ: Reflections on Orthodox Late Medieval Representations', in David Aers and Lynn Staley, *The Powers of the Holy: Religion, Politics and Gender in Late Medieval English Culture* (University Park: Pennsylvania State University Press, 1996), pp. 15–42.

first line: 'Regina celi, qwene of the sowth'. Just as the Bride of the Song of Songs could be read as a symbol of the Church, as well as the Virgin, summoned towards union with God, so the Queen of Sheba was interpreted by some exegetes as the Church, especially the gentiles, gathered from the farthest corners of the earth.[26] The opening line's two titles unite Mary's celestial and mortal affinities, as do water and blood, line 25.

Any poetic success this lyric has cannot be on the basis of emotive writing, dramatic action, or any particular splendour as a hymn of praise, but for its virtuoso play of marian allusions, titles, and images, and the highly original manipulation of focalization alternating between speakers, and between Mary and the human suppliant, which accompanies and dramatizes the rapidly shifting identities it gives to Mary. The wonder the poem evokes, and offers as its homage to Mary, is primarily sheer intellectual amazement and the multiplicity of simultaneous identities it is able to accord to Mary through intermingling exegetical references, images, and titles. Its capacity to act as a prayer for intercession lies in the learned ingenuity with which it shows Mary's desire for the sinner's redemption to be a theme which is an integral part of the typological symbolism of the Assumption. There is, however, something disturbing about the way a poet can move between so many different designations for Mary, without much sense of a unifying central figure: what unifies the text is the network of allusions and images, as well as the motive of religious need that prompts such ingenious praise in the hope of winning Mary's benevolent concern. It shows up the alienations and fragmentations involved when power depends on typology, and its poetic success derives from exploiting these. The kind of power attributed to Mary in the Assumption, Judgement, and Coronation, power allegedly written in the cosmos and through time, is primarily a set of significations: of readings.[27] That is perhaps why in the later Middle Ages, when interest shifted from the Nativity and Crucifixion, biblical events where Mary plays a part, to the Assumption, Coronation, and Judgement, in which her powers are derived from typology, we find titles, metaphoric formulas, and collage playing so large a role in marian praise.

---

[26] *Lexikon der Christlichen Ikonographie*, ed. by Ewald Kirschbaum, 7 vols (Rome and Freiburg: Herder, 1965–74), IV (1972), pp. 2–3.

[27] The Assumption hymn 'Quae est ista' is based precisely on this fact: it lists the exegetical interpretations which create the claims for a Mary who is Queen of Heaven, advocate, and whose identity and power are inscribed throughout the Bible, Dreves, *Jahrtausend*, II, 256–57.

Chaucer's *ABC*, an infinitely more powerful and controlled work, opens with an invocation to Mary of more radical originality than may first appear, though it lacks the startling eccentricity of 'Regina celi, qwene of the sowth'.[28] The stanzas of this alphabetic prayer employ marian titles and types but they are not recondite—'Haven of refut', 'queen of misericorde', burning bush, well of pity, and so on—though Chaucer interweaves familiar images with unostentatious complexity. It opens, however, like this:

> Almighty and al merciable queene,
> To whom that al this world fleeth for socour,
> To have reless of sinne, or sorwe, and teene,
> Glorious virgine, of all floures flour,
> To thee I fle, confounded in errour. (ll. 1–5)[29]

Chaucer's translation departs from the opening of its source, Deguileville's prayer to the Virgin in the *Pélerinage de vie humaine*: 'A toi, du monde le refui'.[30] In Chaucer's equally original conclusion, he repeats the word *merciable* and the double alliteration on the letters *m* and *a*:

> Now, ladi bryghte, sith thou canst and wilt
> Ben to the seed of Adam merciable,
> Bring us to the palais that is bilt
> To penitentes that ben to merci able. Amen. (ll. 181–84)

'Adam merciable' and 'merci able' give us *a/m* and *m/a*, the final words forming a *rime riche* variant on 'al merciable' in lines 1 and 182. While creating a typically 'Ricardian' circularity through these new first and last lines, Chaucer was perhaps influenced by the idea of a rosary, or by Deguileville's comment that his alphabetic Latin prayer 'Ave benedic-

---

[28] See William E. Rogers, *Image and Abstraction: Six Middle English Religious Lyrics*, Anglistica, 18 (Copenhagen: Roskilde and Bagger, 1972), pp. 82–106; Alfred David, 'An ABC to the Style of a Prioress', in *Acts of Interpretation: The Text in its Contexts. Essays on Medieval and Renaissance Literature in Honor of E. Talbot Donaldson*, ed. by Mary J. Carruthers and Elizabeth D. Kirk (Norman, OK: Pilgrim Books, 1982), pp. 147–57; Georgia Ronan Crampton, 'Chaucer's Singular Prayer', *Medium Aevum,* 59 (1990), 191–213; Helen Phillips, 'Chaucer and Deguileville: the *ABC* in Context', *Medium Aevum*, 61 (1993), 1–19.

[29] Quotations from Chaucer are from *The Riverside Chaucer*, ed. by Larry D. Benson, (Boston: Houghton Mifflin, 1987). *Teene*: injury, pain, vexation.

[30] *Le Pélerinage de vie humaine*, ed. by J. J. Stürzinger, Roxburghe Club (London: Nichols, 1893), ll. 10,895–11,192, pp. 338–49. See Phillips, 'Chaucer', pp. 1–6.

tissime' constitutes a crown for the Virgin and her son.[31] The play on *a/m* and *m/a,* at beginning and end, may celebrate *Ave Maria,* the reversal of letters perhaps reflecting the motif of Mary herself reversing Eve's sin, in the words 'Ave Maria'.[32]

There is no mystery about Chaucer's choice of the title 'al merciable queene' in his first line: an alphabet prayer has to have *a* in its first line and 'merciable' foregrounds Mary's paramount attribute, while the *a/m* alliteration allows the first letter of Mary's name to be celebrated, together with *a,* line 1, and also suggests *Ave Maria* (the alphabet, Creed, Lord's Prayer, and *Ave Maria* formed together the materials for elementary reading). The phrase echoes titles like 'mater misericordiae', 'regina misericordiae', common in hymns and lyrics, and also the prayer beginning 'O Royne de misericorde' ('O Queen of mercy') which Deguileville added to the second recension of his *Pèlerinage.*[33]

The puzzle is the word 'almighty'. Mary is not almighty: only God is.[34] Conceivably Chaucer derived this heterodox title from an eccentric theological source, perhaps the *Mariale* which, being attributed to Albert the Great, acquired some circulation. This devotes a chapter to Mary's omnipotence, claiming the Son has given her an omnipotence equal to his own, in heaven, earth and hell: 'The power of mother and son are one and the same'. It includes other extreme statements: 'Our Mother, who art in heaven, give us our daily bread'; 'In the sacrament of her Son we also eat and drink her flesh and blood'.[35] A. G. Rigg suggests that the recherché

---

[31] Found in two manuscripts at the end of his *Pèlerinage de l'âme,* ed. by Stürzinger, p. 384. He wrote other alphabetic prayers and acrostic poems on 'Maria' and 'Ave Maria'; Stürzinger, *Pèlerinage de l'âme,* pp. 383–85.

[32] *Ave Maria* was sometimes inscribed on rings, Charles Oman, *British Rings 800–1914* (London: Batsford, 1974), p. 119, notes on 74G, 75A–E. Alphabet prayers predate Christianity: Psalm 119 is the best-known example; they were especially associated with Mary; see Dreves and Blume, XV, pp. 321–409.

[33] Chaucer probably knew the second recension; see Phillips, pp. 6–7, 16, for further possible links.

[34] 'Regina celi', l. 35, reads 'Goddis moder omnipotent', but grammatically this means 'mother of omnipotent God'. There were marian reformulations of the *Te Deum, Confiteor* and Athanasian Creed: Mone, vol. I, p. 501; F. J. E. Raby, *A History of Christian-Latin Poetry from the Beginnings to the Close of the Middle Ages,* 2nd edn (Oxford: Clarendon Press, 1953), p. 375; Gray, *Themes and Images,* pp. 83–85.

[35] *Mariale,* 10, 1, 8; 2.2.3, quoted in Graef, I, p. 451. The whole text of the *Mariale* is found in Albertus Magnus, *Opera Omnia,* ed. by August Borgnet, 38 vols (Paris: Vivès, 1890–99), XXXVII.

metaphors in some fourteenth-century English Latin marian lyrics perhaps reflect another heterodox marian text, Richard of St Laurent's *De laudibus beatae virginis*. Nevertheless, nothing else in Chaucer's poem suggests a taste for, or influence from, eccentric theological source-texts.[36]

The inspiration for adding 'almighty' to 'al-merciable' may be a familiar phrase, 'Omnipotens et misericors...', found in many prayers in the medieval liturgy, addressed not to Mary but to God. The impetus for importing this phrase into Chaucer's prayer to Mary could have come from two aspects of his approach to translating Deguileville: the stronger liturgical colouring he brings to his version and his emphasis on the theme of penitence.[37] The combination 'omnipotens et misericors' would be familiar particularly from formulas of Absolution: 'Absolutionem et remissionem omnium peccatorum vestrorum... tribuat vobis omnipotens et misericors Deus'.[38] Perhaps Chaucer, with the theme of the penitent praying for mercy in mind, remembered the comforting words of the Absolution and redistributed them from God, who grants mercy, to Mary whose privilege is to intercede for it. Amid several references to penitence, Chaucer identifies his speaker explicitly as a penitent:

> To you my soule penitent I bring. (l. 141)

If Chaucer's poem is focalized from the position of a penitent involved in the liturgical dialogue of pleading for absolution, that supplies a context in which the words of the liturgical response to such a plea—the words of the Absolution—might come to seem an appropriate expression of the powers which, through Mary's mediation, the speaker invokes most fervently. We must never forget that the titles with which Mary is praised are also, and primarily, titles by which her help is invoked. Chaucer's concluding lines, quoted earlier, also look forward to the achievement of forgiveness: 'Now, ladi bryghte, sith thou canst and wilt [...]', lines 181–84.

---

[36] 'Anglo-Latin in the Ricardian Age', in *Essays on Ricardian Literature in Honour of J. A. Burrow*, ed. by A. J. Minnis, Charlotte C. Morse, and Thorlac Turville-Petre (Oxford: Clarendon Press, 1997), pp. 121–41 (p. 129).

[37] Rogers, pp. 105–06 stresses the greater prominence of the theme of penitence in Chaucer.

[38] 'May omnipotent and merciful God grant you absolution and remission of all your sins', *The Lay-Folks Mass-Book*, ed. by Thomas F. Simmons, EETS 71 (1879), p. 92; *The Use of Sarum*, ed. by W. H. Frere, 2 vols (Cambridge: Cambridge University Press, 1898), I, p. 64; it occurs in vernacular prayers too, e.g. IMEV 10.1C, 'Almyghty god of mercyes moste'; 9.56, 'Eterne, omnipotent, mercifull *and* iuste'.

Other late medieval prayers besides the Absolution link omnipotence and mercy:

> Souervayne, immortal, everlastyng god,
> Almyghti, most mercyful, verray welle of grace [...]
>
> Almyghty god of mercyes moste [...]
>
> Eterne, omnipotent, mercifull and iuste [...][39]

The word *praepotens*, 'outstandingly powerful', which falls short of omnipotence, is sometimes used of Mary; the *O intemerata* calls her 'incomparabilis virgo' and one version also call her *praepotentissima.*

When John Marion in the fifteenth century imitated Chaucer's *ABC*, he avoided that heterodox 'almighty':

> All-merciable and gracious quene
> To whom all this world fleeth for socour... [40]

Chaucer's first line, without the problematic 'almighty', is also perhaps echoed in the fifteenth-century cento 'O merciful and O mercyable...', extant in three manuscripts and printed in Stow's Chaucer, 1561.[41]

'Almighty and most merciful Father' opens the Anglican General Confession which in the *Book of Common Prayer* replaced the pre-Reformation Confiteor with its references to Mary and the saints. Clearly the phrase has been transferred to the new English Confession from the old Latin Absolution, but curiously Cranmer seems not only, like Chaucer, to have added an intensifier to his second term, *merciful*, producing a first line with something of the swing of Chaucer's penitent's prayer to Mary, but also introduced as the next words the image 'we have erred and strayed from thy ways like lost sheep', which is drawn from Psalm 119. 176, and which is an alphabet psalm. Was Cranmer inspired by Chaucer's *ABC*?

Chaucer's double alliteration, *a* and *m*, may be a compliment to Anne of Bohemia, fusing veneration to two queens, sacred and secular. Chaucer's compliments in *Troilus*, I. 171, 'Right as oure firste lettre is now an A', and the *a* in the *Legend of Good Women*'s 'Alceste' and 'Hyd Absalon thy gilte tresses' suggest the possibility. The intertwining of the earthly and heavenly queen in the context of the theme of mercy would

---

[39] IMEV 8.73, ll. 1–2; 10.1C, l. 15; 9.56.

[40] MacCracken, pp. 53–56.

[41] IMEV 2510.

harmonize with contemporary assumptions about queenship.[42] The addition of *a* to the *m*, Anne to Mary, could be compared to Richard II's tendency to merge his own kingship with the court of heaven, as in his impaling of his own arms with those of St Edward, his promotion of what critics saw as quasi-divine forms of royal address, his portraiture in Christlike 'maiestas' pose in the Westminster Abbey portrait and in the Wilton Diptych, where the King and Mary are the dual poles of the design, and the boundaries between English royalty and the court of heaven are blurred.[43]

Whether any of these factors influenced Chaucer, his addition of 'almighty', his theological mistake, reflects the gap between popular understanding of Mary's power and theological definitions of her power as limited and dependent: the poet's originality arises from ambiguous and unstable elements within the concept of the Queen of Heaven.

The last lyric considered here, 'In a tabernacle of a toure', opens with two images common in the lexicon of marian titles and images: 'tabernacle' (she is tabernacle of the trinity), tower (tower of ivory), and 'moon' (she is 'pulchra ut luna', from Song of Songs 6):

> In a tabernacle of a toure,
> As I stode musyng on the mone,[44]

but they are disconnected here from the figure of Mary and relocated as part of the background setting seen by the earthly spectator as he gazes up towards her. And 'Quia amore langueo', used as the lyric's refrain, refers here not to her union with the celestial Bridegroom but her own concern for earthly sinners.[45] Mary's identity shifts rapidly from being a 'crowned queene, most of honoure', line 3, the object of veneration, to a more than usually active, vehement subject, a wooer of humanity; we begin with the speaker gazing at Mary as celestial queen, in a tabernacle like a statue, a static object of an adoring gaze, but what follows is Mary's own energetic

---

[42] See Paul Strohm, 'Queens as Intercessors', in *Hochon's Arrow: The Social Imagination of Fourteenth-Century Texts* (Princeton: Princeton University Press, 1991), pp. 95–119.

[43] See *Chaucer's Dream Poetry*, ed. by Helen Phillips and Nick Havely (London and New York: Longman, 1998), pp. 294–300; and Phillips, 'Literary Allusion in Chaucer's "Hyd, Absalon, Thy Gilte Tresses Clere"' *Chaucer Review*, 30 (1995), 134–49; 'Politics and Register in the *Legend of Good Women*', *Chaucer Review*, (forthcoming).

[44] Brown, *Fourteenth Century*, no. 132, pp. 234–37.

[45] 'For I am sick of love', Song of Songs, 5. 8.

concern for humans.[46] The text, abounding in questions, exclamations, sudden twists and turns of emotional persuasion, uses all the rhetoric of cajoling motherhood. Mary presents her own titles as arguments in her own armoury of rhetoric to urge penitence:

> I am hys vokete to voyde his vyce; (l. 10)

> Moder of mercy I was for the made; (l. 33)

Mary's Assumption here, as in 'Regina celi, qwene of the sowth', becomes a two-way movement towards divine/human union; she is raised up to heaven only to turn her attention, in pleading, to earth:

> Why was I crouned and made a qwene?
> Why was I called of mercy the welle? (ll. 81–82)

Her own gaze turns earthwards, seeking the human:

> I loue, I loke when man woll craue, (l. 18)

> O wreche in the worlde, I loke on the,
> I se thy trespas day by day (ll. 25–26)

Not least among the many achievements of this poem is its transformation of the titles that so often in late medieval lyrics diffuse and divert Mary's power, and the gaze that so often appropriates, into vehicles for a Mother of Mercy who, herself, acts, speaks, looks, and woos with vigour. To a great extent, marian titles function themselves as objects of devotion. Frequently, and at their most characteristic, they declare a supra-normal entity which, like the divine in general and the Christian Virgin-Mother in particular, unites contradictions, contains paradoxes, and has the power to stir, enchant, and mystify the worshipper. They do, however, move the vision of female power towards the safely abstract and the linguistic. Their initial awe-inspiring strangeness proves to be a mystery that dissipates once theological and biblical references are decoded: this decodability recoups that potential awe for a female cosmic power back securely into the authority of clerkes.

---

[46] See Woolf, pp. 301–02.

The 'Querelle des femmes': A Continuing Tradition in Welsh Women's Literature

CERIDWEN LLOYD-MORGAN

The 'Querelle des Femmes' is one of the most familiar medieval themes of European literature and was embraced enthusiastically by writers such as Walter Map, Jean de Meung, Lydgate and Boccaccio.[1] From the twelfth century onwards, a strong antifeminist streak emerges in both Latin and vernacular literature, secular as well as religious, which in due course was countered by those taking a more positive attitude towards women and their role in society. Both the Christian Church and the scholarly traditions of the university contributed to the development of this debate, both of them powerful institutions dominated by men, with considerable overlap in terms of training and interest. Although the participants in this—often largely rhetorical—debate were usually men, Christine de Pisan provides a well-known exception to the rule. However, she was not the only woman to speak out in defence of her sex, for Welsh literature provides some notable female voices responding to this tradition of literary misogyny.

Medieval Wales was not immune to antifeminism of a generalized kind, which is easily discernible in the work of the poets, the obvious example being that of Dafydd ap Gwilym in the mid-fourteenth century. Despite the publication of a pioneering article by the Dutch scholar Theodore M. Chotzen in 1931,[2] the impact of the European antifeminist

---

[1] For a selection of relevant texts, see *Woman Defamed and Woman Defended. An Anthology of Medieval Texts*, ed. by Alcuin Blamires (Oxford: Clarendon Press, 1992).

[2] Theodore M. Chotzen, 'La "Querelle des femmes" au Pays de Galles', *Revue celtique*, 48 (1931), 42–93.

tradition on Welsh literature has received comparatively little attention. It is striking that no examples of a literary debate on the subject survive from his time or earlier. This is perhaps curious, for in Welsh the literary dialogue or debate is a very ancient tradition. In the oldest Welsh poems and prose tales the dialogue is a common feature, as witness the 'Pa gur' poem in the Black Book of Carmarthen and the very similar debate in the Middle Welsh prose tale of *Culhwch ac Olwen*. In early poetry the *ymddiddan* (lit. 'conversation' or 'discussion') and *dadl* (lit. 'argument') are often used to present arguments of a religious nature, for example in 'Ymddiddan Arthur a'r Eryr' ('Dialogue of Arthur and the Eagle') and 'Dadl y Corff a'r Enaid' ('Argument between the body and the soul').[3] The poetic debate or *ymryson* (which can be compared in terms of form, at least, with the *tenso* of the Occitan poets), was used for a variety of themes and has remained extremely popular, even into the twentieth century. Despite the existence of such poetic forms ideal as vehicles for the debate on women, however, we have to wait until around 1500 to find a Welsh example, but it is a remarkable case, as Marged Haycock and Llinos Beverley Smith have shown in two articles published in 1990 and 1993 respectively.[4] This example involves two poets: one male, Ieuan Dyfi, and one female, Gwerful Mechain, the only medieval Welsh woman poet for whom we have a substantial corpus of surviving work.[5] Both were active in the late fifteenth and early sixteenth century. Most of the extant poems of Ieuan Dyfi reflect his obsessive feelings for a woman called Anni Goch ('Annie the Red' or 'Red-haired Annie').[6] The earliest of these poems, all composed in the *cywydd* form,[7] express the intense joy

---

[3]   See *Blodeugerdd Barddas o Ganu Crefyddol Cynnar*, ed. by Marged Haycock (Llandybïe: Cyhoeddiadau Barddas, 1994), pp. 203–33, 297–312. On the *ymddiddan* form see also below, p. 109 and n. 24.

[4]   Marged Haycock, 'Merched Da a Merched Drwg: Ieuan Dyvi v. Gwerful Mechain', *Ysgrifau Beirniadol*, 16 (1990), 97–110; Llinos Beverley Smith, 'Olrhain Anni Goch', *Ysgrifau Beirniadol*, 19 (1993), 107–26.

[5]   For a general introduction in English to the life and work of Gwerful Mechain, see Ceridwen Lloyd-Morgan, 'Women and their poetry in medieval Wales', in *Women and Literature in Britain 1150–1500*, ed. by Carol M. Meale, 2nd edn (Cambridge: Cambridge University Press, 1997), pp. 183–201. For a more detailed study of the poet and her work, see Nerys Howells, 'Astudiaeth destunol a beirniadol o farddoniaeth Gwerful Mechain' (unpublished doctoral thesis, University of Wales, Aberystwyth, 2000).

[6]   Twelve poems attributed to Ieuan Dyfi are included in *Gwaith Huw Cae Llwyd ac Eraill*, ed. by Leslie Harries (Cardiff: University of Wales Press, 1953), pp. 124–43.

[7]   The *cywydd* is one of the major metrical forms in Welsh, extremely popular from the fourteenth century onwards, consisting of a series of rhyming couplets, following

of reciprocated love, but then he begins to feel that she has become cool towards him, and he becomes angry and tormented. In this mood he turns for consolation to thoughts of those other men who have suffered because of women, and his *cywydd* 'I Anni Goch' provides a typical selection of *exempla* in the true 'querelle des femmes' tradition.[8] Gwerful Mechain then picks up the challenge and composes a powerful riposte to Ieuan Dyfi, defending Anni Goch herself and the entire female sex against the male poet's tirade.[9]

But this debate is no simple poetic exercise. Thanks to Llinos Beverley Smith's research in the records of the Consistory Court of the diocese of Hereford we now know that Ieuan Dyfi speaks here with his own voice, not that of a literary persona adopted as a convenient device. The fact that Anni Goch herself existed and had apparently been Ieuan's lover, gives extra piquancy to the exchange.[10] The jurisdiction of the diocese of Hereford covered some of the parishes on the Welsh side of the Border, and the records of the deanery of Leominster for the year 1501–02 note that a certain 'Ieuanus Dovy', from the parish of Norton in Radnorshire, then unmarried, had been first summoned to the church in Radnor on 12 July 1502, accused of adultery with a woman called Agneta Goze alias Lippard, obviously none other than Anni Goch herself.[11] Initially she denied adultery, but later claimed that Ieuan had raped her; he eventually confessed to unlawful intercourse with her. The story took a new turn in 1517, when John Lippard of Norton, apparently an Englishman, was accused of setting aside his legal wife, Anna Goze, and entering into a clandestine marriage with a woman called Katerina. Lippard was ordered to take Anni back, but he was unwilling to do so, claiming that she had conspired to cause his death (*machinata est mortem suum*); the court was also told that Lippard had sold Anni to Ieuan Dyfi (*cui maritus suus eam vendidit*: 'to whom her husband sold her'). This, of course, meant that Lippard felt he was free to remarry, with or without the blessing of the

---

particular rules as to line-length, placing of accent, and the use of *cynghanedd* (a complex system of alliteration in precise relationships to the main accents in the line, together with the use of internal rhyme).

[8]   *Gwaith Huw Cae Llwyd ac Eraill*, pp. 129–32.

[9]   For text and discussion see Marged Haycock, 'Merched da a merched drwg', to which I am greatly indebted.

[10]   Smith, 'Olrhain Anni Goch', esp. pp. 113–19.

[11]   In records relating to Wales, the Welsh 'ch' is usually represented by '3', often transcribed as 'z'.

Church, though by February 1518 he had started proceedings for divorce against Anni. Such a well-documented case of wife-selling in medieval Wales is rare, but serial monogamy without ecclesiastical sanction was apparently not uncommon.

Apart from the personal tensions involved, this case raises important questions relating to the Church's attempts to control and police sexual relationships in a community with secular traditions at odds with the laws and rituals of the Church, a matter which Llinos Beverley Smith explores at length. But this tale also clearly touches on the more complex issues of the nature of gender roles and the power balance within relationships, possibly compounded in this case, which straddles the Border, by political, cultural, and linguistic factors, especially since at least one of the protagonists, John Lippard, seems to be English. Such is the explosive background to the poetic debate between Ieuan Dyfi and Gwerful Mechain.

Ieuan's poem opens with an exemplum from Welsh tradition, as he compares himself with Merddin Wyllt, the poet Merddin or Myrddin, who corresponds to Merlin, and who went mad and was finally enslaved by a woman.[12] Here Ieuan blames his lover for driving him out of his senses. 'Merddin Wyllt am *ryw ddyn* wyf' ('I am like Merddin the Mad because of *some person*' [my italics]), he complains, unable even to bring himself to name her.[13] From the very first line, therefore, Ieuan sets his own experience on a par with that of famous men in history and legend, following what had become a common pattern in other European literatures in the Middle Ages, where these *exempla*, like the nine worthies, often fell into three categories: Classical, Jewish, and Christian. Here the division is still threefold but the categories are Welsh, biblical

---

[12] The story of Myrddin being imprisoned through the wiles of a woman is not explicitly attested in early Welsh tradition. Although his name is linked with that of a woman, Gwenddydd, in some sources she is represented as his sister. Later, however, the popularity of French romance in Wales led to the story of Viviane/Nineve influencing the native literature. The French *Prose Merlin* was probably available in Wales by the late fourteenth century, and the first unambiguous allusion to the continental version of the story is in a poem of uncertain authorship, possibly by Rhys Goch Eryri (*fl.* early fifteenth century), which refers to Myrddin being imprisoned under a rock for love of a woman. See *Trioedd Ynys Prydein*, ed. by Rachel Bromwich, 2nd edn (Cardiff: University of Wales Press, 1978), pp. 469–74, 559–60, and *Cywyddau Iolo Goch ac Eraill*, ed. by Henry Lewis, Thomas Roberts and Ifor Williams (Cardiff: University of Wales Press, 1937), no. cxi, p. 335, ll. 15–20.

[13] *Gwaith Huw Cae Llwyd ac Eraill*, p. 129, ll. 1–4.

(Old Testament only), and Classical. After beginning with Merddin Wyllt, Ieuan continues with first biblical and then Classical *exempla*: Samson and Solomon (though, curiously, not Adam and Eve, who usually figure in such lists in other languages), followed by Jason and Medea, Alexander, Brutus, Hercules, Paris, and Ovid. All Ieuan's *exempla*, as Marged Haycock has stressed, are centred on men and their sufferings: only a few of the women are actually named. This is surely deliberate, for naming the women would humanize and individualize them.

Although the consistory court records indicate that Ieuan Dyfi was resident in Radnorshire at the time of the court cases, his name reveals his origins on the Montgomeryshire-Merionethshire borders.[14] Gwerful Mechain, who responded to his diatribe, was from Montgomeryshire and appears to have lived there for most if not all of her life, and it seems likely that she and Ieuan had long known each other from poetic circles in that area. The fact that she heard his poem and composed a reply indicates that the poetic community in one area could be very well informed about events in other parts of the country; although at this late date the traditional system of patronage was beginning to break down, some poets still kept to their old peripatetic ways, travelling from one patron's house to another. However, we do not know how soon after its composition Ieuan Dyfi's poem came to Gwerful's ears and how quickly she responded.

In her poem, like Ieuan's comprising some eighty lines, Gwerful Mechain comes to the defence of Anni Goch in particular and women in general (see Figure 1). She produces her own list of examples, similarly drawn from the three traditions: Welsh, biblical, and Classical. From the Classical world she cites Dido, whilst the Welsh *Brutiau* have provided four examples: Wenddolen (the Guendoloena of Geoffrey of Monmouth), daughter of Corineus, and Marsia, wife of Cuhelyn, both of whom ruled kingdoms during their son's minority; Tonwen, wife of Dyfnwal Moelmud, and Genuissa, wife of Gweirydd, who both brought peace between warring factions. From Scriptural tradition she takes the mother of Judas and the wife of Pontius, both virtuous women who foretold the truth but whose menfolk did not heed them. Other examples cited include Elen ferch Coel (the Helena who discovered the True Cross), Susanna, who was falsely accused of adultery by two men and so was a very appropriate case in the circumstances, and finally Sibyl, who prophesied

---

[14] The border between the two former counties is defined in places by the river Dyfi (*anglice* Dovey).

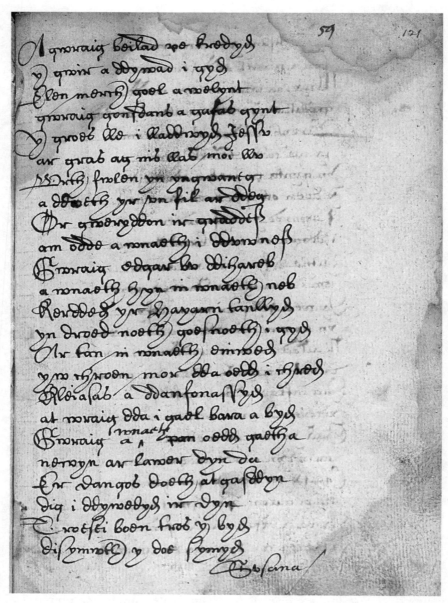

Figure 1. Part of Gwerful Mechain's cywydd *in defence of Anni Goch
(Aberystwyth, National Library of Wales, Peniarth MS 99, p. 121).*

the Day of Judgement. Interestingly, Gwerful does not mention the Virgin
Mary, perhaps because she is normally presented as the counterpoint to
Eve, whom Ieuan omits from his list. Recently, however, Jane Cartwright
has suggested that as all the women mentioned by Gwerful are chosen for
their active achievements in a non-domestic context, not for motherhood
or for conventionally feminine, passive virtues, the Virgin would have
been an inappropriate choice.[15] Gwerful concludes her poem with a more
direct attack on Ieuan Dyfi, answering his accusations against Anni Goch
by pointing out the hypocrisy of his double standards:

> Dywed, Ifan, 'rwy'n d'ofyn
> Yn gywir hardd, ai gwir hyn?
> Ni allodd merch, gordderchwr,
> Diras ei gwaith, dreisio'i gŵr!
> [...]
> Gad yn wib, godinebwr,
> Galw dyn hardd yn gledren hŵr.

(Tell me, Ieuan—I'm asking you in all sincerity—is this true? You philanderer,
no woman, however lewd, was ever able to rape her husband! [...] You
adulterer, leave off at once from calling a fine being a stingy whore).[16]

No doubt the audience who first heard these poems would have been
aware of the events that lay behind them. But by using the literary
tradition of the 'querelle des femmes' to express his bitterness against
Anni Goch, and thus—perhaps unintentionally—inspiring Gwerful
Mechain to respond in terms of the same discourse, Ieuan Dyfi had
sparked off a debate whose interest extended beyond their immediate
circle and time. The poems remained popular, for at least thirty-four
manuscript copies of Ieuan Dyfi's poem have survived and at least five
copies of that by Gwerful,[17] fewer, perhaps, but in view of the general
rarity of manuscripts of women's poetry, this is a good score, and they
testify to her poem being copied from the sixteenth to the eighteenth
century. Curiously, the two poems do not appear together in any extant
manuscript, despite both poets being from the same region, but early

---

[15] Jane Cartwright, *Y Forwyn Fair, Santesau a Lleianod. Agweddau ar Wyryfdod a
Diweirdeb yng Nghymru'r Oesoedd Canol* (Cardiff: University of Wales Press, 1999), pp.
33–34.

[16] Marged Haycock, 'Merched da a merched drwg', p. 105, ll. 63–6, 69–70.

[17] See the lists given by Leslie Harries in *Gwaith Huw Cae Llwyd ac Eraill*, p. 129, and
Marged Haycock in 'Merched Da a Merched Drwg', p. 103, n. 38.

manuscripts of Gwerful's work are scarce and little is yet known of the circumstances of their production.

Since Welsh vernacular texts throughout the medieval period reveal knowledge of major European literary trends, it may seem curious that this kind of debate should have arrived so late, unless, of course, there were other examples which have simply not survived. It is true that under the native law-codes the status of women in Wales differed from that in other European countries, and they enjoyed some privileges not available to their English or continental sisters, but even by the thirteenth century the Welsh laws reflected tradition more than any contemporary reality. More significant might be the absence of a university-based scholastic tradition and above all the unique political and linguistic factors affecting the relationship between the ecclesiastical establishments and the secular population, which meant that the latter confronted conflicting rather than consistent attitudes, with some sections of the Church supporting the Welsh in their wars with the English and others operating as the arm of the English crown.[18]

The theme of bad and good women, used to make general statements to condemn or praise the entire sex, did not vanish with the end of the Middle Ages in Wales, and Theodore Chotzen was amazed to find the debate still current in Welsh texts of the sixteenth century (by men), describing it as the 'résurrection surprenante' of a 'controverse ... moyen-âgeuse'.[19] But as late as the seventeenth century it was still very much alive, for it emerges in another poetic debate between a man and a woman, that between Jane Fychan or Vaughan, on the one hand, and Cadwaladr y Prydydd or Huw Cadwaladr on the other. Jane Vaughan was from Llanuwchllyn, near Bala in Merionethshire, and was probably born in the 1590s. She married Rowland Vaughan of Caer-gai, a member of one of the most important families in North Wales, and they had at least six surviving children.[20] On top of her heavy domestic responsibilities, Jane had to bear the consequences of her husband's political affiliations.

---

[18] On the law-codes, see *The Welsh Law of Women*, ed. by Dafydd Jenkins and Morfydd Owen (Cardiff: University of Wales Press for the Board of Celtic Studies, 1980); on the Church, see Glanmor Williams, *The Welsh Church from Conquest to Reformation* (Cardiff: University of Wales Press, 1976).

[19] Chotzen, p. 93.

[20] See the article on Rowland Vaughan in *The Dictionary of Welsh Biography down to 1940*, ed. by John Edward Lloyd and R. T. Jenkins (London: Honourable Society of Cymmrodorion, 1959), and references there given.

In the English Civil War Rowland Vaughan played a prominent part on the Royalist side and as a result, their home, Caer-gai, was burned to the ground by Cromwell's soldiers in 1645. Rowland was imprisoned and lost his house and his estates. In his lifetime and beyond he was respected as a poet and translator, his works being mainly of a religious or political nature, but his wife too had literary inclinations. Of the two surviving examples we have of poetry ascribed to Jane Vaughan one is religious, but the other, which continues the medieval antifeminist debate, is in a lighter vein.[21]

Here the argument on the sexes takes a rather different form to that of the interchange between Ieuan Dyfi and Gwerful Mechain. Whereas in that instance the man's poem came first, as a response to his own situation, evoking a riposte by the woman poet, this later case seems to be more of a planned literary exercise. It is a single poem where each participant contributes alternate verses. There are plenty of earlier models for this structure, for example an erotic dialogue between Gwerful Mechain and her own lover, Dafydd Llwyd o Fathafarn, with alternate stanzas by each.[22] In our seventeenth-century example the debate is initiated by the woman, but in the form of a general warning to young women not to get married. Although those manuscripts which specifically name Jane Vaughan refer to her by her married name and as of Caer-gai,[23] in the poem itself she takes the voice of the young, unmarried girl. Playing on the difference between her marital status in real life and in the persona presented in the poem would have added an extra, amusing dimension when the poem was received by her contemporaries or later by those who remembered her. This is in keeping with the general tone of the poem, which is light-heartedly satiric, in stark contrast to the bitter-ness and anger in the medieval poems discussed earlier. That this is above all a poetic exercise is again suggested by the title 'Ymddiddanion': in

---

[21] The religious poem ('O f'arglwydd Dduw trugarog tydi sy'n un a thri...' ('O, my merciful God, you who are one and three')) is preserved in Aberystwyth, National Library of Wales, MS Brogyntyn I.3, p. 625.

[22] See *Gwaith Dafydd Llwyd o Fathafarn*, ed. by W. Leslie Richards (Cardiff: University of Wales Press, 1964), p. 178, and *Canu Maswedd yr Oesoedd Canol/Medieval Welsh Erotic Poetry*, ed. by Dafydd Johnston, 2nd edn (Bridgend: Seren, 1998), p. 45.

[23] National Library of Wales, MS Peniarth 125 (p. 273); University of Wales Bangor, MS Bangor 421 (p. 470); London, British Library, MS Add. 15005, fol. 113[v]. Variant versions of the poem exist without any attribution, whilst in two other cases the dialogue is attributed to two male poets with one taking the part of the woman, raising different questions of role-playing and irony.

Welsh this can refer to various types of dialogue, sometimes too a kind of
narrative, but in the poetic context it usually involves an element of
debate or argument.[24]

The poem begins with an address to young girls in which Jane
Vaughan advises them not to marry, but to remain in their happy single
state. Cadwaladr answers that marriage has been ordained by God as the
proper state for both men and women, especially when the woman brings
with her a good dowry, but Jane dismisses this. Men, she declares, speak
sweet words and behave kindly when they are courting, but once they are
married they show their true colours, shout at their wives and abuse them:

> Mae llawer mab yn medru ymddwyn,
> Er ynnill clod, o fod yn fwyn,
> Yn deg ei raen fel un o'r wyn
> Fo draetha ei gŵyn yn dirion;
> Pan darffo ymrwymo ag effo yn gaeth
> Fo dru at waeth 'madroddion,
> Yn bloeddio a'i lais fel blaidd o'i le
> Dan dawli geirie geirwon.

(Many a young man can behave as if kindly, so as to be praised: he appears
as gentle as a lamb, and tells his tale tenderly, but once you are firmly
bound to him he changes his tune, shouting out with a voice like a wolf and
hurling harsh words). (Aberystwyth, National Library of Wales, MS
Cwrtmawr 204B, fol. 54).

This particular argument is found in other poems by women in the seventeenth and eighteenth centuries, many of which are concerned with the
problems of marriage and gender roles, and it became a favourite topos
among female poets composing in Welsh.[25] In this instance it provides a
context for the male poet to introduce the familiar list of *exempla* of bad
women. Since Jane Vaughan has criticized men's behaviour, Cadwaladr
attacks the women, invoking examples from the Bible and Classical
tradition:

---

[24] See above, p. 102, and cf. Brynley F. Roberts, 'Ystoria', *Bulletin of the Board of Celtic
Studies*, 26 (1974), 13–20, esp. p. 17 and n.1. Sioned Davies has stressed the importance
of the *ymddiddan* as a form of entertainment, see her *Pedeir Keinc y Mabinogi*
(Caernarfon: Gwasg Pantycelyn, 1989), 37–39, and *Crefft y Cyfarwydd* (Cardiff:
University of Wales Press, 1995), pp. 189–91.

[25] A good example is that by Marged ferch Ifan in the mid-eighteenth century manuscript
National Library of Wales MS, Cwrtmawr 128, p. 165, where the fifth stanza gives a very
similar account of a husband's behaviour.

> Trwy wraig y syrthiwyd Adda i lawr,
> Trwy wraig y sommwyd Samson gawr,
> O achos merch oedd deg ei gwawr
> Yr aeth Troia Fawr yn wreichion.
> A'i ddwy ferch a feddwodd Lot
> O ddiffyg canfod dynion,
> O nid uch chwi, ferch, yn ddifai,
> Gogenwch lai ar feibion.
> (MS Cwrtmawr 204B, fol. 54)

(Because of a woman Adam suffered the Fall, because of a woman the giant Samson was deceived, because of a girl's fair face great Troy went up in smoke. And Lot's daughters made him drunk, because they couldn't get a man—oh, you women are not blameless, so don't revile men so much).

The example of Adam and Eve was very common in the medieval tradition of the 'querelle des femmes' in Europe generally, although, as noted above, it is absent from Ieuan Dyfi's list. Here Adam's fall forms a couplet with that of Samson, who, as we have already seen, does appear in Ieuan's list and indeed elsewhere. Lot is yet another biblical example, whilst the unnamed Helen is blamed for the war of Troy. It is worth noting that here, as in Ieuan Dyfi's *cywydd*, the women themselves are not named in the lists of men who were betrayed or destroyed by women. The only woman whom Cadwaladr does name in this debate is Sara (the wife of Abraham in the Old Testament), whom he presents as an ideal of conjugal happiness. This image has no attraction for the woman poet, whose response is that she would prefer to live like that mythical bird the phoenix, alone, outside society.[26] The fact that the phoenix reproduces itself asexually—the new bird rising from the ashes of the old—may suggest misgivings about the consequences of the sexual activity which is central to the state of matrimony. Perhaps it would be taking speculation too far to suggest that an audience knowing that Jane Vaughan was married, and perhaps already a mother, would find this reference especially ironic. But the risk of death in childbirth may be behind the contention in a later stanza that it is the men's fault that too many young women go too soon to the grave.

---

[26] 'Mi fydda byw fel Phenics gynt/Mi gymra helynt hylwydd.' ('I shall live like the Phoenix of old, I shall take a fortunate course.') (National Library of Wales, MS Cwrtmawr 204B, fol. 54ᵛ).

The poem concludes in National Library of Wales, MSS Cwrtmawr 204 and Peniarth 239 with the man promising not to say unpleasant things about young women, but immediately devaluing that promise by describing them—again in the biblical tradition—as the weaker vessels. And men do love women, he adds, even those women with a sharp tongue. Women's tongues may be sharp sometimes, but this man's tongue is clearly forked!

In the various manuscript copies of the *Ymddiddanion* between Jane Vaughan and Cadwaladr, the order of the stanzas and even of couplets varies, and there are several major variants within the lines. This textual fluidity, instability even, is similar to that found in the folk-song tradition throughout the British Isles and also in other countries, where formulae or whole stanzas can be introduced at an appropriate point within a song, especially as part of a narrative or as a commentary. In this context it should be noted that one manuscript of our poem, British Library, MS Add. 15005, adds the note 'ar y gainc "Niw Mervles"'—it is to be sung to the tune of a popular air imported from England, called 'New Marvels'. Another copy, in National Library of Wales, MS Peniarth 239B, suggests: 'ar y don a elwir Amaryllis' (to the tune called Amaryllis). It is very common in manuscripts of the seventeenth and eighteenth centuries in Wales as, indeed, in England, for a tune to be noted in this way, and popular airs were used as a model or pattern by poets when composing. This appears to have been especially true for Welsh women poets during this period: from the secular poet Angharad James to the hymn composer Ann Griffiths, both of whom used common tunes, traditional or imported, and relied mainly on oral transmission of their work despite possessing a high degree of literacy.[27]

This oral dimension, including public performance of poems and producing verses to order on the spur of the moment in a poetic contest, has remained important well after the advent, in the nineteenth century, of widespread literacy in Wales. This may account for the persistence into the late nineteenth century of the antifeminist *exempla* first encountered in Welsh around 1500. This late survivor occurs within a short story by Ellen Hughes, better known by her pen-name Elen Engan, a feminist and temperance activist, poet and prose-writer. In 1896 she published a story called 'Camgymeriad Morfudd Prys' ('Morfudd Prys's mistake') in

---

[27] See Ceridwen Lloyd-Morgan, 'Oral composition and written transmission: Welsh women's poetry from the Middle Ages and beyond', *Trivium*, 26 (1991), 89–102.

Cymru, one of the most widely-read magazines in Welsh at the time.[28] The story is notable for various reasons, but within the present discussion its main interest lies in its striking echo of the earlier lists of antifeminist *exempla*.

At a crucial point in the narrative Morfudd Prys is made to feel that her relationship with her suitor has had a deleterious effect on both his character and his career. She has a terrible nightmare in which she sees him being tormented by two horrible demons. Worse still, they point to Morfudd and start to sing:

> ... yna dechreuasant adrodd bob yn ail llinell ryw hen rigwm a glywsai Morfudd yn ei phlentyndod. Ymmhen ychydig, canasant ynghyd y llinellau,—
>
> Merch a daflodd Adda i lawr,
> Merch a dwyllodd Samson gawr. (p. 191)

(... then they started to recite alternate lines of an old rhyme that Morfudd had heard in her childhood. Soon they both sang together the following lines:

> It was a woman who caused Adam's downfall,
> It was a woman who deceived the giant Samson).

The rest of the story need not concern us, but it is worth focusing on this rhyme. First of all, it is presented as verse from the oral tradition, for it is a rhyme which Morfudd had *heard*, not read, in her childhood. Moreover, it preserves the form of the *ymddiddan*, for the demons recite alternately. Furthermore, the couplet that is quoted is almost identical to that used in the seventeenth-century example: the only difference lies in the two verbs, which remain semantically identical to those in the earlier poem.

This late example poses a number of questions, notably, how to account for this survival, and whether the particular *ymddiddanion* in which Jane Vaughan took part were still alive in the oral tradition in late nineteenth century Wales. I have already suggested that at least some parts of the seventeenth-century text were 'floating verses' which were widely known and could be borrowed, with or without adaptation, to fit into new poems, especially in cases of extempore composition, perhaps as part of a poetic competition. One possible explanation is that the list of *exempla* in the seventeenth-century poem itself became just such a floating verse, widely known throughout north-west Wales at least, and like many other verses, was preserved in the end as a rhyme for children,

---

[28] *Cymru*, 10 (1896), 184–93.

once adults began to turn increasingly to the written word. It is probably no accident that the surviving couplet contains *exempla* drawn from the Bible, for one of the consequences of the success in Wales of the nonconformist denominations, with their emphasis on the reading and study of Scripture, was that by the end of the nineteenth century the Welsh-speaking population was probably more familiar with the Bible than with indigenous, secular literature.

It is not exceptional within the Welsh literary tradition in the Middle Ages and beyond to find themes common in French, English, or other European literatures but following a slightly different pattern. The apparently late arrival of the 'querelle des femmes' and its remarkable persistence into very recent times provide yet another case to prove that rule. More than that, however, each of our three examples reflects how women involved in the production of literature turned what was essentially a debate initiated by men to their own uses, not only refuting men's accusations but providing evidence of men's injustice to women and invoking more positive images of the female sex. Furthermore, the transformations to the form and content of that debate as represented by Gwerful Mechain, Jane Vaughan, and Elen Engan, represent in microcosm broader changes that took place in the relationship between poet and audience and between oral and written modes of literary composition and transmission as well as in the social and cultural life of women in Wales from the Middle Ages to the nineteenth century.

Reading Constructed Narratives:
An Orphaned Medieval Heiress
and the Legal Case as Literature

NOËL JAMES MENUGE

Some time during the year of 1342 or 1343,[1] a young woman of about fifteen years of age met her betrothed in a field in Yorkshire and married him by a stone known as 'stoupandstone'.[2] The marriage was apparently celebrated by mass some two years later, followed shortly by the birth of a son, and then by a daughter.[3] This couple might have lived happily ever after and we be none the wiser about their lives were it not for the sudden and unexpected death of the young woman's husband, which precipitated an extraordinary series of events preserved in almost twenty large sheets

---

[1] This article was originally inspired by a conversation with Felicity Riddy in 1997, when she questioned me with great enthusiasm about the life of Constance de Skelmanthorpe, a fourteenth-century ward and heiress, and my reading of her circumstances (as found in the legal case CP E 62: de Hopton c. del Brome). She questioned my then reading of the legal case as that of an autonomous woman fighting for her own rights, and suggested, experimentally, that I consider Constance as much an imaginative construction as the romance wards with whom I had previously been working. This article I hope does some justice to her suggestion.

[2] See the testimonies of Joan, daughter of John, son of Alice de Denby, and Elizabeth, daughter of Clarissa de Denby in the cause of William, son of Adam de Hopton c. Constance de Skelmanthorpe, daughter of Walter del Brome. This case can be found in the Borthwick Institute of Historical Research, York, under the classification of CP E 62 (1348). The transcription and parts of the translation, which I have checked, were kindly undertaken by Mrs Lisa Liddy. Unless otherwise stated, the translations are hers. Where they are mine I signal this with (NM).

[3] CP E 62 (1348), deposition of Adam de Helay.

of legal Latin. The case of William, son of Adam de Hopton c. Constance de Skelmanthorpe, daughter of Walter del Brome,[4] allows us to examine in some detail legally constructed moments from the life of Constance as ward, wife, mother, widow, wife, and yet again wife. By reading these documents we seize an opportunity, not only to examine the legal case for what it can tell us about legal practice but also for what it can tell us about the strategies of at least one young medieval woman in her quest for the restitution of her personal legal rights. In so doing, I shall first outline the details of her life that we have from the case, acknowledging that much of interest to us, such as her allegation that her first husband was murdered, and the circumstances of her third marriage, will not be found there. Then I will suggest ways in which we may read the legal narrative.

Who was Constance de Skelmanthorpe? From the narrative details of the mid-fourteenth century marriage litigation case in which she appears we learn that she was an orphaned heiress in ward to one William de Hopton, possibly a burgess in the city of York, sometime prior to 1348, when the case was heard.[5] It seems that on reaching the age of fourteen or fifteen Constance contracted marriage with one John de Rotherfield (the marriage ceremony at 'Stoupandstone'), probably against the wishes, or without the knowledge, of her guardian. Witnesses described the marriage as affectionate, and the two children born from it, John and Nancy, as loved and well cared for.[6]

Constance's witnesses delivered a narrative which showed a peaceful and loving family life, yet John de Rotherfield was murdered. It was not openly suggested by whom, yet shortly before this event Constance was abducted and forced back into custody by her erstwhile legal guardian, Adam de Hopton. Constance and witnesses for the defence stated that he then forced her into a marriage with his nine-year-old son William against her will, through the illegal act of 'force and fear'.[7] Apparently Adam de

---

[4]   CP E 62 (1348).

[5]   CP E 62 (1348). A will survives in York, Borthwick Institute of Historical Research, Archbishops Register 12, fol. 33ʳ belonging to one Adam de Hopton. It is dated 1383, and could therefore have been the will of Constance's sometime guardian. In the margin next to his name is the title 'Bur' (i.e. burgess).

[6]   See the depositions of Adam de Helay and Richard de Helay, CP E 62 (1348).

[7]   Canon law allowed that if marriages were brought about by 'force and fear', that is, when unreasonable force caused '*metus qui cadere potest in constantum virum/ mulierum*' ('the fear that can fall upon a constant man/woman'), then they could be annulled.

Hopton did so in order to regain or maintain custody of Constance's inheritance, which, as she was legally married to John de Rotherfield (as she and various witnesses attest) should have been returned to Constance and her husband on their marriage.[8] It is possible that Adam de Hopton held custody of it throughout her first marriage; it is certain that he had custody of it during this second, apparently undesired, union. Constance did not bring a case of her own to annul this marriage, nor did she bring a suit to reclaim her inheritance. Instead she escaped from the custody of Adam de Hopton, and married for a third time, to one William Bosevill.

It is all too easy to read the events described in legal cases as absolute fact,[9] or to distort the depositions and statements we find within legal cases by elaborating them into further narratives containing assumption, hypothesis, and surmise which are of our own making.[10] We must realize that the narratives which these legal texts contain are driven by motives and allegiances which we cannot always know about, and thus any statements of so-called fact within these cases will in many cases be tendentious, or even false. Truth for our purposes, however, is of

---

Reasonable force was allowed: Richard Helmholz, *Marriage Litigation in Medieval England* (Cambridge: Cambridge University Press, 1974), pp. 90–94; James A. Brundage, *Law, Sex and Christian Society in Medieval Europe* (Chicago: University of Chicago Press, 1987), pp. 335, 345, 454.

[8]   For ages at which female wards could inherit, and could marry and inherit, see esp. Sue Sheridan Walker, 'The Feudal Family and the Common Law Courts: The Pleas Protecting Rights of Wardship and Marriage, *c*. 1225–1375', *Journal of Medieval History*, 14 (1988), 13–31, (p. 15), and Nicholas Orme, *From Childhood to Chivalry: The Education of the English Kings and Aristocracy 1066–1530* (London and New York: Methuen, 1984), p. 7. For primary sources on this matter see esp. *The Treatise on the Laws and Customs of England Commonly Called Glanvill*, ed. by G. D. G. Hall (London: Nelson, in association with the Selden Society, 1965), VII, 12. p. 85; Henry de Bracton, *On the Laws and Customs of England*, ed. by G. E. Woodbine, 4 vols (Cambridge, MA: Belknap Press, 1968), vol. 2, pp. 255, 257.

[9]   See Paul Strohm, *Hochon's Arrow: The Social Imagination of Fourteenth-Century Texts* (Princeton: Princeton University Press, 1992), pp. 122 on 'public facts in private terms', and p. 133 for notions of the 'real' embodied in the so-called fact in legal cases. See also Elizabeth S. Cohen, 'Court Testimony from the Past: Self and Culture in the Making of Text', in *Essays on Life Writing: From Genre to Critical Practice*, ed. by Marlene Kadar (Toronto: University of Toronto Press, 1992), pp. 83–93.

[10] For an extreme example of this, see Barbara A. Hanawalt, *Growing up in Medieval London: The Experience of Childhood in History* (Oxford: Oxford University Press, 1993) and some of the narrative fictions she herself creates and imposes upon the material she uses.

secondary importance: what concerns us here is how and why the narrative is constructed in the way that it is. The statements of both litigants and witnesses are narratives conditioned by the nature and ordering of the legal process, as I shall explain below. Although they may offer apparently spontaneous incidental material which is vital for the social historian, they are, as we shall see, controlled and structured both by legal formulae and litigants. If we question their value as simple truth, as we do literary works, then we reveal more of what they have to tell us than the surface story.

Here, following the examples of Kathryn Gravdal and Paul Strohm, I consider the possibility of reading legal cases in themselves as types of consciously constructed narrative fictions.[11] These fictions allow us to interrogate legal sources to uncover their deeper narrative structures.[12]

By 'narrative fictions' I mean the version of the truth which a given narrator, for example a litigant, a witness, or a lawyer, gives. In effect, those who provide the narrative are authors.[13] This notion of authoring implies control over the narrative, as in the plaintiff's original accusations against the defendant. However, witness statements, for instance, are not always freely given; often the narrative is controlled by the questions asked. I shall explain this in further detail below.

Individual authors may try to gain control over past events through the acts of speech and rehearsal. In order to win their cause, plaintiffs and defendants will structure and re-structure recalled events to fit the resolution of the case they are seeking. In so doing, they seek to maintain authority in a situation in which, at the time, no-one but the court has control. They recreate a history; they reinvent the story of their lives for an audience of lawyers and judges who will, in their own turn, decide upon the narrative which best fits their own reading of the story as presented by all parties. In this way, all those involved with a legal case in

---

[11]   Kathryn Gravdal, *Ravishing Maidens: Writing Rape in Medieval French Literature and Law* (Philadelphia: University of Pennsylvania Press, 1991), and Strohm, *Hochon's Arrow*.

[12]   For a consideration of how such fictions may inform us about the society from which they come, see P. J. P. Goldberg, 'Fiction in the archives: the York cause papers as a source for later medieval social history', *Continuity and Change*, 12 (1997), 425–45, esp. p. 435. He writes with particular reference to narrative fictions in the marriage causes, of which CP E 62 is one.

[13]   On female authoring in the sense that I use it here see Sidonie Smith, *A Poetics of Women's Autobiography: Marginality and the Fictions of Self-Representation* (Bloomington and Indianapolis: Indiana University Press, 1987), pp. 3–19.

court will author a combined narrative. The authority of the judge will determine which of these cumulative fictions represents 'the truth'.

A society's 'deeper narrative structures' might include notions of authority, personal networks, hidden narratives, and even literary models upon which participants in a legal case might base their actions or stories.[14] Authority can mean the authority of the judge, but may also mean the personal authority of participants, whose status might influence a judgement. Here gender is crucial. William as a minor and Constance as a female may both be subject to masculine authority, but William's case can be brought when he outgrows his dependent status, whereas Constance's marriages may be seen merely as a choice of dependency. Witnesses strive, in many cases, to impress their social standing and moral authority upon their narrative, as we shall see in one example below; litigants might choose their witnesses according to such status. Participants might also look to 'auctorite' in the written sense, in order to impress a judgement. For example, in de Hopton c. del Brome, one of the witnesses is a clerk; thus both the authority of his position and his learning mark him out as a superior witness.

Connected with notions of status is the personal network which litigants employ in order to gain for themselves suitable witnesses.[15] Finally, there is the hidden or alternative narrative which lies underneath the reason for the case. De Hopton c. del Brome is a case about marriage rights, but it is also a case about the question of female autonomy and property rights. These are the deeper structures which I seek to find within the case. They are structures which indeed run deep within medieval society.[16]

In what remains the best secondary source on the subject, *Marriage Litigation in Medieval England*, Richard Helmholz explains the formulaic

---

[14] See Gravdal, esp. chap. 5, 'The Complicity of Literature and Law', p. 135 and Noël James Menuge, 'Female Wards and Marriage in Romance and Law', in *Young Medieval Women*, ed. by Katherine J. Lewis, Noël James Menuge, and Kim M. Phillips (Stroud: Sutton, 1999), pp. 153–71.

[15] For a background to the notion of networks, see Philippa C. Maddern, '"Best Trusted Friends": Concepts and Practices of Friendship among Fifteenth-Century Norfolk Gentry', in *England in the Fifteenth Century: Proceedings of the 1992 Harlaxton Symposium*, ed. by Nicholas Rogers (Stamford: Paul Watkins, 1994), pp. 100–117.

[16] For questions of consent in marriage in this case, which I do not discuss in detail here, see Menuge, 'Female Wards and Marriage in Romance and Law'.

structure of cause papers.[17] A cause paper such as de Hopton c. del Brome would consist, in its written form, of several sections: the libel, followed by the positions, the interrogatories, the depositions, and finally the sentence.[18] Each of these sections (although not found in all marriage causes) served a particular purpose in canonical court actions, and as Helmholz notes, formed 'the basic ingredients of a marriage case' (p. 13). Thus they also formed the integral narrative structure of the document as a whole. Furthermore, they helped determine the way in which the resulting 'narrative fictions' were shaped, through the basic formulae they followed.

The libel stated the petition of the plaintiff, and his or her cause and action within the case. William, son of Adam de Hopton, brings his suit to enforce his alleged marriage to Constance, sometime in ward to his father. In his libel Constance is summarily petitioned to appear at court and to be compelled to stay with 'the same William her husband' because 'the same William and Constance by words of present consent mutually and lawfully contracted marriage...in the presence of the said William and other faithful men'.[19]

Following the libel the defendant would give a general answer to the allegation. This could take the form of an admission or a denial, or an admission with an 'exceptance'. While refuting most of Adam de Hopton's allegations, Constance does admit that the marriage between them took place, but that various factors, as I shall discuss below, rendered it invalid.

After the libel we find the positions, in which the separate parts of the plaintiff's case were set out in more detail, and addressed to the defendant, who would have to answer each of the positions as put. Positions were introduced to determine areas of conflict in the case. It was only those positions which the defendant denied which then had to be further proven, as 'questions of fact'.[20] This was done solely through an examination of the witnesses.[21]

---

[17]   Richard Helmholz, *Marriage Litigation in Medieval England* (Cambridge: Cambridge University Press, 1974).

[18]   See further Helmholz, *Marriage Litigation*, esp. pp. 11–22.

[19]   CP E 63 (1348). Probably through an error we find this libel on the last page of the document.

[20]   Helmholz, *Marriage Litigation*, p. 15.

[21]   Ibid.

Following the positions and possible counter-positions on the part of the defendant were the articles, a set of statements submitted to the judge or to an examiner appointed by the court, in order that witnesses might be questioned on those positions which were not considered proven. The composition of the articles by canon lawyers introduced still another element of authoring. These articles were based on conflict between the stories of the plaintiff and the defendant, and so in effect, their original statements controlled what questions would be asked of the witnesses. To a certain degree, then, the litigants could decide what the witnesses were examined upon; in a sense they devised the narrative structure of the witness statements.[22]

The interrogatories, following the articles, were used by the judge of examiner to question the witnesses of the plaintiff. The interrogatories were introduced by the defendant specifically to undermine the case of the plaintiff, by destroying the credibility of the plaintiff's witnesses, and by extracting positive evidence for the defendant by introducing new material. Helmholz notes that 'they were prepared by the defendant after he had seen the articles, and were in fact framed specifically to meet them' (p. 18). Sometimes, as in the case of de Hopton c. del Brome, the plaintiff would also introduce his own interrogatories. Their purpose was almost to 'second-guess' the witness: for example, they might instruct the judge 'that if a witness says such a thing [in answer to the articles], then ask him such another thing', and so on. Thus the defendant, through his lawyer, also had an opportunity to construct a carefully planned framework in which the narratives of the witnesses would help to formulate the 'plot' of his or her particular defence.

Given that the heaviest onus for proof was laid upon the witness statements, it is no surprise that the plaintiff and the defence had to create their respective structures for questioning very carefully.[23] Aside from the chance (not to be relied upon) that the judge or examiner might ask further questions than those put by the opposing parties, it was up to those parties to extract the desired information, or narrative. There was no questioning of the witness on the stand in the consistory court of the Middle Ages; questions to be put would have to be carefully framed

---

[22] Helmholz points out that the judge or examiner could question the witness beyond the content of the formal articles, and also notes that in some instances they were not used: Helmholz, *Marriage Litigation*, pp. 17–18. Constance puts forward her own articles as part of her defence.

[23] Ibid., p. 15.

beforehand, and in one go. Careful anticipation of the opposition's possible narrative would be a necessary part of the process.

Witness statements, or depositions, were taken in private, with the scribe either taking notes to be recorded later, or inscribing the documents at the time of questioning. This was so that the depositions could be read out in court. Apparently this was the first time that the parties to the case would hear the testimonies. This public reading of the depositions was followed by the pronouncement of sentence by the judge. This public reading of selected and selective legal narratives is a type of aural literary occasion: the libel provides the opening to the plot, the depositions provide the development, both of plot and of character, and the sentence necessarily provides the conclusion, and resolution. Thus we see litigants, lawyers, and witnesses creating narratives in real time, while referring to an imagined, or remembered past, both during the creation of the narrative, and during its recitation.

How then may we, or should we, read the constructed narrative of Constance de Skelmanthorpe? While on the surface we see that it concerns a marriage dispute, we can also see a gender struggle between Constance and William, centred around the control of her property.[24] What we have is female legal vulnerability versus male dominance. What we should be reading for is how Constance constructs herself, and what strategies she employs to overcome such weakness. Marriage is the only legally valid subject of Constance's defence, although underneath it we might detect her own struggle for proprietal independence from her guardian.[25]

The first we learn of Constance as the case survives today is through the positions of William de Hopton, where he states through his proctor

> that Constance at some time consented to have the said William as in marriage...that [the marriage] took place by words of mutual and consensual expression...that it took place legitimately by law...that the aforesaid Constance often in the presence of the said William has confessed this marriage contract...that [it took place] voluntarily...[26]

and so on. In total the proctor of William de Hopton placed seventeen positions against Constance with regard to the alleged marriage between her and William de Hopton. She denied them all.

---

[24] For a similar exposition of the dynamics of gender and property in the case of Elizabeth Wauton, see Strohm, *Hochon's Arrow*, pp. 128–33.

[25] In her positions Constance stated that she only allowed herself to be forced into the marriage because Adam de Hopton still held her property.

[26] CP E 62 (1348).

The first reason we are given for the suit, in terms of canon law, is that William has reached the age of fourteen. According to canon law, infants who married before the age of canonical majority, that is, the age of consent (twelve for girls and fourteen for boys) must have the marriage ratified upon attaining such age.[27] Therefore William sought to have the marriage enforced, because he was now legally able to consent to it. He was also now able to enjoy Constance's lands, as her legal husband. Constance had meanwhile remarried one William Bosevill, having apparently decided for herself that her marriage to William de Hopton was invalid. Thus William de Hopton needed to prove his alleged prior claim to Constance, or lose her, and her land, to his rival. The murder of John de Rotherfield had also freed him to pursue this action: with her first husband dead, Constance would find it more difficult as a young woman alone to prove her contention that she was already married at the time of her alleged contract with William de Hopton.

William's suit was that the marriage was lawful and consensual, and should therefore stand. He had no other points to argue. The articles put forward by William de Hopton's proctor state that the witnesses should be asked if the marriage between William de Hopton and Constance was legitimate, included marital affection, willing marriage, and resulting cohabitation 'through words of mutual and present consent'.[28] Thus William is constructing positive evidence for himself, and thereby his own plot, through his witnesses. The plaintiff's witnesses ask us to take seriously the likelihood that a fourteen- to fifteen-year-old girl and a nine-year-old boy would not only consummate a marriage, but live together happily as man and wife, although the 'wife' deserted the marriage as soon as possible in order to marry another man. Consummation might indicate ratification, or at least acceptance of the union; as indeed might affectionate behaviour, and willing cohabitation. The marriage would thus be more difficult to annul.

There is further significance in William de Hopton's articles to establish that the 'couple' lived together with marital affection. Accord-

---

[27] Canon law allowed infants to contract marriage from the age of seven. Not only was ratification necessary upon reaching canonical majority, but so was consent or dissent. In the case of dissent it had to be given in public and before an ecclesiastical court: Helmholz, pp. 98–100.

[28] CP E 62 (1348). On mutual consent and words of present and future consent see Brundage, *Law, Sex and Christian Society*, pp. 299–416, and M. M. Sheehan, 'The Formation and Stability of Marriage in the Fourteenth-Century: Evidence of an Ely Register', *Mediaeval Studies,* 33 (1971), 228–63, pp. 236–38, respectively.

ing to canon law, the term '*maritalis affectio*' denoted not only affection within marriage, but also the willingness to transfer goods and land within the union.[29] By getting witnesses to testify that Constance treated him with 'marital affection', William de Hopton constructs for them and for himself a narrative which includes his sanctioned ownership of her land.

In a corresponding passage from Constance's positions, her defence proctor puts it that the marriage between Constance and her guardian's nine-year-old son William took place

> through fear, terror and force by the said Adam de Hopton, guardian of the same Constance and natural father of the said William, towards the same Constance [and William] who mutually objected and resisted and disagreed with the alleged contract [which was forced by] striking, holding, and forcing and compelling them...[30]

In total, her defence proctor introduced twenty-six positions, in which Constance not only denied everything that William de Hopton alleged, but gave much fuller information concerning her previous and current marital status, and the conditions under which she was allegedly forced to marry William de Hopton. Her defence is more complex than William's attack. Because of her gender, it needs to be. William merely tried to enforce his marriage with her; Constance resisted by alleging pre-contract, consanguinity, force and fear, and current marriage to someone else. This barrage of impediments to marriage is an attempt to ensure escape from it, which would have been necessary for Constance to have her property re-instated. Her marriage to William Bosevill may have been a means of not only escaping the de Hopton marriage, but possibly also of forcing William de Hopton to bring a suit of enforcement against her, thus giving her a chance to ensure that her marriage into the de Hopton family was legally dissolved. This would have been a huge gamble, but Constance's defence displays a determination which is either driven by truth, or by a sound understanding of the law, and of how it can be manipulated by a combination of the two.

So William's narrative is one which only mentions his marriage to Constance, and asserts that it was valid. Constance's narrative is one which first establishes William's blood relationship with John de

---

[29] J. T. Noonan, 'Marital Affection in the Canonists', *Studia Gratiana,* (1967), pp. 505–19 (p. 506).

[30] CP E 62 (1348).

Rotherfield, and then stresses that Constance was married to this same John de Rotherfield, thus making the second marriage invalid because of consanguinity.[31] Next she has it put that the marriage to John de Rotherfield not only took place before the forced marriage to William de Hopton, but that it was consummated and produced children, confirming the contract in law between them'.[32] Furthermore, it is put that she and John lived together as man and wife and treated each other with 'mutual marital affection'. Her later claim that marriage to William de Hopton was forced because her guardian held her property suggests that he wrongfully seized it from her. If her marriage to John could be proven valid, then Adam de Hopton would have to return her land.

Next it is put that Constance was abducted and forced into marriage with William while 'the said John was alive'.[33] Besides asserting a pre-contract with John which would invalidate the de Hopton marriage,[34] Constance argued that William was not within 'marriageable years for contracting marriage when it was undertaken'.[35] After further alleging force and fear, Constance went on to state that during the alleged marriage between herself and Adam de Hopton she was kept in 'the bound custody and care of the said Adam'.[36] Finally it was stated that she was now lawfully joined in marriage to William Bosevill, a marriage which she had only entered into after hearing of the death of her first husband John.

Constance can thus be seen to present herself simultaneously as a wronged ward, a faithful wife, and as a woman who recognizes her rights

---

[31] Until 1215 canon law held that persons within seven grades or degrees of kinship could marry. By Lateran IV (1215) the degrees were limited to four: James A. Brundage, *Medieval Canon Law* (New York: Longman, 1995), p. 75, n. 5. It is therefore important that witnesses such as Adam de Helay (a church clerk, and therefore knowledgeable in such matters) stated that Constance and William de Hopton were within two grades of consanguinity, causing the marriage to be illegal and invalid.

[32] CP E 62 (1348). On ratification by intercourse see Sheehan, 'Formation and Stability', p. 237; Helmholz, *Marriage Litigation*, pp. 34–37.

[33] CP E 63 (1348).

[34] On pre-contract, see Helmholz, *Marriage Litigation*, pp. 60, 67, 69, 76–77.

[35] CP E 62 (1348). The age of consent was based on the ability to procreate, although notions concerning psychological maturity, as well as physical, are also important here. On this, see Kim M. Phillips, 'The Medieval Maiden: Young Womanhood in Late Medieval England (Unpublished D.Phil. Thesis, University of York, 1997), esp. pp. 31–41.

[36] CP E 62 (1348).

regarding mutual consent and choice of marriage partner. And even as she constructs herself in her own testimony as an independent young wife who knows her legal and personal rights with regard to marriage, she also constructs herself as someone who is vulnerable under the law as her sometime guardian uses it. However, in continuing to construct herself so, her narrative becomes that of a person who merits just treatment by the court because of this vulnerability, of someone who should be released from the greed of the de Hoptons.

The plot is determined for the witnesses and the court by the plaintiff and the defendant and by the positions which their libels necessarily create. The rest of the plot is expanded and developed by witnesses in answering the predetermined questions. Given that the final judgement rests upon these statements, the direction given by the litigants to the answers of the witnesses is as important as the careful construction of the litigants' own narratives.

There are a total of nineteen witness depositions in the document as it survives today. Due to space I shall examine in detail only selected elements of one key testimony (thus constructing my own selective narrative) in order to assess, briefly, how witnesses might shape their own narratives, while conforming to the narrative structures set out for them by the plaintiff and the defendant. The deposition I shall discuss here is that of the first witness, one Adam de Helay, 'sixty years old and more as he believes', who deposed in favour of Constance on every point. Essentially he is her chief witness.

His first statement was that William de Hopton and John de Rother-field (and therefore Constance if her marriage to John is established) are within 'the second grade of consanguinity from each other laterally as he believes', adding the information that he is a (church) clerk, and therefore 'knows that the grade of consanguinity is the increase between parents by reason of blood' as he puts it in impressively technical language.[37] Secondly he deposed that the marriage between John and Constance was contracted 'by words of mutual and present consent', and that it was also at some time 'celebrated before the Church'. He continued:

> then he knows that afterwards they joined together carnally and this he knows because they begot after the said marriage between them two children, viz. one son named John who is now dead and one daughter named Nancy who still lives...[he knows that the children were theirs

---

[37] Deposition of Adam de Helay, CP E 62 (1348).

because] he often saw and knew the same John and Constance to nurture, care for and hold the aforesaid infants as theirs.[38]

Concerning the marriage between John and Constance he deposed that as well as being lawful, and celebrated in front of the Church, he 'very often saw the said John and Constance living together in house and bed and with mutual marital affection', and also that 'he heard the aforesaid John on the day of his death in the presence of many faithful men make it that the said Constance was his lawful wife and this he asserted on danger to his soul'.[39] As a church clerk, Adam de Helay carries an authority concerning marriage under canon law which other witnesses of less status and experience would not. In choosing him as her chief witness Constance shows herself to understand the importance of his status in helping her to prove her case. This witness provides Constance with a social and legal power which she may not have enjoyed on her own or with witnesses of lesser status.

Constance and her lawyer frame some information through her interrogatories (for example, her third interrogatory questions the witness as to the nature of her marriage with John de Rotherfield, i.e. if it was consummated, if there were children and if they held each other with and 'lived in marital affection')[40] yet they do not instigate the interesting information that Adam de Helay himself volunteers. They do not ask for information concerning John's death-bed oath, they do not ask how the children were treated, and they do not ask for the rather remarkable information that Adam de Helay himself married William de Hopton and Constance, and helped Adam de Hopton to coerce them into marriage through force and fear. This is where he plays Constance's trump card. By announcing that he was the cleric who married them, he is able to give first-hand clerical authority that the marriage was invalid. He testified that Constance utterly refused and rejected the marriage, and would not repeat the words of matrimony. Moreover, he stated that William de Hopton also resisted the marriage, and that 'the said Constance at no time consented in any way and did not cohabit with him [William] except in as far as 'the said Adam held her by her care'.[41] And more tellingly, he underlines the property motive by his statement that 'Adam de Hopton

---

[38]   Deposition of Adam de Helay, CP E 62 (1348).

[39]   Deposition of Adam de Helay, CP E 62 (1348).

[40]   CP E 62 (1348) (NM).

[41]   Deposition of Adam de Helay, CP E 62 (1348).

father of the said William once had care and custody of the said
Constance and her land'.[42] By this insertion he becomes the male
authority Constance needs to prove that her property should now be her
own; that Adam de Hopton only had rights to it once.

Finally, Adam de Helay gave authority for the marriage between
Constance and William Bosevill:

> the banns having first been published before the church, the same William
> and Constance contracted marriage and celebrated it in the church and
> afterwards he often saw and knew them to live together, and behave and
> treat themselves mutually with marital affection as lawful man and wife
> and from that he knows that they are lawfully coupled...[43]

This is by far the most authoritative and lengthy witness account within
the case. Although other depositions are also important, many amount to
only a paragraph or more. It is true that William, for his part, had
witnesses who testified that he was married to Constance lawfully, but
among his witnesses he had none as powerful as Adam de Helay, and
their evidence is frequently weakened by their inability to answer many
of the articles, chiefly those concerning the nature of Constance's other
marriages.

Constance would not have found herself in this position had she been
male: she could have married where she chose, when she came of age.[44]
However, if we choose to read the case as I have suggested, then we see
that the position of women such as Constance is indeed a vulnerable one,
but also that a clever woman with good legal advice need not be a
helpless victim. Constance wins by displaying her sound knowledge of
her legal rights, position, and options, and through the careful choice of
her chief witness. Her example shows us that gender need not be an
ultimate handicap where property and litigation is concerned; she
demonstrates empowerment through her self-construction as an
autonomous legal being, while at the same time demonstrating clearly for
the legal audience that this autonomy has been wrongly contained and
controlled.

The canonical resolution of the case is that Constance's marriage to
William de Hopton is proved unlawful, and that her marriage to William
Bosevill is proved valid. One conclusion we may draw from this is that

---

[42] Deposition of Adam de Helay, CP E 62 (1348).

[43] Deposition of Adam de Helay, CP E 62 (1348).

[44] On this see Bracton, *On the Laws and Customs of England*, vol. 2, p. 257.

whether or not Constance was telling the truth, in terms of the legal narrative she was the better author. Marriage cases, and most likely other legal cases, were not won and lost upon legal circumstance, convention, and technicalities alone, but also upon the skill with which events were narrated, key details brought to prominence, and background detail convincingly sketched. The power of the narrative lies, if it is successful, in its composition, and it would be reasonable to suggest that outcomes of such legal cases depended for their resolution, in large part, like literature, upon the power of the narrative.

The Origins of Criseyde

SALLY MAPSTONE

We start in Scotland. At some point in the 1470s–90s Archibald
Whitelaw, secretary to King James III or King James IV, or someone in
Whitelaw's circle using a similar quasi-humanist hand, was reading a
manuscript copy of the *Ilias Latina*, the Latin verse recension in which
the *Iliad* was known in the Middle Ages.[1] Coming upon the early
reference (ll. 12–13) to the priest Chryses weeping at the removal of his
daughter to be Agamemnon's concubine, Whitelaw, or his contemporary,
made the curt marginal gloss, 'nate est creseidis' (fol. 57^r), this is of the
daughter Cresseid, or effectively, this is of Cresseid as daughter. Chryses'
daughter is not in fact named in this couplet, but when her name does
appear in the *Ilias Latina* its Latin form is Chryseida.[2] Why should a
Scots commentator at this period have been interested in Chryseida, or, as
he notably would have it, Creseida, a figure vital to the opening of the
Iliad, but not thereafter a major player within it? The Scots form of the
Latinized name inevitably brings to mind the Cresseid of Robert
Henryson's *Testament of Cresseid*, a poem which was probably written

---

[1]   Edinburgh, National Library of Scotland, Advocates MS 18.4.8. See R. J. Lyall, 'Books
and Book Owners in Fifteenth-Century Scotland', in *Book Production and Publishing in
Britain 1375–1475*, ed. by Jeremy Griffiths and Derek Pearsall (Cambridge: Cambridge
University Press, 1989), pp. 239–56 (p. 248); I. C. Cunningham, 'Latin Classical
Manuscripts in the National Library of Scotland', *Scriptorium*, 27 (1973), 64–90 (pp. 75–
76); P. K. Marshall, '*Ilias Latina*', in *Texts and Transmission: A Survey of the Latin
Classics*, ed. by L. D. Reynolds (Oxford: Clarendon Press, 1983), pp. 191–94.

[2]   *Poetae Latini Minores*, II, ed. by Æ. Baehrens (Leipzig: Teubner 1881), p. 8; for
Chryseida see, e.g., lines 23 (p. 8), 56 (p.10).

by 1492.[3] What this Scottish gloss may show is one aspect of the main point I wish to make about the origins of Criseyde.[4] This is that writers, and readers, in the Middle Ages could meaningfully connect later Criseydes with their two originally Homeric predecessors, Chryseis and Briseis, whom they would have encountered in a variety of works descending from the *Iliad*, despite the fact that the literary life-stories of earlier and later Criseydes differed.

There are two reasons for stressing this connection. Firstly, because it was a suggestive one to several of the writers whose works lie behind Chaucer's *Troilus and Criseyde* and Henryson's *Testament*; and secondly, because the connection has been so persistently denied by those who have written about the history of Chaucer's Criseyde. The standard argument is characterized by the statement with which one of the most recent studies of 'The Birth of Criseyde' begins: 'The figure of Briseis-Cressida, the lover of Troilus, is unknown in classical and medieval literature'.[5] Benoît invented the story of Briseida's relationship with Troilus, certainly, but important elements in his shaping of Briseida within it surely came down to him from antiquity; Briseis was not entirely unknown to him.

To illustrate the backdrop to this contention, I will summarize what we know about Chryseis and Briseis from the *Iliad*, and then look at the treatment of Briseis by the classical writer who most significantly influenced medieval conceptions of her: Ovid. Chryseis engaged the interest of writers in the Middle Ages less—for reasons that relate to one of the major concerns in this essay: she had little literary tradition of a distinctive speaking voice.

It is with the fate of Chryseis that the *Iliad* famously opens. She is the daughter of a Trojan priest, Chryses; she has been captured by the Greeks during their plundering of her city. Her father appeals to them to ransom her back, and the Greeks are largely willing to do so, but their leader, Agamemnon, who has taken Chryseis as a concubine, refuses. Chryses

---

[3] This is on the assumption that *The Spektakle of Luf*, dated 1492, refers to the *Testament* (and to 'Cresseid'), and not vice versa. See *The Poems of Robert Henryson*, ed. by Denton Fox (Oxford: Clarendon Press, 1981), p. xix.

[4] Chaucer's form is used as the generic in this essay.

[5] Roberto Antonelli, 'The Birth of Criseyde—An Exemplary Triangle: "Classical" Troilus and the Question of Love at the Anglo-Norman Court', in *The European Tragedy of Troilus*, ed. by Piero Boitani (Oxford: Clarendon Press, 1989), pp. 21–48 (p. 21); cf. Stephen A. Barney in *The Riverside Chaucer*, ed. by Larry D. Benson (Oxford: Oxford University Press, 1987), p. 1023.

prays to the god Apollo and the Greek host is afflicted with plague. After the intervention of the soothsayer Calchas (here a Greek), who urges the return of Chryseis to appease Apollo, Agamemnon agrees to her ransom. But he asks a price for this. One of the other Greek chieftains, Achilles, has as a slave a beautiful widow called Briseis, daughter of Briseus, whom he had made his captive during the sacking of her city, Lyrnessos. Agamemnon demands *her* in return for giving up Chryseis. There ensues a mighty tangle between Agamemnon and Achilles, which culminates in Achilles' refusal to participate in the siege of Troy. Only after the death of his best friend Patroklus does Achilles re-enter the fighting; and then as a mark of the ending of the quarrel with Agamemnon, Briseis is returned to him.

Briseis is given little definition in the *Iliad* until book XIX. She is of course a possession prized enough to be fiercely contested, and she is beautiful, the fair-cheeked Briseis.[6] But not until after the death of Patroklus do we gain any sense of her conception of things. The sight of his corpse provokes in the returned Briseis a short, intense, and revealing lament. Patroklus, it emerges, was a sort of champion to her. After the death in one day at the siege of Lyrnessos of her husband and three brothers, it was Patroklus who urged in her the hope that he could make her Achilles' future wife. With his death that hope fades. And indeed Achilles speaks of her at this time with a harshness that distinguishes between the love he feels for his dead friend Patroklus, and the desire he felt for Briseis—what he is doing is blaming the woman rather than himself for events that have led to his friend's death: 'We [Achilles and Agamemnon] quarrelled together for the sake of a girl in soul-perishing hatred. I wish Artemis had killed her with an arrow beside the ships on that day when I destroyed Lyrnessos and took her'.[7] Briseis shows a consciousness of this rejection in the dismal future she anticipates, and the way in which she tears at her breast and face before she speaks: 'So

---

[6] 'Fair-cheeked' is the recurrent term in Homer, e.g. I. 184, 323, 346, XIX. 246, XXIV. 676: Homer, *The Iliad*, ed. by A. T. Murray, 2 vols (London: Heinemann, 1924–25). 'The beautiful Briseida' seems to have become a stylization, as in the *Briseida formosa* of Dares (*Daretis Phrygii De Excidio Troiae Historia*, ed. by Ferdinand Meister (Leipzig: Teubner, 1873, p. 17)) and Propertius (elegy II. 8, 35; *Elegies*, ed. by G. P. Goold, (Cambridge, MA: Harvard University Press, 1990), p. 144). For other references see *Paulys Real-Encylopädie*, III, ed. by Georg Wissowa, (Stuttgart: Metzler, 1899), cols 856–57. Henryson's persistent 'fair Cresseid' may owe a conscious debt to that tradition.

[7] See *The Iliad of Homer*, trans. by Richmond Lattimore (Chicago and London: University of Chicago, Press, 1969), p. 393; original, XIX. 56–60.

evil in my life takes over from evil for ever'.[8] Though she has been restored to Achilles, her lament is delivered from a position once more insecure. Moreover, it is received only by other women: the Greek lords are gathered around Achilles, and he and they are oblivious to Briseis's speech.

Manifestly, both Chryseis and Briseis have things to link them to medieval Criseydes, even though those later Criseydes have another story. Chryseis through her ransom, her priestly Trojan father, and the connection with Calchas; Briseis through her ransom, her widowhood, her beauty, and her role as the disputed love-object of two men. Their similarity in situation is enhanced by their closeness in names. Though it will be argued here that Criseyde is essentially Briseis's descendant, it seems entirely possible that Briseis's and Chryseis's close association led both Benoît de Saint-Maure and Boccaccio to blend elements from the representation of the classical Chryseis into the reconstructed medieval Briseida. Benoît makes Calchas a Trojan priest, and Briseida his daughter,[9] inventions possibly prompted by the fact that in Dares and the *Ilias Latina* Chryseis is the daughter of a Trojan priest and her release is effected by Calchas. Boccaccio's alteration of Briseida's name to Criseida may have been influenced by his misreading of a reference to Chryseida as Calchas's daughter in Ovid's *Remedia Amoris*.[10]

It was, though, Briseis who caught the attention of post-Homeric writers. It is important, however, that from early on a range of ways of seeing her existed. In part these divided between those who saw Achilles' love for her as an admirable passion, and those who saw it as at odds with the waging of war.[11] It is that latter view that is expressed, for instance, in the *Ilias Latina*. But for the other main ways of conceiving of Briseis, all primarily responding to the *Iliad*,[12] we must turn to Ovid.

---

[8]   Ibid., p. 400; XIX. 290.

[9]   See Léopold Constans, *Le Roman de Troie*, 6 vols, Société des Anciens Textes Français (Paris: Firmin-Didot, 1904–12), VI, p. 251; also R. M. Lumiansky, 'Calchas in the Early Versions of the Troilus Story', *Tulane Studies in English*, 4 (1954), 5–20.

[10]   *Remedia Amoris*, ll. 469–75, pp. 208–10 in Ovid, *The Art of Love and Other Poems*, ed. by G. P. Goold, 2nd edn (Cambridge, MA: Harvard University Press, 1985); E. H. Wilkins, 'Criseida', *Modern Language Notes*, 24 (1919), 65–67.

[11]   Katherine Callen King, *Achilles: Paradigm of the War Hero from Homer to the Middle Ages* (Berkeley: University of California Press, 1987), pp. 172–74.

[12]   See Howard Jacobson, *Ovid's Heroides* (Princeton: Princeton University Press, 1974), p. 21.

The dominant work is the *Heroides*, in which collection of epistles from separated or unhappy lovers, Briseis's letter to Achilles is the third. Ovid creates a Briseis who writes as Agamemnon's troubled and lonely captive, describing herself in the opening line as 'rapta Briseide', and as a woman brought by events to see her greatest security as lying in the restoration of another relationship in which she is captive, with Achilles, the man responsible for the death of her husband and brothers.[13] As one of the more perceptive commentators on her epistle writes, 'fear, not jealousy or anger, is her predominant emotion'.[14] Briseis's letter is presented as composed while she is still separated from Achilles, and after he has refused Agamemnon's delegation offering him Briseis back along with a host of other presents, and is threatening to leave the siege completely and go home. The *Iliad* is the major source, but such is the sophistication of Ovid's appropriation of it that Briseis's letter also covers material, including her lament in the *Iliad*, that in the Homeric work takes place after her unhappy restoration to Achilles. The effect is dramatically to foreground Briseis's way of seeing, producing another reading of the events of the *Iliad*.

The fluidity of the Ovidian Briseis's response to, so to speak, her earlier self, and her earlier literary history, is enhanced by the fact that she has access in the *Heroides* to material from the *Iliad* in the narration of which in that work itself she is not a participant. Thus Briseis's attempts to persuade Achilles to return to the fray and in so doing accept her back from Agamemnon include allusion to the story of Meleager, which in the *Iliad* book IX is narrated at a dinner served by Achilles and Patroklus in Achilles' tent. There it is told to him by his former tutor Phoenix, part of an embassy sent from Agamemnon to try to get Achilles to resume arms.

In attempting to persuade Achilles to recover her, the Briseis of the *Heroides* thus makes reference to a story already used in the *Iliad* in that connection. But this is a complex intertextuality. Briseis tells the Meleager story differently from Phoenix and both of them suppress elements in it. In Phoenix's account Meleager defends the city of Calydon during the wars between the Calydonians and Kouretes against the chaos caused by a ravaging boar sent by Artemis because Oeneus, Meleager's father, has neglected to pay tribute to her. Meleager kills the boar; the

---

[13] Ovid, *Heroides and Amores*, ed. by G. P. Goold, 2nd edn (Cambridge, MA: Harvard University Press, 1986), p. 32.

[14] Jacobson, p. 35.

next part of the story is obliquely told, for reasons that will become clear, but it is apparent that there is a dispute over the relics of the boar, during which Meleager kills one of his maternal uncles; at which his mother, Althaea, curses him. When the wars flare up again, Meleager withdraws from the battle out of anger at his mother, being only persuaded belatedly into the action by his wife Cleopatra when things are desperate and the city afire. He thus forfeits the enjoyment of the gifts offered to him by his family and friends in attempts to get him to take up arms. The inference is that he also loses out on the enjoyment of the gifts because his mother's curse takes effect. What Phoenix's account conspicuously plays down are details known to us from other Greek sources, and later from Ovid's own *Metamorphoses* (book VIII),[15] where they receive one of their most memorable statements. There Meleager's mother's wrath is due to his murder of two of his uncles, her brothers, because they object to his wish to give the boar's head to Atalanta, with whom he has fallen in love. Ovid further relates how Althaea has retained a piece of kindling which she had rescued from the flames at Meleager's birth when the Fates had decreed that Meleager's life would last only as long as the wood took to burn. Torn between the instincts of a sister and a mother Althaea agonizes about whether to forgive Meleager or not, but finally she casts the brand into the flames. A long way off, Meleager dies, and in due course Calydon falls too.

These details are far less to Phoenix's purposes in the *Iliad* than the point about regrettable delaying and rejection of gifts; he does not want to suggest, after all, that Achilles is cursed, rather that he is of a comparable warlike magnitude to Meleager. They are also less to Briseis's purpose in the *Heroides* too, since the point of the story, as she tells it, is the crucial role played by Meleager's wife in persuading him back to battle—the moral being that there is nothing wrong in listening to a woman's pleas (with the sub-text, I would like to be your wife, even though I am a slave).[16] Briseis actually says nothing at all about the boar hunt. But she does refer to the mother's curse in close proximity to the particular female reading that she is imparting to the story, though she too does not

---

[15] See Ovid, *Metamorphoses, Book VIII*, ed. by A. S. Hollis (Oxford: Oxford University Press, 1970), pp. 66–68.

[16] For an analysis of this epistle as a disturbing parody of the posture of *servitium amoris*, in which Briseis's status as a high-born slave is crucial, see Florence Verducci, *Ovid's Toyshop of the Heart: Epistulae Heroidum* (Princeton: Princeton University Press, 1985), pp. 88–121.

follow its implications through: 'By the prayer of his wedded wife was
the son of Oeneus roused to arms. It's only something I've heard, but it is
well known to you. Reft of her brothers, a mother cursed the hope and
head of her son....'[17] It would be easy to argue that the organization of
material through its emotional meaning to Briseis rather than through
chronology is privileging a female reading that dehistoricizes the story.
But Briseis's argument can be read as both intentionally more subtle and
in its own desperate way more conservative than that. She both
diminishes her own access to the story, 'res audita mihi', and indicates
that what she is saying endorses an interpretative *status quo,* 'nota est
tibi'. In other words, Briseis suggests that her reading is one that Achilles
should find acceptable: her role, like the role of Meleager's wife, is one
supportive of the historical, public enterprises in the wider world in
which Meleager and Achilles are situated.

The ironies here are extensive, however, and work against the very
conservatism that Briseis strives for. Hanging over the Meleager example
is the grimness of Meleager's own fate at the hands of a woman, that even
lurks behind Phoenix's very masculine retelling of it in the *Iliad.* Shortly
before her reference to the story Briseis tells Achilles, 'You were my
master, you my husband, you my brother'.[18] The plethora of domestic
roles in which she has thus situated herself in relation to him inevitably
invites comparison with the contradictory roles in which Althaea found
herself, and contributes to the impression that Briseis exists in a
disturbing and unresolved relation to the only male figure who can make
sense of her life. Ovid renders this Briseis as a woman haunted by the
destruction of her own family and forced into constructing bonds with its
destroyer that are fraught with conflict. Further informing the Meleager
story's association with Briseis is the fact that in the *Iliad* Phoenix's
narration to Achilles is unsuccessful in persuading him either to take back
Briseis or resume his role in the war. And, as Verducci notes, insofar as
the time-scheme of this epistle can be gauged, it is also a story which
Achilles had only heard the day before, and it did not move him then.[19]
Briseis's hortatory example in the *Heroides* carries the constraints of its

---

[17] Heroides, pp. 38–39 (ll. 92–94).

[18] Ibid., l. 52 (p. 36), 'tu dominus, tu vir, tu mihi frater eras'. Verducci sees here a
reference to Andromache's parting from Hector in the Iliad, and argues that the
intertextuality works powerfully against Briseis (pp. 111–12).

[19] Verducci, p. 115.

own literary history, and underwrites the profound sense of loss, estrange-
ment, and failure in her epistle.

It thus seems inappropriate to call this Briseis a 'sentimentalize[d]'
Briseis.[20] To emphasize the pathos of her situation is not Ovid's primary
concern. The depth that he imparts to his Briseis comes from something
that is to be a marked feature of her descendants: from the start, the
complex way in which Briseis interacts with her own literary history
makes her own reading of it one that both endorses and qualifies its
traditional interpretations. This is also, strikingly, not dominantly the
letter of a woman in love. It is the letter of a woman coping with
situations far from her own making, at once accusing and inviting the
only person who can give meaning to her existence.

It is stressed in this letter, as it is in the *Iliad*, that Agamemnon had
never taken Briseis into his bed while she has been in his power. Briseis
points out that Achilles would not like to be asked whether he had kept
his vow to her, whereas 'if I prove false, desire never to see me again!'[21]
It might be argued that it is precisely this aspect of constancy that distinguishes the Ovidian Briseis from the later characters that share her name.
But this was not the only Ovidian reading of Briseis's sojourn with
Agamemnon. In the *Remedia Amoris* Ovid suggests that it is unimagin-
able that Briseis did not give Agamemnon the pleasure she gave
Achilles—and that this is precisely what so distressed Achilles. This is
consonant with his suggestion in the *Ars Amatoria* that Briseis felt a
wanton enjoyment with Achilles in being caressed by hands that had been
engaged in bloody battle.[22] Passages like this gave signals to later writers
that Briseis could be variously interpreted. We have seen in the *Heroides*
the way her own narrative interacts with her literary past; her presentation
in the Ovidian corpus suggests a further area of divergence, over precisely
the issue that was to become such a central one for subsequent Briseidas
and Criseydes: her constancy.

The story of Troilus and Briseida's love-affair and her betrayal of
Troilus for Diomede does indeed first appear in Benoît de Saint-Maure's

---

[20] E. Talbot Donaldson, 'Briseis, Briseida, Criseyde, Cresseid, Cressid: Progress of a
Heroine'; in *Chaucerian Problems and Perspectives*, ed. by Edward Vasta and Zacharias
P. Thundy (Notre Dame: University of Notre Dame Press, 1979), pp. 3–12 (p. 4).

[21] *Heroides*, p. 40, l. 110, 'fallentem deseruisse velis'.

[22] *Remedia Amoris*, ll. 783–84, pp. 230–31; *Ars Amatoria*, II. 713–16, pp. 114–15, in
Goold (ed.), *The Art of Love*.

Roman de Troie of *c.* 1165,[23] where the relationship is one of four love pairings woven through the poem. Benoît's poem extensively fills in the outline of its allegedly eye-witness, and thus pre-Homeric, sources, which were in fact composed originally in Greek, much later than Homer, and translated into Latin several centuries later: Dares' *De Excidio Troiae Historia*, from which Benoît mainly worked, and Dictys's *Ephemeridos Belli Troiani*, with which Benoît supplemented Dares.[24] The standard critical line on where Benoît got his Briseida from is, as I have indicated, that he didn't, that he got the name from Dares but no more, since in Dares' account all that survives of the Homeric Briseis is the portrait of her that concludes the group of twenty-nine portraits which Dares includes in his history (and which inaugurates the line of descent which will eventually produce Chaucer's portraits of Troilus, Criseyde and Diomede). Dares has nothing more of Briseis's history, and thus it is argued that because Benoît didn't know Briseis's past he felt free to devise one for her, involving Troilus, and responding to the suggestion in Dares' (wholly approving) portrait of Briseis that hers was a winning disposition as well as one modest and kindly.[25]

The critical orthodoxy has changed little in the past twenty years. E. T. Donaldson, often a perceptive inquisitor of the history of Criseyde, remarks with puzzlement that 'It is interesting that Benoît, who certainly didn't know who Briseida had originally been, should have assigned her her original Homeric role of a woman who is shuttled involuntarily from one man to another. I suppose it was just chance, plus the obvious analogy to Helen that led him to do so'.[26] More recently, Barry Windeatt sees it very similarly: 'In inventing his story Benoît effectively assigned Briseida her original Homeric role of a woman passed involuntarily from one man to another, *although* [my emphasis] Benoît's Briseida has no connection—other than through the misunderstanding of a name—with Briseis, the concubine of Achilles, or with Chryseis, the daughter of

---

[23] On its dissemination see Marc-René Jung, *La Légende de Troie en France au moyen âge*, Romanica Helvetica 114 (Basel and Tübingen: Francke, 1996).

[24] For Dares see n. 6 above; Dictys Cretensis, *Ephemeridos Belli Troiani Libri*, ed. by W. Eisenhut (Leipzig: Teubner, 1973).

[25] Dares, p. 17; see Constans at VI, p. 249, and Aimé Petit, *Naissances du Roman: Les techniques littéraires dans les romans antiques du xiie siècle*, 2 vols (Geneva: Slatkine, 1985), I, pp. 546–47.

[26] Donaldson, p. 5.

Chryses, priest of Apollo, who figure in the *Iliad*.[27] As we have seen, however, the connection to be made is less immediately with the *Iliad*, than with the Ovidian corpus responding to it.

For it is hard to accept that Benoît knew nothing at all about Briseida's pre-history, even if Dares didn't tell him anything. Before we even approach Ovid, we should note that Dictys's work had a more detailed account of the Achilles and Agamemnon quarrel, though here the Briseis character is known as Hippodamia, and Chryses as Astynome.[28] Benoît indeed has Ajax give a lengthy narration of this episode in the latter part of the *Roman de Troie* after the death of Achilles.[29] However, the fact that Benoît knew the Briseis story from Dictys with Briseis as Hippodamia does not prove that he was unacquainted with her role as Briseis in other texts. He is very likely to have known the *Ilias Latina,* which was a school text in the twelfth century.[30] Even more relevantly, so was Ovid's *Heroides.*[31]

The *Roman de Troie* is one of a group of *romans d'antiquité* in which a powerful Ovidian influence is unmistakable. It is transmitted through a conception of love as both overwhelming and foolhardy, and through stylistic and expressive mannerisms, including the monologue and epistle, which create a sense of interior depth in the speaker or writer. The *Heroides* is a significant text here. However, despite the acknowledgement of this by commentators on the *Roman de Troie*,[32] there is still a reluctance to make the Briseis/Briseida connection. Thus Barbara Nolan observes that the Troilus/Briseida relationship is the only one of the four

---

[27] Barry Windeatt, *Troilus and Criseyde*, Oxford Guides to Chaucer (Oxford: Clarendon Press, 1992), p. 78.

[28] See *Paulys Real-Encylopädie*, VIII, ed. by Wilhelm Kroll (Stuttgart: Metzler, 1913), col. 1729.

[29] Lines 26640–7038, IV, pp. 191–212. For Dictys see pp. 32–33, 42–46.

[30] Marshall, p. 191.

[31] Ralph H. Hexter, *Ovid and Medieval Schooling: Studies in Medieval School Commentaries on Ovid's Ars Amatoria, Epistolae ex Ponto, and Epistolae Heroidum*, Münchener Beiträge zur Mediävistik und Renaissance-Forschung, 38 (Munich: Arbeo-Gesellschaft, 1986), esp. pp. 137–210.

[32] For example, Petit, I, pp. 364–412; Reto R. Bezzola, *Les origines et la formation de la littérature courtoise en Occident 500–1200*, pt 3 (Paris: Champion, 1963), pp. 281–83; Inez Hansen, *Zwischen Epos und Höfischem Roman: Die Frauengestalten im Trojaroman des Benoît de Sainte-Maure*, Beiträge zur romanischen Philologie des Mittelaters, 8 (Munich: W. Fink, 1971), pp. 86–90, 99–101, 106–47.

in the *Roman* without any precedent, and goes on to suggest that Benoît 'drew ideas for the character of Briseida' from Ovid's portrayal of Helen in her letter to Paris in the *Heroides*.[33] The Helen link is undoubtedly significant, but I want to propose that since Benoît knew the *Heroides* as well as that, he also found suggestive things in the Briseis there to carry over into the creation of his own Briseida.

The major *difference* between the Briseis of the *Heroides* and the Briseida of the *Roman*, however, beyond the attachment of one to Achilles and the other to Troilus, is that Ovid's Briseis is constant in her affections and Benoît's Briseida is not. However, we have noted that Ovid himself had suggested, in works which we can again be sure that Benoît knew,[34] that Briseis was susceptible to different interpretations. We have also noted that Ovid presents Briseis in the *Heroides* as a figure of conflicting emotions, *sollicita Briseida*, trying to reconcile herself to her past, and to Achilles, and trying further to resolve the question of whether she has been constant to Achilles or not. In my view, all these elements have an impact on Benoît's shaping of her story as Troilus's lover, and the complex shading of her speaking voice in the poem. They are accompanied by a further aspect of Ovidian transmission in the Middle Ages which markedly influenced the construction of Benoît's narratorial voice in these parts of the *Roman*. Medieval commentaries on the *Heroides* commonly read Briseis in a strongly reproving light, rebuking her for 'profaning the memory of her husband and brothers by loving their murderer'.[35] It has been well observed that 'this Briseis, like the fourteenth-century Criseyde, is emblematically "untrewe"'.[36]

The *Roman de Troie* gains much of its narrative complexity by a contrapuntal movement between the self-expression of the protagonists, frequently through monologue, and the commentary supplied by the narratorial voice. This is especially present in the characterization of Briseida, and is a movement that was highly influential on later renditions of the Criseyde story. It is a pattern centred on how she speaks for herself and how she is spoken about. In the *Roman,* Benoît's narrator has a series of uncompromising antifeminist judgements upon Briseida that initiated

---

[33] Barbara Nolan, *Chaucer and the Tradition of the 'Roman Antique'*, Cambridge Studies in Medieval Literature, 15 (Cambridge: Cambridge University Press, 1992), pp. 109–14 (p. 112).

[34] Amply demonstrated by Nolan, pp. 76–77, 99–104, 106–17.

[35] Hexter, p. 179.

[36] Ibid.

the literary reputation she gained as a type for fickle womanhood.[37] Yet
the overall picture of Briseida that emerges from the poem is a more
developed and contradictory one than such narratorial remarks imply. For
the speeches afforded to Briseida, culminating in a final monologue, set
up a tension between her own self-presentation and the narratorial view of
her, a sort of fragmentation of her depiction[38] which is to be repeated over
the next four or five hundred years, particularly, and paradoxically, in
those works which seek to impart more complexity and sometimes more
sympathy to her representation.

Briseida's last monologue is one that gives many things to Criseyde's
final spoken words (her really final words are written) in book V of
Chaucer's poem. It is approached by a series of speeches mostly with
figures other than Troilus—Diomede, his servant, her father, finally with
herself—which convey unsure or veiled motivation in her behaviour, as if
the movement from Troilus to Diomede is far from a foregone
conclusion, but which are persistently countered by following narratorial
statements which suggest that Briseida is easily read as a deceitful
woman. Thus after Briseida's arrival at the Greek camp and her reproach
to Calchas for his treachery, the narratorial voice comments that she will
soon be appeased: 'Their minds are indeed quickly changed, and lack
both sincerity and constancy, and their hearts are most vain and fickle.'[39]
With her final speech however, when everyone knows that she has
betrayed Troilus (her affair with whom was already public knowledge),
the pattern of letting Briseida speak and then passing judgement upon her
is reversed, with the narratorial reading coming in even before she has
begun her monologue. The desire is palpably to limit the interpretation:
'[S]he knows well that she is acting despicably. She has abandoned
Troilus most unjustly and treacherously, and knows that she has behaved
very badly and greatly wounded a man who is fair, noble, and valiant, and

[37] Gretchen Mieszkowski, 'The Reputation of Criseyde, 1155–1500', *Transactions of the Connecticut Academy of Arts and Sciences*, 43 (1971), 71–153.

[38] Cf. Felicity Riddy: '"Abject Odious": Feminine and Masculine in Henryson's *Testament of Cresseid*', in *The Long Fifteenth Century: Essays for Douglas Gray*, ed. by Helen Cooper and Sally Mapstone (Oxford: Clarendon Press, 1997), pp. 229–48.

[39] Quotation is from the translations by N. R. Havely in *Chaucer's Boccaccio* (Cambridge: D. S. Brewer, 1980), p. 175; for the original, *Roman de Troie*, II, p. 328, ll. 13862–64; in the Old French the references are to 'corage tost müé' and 'li cuer vain e muable', phrases which Chaucer may have recalled in his portrait of Criseyde in V, ll. 825–26.

superior as a soldier to all of them. And she says to herself in her thoughts
...'.[40] But Briseida's reflections pass far beyond this description. Instead,
her speech offers a vivid picture of changing moods, in which we see a
woman interrogating her own history, trying to make sense of a past
which destabilizes her sense of where she is now emotionally: 'Often I'm
at ease, and often I'm troubled; often things seem really to be going as
well as I would wish; often my eyes grow full of tears'.[41] Her moods
alternate between misery, self-justification, and a resolute, if rather weary,
optimism. The honesty of the self-reflection may well be unattractive—
Benoît is hardly seeking to exculpate her—but it reacts against the more
morally restricted role assigned to her by the narratorial commentary.

Of course this is not directly Ovid's Briseis. Briseida turns determined-
ly in the direction of a new love in a manner antithetical to that espoused
by Briseis in the *Heroides*. But the choice for this most powerful
statement of her emotions, of the monologue, a genre close to the epistle,
and the way in which the conflicts in her interpretation of herself generate
a subtlety in her presentation that is not pathetic but disturbing, do
suggest that Benoît took more from the Briseis of antiquity than is
normally recognized. His Hippodamia has the originally Homeric
Briseidian role. His Briseida has aspects of her Ovidian colouring.

Benoît is the first of a group of writers who utilize to great effect this
contrast between what Criseyde may say and what may be said of her,
notably Chaucer, Henryson, and Shakespeare. The opening up of a sense
of space between what Briseida says of herself and the judgement the
narratorial voice passes upon her was something that Benoît's poem gave
to Chaucer, though of course Chaucer's narrator is very much Criseyde's
defender. The celebrated ambiguity of Chaucer's Criseyde owes a lot to
Benoît's Briseida. There are also things to suggest that Chaucer himself
looked back to Ovid's own Briseis, perhaps encouraged by connections
he picked up in Boccaccio and Benoît. The intense fearfulness of his
Criseyde parallels the anxiety of the Herodian Briseis. There is one
specific moment when both write or speak of themselves as captives,
where Chaucer, in a speech added to his Boccaccian source, could be
quite closely recalling the Ovidian figure:

> Often I have wished to deceive my guards and return to you,
> But the enemy was there to seize upon a fearful woman.

---

[40] Havely, p. 180; *Roman*, III, p. 290, ll. 20229–37.

[41] Havely, pp. 180–81 (adapted); *Roman*, III, p. 204, ll. 20314–15.

Should I have gone out by night, I feared I should be taken,
And delivered over a gift to some one of the ladies of Priam's sons.
    (ll. 17–20)[42]

And if that I me putte in jupartie
To stele awey by nyght, and it bifalle
That I be kaught, I shal be holde a spie;
And elles—lo, this drede I moost of alle—
If in the hondes of some wreche I falle,
I nam but lost, al be myn herte trewe... (V. 701–06)[43]

By contrast, writers who give Criseyde a more restricted means of expression, through narratorial commentary rather than her own voice, notably Guido delle Colonne[44] and Lydgate, endorse a clearer antifeminist reading of her. Boccaccio comes somewhere in between these two camps because he gives her a great deal of voice while she is faithful and then removes it decisively from her and brings in narratorial antifeminist commentary when she has become unfaithful.

Boccaccio, in fact, was the first writer to make Criseyde, his Criseida, a widow—as well as being probably the first to give her love affair with Troilus a history, Benoît and his successors having inaugurated its narration at the point when Briseida has to leave for the Greek camp. Making Criseida a widow fits with Boccaccio's reshaping of the story's protagonists into more sexually experienced people, but it is an element in *Il Filostrato* that could mean that he too recalled Ovid's widowed Briseis.[45] Both Boccaccio and Chaucer knew the *Heroides* well.[46]

Another link between *Il Filostrato* and the *Heroides* takes us back to Meleager and the boar. In part 7 of *Il Filostrato* the desolate Troilo dreams that he is in a wood through which he sees a boar charging; Criseida appears and the boar tears out her heart, which does not seem to pain her but to give her pleasure. Awakened rudely, Troilo summons Pandaro, and immediately interprets the boar as Diomede, descended from the boar-killer, who is of course Meleager—though he is not at this

---

[42] *Heroides*, ll. 17–20, p. 32.

[43] *The Riverside Chaucer*, p. 569.

[44] See R. M. Lumiansky, 'The Story of Troilus and Briseida according to Benoît and Guido', *Speculum*, 29 (1954), 727–33.

[45] Cf. Hexter, p. 179, n. 98.

[46] Nolan is willing to see a connection between Boccaccio's Criseida and the Briseis of Ovid's *Ars Amatoria* (p. 141).

point so named in Boccaccio's poem.[47] Critical comment on this passage tends to concentrate on Troilo's ready connection of Diomede and the boar, and the suggestion thus in *Il Filostrato* that Diomede has taken Criseida's heart without her objection. What has gone unnoticed is the small link back to the use of the same episode, though far from the same details, by Ovid's Briseis.

First, though, Chaucer's version (*Troilus* V. 1233–60). Here in Troilus's dream the boar, distinguished not as in Boccaccio by its grand size overall, but by its 'tuskes grete' is sleeping in the heat of the sun in the forest. And in an embrace with it and smothering it with kisses ('kyssyng ay') is Criseyde. The sight of this wakens Troilus, who summons Pandarus and cries out in agony that Criseyde has betrayed him; but he does not produce the identification of the boar as Diomede—this comes later, from his prophetic sister Cassandra. Discussion of this scene has again focussed on the interpretation of the boar, since its lack of immediate identification with Diomede frees up other possibilities: not just explicitly in the text that, as Pandarus rather desperately suggests, this nice old boar is Criseyde's father, whom she is kissing because she is pleased to see him again, but also that Chaucer may be implicitly setting up some identification of the boar with Troilus himself, as ill-fated lover. Cassandra's interpretation of the boar as Diomede also politicizes this part of the poem, and she delivers a version of the Meleager narrative in explanation, for which the dominant source is *Metamorphoses* VIII, and for which there is no precedent in *Il Filostrato*. This links the story to the Theban context of feuding and doom that underscores much of *Troilus and Criseyde*. The boar scene is clearly susceptible to a number of different modes of reading—Troilian, Pandarian, Cassandrian, and those others thereby generated for readers.[48]

My concern is rather to ask what Chaucer thought he was doing with Criseyde here. There is, in this connection, a nice textual difficulty in the opening of the stanza that describes the embrace between the boar and

---

[47] Translated by Havely, pp. 88–89; the original is provided in Geoffrey Chaucer, *Troilus and Criseyde*, ed. by B. A. Windeatt (London: Longman, 1984) pp. 512–20.

[48] See David Anderson, 'Cassandra's Analogy: *Troilus* V, 1450–1542', *Hebrew University Studies in Literature*, 13 (1985), 1–17; Winthrop Wetherbee, *Chaucer and the Poets: An Essay on 'Troilus and Criseyde'* (Ithaca, NY: Cornell University Press, 1984), pp. 128–34; Lee Patterson, *Chaucer and the Subject of History* (Madison: University of Wisconsin Press, 1991), pp. 129–32; Jane Chance, *The Mythographic Chaucer: The Fabulation of Sexual Politics* (Minneapolis: University of Minnesota Press, 1995), pp. 1616–24.

Criseyde. One group of witnesses reads 'faste in his armes folde', the reading preferred by most editors; another group omits the pronoun, suggesting, presumably, that the boar and Criseyde are bound in a mutual embrace; and the last group reads 'faste in hire armes folde'.[49] This, writes Windeatt, 'makes awkward sense',[50] but as Criseyde is the one who is kissing the sleeping boar, isn't it perhaps just as sensible to see her embracing it as being embraced by it? An image of Criseyde held fast by a somnolent pig but willingly kissing it generates a sense of enforced but not unenthusiastic compliance that fits with the image of Criseyde's relationship with Diomede that many readers want to take from the poem. To have the slumbering boar (and is this post-coital slumber?) folded in Criseyde's arms as she kisses him would suggest that Criseyde is very much the active partner, something apparently antithetical to editors. The ambiguity in the textual variants here points up the difficulties of interpreting Criseyde in the last part of the poem. Cassandra's omission of any interpretation of Criseyde's role in Troilus's dream indicates that she is easily read, but this is surely not the case. And Criseyde's closeness to the boar in this scene also establishes a potential link between her and Meleager, and the Meleager story.

Such a link casts a shadow over Criseyde and suggests she is bound up with a complex of conflicts in her familial and love relationships. Moreover, though so strongly indebted to the *Metamorphoses*, Cassandra's account notably truncates the denouement: 'But how this Meleagre gan to dye/Thorugh his moder wol I yow naught telle,/For al to longe it were for to dwelle' (V. 1482–84). The mother's curse is also alluded to, but not dwelt on, in Briseis's account in the *Heroides*. In both that work and in Chaucer's *Troilus* the association of Briseis and Criseyde with the Meleager story does not bode well for either woman, but also suggests that neither of them can be read in a straightforward way.

If then, Boccaccio made the initial connection back to the Meleager episode and to Ovid's Briseis, Chaucer greatly extended that potential. Whether Meleager finally relates to Diomede, Troilus, Criseyde, or all three, is thus left unclear in this part of *Troilus* and contributes to the perception in book V that interpretation is a highly complicated act, particularly concerning figures with literary traditions that contain their own ambiguities. The idea that interpretation is thus a complex *moral* act

---

[49] Windeatt, as n. 47, p. 515.

[50] Ibid.

is certainly something Chaucer wanted his readers to think about, as did Robert Henryson, who saw all sorts of possibilities for Criseyde in the dark world of book V of *Troilus* beyond the desire to show what finally happened to her. And medieval readers were perhaps more sensitive to characters casting long literary shadows than we sometimes allow them to be. When Whitelaw (the hand here is definitely his), commented on a later part of the *Ilias Latina* where Diomede wounds Venus when she is removing Aeneas in a cloud from the Greek warrior, 'Dyomedes in hoc loco vulnerat venerem'[51] he was making an ironic little comment on how it was often the other way round. This interest in Diomede on the part of a Scottish reader prompts one to think again of Henryson's poem. The *Testament* indeed gains much of its structure from a series of Cresseidian speeches, and, strikingly, Cresseid's final speaking act, is, like Criseyde's in Chaucer's *Troilus*, a written one. Criseyde writes to Troilus; Cresseid writes her testament. This brings to mind once more the written world of letters in the *Heroides*. It seems to me closing a door quite unnecessarily to suggest that Henryson and Chaucer did not look back to the Ovidian Briseis when they gave their Criseydes this form of last word.

---

[51] Fol. 68^r; 'here Diomede wounds Venus'.

II. Matters of Conduct

Chaucer and the French Tradition Revisited: Philippe de Mézières and the Good Wife

CAROLYN P. COLLETTE

For most of this century Chaucer's relationship to the subjects and conventions of French vernacular literature has been traced through two lines of descent: one, the elegant and highly formalized court poetry of Machaut, Deschamps, and Graunson, appears in Chaucer's earlier poetry, short lyrics, and, of course, the romance of Troilus. A second tradition, which Charles Muscatine termed the bourgeois tradition located in the 'mime, the beast epic, the fable,' a literature 'traditionally humorous, and lightly didactic,' appears in the fabliau and stories of merchants, friars, and animals, in *The Canterbury Tales*.[1] But Chaucer was aware of and influenced by a third kind of tradition in late fourteenth and early fifteenth century French literature. This tradition, appearing in the popular French genre of advice books for and about wives, in collections

I am grateful to Nadia Margolis, Elizabeth Petroff, and Sherry Reames for help with the research for this article.

[1] See Charles Muscatine, *Chaucer and the French Tradition* (Berkeley: University of California Press, 1969), p. 58. Chaucer scholarship has historically identified and separated two continental influences on Chaucer's work, the French and the Italian. Working with Philippe de Mézières makes it clear that the separation of French and Italian literary influences distorts the true nature of late medieval intertextuality on the subject of literature for and about women. On the influence of French literature on Chaucer see Haldeen Braddy, *Chaucer and the French Poet Graunson* (Baton Rouge: Louisiana Sate University Press, 1947), James I. Wimsatt, *Chaucer and His French Contemporaries: Natural Music in the Fourteenth Century* (Toronto: University of Toronto Press, 1991). William Calin, *The French Tradition and the Literature of Medieval England* (Toronto: University of Toronto Press, 1994).

of stories in which female virtue grounded in prudence and self-control benefits the immediate domestic and also the wider public spheres, constitutes the literary topos of the good wife. The influence of this subject appears in some of the most debated and some of the most passed-over of *The Canterbury Tales,* in the stories of Prudence and Melibee, St Cecilia, and Griselda, stories Chaucer tells either in his exalted *rime royalle* form, or in the prose which he selects for religious and philosophical subjects. While a great deal of attention has been paid to Chaucer's women, this particular line of influence and tradition has so far been largely overlooked.

Exemplary and cautionary stories of and for women existed in many collections throughout the Middle Ages, of course. Three features mark the late medieval French versions of this kind of narrative as a particular genre or tradition: first they are closely tied through dedication and patronage to the highest levels of French nobility. Second, the tales that comprise this genre focus on married women's behaviour rather than on single-women's virginity as an important arena of female virtue. Third, they are imbued with a strong socio-political dimension manifested in the assumption that the good wife bears a responsibility for creating domestic harmony through virtues which can also be called upon to promote the common good.[2]

This genre is usually associated with Christine de Pizan, who developed and in a sense perfected, but did not initiate it. Many of the ideas she would express so forcefully in the *Cité des Dames* and much of her thinking about how women's virtue connects the domestic and the public spheres and the importance of the virtue of prudence to the wise noble woman in the subsequent *Le Livre des Trois Vertus*, were anticipated in a more conservative form in *Le Livre de la Vertu du sacrement de mariage et du reconfort des dames mariees* (1384–89) of Philippe de Mézières, a prominent courtier at the court of Charles V where Christine's father was court astrologer. Jean-Louis G. Picherit makes a strong case for Philippe's influence on Christine's thinking about

---

[2]   Based on the Book of Proverbs 31. 10–31, and Ecclesiasticus 26, the topos of the good wife is generic throughout the Middle Ages. Late medieval Europe, however, developed a particular interest in this topos: see Silvana Vecchio, 'The Good Wife', trans. by Clarissa Botsford, *A History of Women in the West: II Silences of the Middle Ages*, ed. by Christiane Klapisch-Zuber (Cambridge, MA: Harvard University Press, 1992), pp. 105–35 (p. 107). On the subject of good wives and medieval expectations of female behaviour, see Felicity Riddy, 'Mother Knows Best: Reading Social Change in a Courtesy Text', *Speculum*, 71 (1996), 66–86.

marriage and married women. While scholars have previously recognized connections between his *Songe de vieil Pelerin* and her *Livre de la Mutacion de Fortune*, Picherit maintains that their common interest in married women's behaviour forms an even more fundamental connection: 'Among the points they have in common two seem to have an especially important place in the work of Christine de Pizan and Philippe de Mézières. They concern the defence of marriage and of the married woman, and the pre-eminent place accorded to the Virgin Mary.'[3] Just as Philippe de Mézières's work helps delineate the tradition within which Christine wrote, it can also help define the field of reference and the literary *sociolect* in which Chaucer's stories of Prudence, Cecilia, and Griselda were written and received.

A good deal of circumstantial detail suggests that Philippe de Mézières was a familiar figure in Chaucer's world, as his 1395 *Epistre au Roi Richart*, urging peace and a royal marriage between Richard II and Isabel, daughter of Charles VI, suggests. Joan Williamson, de Mézières's twentieth-century editor, points out that he had led an extremely public life, serving six kings in Europe and the Mediterranean area. In his later years he was Charles V's most trusted counsellor, and he was tutor to Charles VI.[4] The chivalric order he founded, the *Chevalerie de la Passion de Jhesu Crist*, included what Williamson terms some of the 'most illustrious names in Europe'.[5] Philippe also vigorously advocated the cause of Leo VI, the last King of Armenia who visited the English court in 1386 trying to gain economic and military support to regain his kingdom. Trying to organize a new Crusade to support that displaced monarch and recapture the Middle East from Islam involved Philippe de Mézières in extensive negotiations and petitions on both sides of the Channel.[6]

---

[3] 'De Philippe de Mézières à Christine de Pizan', *Le Moyen Français*, 13 (1983), 20–36 (p. 23). All translations are mine unless otherwise noted.

[4] Joan B. Williamson, 'Philippe de Mézières' Book for Married Ladies: A Book from the Entourage of the Court of Charles VI', *The Spirit of the Court: Selected Proceedings of the Fourth Congress of the International Courtly Literature Society (Toronto, 1983)*, ed. by Glyn S. Burgess and Robert A. Taylor (Cambridge: D. S. Brewer, 1985), pp. 393–408 (p. 395).

[5] Williamson, 'Book for Married Ladies,' pp. 395–96.

[6] For Leo VI in England, see *The Westminster Chronicle (1381–1394)*, trans. and ed. by L. C. Hector and Barbara F. Harvey (Oxford: Clarendon Press, 1982), p. 155. On Philippe de Mézières, the Order of the Passion, and the English court see Maurice Keen, 'Chaucer's Knight, the English Aristocracy and the Crusade,' in *English Court Culture in the Later Middle Ages*, ed. by V. J. Scattergood and J. W. Sherborne (New York: St Martin's Press,

But more than reputation links Chaucer to Philippe, for both contributed to a body of ethically-centred court literature that appeared in both England and France during this period. Writing in the last quarter of the fourteenth-century, Philippe de Mézières constructed himself as a reclusive persona and a public voice, as he withdrew from public life to the convent of the Celestines. Although in his later years he described himself in his writings as 'le povre, viel solitaire,' his withdrawal from court life was more physical than mental, as his literary output suggests. Jacques Krynen singles out de Mézières as the writer who most cogently developed and expressed a theory of responsible kingship, what Krynen terms 'la royauté-fonction publique,' during the later fourteenth century. He describes Philippe de Mézières as ceaselessly calling Charles VI's attention to the fact that 'the splendour of his royal dignity has no other justification than the pursuit of the welfare of his subjects';[7] he sought to school Charles VI in the moral foundations of power, recommending the 'dictez vertueulx' (moral poems) of Deschamps to the young king, as well as other 'escriptures vrayes, honnestes et catholiques, tendans a bonne édification.'[8]

His moral writings directed to the highest levels of the aristocracy form part of a shift of literary focus away from a vernacular court literature focused on the self and the self's emotions, toward a courtly vernacular literature focused on social relations. French scholars tie this flowering of instructive vernacular literature written in court circles to the deteriorating political situation after the death of Charles V. Joël Blanchard describes the period as characterized by a shift in poetic consciousness and attention, from the self-centred to awareness of the external:

> For the first time the poet posits in a form both allegorical and dramatic the problem of the existence of an object outside of and beyond himself, not the promptings of his heart, but a consideration for that which is not him.[9]

1983), pp. 45–61 and the introduction to G. W. Coopland's dual language edition of Philippe de Mézières's *Letter to King Richard II* (New York: Barnes and Noble, 1976).

[7] Jacques Krynen, *Idéal du prince et pouvoir royal en France à la fin du Moyen Age (1380–1440): étude de la littérature politique du temps* (Paris: Picard, 1981), p. 327.

[8] Jacqueline Cerquiglini-Toulet, *The Color of Melancholy: The Uses of Books in the Fourteenth Century*, trans. by Lydia G. Cochrane (Baltimore: Johns Hopkins University Press, 1997), p. 149.

[9] Joël Blanchard, 'L'Entrée du poète dans le champ poétique au xve siècle,' *Annales E.S.C.*, 41 (1986), 43–61 (p. 47).

Daniel Poirion puts it slightly differently, seeing a moral dimension inherent in all court-based literature of the time.[10]

Anne Middleton has identified a similar development in England. She places Chaucer among a group of men who lived at the centre of the royal court, and who, like their French counterparts, created a literature of instruction and edification for the aristocracy, a literature designed, as Middleton says, to 'exemplify an ideal of communal responsibility founded [...]in an altruistic and outward turning form of love that might be called "common love" to emphasize its symmetry and contrast with that singular passion which expresses itself in literature in the inward self-cultivation sometimes called "courtly love".'[11] The voice of this public poetry was, she says, 'pious, but its central pieties are worldly felicity and peaceful, harmonious communal existence' (p. 95). Stories of good wives and domestic relations form an important, if not fully recognized, topos in this literature of commonweal.

Philippe de Mézières conceived of public and social good as rooted in the morality and virtue of the individual, in turn grounded in religious faith. His goal was a society structured by reciprocal bonds of duty and obliga-tion. Noble women no less than men bore a responsibility for promoting harmonious social patterns; they could do so most effectively by reflecting on the life and Passion of Christ, by denying destructive self-will, and by working within their marriages to create harmony. Written in the late 1380s (1384–89) and dedicated to Jehanne de Chastillon, wife of his patron Pierre de Craon, *Le Livre de la vertu du sacrement de mariage* (preserved in a unique manuscript Paris, Bibliothèque Nationale MS fr. 1175) presents an extended discussion of the interconnected religious, moral, and social dimensions of marriage. While de Mézières focuses on individual instances of good and bad behaviour, the clear purpose of his book, as Joan Williamson has pointed out, is 'the smooth functioning of society'.[12]

Although we have only a single extant copy, it is clear from the way Philippe writes of his potential audience as primarily, but not exclusively, women, that he is writing a book he hopes will instruct a wide audience in the public implications of private morality. The title he gives his work

---

[10] Daniel Poirion, *Le Moyen Age II: 1300–1480* (Paris: Arthaud, 1971), p. 91.

[11] Anne Middleton, 'The Idea of Public Poetry in the Reign of Richard II,' *Speculum*, 53 (1978), 94–114 (pp. 95–96).

[12] 'Book for Married Ladies,' p. 404.

addresses it to the 'reconfort des dames mariees et de tout bon Crestien.'[13] The introduction to chapter twenty-four of book three announces that the chapter is written for both husbands and wives: 'Du reconfort en especial des hommes mariés et comment l'omme en son mariage se doit confourmer aux vertus morales du fin rubin [Jesus Christ] et la femme mariee au fin dyamant [Virgin Mary]' (Le Livre, p. 308).[14] Philippe's frequent reference to his audience/subject as 'femmes mariees' indicates that he imagined a large audience which would benefit from his advice.

Comprising four books, the Livre is an extensive allegory of the spiritual marriage between Christ and the Church, between Christ and the human soul, as well as an anatomization of the sources, manifestations, and cures for female marital discontent. The work describes married women as simultaneously spiritual brides of Christ and physical wives of real men, thereby connecting religion to ideal social behaviour, and placing the wife in a complicated and highly restricting net of obligations. In part to express a sense of marriage as a series of complex, intersecting duties, Philippe structures his work through elaborately intertwined metaphors drawing on alchemy, lapidaries, optics, pilgrimages, and medicine, as he seeks to define and remedy what is wrong with the woman who is 'unhappy and ill' ('la dame malcontente et malade', Le Livre, p. 262) in her marriage. Through numerous comparisons and examples which posit Jesus as the ideal spouse and the Virgin Mary as ideal wife and mother, he instructs his female audience in the dangers of wilfulness, of giving in to unhappiness, luxurious living, and pride. He draws most of his examples from the Bible and from history, taking others from legend and myth. While his purpose in adducing his copious examples is primarily to show how wives ought and ought not to behave in domestic relations, he cites a number of examples of noble wives whose behaviour led directly to disastrous political results. One such story is that of the fictional Rosamund, daughter of the King of the Lombards, who was forced to marry her father's murderer, a king who made her drink from a cup fashioned out of her dead father's skull. She took revenge upon her husband, seducing one of his knights whom she persuaded to kill her husband; subsequently she became a serial

---

[13] 'to the support of married women and all good Christians', Philippe de Mézières, Le Livre de la Vertu du Sacrement de Mariage, ed. by Joan B. Williamson (Washington, DC: Catholic University of America Press, 1993), p. 47.

[14] Of comfort particularly for married men and how the man in his marriage ought to embody the moral virtues of the perfect ruby and the married woman those of the perfect diamond.

murderess, poisoning her second husband because of lust for a third man, spreading yet more death and social instability. In a story so fraught with horror and justifiable motives for revenge, it may surprise a modern reader that Philippe interprets it as an example of the ill effect of female desperation in marriage, a kind of illness which could have been either avoided or cured (*Le Livre*, pp. 238–39). Rosamund's personal situation, while pitiable, he contends, was one she should have overcome, for her own sake as well as others.[15] His story of Joan of Naples provides a hortatory example of the dangers of unfettered female imagination to the body politic. She fell prey to a *frenesie*, an illusion that when her husband, King Andrew, came to her bed, he appeared to her in the form of an ass ('il li sambloit de son seigneur et mari quant il estoit couchiéz avec lui que ce fut un asne', *Le Livre,* pp. 236–37). From this *frenesie* came the ruin of the monarchy, as the barons, seeking to please the queen, villainously murdered the innocent king: 'dont tant de maulx avindrent que les barons du royaume, cuidans plaire a leur royne, par l'enortement d'une contesse de Cabane, murdrirent leur seigneur innocent et de tres vilaine mort' (*Le Livre*, p. 237).[16] Such stories clearly reflect anxiety about the indirect but real influence women exerted over male bonds that formed the basis of political power. Eric Hicks has observed that late medieval French culture was a culture in which women were excluded from affairs of state by law, but were everywhere present by force of circumstance.[17] The stories Philippe tells reflect an anxiety that women might indeed insinuate themselves into affairs of state, and that their private passions could result in disastrous public consequences.

---

[15] In this de Mézières anticipates Christine de Pizan's advice in *Le Livre des Trois Vertus* to the noble princess married to a brutish husband: that 'wisdom and prudence' lie in 'dissembling wisely' (*Le Livre des Trois Vertus*, ed. by Charity Cannon Willard and Eric Hicks (Paris: Champion, 1989), pp. 54–56).

Philippe de Mézières's attitude toward unhappy women is that the *malcontente* woman is necessarily a *malade* woman whose illness needs a suitable medicine. Christine, in contrast, recognizes that women may very well be unhappy for a variety of reasons beyond their control; nevertheless she, too, advises the unhappy woman to deal with and solve her problems quietly and privately.

[16] ...from which so many ills arose that the barons of the realm, thinking to please their queen, at the goading of a Countess of the Cabane [laundry], murdered their innocent lord by a villainous death.

[17] Eric Hicks, 'Une femme dans le monde: Christine de Pizan et l'écriture de la politique,' in *L'hostellerie de pensée: études sur l'art littéraire au Moyen Age, textes réunis par Michel Zink et Danielle Bohler*, ed. by Eric Hicks and Manuela Python (Paris: Sorbonne, 1995), pp. 233–43 (p. 234).

But just as inordinate passion and lack of self-control could damage the fabric of social relations, so female virtue could sustain and strengthen it. Within a general frame of moralization illustrated by women-focused exempla, Philippe constructs themes and stories about good wives that serve to illustrate virtues fundamental to private and public harmony. Early in the text, as he lays out the terms of his argument, Philippe establishes the fundamental nature of female prudence as a gift of the Holy Spirit, and modelled by the Virgin: '...par laquelle prudence elle avoit plaine science et sapience acquise par grace et infusé par le Saint Esperit; dont elle estoit maistresse de cognoistre les choses passees, de considerer et contempler les choses presentes, et reguler toutes ses euvres selonc Dieu, faisant le bien et laissant le mal, et par sa grant prudence discrete moderer les choses a avenir' (*Le Livre*, pp. 169–170).[18] Later he describes Prudence as the chief of the four cardinal virtues, 'who knows and marks all that is necessary to do and makes provision and preparation against the ills and maladies which are or which might come in the future' ('provision et preparation contre les maulz et maladies', *Le Livre*, p. 262). Philippe's definition of Prudence is essentially the broad conventional definition: Prudence is foresight built on knowledge of the past and ability to use that knowledge effectively in coping with the future. At the very time that he wrote, the concept of Prudence, once defined and discussed in texts that generally assumed a male audience, was developing a decidedly female dimension. His work both reflects and helps to shape this new dimension, for like Christine de Pizan, he places female prudence at the heart of effective social relations.

By the late fourteenth century Prudence was no longer primarily a virtue for men to employ in statecraft; instead, the idea of Prudence had been expanded to include social and political relationships, particularly within households. Prudence, once a virtue of action based on foresight in the world of governance, began to suggest the idea of circumspection and intelligence in managing human relationships within households.[19] The history of Albertano of Brescia's story of Prudence and Melibee attests to this evolution. The *Histoire Littéraire de la France* notes that over time

---

[18] ...by which prudence she possessed full knowledge and wisdom acquired by grace and infused by the Holy Spirit through which she mastered knowing things past, considering and contemplating things present, and regulating all her works according to God, doing good and avoiding evil, and by her great, discreet prudence, moderating those things to come.

[19] J. D. Burnley, *Chaucer's Language and the Philosopher's Tradition* (Cambridge: D. S. Brewer, 1979), pp. 51–57.

the story itself changes, citing as evidence the story's appearance in *Le Menagier de Paris*'s compilation and in *Le Livre du Chevalier de la Tour Landry*.[20]

The emphasis Philippe places upon Prudence helps contextualize Chaucer's 'Tale of Melibee,' a version of the popular story of Prudence and Melibee. Chaucer's narrative presents Dame Prudence acting and speaking in just the ways that Philippe would approve. Prudence works to counter 'les maulz et maladies' of the injury her husband has received as she counsels her husband against violence, toward peace, and as she moves to broker peace between her husband and his enemies. As I have argued elsewhere, Chaucer's Prudence follows the pattern of speech and action Christine de Pizan advises as ideal for a noblewoman in *Le Livre des Trois Vertus*; she brokers peace between Melibee and his enemies, bides her time, speaks carefully and wisely to her husband, and looks after his welfare, both domestic and political.[21] Philippe de Mézières's work, together with Christine de Pizan's, demonstrates that in the social and literary culture of late medieval France, Prudence was a female virtue necessary to the smooth running of households, the foundation of a noblewoman's ability to advise her husband wisely and mediate on his behalf. Whatever else is going on in Chaucer's tale, the scenes and actions it narrates conform in language and spirit to the principle that the wise wife will be prudent in counselling her husband and seeking to remedy past injuries while planning for a peaceful future.

In valuing female prudence as the ability to look outward, beyond the self, Philippe characterizes the unhappy married woman as preoccupied with a kind of self-absorption that negates her power of thoughtful analysis and wise expectation. He spends a great deal of time discussing the dangers of inordinate self-will, and inordinate desires for luxury: he describes *malcontentes* as women who have 'un appetit et desir desordené' for honours beyond their merit. Such women possess 'an insatiable appetite for many beautiful robes, for grand apparel and splendid jewels, and beautiful adornment', wish 'to do nothing and to sleep late into the morning, to drink and to eat much of expensive and delicious dishes...and briefly, such a malcontent woman has the appetite of a dog ('un appetit canin') which can never be sated' (*Le Livre*, p. 232). The woman so given to luxury and pleasures of the flesh is subject to a

---

[20] *Histoire Littéraire de la France*, 37 (1938), p. 502.

[21] 'Heeding the Counsel of Prudence: A Context for the *Melibee*', *Chaucer Review*, 29 (1995), 337–49.

terrible fate, to physical and spiritual destruction, and to loss of reputation: her private sin becomes a public matter (*Le Livre*, p. 292). Such a
woman becomes a danger not only to herself but to others, offering an
undefended place for the devil's work in her marriage (*Le Livre*, p. 292).

One ideal example Philippe offers of how a good wife overcomes the
trammels of luxury and idleness that may destroy herself and others is the
story of St Cecilia. The legend of St Cecilia was a popular one, particularly in the Italian-French literary culture of which Philippe was part.[22] It
appeared in a number of venues in addition to hagiographic collections,
notably in thirteenth- and fourteenth-century texts including the preaching
of Jacobus de Voragine and the writing of Thomas of Chobham and
Pierre Dubois, all of whom cited it as an example of ideal wifely
behaviour in large part because it exemplified St Paul's assertion in I
Corinthians 7. 12–16 that an 'unbelieving husband is sanctified by a wife
with faith'.[23] As Sharon Farmer has shown, Chobham's 1215 *Manual for
Confessors* argued that women were powerfully able through words and
actions in the privacy of the bedchamber to 'correct the moral and
economic behaviour of their husbands' in the public sphere.[24] The cult of
St Cecilia current in Italian and French intellectual circles from the
thirteenth century through the Renaissance was not merely an example of
a glorious martyrdom, it was a pattern of idealized wifely behaviour.
Sherry Reames calls attention to this shift of focus as it notes a tendency
to 'domesticate' Cecilia's legend in the late Middle Ages: 'Indeed, one
would hesitate to call her a hero at all on the basis of many of these
breviaries, since they do not allow her to do anything except convert her
own husband in the privacy of their bedroom, eventually refuse the
persecutor's order to sacrifice, and somehow acquire a group of female
followers whom she commits to the Pope when she dies'.[25] Reames notes
that in the later Middle Ages saints' lives in general were 'apparently

---

[22] See Joan Williamson, 'The French-Italian World of Philippe de Mézières in 1370,'
Romance Languages Annual, 3 (1992), 140–45.

[23] Vecchio, p. 116.

[24] 'Persuasive Voices: Clerical Images of Medieval Wives,' *Speculum*, 61 (1986), 517–
543 (pp. 517, 539).

[25] '*Mouvance* and Interpretation in Late-Medieval Latin: The Legend of St Cecilia in
British Breviaries,' *Medieval Literature: Texts and Interpretation*, ed. by Tim William
Machan (Binghamton: Medieval and Renaissance Texts and Studies, 1991), 159–189 (p.
188).

being revised and updated—brought into closer line, that is, with the values and expectations of the revisers' own culture'.[26]

Philippe does indeed seem to adapt the story of Cecilia to reflect the values and expectations central to his work and the culture that shaped it. He abbreviates it and strips it of its more dramatic elements, and of characters extraneous to the domestic setting of Cecilia's bedchamber:

> Ceste glorieuse vierge et espouse de Jesu Crist, le jour de ses noces et touzjours aussy, portoit en sa poitrine l'Evangile de Jesu Crist et si portoit a sa char nue la haire, mais par dehors elle estoit vestu de drap d'or et bien paree. Ceste noble dame vierge fu mariee a un grant prince de Romme appellé Valerien, riche, josne et tres bel. Et quant vint la nuit des noces et elle fu couchie avec son biau mari, elle sot tant dire et tant preschier a son mari qu'elle demoura vierge. Et converti son mari a la foy crestienne par le moyen de l'angele qui apporta en la chambre les belles roses vermailles— et si estoit plain yver—segnefiant le martire du noble prince Valerien et de Tiburcius son frere, que la vierge aussy converti, et les fleurs de lys aussy que l'angele apporta segnifoient la virginité de la vierge Cecilie et la chasteté de son mari et de son frere, qui furent vrays martirs et la vierge aussi. (*Le Livre*, p. 274)[27]

Philippe emphasizes various elements of the story to support his major contentions about what constitutes a good wife. Later, in drawing the moral of his story, he recapitulates the major points of his compressed narrative, this time concluding that Cecilia's great act is to reject the luxury her life offers. The hair shirt she wears on her wedding day, one of the traditional elements of the legend, becomes an important sign of her scorn of luxury and material ease. He says of her, that she 'carefully kept herself from becoming swollen or puffed up ('ydropique ne...enflee'), however well adorned she was externally' (*Le Livre*, p. 274). For

---

[26] Reames, p. 189.

[27] This glorious virgin and spouse of Jesus Christ, the day of her wedding, as always, carried in her heart the gospel of Jesus Christ and indeed she wore a hair shirt next to her naked flesh, but externally she was clothed with a cloth of gold, beautifully ornamented. This noble lady virgin was married to a great prince of Rome called Valerian, rich, young, and very handsome. And when their wedding-night came and she was in bed with her handsome husband, she so spoke and preached to her husband that she remained a virgin. And converted her husband to the Christian faith by means of an angel who brought into her chamber beautiful red roses—although it was fully wintertime—signifying the martyrdom of the noble prince Valerian and of Tiburtius his brother, whom the virgin also converted, and the lilies also which the angel brought signified the virginity of the virgin Cecilia and the chastity of her husband and his brother, who were true martyrs, as was the virgin also.

converting her husband and brother-in-law, as well as for the humility she demonstrates, she is a mirror to married women, like Christ in her exemplary behaviour:

> Pour ce les dames mariees, aprés l'example et miroir de la Passion du doulx Aignelet occys, se doivent remirer pour desenfler ou miroir de Cecilie, suiant le Cruxefis, qui dit a ses amis, 'Aprenéz de moy qui suis humbles de cuer et debonnaire, et ce faisant vous trouveréz repos en vos ames' [Matthew 11. 29]. (*Le Livre*, p. 274)[28]

Philippe's version of the legend of St Cecilia provides an illuminating analogue to Chaucer's version in 'The Second Nun's Tale,' because of the way both writers link St Cecilia to themes of idleness and luxury. Thomas Connolly's extensive discussion of the cult of St Cecilia, observes that the theme of work as spiritual transformation is central to the legend of this saint whose life was dedicated to converting pagans to Christianity.[29] Clearly Chaucer's language in his prologue is influenced by this tradition, as he stresses the value of 'feithful bisynesse' in creating a 'translacioun' of the story as a bulwark against 'ydelnesse.'[30] But the first four stanzas of the prologue to the tale warn against *ydelnesse* in language that echoes Philippe's condemnation of women who give themselves over to luxurious living. The Second Nun warns against 'The ministre and the norice unto vices/Which that men clepe in Englissh Ydelnesse/That porter of the gate is of delices' for the Feend 'with his thousand cordes slye' waits to catch those who give in to the temptations of luxury, those whom 'slouthe hire holden in a lees/Oonly to slepe, and for to ete and drynke/And to devouren al that othere swynke' (SNP, 1–21). Both Chaucer and Philippe de Mézières connect the story of St Cecilia with the dangers of idleness as much as with the importance of work.

The fact that the story of St Cecilia current in late medieval Italian and French culture was a marriage tale as much as a saint's *legend* suggests

---

[28] Therefore married women, following the example and the mirror of the Passion of the sweet murdered Lamb, in order to be less proud, ought to look into the mirror of St Cecilia, following the Crucifix, who says to his friends, 'Learn from me, I who am humble in heart and meek, and in so doing you will find repose in your souls.'

[29] *Mourning into Joy: Music, Raphael and Saint Cecilia* (New Haven, CT: Yale University Press, 1994).

[30] 'Second Nun's Prologue,' 22–25; all citations of Chaucer's work are from Geoffrey Chaucer, *The Canterbury Tales,* in *The Riverside Chaucer,* ed. by Larry D. Benson, 3rd edn (Boston: Houghton Mifflin, 1987).

that Chaucer's audience may have contextualized the tale quite differently
from the way we do. In 1960 Donald Howard proposed that the tale is
actually a fitting conclusion to the marriage group because medieval
culture regarded virginal marriage as the highest form of marriage.[31]
Philippe de Mézières's version suggests another way in which the tale
may continue the theme of marriage, as an example of an ideal form of
wifely care for and counsel of her husband and his circle, the topic that
Chaucer introduces in his 'Tale of Melibee.'

The legend of St Cecilia represents one kind of female virtue, the
chaste wife who creates a chaste, spiritually-centred marriage. This is the
kind of ideal marriage Philippe acknowledges as a rarity. He therefore
chooses an example of a married woman to epitomize ideal female virtue
in a consummated marriage—Griselda. From the very beginning of *Le
Livre*, Philippe refers to Griselda as exalted above all other exemplars of
female virtue. At the end of the prologue Philippe records the extended
title of his work as *De la Vertu du sacrement de mariage espirituel et
reconfort des dames mariees et de tout bon Crestien par un devot
example de la Passion de Jesu Crist et du miroir des dames mariees, la
noble marquise de Saluce. (Le Livre, p. 47),*[32] placing Christ's passion
and Griselda's patient endurance on an equal plane. He structures the
work so that the story of Griselda functions as a point of climax in respect
to form and theme. Griselda's is the story of a woman whose 'constance
et loyaulté, amour et obedience' to her husband and to Christ 'surmonte et
nature et toute femme mariee vertueuse dont les histoires anciennes et
croniques faissent aucune mencion' (*Le Livre*, p. 356).[33] Moreover, he
says, this story encompasses and surpasses all the previous examples of
appropriate female behaviour in the work. To encourage women to
emulate her, Philippe maintains that Griselda was a historical figure, not
merely a fictional idea: 'Et est la dicte histoire publique et notoire en
Lombardie et par especial en Pieumont et ou marquisie de Saluce et
reputee pour vraye' (*Le Livre*, p. 358).[34] Griselda is greater than any of

---

[31] 'The Conclusion of the Marriage Group: Chaucer and the Human Condition', *Modern
Philology*, 57 (1959–60), 223–32.

[32] Concerning the Virtue of the Sacrament of spiritual marriage and of comfort for
married women and for all good Christians by means of a devoted example of the Passion
of Jesus Christ and of the mirror of married women, the noble marquise of Saluzzo.

[33] ...surmounts both nature and all virtuous married women of whom ancient chronicles
and histories make any mention.

[34] And the said story is well-known and famous in Lombardy and especially in Piedmont
and in the marquisate of Saluce is believed to be true.

the nine worthy women of great virtue who did wonderful things in the
world, such as the warrior queen *Semiramis, royne des Assiriens* who,
after her husband's death conquered India and Ethiopia 'a l'espee' which
her husband in his lifetime had been unable to achieve (*Le Livre*, p. 356).
Great as this accomplishment was, Griselda's is greater, for through
valour and invincible courage she conquers herself, a matter 'of greater
merit than conquering others' ('de plus grant merite que n'est de vaincre
autrie', *Le Livre*, p. 357). In this she epitomizes all the ideal examples he
has adduced. For Philippe self-control is the paramount female virtue.

The story Philippe presents conforms in terms of theme and action to
all the other versions of the period. Nevertheless, as with the story of
Cecilia, he is careful to emphasize elements of the action and of
Griselda's character that reinforce and illustrate his larger theme, the
social value of female virtue rooted in self-control. Griselda is humble,
happy, a patient daughter to her aged father; she manifests self-control,
for she is also quite specifically not the sort of woman to desire luxury.
She is unaccustomed to a soft and delicate diet and rich thing ('choses
riches, molles et delicatives') but has a virtuous heart full of humility and
wisdom (*Le Livre*, p. 361). When she agrees to marry Walter she is
transformed physically by the rich vestments, rings, coronals, and jewels
bestowed upon her, but she herself is made 'honteuse et esbahie'
(embarrassed and overwhelmed) by the whole process (*Le Livre*, p. 363).

Philippe devotes a comparatively extensive section of his story to
describing her success as a marquise. Not only does she seem to have
been nurtured in a palace rather than a poor hut, but she is also loved,
honoured by all for her conduct and her sweet and wise words which
drew the hearts of all; both immediate subjects and 'seigneurs et dames'
from all over the countryside come to be with her (*Le Livre*, p. 364). Her
virtue is a public virtue, for when Walter is absent she manages affairs of
state as well as she manages her household; conforming to the ideal of a
noble woman exercising power, she is what Christine calls a
moyeneresse, she mediates disputes:

> ...la marquise non tant seulement du gouvernement de l'ostel et de ce qui
> appartient aus dames sagement et diligamment s'entremetoit, mais quant le
> cas si offroit es office de la chose publique, en absence de son seigneur,
> elles les adreçoit en apaissant les debas et discordes des nobles par ses
> doulces et meures paroles, par si bon jugement et si grant equité.... (*Le
> Livre*, p. 364).[35]

---

[35] ...the marquise [exercised] not only the government of the household and of that which
pertains to women wisely and soberly to be involved themselves, but when the circum-

Given this emphasis on her role as public mediatrix, it is not surprising that Walter's tests present her choice as one between her own will, located in her love for her children, and the common good. Walter cites public anger and his own desire 'vivre en pais avec' his people as rationales for his action (*Le Livre*, pp. 365, 368). The compulsion of civic harmony drives her submission, as much as her promise to Walter. When she is asked to surrender her children she chooses between her will and the public good.

Born to poverty, Griselda, it seems, has schooled herself to subordinate her will; she is thus a perfect wife and a perfect political subject, always modelling loyalty to her lord. She hears rumours that Walter will take a second wife, but shows no outward emotion, although, Philippe tells us, she suffers internal distress: ('fu tourblee en son cuer', *Le Livre*, p. 370). However, her self-control exemplifies the ideal of feminine behaviour, for she soon masters her dismay: 'having once honestly deliberated about herself, her people, and her fate, she took heart, awaiting all that he to whom she had completely submitted herself ('s'estoit sousmise') wished to ordain' (*Le Livre*, p. 370). When Walter tells her he plans to take a second wife, for political reasons, she expresses her perfect contentment in returning to her father (*Le Livre*, p. 371), and, on returning home instructs the lords and ladies who have accompanied her to Janicula, to love and loyally serve Walter (*Le Livre*, p. 372); she remains with her father 'en merveilleuse humilité' without outward sign of distress (*Le Livre*, p. 372).

As the narrative approaches its conclusion, Griselda's virtues of good works, self-control, and humility are augmented by a new focus on how she manifests the virtue of Prudence in returning to prepare the palace for Walter's new bride. Because this is such a painful moment in the story, modern readers and critics tend to pass over it, cringing at the thought of the abasement Griselda endures. Yet it bears consideration, for in sweeping and preparing the domestic space of Walter's household, Griselda is also preparing a public space that will witness a new marriage, a new dynamic in the polity of Walter's domain. Philippe stresses the public nature of her action in emphasizing the public response to it. In sweeping and cleaning dressed as a maid, Griselda is on display; she seems to all who behold her 'une femme de grant honnour et de

---

stances warranted in the office of public affairs, in the absence of her husband, she addressed and mollified the debates and discords of the nobles by her gentle and sober words, by excellent judgement and great fairness....

merveilleuse prudence' (*Le Livre*, p. 374). The guests who arrive with the wedding party make the same connection; under the poor clothing they see 'majestic nobility, worthy deportment and prudence' ('une majesté d'onnour, de bonnes meurs et de prudence, *Le Livre*, p. 375). At the very conclusion of the story Griselda in her triumph is said to seem more the daughter of an emperor or of Solomon than of Janicula (*Le Livre*, p. 377). Even the humblest of domestic actions, if well performed, send public messages.

While it differs in many significant ways, Chaucer's story of Griselda emphasizes the same element of self-control that Philippe does as central to Griselda's virtue. A recurrent rhyme of *wille/stille* calls attention to Griselda as unflinching and unchanging in her faithfulness to her promise to Walter in passages like these: 'And with sad contenance kneleth stille/Til she had herd what was the lordes wille' (ClT, ll. 293–94); 'And as a lamb she sitteth meke and stille,/And leet this crueel sargeant doon his wille' (ClT, ll. 538–39); Walter picks up the theme as he explains how he secreted their children: 'But for to kepe hem pryvely and stille,/Til I thy purpos knewe and al thy wille' (ClT, ll. 1077–78). The stanza that concludes the Envoy 'in most of the manuscripts that preserve it'[36] also repeats the rhyme in its concluding couplet, as if to emphasize its thematic importance. Griselda manifests an unwavering self-control so great that she has seemed without agency, like a stone, to many modern Chaucer critics, who have noted that at the moment when she is allowed to express her feelings, at her reunion with her family, she faints away (ClT, l. 1079). Chaucer's conclusion is less sure than Philippe's as he complicates the moral by refusing to fix it. He opens the conclusion to indeterminacy, by saying it would be *inportable* should wives want to pattern themselves after Griselda. Like Philippe's, Chaucer's Griselda is a woman whose virtue and constancy, an aid to her husband and his people, is rooted less in strength of purpose than in strength of self-control.[37]

---

[36] Benson, p. 153.

[37] Philippe de Mézières counted Petrarch among his friends; his close translation of Petrarch's Latin into French provided a major French version of the story, one that Christine is thought to have used, but changed significantly. De Pizan's Griselda is a model of strength of purpose, rather than of faithfulness to her word. A different dynamic appears in the 1395 play 'L'Estoire de Griseldis' in which Griselda appears within a context of class and community. See *L'Estoire de Griseldis*, ed. by Barbara M. Craig (Lawrence: University of Kansas Press, 1954).

Philippe de Mézières's version of the story calls attention to Griselda's strength and goodness as an ideal combination of virtues. Just as his version of the St Cecilia story heightens our awareness of elements of Chaucer's version, so his emphasis on Griselda as an epitome of virtue calls attention to the likelihood that for Chaucer, too, Griselda's virtues comprised an ideal pattern of human behaviour. Among the remedies for the seven deadly sins in 'The Parsons' Tale' we find many of Griselda's habits: she exhibits the humility that is an antidote to pride (ParsT, ll. 474–82), she loves her enemies and prays for those who, like Walter, do her ill, a remedy for envy (ParsT, ll. 513–31) ; she exhibits the patience that is prescribed as a remedy to ire (ParsT, ll. 653–76); she manifests the 'constaunce, that is stableness of corage[...]in mouth, and in berynge, and in chiere, and in dede' (ParsT, l. 736) that is a kind of fortitude that overcomes sloth; her humility and what Chaucer calls her 'attemperance' mean that she is never gluttonous or avaricious, and, of course, she is entirely chaste.

Philippe de Mézières's book on marriage and good wives shows that even before Christine de Pizan, an exact contemporary of Chaucer's dealt with the idea of marriage and the good woman in terms and stories that indicated the public nature of the marriage bond, and, within that bond, the power of women to stabilize and destabilize elements of society through virtue and through uncontrolled will. *Le Livre du sacrement de mariage* offers a way to contextualize the idea of marriage and good wives in *The Canterbury Tales* more broadly than has historically been the case, thinking not so much of individual tales in terms of their sources but more in terms of their analogues in the Anglo-French culture of Chaucer's time. In the case of the specific stories I have touched on here, such reading across culture means expanding our sense of how marriage figures in Chaucer's work. It means moving beyond our assumptions of a marriage group or marriage tales that can be understood in terms of affective relationships or of individual psychology. It means thinking of marriage as a social institution that sustains the larger polity. Chaucer's own 'Tale of Melibee', coming at the centre of the tales, demonstrates his awareness of the fundamental importance of prudence as a female virtue dedicated to the smooth functioning of households, a subject emphasized by Harry Bailly's constant references to his own wife. 'The Second Nun's Tale' echoes the kind of sentiment that Philippe de Mézières expresses in his apprehension that noblewomen will turn inward, abandoning their duty toward their husbands. Like Philippe de Mézières's Cecilia,

Chaucer's St Cecile enacts what his audience would have recognized as an age-old pattern of ultimate wifely behaviour, demonstrating such excellent care for her husband that she brings about his salvation. The story of Griselda, when read in the context of its French versions, reveals the political theme at its heart: as a good wife Griselda subordinates her own will and desire to the political necessities of her husband's life, working to ensure his success.

The French tradition of the late fourteenth and early fifteenth centuries includes a body of literature about good wives and their centrality in the process of creating social harmony both within and beyond their marriages. Chaucer's audience in the later Middle Ages would have been aware of this tradition, and would have used it to contextualize his stories of good wives as more than cautionary tales of female deportment. It is time that modern readers of Chaucer's work did, too.

Fashioning the Puritan Gentry-Woman: Devotion and Dissent in *Book to a Mother*

NICHOLAS WATSON

> I seche a youthe that eldeth noght
> I seche a lyf that dyeth noght
> I seche joye withowte drede
> I seche rychesse withowte nede
> I seche ful blisse withowte stryfe
> And therfore thus I led [lead] my lyf.[1]

At some time probably during the 1370s—while Langland was working on *Piers Plowman*, and John Wyclif was writing treatise after treatise on church reform, and John Ball was preaching his seditious way around southern England—a fiercely puritanical priest from the west Midlands wrote an epistolary treatise to his widowed mother. Like other treatises of its kind, it was not meant for her alone, imagining, indeed, all serious Christians as potential readers. But even though the priest's responsibilities to this general audience were important to him, he did really write for his mother instead of making her a mere pretext, often referring to her in ways only she could follow, and always thinking of her situation. As a result, his treatise opens windows on a pious way of being in the world we might otherwise hardly know about, one which, in its alignments with what usually seems the male world of Lollardy, is different from those we associate with late-medieval gentrywomen.[2]

---

[1]   Verse scribbled on the flyleaf of the Laud manuscript containing *Book to a Mother*.

[2]   Felicity Riddy describes English gentrywomen's devotional circles in '"Women Talking About the Things of God": A Late Medieval Sub-Culture', in *Women and Literature in Britain, 1150–1500*, ed. by Carol M. Meale (Cambridge: Cambridge University Press, 1993),

This treatise, edited as *Book to a Mother*,[3] survives in a group of four manuscripts (copied *c.* 1400) from the south-west Midlands. These are characterized by a startling tendency to include mainstream devotional texts alongside texts advocating religious reform. Many of the contents of the manuscripts are unexceptionable: in Oxford, Bodleian Library, MS Bodley 416 the work occurs with *The Mirror of Holy Church*, and can be linked to the milieu in which the Vernon manuscript was copied;[4] in London, British Library Additional MS 30897 it appears with *Pore Caitif* and an explication of the *Ave Maria*; and Oxford, Bodleian Library Laud Miscellaneous MS 210 also contains a roster of devotional classics from *The Abbey of the Holy Ghost* to Rolle's *Form of Living*. Yet not only does the Laud manuscript also contain *The Life of Soul*, which has clear affinities with Lollard writing,[5] it includes a discussion of kingship and a treatise on clerical poverty which argues that preachers should work for their living and advocates an end to expensive religious ceremonies.[6] The third work in MS Bodley 416 is a treatise on holy days similarly radical in attitude;[7] the *Ave Maria* exposition in the Additional manuscript follows Lollard practice by expounding only the verses for which there is scriptural warrant; while the fourth manuscript of the *Book*, British Library Egerton 826, was copied by a scribe who also supervised the production of a Wycliffite New Testament.[8] The people who compiled

---

pp. 104–27, a classic article to which this paper's evocation of an apparently different religious subculture, also involving women, is intended as an addendum and tribute.

[3]   *Book to a Mother: An Edition with Commentary*, ed. by Adrian James McCarthy, Salzburg Studies in English Literature, Elizabethan and Renaissance Studies 92: Studies in the English Mystics 1 (Salzburg: Institut für Anglistik und Amerikanistik, 1981). I have checked extended quotations against the relevant manuscripts, and repunctuated the text, as well as substituting 'th' for *thorn* and 'gh' or 'y' for *yogh*, and regularizing the use of *u* and *v*, *i* and *j*.

[4]   See Ralph Hanna III, 'The Origins and Production of Westminster School MS. 3', *Studies in Bibliography*, 41 (1988), 197–218.

[5]   *Þe Lyfe of Soule: An Edition with Commentary*, ed. Helen M. Moon, Salzburg Studies in English Literature, Elizabethan and Renaissance Studies 75 (Salzburg: Institut für Anglistik und Amerikanistik, 1978).

[6]   'De duodecim [there are actually 23] justitiae actibus ad regem spectantibus', Laud MS, fols 133^r–134^r; 'Here begynneth materes of Holy Wryt that is nedeful to be knowen', fols 168^r–174^v.

[7]   Bodley MS, fols 106^v–109^v.

[8]   Alan J. Fletcher, 'A Hive of Industry or a Hornets' Nest? MS Sidney Sussex 74 and its Scribes', in *Late-Medieval Religious Texts and Their Transmission: Essays in Honour of A. I. Doyle*, ed. by A. J. Minnis (Cambridge: D. S. Brewer, 1994), pp. 131–55.

these manuscripts thus shared an interest in reformist and devotional modes of thought that modern scholars have always treated in isolation from one another. This interest is mirrored in the *Book* itself.

Book to a Mother runs to around sixty thousand words and was likely addressed to a reader in the West Midlands, close enough to the marches for allusions to Welsh to be meaningful (79.24–80.4). The work's exact date is hard to establish. Satirical references to the fashionably impractical footwear known as 'cracowes' (e.g., 48.18) suggest it was written no earlier than the 1360s,[9] and it cannot have been finished later than the 1390s, when the manuscripts were copied. The dating to the 1370s is James McCarthy's, who argues that a tirade against the 'reynynge of wommenliche men that ben overcome with Heredias [...] as Heroud was' (195.16–18) alludes to Edward III's relationship with Alice Perrers.[10] This seems likely in view of the way the work's discussions parallel without alluding to Lollard attitudes. Although it approves of confession and image veneration,[11] the work nonetheless defines the Church as 'alle that schulle be saved' (2.1–2) and conveys a sectarian view of the world as a place of wickedness in which true Christians are a beleaguered minority; it disapproves of religious orders and the abuse of learning; and its translations from the New Testament offer a precedent for the Wycliffite Bible.[12] Although we cannot be sure, the *Book* may thus be a rare vernacular example of reformist prose from before the explosion of writing that accompanied the rise of Lollardy. Since it also originates from the south-west Midlands and so may promise insights into the milieu in which *Piers Plowman* was written, and since few works of its controversialist cast can clearly be associated with women,[13] an extended description is warranted.

---

[9] For the introduction of 'cracowes' into England, see Richard Firth Green, 'Jack Philpot, John of Gaunt, and a Poem of 1380', *Speculum*, 66 (1991), 330–41; Frances Grew and Margrethe de Neergaard, *Shoes and Patterns* (London: HMSO, 1988), pp.115–17.

[10] McCarthy, *Book to a Mother*, pp. xxx–xxxiv, citing the *Fasciculi zizaniorum* for a clear reference to Edward as Herod. Edward III died in 1377.

[11] See 15.9–12 (sacraments), 39.7–40.6 (images). For the image controversy, see Margaret Aston, *England's Iconoclasts, 1: Laws Against Images* (Oxford: Clarendon Press, 1988).

[12] On the work's relationship with Wycliffite thought, see also Fletcher, 'Hive of Industry', pp. 153–54, and the discussion in McCarthy, *Book to a Mother*, pp. xlvi–lvii. For its relationship with Wyclif's early theory of dominion, see note 21 below.

[13] One manuscript of *The Life of Soul* addresses the work to a nun, and at least two other reformist prose works were addressed primarily to women. See *Book for a Simple and Devout Woman: A Late Middle English Adaptation of Peraldus's 'Summa de Vitiis et Virtutibus' and*

READER AND AUTHOR

Looking at the textual personae the work develops for its author and intended reader and at its larger metaphoric and thematic concerns, it is possible to develop a portrait of its social context; indeed, the *Book* is remarkable for the intensity with which it responds to the circumstances of its first reader's life. This reader is a widow who has come down in the world and lives in relative poverty. The son refers to her repeatedly as 'my leve [beloved] dere moder' (16.1, etc.), holds out the hope that at death she will 'stie [rise] up with angelis harpinge with gret melodie ... to thine two hosbondis, Crist and mi fadir' (30.5–6), tells her to 'lerne wel of holi Anne hou thou schalt be a goode widwe' (52.9), and warns her not to grieve for the loss of 'the pompe ... that thou livedest inne in thi youthe' (58.25–59.1). She does not live alone (45.13–14), but while she could be living in a hospital or as a vowess[14] she is not a nun (he calls her widow several times); and she does not reside with nuns, judging by her son's hostility towards them: he attacks the schemes 'somme wommen of religioun' devise to make money by teaching 'curtesie' to 'ony lordis doughtres or sones' (56.21–19), disdains the way convents allow a nun 'to be a good womman in o side of a wal and in that other side a schrewe' (124.11–12), and compares 'false feynynge nonnes' to whores (194.15, 11). Despite references to monastic life, this is explicitly a treatise designed for those who are living, and intend to go on living, in the world.

Such an emphasis on the laity is most strongly evoked through the network of references to family relationships throughout the treatise. The work is an extrapolation of Matthew 12. 50 ('for Crist seyth, *he that doth his fader wille is his brother, suster and moder*', 1.3–4), and a fulfilment of the 'ferthe heste of God that comaundeth to worschipe fader and moder' (16.5–6). Naturally, it thus uses references to 'fader ... sones ...

Friar Laurent's 'Somme le Roi', ed. by F. N. M. Diekstra, Mediaevalia Groningana 24 (Groningen: Forsten, 1998), written for a laywoman; *Þe Pater Noster of Richard Ermyte: A Late Middle English Exposition of the Lord's Prayer*, ed. by Florent G. A. M. Aarts (Nijmegen: Janssen, 1967), written for a nun. For the 'puritan' tradition in which these works participate, see Nicholas Watson, *'Ancrene Wisse*, Religious Reform, and the Late Middle Ages', in *A Companion Guide to 'Ancrene Wisse'*, ed. by Yoko Wada (Cambridge: D. S. Brewer, forthcoming).

[14] For hospitals, see Nicholas Orme and M. Webster, *The English Hospital 1070–1570* (New Haven: Yale University Press, 1995); for vowesses see Mary Erler, 'English Vowed Women at the End of the Middle Ages', *Mediaeval Studies*, 57 (1995), 155–203.

doughtres ... moder ... brother ... sister ... child' (16–17) as colours in its metaphorical palette. But the son also alludes to family life in unusual detail. He tells stories about Tobit and his wife Sarah's efforts to live holy lives in the evil city of Nineveh (65.18–86.8) and recounts the martyrdom of St Lucy as a family drama between Lucy, her holy mother, and her worldly father (94.15–96.19); he reminds his mother to 'prei bisiliche that thi children mowe [may] come with the to the blisse of hevene' (70.1) and alludes to his mother's patron saint Andrew as 'thi fadir' (37.16–17). On the negative side, the treatise is consistently rude about cousins (66.26– 67.1,126.12–13, 4), attacks sex before marriage, implying that illegitimate children are as 'cursede' as the acts that produce them, and reserves bitter venom for fathers who rejoice in many children (78.5–9) but teach them 'to despise God ... with gret othis and lecherouse wordes and wicked werkes' (71.11–12). None of this polemic serves a clear biographical theory—although the work's harsh view of lawyers and advice that 'a man [person] shulde not withstonde [resist] though men tok of him his goodis or diden him bodilich harme' (73.7–8) is suggestive of the problems the mother may have faced, perhaps as a result of her widowed state.[15] But it does seem that she must continue her life of devotion, and whatever parental and grandparental duties are left her, in a hostile and materially reduced environment.

The son for his part is a friar or country priest, who hears confession (64.3–6) but disdains those who 'preche in grete citees among grete lordis' rather than 'to simple folk in litele tounes' (127.6, 4–5), as did Christ. His address to his mother affirms their common rural background. Christian souls are compared to oxen, with Christ as plowman and 'forwe [furrow or lead] oxe' who 'draweth with us undur the same yok'. A bad Christian is 'on schrewede [spiteful], untame oxe that is a thrustere', useless for ploughing purposes and worth only to 'ben kept to larder' (104.21–2, 107.12–13, 21).[16] The priest also thinks of himself as a purist

---

[15] For widows' property, see Christine Carpenter, *Locality and Polity: A Study of Warwickshire Landed Society, 1401–1499* (Cambridge: Cambridge University Press, 1992), chapter 4.

[16] 'Forwe oxe' (the lead ox on the side where the furrow is cut?) is unrecorded in *MED* or *OED*; Wright's *English Dialect Dictionary* records *farest*, used of horses (West Midlands). The passage gives *MED* its only example of 'thrustere', found in a barely-related sense in the *Dialect Dictionary*, and uses other terms not otherwise recorded in religious contexts, according to *MED*: 'drivere', where the *Book* precedes the earliest recorded use in *MED*, and 'holdere' (104.23), whose only earlier recorded use, from 1296, is in an estate record. The presentation of plowing is far more realistic than in *Piers Plowman*: thus Christ's yoke is 'smothe, not hurtinge neckes of meke men' (103.17–18), but proves too heavy for the wicked,

who, 'despisinge grete othes, as God techith,' says '"ye" and "nay" and
"sothlich"', and is avoided by 'grete clerkes', who taunt him by calling
him 'on of the sotheleches' (79.9–11)—'one of the people who say
"truly"'—a milksop. He has access to a number of vernacular and Latin
books (a Bible, a *Legenda aurea*, excerpts of Augustine, Gregory,
Bernard). McCarthy is right to associate some of his teachings with
Oxford:[17] the priest may have used university connections to find a
benefice or curacy. Yet the priest also states that he hoped to become a
canon, but that the 'twenti marc' his mother offered the order was too
little, as 'thei wolde not receive me lasse than twenti pound' (122.15–17).
The economic implications are unclear, but twenty marks is not a big
dowry for a man entering religious life, and the setting this implies for the
treatise seems closer to the lower than to the middle or upper gentry.[18]

Perhaps this is why the attacks on the wealthy's accoutrements, despite
being knowledgeably specific in their vocabulary, are so secure in their
defiant underprivilege. Not only are 'proude squyers with baudrikes,
gurdelis, lacis, colers abouten the neckes, ne with long cracowes'
condemned (48.17–18). Mary and the Christ child here are poor folk who
own no 'gaiye coverelites ne testres, curtynes, docers [pillows],
quischines [cushions]; calabre, meniver ne othir pelure [kinds of fur], ne
panter, ne boteler, ne curiouse [fancy] cokis' (49.16–18), and the treatise
has as little good to say about those who rule the land as it does about
'alle corsede popis, cardinallis, bishopis, prelatis, prestis, freris, monkes,
chanouns, {nunnes}' (90.15–17).[19] Where Christ, 'oure duke'(110.9),[20]

'for the neckes of suche folk be so sore gallid' (107.16–17). On ploughing, see *Agriculture in the Middle Ages: Technology, Practice, and Representation*, ed. by Del Sweeney (Philadelphia: University of Pennsylvania Press, 1995).

[17] McCarthy, *Book to a Mother*, p. xxvi, citing the work's articulation of a version of the 'theory of dominion' (see note 21), and its predestinarianism, especially its early definition of the church as 'alle that schulle be saved' (2.1–2) (the phrase is omitted in MS Egerton 826).

[18] For gentry incomes, see Christopher Dyer, *Standards of Living in the later Middle Ages: Social Change in England c. 1200–1520* (Cambridge: Cambridge University Press, 1989), pp. 27–48, and Nigel Saul, *Knights and Esquires: The Gloucestershire Gentry in the Fourteenth Century* (Oxford: Clarendon Press, 1981). In the passage, the difference between twenty marks and twenty pounds is that between acceptable and unacceptable expenditure on the son's career. According to Dyer's and Saul's figures, this would tend to suggest a gentry family of modest means.

[19] 'Nunnes' is added here from the Egerton manuscript.

[20] *MED*, s.v. *duk*, has some ten citations in which the word refers to Christ; all but one are from Wycliffite sources.

spent his time with the poor, in the earthly kingdom virtue is almost destroyed (195.17–20). Indeed, the work places the viability of secular government itself into question by insisting that all legal practice is wrong, that 'worldlis lawe is of contrarie condiciouns' to 'Cristes lawe', and that those in a state of sin have no right to 'ony thing of the world but it were to helle' (75.9–20).[21] While this discussion shows traces of academic origins, it seems the son, and perhaps his mother, have been radicalized by their difficulties to the point where they identify almost naturally with the poor and feel indignation against the social and ecclesiastical apparatus. Echoes of Langland abound here, as do echoes of the rebellion of 1381.[22]

STRUCTURE AND GENRE

First reading of *Book to a Mother* leaves a disorderly impression of a work heaving with polemical digressions from a rambling line of argument that itself lacks any sustained depiction of the way of life it advocates. The impression is made worse by the absence of devices that were slowly becoming routine in prose texts—formal title, table of contents, chapter divisions[23]—and by an approach to sentence-structure that sometimes makes punctuation impossible. The work begins clearly, with a list of catechetical information; many of its sections (which tend to begin 'my leve dere moder') are held together by a body of imagery or

---

[21] See also 73.16–18. The opposition between divine law and worldly laws resembles a radical development of the 'theory of dominion' articulated by Wyclif in *De civili dominio*. See Margaret Aston, '"Caim's Castles": Poverty, Politics, and Disendowment', in *Faith and Fire: Popular and Unpopular Religion, 1350–1600* (London: Hambledon Press, 1993), pp. 95–131, and Anne Hudson, *The Premature Reformation: Wycliffite Texts and Lollard History* (Oxford: Clarendon Press, 1988), pp. 359–62, citing a discussion from the Wycliffite Sermon Cycle.

[22] For the rebellion, see Steven Justice, *Writing and Rebellion: England in 1381* (Berkeley: University of California Press, 1994), especially chapter 2.

[23] For textual apparatus in vernacular books, see George Keiser, 'Serving the Needs of the Reader: Textual Division in Some Late-Medieval English Texts', in *New Science out of Old Books: Studies in Manuscripts and Early Printed Books in Honour of A. I. Doyle*, ed. by Richard Beadle and A. J. Piper (Aldershot: Scolar Press, 1995), pp. 207–26. *Book to a Mother* has an opening colophon and its manuscripts contain rubrics and divide sections with large capitals. But apart from side-notes in the Additional and Laud MSS, the only attempt to articulate the work's structure is a set of phrases written over the head of certain pages in the Egerton MS—e.g., 'To be Cristis modir. sustir and brothir' (fol. 15ʳ; see 17.18ff.).

argument; and much of the work loosely narrates the life and teaching of Christ, until the later sections, which give fluent translations of portions of John's gospel and the New Testament epistles. But we are far from the careful subdivisions of an *Ancrene Wisse*.

However, closer investigation suggests that the work's lack of tight organization is systematic, expressions of a belief (basic to the *Book*'s thinking) in the corrupting potential of all external forms, including literary ones. Such a belief is obvious in the author's suspicion of clerics, nuns, and others with pretensions to holiness and lies behind his attacks on worldly riches, which vainly mimic heavenly wealth. But the fear that the outer sign is always on the point of perverting itself into a simulacrum of the inner reality it represents—perhaps the most important attitude late medieval affectivity shares with Lollardy—has also found its way into the work's account of its genre and purpose, and even into its presentation of the status of its own words as vehicles for conveying truth.

The work's clearest account of itself is in an early passage that forms part of a discussion of Christ as a 'book' the author wants to give his mother. The author explains that he is not providing a standard rule for his mother, with vows, prayers, and so on, because the order he wishes her to join is not an official religious order but rather 'Cristes religioun', to which all good Christians belong:

> Mi leve dere modur, to speke more opunliche [clearly] to the of the bok that I ches [chose] bifore alle othire for the ...: this bok is Crist, Godis sone of hevene, with his conversacioun [manner of living] thre and thrytti wyntur, i-write withinne and withoute with humilite to hele Adames pride and oures, with wilful poverte to hele the synne of proprete [property], with chastite to hele fleschlich lustis. And so he, with his conversacioun, is to alle that wollen [wish to] be saved the beste remedie and the beste rule and the beste mirour that mai be to overcome synne. And therfore, furst studefastliche thenk thou [intend] to rule thine thoughtes and thine wordis and werkis aftir his, and specialli that thou be write withinne and withoute with thulke thre [i.e., humility, poverty, chastity] as Crist was. For withoute hem mai no man holde Cristes religioun [religious rule of life]. (31.1–14)

After citing Christ as the true exemplar of the monastic virtues of humility, poverty, and chastity, this passage invokes three genres of religious writing which, it implies, between them cater to the whole of life—thoughts, words, and deeds. The genres are: for 'thoughtes', the 'remedie' (*remedia*), didactic writing about temptation, such as *The Book of Tribulation* in the Laud manuscript; for 'wordis', the 'rule' (*regula*), rules for nuns or broader prescriptive texts such as *Ancrene Wisse*; and for 'werkis', the 'mirour' (*speculum*), encyclopaedic discussions of the faith like *The Mirror of Holy Church* in the Bodley manuscript, or lives of Christ. These are the genres within which *Book to a Mother* is written.

Yet the 'bok' which the author says he has chosen for his mother is at least fivefold. First, it signifies Christ, 'with his conversacioun', who perfectly fulfils the aims of the three genres (Rule, Remedy, and Mirror); second, the Bible; and third, *Book to a Mother* itself. Fourth, it also represents salvation—the book with seven seals in Revelation (24.19–25.21), the pearl of great price (21.13–15)—as the goal of these first three books. Thus the reader is told that poverty is no excuse for not buying this book (salvation), since the 'same bok' (the Bible) 'techeth how a man may bigge [buy] and lerne him' [Christ] 'with a litel cold water' [baptism] (18.1–4). (Indeed this book of salvation defies the usual rules, since it is 'lerned, bought, and sold' not in an amassing of intellectual or material wealth but in the act of 'forsakynge propurte'; 22.15–16). Fifth, and most important, the book is the reader, imaged as parchment onto which humility, poverty, and chastity must be 'write withinne and withoute' by herself. To do this, she must 'lerne this bok' by 'chewing' Christ's life in meditation (32.12–14), making sure her book accurately copies its exemplar, 'and ther it doth not, scrape it out with sorow of herte and schrift of mouthe and satisfaccioun' (38.20–2). Her pen is love, sharpened by the knife of fear of hell, and full of the ink of God's grace (38.26–39.6), with which implements 'thou maist lerne aftir thi samplerie [exemplar] to write a feir trewe bok and better konne [understand] holi writ than ony maister of divinite that loveth not God so wel as thou' (39.7–9).[24] This conflation of reader, text, and Christ drastically disrupts the division between inner and outer, prescription and inscription, literary genre and Christian living.

Book to a Mother thus announces itself as a composite text that both uses and deconstructs several genres of didactic writing by showing how they find their summation in Christ. The work is itself a 'samplerie', an exemplar of the works and words of Christ for the reader to write in her heart, after she has learned to 'thenke ofte and loke inwardlich in Crist'

---

[24] As with the account of ploughing (see note 16), the language here is precise, presupposing the reader's knowledge of how parchment books were copied and corrected, how quill pens were kept sharp, and the function of an exemplar. For 'samplerie' in the sense 'exemplar' clearly intended here, see *Piers Plowman* B 12.101–02.

(38.2–5): a process understood to involve both feeling and thinking, and
to lead to the adoption of a deliberately severe style of personal and
public life. But the author's book, like the Bible, can serve only a
mediating function. 'For who loveth best God, can [understands] best holi
writ. For bokis that men wryten ben not holi wryt, but as ymages ben holi
for thei bitokeneth holi seintes. But Crist, Godis sone, he is verreiliche
[truly] holi writ, and who that lovith him best is best clerk' (39.9–13). It
follows that while *Book to a Mother* needs to include a good deal of the
Bible within it, it can substitute for the Bible as an exposition of 'God's
law', since both texts are only pointers to Christ. It also follows that to
serve as an effective pointer the book must, as a structure always in
danger of substituting for the reality it represents, seek to disappear. This
is why *Book to a Mother*, despite its sophisticated awareness of genre and
dazzling use of metaphor, seems to work so hard *against* the temptation
of formal coherence.

COMMANDMENTS AND COUNSELS

Dislike of formalism does not in itself make a work radical. The notion
that a text must point the reader beyond itself is given classic expression
in the prologue to Anselm's *Prayers and Meditations*, which advises
readers to use Anselm's written words as a stepping-stone to personal
prayer,[25] while late-medieval devotional writers, as they became more
conscious of the laity, regularly invoked the divide between inner and
outer to argue that professional status is of no importance compared to
inner state. In this sense, *Book to a Mother* is part of a group of texts that
include manuscript companions like Rolle's epistles, *The Abbey of the
Holy Ghost*, and *The Mirror of Holy Church*. Yet *Book to a Mother* takes
its opposition to external forms very far and in directions few vernacular
works before the Lollards envisaged, both in its theology and in its tone.
Not only does the *Book* resist being tied down by the generic conventions
of Remedy, Rule, and Mirror; its opening sequence undercuts the very
opposition between 'active' Christians (the *mediocriter boni*) and

---

[25] See *The Idea of the Vernacular: An Anthology of Middle English Literary Theory, 1280–
1520*, ed. by Jocelyn Wogan-Browne, Nicholas Watson, Andrew Taylor, Ruth Evans
(University Park: Pennsylvania State University Press, 1999), pp. 212–13. Compare Nicholas
Watson, 'Conceptions of the Word: The Mother Tongue and the Incarnation of God', *New
Medieval Literatures*, 1 (1997), 85–124.

contemplatives (the *perfecti*) epistolary treatises often relied upon to create the aura of shared privilege they evoke.

The genre of the 'remedie' includes not only works like William Flete's *Remedies Against Temptation*, aimed at an advanced audience, but also the texts written in response to Archbishop Pecham's celebrated *Syllabus* of 1281, with its list of the information necessary to salvation: the *Pater noster* and *Ave Maria*, the creed, the commandments, the sins and their remedies, the works of mercy, and so on. As a letter of direction that anticipates both specific and general readerships, there is an expectation that *Book to a Mother* will give a broader array of remedies than the mother requires, providing basic information for the work's less prepared lay readers before moving on to her specific needs. A prologue in what the Laud manuscript treats as three sections—two addressed to the general reader, one to the mother—nods at this structure. But the contents of the sections undercut it.

First, general readers are defined in a way that makes no distinction between them and the specific one. As the book's opening states, 'to knowe the bettere my purpos in this boke, wite [know] ye wel {alle} that I desire everych man and womman and child to be my modur. For {my wille is that thei don the fadur wille [father's will] of hevene; as} Crist seyth {that uch} [each] that doth his fader wille is his brother, sister and moder' (1.1–4).[26] Echoing Christ's rejection of the ties of kinship in Matthew 12. 50, this opening throws the work open to a notionally universal Christian audience.

Second, although the catechetical lists that follow this opening are clearly based on Pecham's *Syllabus*, the opening sections fail to confine themselves to catechesis, offering radical interpretations of many items on the lists. Thus the Church is the invisible Church of the predestined; the first deed of mercy (feeding the hungry) is interpreted as giving spiritual food to these same predestined by preaching, martyrdom, and secret penance (5.1–21); and the exposition of the gifts of the spirit and the beatitudes turns into an account of the perfect soul based on the Song of Songs, of the wine-cellar into which the bridegroom leads the bride, and of the spiritual drunkenness that follows (10.13–13.6).

Third, while the *Book* first seems to accept the traditional distinction between ordinary Christians who follow God's commands (symbolized by Martha) and special ones who also follow his counsels (symbolized by Mary) (3.15–4.7), the distinction is soon vigorously attacked:

---

[26] Bracketed words are added to the Laud MS from MS Egerton 826, fol. 1ʳ.

> Therfore, my leve moder, while thou maist be siker [safe], chese his blessynge and fle his curs: that is, chese to fulfille his counseiles whan it is lightere [easier] and lasse travel [work], ... and bettere to the than to bisye the, as thou hast do heretofore, aboute many thynges. For Crist undernome [reproved] Martha for sche chese not the lightere and the best part, as Mary dide. Therfore, moder, be sory that thou hast taryed [delayed] so longe fro chesynge of the best part. For Crist seide to Martha that o thyng is necessarye, that is, forte forsake alle thynge for Cristes love. And bot a man chese the best part while he is in this world, he schal never come in hevene ... (20.1–16)

Because 'one thing is necessary', to be in charity with Christ (Luke 10. 38–42), it seems Martha will actually be damned unless she becomes Mary before death (an extremely unusual interpretation of the story): only those who give their all to Christ, following his counsels as well as commands, can hope for salvation. This assertion undercuts any idea that observing a catechetical minimum can ever be enough by making nonsense of the notion, fundamental to exegesis of this passage of Luke, that different classes of Christian attain different levels of heavenly reward in different ways.[27] Where the layman for whom Hilton's *Mixed Life* was written is encouraged to think of himself as better than active Christians but not so holy as contemplatives,[28] here the widow and those who read with her find themselves in a world in which the only viable form of religious life is one of radical holiness, in which sin is remedied only by perfect living, not by mere obedience to the commandments. Following this logic—which in practice restricts its notionally universal audience to a group of like-mindedly austere readers—the *Book* asserts that the only remedy for sin is the rigorous imitation of Christ.

TRUE RELIGION

Having dispatched the distinction between ordinary Christians and the perfect, the work has no place for the professional religious life, and so cannot function as a 'rule' in an ordinary way. As we saw, it does invoke

---

[27] For the many different ways of understanding the Martha-Mary story (none quite like this), see Giles Constable, *Three Studies in Medieval Religious and Social Thought* (Cambridge: Cambridge University Press, 1995), part 1 ('The Interpretation of Martha and Mary').

[28] See *Walter Hilton, On the Mixed Life*, ed. by S. J. Ogilvie-Thomson, Salzburg Studies in English Literature, Elizabethan and Renaissance Studies 92: Studies in the English Mystics 19 (Salzburg: Institut für Anglistik und Amerikanistik, 1986).

the Benedictine vows of humility, poverty and chastity and obedience, later adding the cardinal virtues, 'a cloister of foure stronge wallis' which it explicitly equates with 'Seint Benettis rule' (120.26–121.1). But the rule in this book applies to all Christians, and so can neither impose liturgical and sartorial requirements nor approve of these requirements. Where *The Abbey of the Holy Ghost* dwells lovingly on convent life as it tells the lay reader how to build a cloister in her heart, *Book to a Mother* is persistently ambivalent about its use of monastic metaphors:

> Modur, if thou kepe wel this cloister and holde the therinne to thi lives ende, Crist, that is abbot and priour of this cloister, wol ever be therinne with the where-evere thou be and teche the his religioun [religious rule of life], that is, mekenes and humilite. ... Therfore be thou obedient to his rule, whatevere he conseileth and hoteth [commands] the to do. For his religioun is most parfit bi hereself [itself], and evere schal laste in hevene, and non other mai be good withoute this. For what abite ther ben of ony religioun, customes, signes, or ony other serimonies, but thei acorde with Cristes religioun and helpe therto, thei ben noiouse [bad], and better hit were to leve suche ordynaunces of men. Therfore his religioun is most general—for alle men ben bounde to holed hure [hold to it] on peine of dampnacioun; and most fre ... Iblessed be Crist with his fre covent that it is so ordeined! (122.1–18)

This rule is a matter of living life in obedience to Christ's words in the gospels, and cannot be tabulated like other rules. Indeed, the author thinks of monasteries and other church institutions not in a hierarchic relation to the world of the laity but as fully bound up in that world, often by simony and social élitism. Theologically, this position leads to a silence over purgatory and a lack of interest in confession and liturgical observance. Rhetorically, it leads to satire, as he vituperates everything that fails to follow Christ, especially when it pretends to do so. Indeed, it is by satire against lawyers (who consider human law more important than divine), clerics (who mistake learning for godliness), the rich, and all hypocrites, that one of the work's functions as a rule—to separate the reader from the world—is fulfilled: by its depiction of a situation in which 'the moste part of this world is ablend [blinded], bothe lewed and lered, religiouse and seculers, fro the leste degre to the pope' (74.26–75.2). Although all who wish to be saved must follow Christ's rule, the work constantly suggests that to do this is to step outside the practices that make up most contemporary religion—for Christ's rule in part works by showing up the inadequacies of other forms of living, attacking the hierarchies that confine a notionally uneducated lay woman to a lowly rung of the

religious life. (To Christ, 'the lowere ... the bettur welcome', 123.1–2).
And if the rule seems judgmental, the reader is told—in a defence of
satire that cuts through much agonized discussion of the issue in *Piers
Plowman*—to judge the wicked for what they are: 'Crist juggede and
cursede muche in this world, and taughte forte jugge to destruye sinne
ther as [where] hit is opene agenus his hestis [commandments]' (72.23–
5). Just as the son's use of the book image makes his mother into a writer
as well as reader, playing down his role as instructor, so he here dispels
any notion that learning allows him a preacherly privilege of denouncing
others she is denied. Even the learned are reproved by this militant
meekness: since Latin is only 'a langage, as Walsch and Englisch', and
just as speaking Welsh does not make someone 'the grettur clerk but he
kepe Godis hestis', neither does knowing Latin, which people can 'teche
a pie or a jay to speke' (79.24–80.5). Stridently aware of his worth, far
more concerned to nurture his intimacy with his mother through righteous
anger than to inculcate traditional feminine virtues of silence and
abjection, the *Book*'s author does not use the sort of language rules for
women generally used to preach holiness to readers.

CHRIST'S CONVERSATION

If Christ is the rule for true Christians to follow, his life and
'conversacioun' have to be at the centre of *Book to a Mother*. Thus a
version of the *vita Christi* genre, related to works like Johannes de
Caulibus's *Meditationes vitae Christi*, dominates the middle part of the
work, and is the thread on which many of the passages I have quoted are
strung.[29] The author works his way through Christ's life, sometimes using
a standard meditative formula for bringing episodes to mind by telling the
reader to 'thenk' episodes by identifying with its central characters
(especially women); and long passages sound similar to (and may derive
from) devotional classics like Bernard's sermons on the nativity.

Two things, however, are remarkable about the work as a devotional
vita Christi for a woman reader. First, the narrative is often interrupted by
discussions not only of what the reader should learn from Christ's deeds
and words but of how these words condemn the world in which she lives:
thus Christ's authority lies behind the satirical passages that do so much

---

[29] For a succinct discussion of *vitae Christi*, see *Nicholas Love's 'Mirror of the Blessed Life
of Jesus Christ'*, ed. by Michael G. Sargent (New York: Garland, 1992), especially pp. ix–xx.

to situate reader and writer as members of the small company of the elect. Second, the emphasis throughout is less on the reader's affective responses to Christ—although these are important—but on the *meaning* of what he does and says. This brings the *vita Christi* ever closer to biblical translation with commentary. Indeed, the later parts of the work present an abbreviated version of the New Testament epistles, moving beyond Christ's teachings to those of his principal disciples, who share with him the office of the 'sixe highe justices of the heiest king, fadur and emparour of hevene, erthe, and helle: Crist, Jon, Jude, Jame, Petur, and Poul' (191.1–3).[30] The emphasis on Christ as teacher also has another effect, startling in a devotional work for a woman, that there is only a brief account of the passion (147.8–149.5), just as there is no redemption theology beyond the requirement to follow 'Cristis hestes' (191.11).

It is not clear what these emphases and omissions would have meant in the 1370s. Wyclif's *De civili dominio* uses language close to the *Book* in describing the 'life of Christ as the exemplar and ground, without which Christian living (*conversacio*) is worthless',[31] while the text's emphasis on poverty could be taken to echo Wyclif's narrower call for the clergy to imitate Christ's poverty. But whatever these parallels suggest, if we think of the *Meditationes vitae Christi* as offering a typical account of how a work in this genre catered for women readers—by leading them away from the world in devout contemplation of Christ's life—it is apparent that the *Book* offers something different: a set of intellectually demanding reflections that constantly return the reader to the world in which she lives, inculcating an attitude not of devotion but of boldly public condemnation. In this general sense, at least, we are close to an early Wycliffite and later Lollard attitude to *imitatio Christi*, where, as David Aers has recently insisted, it is Christ as teacher and doer of good that dominates, not the crucified and passive Christ of the passion meditations of the period.[32] The mystical identification with Christ the work still

---

[30] This part of the work has an unexplored but fairly clear relation with two similarly early biblical paraphrases: *The Life of Soul* and the text Anna Paues edited as *A Fourteenth-Century English Biblical Version* (Cambridge: Cambridge University Press, 1904).

[31] 'Vita Christi est exemplar et fundamentum sine quo fundante et exemplante non potest esse christiani conversacio virtuosa, sed sine conversacione virtuosa non potest christianus venire ad patriam, ideo, nisi secutus fuerit hunc priorem'; *Iohannis Wycliffe Tractatus de civili dominio*, ed. by R. L. Poole and J. Loserth (London, 1885–1904), 3: 50.

[32] David Aers and Lynn Staley, *The Powers of the Holy: Religion, Politics, and Gender in Late Medieval English Culture* (University Park: Pennsylvania State University Press, 1996), chapters 1–3.

advocates was seldom directed to a more overtly political end than it is
here.

CONCLUSION

Steven Justice and others have rightly expressed suspicion of the way
John of Gaunt and wealthy lay Lollards sponsored a movement that
preached poverty, Justice seeing Wyclif's advocacy of a redistribution of
ecclesiastical wealth as no more than preparation for a cash grab by his
patron.[33] But there was a lay milieu in which poverty was neither an
impossibility nor a mere fact of life but a threat and potential choice, a
milieu to which Langland may also have belonged, and whose attitudes
are richly articulated by *Book to a Mother*. It is here, I suggest, as well as
in the impact of Wyclif himself, that we can look to find much of the
ethical energy that drove the early Lollard movement and other late
fourteenth-century types of reform. *Book to a Mother*, apparently written
just before the Lollard movement got going, can give us information
about this milieu we may not be able to get anywhere else. Focussed
around the concerns of a woman reader—unlike any major Lollard
work—and acting as a bridge between what we think of as the separate
worlds of devotion and religious dissent, the text may be an unexpectedly
important piece of the jigsaw puzzle of medieval English literary history.
And whether or not this is so there is something that matters here:
thoughts and feelings as impassioned as anyone's, as the good son
imagines his mother willy-nilly into holiness, rewriting the intimate and
ancient form of the epistolary treatise to suit his and (he believed) her
purposes, while squeezing his idea of humble living through the narrow
gap his puritanical anger at the world had left open. 'And this [meekness],
my leve dere modur', as the work ends, 'was Cristes lessoun that he
clepede [summoned] alle to lerne of him. Therfore to him herynge
[praise], joye and worshup in wordlis of wordles. Amen, Amen, Amen.'
(204.8–10).[34]

---

[33] Justice, *Writing and Rebellion*, pp. 75–90.

[34] Versions of this paper were given at the Kalamazoo International Congress, May 1996,
and at the Medieval Academy Annual Conference, Stanford University, March 1998. I thank
Alison Conway, Richard Green, Fiona Somerset, and Jocelyn Wogan-Browne for their help.

Bodily Walls, Windows, and Doors:
The Politics of Gesture in Late Fifteenth-Century English Books for Women

KIM M. PHILLIPS

As a small girl growing up in the Morocco of the 1940s, feminist author Fatima Mernissi was much puzzled by the concept of the harem. Fatima herself lived in Fez, in strict enclosure, with the extended family group dwelling together in apartments facing onto a central courtyard. The complex was accessible by a single gate kept locked and under the constant guard of a doorkeeper.[1] Her maternal grandmother, with eight co-wives, also lived in a 'harem', but on a farm in the countryside, and without the strict physical barriers of walls, gates, and doorkeepers. They spent their days outdoors in the garden, or further afield riding on horseback, even fishing and swimming in a nearby river. How could these two arrangements, so different in the degree of freedom of movement offered to women, be known equally as 'harems', wondered the young Mernissi (pp. 41–52, 57–58)? Her grandmother provided the answer. The harem need not necessarily be composed of four constraining walls. Rather, as an aspect of the sacred frontier separating men and women, it is composed not only of a physical system of walls, gateways, and doorkeepers, but also *mental* walls and gateways which can be erected or passed through by way of clothing, veiling, speech, body language, and

Warm thanks to Arlyn Diamond and Rosalynn Voaden for criticism and encouragement on drafts of this article, and to Martin Jones for first alerting me to the crucial importance of spatial elements in social relations.

[1] Fatima Mernissi, *The Harem Within: Tales of a Moroccan Girlhood* (London: Bantam, 1995).

eye contact. 'Once you knew what was forbidden, you carried the harem within' (pp. 64–66).

Late medieval Englishwomen, particularly young unmarried women of high social status, have sometimes been thought by modern scholars to have led physically cloistered lives similar to that of the young Mernissi in Fez.[2] Such claims have been exaggerated and are belied by textual evidence, which shows for example the mingling of male and female servants of noble status within such households, and by the words of male travellers to England in the later fifteenth century which tell of feasts and dances at which male and female guests and servants mixed sociably.[3] To what extent, though, were the gender politics of space in English noble houses affected by a notion like that of the 'harem within'? That is the question prompting this examination of gestural interaction of men and women in five late-fifteenth-century books read by or aimed at women. Rather than looking at bricks and mortar, walls, windows, and doorways, my focus is on bodily boundaries—those composed of etiquette, posture, body language, and gaze. Cultural historians and literary critics have found the term 'gesture' the most useful to encompass this range of physical 'languages', and I shall follow them in adopting this term here.[4] I

---

[2]   Roberta Gilchrist, 'Medieval Bodies in the Material World: Gender, Stigma and the Body', in *Framing Medieval Bodies*, ed. by Sarah Kay and Miri Rubin (Manchester: Manchester University Press, 1993); Roberta Gilchrist, *Gender and Material Culture: The Archaeology of Religious Women* (London: Routledge, 1994), pp. 167–69; Nicholas Orme, *From Childhood to Chivalry: The Education of the English Kings and Aristocracy 1066–1530* (London: Methuen, 1984), pp. 31–32.

[3]   Kim M. Phillips, 'The Medieval Maiden: Young Womanhood in Late Medieval England' (unpublished doctoral thesis, University of York, 1997), pp. 86–96; *The Travels of Leo of Rozmital 1465–7*, ed. by Malcolm Letts, Hakluyt Society, 2nd series, 108 (Cambridge: Cambridge University Press, 1957), pp. 45–47; C. L. Kingsford, ed., 'The Record of the Bluemantle Pursuivant', in *English Historical Documents 1327–1485*, ed. by A. R. Myers (London: Eyre and Spottiswood, 1969), p. 1177.

[4]   Werner Habicht defined gesture as 'all physical motions or positions of the body which have a meaning but do not serve a practical purpose', *Die Gebärde in englischen Dichtungen des Mittelalters* (Munich: Bayerische Akademie der Wisschenschaften, 1959), p. 8, quoted by Barry Windeatt, 'Gesture in Chaucer', *Medievalia et Humanistica*, 9 (1979), 143–61 (p. 143). For medieval gesture see also Robert G. Benson, *Medieval Body Language: A Study of the Use of Gesture in Chaucer's Poetry*, Anglistica 21 (Copenhagen: Rosenkilde and Bagger, 1980); Jean-Claude Schmitt, *La Raison des Gestes dans l'Occident Médiéval* (Paris: Gallimard, 1990), and his essay 'The Rationale of Gestures in the West: Third to Thirteenth Centuries' along with others, in *A Cultural History of Gesture: From Antiquity to the Present Day*, ed. by Jan Bremmer and Herman

will argue that the two printed texts of my study offer a more constricting or conservative model of gestural interaction between the sexes than the three manuscript romances, and will attempt to locate these differences in the values and intents of the texts' authors and audiences.

The three romances are chosen for their important links with moderately high status women readers. The prose *Merlin* in Cambridge University Library MS Ff. 3.11, though probably produced around 1450, was in the possession of Elyanor Guldeford, member of a rising Kentish gentry family, in the last years of the fifteenth or early years of the sixteenth century.[5] *Sir Degrevant* from Cambridge University Library MS Ff. 1.6 (the 'Findern Manuscript') is well-known for the inclusion of the signatures of Elisabet Coton and Elisabet Frauncys, and it has been speculated that these two Derbyshire gentlewomen collaborated as scribes of the romance.[6] *Generydes* from Cambridge Trinity College MS O.5.2 is in a manuscript thought to have been owned by Anne Knevet, daughter of a Norfolk gentleman, at the time of her marriage to John Thwaites

---

Roodenburg (Cambridge: Polity Press, 1991); Moshe Barasch, *Giotto and the Language of Gesture* (Cambridge: Cambridge University Press, 1987).

[5] *Merlin, or The Early History of King Arthur*, ed. by Henry B. Wheatley, EETS, OS 10, 21, 36, 112 (London, 1865, 1866, 1869, 1899), reprinted as two volumes (Liechtenstein: Kraus, 1973). Carol M. Meale, 'The Manuscripts and Early Audience of the Middle English *Prose Merlin*', in *The Changing Face of Arthurian Romance: Essays on Arthurian Prose Romances in Memory of Cedric E. Pickford*, ed. by Alison Adams, Armel H. Diverres, Karen Stern and Kenneth Varty (Cambridge: D. S. Brewer, 1986). In researching this essay I have been indebted to Dr Meale's meticulous studies of book ownership by medieval English women. See especially '"…alle the bokes that I haue of latyn, englisch, and frensch": Laywomen and their Books in Late Medieval England', in *Women and Literature in Britain 1150–1500*, ed. by Carol M. Meale (Cambridge: Cambridge University Press, 1993), and '"Gode men/ Wiues maydnes and alle men": Romance and Its Audiences', in *Readings in Medieval English Romance*, ed. by Carol M. Meale (Cambridge: D. S. Brewer, 1994).

[6] *The Romance of Sir Degrevant*, ed. by L. F. Casson, EETS, OS 221 (London, 1949). Kate Harris, 'The Origins and Makeup of Cambridge University Library MS Ff.1.6', *Transactions of the Cambridge Bibliographical Society*, 8 (1983), 299–333, revising views established by R. H. Robbins, 'The Findern Anthology', *PMLA*, 69 (1954), 610–42. See also *The Findern Manuscript*, ed. by Richard Beadle and A. E. B. Owen (London: Scolar, 1977), pp. vii–viii. John J. Thompson advises caution on the question of whether the women acted as scribes, 'Collecting Middle English Romances and Some Related Book-Production Activities in the Later Middle Ages', in *Romance in Medieval England*, ed. by Maldwyn Mills, Jennifer Fellows and Carol M. Meale (Cambridge: D. S. Brewer, 1991), esp. pp. 34–35.

sometime between 1480 and 1490. There has been some speculation over the possibility that this romance was the work of a woman author, but this remains no more than hypothesis.[7] The two printed works from Caxton's workshop are also linked to women. Caxton claims that he made his translation of *Blanchardyn and Eglantine* (*c.* 1489) at the commandment of Lady Margaret Beaufort, who had given him a French version, for the purposes of instructing 'yong noble gentylmen & wymmen', but especially 'for gentle yonge ladyes & damoysellys, for to lerne to be stedfaste & constaunt in their parte to theym that they ones haue promysed'.[8] His *Book of the Knight of the Tower* (1484), a courtesy text rather than a romance, seems to have been produced with similar intent. Caxton's prologue here, too, claims that he made the translation at the request of a certain 'noble lady' in order to help gentlemen and women in teaching their daughters to 'gouerne them vertuously in this present lyf'.[9] I shall posit two key differences between the three manuscript texts and two printed works which explain their different views on gestural interaction between young men and women: one, that where the manuscript romances represent texts which women *wanted* to engage with, the printed works represent texts which others thought they *should* engage with; and two, that the manuscripts purvey an older set of feudal values, in which behaviour appropriate to station is elevated above concerns of sexual propriety, while the printed works address a newer audience in which status concerns are still strong but modified by a strengthening code of sexual propriety.

These texts are chosen partly for their links with women readers, but also for their function in either modelling or, in the case of the printed works, policing women's conduct, especially in the company of men. I do not claim that the representations of gestural interaction were meant to be literally imitated by women readers, but rather that the values they

---

[7] *Generydes*, ed. by W. Aldis Wright, EETS, os 55 and 70 (London: Trübner, 1873–1878). Wright suggests possible ownership by Anne Knevet on the basis of the manuscript's heraldic decorations in particular, and this argument is explored and supported, though cautiously, by Derek Pearsall, 'Notes on the Manuscript of Generydes', *The Library* 5th series, 16 (1961), 205–10. On female authorship see Carol. M. Meale, 'The Morgan Library Copy of *Generides*' in Mills, Fellows, and Meale, *Romance in Medieval England*, pp. 95–96, n. 30.

[8] *Caxton's Blanchardyn and Eglantine, c. 1489*, ed. by Leon Kellner, EETS, ES 58 (London: Trübner, 1890), p. 1, ll. 11–12, 18–21.

[9] *The Book of the Knight of the Tower*, trans. by William Caxton, ed. by M. Y. Offord, EETS, ss 2 (London: Oxford University Press, 1971), p. 3.

embody were being endorsed. *The Book of the Knight* is perhaps the most obviously didactic. The social purposes served by romances are more heavily veiled, but probably no less important ideologically. Felicity Riddy has pointed to romances' role as, amongst other things, helping their readers to learn 'how to lead good lives', how to model their conduct and their manners.[10] Arlyn Diamond has placed greater emphasis on the genre's capacity for modelling happy lives, by allowing lovers' fantasies of escape from the emotional confines of medieval marriages.[11] How does the interplay of genre, intent, and audience influence representation of a range of gestures: posture, gaze, greetings, taking another's hand, embracing, and kissing?

Maintaining a still and upright posture, and keeping the head still and gaze level, are recognized as important aspects of deportment in courtesy literature. The Knight of the Tower makes much of these elements of feminine conduct:

> How yonge maydens ought not to torne their heedes lyghtely here ne there......be ye not like ne semblable the tortuse ne to the Crane. Whiche torne their visage and the heede aboue their sholders/ and wind their hede here and there as a vane. But have youre regard and manere stedfast lyke as the hare hath/ which is a beest that seeth alwey to fore hym euen right forth. Withoute tornyng of his heede here ne there. Alwey see that ye be stedfast in lokyng playnly to fore you And yf ye wylle loke a syde/ torne youre vysage & youre body to geder/ And so shalle ye hold you in youre estate more ferme & sure For they be mocqued that so lyghtely cast their sight and hede and torne their vysage here and there (cap. 11, p. 25).

A princess, he says, was passed over as a potential bride for the king of England because she lacked a steadfast manner, and constantly turned her head and gaze about. Her sister was rejected for being too talkative, while their youngest sister was judged most eligible, despite her lesser beauty, because of her little speech and 'ferme/ & humble' regard and sight (cap. 12, p. 26).

Concerns about the maintenance of class identity partly drive the Knight's words here. This is implied by his statement that still demeanour ensures that one is held in one's 'estate more ferme & sure', and suggested strongly by comparison with contemporary courtesy books for

---

[10] Felicity Riddy, *Sir Thomas Malory* (Leiden: Brill, 1987), pp. 17–23.

[11] Arlyn Diamond, 'Unhappy Endings: Failed Love/Failed Faith in Late Romances', in Meale, *Readings in Medieval English Romance*, pp. 65–81 (esp. pp. 70–71).

adolescent noble youths who went to serve in the households of the elite. In these, instructions to refrain from looking all around but rather to keep a forward gaze and steadfast posture are common. For example, the author of 'The Babees Book' from a 1475 manuscript advises 'caste nouhte your syhte/ Aboute the hovs, but take to theyn entent/ With blythe vysage and spiryt diligent', and also to keep one's head, hands, and feet still.[12] These courtesy books also make clear that *downcast* head and gaze are socially undesirable, and are traits associated with persons of lower status.

> Who-so speke to thee in ony maner place,
> lumpischli caste not thin heed a-doun
> but with a sad cheer loke him in the face.[13]

It is 'lumpish', or 'rude' as another manuscript of the text has it[14]—in other words ill-bred or servile—to cast one's head and gaze down. The Knight advises his daughters to be like the hare which 'seeth alwey to fore hym euen right forth' and 'stedfast in lokyng playnly to fore you' (cap. 11, p. 25). This level head and gaze, perhaps surprising as a desirable feminine trait, seems linked firmly to concerns about status: I have not yet encountered any textual indication that it was considered desirable for maidens or ladies to maintain a downcast, coy posture with men.[15] Rather, a calm, steady and direct manner constituted good deportment, incorporating notions both of proper femininity and superior social status.

But the Knight is also strongly motivated by anxiety about feminine sexual purity. Looseness of posture in the head, neck, and shoulders and flighty gaze are read as looseness of character in a woman. Through lack of 'mayntene'—firm demeanour—a young woman in male company

---

[12] 'The Babees Book', in *The Babees Book, etc.*, ed. by Frederick J. Furnivall, EETS, OS 32 (London, 1868), pp. 3–4. See also in the same volume, 'Urbanitas', p. 13; 'The Young Children's Book', p. 21; 'Stans Puer ad Mensam', p. 27.

[13] 'Stans Puer ad Mensam', p. 27. See also 'Babees Book', p. 3; 'Urbanitas', p, 13; 'Young Children's Book', p. 21.

[14] 'Stans Puer ad Mensam' (MS *c.* 1460), p. 26.

[15] Discussing women of lower social status, Barbara Hanawalt interprets a passage from the popular conduct text 'How the Good Wife Taught her Daughter' as an instruction to young urban women to keep their eyes downcast while walking through town, 'At the Margins of Women's Space in Medieval Europe', in *Matrons and Marginal Women in Medieval Society*, ed. by Robert R. Edwards and Vickie Ziegler (Woodbridge: Boydell Press, 1995), pp. 5–6. However she seems to have misread the passage concerned.

opens herself up, imparts an impression of availability. Jean-Claude Schmitt has remarked that medieval culture saw the human self as composed of both soul and body, inner and outer, and that gesture was thus of crucial importance because it 'figured, or better, *embodied* the dialectic between *intus* and *foris* since they were supposed to express without the "secret movements" of the soul within'.[16] Without claiming that the Knight is necessarily working from any universal medieval theory of psychology and body language, it does seem that he is linking outer looseness of the body to inner looseness of the character, and that in the case of women this has a specifically sexual connotation. He tells of a young woman courted by himself and rejected because she had an 'eye quyck & lyght' and spoke frivolously, and had 'grete malepertnes &... lyght manere', and who within a year and a half 'was blamed' and died soon after, presumably as just recompense for her sinful ways (cap. 12, pp. 27–28). In young women lack of steady posture and gaze could easily be equated with unchastity.

These twin concerns—with expression of social status, and of sexual respectability—become a point of conflict for the Knight in considering the female gaze. As already indicated, a level and firm gaze constituted one aspect of respectable feminine behaviour, a bodily wall, where a flighty and curious gaze opened a bodily window in interaction with men, inviting improper intimacy. But despite its links with proper class conduct, the gaze is fraught with dangers in gender relations. 'Sybylle sayth that the fyrst signe or token of loue is the loke or beholdyng/ And after the amerous loke they come to the kyssynge/ and thenne the dede or faytte' (cap. 133, p. 175). The look sets up a domino effect which begins with a glance and ends in deadly sin.

In the three manuscript romances, the gaze carries similar overtones of intimacy, but without the censorious tone of the Knight. The gaze serves as a narrative device by which the hero and heroine of the tale become aware of and desire one another, and there is no suggestion that it is always the woman who is objectified by a possessive male gaze. Female characters gaze with equal pleasure upon the beauty of men. The meeting of Sir Degrevant and Melidor in the earl's hall provides occasion for mutual and admiring gaze:

> the knyth hoves in the feld, [waits in the field]
> Bothe weth ax and with sheld,

---

[16] Schmitt, 'Rationale of Gestures', p. 60.

the Eorlus doughter be-held
That borlich and bolde; [massive and bold man]
For he was armed so clen
With gold [and] azour ful schen, [azure]
And with his trowe-loues bytwen [true-love flowers]
Was ioy to be-hold.
She was comlech y-clade,
To ryche banre[ttes] hur lade, [two noble knights bearing banners]
All the beut[e] sche hade
That frely to folde. [noble-looking woman]
Wyth loue she w[o]ndes the knyght (ll. 465–77). [wounds]

Clarionas looks directly and with pleasure upon Generydes at their first
meeting, when he enters her chamber to serve her:

This fayre lady behelde Generydes,
In stedefast wise on hym she cast her eye,
All his maners so wele it did hyr plece, [please]
That she constreyned was in certeynte
To loue hym best, it wold non other be. (ll. 687–91)
       (See also ll. 471–76)

The prose *Merlin* contains many instances of desire resulting from the
gaze of men upon women or women upon men. When the maidens carry
out their apparently conventional task of disarming, washing, and
dressing the knights, the male bodies are offered to the view of young
women, who do not lose the opportunity to appraise them:

[after a tournament] on that other parte wente Gawein and his felowes hem
for to vn-arme in oon of the Queenes chambres that was assigned for hem
to repeire; and when thei were vn-armed and waissh, thei clothed hem
richely, and yef thei were well serued it nedeth not to aske, ffor ther were
ladyes and maydenes hem for to serue grete foyson [abundance]. Ther was
Segramor moche be-holden of oon and of other, ffor he was a feire knyght
and semly, and so was also Dodinell le sauage; these tweyne were sore
preised of alle that hem be-helden (p. 499).[17]

The texts' presentation of male bodies for the gaze of fictional women
and actual readers could well be caused by the (at least partly) female

---

[17] See also *Merlin*, pp. 225 and 607. That it was acceptable for men to undress for bed in
the presence of maids is suggested on p. 466. For examples of women as the subject of the
male gaze see e.g. pp. 226, 671. *Blanchardyn and Eglantine* also contains a scene in
which maidens disarm and robe the young knight Blanchardyn, p. 50, ll. 21–26, causing
Eglantine some dismay.

audience, although descriptions of masculine beauty and sexual attractiveness are hardly uncommon in romances generally. The sexually appraising female gaze is present in *Blanchardyn and Eglantine* too, but wreathed about with more anxiety, as Eglantine worries that the Provost's daughters will distract Blanchardyn: '[Promise that] they forebere hem self to the smylynges and fayre shewes of their eyen, whiche wauntonly they caste full often vpon that yonge knyght' (ll. 30–32). The gaze thus has meanings which vary not only according to its function as a marker of class or gender identity, but also according to the tone and audience of particular texts. In the three manuscript romances it can function without censure as a window to greater interaction and intimacy between male and female characters, while the printed romance and conduct book would prefer that that window be kept shuttered.

The evidence so far presented suggests that while concerns of behaviour appropriate to social status are foremost in representations of gesture in the three manuscript romances, these are often overridden by anxiety about feminine sexual purity in the printed works. This can also be demonstrated by examining a range of gestures which could all be incorporated under the heading 'greeting', though they perform other functions as well. It is of interest here that forms of greeting are not noticeably gendered in the textual representations examined. Gender-specific forms of greeting associated with European aristocratic culture of later centuries—such as a man kissing a woman's hand, or the curtsey for a woman and bow for a man—are absent both from these texts and, it seems, from Middle English texts in general.[18] With greetings the emphasis seems firmly on concerns of courtly conduct, but in some instances anxieties about physical interaction between men and women may colour the meanings of such gestures.

---

[18] Men do not kiss the hands of ladies in these texts. A search of the terms 'hand and kiss' in the *Literature Online* database of fifteenth-century verse turned up only five references to hand-kissing, and of these only two involved a man kissing a woman's hand. In neither of these two instances was the hand-kiss a secular form of greeting. The *Literature Online* database can be found at http://lion.chadwyck.co.uk. The bow, according to the examples listed in the *Middle English Dictionary*, could be used as a greeting, but was primarily a gesture of humility, whether used in worship or to indicate social submission, *Middle English Dictionary*, ed. by Hans Kurath, Sherman Kuhn and Robert E. Lewis (Ann Arbor: University of Michigan Press, 1952–), s.v. 'bouen'. The later 'curtsey', probably an adaptation of the medieval gesture of kneeling on one knee, came gradually to be restricted to women, *The Shorter Oxford English Dictionary* (Oxford: Clarendon Press, 1973), s.v. 'curtsey'.

The 'salue', in its variety of forms, held an important place in the codes of courtly conduct. The exact form which it took, and some idea of which forms were more courteous than others, is difficult to discern as the texts frequently say little more than, as with Blanchardyn's manners, he gave 'a gracyouse and honourable salutacion to them all where he went forth by', earning the admiration of all (but particularly that of ladies and gentle-women) as he passed (ll. 11–17), or as with a lady who came into Arthur's hall and 'salued the kynge right curteisly as she that was connynge and wele taught' (p. 635). But it is clear that to offer no form of salutation was to offer deep offence, as Gawein found when he passed a lady in a forest, too pensive to offer greetings, and she rode after him saying "'thou art the most vileyn knyght that euer I mette in my lif...that thou deynes not me ones to salue ne to speke a worde'" (p. 690). The salue could take the form of a bowed head, kneeling, prostration, or words,[19] a raised hand to hip, chest or chin height, palm forward,[20] a doffed hat or cap,[21] or standing if one was sitting (*Merlin*, pp. 361, 499). There is nothing to suggest that any of these gestures were gender-specific, as most of them can be found performed by both men and women in the texts examined. Concerns about proper courtly behaviour are foremost.

Gestures of greeting which involve bodily contact complicate this, however, and constitute a bodily window, or even a doorway, in the interaction of men and women. These include taking hands, embracing, and kissing. The Knight was alert to potential dangers of touching. The fifth of the nine follies of Eve, he said, was that 'she took and touched the fruyte/ It hadde be better that she had had no handes/ for ouermoche peryllous was the touchynge of it'. One must refrain from touching any perilous delight, 'For foolisshe touchyng chaufeth and enflammeth the herte' (cap. 43, p. 66). Yet welcoming guests by taking them by the hand was a mark of great courtesy and respect, and one which was appropriate between men and women. At the Provost's house Blanchardyn is greeted by the Provost's daughters, who take him by the hands and lead him in to dine. Then they take him to a chamber to disarm and robe him (ll. 18–26).

[19] *MED*, s.v. 'saluen', 'salut', 'salutacioun', 'saluten'.

[20] See Kathleen L. Scott, *Later Gothic Manuscripts*, vol. 6 of J. J. G. Alexander, general ed., *A Survey of Manuscripts Illuminated in the British Isles* (London: Harvey Miller, 1996), part 1, nos 428, 440, 443, 444.

[21] *Book of the Knight*, cap. 10, p. 24; 'Urbanitas', p. 13, 'Young Children's Book', p. 25, 'The Boke of Curtasye', p. 299; Scott, *Later Gothic MSS.*, part 1, no 366.

Gawein is welcomed into the hall after a tournament by Arthur and Gonnore, and the king 'toke sir Gawein be the right hande, and the queen toke hym by tother hande and wente to sitte alle to-geder' (*Merlin*, p. 499). This example points to what is clear from other passages: that for men to hold one another's hands was non-sexualized courtly behaviour. 'As soone as thei were a-raied, thei [Gawein's knights] com in to the halle two and two to-geder, holdinge be the handes oon after a-nother'; 'ther com vp xij princes full richely be-seyn, and clothed in riche clothes of silke, and com two and two holdinge eche other be the handes'; 'Ther was many a baron hir to conveien holdinge be the hondes two and two' (*Merlin*, pp. 499, 639, 453).[22] Taking of the hands in these texts seems to indicate a chivalric fraternity.

The Knight's anxiety about touch and inflamed desire seems largely borne out, yet without censure, in *Sir Degrevant* when the lovers, alone together at last in Melidor's chamber, embrace and kiss enthusiastically as a prelude to their (passionate, if unconsummated) first night together (ll. 1377–84). In *Generydes* the hero and Clarionas are reunited after long separation with a passionate embrace and kiss (ll. 6883–84). The embrace holds no necessary sexual overtones, however, but could indicate only a warm degree of courtesy and hospitality between men and women, or chivalric fraternity, as when Gawein and Nascien embrace when the latter yields during a tournament (*Merlin*, p. 458).

But it is with the kiss, with its complex of meanings in late medieval texts, that this brief examination of gesture shall end. The kiss could certainly constitute a bodily doorway by which men and women could achieve a potentially hazardous degree of intimacy, risking stepping over the threshold of decency. The Knight says he is quoting his wife's anxiety about the act: 'the wyse lady Rebecca whiche was ryght gentylle and noble/ sayth/ the kyssynge is nyghe parente and Cosyn vnto the fowle faytte or dede...& I lete you know that me semeth that assone as they suffre them to be kyssed they put them self in the subiection of the deuyll...And thus as one kyssynge draweth to hym another/ And as the fyre kyndeleth a strawe/ and fro that strawe it cometh/ and kyndeleth another/ & thus atte last the bedde is a fyre & the hows also' (cap. 133, p. 175). The plot of *Blanchardyn and Eglantine* hangs on precisely this gesture, when Eglantine takes offence at a kiss which Blanchardyn dares

---

[22] For another example of knights holding hands see *The Romance of Guy of Warwick*, ed. by Julius Zupitza, EETS, ES 42, 49 and 59 (London: Trübner, 1883, 1887, 1891), p. 185.

to snatch from her. She is only slowly persuaded not to treat the gesture as dishonouring. The kiss, in these printed works, is dangerous when performed between men and women.

The kiss signals a variety of relationships and behaviours in the manuscript romances. It could indicate warm welcome between two with a close relationship, as when Gonnore rushes open-armed to greet Arthur, her betrothed, in a public street and kisses him on the mouth (*Merlin*, p. 448). It could indicate proper courteous conduct, as when Clarionas kisses Generydes once he has finished serving her at their first meeting (*Generydes*, ll. 704–05), or when in *Generydes* Sir Darell takes leave of Lucidas 'And curtesly of hir his leve he toke/ With kysseng fele [many] as witnes[eth] the book' (ll. 6700–01). It could be a courtly gesture of reconciliation, as when Sir Degrevant finally makes his peace with the earl and they kiss in recognition of this (*Sir Degrevant*, l. 1819). On the other hand, it could indicate proper conduct while containing some reminder of sexual intimacy, as when Arthur meets his sister, with whom he had previously had sex, 'and thei kissed as brother and sister' (*Merlin*, p. 374). Or it could stand fully for sexual love in the moments when the lovers, their obstacles surmounted, can come together at last (*Sir Degrevant*, p. 81, l.1384; *Generydes*, p. 219, ll. 6883–84). The pattern so far noticed in the manuscript romances, with their less censorious or anxious view of gestural interaction between men and women, is apparent when Arthur gathers his betrothed to him, 'and kissed hir swetly as yonge peple that full well to-geder loved'(*Merlin*, p. 323).

The kiss is such an important and well-documented gesture in elite English medieval culture that it allows for a discussion of changes in meaning over time: changes which will help to illuminate the general patterns raised here. J. Russell Major has studied the decline of the use of the kiss in feudal rituals of homage from the fourteenth to the sixteenth centuries, and argued that its increasingly erotic implications, reflected in the increasing anxiety expressed by detractors of the feudal kiss, contributed significantly to its eventual erasure from the ceremony.[23] In the late

---

[23] J. Russell Major, '"Bastard Feudalism" and the Kiss: Changing Social Mores in Late Medieval and Early Modern France', *Journal of Interdisciplinary History*, 17 (1987), 509–35. On the kiss see also Willem Frijhoff, 'The Kiss Sacred and Profane: Reflections on a Cross-Cultural Confrontation', in Bremmer and Roodenburg; Nicolas James Perella, *The Kiss Sacred and Profane: An Interpretative History of Kiss Symbolism and Related Religio-Erotic Themes* (Berkeley and Los Angeles: University of California Press, 1969), pp. 210–36.

fifteenth-century manuscript romances I discuss, the kiss retains a sense of propriety and signalling of status, while its sexual implications are acknowledged without censure. The apprehension about the kiss expressed by the printed texts models an ideal of restraint in areas of class and gender interactions, and is perhaps responding to the newer anxieties noted by Major.

The different attitudes to gestural interaction demonstrated in these five texts are, I would argue, linked to wider sets of values relating to status and gender. In comparison with the printed works, the manuscript works seem conservative in their concern for social status, but more expansive in their playful approaches to interaction between men and women. In the context of the late fifteenth century, the values expressed within the manuscript works seem above all traditional or nostalgic. The courtly world which they evoke was one which their female readers would have been more likely to associate with a romantic and mythical past than with their daily experiences. The works would foster fantasies of gracious living and courtly loving, and perhaps such fantasies were particularly appealing to the women with whom the works are linked. Elyanor Guldeford was a member of a family which occupied gentry status but was fast rising in court circles and demonstrated a taste for lavish art and music as well as courtly literature.[24] Anne Knevet and Richard Thwaite's marriage is symbolized in the richly decorated book that was made of their separate works, thus placing *Generydes* in a more high status manuscript than is usually associated with romances.[25] Elisabet Coton and Elisabet Frauncys were actively engaged in the production of a manuscript which is now viewed as a repository of refined courtly literature.[26] At the end of the fifteenth century the texts which apparently appealed to these four provincial, yet socially or culturally aspiring gentrywomen, were suffused with nostalgia for an imagined feudal past. That lost era is represented through these romances as one which worried most about status, and modelled behaviour accordingly, while offering a more expansive view of gender interaction and women's agency.

William Caxton, however, had some inkling of which way the wind was blowing. *Blanchardyn and Eglantine* and *The Book of the Knight*,

---

[24] Meale, '*Prose Merlin*', pp. 100–11.

[25] Riddy, *Malory*, p. 14.

[26] Riddy, *Malory*, pp. 14–15.

though their prologues lay claim to an intended noble audience, would probably have been intended to appeal to the wider audience which print fostered.[27] We have seen that the printed works retain some interest in maintenance of status roles, but are most concerned with gender and sexual respectability. This combination of old and new tastes marks the era. As fifteenth-century parvenus built new castles which harked back to a chivalric age, but which were built of fashionable brick or with large and elegant windows, new readers at the end of the fifteenth century adopted elements of courtly behaviour as ideals but adapted them according to their particular concerns. The middling status parental or guardian figures who are Caxton's target audience here may have had illusions of gentility guiding their own choice of reading material, but when choosing for their daughters they brought a strong sense of bourgeois respectability into play.[28] It was these daughters, more than those of the aspiring gentry, who had impressed upon them the importance of a 'harem within'.

---

[27] On Caxton's audience see Riddy, *Malory*, pp. 8–11; H. S. Bennett, *English Books and Readers, 1475–1557* (Cambridge: Cambridge University Press, 1952), pp. 54–55; Lotte Hellinga, *Caxton in Focus: The Beginning of Printing in England* (London: The British Library, 1982), pp. 101–02.

[28] The notion of fifteenth-century 'bourgeois respectability' is explored by Felicity Riddy in 'Mother Knows Best: Reading Social Change in a Courtesy Text', *Speculum*, 71 (1996), 66–86.

Chaucer's Criseyde and Feminine Fear

ALASTAIR MINNIS AND ERIC J. JOHNSON

In his 1936 monograph *The Allegory of Love*, C. S. Lewis offered a view
of the character of Criseyde which presented subsequent criticism with a
major challenge. For him, Chaucer's heroine was

> a tragic figure in the strictest Aristotelian sense, for she is neither very
> good nor execrably wicked. In happier circumstances she would have been
> a faithful mistress, or a faithful wife, an affectionate mother, and a kindly
> neighbour—a happy woman and a cause of happiness to all about her—
> caressed and caressing in her youth, and honoured in her old age. But there
> is a flaw in her, and Chaucer has told us what it is; 'she was the ferfulleste
> wight that mighte be'. If fate had so willed, men would have known this
> flaw only as a pardonable, perhaps an endearing, weakness; but fate threw
> her upon difficulties which convert it into a tragic fault, and Cryseide is
> ruined.[1]

Generations of critics have echoed, amplified or rejected these views.[2]
And yet, little attempt has been made to relate Criseyde's emotions either

---

[1] *The Allegory of Love: A Study in Medieval Tradition* (Oxford: Oxford University Press,
1936), pp. 189–90.

[2] See especially Robert P. apRoberts, 'Criseyde's Infidelity and the Moral of *Troilus*',
Speculum, 44 (1969), 383–402; Elizabeth R. Hatcher, 'Chaucer and the Psychology of
Fear: Troilus in Book V', *English Literary History*, 40 (1973), 307–24; Maureen Fries,
'"Slydynge of Corage": Chaucer's Criseyde as Feminist and Victim', in *The Authority of
Experience: Essays in Feminist Criticism*, ed. by Arlyn Diamond and Lee R. Edwards
(Amherst: University of Massachusetts Press, 1977), pp. 45–59; Mark Lambert, '*Troilus,
Books I–III: A Criseydan Reading*', in *Essays on Troilus and Criseyde*, ed. by Mary Salu
(Cambridge: D. S. Brewer, 1979), pp. 105–25; David Aers, *Chaucer, Langland and the
Creative Imagination* (London: Routledge and Kegan Paul, 1980), pp. 117–42; Carolyn

to the medieval psychology and ethics of fear or to fear's position within late medieval cultural constructions of woman's nature. In our opinion, the type of fear which Criseyde possesses is in itself morally neutral (what she proceeds to do after its inception being a different, though of course related, issue). Chaucer attributes to her a natural response to situations which she feels are, to cite St Thomas Aquinas's description for the object of fear, 'disagreeable and overwhelmingly threatening'. Furthermore, at certain points in *Troilus and Criseyde* Chaucer seems to be opposing feminine fear to the blatantly misogynistic inscriptions of woman's inconstancy which are offered by all previous versions of the tale. In brief, through Lewis's criticism of her character Criseyde has 'falsly ben apeired'.

Feminine fear as emotion and motivation is in short supply in the three major sources of Chaucer's poem, Benoît de Saint-Maure's *Roman de Troie* (*c*. 1155–70), Guido delle Colonne's *Historia Destructionis Troiae* (1287), and Giovanni Boccaccio's *Filostrato* (*c*. 1335–40).[3] Benoît, who first fleshed out the character of Briseida/Criseyde, briefly states that she is 'very timid' (*mout vergondose*, l. 5287) but concentrates on the related themes of (temporary) female power and (perennial) female shame. At the outset we are told that the heroine's 'heart was not constant' (*sis corages li chanjot*, l. 5286; presumably the source of Chaucer's description of her as *slydynge of corage* at V. 825).[4] Guido delle Colonne, who produced an amplified Latin version of Benoît's *Roman,* went even further. The phobic misogyny of the *Historia Destructionis Troiae* condemns Briseida's infidelity as symptomatic of the universal untrustworthiness of the female sex: 'It is clearly implanted in all women by nature not to have any steady constancy.'[5]. Boccaccio's *Filostrato* clearly bears the imprint of Guido. At the end of its narrative Troiolo becomes an *exemplum* of the foolish man who has been led astray by one of those young women who

---

Dinshaw, *Chaucer's Sexual Poetics* (Madison: University of Wisconsin Press, 1989), p. 62; and Barry Windeatt, *Oxford Guides to Chaucer: Troilus and Criseyde* (Oxford: Clarendon Press, 1992), pp. 285–86.

[3] On the development of the story see Gretchen Mieszkowski, 'The Reputation of Criseyde: 1155–1500', *Transactions of the Connecticut Academy of Arts and Sciences*, 43 (1971), 71–153.

[4] *The Story of Troilus*, trans. by R. K. Gordon (New York: Dutton, 1964), p. 5.

[5] *Historia Destructionis Troiae*, XIX, ed. by N. E. Griffin (Cambridge, MA: Medieval Academy of America, 1936), p. 164; trans. by Mary E. Meek (Bloomington: Indiana University Press, 1974), p. 157.

are 'inconstant and eager for many lovers'.[6] Boccaccio was the inventor of the exchange between Pandaro and Criseida which corresponds to the episode in Book II of *Troilus* wherein she is described as the *ferfulleste wight*. In the relevant scene in *Il Filostrato* Criseida is very much the urban sophisticate who emulates the behaviour of her social peer-group ('I know of no woman in the city who does not have a lover') and embarks on her affair with utter confidence: 'welcome this sweet love, [...] and satisfy his burning desire'[7]. Her language is often that of the Ovidian merry widow who is keen to gather rosebuds while she may.[8] She thinks briefly of marriage, but brushes the idea aside: there's a war on, and so this isn't the time to take a husband. Besides, 'to keep one's freedom is much the wiser course. [...] Water gained by stealth is a much sweeter thing than wine that can be taken freely—and so in love the pleasure that remains secret far excels that of constantly embracing a husband'.[9] Here Boccaccio deploys discourses which pave the way for the ultimate condemnation of his unworthy heroine on the charge of inconstancy.[10]

Chaucer changed this quite radically—his Criseyde gives Troilus her love through decorous process and in no sudden manner—as he did the scene in which Criseida tries to make Troiolo feel better about her imminent departure to the Greek camp. Gone is one of Criseida's major arguments against elopement, namely that their love will last only if it 'be enjoyed by stealth'. Chaucer may have felt that this statement indicated a demeaning interest in prompt physical gratification which was inappropriate to the figure he was reconstructing, however much it fitted the

---

[6] *Chaucer's Boccaccio*, trans. by N. R. Havely, rev. edn (Cambridge: D. S. Brewer, 1992), p. 101.

[7] Havely, *Chaucer's Boccaccio*, p. 38. There are, to be sure, a few token fears: 'The fearfulness that was preventing Criseida from reaching a decision fled away as she admired his manners....' (p. 39).

[8] With Criseida's reaction to Pandaro cf. especially the *capite florem* passage in *Ars amatoria*, III. 59–80. For discussion see Barbara Nolan, *Chaucer and the Tradition of the 'Roman Antique'* (Cambridge: Cambridge University Press, 1992), pp. 119–54. In her view Boccaccio here 'concerns himself with the strategies and the folly of illicit, secret, Ovidian love and the treachery of women' (p. 120).

[9] Havely, *Chaucer's Boccaccio*, p. 38.

[10] Cf. Nolan, *Chaucer and the 'Roman Antique'*: 'The Criseida who emerges under his pen—a widow, well-schooled in the strategies of love, a writer of empty letters—is no paragon of virtue. She falls easily and often in just the way Ovid and his medieval successors suggest women will' (p. 141).

character that Boccaccio was preparing for a fall. One of the many things Chaucer introduced at this point was Criseyde's pronouncement—in the context of a condemnation of the 'coward herte' of her father Calkas— that 'Drede fond first goddes' (IV. 1408), i.e. the origin of the pagan gods was in human fear.[11] Given Chaucer's obvious desire to exploit the genre of the *roman antique*, thereby emphasizing the historical context in which his pagans lived and loved, it could be argued that Criseyde's exempli- fication of, and interest in, the fear motive is a crucial facet of the poet's realization of pagan antiquity.[12] Thus, in his characterization of Criseyde, as in his depiction of Calkas, priest of Apollo, Chaucer made specific and personal the emotion of fear which was supposed to permeate pagan society and was at the very root of pagan religion. But this does not resolve the matter entirely. Criseyde's fear, as described in Book II of *Troilus*, does not come across as a quintessentially and exclusively pagan phenomenon; rather the impression is given that this woman would be *the ferfulleste wight* no matter what time she was living in, and whatever external forces were there to threaten her.

It would seem, therefore, that Criseydan fear cannot be located within the matter of Troy as Chaucer knew it, and neither can its significance readily be explained through reference to the potentialities of the *roman antique* genre. Little wonder that C. S. Lewis singled out this emotion as a careful contrivance on Chaucer's part, and the key to his character's subsequent behaviour. However, his reading of Criseyde in terms of Aristotelian tragedy is quite anachronistic. Those few late-medieval scholars who knew about the *Poetics* re-cast Aristotle's doctrine in a mould very different from the one which Lewis assumed. Unfortunately, this medieval re-casting offers nothing that might help determine the significance of feminine fear in *Troilus*. No pointers may be found in Hermann the German's translation of Averroes's 'Middle Commentary' on the *Poetics* (1256), the best-known medieval version of Aristotle's work.[13] Even more importantly, Lewis's radical gender-shift—his tacit

---

[11] This statement probably derives from Petronius's *Primus in orbe deos fecit inesse timor,* a *sentence* included, for example, in Robert Holcot's highly popular commentary on the book of Wisdom (1334–36), which Chaucer may well have known. Cf. *Sapientiae regis Salomonis praelectiones* (Basel: n.p., 1586), pp. 540–41.

[12] As argued by A. J. Minnis, *Chaucer and Pagan Antiquity* (Cambridge: D. S. Brewer, 1982), pp. 82–93.

[13] See *Medieval Literary Theory and Criticism c.1100-c.1375: The Commentary Tradition*, ed. by A. J. Minnis and A. B. Scott, rev. edn (Oxford: Clarendon Press, 1991), pp. 278–79.

admission that a woman can be the 'neither very good nor execrably wicked' tragic protagonist—is unprecedented in either Aristotle or Averroes/Hermann.[14]

Having drawn a blank here, we may now proceed to address the problem by reference to late-medieval accounts of the psychology and ethics of fear. A useful point of departure is provided by John Lawlor's remark that in Criseyde's case fear exists 'in its least obvious and most insidious form', this being 'the fear of dispossession or dislocation, the mere terror of change over the wish to be left alone', from which he concludes that Chaucer's decision to emphasize Criseyde's fearfulness limits the degree of her character's development and effectiveness and prevents us from making much of her.[15] But, while it may be accepted that the fear which Criseyde feels helps to define her character, it is hardly insidious and by no means rare. Rather, dispossession (or privation, *privatio*) was in Chaucer's day deemed to be one of fear's most common antecedents, and the discourse which he uses to describe Criseyde's fearful state does not simplify her character but, in our view, enriches it by adroitly drawing on certain medieval intellectual traditions concerning dread.

Scholastic analyses of fear did not see it simply as a single general emotional response to danger, but as a system of different species that could signify almost any moral, physical, or spiritual state depending on which particular type of fear an individual experienced at any given time. Fear was commonly divided into three specific branches: natural, culpable, and laudable.[16] Central to all of these was the notion that the privation of loved objects was fear's ultimate cause:

> ... if someone loves something good, then it follows that the privation of such a good will be evil, and consequently one should fear this same evil. Indeed, fear... looks back to the evil from which it flees which is opposed

---

[14] Neither can any anticipation of it be found in the second of the avant-garde discussions of tragedy to date from the later Middle Ages, Nicholas Trevet's commentary on Seneca's tragedies. Trevet's general prologue merely offers a version of Isidore of Seville's pronouncements in the eighth book of the *Etymologiae*, the same account which Chaucer was to echo in the *Prologue of the Monk's Tale (Canterbury Tales,* VII. 1973–81). Cf. Minnis and Scott, *Medieval Literary Theory*, pp. 343–44.

[15] John Lawlor, *Chaucer* (London: Hutchinson, 1968), p. 76.

[16] St Bonaventure, *Commentaria in Quatuor Libros Sententiarum Magistri Petri Lombardi*, Lib. 3, dist. 34, dub. 2, respon., in *Opera Omnia* (Quaracchi: ex typ. Collegii S. Bonaventurae, 1882–1902), III. 768.

to some loved good. And thus fear is born from love, whence Augustine says.. .. it may not be doubted that there is no other cause of the act of fearing (*metuendi*) than lest we lose that which we love, or what we are adept at, or that we do not obtain what is hoped for.[17]

Culpable fear was the result of an excessive and overpowering love for one's own life or possessions at the expense of all else, while laudable fear arose from the free exchange and sharing of selfless love between God and good Christians. We will argue that Chaucer's use of fear in his characterization of Criseyde does not draw upon either of these definitions. Instead, it stems directly from interpretations of natural fear, commonly defined as the reflexive concern for one's personal well-being in moments of difficulty or danger.

Throughout the later Middle Ages, the basic definition of natural fear remained largely unchanged. Peter Lombard defined *timor naturalis* as the specific type of fear 'which is in everyone, in which death is feared and punishment dreaded'.[18] Approximately one-and-a-half centuries later, the anonymous *Speculum Morale* (a popular Dominican compilation heavily indebted to St Thomas Aquinas) addressed the relative values of different types of fear, stating that fear's laudability or culpability depends on whether it is reflexive or wilful. *Timor naturalis* is described as a type of fear 'in which someone naturally fears whatever is contrary to nature or unpleasing: it is not meritorious, nor is it demeritorious, it is indifferent because it is not subject to free will'.[19] Natural fear, then, cannot be subject to moral judgment because it has no moral value. Therefore, if Criseyde's fear is naturally reflexive, Lewis's attempt to label it as a flaw or fault must be fundamentally mistaken.

At the beginning of the poem Criseyde's fear seems to be of the purely natural, and hence morally neutral, type. Her emotion arises reflexively as a result of her father's sudden and treacherous desertion, an act that

[17] *Speculum Morale*, Lib. 1, pars 1, dist. 28 (Douai: ex typ. Baltazaris Belleri, 1624; reprinted Graz: Akademische Druck u. Verlagsanstalt, 1964), p. 103. On fear as directly contingent on love, see further Bonaventure, *Comment. in Lib. Sent.*, Lib. 3, dist. 34, art. 1, qu. 3, conclusio/respondeo 4 (III. 760), and Aquinas, *Commentum in Quatuor Libros Sententiarum*, Lib. 3, dist. 34, quaestiunc. 2, in *Opera omnia* (Parma: P. Fiaccadori, 1852–72), VII. 392. An analysis of the operation of different kinds of fear specifically within *fin amor* is beyond the scope of this paper.

[18] *Libri sententiarum*, Lib. 3, dist. 34, ch. 9 (Grottaferrata: Editiones Collegii S. Bonaventurae, 1971–81), II. 198.

[19] *Speculum Morale,* Lib. 1, pars 1, dist. 26 (col. 78).

abandons her to an uncertain fate at the hands of the potentially vindictive Trojans. The situation in which she finds herself is both unusual and unexpected, two conditions which, it was understood, contributed to the arousal and propagation of fear: 'the fact that ... a future evil is sudden and unusual further weakens a man, distracting him from the measure he might take in preparation for fending off future evil'.[20] Criseyde had no warning of her father's treacherous plan, and the fearful anguish she feels because of it augments her fear and throws her into a state of confusion. She has no idea how to react to her new situation, and, finding herself alone and believing that she may be held accountable for her father's actions, justifiably fears for her own life. At the very outset, then, Criseyde is associated with fear. But there is nothing necessarily or self-evidently negative about it. She does not wilfully choose to fear; she simply does so instinctively in response to her sudden privation and uncertain future. The dread Chaucer describes in these lines seems to parallel the standard definitions of *timor naturalis*, and thus firmly locates Criseyde's emotion in the morally neutral sphere of natural fear.

The unexpected loss of her father is traumatic enough. However, Chaucer accentuates the degree of her privation, her solitary 'redeles' state and the fear it promotes, by drawing attention to the fact that she is a widow and 'allone / Of any frend to whom she dorste her mone' (I. 97–98); (the friends and ladies-in-waiting who surround her in Book II are kept out of the picture here). She has no-one in whom to confide, no-one to help her rationalize her fears. As a result, her dread steadily intensifies until she becomes 'Wel neigh out of hir wit for sorwe and fere' (I. 108). One of the traditional means of mitigating fear is denied to her. As Aquinas notes, it is when people are afraid 'that they are especially anxious to deliberate'.[21] Intense fear, he says, encourages one to seek counsel, but despite this it often disturbs rational thought to such a degree that counsel can be ineffective. Deliberation and counsel mitigate fear by analyzing prospective danger and discovering a way to avoid it, but Criseyde, in her growing dread and utter loneliness, has no immediate or familiar recourse to this action. The intensity of her fear prevents her from knowing 'what was best to rede', and thus she herself is unable to lessen her dread. Criseyde does the only thing she can do: she puts her

---

[20] Aquinas, *Summa theologiae*, 1a 2ae 42, art. 5, in the Blackfriars edition and translation (London and New York: Eyre and Spottiswoode, McGraw-Hill, 1964–81), XXI. 49–51.

[21] Aquinas, *Summa theologiae*, 1a 2ae 44, 2; Blackfriars edn, XXI. 65–67.

life in the care of another. Hence her tearful supplication and prostration before Hector.

Included in Criseyde's growing sense of *timor naturalis* is an additional, yet related, type of fear: her dread of the shame which results from Calkas's perfidious act. We are told how she is constantly exposed to remarks about his 'falsnesse and tresoun' (l. 107), which directly contribute to her heightened emotional state, and here we are first made aware of her possession of what, in scholastic tradition, commonly could be referred to as either *timor erubescentiae* (embarrassment) or *timor verecundiae* (shame). These two fears were considered to be specific parts of *timor naturalis*, both of which focused on the possibility of disgrace. *Timor erubescentiae* developed when one feared disgrace arising from an uncompleted act; *timor verecundiae*, on the other hand, was a direct response to a disgraceful act one had already committed.[22] Each of these fears was deemed a natural and reasonable response to the threat of potential disgrace. Criseyde's early sense of shame for her father's treachery transforms, later in the poem, into the fear of other types of shame, such as the disrepute which might arise should people become aware of her illicit relationship with Troilus. The shame and fear Criseyde experiences in the poem therefore relate, in the main, to perceived culpability, but this emotion is far from being culpable in itself. It consistently adheres closely to the general scheme of *timor naturalis* and is nothing more than a natural response to unpleasant and threatening objects and events.

In Book II of *Troilus* Criseyde's fear intensifies, but it does not seem to be any more culpable than it was in Book I. She becomes the 'ferfulleste wight' because a number of specific, and very real, fears merge.[23] First is her fear of the unknown: she is unsure what to expect from a relationship with Troilus, and worried about doing something which might disturb her already precarious position within Trojan society. Second is, perhaps, her fear of death, this time not her own but Troilus's and Pandarus's, and the privation such losses would bring. (We say 'perhaps' because bullying threats of male death are a predictable strategy in the game of love, and Criseyde's response is robust: she spiritedly assures Pandarus that such

---

[22] Aquinas, *Summa theologiae*, 1a 2ae 41, 4; XLII. 35. See also Aquinas, *In Sent*. Lib. 3, dist. 34, art. 1, quaestiunc. II. 4 (VII. 391); and Bonaventure, *In Sent*. Lib. 3, dist. 34, dub. 3 (III. 769–70).

[23] Cf. Aers's discussion of her 'well-founded' fears at this point: *Creative Imagination*, p. 122.

talk will not force her to act against her own volition.) The third type of fear is her fear of shame, as she is reluctant to be held responsible for any extreme action which the two males in question might undertake.

> ... for the harm that myghte ek fallen moore,
> She gan to rewe and dredde hir wonder soore... (II. 54–55).

Such fears help convince Criseyde that she should at least explore the possibility of a relationship with Troilus.

We have already seen that fear was commonly understood to arise from love.[24] However, in some cases love could arise from fear, as Aquinas tells us:

> Fear is also secondarily concerned with the possible source of such an evil [from which one shrinks] and in this respect it is fear which may accidentally lead to love... a spark of hope is struck and this blazes into love... At first we hate an agent from whom we expect trouble; later, if we have reason to hope for some favour from him, we may begin to love him.[25]

Criseyde's 'conversion' in Book II, lines 449–76 represents the end of the process Aquinas describes here. Dread of separation and privation and fear of death have helped to promote her growing love for the pining knight, and subsequently they will encourage acceptance of him. Her all-encompassing terror in Book I had led Criseyde to seek Hector's protection, and his willingness to look after her interests had struck her first spark of hope. (Significantly, Pandarus recommends Troilus to her as 'Ector the secounde', II. 158). By his pleas (and threats) Pandarus fans this spark to life, and when Criseyde finally sees Troilus the sputtering fire of her fearful hope bursts into the full flame of love. Once she resolves to accept Troilus's affection, no matter how afraid she might be, or how adamantly she maintains that her heart cannot truly love against its will, she begins to perceive the first lessening of her dread. And in Book III we are assured that Troilus has become to her 'a wal /Of stiel, and sheld from every displesaunce'; hence 'she was namore afered' (III. 479–82).

If Criseyde's fear is judged to be culpable because it eventually prompts her to accept Diomedes as a lover, then it should also be

---

[24] Cf. the quotations from the *Speculum Morale* and the *Sentences* commentaries of Bonaventure and Aquinas in note 17 above.

[25] *Summa theologiae*, 1a 2ae 43, 1; XXI. 57.

regarded as culpable when it impels her to seek Hector's protection and when it encourages her to return Troilus's love.[26] In each and every case her dread has one and the same motivation: it depends upon her natural fears of death, shame and privation, and although it may indirectly lead her to betray Troilus it can hardly be identified as some 'fundamental flaw' in her character. In Criseyde fear arises, exists, and functions reflexively, and strictly according to the dictates of nature.

It could be objected that, while natural fear in itself may be morally neutral, it can prompt actions which are definitely immoral, such as fornication (which is how Robertsonian readings of *Troilus and Criseyde* regard the heroine's future actions, first with Troilus and subsequently with Diomede, faithlessness compounding the guilt of the latter offence). This approach, it may be noted, shifts the ground far away from Lewis's location of fear as fatal flaw, the site on which our arguments thus far have rested. However, as a basis of interpretation it is theoretically possible. D. W. Robertson's claim that Criseyde's fear is 'always self-centred and never actually involves the fear of violating any higher principles'[27] finds support in moral-theological condemnations of disordered fear. As long as fear is subject to reason it is either blameless or, at the worst, no more than an easily shriven venial sin. But disordered fear which affects the rational appetite, and involves free choice, is definitely a mortal sin. Judged by such criteria, Criseyde does not fare very well. The admonition of I John 4. 18 could be directed at her: 'he that feareth is not perfected in charity'. Her fear may thereby be identified as an impediment to any prospect she has of a good spiritual life. Moreover, she fears the wrong things, thus falling foul of the injunction of Matthew 10. 28 ('And fear ye not them that kill the body, and are not able to kill the soul...'), which was interpreted as meaning that the things of this world should not be feared but rather those things which threaten the spiritual life. Criseyde's fear falls far short of this religious ideal.

The obvious retort to this is that Criseyde is 'naught religious' (i.e. is no nun, II. 759): this ideal is not relevant to Chaucer's text, which espouses values far more pluralistic and contested than the vendors of patristic exegesis would allow. However, it is possible to engage the

---

[26] There are enormous interpretative problems here, of course—we will return to the central issue later, on p. 211, in the light of our following discussion of the gender politics of feminine fear.

[27] *A Preface to Chaucer: Studies in Medieval Perspectives* (Princeton: Princeton University Press, 1962), p. 483.

Robertsonians on their own ground. Far from seeing morally-neutral fear as the prelude and prompt to behaviour which goes far beyond the terms of that neutrality to become liable to moral condemnation, rather the converse may be true—fear could *lessen* blame and guilt. Aquinas talks about how causes which 'weaken judgment, such as ignorance, or which interfere with the free motion of the will, such as sickness, force or fear, lessen sinfulness, just as they lessen voluntariness. For if an action is altogether involuntary there can then be no sin'.[28] Similarly, in his later *quaestio* 'Does fear clear us from sin?' he declares that sin is lessened to a certain degree 'because what is done under the influence of fear is not a wholly voluntary act'. Such actions are, as Aristotle says, 'part voluntary and part involuntary' (*Ethics* III. 1. 1110a11).[29] Now, the degree to which Criseyde experiences dread can indeed be seen as an impediment to what might be deemed proper or honourable ethical behaviour. But it would be difficult to regard this as an all-determining 'fatal flaw' because her actions are never, in our view, wholly voluntary in the terms here laid out by Aquinas. Chaucer may therefore have intended her dread to be a mitigating factor in her guilt rather than, as Lewis and others suppose, the seed from which her betrayal grows.

The scholastic discussions on which we have been drawing are, inevitably, androcentric; man is the measure of all morality. Female fears are not specifically addressed. However, no doubt our schoolmen would have protested that they were dealing with universal *human* emotions, their doctrines being as relevant to women as to men. Furthermore, they would have been obliged to admit that, given the common belief that woman was the weaker vessel, certain fears were more likely to be felt (or, more likely to be felt in large measure) by women. An exceptional text puts such assumptions into words, but goes far beyond them in making the case that a certain kind of *timor naturalis* is not only naturally but also admirably feminine. Here we refer to Christine de Pizan's *Epistre au dieu d'amours* (1402), which contains a description of the distinctive characteristics of men and women with emphasis on the virtues of the female sex. Christine declares that woman does not kill, wound, or mutilate, foster any treasonous misdeeds, steal gold or silver, cheat others out of their inheritance through bogus contracts, and the like; indeed, her greatest fault can cause but little harm. And if someone were

---

[28] *Summa theologiae,* 1a 2ae 73, 6; Blackfriars edn, XXV. 77.

[29] 2a 2ae 125, 4 reply; Blackfriars edn, XLII. 71.

to say that female traits and qualities (*condicions et taches femenines*) are not inclined towards things like that—such as making war, murdering, and so forth—and therefore women deserve no special credit for abstinence from those activities, Christine would utterly agree with them. That claim would in fact reinforce her own view, for the essential nature of woman involves the qualities of gentleness, compassion—and fear.

> For woman's nature is but sweet and mild,
> Compassionate and fearful (*paoureuse*), timorous
> And humble, gentle, sweet, and generous,
> And pleasant, pious, meek in time of peace,
> Afraid of war, religious,[30] plain at heart.
> When angry, quickly she allays her ire,
> Nor can she bear to see brutality
> Or suffering. It's clear those qualities
> By nature make a woman's character (*condicions de femme*).
>   (ll. 668–76)[31]

In the Middle English translation of this poem which Thomas Hoccleve made three years after de Pizan had written it, the above passage is rendered as follows:

> Wommanes herte/ to no creweltee
> Enclyned is/ but they been charitable
> Pitous/ deuout/ ful of humilitee
> Shamefast/ debonaire and amiable
> Dreedful/ and of hir wordes mesurable
> What womman thise hath nat per auenture
> Folwyth nothyng the way of her nature. (ll. 344–50)[32]

In brief, the 'custume and vsage' of woman is to be, *inter alia*, compassionate, humble, modest, timorous, and judicious in speech, and any woman who does not have these qualities is going against her very self; without them she cannot please the promptings of her nature. This puts the fear so elaborately described in Book II of *Troilus* in a very different light. Chaucer's attribution of fear to Criseyde, particularly in Book II, could have been a commendatory strategy, a vital part of his reaction

---

[30] *Religïeuse*, in the sense of 'devout' or 'pious'.

[31] *Poems of Cupid, God of Love. Christine de Pizan's 'Epistre au dieu d'Amours' and 'Dit de la Rose'; Thomas Hoccleve's 'The Letter of Cupid'*, ed. by T. S. Fenster and M. Carpenter Erler (Leiden: Brill, 1990), pp. 66–67.

[32] Fenster and Carpenter Erler, *Poems of Cupid*, p. 194.

against, and critique of, the fickle and wanton women he had found in the narratives of Benoît, Guido, and Boccaccio. Chaucer tried to extract 'the venym of so longe ago'[33] from those texts and substituted an emotion which, in his view, helped to affirm Criseyde's superlative womanliness: this heroine excels in so many of the virtues traditionally associated with the courtly lady, so why not bestow upon her in large measure the *condicion* of fear?

Moreover, Criseyde's *condicions et taches femenines* are complementary to masculine characteristics, which Chaucer depicts (through the exemplary figure of Troilus) in a far more positive manner than de Pizan had adopted. Indeed, the complementarity of normative female and male behaviour[34] is often illustrated in Criseyde's encounters with men. Take her appeal to Hector, for instance. Chaucer depicts her in the inferior subject-position—quite literally, as she kneels in front of the man whose favour she must win in order to protect her in Troy (I. 108–25). Criseyde's 'fere', 'pitous vois', and tender weeping here have their desired effect.[35] Hector assures her of his sympathy and support. Criseyde can remain in Troy as long as she likes, enjoying as much honour as she had when Calkas dwelt there. She will be free from the threat of physical violation—'And youre body shal men save'—insofar as this lies in his power. And he is, of course, a very powerful man indeed. Criseyde takes her leave, goes home quite reassured, and 'held hir stille'—lives discreetly, enjoys the social life which is appropriate for a woman of her status, and preserves her reputation (ll. 126–33).

A similar pattern is present in a social exchange of a very different kind, namely the lovers' first sexual encounter as described in Book III. 1093–323.[36] Troilus's exemplary manliness is carefully established. As he swoons Pandarus exclaims 'Is this a mannes herte?' A few moments later, Criseyde expresses the same attitude in the remark, 'Is this a mannes game?'. But such behaviour is not damagingly 'feminine' or 'effeminate';

---

[33] To borrow a phrase from Chaucer's *Legend of Good Women*, l. 2241.

[34] For a medieval account of gender complementary see William of Aragon's *De nobilitate animi*, as discussed by A. J. Minnis, 'From Medieval to Renaissance? Chaucer's Position on Past Gentility', *Proceedings of the British Academy*, 72 (1986), 205–46 (p. 222, n. 2 and p. 244, n. 1).

[35] See especially Aers's discussion of this episode; *Creative Imagination*, p. 120.

[36] See Aers, *Creative Imagination*, pp. 127–28, and E. T. Hansen, *Chaucer and the Fictions of Gender* (Berkeley and Los Angeles: University of California Press, 1992), pp. 150–51.

ALASTAIR MINNIS AND ERIC J. JOHNSON

rather, Troilus's response manifests his highly-strung aristocratic sensitivity—providing of course that he does not indulge it too long. There is no risk of that here, and soon he is displaying his manly vigour by demanding of Criseyde, 'Now yeldeth yow!' The force of Troilus's male desire is emphasized when Chaucer likens him to a sparrow-hawk which has caught a lark in its claws (ll. 1191–2). Such aggression, it would seem, is understood as being at once erotically potent and socially acceptable.[37] For her part, Criseyde is all a-tremble -

> Right as an aspen leef she gan to quake,
> Whan she hym felte hire in his armes folde (ll. 1200–01)

—as she accepts the ardour of her entrapping and enfolding lover. She is now playing the passive sexual role, displaying a version of her fearfulness which is sexually motivated and clearly attractive to manly Troilus. Once again, she is embodying to a superlative degree a traditional female 'condition' in Christine de Pizan's sense. Statutory female behaviour provokes passion in Troilus just as, in different social circumstances, it provoked pity in Hector. In both cases Criseyde is the 'wommanliche wif'[38] *par excellence*.

It would seem, then, that fear is too general a feminine (and indeed, human) emotion to be pressed into service as the distinguishing 'fatal flaw' which explains the actions of one individual woman, Chaucer's Criseyde.[39] And if flaw it be, then the whole of womankind would be flawed, doomed to a life of infidelity and deceit: to which one can respond in several ways. First, that such an ubiquitous failing could not function as a 'fatal flaw' as Aristotle defined it (however relevant or useful we deem that definition to be). Secondly, it would be very difficult to suggest that Chaucer's text was postulating the endemic faithlessness of womankind, given Chaucer's consistent rewriting of his blatantly

---

[37] See especially David Aers, *Community, Gender, and Individual Identity: English Writing 1360–1430* (London: Routledge, 1988), pp. 128–31, and Jill Mann, *Geoffrey Chaucer*, Feminist Reading Series (Hemel Hempstead: Harvester Wheatsheaf, 1991), pp. 108–110. In our view, Aers overstates the violence in this passage (in raising the spectre of 'strange fantasies of rape'), while Mann undervalues it.

[38] As Troilus calls her on two occasions (III. 106 and 1295).

[39] Cf. apRoberts, albeit speaking of human fear in general: 'there is nothing in Criseyde's fear which the reader will feel as peculiar to her. It has not the individually marked quality of the tragic flaw' ('Criseyde's Infidelity', p. 385). And, 'It is necessary to the central effect of the poem that the reader should not feel Criseyde's fear to have a unique quality—that he should feel it to be a fear common to humanity' (p. 385, cf. p. 394).

antifeminist sources.[40] The changes which Chaucer made to the earlier
constructions of Criseyde seem to point in one and the same direction.
Chaucer may declare that he does not wish to chide 'this sely womman /
Forther than the storye wol deyvse' (V. 1093–94), but in fact he goes
much further than any of the earlier versions of the 'storye' in presenting
her in a positive manner, especially in the earlier books of the poem. And
his attribution of fearfulness to Criseyde may be regarded a part and
parcel of that idealizing, antimisogynistic strategy.

This approach certainly helps to account for one of the most curious
differences between Books II and V of *Troilus and Criseyde*. It is hardly
surprising that so much attention should be paid to Criseyde's fear in
Book II, given that this is the section of Chaucer's poem in which her
interiority is explored in extraordinary detail. As Barbara Nolan says,
Book II 'belongs to Criseyde and her world—her domestic spaces, her
life with her ladies-in-waiting, her comfortable daily round of activities,
the private recesses of her mind'.[41] In the public, militaristic male world
of Book V, in sharp contrast, we are given very little insight into
Criseyde's mind: and the discourse of feminine fear is notably muted.
This may seem somewhat strange, given that here the narrative duplicates
the situation in which Criseyde was placed at the very beginning of the
poem: once again she is 'allone and hadde nede / Of frendes help' (V.
1026–27). Now she is living among the very Greeks whom she professed
(in Book II) to fear so much, and being assailed by Diomede's love
entreaties on the one hand and on the other by his—and her father's—
bleak view of the future of Troy. Many motives of fear are here, at least
as many as existed in Books I and II, if not more. And yet—here is the
main thrust of what Book V has to say on the subject:

> And if that I me putte in jupartie
> To stele awey by nyght, and it bifalle
> That I be kaught, I shal be holde a spie;
> Or elles—lo, this drede I moost of alle—
> If in the hondes of som wrecche I falle,
> I nam but lost, al be myn herte trewe. (ll. 701–06)

Criseyde's fears of what might happen should she attempt to return to
Troy under cover of darkness—either being deemed a spy or being raped,

---

[40] See for example Chaucer's transformation of Guido delle Colonne's Medea, which
forms part of his *Legend of Good Women*. This is discussed by A. J. Minnis, *Oxford
Guides to Chaucer: The Shorter Poems* (Oxford: Clarendon Press, 1995), pp. 367–78.

[41] *Chaucer and the 'Roman Antique'*, p. 237.

robbed, or murdered by some 'wrecche'—seem well-founded.[42] But little is made of them. The 'ferfulleste wight / That myghte be' fails to rematerialize.

Why is this? Perhaps because, for Chaucer, Criseyde's fear was a vital part of her rehabilitation in Book II of the poem, in marked contrast to the negative character-traits she displays in Boccaccio's *Filostrato*. Hence Chaucer's positive discourse of fear as part of ideal femininity had no place at the end of his poem. For in Book V he had no choice but to recognize that 'Criseyde was untrewe' (V. 1774); all the compassion in the world (and his narrator's 'routhe' concerning her situation is heavily emphasized) cannot alter that fact. Yes, she was *slydynge of corage* (V. 825), but only at this very late stage does Chaucer make that damning point which, as already noted (p. 200 above), Benoît had introduced quite early in his narrative. It is not to be found in Book II of Troilus; it is, as it were, kept well away from the language of Criseydan fear, and therefore there is no reason to follow Lewis's linking of the two in terms of cause and effect. Indeed, *slydynge corage* does not fit easily into any of the different discourses of fear which operate in previous parts of the poem: the socially normative female fear of Book II, the timorous sexual role-playing of Book III, or the historicizing of pagan fear of Book IV.

But is it really a 'damning point'? There are good reasons for reaffirming the traditional view that this is indeed the case, particularly in view of David Burnley's demonstration that in Middle English the terms *slydyr* and *slydynge* are 'associated with wandering from the right moral path, or with falling into sin'.[43] And yet—in Chaucer's text the phrase *slydynge of corage* does not function within a rhetoric of condemnation but rather constitutes a simple statement of fact that is lacking in depth of interior analysis. After all, considered in itself, it need not mean a 'decrease in courage' in moral terms but may rather refer to a 'change of heart' in the sense of a loss of 'inclination' or 'desire'—of the desire to return to Troilus, for instance.[44] Then again, far from serving an account that

---

[42] Cf. Aers's view; *Creative Imagination*, p. 135.

[43] J. D. Burnley, 'Criseyde's Heart and the Weakness of Women: An Essay in Lexical Interpretation', *Studia Neophilologica*, 54 (1982), 25–38 (p. 29).

[44] Cf. *MED*, 'corage', where the heart is described as 'the seat of the emotions, affection, attitudes, and volition; heart, spirit; disposition, temperament'. Compare also H. A. Kelly's positive reading of *slydynge of corage,* which he understands as something like 'easily moved', the expression being meant as 'an amplification of Criseyde's pitying and tenderhearted nature' (*Chaucerian Tragedy* (Woodbridge: Boydell and Brewer, 1997) p. 127).

claims knowledge (historical or moral) of Criseyde, *slydynge of corage* is part of a passage that indicates how much of an enigma this woman is— the narrator does not even know her age (V. 826). This is not, of course, to refuse acceptance of the textual truth that 'Criseyde was untrewe'. But it is one additional argument against the facile assimilation of the psychology of female fear to the morally culpable inconstancy of woman. For such reasons we would question Burnley's conclusion that, on the whole, 'Chaucer's conception of femininity' in the poem 'is one of moral weakness'.[45] Rather, Criseyde's 'behaviour, as both motive and effect, has a complexity and texture that resists reduction to *any* simple explanatory formula, whether antifeminist or more disinterestedly philosophical'.[46] Misogynist clichés stand ready to categorize and control her, but Chaucer's text refuses to allow them interpretative hegemony.

In sum, in searching for reasons for Criseyde's infidelity, there is no reason to treat fear—or at least fear as inscribed in Book II of *Troilus*—as the prime suspect. On the contrary, one might go so far as to say that if Criseyde is the fearfullest wight that might be, that is an aspect of Chaucer's attempt to depict her as one of the most wonderful women that might be: a creature who presents quintessential femininity in direct opposition to ideal male characteristics, a 'wommanliche wif' who possesses in abundance all the *condicions de femme* and who is highly desirable sexually in a way which is unthreatening to men (in marked contrast to the emasculating Briseida).[47] Indeed, fear is almost a virtue in a woman, or at least a condition which functions in association with female virtues, as we see from Christine de Pizan's list—hardly a fatal flaw!

This is, of course, an essentializing view of woman. More precisely, one essentializing view (of the culpably fickle female) has been replaced with another (of the attractively fearful female). As such it could be deemed to form part of that discourse which, while apparently empowering women by putting them on a pedestal, actually diverts them 'from history by the annihilation of the identity of individual women, hidden behind the requirement of discretion and the anonymity of the

---

[45] Burnley, 'Criseyde's Heart', p. 37.

[46] Here we apply to Criseyde what Lee Patterson has said of Benoît's Briseida; see *Chaucer and the Subject of History* (London: Routledge, 1991), p. 119.

[47] On Criseyde's exemplary femininity as unthreatening see especially E. T. Hansen, *Chaucer and the Fictions of Gender* (Berkeley: University of California Press, 1992), pp. 158–62.

domna' as depersonalizing, disenfranchising object of male worship.[48] However, surely Chaucer's attempt at a culturally positive reconstruction of Criseyde (in at least parts of his poem) should not be set at naught because the images of good womanliness presented therein are nowadays highly problematic. Shakespeare's King Lear said of the dead Cordelia that 'Her voice was ever soft, / Gentle and low, an excellent thing in woman'.[49] By the same token—and with full recognition of similar ironies—we could say that feminine fear was an excellent thing in Chaucer's Criseyde.

---

[48] R. Howard Bloch, *Medieval Misogyny and the Invention of Western Romantic Love* (Chicago and London: University of Chicago Press, 1991), pp. 196–97. See further Aers, *Community, Gender*, p. 138.

[49] *King Lear*, V. 3.

How Margaret Blackburn
Taught her Daughters: Reading Devotional
Instruction in a Book of Hours

PATRICIA CULLUM AND JEREMY GOLDBERG

Primers or books of hours constituted by far the most widely disseminated texts during the later Middle Ages in England. Members of the aristocracy often possessed several, itself an indicator that they had a variety of functions or of users. Numbers of such aristocratic manuscripts are well-known by reason of their illuminations. Probate evidence suggests that mercantile families and, more rarely, artisans also possessed such books, but how far these survive has hardly been explored.[1] Books of hours, principally Latin texts, thus circulated amongst persons whose levels of vernacular literacy, let alone Latinity, must often have been limited. This begs important questions about how such texts were used and by whom. This present essay will address these questions tangentially by focusing on the so-called Bolton Hours (York Minster Library, MS Additional 2). This manuscript is doubly interesting because, though clearly a prestige object, it is not apparently aristocratic in terms of patronage and it is provincial in terms of workmanship.

The Bolton Hours cannot be precisely dated, nor are the original owner or owners recorded. That it contains a commemoration, a hymn, and two different illuminations of Richard Scrope, the martyred archbishop of York and focus of a politically-charged local cult, suggests a date after his

---

[1]   Jeremy Goldberg, 'Lay Book Ownership in Late Medieval York: The Evidence of Wills', *The Library*, 6th series, 16 (1994), 181–89.

execution in 1405.[2] The hours are compiled according to the York Use and St Peter, patron of the cathedral church, and William of York, the cathedral's only 'official' saint, are prominent within the first grouping of illuminations of saints contained between fols 32[v] and 41.[3] Indeed the manuscript is in some ways a picture book. It contains many more illuminations than is normal for a book of hours.[4] These include forty-seven full-page illuminations largely contained in four groupings separate from the text of the hours, an arrangement found elsewhere in a small number of hours of the end of the fourteenth and early years of the fifteenth century. Several of these have York connections and may thus have influenced one another.[5] It is striking that whereas many of the text gatherings show some wear, particularly to the edges and lower part of the page, the miniatures are in almost pristine condition. This suggests that the reader held the book open by the text pages in order more clearly

---

[2]   Richard Scrope's role in the Percy-inspired rebellion of 1405 is discussed in Peter McNiven, 'The Betrayal of Archbishop Scrope', *Bulletin of the John Rylands Library*, 54 (1971), 173–213.

[3]   Neither Richard Scrope nor William of York is commonly found in books of hours. Scrope memorials are found in York Minster Library, MS Add. 67, fol. 102 and Cambridge, St John's College, MS 129, fol. 163. Although this last follows the Sarum Use, it may have had a Yorkshire patron. The former is almost certainly a York manuscript and contains memorials to Saints Blaise, William, Ninian, and John of Beverley. See also n. 5.

[4]   Kathleen Scott, *Later Gothic Manuscripts, 1390–1490*, 2 vols (London: Harvey Miller, 1996), II, 120. The authors owe much to Scott's study and to the iconographic index of the late Peter Newton held in the King's Manor Library of the University of York.

[5]   These are (A) Boulogne-sur-Mer, Biblothèque Municipale, MS 93; (B) London, British Library, MS Royal 2 A. xvii; (C) Rennes, Bibliothèque Municipale, MS 22; (D) Oxford, Bodleian Library, Lat. liturg. f. 2; (E) Oxford, St John's College, MS 94; (F) Aberystwyth, National Library of Wales, MS 17520. Only (F) has no apparent York or regional connection. (E) is by John Lacy, a Newcastle Dominican and may post-date the Bolton Hours by a few years. (A) follows the York Use and is late fourteenth century. (B) and (C) were originally part of the same manuscript, a psalter rather than a book of hours, made for an aristocratic lady within the diocese of York and probably contemporary with the Bolton Hours. Like the latter (fol. 123), it contains a miniature of a lady before her guardian angel (fol. 26). (D) is a Franco-Flemish product of *c.* 1400, but which came into the hands of a York patron who then added a suffrage to Richard Scrope (fol. 147). Morgan has described similarities 'in text contents and choice of subject matter' between the Bolton Hours, (A), (D), and another manuscript (Cambridge, Trinity College MS O. 3. 10), also a psalter, associated with York of similar date: Scott, *Later Gothic Manuscripts*, II, 32, 373–79, 62, 117–19, 128–29, 132–34; Nigel Morgan, 'Longinus and the Wounded Heart', *Wiener Jahrbuch für Kunstgeschichte*, 46–47 (1993–94), 508–18.

to see and meditate on the miniature images. This appears particularly to be the case with the image of St Anne (fol. 35).

On stylistic grounds Scott suggests that the manuscript is 'not much later than *c.* 1415'. Certainly the head dress of the woman (fols 33, 40ᵛ, 78) is akin to high fashion of the end of the previous century.[6] Similarly the design of the panels that frame the illuminations of saints is strikingly reminiscent of Oxford, Bodleian Library, MS Bodley 581 dated to (or after) 1391. The prominence of Richard Scrope may also suggest a date closer to 1405 than later, nor need the inclusion of St Bridget of Sweden post-date the founding of Syon.

Additional iconographical and stylistic evidence noted by Scott strengthens the view that the Hours were made in York. The representation of the Virgin seated next to God, rather than the more conventional coronation iconography, is found again in Boulogne-sur-Mer, Bibliothèque Municipale MS 93, itself connected with York. Miniatures of a priest hearing confession are likewise found only in these two manuscripts. Similarities of style are also to be found in the work of the artist of the first four illuminations (fols 12ᵛ, 13ᵛ, 14ᵛ, 15ᵛ) of an almanac and calendar (Cambridge, Trinity College MS R. 15. 21) dated to 1408 and associated with York, in the historiations of Cambridge, Trinity College MS O. 3. 10 (a calendar and psalter of similar date following the Use of York), and that of the Bolton Hours itself.

The stylistic and historical evidence that the manuscript was produced in York in the early fifteenth century seems compelling, but internal evidence suggests specific Dominican workmanship. Full-page illuminations of St Dominic (fol. 185) and Peter of Milan, otherwise Peter Martyr (fol. 105), are most unusual. Only the Taymouth Hours (London, British Library, MS Yates Thompson 13) of about a century earlier contains similar iconography. On the verso of the Peter Martyr illumination is found Mary Magdalene. Together these demonstrate a Dominican connection, since the York priory incorporated an earlier chapel of St Mary Magdalene, and a relic of her right hand, which had reached out to touch the resurrected Christ, came into the possession of the York Dominicans sometime during the later fourteenth or early years

---

[6] Women's head-dresses are the fashion items most likely to suggest accurate indicators of date. The figures are also characterized by bag sleeves closed at the wrists and necklines just below the neck. These were high fashion just before the turn of the century, but remained fashionable for some time after. Cf. Margaret Scott, *A Visual History of Costume: The Fourteenth and Fifteenth Centuries* (London: Batsford, 1988), esp. 48–58.

of the fifteenth century.[7] As will become clear, it is significant that the location of the Dominican house by Toft Green behind Micklegate within the south-west corner of the city walls made it the nearest, or at least the most accessible, of the city's friaries to the mercantile Blackburn family.[8] The devotion to Richard Scrope so apparent in the manuscript may have been shared by the York Dominicans; one of their number, friar William de Thorpe, had evidently been implicated in the 1405 rebellion for which he was given a royal pardon the following year.[9]

The only internal evidence for the identity of the craftsmen who produced this manuscript is the scribe's reference to himself on fol. 122^v as '*Johannes nomine felix*', an identity that is at least suggestive of a religious.[10] We know that friars did produce various liturgical manuscripts and *horae*. Thus the Dominican John Siferwas is associated with the Lovell Lectionary and the Sherborne Missal. A particularly apposite example, however, is Oxford, St John's College, MS 94, dated 1420 and hence almost contemporary with the Bolton Hours, the work of John Lacy, a Dominican anchorite of Newcastle. This has some similarity of layout to the Bolton Hours in its grouping of numbers of full-page illuminations and is one of the few extant Hours containing illuminations of St Sitha.[11]

The manuscript may have been made in York for local use, but the clearest evidence to tie it to specific York patrons comes from the obits

---

[7]   *Victoria History of the Counties of England: County of York*, ed. by William Page, III (London: Constable, 1913), pp. 283, 285.

[8]   Margaret Blackburn left 10s. to the York Dominicans, but only 20s. to be divided among the other three orders. She also left a coconut to friar Nicholas Wattre. Nicholas Blackburn senior likewise remembered Wattre and left 40 shillings to friar John Orre. Nicholas Wattre, marked with a contraction in the registered copy of Nicholas Blackburn's will, was probably Nicholas de Watreford, a Dominican ordained priest in the York friary in 1402. John Orre can be identified as a Dominican from the will of Margaret Ottryngton: Borthwick Institute of Historical Research (hereafter BIHR), Prob. Reg. 2 fol. 605; 3 fols 415^v, 426^v; Alfred Emden, *A Survey of Dominicans in England* (Rome: Instituto Storico Domenicano, 1967), 318–19.

[9]   *Victoria History: County of York*, III, 285; *Calendar of Patent Rolls Henry IV vol. III 1405–1408* (London: HMSO, 1907), 193.

[10]   John called '*felix*' (i.e. lucky, happy, fortunate etc.).

[11]   The feast of St Sitha (otherwise Zita) has also been added to the calendar. In addition to John Lacy's hours, memoria and illuminations of St Sitha are found in the Kildare Hours (fol. 83) and in some later fifteenth-century hours, e.g. London, British Library, Add. MS 54782 (Hastings Hours), fol. 66^v.

written into the calendar. These include those of John and Alice Bolton. There are additional obits to Agnes Lond' and Thomas Scauceby. John Bolton (d. 1445) was a leading merchant in York during the first part of the fifteenth century where he held office as mayor and as MP.[12] Agnes Lond' has not been identified, but Scauceby was a York mercer closely connected to the Blackburn family.[13] Alice Blackburn, Lond', and Scauceby are all recorded as having died in the autumn of 1472, long after the likely date of production of the hours.[14]

The calendar demonstrates that the Hours came into the possession of a person or family with close ties to John and Alice Bolton during the course of the fifteenth century, but these entries post-date the original production of the manuscript. To identify the original patrons, we need to look back a generation. At the same time we should not assume transmission from father to son; probate evidence demonstrates the comparative frequency with which books, not least primers, passed through the female line, and the form of the prayers within the book show that it was made for a woman.[15] There is internal evidence to suggest that this was a book passed between a mother and her daughter or daughters.

---

[12] John Bolton lived within the parish of St John at Ouse Bridge End, whose church was located at the junction of North Street with Micklegate. He had a brother, Robert, also a merchant, who predeceased him: BIHR, Prob. Reg. 2 fol. 107[v] (John Bolton); 3 fol. 463[v] (Robert Bolton).

[13] Scauceby or Scawceby (not Scanceby as transcribed by Scott) was a man of substance. He married twice. Only the first name of his widow (Isota) is known. He owned a messuage in Thursday Market, but also property in Micklegate and North Street. He made bequests to two sons of Joan Blackburn (the widow of another of Margaret Blackburn's children) and required that they be under the guardianship of his older brother William. His will was made in September 1471 and supposedly proved in December. Either this is an error and the will was proved in 1472 or, more likely, the obit in the calendar of the Hours is inaccurate: BIHR, Prob. Reg. 4 fol. 169.

[14] There was a plague epidemic in York during the second half of 1471 into the early months of 1472. Levels of mortality were falling by the period of the three deaths recorded in the calendar. It may be that these deaths actually occurred in 1471 and the obits are miscalculated (see note 13 above): Jeremy Goldberg, 'Mortality and Economic Change in the Diocese of York, 1390–1514', *Northern History*, 24 (1988), 47.

[15] Susan Gloag Bell, 'Medieval Women Book Owners: Arbiters of Lay Piety and Ambassadors of Culture', in *Women and Power in the Middle Ages*, ed. by Mary Erler and Maryanne Kowaleski (Athens: University of Georgia Press, 1988), 162–66; Goldberg, 'Lay Book Ownership', 185–87, 189; Anne Dutton, 'Passing the Book: Testamentary Transmission of Religious Literature to and by Women in England 1350–1500', in *Women, the Book and the Godly*, ed. by Lesley Smith and Jane Taylor (Cambridge: D. S. Brewer, 1995), pp. 41–54.

The three single patronal figures found in the illuminations are all female. Locating these in the context of the family of father, mother, son, and daughter represented in devotion before the Trinity (the first full-page illumination, fol. 33), two appear to represent the mother, one the daughter. Evaluating this evidence, Scott concludes, 'whatever family is shown with the Crucifix-Trinity, the mistress of the household was apparently the guiding hand in the production of the book'.[16] This observation may be taken further; both the illumination of the mother kneeling in veneration before St Sitha and the iconographically unconventional illumination of St Anne and the Virgin make sense of mother-daughter patronage.[17]

The Trinity as a devotion seems to have had high-status connotations. It was, for example, Edward the Black Prince's particular devotion. The Trinity guild was the pre-eminent guild of Coventry and had a membership composed exclusively of persons of wealth and standing within the city.[18] Similarly in York the Trinity guild, associated with the hospital of that name, drew its membership from a mercantile élite. The inclusion of donor figures on a Trinity page within books of Hours is likewise not unusual, but only in the context of aristocratic ownership, as for example Oxford, Keble College, MS 47, fol. 13^v where aristocratic ownership is marked by the use of heraldry.

The Crucifix-Trinity was also a specific devotion of the Blackburn family. Nicholas Blackburn senior asked to be buried before the crucifix in York Minster and Margaret, his wife, was later buried beside him. The Blackburn memorial window in All Saints, North Street contains an image of the Crucifix-Trinity with the donor figures arranged on either side. Here Nicholas and Margaret are depicted, Margaret at prayer with an open service book before her, Nicholas with a prayer scroll addressed to the triune King.[19] We may note finally that Joan, the widow of John

---

[16] Scott, *Later Gothic Manuscripts*, II, 120.

[17] For St Sitha see Sebastian Sutcliffe, 'The Cult of St Sitha in England: an introduction', *Nottingham Medieval Studies*, 37 (1993), 83–89. It may also be that the miniature of St Bridget may be similarly understood: see n. 61 below.

[18] Charles Phythian-Adams, *Desolation of a City: Coventry and the Urban Crisis of the Late Middle Ages* (Cambridge: Cambridge University Press, 1979), 124–26. The Trinity guild of Lynn may have performed a similar function: *The Book of Margery Kempe*, ed. by Sanford Meech and Hope Emily Allen, EETS, os 212 (London: Humphrey Milford, Oxford University Press, 1940), 9, 358–59.

[19] BIHR, Prob. Reg. 2 fol. 605. The Trinity panel and donor figures of the present east window of All Saints are much restored, but represent the original glazing noted by Henry

Blackburn, the son of Nicholas and Margaret, left a maser with an image of the Holy Trinity at her death in 1446.[20]

The family figures before the Crucifix-Trinity wear civilian dress and no armorial bearings are apparent here or elsewhere.[21] This is consistent with the supposition that they represent a mercantile family and hence the family who first commissioned the book. As such this constitutes the earliest representation of a family group within a book of hours. The figures are representative of status and kinship rather than actual portraits; the single male and female child stand for all the children of the family. Each figure carries a scroll which represents one line of a prayer. The family is thus symbolically united in prayer to the Trinity, the '*trinus deus*' of the mother's scroll,[22] which concludes with the daughter's line '*Premia qui prestas nos castas fac et honestas*'.[23] As Felicity Riddy has observed, this petition, worded in the feminine gender, is specifically apposite for the women in the group, and perhaps particularly for the daughter onto whose scroll this line is written.[24] The good name of the family rests in part on the chastity and reputation (understood in sexual terms) of the female members of the family, though the menfolk share in that responsibility since they ought to protect their wives, daughters, and female siblings.[25]

We have a number of further clues as to the identity of this family. Alice Bolton, one of the persons whose obit is recorded in the calendar, was born Alice Blackburn. She was the daughter of Margaret Blackburn (née Ormeshead), and her husband, Nicholas, another leading merchant and mayor of York in 1412, who hailed in the first instance from Richmond and originally from Blackburn (Lancs.).[26] Nicholas had a

---

Johnston in 1670. The glass can be dated between 1412 and 1427: Eric Gee, 'The Painted Glass of All Saints' Church, North Street, York', *Archaeologia*, 102 (1969), 151–202.

[20] BIHR, Prob. Reg. 2 fol. 141.

[21] Heraldry is common in books of hours, but is probably restricted to books owed by the aristocracy.

[22] 'The triune God'.

[23] 'You who grant gifts, make us chaste and honest'.

[24] Paper given at conference on 'Women in the Christian Tradition', Seefeld, Austria, October 1998.

[25] E.g. brothers can be found protecting their sisters by obliging lovers to enter into contracts of marriage: BIHR, CP E 26, F.200.

[26] Nicholas Blackburn was probably born in Blackburnshire—his will mentions 'my cosyn' Alison Strynger of the parish of Blackburn. He moved to Richmond, probably

particular devotion to Cuthbert, reflected in his generous gift in 1425 of
'x *li.* of gold whilk sall be warede in a memoriall Jowell' to the feretory
of the saint in Durham, and this makes sense of the full-page illumination
of the saint.[27] Their family home was in the parish of All Saints, North
Street of whose church they were major patrons.[28] It is not known when
Alice or her sisters were born, though it was almost certainly at some
point within the decades of the fourteenth century or early years of the
fifteenth. She and her two sisters may have been children when the

---

through a common Duchy of Lancaster connection. Blackburnshire was part of the Duchy
estates and John of Gaunt held the Honour of Richmond between 1342 and 1372. When
admitted to the franchise of York in 1397–98 he was described as 'de Richemund', which
implies that he had not then fully relocated to York. His will shows close links with
Richmond and Richmond traders long after his removal. In 1412, the very year he was
mayor of York, he founded a chantry at the altar of St Mary in the parish church of
Richmond. That his sons John and Nicholas were first admitted to the franchise in 1402–
03 suggests that they was born *c.* 1382 and hence that Nicholas married Margaret prior to
his removal. Further evidence of these connections, and the family's patronage, are the
presence of an anchoress named Blackburn in Richmond at the end of the fourteenth
century, and of a clerk named Thomas Blakburn and a chantry priest named John de
Richmonde within the Blackburns' parish church of All Saints, North Street: Patrick
Shaw, *An Old York Church, All Hallows in North Street* (York: The Church Shop, 1905),
p. 94; Peter Wenham, 'The Chantries, Guilds, Obits and Lights of Richmond', *Yorkshire
Archaeological Journal*, 38 (1952–55), 199; Peter Wenham, 'The Anchoress of Richmond,
North Yorkshire', in *A Richmond Miscellany*, ed. by Peter Wenham and Jane Hatcher,
North Yorkshire Record Office Publications, 25 (Northallerton: North Yorkshire County
Record Office Publications, 1980), p. 53; *Register of the Freemen of the City of York I:
1272–1588*, ed. by Francis Collins, Surtees Society, 96 (Durham: Andrews, 1897–1900),
98, 105. Saints Cuthbert and John of Beverley are also depicted in the Kildare Hours of *c.*
1425 manufactured in Rouen probably for a Yorkshire patron (New York, Pierpont
Morgan Library, MS M. 105, fols 51, 54). A memorial to St John of Beverley is also found
in Cambridge, St John's College, MS 129, fol. 29.

[27] Barrie Dobson, *Durham Priory 1400–1450* (Cambridge: Cambridge University Press,
1973), p. 29.

[28] Further evidence of York patronage are the memorials to John of Beverley and to John
of Bridlington, and illuminations of Saints Martin, Leonard, and Blaise, all of which are
unusual within the context of a book of hours, make sense in respect of York patronage.
The feast of St Blaise was the day on which the city's mayors took office, whereas the
feast of St Martin, known as Martinmas, was the customary date for hiring servants and
leasing property within the region. Nicholas Blackburn senior also had rights of presentation to two chantries in the nearby church of St Martin in Micklegate. Leonard was the
patron of the city's principal hospital. The very number of miniatures is, furthermore, a
reflection of the dedication of the parish for which there is otherwise no specific
iconography.

manuscript was made and it is our contention here that the daughter depicted before the Trinity (fol. 33) and again singly in devotion before Richard Scrope (fol. 100^v) is representative of these. To take this one stage further, the Hours were commissioned by Margaret Blackburn to use with her then unmarried daughters Isabel, Alice, and Agnes. They are then as much the Blackburn Hours as the Bolton Hours and how or when they passed to Alice is unclear.[29]

Though this is in some ways a family book, it is especially a book for a mother and her daughter (or daughters). This is apparent in two ways. First, the only other representations of kneeling devotional figures contained elsewhere within the manuscript are of the mother figure (before St Sitha, fol. 40^v, before St Michael, fol. 123) and of the daughter (with hair unbound wearing a maiden's circlet in prayer before Richard Scrope, fol. 100v). Second, the mother kneeling in devotion before St Sitha may, echoing the words of the prayer jointly addressed to the Trinity, have had the welfare and chastity of her daughter specifically in mind. The cult of St Sitha, the servant saint and virgin, was transmitted from Lucca some time in the fourteenth century, but seems to have enjoyed a particular popularity in England during the century-and-a-half prior to the Reformation. Her cult may be seen to have a variety of meanings and to have perhaps appealed to a variety of audiences. On one level she was understood, by reason of an iconography that often depicts her with keys at her side, to be helpful in finding lost keys and by extension lost valuables. This is of course a perspective that Lollard commentators and later critics of 'superstitious' practice tell us about, but perhaps more importantly, Sitha was a model of feminine chastity and piety. She was also a servant.[30]

---

[29] Agnes may have died as a child (see note 44 below). Isabel probably married before Alice being the older—she is named before Alice in both her parents' wills. Alice was probably the last surviving daughter to leave home. The Hours could have been given to her as a wedding present to use with her own daughters (cf. the Hours of Jeanne d'Evreux, also Bell, 'Medieval Women Book Owners', pp. 165, 184.) King suggests that the manuscript is the primer given by William Revetour, an executor of Nicholas Blackburn, to his goddaughter Isabel, the daughter of Alice Blackburn and her husband John Bolton, however the description of Revetour's primer as '*largum*' does not describe the Bolton Hours: Pamela King, 'Corpus Christi Plays and the "Bolton Hours" 1: Tastes in Lay Piety and Patronage in Fifteenth-Century York', *Medieval English Theatre*, 14 (1996), 54–55.

[30] Michael Goodich, '*Ancilla Dei*: The Servant as Saint in the Later Middle Ages', in *Women of the Medieval World*, ed. by Julius Kirshner and Suzanne Wemple (Oxford: Blackwell, 1985), pp. 119–36; Sutcliffe, 'Cult of St Sitha'; Thorlac Turville-Petre, 'A Middle English Life of St Zita', *Nottingham Medieval Studies*, 35 (1991), 102–05.

Illustration 1 Margaret Blackburn kneeling in devotion before St Sitha. York Minster Library MS Add. 2, fol. 40ᵛ. By kind permission of the Dean and Chapter of York.

In Lucca Zita's cult was promoted by the city government as a means to exercise control over female servants, who formed a potentially disorderly underclass. The social context in late medieval England was very different. Whereas orphaned girls and the socially destitute, a vulnerable and easily exploitable group, constituted the majority of the Italian servant population, in England of the later fourteenth and early fifteenth centuries servants were of both sexes and were drawn from a variety of social backgrounds.[31] It was not just the sons and daughters of peasant labourers who found positions in the households of lords of manors or prosperous merchants. The children of husbandmen, of artisans, of merchants, and of members of both the lesser and greater aristocracy also went into service, often into households of similar social rank. Whilst in service they ceased to be under the watchful eyes of their parents, but through their work and also during their leisure time would have contact with numbers of others persons, both of their own age and older. As such the female servant would as an adolescent or young adult be exposed to a range of temptations whether from worldly-wise older female servants or from sexually predatory male servants or masters. It was for such women that St Sitha could act as a model and as a protector. But she was perhaps a particularly appropriate model for young women from more well-to-do social backgrounds. Indeed it is striking how frequently St Sitha is encountered in aristocratic primers, as for example the Hastings Hours, or in glass or on tombs. Her attire is regularly that of the aristocratic maiden rather than the poor domestic hireling. She may have had a more plebeian cult following, for whom she was a finder of lost objects, but she also had a mercantile and gentry cult for whom she provides both a model of youthful female conduct that was chaste, pious, and charitable, and of service itself.

There are grounds for believing that life-cycle service was a much more significant part of the culture of English society in the hundred years following the Black Death than was the case prior to the advent of plague.[32] This novel social phenomenon created new needs, both social and spiritual. The appropriation of the imported cult of St Sitha served

---

[31] Richard Smith, 'Geographical Diversity in the Resort to Marriage in Late Medieval Europe', in *Woman is a Worthy Wight*, ed. by Jeremy Goldberg (Stroud: Sutton, 1992), pp. 16–59.

[32] This is a consequence of the increased cost of wage labour, but also the reduced cost of maintenance as a consequence of profound demographic attrition.

these needs in much the same way as the creation and circulation of the bourgeois text 'How the Goodwife Taught her Daughter', which Felicity Riddy has written about elsewhere.[33] In the context of the Bolton Hours then we may thus hypothesize that the mother's devotion to St Sitha is to be explained by her desire for the protection, for the virtue, and for the good name of a daughter in service. St Sitha then is a bridge between mother and daughter. Another striking, though iconographically unconventional depiction, which follows soon after the Trinity page, serves to reinforce this reading.

An important miniature featuring the mother figure is contained in the historiated initial at the beginning of the sequence of penitential psalms, one of the most heavily worn pieces of text within the manuscript. This depicts a woman kneeling before her confessor and may thus have served as a prompt to the sort of meditative piety and examination of conscience for which the book of hours as a whole was a vehicle. Here again we may see a Dominican influence, since friars often acted as confessors to the well-to-do, and friar Nicholas Waterford, the Dominican remembered in Margaret Blackburn's will, may well have so acted.[34] The miniature need not, however, have been a prompt to Margaret alone, since she herself could have used it to instruct daughters who had not yet made confession or for whom confession was a new experience.

The illumination on fol. 35 of the Bolton Hours has caused scholars some confusion. Ker describes it as a Visitation. A post-medieval hand that has annotated a number of the illuminations indicates the same. Scott, however, reads this as St Anne with the Virgin accompanied by two other female saints.[35] It is this last reading that we prefer. The problem is that the standard iconography of St Anne with the Virgin represents the two figures close together, Anne standing over Mary and pointing to the text of the open book in her daughter's hand. It is this standard iconography

[33] Felicity Riddy, 'Mother Knows Best: Reading Social Change in a Courtesy Text', *Speculum*, 71 (1996), 66–86.

[34] See note 8 above. Hughes points to the attention paid to confession in the pastoral literature of the diocese of York in the late fourteenth century, and Margaret's apparently heavy use of this part of the Hours suggests that this message reached a wider audience than that which had direct access to spiritual counsellors of the quality of Rolle and Hilton: Jonathan Hughes, *Pastors and Visionaries: Religion and Secular Life in Late Medieval Yorkshire* (Woodbridge: Boydell Press, 1988) especially, ch. 5.

[35] Neil Ker, *Medieval Manuscripts in British Libraries*, 5 vols (Oxford: Oxford University Press, 1969–) IV, 790; Scott, *Later Gothic Manuscripts*, II, 119.

Illustration 2. St Anne instructing the Virgin with the Holy Spirit above. To the right Mary Cleophas and Mary Salome. York Minster Library MS Add. 2, fol. 35. By kind permission of the Dean and Chapter of York.

that, for example, is contained within the present east window of All Saints, North Street, a memorial to the Blackburn family and one of a number of indications of the very special devotion the family had towards the saint.[36] The illumination here shows two nimbed female figures standing to the right of the scene and a dove, representing the Holy Spirit, descending above the two main figures of a mother and daughter. These two last stand facing one another holding an open book between them. This last element is strikingly similar to the otherwise unambiguous St Anne and Virgin found in Boulogne-sur-Mer, Bibliothèque Municipale MS 93, fol. 26, which uniquely introduces those hours, another probable product of a York workshop.[37]

If the figure to the left of the page is indeed St Anne, then it may be possible to read the two accompanying young female saints, depicted with their hair unbound, as Mary's half-sisters, Mary Cleophas and Mary Salome; in other words this iconography conflates the standard English iconography for St Anne with that of the Holy Kindred. The presence of the dove directly above Mary's womb extends this reading in that it reminds the devout reader meditating before this holy picture that, just as St Sitha was the 'famula Jhesu Christi',[38] so Mary was 'ancilla Dei',[39] the pure maiden chosen to bear the Son of God. Thus if the iconography here mirrors that of the Visitation, it is not a consequence of ignorance of the 'correct' iconography, nor an accidental product of the artist's lack of sophistication of draughtsmanship, but rather it is a deliberate and conscious decision. Such a departure from iconographic norms is very unusual and so may say something about the particular intentions of the person or persons who commissioned the manuscript.

---

[36] Nicholas Blackburn established a family chantry in the chapel of St Anne on the rebuilt Foss Bridge, and may even have influenced the chapel's dedication. Both Nicholas and Margaret specifically name St Anne in the preambles to their wills. Few wills of lay York testators include such additions, though St Anne is also noted (alongside St John the Baptist and St Katherine) in the preambles of Richard Russell (d. 1435) and (alongside SS Anthony, Martin, Richard Scrope, and All Saints) Edmund de la Pole (d. ?1448): BIHR, Prob. Reg. 2 fols 169[v] (de la Pole), 605; 3 fols 415, 439 (Russell).

[37] The representation of St Anne teaching the Virgin in Oxford, Bodleian Library, Lat. liturg. f. 2, a manuscript that may be associated with a local family (see n. 5 above), shows the same arrangement of St Anne to the left (here seated) and the Virgin facing her, the book being held in the middle by mother and daughter (fol. 104[v]).

[38] 'The (female) servant of Jesus Christ'.

[39] 'The handmaid of the Lord'.

The illumination of St Anne and the Virgin on fol. 35 thus shows a mother and daughter as if gently embracing, but with an open book at the centre of that embrace. The book thus becomes symbolic of the relationship between mother and daughter. Through the book the mother is able to provide her daughter with a model of piety and conduct, just as St Anne was herself by the early fifteenth century, when the Hours were made, the very model of the modern devout mother.[40] We know, moreover, that primers were often associated with female owners and were regularly transmitted through the female line. To take our suggestion one stage further, we may see the Bolton Hours as commissioned for a mother and her daughter with the implicit assumption that the book would pass from mother to daughter. Alternatively we can read it as being commissioned by a mother for her daughter, or even, granted that the figures in the family group are generic, not specific, by a mother for her daughters. There are a variety of reasons for preferring this last reading.

Books of Hours or primers regularly contained the Paternoster, the Ave, and the Creed, which all youngsters were supposed to learn by rote. Some even contain an alphabet. This is true of the Bolton Hours.[41] These are followed here by a group of such essential prayers as '*in manus tuas*',

---

[40] Wendy Scase, 'St Anne and the Education of the Virgin: Literary and Artistic Traditions and their Implications', in *England in the Fourteenth Century*, ed. by Nicholas Rogers (Stamford: Paul Watkin, 1993), pp. 81–96; Ton Brandenbarg, 'St Anne and her Family', in *Saints and She-Devils*, ed. by Lène Dresen-Coenders (London: Rubicon Press, 1987), pp. 101–27.

[41] Fols 13–14. The text commences with an historiated initial containing the Holy Face. The alphabet (or 'cross-row') is, as is customary, preceded by a crucifix. Trevisa commences his translation of Bartholomew Anglicus (*On the Properties of Things ... a critical text: John Trevisa's translation of Bartholomaeus Anglicus* De Proprietatibus Rerum, ed. by Michael Seymour, 2 vols (Oxford: Clarendon Press, 1975), I, 40) with the following explanatory verse:

Croys was meed al of reed
In the biggynnynge of my book
That is clepid God me spede.
In the firste lessoun that I took
Than I lerned *a* and *be*
And othir lettres by here names ...

Cf. Marie Denley, 'Elementary Teaching Techniques and Middle English Religious Didactic Writing', in *Langland, the Mystics and the Medieval English Religious Tradition*, ed. by Helen Phillips (Cambridge: D. S. Brewer, 1990), pp. 224, 226.

'*confiteor deo et beate maria*',[42] and the Kyrie. The texts contained in these books thus became a teaching aid for the instruction of young children. Mothers had a particular role to play in the early socialization of their children, including we may presume the most basic elements of religious education, but their instruction of daughters extended beyond early childhood into adolescence. St Anne, whose iconography showed her instructing the Virgin, was the model and exemplar of the devout mother who furnishes religious instruction to her daughter. She also provided a model for instruction through the medium of the book.[43] The image of St Anne contained within a book of hours thus reinforced and valorized the very process of reading with mother for which St Anne and the Virgin were the models. The particular iconography of the Bolton Hours, however, shows not one daughter, but three. Margaret Blackburn appears to have had three daughters, two of whom, Alice, later Alice Bolton, and Isabel, who married Brian Sandford, survived to adulthood.[44] If the manuscript was commissioned for the education of these daughters from an early age, rather than specifically for Alice's use as an adolescent already in service or about to go into service, then it becomes easier to date the manuscript to within only a few years of Richard Scrope's execution. This would make better sense both of the stylistic evidence and of the high profile of the Scrope cult apparent within the manuscript.

The evidence that the manuscript was made for a female member or members of the Blackburn family within a decade of the execution of Archbishop Scrope in 1405 is compelling. Alongside the pantheon of York and regional saints presented, the particular prominence given to the Blackburn family cults of the Trinity, St Cuthbert, and St Anne is striking. Other than the family group before the Trinity, the individuals represented in devotion before St Michael and All Angels, St Sitha, and Richard Scrope are all female. So too is the figure represented in the historiated capital representing confession at the beginning of the Penitential Psalms. Each of these three last miniatures seem to have been much used to judge from signs of wear to the page. St Sitha, as we have shown, may have been a personal devotion of the mother figure, representing Margaret Blackburn, who is shown in prayer before her. The

[42] 'Into Your hands', 'I confess to God and the Blessed Mary'.

[43] Bell, 'Medieval Women Book Owners', pp. 163–65; Scase, 'St Anne and the Education of the Virgin', pp. 94–95.

[44] For Agnes see Jenny Kermode, *Medieval Merchants: York, Beverley and Hull in the Later Middle Ages* (Cambridge: Cambridge University Press, 1998), fig. 1, p. 82.

same is true of St Michael and All Angels, who may here represent the cult of the guardian angel. The daughter figure before Scrope, however, to judge by the associated devotion, may be petitioning the saint on behalf of her family as chaste virgin before martyred patriarch.[45]

We have suggested that the so-called Bolton Hours were made for Margaret Blackburn and have argued that she used this book to teach her daughters. The book then may be evidence for what it was she taught her daughters. In addressing this issue we are also able to suggest a specific context for the commissioning of the hours. One of the distinctive features of the Bolton Hours in visual terms is the series of groupings of full-page miniatures depicting saints. Here a range of overlapping identities could be imparted. Margaret Blackburn's personal devotion to her name saint is indicated by the well-thumbed miniature of St Margaret on fol. 123[v]. As just suggested, a family identity is constructed through the prominence given *inter alia* to the Trinity, St Anne, and St Cuthbert. This last also reflects a regional identity for a family that maintained close links with Richmond (and the North more generally) even after its removal to York. Further Richmond associations may be reflected in the choice of miniatures to St Edmund, St Anthony, and St James, all patrons of chapels within the borough.[46] A York identity comes from the presence of so many saints who were known as patrons of York parishes, hospitals (as in the case of St Leonard), or the Minster, but also from the particular devotion to Richard Scrope. A civic identity follows from the depiction of St William, of St Blaise, and of St Christopher, patron of the confraternity from which the city's ruling group were drawn.[47]

The local and regional saints thus provided both a spiritual genealogy and a family history which might be taught to the Blackburn daughters.

---

[45] The Blackburns as leading regional merchants are likely to have known the martyred archbishop. His rebellion enjoyed especial support within York and bills were posted on churches in York and the surrounding region which denounced the oppression of merchants. Richard Scrope was also a member of the Masham branch of the Scrope family whose seat lay within Richmondshire. This sense of shared origin and of identity with place is an important feature of the Hours: McNiven, 'The Betrayal', p. 182.

[46] Wenham, 'Chantries, Guilds, Obits', pp. 311–14, 317. York possessed a hospital of St Anthony, but not at this date. None of these saints were patrons of York churches. There was a well associated with St Sitha in Richmond and the borough's principal chapel was dedicated to Holy Trinity.

[47] Sarah Rees Jones, 'York's Civic Administration, 1354–1464', in *The Government of Medieval York*, ed. by Sarah Rees Jones, Borthwick Studies in History, 3 (York: Borthwick Institute of Historical Research, 1997), pp. 137–38.

Their representation in the Hours created the family as one with deep and widespread roots within the region and so lent them the ancestry and connections they so patently lacked in reality. Besides this testimony to stability, conservatism, and the values associated with the prud'homme, there are also more up-to-date and innovatory elements to the manuscript. Most of these probably derive from Nicholas Blackburn's close associations with the Richmondshire gentry, and so reflect those associations, and at the same time signal the Blackburns' own social aspirations as members of a mercantile élite.[48] This is perhaps true of the family devotion to St Anne, to whom, for example, the chapel of the newly built Scrope castle at Castle Bolton was dedicated.[49] Devotions to the Holy Name of Jesus were likewise known to the Richmondshire gentry through the work of Richard Rolle and subsequently Walter Hilton.[50] The cult of St Sitha may also have been aristocratic in origin, but the most telling,[51] and most innovatory adoption of an aristocratic devotion is that St Bridget of Sweden. Her revelations are known to have

---

[48] We may speculate that the daughters may have been intended to spend time as servants in the households of local gentry. There is circumstantial evidence that Alice Blackburn had served Maud, Countess of Cambridge, since she was left a bequest of £20 against the marriage of one of her daughters. If so, then we speculate further that Alice was in service when Maud was still married to her first husband, John Neville, Lord Latimer of Danby Castle (Yorks., N.R.). She was the sister of William Clifford, one of Northumberland's principal supporters at the time of the 1405 revolt. She married in or before 1406, but the marriage was subsequently annulled on the grounds of his impotence and she married soon after Richard Plantagenet, created Earl of Cambridge about the same time. He was executed a year later (1415) for his role in the Southampton plot: *Testamenta Eboracensia* II, ed. by J. Raine, Surtees Society, 30 (1855), 119, 122; George Cokayne, *The Complete Peerage*, 13 vols (London: St Catherine Press, 1910–40), II, 494; VII, 476; McNiven, 'The Betrayal', p. 191.

[49] The chapel was dedicated in 1399.

[50] The Scropes of Masham, the FitzHughs, and the Stapletons of Bedale all shared an interest in the works of Rolle. The cult of the Holy Name of Jesus seems otherwise to have been established only in the early fifteenth century and not to have achieved popularity until the half century before the Reformation. Interestingly one of the earliest manifestations of the cult may have been the foundation of a chapel in honour of the Holy Name by Richard Scrope whilst bishop of Lichfield: Hughes, *Pastors and Visionaries*, pp. 86–88, 91; Richard Pfaff, *New Liturgical Feasts in Later Medieval England* (Oxford: Clarendon Press, 1970), pp. 62–67, 71–83.

[51] The rededication in 1407 of a chapel with associated relics at Eagle (Lincs.) to St Sitha may be an indication of just how fashionable she was at the time of the creation of the Bolton Hours. Patronage by the Hospitallers here and at St Thomas of Acon, London again suggest aristocratic associations: Sutcliffe, 'Cult of St Sitha', pp. 84–85.

circulated in England from the end of the fourteenth century. Her cult appears to have been particularly championed by Henry, Lord FitzHugh of Ravensworth, a leading figure among the Richmondshire gentry and related also to Richard Scrope.[52] He had visited Vadstena in 1406 to arrange the marriage of Henry IV's daughter, Princess Philippa to the then king of Sweden and subsequently brought some brothers of the Bridgettine order to his manor of Cherry Hinton (Cambs.). Together with his brother-in-law Henry, Lord Scrope of Masham he attempted abortively to establish a Bridgettine house in York, possibly as part of a project for the expiation of Henry IV's sins for the judicial murder of Richard Scrope.[53]

For a 'woman's book', however, the Bolton Hours does not contain many female saints, particularly virgin martyrs, whom Margaret Blackburn might otherwise have been expected to hold up as examples to her daughters. This may be because the manuscript shows comparatively few signs of the imitatory piety we have come to associate with devout laywomen. There are the miniatures of the Five Wounds, a devotion associated with Scrope, the Instruments of the Passion, the Buffeting, and the Deposition, which together with the Crucifix-Trinity suggest a devotion to the suffering Christ. The miniature of the Name of Jesus (fol. 4^v) that originally opened the manuscript seems, however, too clean to have been much used and may suggest that this novel and aristocratic devotion failed to have any great impact on Margaret.[54] Although there are indications of some direct identification between the manuscript's users and other miniatures, particularly in the case of St Anne shown with her three daughters or even in the case of St Bridget, likewise a married woman and the mother of an exemplary daughter, in general the saints

---

[52] Henry FitzHugh, Richard Scrope's nephew, would have been known to the Blackburns; between 1388 and 1395 he leased the Honour of Richmond, including Richmond castle, confiscated from John, Duke of Brittany: Cokayne, *Complete Peerage*, V, 421–25. Elizabeth, Lady FitzHugh was herself an exemplar of a pious lady who provided her daughters with books of hours: Carol M. Meale, "'... alle the bokes that I haue of latyn, englisch, and frensch": Laywomen and their Books in Late Medieval England', in *Women and Literature in Britain, 1150–1500*, ed. by Carol M. Meale (Cambridge: Cambridge University Press, 1993), pp. 130–31.

[53] This came eventually with the foundation of Syon. Hughes, *Pastors and Visionaries*, p. 75; David Knowles, *Religious Orders in England* (Cambridge: Cambridge University Press, 1957), II, 175–77.

[54] This may suggest a tension between the devotional needs of those who commissioned the manuscript and the aspirations of the Dominicans who were involved in its production.

here appear to have been understood primarily as protective and intercessory.[55] Hence it is Margaret Blackburn and not a daughter who kneels before St Sitha; it is the mother who seeks protection for her child, rather than the daughter, a potential servant, who identifies with St Sitha as her ideal role-model.

We may understand this in terms of the multiple functions of the Hours. It was a devotional aid and educational tool for Margaret Blackburn and her daughters. It was also a prestige object designed to impress. This is reflected in the unusual proliferation of illumination and the very extensive use of gold leaf. As a show object it served to demonstrate not just Margaret's piety, but also her status as the wife of a leading York merchant and member of the city's ruling élite. Indeed Nicholas Blackburn's election to the mayoralty in 1412 may even provide a specific context for the commissioning of the manuscript. In this respect the choice of York craftsmen, and hence the creation of a distinctively provincial production, may not represent a lack of aesthetic sophistication or wealth on the part of Margaret Blackburn or her spouse, but a very deliberate choice. It may be noted finally that Alice Bolton (née Blackburn) learned well the lessons her mother taught her, for it would appear that, whilst managing a large household of six children, she took in her widowed mother during her last years.[56]

---

[55] The miniature of St Bridget with scroll labelled *Ecce sponsa Christi* ('Behold the bride of Christ') shows signs of frequent use. She was a singularly appropriate model for Margaret Blackburn to use with her daughters. Bridget was mother to eight children, one of whom, Katherine (Karin), joined her in Rome and subsequently took her body back to Sweden. Katherine was later regarded as the first abbess of Vadstena. The order that Bridget founded quickly earned a reputation for piety and strictness of enclosure which contrasts markedly with that of other houses of nuns as reflected in contemporary visitation material or the poem 'Why I Can't be a Nun' (printed in *Six Ecclesiastical Satires*, ed. by James Dean (Kalamazoo: Medieval Institute Publications, Western Michigan University, 1991), pp. 231–42).

[56] The codicil to Margaret Blackburn's will was made 'in a certain high chamber by the upper part of the hall of the residence of John Bolton [...] in the street called Skeldergate'. Nicholas Blackburn in his own will had desired that his widow be provided 'with the means to live like a gentlewoman ['to fynde hyrre of a gentels Woman lyfolade] so long as she lives and a priest and a servant': BIHR Prob. Reg. 2 fol. 605, 3 fol. 417.

'A Fulle Wyse Gentyl-Woman of Fraunce': *The Epistle of Othea* and Later Medieval English Literary Culture

DOUGLAS GRAY

Although Christine de Pisan's *Epistre d'Othéa la déesse à Hector* (*c.* 1400) is not well known to her modern admirers, it seems to have pleased its medieval readers greatly. The French text survives in over forty manuscripts, together with a number of early sixteenth-century prints.[1] No fewer than three translations of it were made for English readers: that of Stephen Scrope (d. 1472), the stepson of Sir John Fastolf (1380–1459), the famous English captain in the last phase of the Hundred Years War; a version (second half of fifteenth century?) in London, British Library, MS Harley 838 attributed to Anthony Babyngton; and 'the C. Hystories of Troye' translated and printed by Robert Wyer (*c.* 1540). For reasons of space I will confine my discussion to the Scrope translation, which has been well edited by Curt F. Bühler.[2] It seems likely to have been made between 1440–59 and dedicated first to Fastolf (a dedication which is preserved in the version in Longleat MS 253). It was subsequently dedicated to Humphrey Stafford, Duke of Buckingham (d. 1460), in the St John's Cambridge MS copy which was perhaps intended for him, and later (in the New York, Pierpont Morgan Library MS), to a 'hye princesse' (unidentified, but perhaps Anne Neville).

---

[1] Gianni Mombello, 'Per un' edizione critica dell' "Epistre Othea" di Christine de Pizan', *Studi Francesi*, 24 (1964), 401–17, and 25 (1965), 1–12.

[2] *Stephen Scrope. The Epistle of Othea*, ed. by Curt F. Bühler, EETS OS 264 (London: Oxford University Press, 1970). For the other English translations, and a discussion of the date and dedications of Scrope's version, see the Introduction.

The *Epistle of Othea* makes us look again at some areas of literary culture in the later Middle Ages which modern presuppositions and tastes have caused us to neglect. Most obviously, Christine's book and its English versions are examples of that large and influential tradition of moral, didactic, and encyclopaedic works (like Tignonville's *Dits moraulx des philosophes*, also translated by Scrope as *The Dicts and Sayings of the Philosophers*) which are now almost totally ignored, but which clearly enjoyed a large readership in the Middle Ages.[3] Christine's *Othéa* is an excellent example of the tradition. Like the *Cité des Dames* it is a book of wisdom, and allows her to speak in one of her favourite voices, that of a Lady Philosophy, less rarefied perhaps, but no less instructional, with her own distinctive kind of medieval feminist high seriousness. It is a compilation, from a variety of sources (the *Ovide moralisé*, the *Histoire ancienne*, etc.), but is made into a new and interesting work.[4] She did not write her own name into the text in the way she did in her 'art of war' translated by Caxton as *The boke of the Fayt of Armes and of Chyvalrye* (printed 1489 or 1490),[5] and for those English readers who knew only the translation her authorship of *Othea* was obscured, whether by accident or design. In his Preface to the Longleat MS Scrope seems to think of her as its instigator rather than its author: 'this seyde booke, at the instavnce [entreaty] & praer off a fulle wyse gentyl-woman of Frawnce called Dame Cristine, was compiled & grounded by the famous doctours of the most excellent in clerge [learning] the nobyl Vniuersyte off Paris'.[6] Scrope adapted her dedication to Jean de Berry, and refers to him in this Preface. Possibly, taking her protestation of 'the febilnesse/Of my smalle witte' literally, he was fitting her into a cultural pattern (of a 'wise' lady ordering and sometimes organizing the making of a book of moral instruction) which would have been familiar to him: if so, it would suggest that he was not closely familiar with Christine's literary career. Speculations of a less charitable kind are also possible.

---

[3] *The Dicts and Sayings of the Philosophers*, ed by Curt F. Bühler, EETS OS 211 (London: Oxford University Press, 1941).

[4] P. G. C. Campbell, *L'Epitre d'Othéa: Etude sur les sources de Christine de Pisan* (Paris: Champion, 1924); Bühler, *Othea*, pp. xxvi–xxviii.

[5] *The Book of Fayttes of Armes and of Chyualrye*, ed. by A. T. P. Byles, EETS OS 189 (London: Oxford University Press, 1932).

[6] Bühler, p. 122.

In what follows a number of areas of interest will be singled out, notably the way in which the book's treatment of the mythography and stories of classical antiquity may cast light on late medieval humanism both old and new in France and England; the way in which it blends a kind of humanism with the doctrine of chivalry and the literature of advice to knights and rulers (in the Longleat Preface Scrope entitled it 'The Boke of Knyghthode'); and the way this material is fused with Christian doctrine, faith, and conduct. But first a few general remarks on the nature and form of the book. It is a 'book of wisdom', in the tradition of the didactic letter (cf. that of Aristotle to Alexander), which is both 'ancient' (feigned to be sent from Othea, goddess of Prudence to the hero Hector) and 'modern' (being set within a framework of commentary which explains its contemporary relevance). In scope it is a small pictorial encyclopaedia of ancient mythical lore (from a classicist's point of view, of decidedly uneven quality). In form it has the neat mnemonic structure which Christine liked. One hundred exempla have each a threefold structure: a 'texte' in verse, which sets out, often briefly and allusively, Othea's advice to Hector—

> Resemble nat Jason, that man
> The which thorugh Meede the flees wan
> Of goolde, for the which soone aftirward
> He yaf hir right yvil guerdon & harde (LIV)[7]

—then a 'glose' which gives a fuller prose account of the story in question and applies it to the 'good knight' (in this case, that he should not be ungrateful for goodness that has been shown to him, whether from a lady or any person), and caps it with a 'sentence' from an authority (in this case Hermes); and finally an 'allegorie' in prose which sets out its spiritual significance (here, that the 'good spirit' should not be ungrateful for the benefits it has received from its creator), with one or more 'sentences' from Christian authorities (here, St Bernard and the 'wise man', the author of the biblical book of *Wisdom*). As Rosemond Tuve, one of the few who have paid serious attention to the work (and saw in it valuable material for later allegory), notes, 'the Glose has to do with building a character (preparing the Good Knight to enter the moral tournament of life)', while in 'the simultaneous second reading, the Allegorie...' the 'Good Spirit .. reads in figures the reminder of its true

---

[7] 'Do not be like Jason, that man who won through Medea the golden fleece for which he soon afterwards gave her an evil and cruel repayment'. All quotations are from Bühler's edition: the exempla are indicated by Roman numerals.

condition as a creature, sometimes seeing its need of rescue, often seeing in the figures a repetition of the news of its way of deliverance or some definition of the nature of this deliverance'. The effect is entertainingly like that of the *Ovide moralisé* (from which many of the stories are derived), or Aesop's fables with commentaries, or biblical commentaries or scholastic handbooks of doctrine. Tuve put it well: 'the originality of this use of classical materials is to shape a scheme so thoroughly familiar in the handbooks, for it surprises, provides new realizations of the meaning of old doctrines and mnemonically is quite amusingly efficacious'.[8]

It is indeed attractive as well as uplifting. There is a pleasing mixture of prose and verse, and of different literary types—emblematic verses, narratives in prose, commentaries. It is highly patterned work. The largest pattern consists of the hundred exempla (or 'auctoritees', as they are called in the text), in which the moral teaching is encapsulated, similar to the technique used in the *Cité des Dames*. They are little stories in miniature, and also aphorisms, like those Christine uses in her *Les Enseignemens moraux* and its sequel *Prouverbes moraux* (c. 1402) to educate the young in ethics (this work too was translated into English in the fifteenth century, by Earl Rivers, and printed by Caxton in 1477).[9] The exempla are both positive and negative, so that Hector is advised to follow X (e.g. Mars, Jupiter) or avoid Y (e.g. Venus, Midas, Narcissus). Occasionally the two are combined in one: XXXIX tells him to believe Aesculapius but not Circe. There are smaller patterns within this framework. At the beginning the exempla are arranged in sets—the cardinal virtues (II–V), the seven planets, and other gods (VI ff.); the Seven Deadly Sins (XVI ff); the articles of the faith (XXIII ff.); the ten commandments of the faith (XXXV ff.); but this is not carried through to the end. Later in the book there is the occasional repetition of a main figure (Corinis XLVIII and LII), or of some point made earlier ('Saturne, as I haue seid afore, is a planete hevy and slowe' LI, or 'Leomedon, as I haue seide afore, was king of Troye' LXI).

---

[8]   Rosemond Tuve, *Allegorical Imagery. Some Medieval Books and Their Posterity* (Princeton: Princeton University Press, 1966), pp. 34–41. See also Tuve, 'Notes on the Virtues and Vices', *Journal of the Warburg and Courtauld Institutes*, 26 (1963), 264–303, 27 (1964), 42–72.

[9]   *Morale Prouerbes, composed in French by Christyne de Pisan, translated by the Earl Rivers, and reprinted from the Original Edition of William Caxton, A.D. 1478*, ed. by William Blades (London: Blades, East & Blades, 1859).

The first element of the threefold pattern of the 'auctoritee', the verse
'texte' which is its nucleus, is often emblematic and allusive. Each one is
a 'speaking picture' intended to be accompanied by an illustration, rather
in the way in which fables are sometimes presented. The French work is
in fact an 'illustrated poem' or *Bildgedicht*, a type that was very popular
in the fifteenth century in both France and England.[10] This pattern is
obscured in the manuscripts of Scrope's translation (the St John's MS has
six miniatures, Pierpont Morgan has only three surviving, while Longleat
has spaces left for the illustrations), and readers of the modern printed
edition need to imagine illustrations for the 'textes' (e.g. Orpheus with his
harp and Eurydice at the gates of hell, LXX). Their absence increases an
allusiveness already strongly present (sometimes adding a pleasingly
enigmatic quality): thus XX opens 'In no wise striue with no
frosschis,/Ne defoule the not in theire brothis'; (XLV) 'Knowing that this
Pasiphe was a fool..'; (XXX) 'Be-ware in what place so that it be,/In the
noyse of floytes slepe not ye..'[11]

The 'glose' offers an *expositio ad sensum* which, as well as explaining
the relevance of the 'texte', also gives a brief narrative, making it into a
little fable. These are of uneven literary quality, but some are well told
(e.g. Piramus and Thisbe, XXXVIII; Leander, XLII; Actaeon, LXIX), and
Scrope's prose usually does justice to the material: Pygmalion (XXXII)
'made an ymage after a womman of souereyne beaute. When he had ful
made it, loue, the which subtilli can rauysch hertis, made him to be
amorous vppon the ymage, so that for hire he was vexid with wois of
loue, ful of clamoures and pitous sighynges that he made to it; but the
ymage, which was of ston, vnderstoode him not.'[12]

The 'allegorie', an *expositio ad sententiam*, breaks open the hard shell
of the nut (in the traditional image) and lays bare the sweetness of the
doctrine concealed within it. As often in this type of literature, the

---

[10] Douglas Gray, *Themes and Images in the Medieval English Religious Lyric* (London:
Routledge & Kegan Paul, 1972), pp. 50–55, and *Robert Henryson* (Leiden: Brill, 1979),
pp. 58–62. (Plates 2–7 show examples of illustrated fables, Plate 13 Orpheus and Eurydice
at the gates of hell from a French text of *Othéa*). On the surviving English illustrations, see
Bühler, pp. xiv–xv and references.

[11] XX 'In no way contend with frogs, nor pollute yourself in the waters they inhabit';
XXX 'Be careful wherever you are not to sleep to the sound of flutes'.

[12] XXXII: '[Pygmalion] made a statue representing a woman of surpassing beauty. When
he had completed it, love, which can subtly ravish hearts, made him enamoured of the
statue, so that for its sake he was troubled with the pains of love, full of complaining and
piteous sighings which he made to it, but the statue, which was of stone, did not
understand him.'

interpretation may be clear and obvious (as in the Jason example quoted above, or in the association of Bacchus with gluttony in XXI), but may also be unexpected 'dark' or 'imposed' allegory, of a kind that strikes the modern reader as odd and arbitrary, but which seems to have delighted medieval commentators, and, presumably, their readers. So Actaeon is the true penitent. The 'glose' to the story of Leander (XLII) notes the dangers of 'delite' reasonably enough, but the 'allegorie' rather abruptly turns aside: that a man should not set too much store on his 'plesaunce' is to be understood by the commandment, thou shalt not bear false witness against thy neighbour.

The general moral advice which emerges is usually sensible and down to earth. 'Avaunte the nought' is the moral of the story of Arachne (LXIV); the story of Paris (LXVIII) warns the good knight not to base great enterprises on 'avisiones' [prophetic dreams] or 'lewde illusiones' [vulgar illusions]; that of Piramus (XXXVIII) not to trust that anything is certain until the truth is known—with the somewhat unromantic thought that the good knight should not give faith to a little token. The treatment of love and passion is interesting. Not surprisingly, the good knight should not make Venus his goddess (VII). The example of the virtuous Penthesilea (XV), the Amazon queen who avenged Hector's death 'with a greete hoost of fulle cheuallerous gentilwommen', teaches the good knight to love and praise 'every vertuous persone, and namely a womman strong in vertu of witte and conscience'. He is firmly told, 'Assot the not in loue of straunge kinde' ('Do not become infatuated with a foreign love')—as Achilles did with Polixena (XCIII)—'for be ferre [distant] loues comyth myche harme'. The dangers of excess are illustrated by an especially intriguing example:

> If thou wilt yeve the to Cupido,
> Thin hert and all abaundon hir-to
> Thinke on Cresseidis newfangilnes,
> For hir herte hadde to myche doubilnes (LXXXIV)[13]

Christine knew the story of Briseid only from French sources, but evidently her English translators knew Chaucer's version: Wyer remarks, 'Bryseyde (whom mayster Chaucer calleth Cressayde, in his Boke of Troylus'.[14] (One wonders if this severe view of Briseid/Criseyde had

---

[13] 'If you want to give yourself to Cupid and abandon your heart and everything to her [i.e. your lover], ponder Criseyde's newfangledness, for her heart had too much doubleness.'

[14] Bühler, p. 184. In the 'allegorie' she is vainglory, Christine describes Troilus (LXXX) as 'a childe & the yongist of Priantys sones'.

some part in the general decline in estimation of Chaucer's heroine.) But virtuous love has its place in the education of the knight:

> With Cupido, the yong and the ioly,
> It plesith me that thou queynte the truly.
> The god of batayle it plesith also;
> Yit be good mesure it oughte to be do (XLVII)[15]

and the 'glose' repeats that 'it sittith not much amys for a yonge knyghte to be amorous vppon a wise wurschipfull lady', with moderation. This is supported by 'a philozophre' who says that 'to loue with good corage, it cometh of noblesse of herte' (Cupid is then allegorized as penance). One or two of the 'auctoritees' are rather more permissive than we might expect, like Mars and Venus (LVI):

> If that loue vn-to the make schorte the nyhte,
> Bewar Phebus noye the not with his myht,
> Wherbi thou maist be take and teid
> In Vulcans lyemes and ouer-leid

—though this is taken to signify that a good knight should not be 'overlaid' by forgetfulness of time, and, *allegorice* that the good spirit should keep himself from the watches of the fiend.[16] One of the expositions of Daphne (LXXXVII)—the good knight should pursue Daphne—is 'it myght happe that some myhti man with longe traveil suwed [pursued] a lady, in so myche that with his great pursute he come to his will vndir a laurere [laurel-tree], and for that cause fro thens-forth he loued the laurere & bare it in his deuice [heraldry], in signe of the victorie that he had of his loue vndir the laurere'. Part of the message of Semele (LXII) is also rather worldly: 'If it happe thou be of loue dotid [besotted with love],/Be-ware at the leest to whom thou telle it ...'

The treatment of ancient myth and story quite clearly reflects the older 'medieval humanism' rather than the newer philological humanism of Italy that was slowly spreading into the north.[17] There is much less

---

[15] 'It pleases me that you acquaint yourself in the proper way with Cupid, the young and amorous. It pleases the god of battle too, but it ought to be done in moderation.'

[16] 'If love makes the night short for you, beware lest Phoebus vex you with his power, whereby you may be caught and tied in Vulcan's shackles and captured.'

[17] Douglas Gray, 'Humanism and Humanisms in the Literature of Late Medieval England', in *Italy and the English Renaissance*, ed. by Sergio Rossi and Dianella Savoia (Milan: Unicopli, 1989), pp. 25–44.

insistence on the difference between the ancient and the contemporary worlds. The ancient heroes and places are 'medievalized' (just as they were in their appearance by contemporary Northern artists), and the strange is made familiar: Ulixes is 'a baron of Grece' (LXXXIII); Ajax is 'a good knyht of his hande' [valorous] (XCIV); Minos 'as poetis seyn, is a justicer [judge] of helle, as a prouost or a chef bailie [bailiff], and a-fore him is broughte alle <the soules> descending in-to that valeye' (IV); Ylion is the maister dongeon [chief tower] of Troye' (XCVII). Scrope even transforms the name of Perseus into Percyualle (V, LV).

In one area, that of religion, there is a clear awareness of difference. The ancient poets, we are told, who worshipped many gods, held the planets for gods and named the days of the week after them (VI), and the approach to gods is firmly euhemeristic: since the ancients 'hadde a custom to wurschip all thing which aboue the comune course of thinges had prerogatif [superiority] of some grace, many wise ladies in theire tyme were callid goddesses'; (I). So Minerva 'was a ladi of grete connynge [knowledge] and fonde [discovered] the crafte to make armure' (XIII); Bacchus 'was the man that first planted vynes in Grece; and whanne they of the cuntre felte the strengthe of the wyne, the which made <them> dronken, thei seide that Bacchus was a god' (XXI); and in the reign of Augustus the universal peace was attributed by ignorant people and misbelievers to the emperor's goodness, so that they wanted to worship him as a god - but it really came about because Christ was at that time on earth and as long as he was on earth there was peace over all the world (C).

These ancient errors are taken care of by allegory: 'as yit at that tyme God hadde not openyd the yate [gate] of merci. But we Cristen men and wommen, now at this tyme be the grace of God enlumyned [enlightened] with verrey feith, may bringe ayen to morall mynde [bring back to moral recollection] the opynyones of ancient pepill, and there-vppon many faire allegories may be made.' But Christine's 'textes', though purporting to be addressed to Hector, are also read as addressed to the good knight and the good spirit, and thus once or twice produce apparently odd pieces of exemplary advice: thus, the 'texte' of XXXIII enjoins the reader, 'haunte [frequent] thou the temple and wurschip .. / The goddes of heuene', and in XXXIII the reader is told to 'halowe' [honour] the feast of Neptune. (In both cases the 'glose' offers a discreet correction by way of explanation: 'that is to seye, the chirch and the mynystres thereof', and to 'take a singulere [special] deuotion to some seinte be deuoute prayers'. I suspect that this is not an example of literary awkwardness, but rather of the enthusiastic involvement of 'medieval humanism' with ancient story and its characteristic emotional closeness to it.

The attitude is noticeable throughout the work. The first lines of the first unit of the threefold 'auctoritee' will often directly address Hector and the reader, as in the pattern 'governe thou thi tonge aftir Saturne' (LI). Some examples are more enthusiastically involved and allusive: 'yelde [return] Helaine ayen if asked she be' (XLIII); 'Ayens [against] Amphoras sadde [wise] counsell ../ Go not to distroye ../ To Thebes ne the cite of Arges,/ Assemble noon oste ..' (L); 'kepe the wel fro <the> serpent Gorgon' (LV); 'I sey: go nat to the yatis of helle / For to seke Euridice' (LXX); 'With Athalentas strive thou not now, / For sche hath grettir talent than thow' (LXXII); 'Hate Calcas & his fals deceites' (LXXXI); 'When thou has killid Patroclus, / Ware of Achilles ..' (LXXXV): '.. Take thou good hede of the hors of tre' [wooden horse] (XCVI). Such vivid and often enigmatic openings ensure that the book is never boringly didactic.

The moral advice to the good knight and the good spirit has, as Tuve pointed out, a distinctly 'Spenserian' quality. In both 'glose' and 'allegorie' knighthood (earthly and spiritual) is a constant theme. It is announced at the beginning—'we may calle mankyndli lif verrai chyualrie' ('we may call human life true chivalry') and its equivalent is 'goostli [spiritual] knyghthood' (l)—and is repeated again and again. Perseus was 'a righte good errant myghti knyghte', and 'a good knyght' should follow him and gain 'wurschip' while 'the chivallerous spirite should desire a good name among the saints of heaven' (V). The example of Ceres (XXXIV) teaches the good knight to be 'habundaunte to alle persones and to yeue his helpe and comforte ..'—as Aristotle says, 'be a liberall yeuerre [giver] and thou schalte haue frendes'. He should not be over-trusting in himself but 'schuld doute that he myhte happe amys be some fortune and yet be sympiller than he is' ('should fear that he might fare badly by some turn of fortune and become of more humble rank than he currently is')—as happened to Cyrus, who fell victim to the Amazon queen Thamaris, 'the which was experte & subtill in crafte of armes' (LVII).[18] That Hercules accompanied Theseus and Protheus to Hell (XXVII) shows that 'a good knyghte schulde not fayle his felawe for no maner of perill that myht be'—and so forth.

Sometimes the advice is specifically military: the good knight should not be deceived by his enemies (as the Trojans under Laomedon were,

---

[18] As Bühler (p. 166) points out, this seems to have been a favourite story of Christine's; cf. *Cité* 1, 17, 2–3.

LXVI); Paris was not 'condicioned' to arms but to love (LXXXV), and so
the good knight 'scholde not make a cheuentayne [chieftain] of <his ost,
ne> of his bataillis, a knyht the which is not apte to armys' (with a
supporting quotation from Aristotle to Alexander): he should take care
not to be deprived of his arms in battle (XCI). Christine of course knew
something of the art of war. Sometimes the advice concerns the duties of
a ruler—the material used in advice to knights often overlaps with that in
advice to princes. In *Othea* this is specifically marked in those early
examples which illustrate the cardinal virtues, which are, it is said
explicitly, 'necessarie to good policie' (I). Thus in IV it is said of justice
'.. if soo be thou wilte thiself enhaunce,/ To kepe trewe justice thou most
the avaunce./ Ellis arte not wurthi an helme to were / Ne for to gouerne a
reaume nowhere'.[19] And the 'allegorie' insists that it is necessary to 'the
chyualerous spirit that wil come to the victorious blisse', citing St
Bernard on his duties to three 'maner of pepil'—to 'thi souerayne, thi
fellawe and thi subiecte'. Later, in the 'glose' to Memnon (XXXVI), the
remark that 'every prince and good knyghte which hath kyn, be thei neuer
so litill or pore, so he be good and trewe, he schulde loue him [them] and
supporte him [them] in his dedis, and in especiall whan he felith him
[them] trewe to him. And it happith som tyme that a grete prince is bettir
loued and more trewli of his poore kyn than of a ful myghti man' could
come straight from a 'Mirror' for a prince. I think that this shows the
flexible nature of the material in books of wisdom, and how the pervasive
'advice to princes' type of literature can be used in different contexts.

Othea seems to have interested a fairly wide range of readers. Its
various dedicatees are a rather grand group—Jean de Berry, Fastolf,
Buckingham and the 'hye princesse'—and the French 'Le traittie Othea'
appears in a splendid manuscript (London, British Library, MS Royal 14
E.ii) made at Bruges for Edward IV. Yet its readers were not restricted to
these circles. John Paston II possessed 'a boke de Othea, text and glose'
and presumably the Wyer printed version reached an even wider
audience.[20] Scrope's Preface in the Longleat MS addressed to Fastolf
(which says that he undertook the translation 'be the suffraunce off yowre
noble and good ffadyrhode & by yowre commaundementes'), having

---

[19] 'If it is the case that you want to exalt yourself, you must put yourself forward to keep
true justice. Otherwise you are unworthy to wear a helm or to govern a kingdom
anywhere.'

[20] *Paston Letters and Papers of the Fifteenth Century*, ed. by Norman Davis (Oxford:
Clarendon Press, 1971), I, p. 518.

praised Fastolf's knightly deeds, draws attention to the book's religious content, and seems to suggest a potentially wide appeal: 'ye schal fynde here .. how and in whatte maner ye, and all othir off whatte astate, condicion or degree he be off, may welle be called a knyght that ouercomyth and conqveryth hys gostly ennemys by the safegard repuignand defence off hys sovle'.[21] The translation's immediate context is that circle connected with Fastolf, which included his secretary William Worcestre, who later was probably Scrope's literary executor, and who also wrote works for Fastolf (the *Boke of Noblesse* and a translation of Laurent de Premierfait's translation of Cicero's *De senectute*). It is a group which forms part of a long and interesting East Anglian literary culture in the fifteenth century, a group both local and with wider interests in London and Europe, interested in the ancient past and in the contemporary world.

The reasons for the apparently wide appeal of *Othea* are not as easy to identify as one might think. Curt Bühler says that 'the chief virtue (and claim to fame) of Scrope's *Othea* is that it epitomizes the culture of the noble and wealthy classes of mid-fifteenth-century England, though no trace of that humanism so soon to flourish can be discovered in this translation' (*Epistle*, p. xxxii, n. 1). This seems to me to underestimate its quality and to be curiously defensive. It is perfectly true that it has no trace of the newer humanism spreading from Italy, the influence of which is clearly present in the two translations by John Tiptoft, Earl of Worcester, which were printed by Caxton along with William Worcestre's 'Tully of Old Age'.[22] No doubt a later English humanist would have thought that Christine's sources were 'blotterature' rather than literature, and the author of the *Letters of Obscure Men* wold have made merry at the expense of her 'allegories'. But it is important to remember that the 'new learning', although of obvious significance, was not the only intellectual strand in late medieval culture, nor did it flourish in isolation. The older patterns of 'medieval humanism' lived on,

---

[21] 'You will find here... how and in what way you, and any other of whatever rank, condition, or degree he may be, may properly be called a knight if he overcomes and conquers his spiritual enemies by the protective and resisting defence of his soul' (Bühler, *Epistle*, p. 122/23–28).

[22] Douglas Gray, 'Some Pre-Elizabethan Examples of an Elizabethan Art', in *England and the Continental Renaissance: Essays in Honour of J. B. Trapp,* ed. by Edward Chaney and Peter Mack (Woodbridge: Boydell Press, 1990), pp. 27–34.

sometimes ignoring it, sometimes domesticating it or cautiously accepting it. The older patterns were very long-lived. Christine, who is a good example of the older 'humanism', can still speak—like Chaucer, Gower, and Lydgate—to writers and readers in mid-fifteenth-century England. They were mostly not interested in writing a purer Latin but in learning from the ancient world. As McFarlane said of William Worcestre: 'he read the classics as he studied modern authors, to use what they taught him. He was less interested in their manner than in their content. The ancients possessed knowledge he was anxious to learn; it never occurred to him to alter his Latin prose in imitation of theirs'.[23] And at the end of the century in France Molinet's *Roman de la Rose moralisé* with its spiritual 'moralités' sometimes allegorizes the ancient heroes in the manner of Othéa.[24]

Othea also cautions us against the simple opposition of 'chivalry' and 'humanism' as rival intellectual systems. In it the older kind of humanism is blended with the doctrine of chivalry and the literature of advice to knights and rulers (in the Longleat Preface Scrope entitled it 'The Boke of Knyghthode', and refers to it also as this 'Boke off Cheuallry'). Worcestre's *Boke of Noblesse* is a much more propagandist work, urging (as the old warrior Fastolf would) the English claim to France, and celebrating earlier English triumphs and heroes - but the ancient world is also drafted into service, and the sections containing ancient exempla (such as Hector) are similar to the 'textes' in *Othea*.[25] Even in Italy, in the midst of the 'new learning', at Mantova, where the Gonzaga library included French *chansons de geste* and romances, Pisanello made 'sinopie' with Arthurian and chivalric themes to glorify the ruler.[26]

That a deeply pious Christianity was characteristic of much northern 'new learning' is not in question. This was often as marked in the case of the older humanism, where there is often a humane piety, with an emphasis on individuals and human experience as a means of knowing

[23] K. B. McFarlane, 'William Worcester: A Preliminary Survey', in *Studies Presented to Sir Hilary Jenkinson*, ed. by J. Conway Davis (Oxford: Clarendon Press, 1957), p. 214.

[24] Three examples are included in *Fleurs de Rhétorique*, ed. by Kathleen Chesney (Oxford: Blackwell, 1950), pp. 16–21.

[25] *The Boke of Noblesse*, ed. by J. G. Nicholas, (London: Oxford University Press, 1860): e.g. on 'the noblesse of Ectour and other mighty kinges of Grece', pp. 20–21.

[26] G. Paccagnini, *Pisanello e il ciclo cavalleresco di Mantova* (Milan: Electa, 1972; trans. by Jane Carroll (London: Phaidon, 1973); R. M. Ruggieri, *L'umanesimo cavalleresco italiano: da Dante all' Ariosto* (Naples: Fratelli Conte, 1977).

God, and on self-knowledge and friendship, and intellectual order.[27] This is found in the many works on virtue and honour to which *Othéa* and *Othea* so clearly belong, and to which. this book of the 'wise gentle-woman of France', among the several of her works that became available to late medieval English readers, made a particular and influential contribution. It is written with a quiet confidence and pride. A woman, says the final 'auctoritee', advised Augustus, and showed him the vision of the virgin and child; and readers seem to have been in accord with its quotation from 'Hermes': 'be not ashamed to here trouthe & good teching of whom that euer seith it, for trouthe noblith [enobles] him that pronounceth [proclaims] it'.

---

[27] James Simpson, *Sciences and the Self in Medieval Poetry: Alan of Lille's "Anticlaudianus" and John Gower's "Confessio Amantis"*, Cambridge Studies in Medieval Literature 25 (Cambridge: Cambridge University Press, 1995).

Elizabeth Clere: Friend of the Pastons

COLIN RICHMOND

Elizabeth Clere is not prominent in the Paston Letters, but she appears in two of the most often cited and it is clear that she was one of the closest friends of Margaret Mautby and Margaret's husband John Paston I. The first of the two letters was written by Margaret to John Paston I from Norwich on Friday 20 April 1453:

> As for tydyngys, the Quene come in-to this town on Tewysday last past after none and abode here tyll itt was Thursday iij after none, and she sent after my cosyn Elysabeth Clere be Sharynborn to come to here. And she durst not dysabey here commandment, and come to here. And when she come in the Quenys presens the Quene made ryght meche of here, and desyrid here to have an hosbond, the which ye shall know of here-after... The Quene was right well pleasid wyth here answere, and reportyht of here in the best wyse, and seyth be here trowth she sey no jantylwomman syn she come into Norffolk that she lykyth better than she doth here.[1]

Queen Margaret of Anjou was three months pregnant, which may have been one reason why her mind was running on marriage. There were, however, other reasons. Margaret was 'an indefatigable patron',[2] who wished to see married off not only her household esquires, but eligible widows too, like Elizabeth Clere whose husband Robert had died in 1446, or Jane Carew whose husband Sir Nicholas had died in 1447 and to

---

[1] *Paston Letters and Papers of the Fifteenth Century*, ed. by Norman Davis, 2 vols (Oxford: Oxford University Press, 1971–76), I, no. 146.

[2] *Letters of the Queens of England 1100–1547*, ed. by Anne Crawford (Stroud: Sutton, 1994), p. 122.

whom the queen wrote a little thereafter asking her to marry another of her household esquires Thomas Burneby.[3] Both ladies ignored her: Jane Carew married the brother of an earl and Elizabeth Clere never again married anyone: it looks as if she was prevaricating if the queen had been happy with her response. Is it possible that in Elizabeth's case Margaret also had one of her household esquires in mind? The brief passage I have omitted from the quotation reads, 'but as for that, he is non nerrere than he was before'—Margaret Paston knew that Elizabeth had not been entirely frank because she also knew whose name had been canvassed as Elizabeth's second husband and knew Elizabeth did not want him. We do not know who he was; we can only guess. A not unreasonable guess might be one of the queen's esquires, Edmund Clere of Stokesby, a cousin of her late husband.[4] How young a widow Elizabeth was in April 1453 is unknown; as she had four children by Robert Clere, she cannot have been younger than the twenty-three-year-old queen; if the interview was, therefore, a trying one Elizabeth came out of it with flying colours and, so to speak, with her powder dry: she was to remain a widow until her death in 1493.

Margaret Paston ends her letter to John with a further reference to Elizabeth, one which also shows her in an attractive light:

> I pray yow that ye woll do yowr cost on me ayens Witsontyd, that I may have somme thyng for my nekke. When the Quene was here I borowd my cosyn Elysabet Cleris devys, for I durst not for shame go wyth my bedys among so many fresch jantyl- womman as here were at that tym.

What necklace then did Elizabeth wear when she went for her interview? It certainly looks as though Robert Clere had been a less parsimonious husband than was John Paston.

---

[3] *Letters of Queen Margaret of Anjou and Bishop Beckington and others*, ed. by Cecil Monro, Camden Society, LXXXVI (London: published for the Camden Society, 1863), pp. 96–98; letters on the same or a similar theme are at pp. 89–90 and 125.

[4] J. C. Wedgwood, *History of Parliament 1439–1509. Biographies* (London: HMSO, 1936), p. 189, has his descent wrong: he was not the second son of John Clere of Ormesby, which would have made him the brother of Elizabeth's husband Robert, but the third son of Robert Clere of Stokesby. But then Edmund of Stokesby was not the Norfolk MP of 1447; it was Edmund Clere of Ormesby (*History of Parliament. The House of Commons 1386–1421*, ed. by J. S. Roskell, Linda Clark and Carole Rawcliffe, 4 vols (Stroud: Sutton for the History of Parliament Trust, 1992), II, p. 582), or of Caister, which is how he will be styled in this paper.

The second letter is from Elizabeth herself.[5] It was to John and is one of the best known of the whole collection. In it she describes, discusses, suggests, advises, and recommends in what seems to us an engagingly direct manner; it may also have seemed so to John, who rather than burn the letter, as Elizabeth asked him to do, kept it. The topic which impelled her, someone outside the family, to intervene in what was a family matter, *the* family matter, was the chance of a marriage for a much-put-upon Elizabeth Paston. She paints a grim picture of a twenty-year-old daughter physically abused by a mother in her late forties, for there is no other way of reading: 'And sche hath son Esterne [since Easter] the most part be betyn onys in the weke or twyes, and som tyme twyes on o day, and hir hed broken in to or thre places'. The urgency of the need to write such a letter, whose discovery to the strong-armed mother Agnes Paston its writer justifiably feared would lose her a good friend's love, was occasioned also by the pressing thought that a suitor for Elizabeth might be lost.[6] In appealing to a brother to be brotherly, Elizabeth Clere was not demanding that he intervene to stop his mother beating up his sister, but that he stop the suitor getting away. Not that Stephen Scrope was on any sort of hook. It is usually thought that it is a measure of Elizabeth Clere's concern for Elizabeth Paston that she urges on John so unlikely a candidate as the fifty-year-old ex-soldier turned writer, particularly in the light of our knowledge that she, exactly like her friend Agnes Paston, preferred thirty-five years of widowhood to another husband. We have almost talked ourselves into the idea that she is saying any man will do to get Elizabeth Paston out of the terrible predicament she is in. On the contrary, she says that is what might happen if the opportunity of a good candidate, like Stephen Scrope, is let slip.

What the second letter reveals is Elizabeth's commitment to her friends, her loving concern for one of them in distress, her risk-taking—women did not often write to men who were neither their relatives nor servants in such a manner (and with such brio)—and that she had a good head for business, for she is as well-informed on Stephen Scrope's landed position as she is knowledgeable about the deplorable situation of Elizabeth Paston. She is not content to be a bystander; she has not averted

---

[5]   Davis II, no. 446. I would like to date this famous letter to 1449, and to the same day, 29 June, as Davis I, no. 18. My reasons for wishing to do so will have to be set out elsewhere.

[6]   Note in this context the letter's last sentence, 'Wretyn in hast on Seynt Peterys Day be candel lyght': Davis II, p. 33.

her face from another's trouble; she has sought to do the right thing. Some, perhaps all, of these qualities, and I do see them as qualities, we shall encounter again. They were, one wants to believe, what endeared her to Margaret and Agnes Paston, for these three women were particularly close.

Elizabeth and Agnes both had houses in Norwich; there they dined or had supper together, probably frequently, perhaps regularly; Margaret sometimes joined them or when she was in town had Elizabeth to dine with her on her own. At any rate that was how it was in 1449,[7] and almost certainly throughout the 1450s, when Margaret's surviving letters to John are few and far between and there are no letters at all from Agnes to her eldest son between 1453 and 1461. In the early 1460s the names of Agnes and Elizabeth are linked by Paston correspondents as if the two lived in and out of one another's pockets, Margaret reporting that she had done John's errands to both as if it were a routine matter, and John III with the royal army at Newcastle-upon-Tyne writing to John II to 'let my grandam and my cosyn Cler have knolage how that I desyiryd yow to let hem have knowlage of the tydyngs in this letyr, for I promysyd for to send them tydyngys'.[8] Both women, not contemporaries but almost contemporary widows, Agnes losing William in 1444 and Elizabeth Robert in 1446,[9] had their own view of Paston affairs, in 1462 sending their hopes, along with Margaret's, that John and William Worcester would be reconciled, and a few months earlier Elizabeth, 'and othere that be yowr frendes', advising him 'that it is right necessary for you to have Hew of Fen to be yowr frende in yowr materes'.[10] It is a simple measure of Elizabeth as the

---

[7] Davis I, p. 233; Davis II, pp. 30–31.

[8] Davis I, pp. 284, 524. It is testimony to the closeness of the two that in 1451 when John Wyndham wanted to learn what Agnes was up to he went to Elizabeth Clere to try to find out: Davis I, pp. 67–68. Compare Elizabeth's casual manner of reminding John Paston of his mother's wishes, casual because they were all used to this way of doing things: Davis II, p. 97, lines 27–28 and 31–32.

[9] Agnes married in 1420, probably aged 18, was 42 when she was widowed in 1444; Elizabeth was married in 1434, for which see below, but at what age is uncertain; in 1410 her parents had a son, for whom also see below, but there was no mention of her at that date; if we assume Elizabeth was also about 18 when she was married then she was a widow of 30 in 1446. In that year Margaret Paston was 24: Colin Richmond, *The Paston Family in the Fifteenth Century: The First Phase* (Cambridge: Cambridge University Press, 1990), p. 120. There was, therefore, a difference in age between the three women when their friendship developed in the second half of the 1440s: Agnes was in her mid-forties, Elizabeth was about 30, and Margaret in her mid-twenties.

[10] Davis I, pp. 275, 281. For 'Hew of Fen', see Roger Virgoe, 'The Will of Hugh Atte Fenne, 1476', *Norfolk Record Society*, 56 (1991), 31–57, and Colin Richmond, *The Paston*

Paston family friend that William II in London in 1454 closes his letters to his brother John I with remembrances to 'myn suster' Margaret and 'myn cosyn Elyzabet Clere',[11] and a more profound one that she bursts into tears in August 1465 because John Paston, in the Fleet prison and during the darkest days of his misfortunes, has heard she has been unfriendly, as Margaret wrote to John: 'She sayth she wote well such langage as hath be reportyd to you of here othere-wyse then she hath deservyd causyth you to be othere-wyse to here then ye shold be. She had to me thys langage wypyng'.[12]

Even more to the point (of friendship) was Elizabeth's willingness to lend to the Pastons in the time of their direst financial need. Nor were the sums paltry: 100 marks sometime before November 1471, £40 in October 1474, and probably a further £100 in the same year. Nor did she and her affable and accommodating son and heir Robert press for repayment, not in Elizabeth's case until another friend of hers having 'lost better than ccc marc... sent to here for money', and Elizabeth being Elizabeth wanting to help out but not having money to hand wrote to Margaret asking for her 100 marks.[13] The generosity of the Cleres to the Pastons needs to be noted: in the first place that it was Elizabeth Clere whom the family turned to, and in the second that she responded in the way she did. Margaret, it might be argued, had no one else to turn to on behalf of John II, the impecunious head of the family, but if that is the case, how much the greater ought to be our admiration for Elizabeth. She stood by her friends of more than twenty years. Who else did? The lending and borrowing does not seem to have soured relations, as proverbially it is said to, although John II no doubt was peeved in 1478 when his mother held up his Clere cousins to him as models of pious behaviour.[14]

Family in the Fifteenth Century: Fastolf's Will (Cambridge: Cambridge University Press, 1996), pp. 20–21, 145, 188.

[11] Davis I, pp. 154, 156. William III when a child may have been boarded out with Elizabeth; at some point not long after John Paston's death, in a letter to Margaret she reported, 'And as for my litel cosyn your sone is a faire childe and a mery, blissed be God': Davis II, p. 351, lines 2–3.

[12] Davis I, p. 316. I have substituted Agnes for Elizabeth in *Fastolf's Will*, p. 145, where, because I have cited the whole paragraph, careful readers will have noted my howler. A 'mother's tears' were, therefore, only in my imagination; it was a Paston friend, perhaps the family's best friend, who cried.

[13] *Fastolf's Will*, pp. 262 and 266 and references there; the quotation is from Davis I, p. 353.

[14] Davis I, p. 330, lines 10–13.

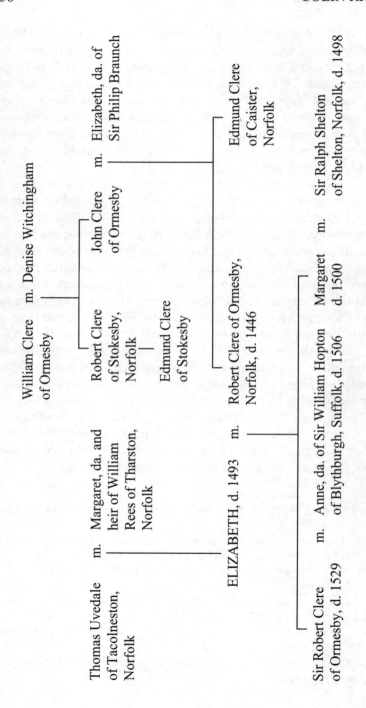

Figure 1. Family tree of Elizabeth Clere.

Paston-Clere relations were not one-sided. John Paston advised and counselled Elizabeth and was probably a member of her council, along with John Heydon and William Jenny.[15] It was to John that she wrote when problems occurred, two specifically. The first concerned the potential over-stocking of a pasture 'called N. lying in the towne of N and longyng to the manor of the same towne', which, unless Elizabeth was wanting to conceal the identity of the place, seems likely to have been Norwich, from where she was almost certainly writing. Hitherto she and her tenants had pastured their animals on the hundred-acre common; now, however, it was being proposed that an old custom be revived and that 'the comoun heerde of the seide towne schuld bryng into the seid pasture his beestys on Lammesse Day to pasturen... And fro that tyme tyl Candelmesse thei seyn that thei wil kepe theron here schepe'; in consequence, Elizabeth and her tenants would have to make shift elsewhere: 'I must put a-wey my takke [the animals of her tenants] and may not kepe there myn owen bestys but if I schuld lese hem for defawt of mete, for the comoun bestys schulde over charge the seide pasture'. Would Paston see to this being discussed 'among lerned men' so that when 'ye come hoom... I may be in very certeynté how I may best be rewled in this mateer', as she had been informed that the new arrangement was to begin at the next Lammas Day, that is 1 August. Elizabeth wrote on 25 May but in which year is entirely obscure.[16]

The second issue on which Elizabeth asked John's advice was her quarrel with the Stewardsons, father and son, William and William junior. Their dispute reached the Court of Chancery in 1451 and was still at issue there in 1454.[17] The letter is long and in its first part offers almost as vivid a picture of her confrontation with one of the Stewardsons in church as does Agnes in a letter of about the same time of hers with

---

[15] For the last two as members of her council, see Davis II, p. 200, lines 40–42.

[16] Davis II, no. 500.

[17] See the memoranda on PRO, Early Chancery Proceedings, C1/18/205a and C1/24/146, appointment of mainpernors for the parties, in the first instance William Lomnour and William White of Norfolk esquires on 17 February 1451 for Elizabeth, and in the second Brian Stapleton of Happisburgh [Hawesborough], Norfolk, and Thomas Warde of Westminster gentlemen on 23 May 1454 for William Stewardson. William White was in the household of John Kemp, Archbishop and Chancellor 1450–1454, and an associate of the Pastons for twenty years or more; for him, see Davis II, sub index, especially I, pp. 58, 170, and the address of II, no. 454; Thomas Dennis in March 1451 said bluntly and with approval, 'He is a gentleman': Davis II, p. 69. To this gentleman and his daughters Elizabeth was deeply attached: as we shall see from her will.

Waryn Herman.[18] No doubt Stewardson and Herman were of similar
status and similar disposition: bloody-minded husbandmen (or yeomen)
who were not going to be put upon by the gentry. Here is the scene in
Ormesby St Margaret church one Easter Saturday in the early 1450s:

> Like it you to wete that Stywardesson came to me on Esterne Even to
> chirch and preide me to be his good mastras, and wold put hym-self in my
> rewle to do as I bidde hym; trustyng, he seid, that I wold take hym to grace
> the rather for his submyssion, for if Judas, he seid, wold an asked grace of
> God he schuld an had it, and for his sake that I had receyved that day that I
> wold take his submyssion. And I lete hym wete that I was in charité, for I
> wold to hym no bodily harm, and I seid if a theef come and robbed me of
> al the good I have on the today and come and asked me for-yifnesse on the
> tothyr day, were it reason that I schuld for-yeve it without satisfaccion?
> And he seid nay.

There are another twenty lines of similar exchanges before they are
through. What was it all about?

It was about a small property in Ormesby, which Elizabeth claimed she
had first option on when it was sold (and duly took), and which the
Stewardsons argued had been legitimately disposed of to William
Stewardson junior. If Elizabeth is to be believed, her opponents forcibly
carried off from the house on the property Thomas Green, the seller,
bound him on a horse, menaced him with a dagger, threatened that they
would 'shete hym thowh' if he did not do as they wanted, and took him to
Islington [Iseldon], where their sister, who had murdered her husband,
lived with 'her paramour'. There he was kept for three weeks before
being taken to London to be shown men fettered and collared with iron
and told that he would suffer the same fate if he did not seal the
documents of sale; he was then brought before a master with a 'furrid
hood', whom afterwards he learned was a Master in Chancery, and duly
sealed, as he also discovered later, a release of all actions against William
Stewardson the younger and an obligation of £20 that Elizabeth would
not implead the Stewardsons either for the property or for their trespass.[19]
That done he was dismissed, and William Stewardson 'gaffe hym nother
peny ne halpeny to goo hom with he havyng an C myle to goo on fote

---

[18] Elizabeth's letter is Davis II, no. 600; Agnes's is Davis I, no. 24. For Warin Herman, see
The First Phase, pp. 8–10.

[19] The kidnapping of Thomas Green occurred in late May or at the beginning of June 1451,
as the release and the bond were enrolled on 21–22 June 1451: *CCR 1447–1454*, pp. 271–
72. Isn't this a perfect illustration of what lurks behind the blandness of an official document?

with ought knewlich or frende be the weye'.[20] Whatever the truth of such a *Black Adder* sort of story and of the double-dealing and beating (or threats of it) alleged against Elizabeth by her opponents, endeavours to arbitrate between them were made by Thomas, Lord Scales, who, calling William Stewardson 'a servaunt of myne', wrote to John Paston to urge such a course on Elizabeth.[21] She seems not to have been keen, telling William Stewardson in Ormesby church:

> and if he had come wyth his maister I wold not a spoke with hym, and for his mayntenaunce he schal fare the wers; and if he come to me in the begynnyng or the lawe was attamed I wold a mad therin an ende my-self... And I seid his maister schuld leve his mayntenaunce, wherof I schuld have right good suerté or ellys we schuld not go thorgh esyly.

What happened, of course, we do not know. Given what is known of Thomas, Lord Scales on one hand, and what we have so far learned of Elizabeth Clere on the other, it is Elizabeth's side we are likely to take: she, it seems most likely, was the injured party.

But: who was Elizabeth Clere? The first thing that needs to be said is that she was no more a Clere than Margaret Paston was a Paston. Margaret was an out-and-out Mautby, probably because she was the Mautby heiress; Elizabeth was almost as thoroughgoing an Uvedale, as she was the Uvedale heiress. I have said 'almost' for two reasons. First,

---

[20] PRO, C1/19/474, 477, 478. The other documents in the case, besides C1/19/475–6 (the Stewardson replications), are C1/18/203–5 and C1/24/146: the latter is a Stewardson petition which sets out the familiar story of the suborning of a feoffee, in this instance, William Stewardson contends, by Elizabeth Clere. The two Stewardsons had been amerced for trespass in the manor court at Ormesby; they countered by impleading Thomas Green for the same offence in King's Bench in Trinity Term 1452, but did not take the case further, for which see Roger Virgoe's notes on PRO, KB 27/765, rot. 39d, in his file on the Clere family: it is owing to the generosity of Roger Virgoe's widow, Norma, that the extensive collection of material on Norfolk gentry families, which Roger had spent more than thirty years accumulating, is for the time being in my possession. Elizabeth also distrained on William Stewardson's own land and wrote to John Paston to learn whether she had been entitled to do so: Davis II, no. 600, lines 45–46. William certainly held a little land from Elizabeth in Ormesby, an acre and three roods to be precise, at a rent of 11d per annum; Richard Wells of Scratby granted her the property, rent, and William's fealty on 10 September 1454: *Cal. Anc. Deeds* IV, A7809. The three witnesses to the transaction were John Paston, Edmund Clere of Horninghall in Caister, and Edmund Clere of Stokesby. Might this not have been part of the settlement of the trouble, even a pre-condition of it, as it post-dates the last Chancery reference by three months?

[21] Davis II, no. 594.

the Uvedales of Tacolneston, Norfolk, were nowhere near so august a county family as the Mautbys of Mautby, or for that matter the Cleres of Ormesby. Secondly, Elizabeth's relations with her husband Robert Clere, her sons, and her daughter were considerably more amicable and harmonious than Margaret Paston's with her husband, sons, and daughters. The Uvedales, their lands apart, are now virtually anonymous.[22] When Elizabeth Uvedale was married to Robert Clere is not documented, but as Robert held his first court jointly with her at Tacolneston in 1434, that year is surely the year of the marriage.[23] Robert knew what he was getting, or at least we have to assume he did; what was Elizabeth Uvedale taking on?

Not, as it turned out, more than she could chew. Although, more speedily than she can have anticipated, there was much to chew. But, as Robert on his premature death in 1446 left all his lands to her for life unconditionally and trusted her with the upkeep of their children, also without conditions, 'having full confidence that if they bore themselves well and humbly to her she would maintain them becomingly', we are bound to assert that he got a very good woman in 1434 and knew it, or that he loved her dearly, or both.[24] Robert is likely to have been much older than Elizabeth, which might have aided her affinity with Agnes Paston (also only half her husband's age) as Robert's parents, John Clere of Ormesby and Elizabeth Braunch, daughter of Philip Braunch, were, it appears, already married in 1389.[25] John Clere was dead by 1415.[26] In September 1422, Ormesby was settled on his widow for life;[27] that was

---

[22] For the landed estate Elizabeth brought to Robert Clere, and its history, see Francis Blomefield *The Topographical History of Norfolk*, 5 vols (Fersfield and Lynn: Whittingham, 1739–75), I, pp. 720–21; III, pp. 44, 108, 204. All four Uvedale estates of Tacolneston, Tharston, Rainthorp Hall in Newton, and the manor of Rusteyn's at Wymondham, are mentioned as being 'of my liflode' in Elizabeth's letter to Margaret written shortly after John's death: Davis II, no. 724.

[23] Blomefield III, p. 108.

[24] *Cal. Anc. Deeds* IV, A7778. Elizabeth's commemoration at Ormesby of the anniversary of her husband's death on the feast of St Peter in Chains [1 August] features in the accounts of that estate, for example, PRO, SC6/942/3, 942/7, 942/8.

[25] *Cal. Anc. Deeds* V, A10438: 'it appears' because there is some doubt about the year.

[26] *The History of Parliament, The House of Commons, 1386–1421*, II, p. 582.

[27] *Cal. Anc. Deeds* IV, A7766. Why then? Confirmation by Robert in April 1430, perhaps when he came of age: *ibid.*, A7640. The first year of Elizabeth's possession of Ormesby, on the death of her mother-in-law, Denise Clere, was 1418–19: PRO, SC6/938/31. This more precisely establishes the date of death of another long-lived widow: William Clere, the husband of Denise, daughter of Sir William Witchingham of Witchingham, Norfolk, had died in 1384.

two years after her second husband, Sir John Rothenhale, had died; the long-living Elizabeth did not die until 1438, so that Robert had to wait some time before he came into possession of Ormesby.[28] Moreover, although in her long and detailed will she was particularly generous to Edmund, her other son by John Clere, Elizabeth was fairly parsimonious where Robert was concerned.[29] Apart from leaving him the household stuff at Ormesby, she bequeathed him no more than a 'pece' called Clarence, with another 'pece', this time of gold, to Elizabeth Clere, his wife.

In a reversal of the usual state of affairs, Robert Clere is a dimmer figure than Elizabeth Uvedale. He was a friend of William Paston I, he and Edmund Clere of Stokesby being associated with William in the initial and crucial stages of the creation of the manor of Paston, and both of them being among William's feoffees.[30] Robert was escheator in 1444 when William died, so was enabled to demonstrate his friendship when the *inquisitions post mortem* were taken in Norfolk and Suffolk in November of that year; indeed, he was as accommodating and as affable as his son Robert was to be twenty years later.[31] He was, as we have already noticed, entirely accommodating as regards Elizabeth when it came to her widowhood; her changed status must have arrived sharply, Robert's will being nuncupative: one of those who testified to it on 3 August 1446 was John Paston.[32] Robert left all his lands to Elizabeth for life and made no provision for his three young sons, William, Thomas, and William, and his daughter Margaret, trusting Elizabeth to see to their upbringing and Margaret's marriage. She was to be sole executrix. What lands did Elizabeth have to support herself and her children, eventually (and perhaps quite shortly) only two of them, William and Thomas dying to leave Robert the sole heir to both his father and mother?

---

[28] The date of her death is established by the Ormesby accounts at the PRO. The account for 1438–39 begins not at Michaelmas, but at All Saints and was the first account of Robert Clere, £99 of arrears being wiped off to give him a clean slate: PRO, SC6/939/13. Elizabeth, therefore, died in the second half of October 1438, her will having been made on 16 October of that year.

[29] NRO, NCC, Reg. Doke, fol. 150ᵛ, dated 16 October 1438, proved 11 July 1441.

[30] *The Paston Letters*, ed. by James Gairdner, 6 vols (London: Chatto and Windus, Library Edition, 1904) II, nos 42 and 48; Davis I, pp. 22–23; *The First Phase*, pp. 3–7.

[31] Davis II, no. 441 and the headnote to no. 437. For William Bondes, the deputy escheator, see *John Hopton*, pp. 196–98.

[32] It is NRO, NCC Reg. Wylbey, fol. 117ᵛ. It was proved in little over a week, on 12 August 1446. It is more accessible in *Cal. Anc. Deeds* IV, A7778.

Besides her own 'liflode, that is to seye Tacolneston, Therston, Reynthorp, [and] Rusteynes in Wymondham', there was Keswick near Norwich and Stratton Strawless between Norwich and Aylsham, which in a letter of 1466 she also includes in 'my liflode'.[33] Keswick and Stratton were two Clere estates left to her for life by her husband, Stratton with remainder to the second son Thomas, Keswick with remainder to the third son Robert. By 1466 Thomas was dead; so was William who had been left the remainder of Ormesby, Winterton, and Freethorp, the three other estates mentioned in her husband's will.[34] In 1464, after the death of her brother-in-law Edmund Clere of Caister,[35] Elizabeth added the two manors of Vaux Hall and Stalham Hall in Burgh St Mary, Norfolk, to the five Clere estates she held;[36] nine years later she settled the two manors on Robert, her son, and his wife Anne, daughter of Sir William Hopton.[37] Elizabeth also bought land: two properties in Winterton and East Somerton (one called Bretons which had been Edmund Clere of Stokesby's, the other called Cookes which had belonged to Thomas Rychers of Somerton) and an estate in [Great] Moulton, Norfolk, formerly William White's.[38] How wealthy a widow her lands made Elizabeth it is impossible to say, but all the indications are that she was certainly better off than her two friends Agnes and Margaret Paston, each of whom as widows had incomes of around £100 a year, and probably that she was far better off than they were.[39]

---

[33] Davis II, no. 724.

[34] She was given seisin of Ormesby promptly: on 20 October 1446 (*Cal. Anc. Deeds* IV, A7774). For the three estates and the Cleres, see Blomefield IV, p. 18; V, pp. 1542, 1569–74.

[35] According to a Roger Virgoe note of NRO, NCC Reg. Jekkys, Administration, fol. 3, administration of Edmund Clere's will was granted to Edmund Clere of Stokesby on 17 April 1463.

[36] See Blomefield, cited in note 34. Her *inquisition post mortem*, naturally enough, reports her as holding no lands whatsoever in Norfolk and Suffolk: *CIPM Henry VII*, I, p. 392.

[37] *Cal. Anc. Deeds* IV, A7760, A7765. It seems likely, therefore, that the marriage took place between January and July 1473.

[38] Elizabeth's will: NRO, NCC Reg. Wolman, fols 133^v, 135. Great Moulton is no distance from Tacolneston and Tharston. For William White, see note 17 above, and for his three daughters, all nuns, see below.

[39] *The First Phase*, pp. 171–72; *Fastolf's Will*, p. 258. The sums named in Elizabeth's will are an indication of her greater wealth: to take a single example, Margaret Paston gave £10 to her son and principal executor, John Paston III, and five marks to each of her other three executors, whereas Elizabeth Clere gave £40 to each of her two executors, her son-in-law Sir Ralph Shelton and Richard Southwell esquire, whom she calls on another occasion, 'my trusted cousin and special friend'.

A little more can be said about Elizabeth as landowner and landlord. We have already noticed her as concerned about the loss of revenue from rights of pasture, attempting, no doubt successfully, to extend her property at Ormesby, and purchasing lands in Winterton, East Somerton, and elsewhere. At Ormesby she seems to have been an improving lady of the manor, entering into two agreements with the tenants, the first in August 1465 rationalizing and consolidating rents and services, the second in January 1466 initiating tenant self-government: they were to choose two or three of their number to settle their differences before resorting to her and the manor court, 'for eschewyng of losses to the common weel of the foreseide tennauntes'.[40] Ormesby was in Norfolk barley country, and Ormesby malt and barley helped make Elizabeth a wealthy woman.[41] The Ormesby estate accounts show that she took a part in the management of the estate and an interest in the sale of its grain, and sometimes its animals, before handing it over to Robert Clere in 1475; in that year Robert took on a forty-year lease, which was still in effect when the accounts come to an end some ten years later.[42]

As a mother Elizabeth seems to have done all that Robert had expected of her. She made, for example, good marriages for her surviving son and daughter. Robert, as we have seen, turned out to be a good man: how much of that was due to his mother's influence it is impossible to know, but clearly she did not spoil him. Robert was married, probably in 1473,

---

[40] *Cal. Anc. Deeds* IV, A6678 (but Roger Virgoe's notes on PRO, E41/24, the original indenture, have 22 August 1461 not 22 August 1465), A7539 (cf. an earlier agreement of 1454: A7769, 7808, 7809, and V, A10098); *Cal. Anc. Deeds* V, A12188.

[41] Robert and Elizabeth Clere lived at Ormesby, so that the accounts dating from Robert's short time there include, although not in detail, household expenses; nonetheless, Robert still sold plenty of malt and barley: PRO, SC6/939/13, 940/2, 940/3, 940/4, 940/5, 940/6. For Ormesby barley, see R. H. Britnell, 'The Occupation of the Land: Eastern England', *The Agrarian History of England and Wales*, III, 1348–1500, ed. by E. Miller (Cambridge: Cambridge University Press, 1991), pp. 61, 63–64; R. H. Britnell, 'The Pastons and their Norfolk', *The Agricultural History Review*, 36 (1988), 132–43 (pp. 133, 138–39).

[42] How active a part a landowner took in estate management manorial accounts seldom reveal. Frequent reference in the Ormesby accounts to the book of the lady, probably a receipt book of some kind as cash liveries were recorded in it, suggests Elizabeth kept her eye on things. The wording of an account of a trading voyage made by John Cok to Holy Island in Summer 1476 suggests that Elizabeth was a principal mover in the enterprise, even at a time when her son Robert had taken on responsibility at Ormesby: the account is added at the foot of the estate accounts of 1475–76, the first year of Robert's forty-year lease (PRO, SC6/942/9), and is fascinating in its own right. It might usefully be published. John Kendall, Elizabeth's receiver-general over a long period, wrote Davis II, no. 768.

to Anne, the daughter of a highly successful career-politician, Sir William Hopton, son and heir of John Hopton of Blythburgh, Suffolk. A little while before that Margaret Paston wondered whether Robert might not be interested in her daughter Anne. Anne had been living in the household of Sir William Calthorpe, but bent upon economy (or so he said) Sir William wished to be rid of her; Margaret continued her letter to John III:[43]

> He seth she waxeth hygh, and it were tyme to purvey here a mariage. I marveyll what causeth hym to write so now: owthere she hath displeased hym or ell he hath takyn here wyth summe diffaught. There-fore I pray you comune wyth my cosyn Clere at London and wete how he is disposyd to here ward, and send me word, for I shall be fayn to send for here and wyth me she shall but lese here tyme; and wyth-ought she wull be the better occupied she shall oftyn tymes meve me and put me in gret unquiete-nesse... Therefore do your parte to help here forth that may be to your wurchep and myn.

There is no doubt that a marriage to the Clere son and heir would have been to the 'wurchep' of the Pastons. It was not to be. It was not until the next generation that a Paston daughter was married to a Clere son, when in 1498 John III's daughter Elizabeth married Robert Clere's son and heir William.[44] There had been talk before that, however, of a marriage between John's son William Paston IV and a daughter of Robert Clere, a man to whom John felt sufficiently close to call brother.[45] In recommend-ing to his brother John the union between the two families, Edmund Paston reveals the great goodwill of Cleres for Pastons: 'I know well this jantylman berythe yow as good mynde as any man alyve, my mastres hys mothere and allso my mastres hys wyve in lyeke wyesse'.[46] Elizabeth, it seems, got on well with her Hopton daughter-in-law, as well as she got on with her son and he with her. Because they did get on well in circumstances much the same as those in which Margaret Paston and her son and heir did not, we have to conclude, and gladly do so, that Elizabeth was as good a mother as she was a woman; as we have already

---

[43] Davis I, p. 348.

[44] *Cal. Anc. Deeds* IV, A7773. The marriage was brief: William died in 1501, on 17 March, according to his brass: Blomefield V, pp. 1576–77.

[45] Twice in one paragraph: Davis I, p. 631. They were both councillors of Elizabeth, duchess of Norfolk: Davis II, no. 835.

[46] Davis I, p. 642.

said: as good a mother and a woman as her son was a good son and a
good man.

A paragraph on Elizabeth's relations with her daughter Margaret, to
whom John Paston sent greetings from Newcastle-on-Tyne in December
1462,[47] will be shorter. Margaret she married to Ralph Shelton esquire of
Shelton, Norfolk, in 1466 or 1467. The wedding took place at Ormesby
and we know who were the most distinguished guests because the
stabling of their horses had to be accounted for: Sir Thomas Brews, I take
it, gave the bride away, while Edmund Bedingfield was the 'best man',
and Thomas Marke, Archdeacon of Norfolk, performed the ceremony.
Provisions for the feast were sought in a variety of places in Norfolk.
What part the nuns of Flixton and Bungay had to play in the marriage-
making, if any, we cannot now determine; they were, however, consulted
by Elizabeth in the course of the accounting year 1466–67.[48] To judge
from Elizabeth's will she was fond both of her daughter and of her
Shelton grandchildren. It is to that will which we finally need to turn.

Elizabeth's will of 13 January 1493 is a model of its kind, its kind
being a wealthy English widow's of the fifteenth century. I do not intend
a comparative study here. Besides, each well-off widow, Thomasin
Hopton say, or Anne Bourgchier, or Margaret Paston, was different from
the next: each was her own woman.[49] Elizabeth Clere was very much
Elizabeth Uvedale. She proclaims that she was in the first line of a will
which runs to nine-and-a-half closely written pages: 'I Elizabeth Clere of
Takelneston'.[50] Having established her identity, she goes on to advertise
her individuality, 'I bewhethe and comende my sowle to my lord god my
maker and savyour etc', which without the 'etc' is a brass-tacks sort of
statement, and with it leaves us pondering an old lady dismissing the
Blessed Virgin and the Saints with an impatient wave of the hand. Let's

---

[47] Davis I, p. 524, lines 54–55.

[48] *Cal. Anc. Deeds* IV, A7885. It was a very local union: Shelton is adjacent to Long
Stratton and no distance from Tharston, both estates of the Rees family; one or other of them
was the former home of Elizabeth's mother Margaret Rees. For the wedding at Ormesby in
1466–67: PRO, SC6/942/1.

[49] Colin Richmond, *John Hopton: A Fifteenth Century Suffolk Gentleman* (Cambridge:
Cambridge University Press, 1981), p. 119ff; 'The Sulyard Papers', *England in the Fifteenth
Century. Proceedings of the 1986 Harlaxton Symposium*, ed. by Daniel Williams
(Woodbridge: Boydell Press, 1987), pp. 199–228 (pp. 214ff). Margaret Paston's will (Davis
I, no. 23) will have to be dealt with at another time.

[50] NRO, NCC Reg. Wolman, fols 131–35ᵛ.

get on with it, we can hear her saying, probably to Robert Stevenson, parson of Tacolneston since 1443, and a very old friend.[51] It was prayers that had to be got on with. Thousands of prayers, Elizabeth intended, were to be offered up on behalf of her soul, her husband's soul, and the souls of her mother and father. At her burial place in the presbytery of Norwich cathedral she had already established a perpetual chantry; by an agreement of 20 May 1478 with the prior and convent a monk was celebrating daily.[52] On the eve of her burial, on the day of her burial, on the seventh day after it and at her month's mind, what seems like all the monks at Norwich, St Benet's at Holm and Bromholm, all the friars of Norfolk, all the nuns of Norfolk and Suffolk, all the priests, choristers, sisters, and poor persons of the hospitals of Norwich, and all the anchors, anchoresses and lepers of Norwich and Yarmouth, were likely to be praying for her departed soul: they were, at any rate, given a generous financial inducement so to do. It should be noted that Elizabeth says not a word about ceremony (let alone ostentation) at her interment, nor about her tomb itself, and nor does she mention the poor attending it. Not for Elizabeth indiscriminate charity or indiscriminate prayers: brisk and businesslike, she knows what she wants, is ready to pay a good price for it, and no doubt anticipated getting it.

Between, so to speak, the eternal, daily, but individual prayer at Norwich cathedral and the communal, immediate, yet temporary prayer of the devout of Norfolk, Elizabeth had made provision as early as 1477 for prayers of a more intense kind to be sustained over a period of two years after her death.[53] Her endowment of these prayers, like that for her perpetual chantry, was to come out of the revenues of her manors of Claydon and Tharston. In 1493 only minor adjustments were made to the provisions of sixteen years before. The profits of Claydon for two years were to provide the salaries (each at £5 6s 8d a year) of three priests, who

---

[51] Appointed rector by her in 1443, says Blomefield III, p. 111; but what of Roger Hayles, rector in 1446, when he was present at Robert Clere's deathbed?

[52] NRO, DCN 4/6: a reference I owe to Roger Virgoe. The endowment was a rent of 66s 8d out of the manors of Claydon and Tharston, the grant of which is dated 16 May 1478 in the will of 1493. The price of the crown's assent to this alienation, it seems to me, was the otherwise curious 'gift' by Elizabeth of an annual rent charge of £20 out of Claydon and Tharston to Richard, duke of York and his wife Anne Mowbray on 27 November 1479: *CCR 1476–1485*, p. 171, another reference I owe to Roger Virgoe.

[53] A will of 17 May 1477 deals solely with the establishment of these prayers: Roger's notes on PRO, Exchequer, T.R. 22/22. The terms are repeated in the will of 1493.

were to pray 'for my sowle and for the sowles of my husbond Robert Clere, Thomas Uvedale my Fadyr, Margarete his wyf my modyr, and all the sowles of myn auncestres and frendes to and for whom I am bounde and beholde to pray fore and for alle christon sowles'. Two of the priests were to celebrate at the altar called Rees's in the Chapel of the College of St Mary in the Fields at Norwich,[54] the third in St Margaret's church at Ormesby 'where my seyd husbond lyethe'. In addition and if the licence could be obtained, Robert Stevenson was to have an annuity of ten marks for life to add to his benefice of Tacolneston, 'he therfore to synge or seye for me and my seyde auncestres and othyr as is above seyd where he wole at his lyberte'. Another seven marks a year was to go to Walter Balle, priest, to celebrate at the College of St Mary for two years in the same fashion as the other two priests, and finally, if the Master of the College agreed to celebrate Elizabeth's mother Margaret's year day during the two years, he was to have 8d, every priest who attended was to have 4d, and every clerk 2d, while two tapers of wax costing 1s were to burn throughout the service. All this was to be funded out of Claydon, whose annual value in 1477 was estimated at just over £27. One year's revenue from Tharston, calculated at a little under £35, was to provide, firstly, for three priests, 'wele disposed and apt to lerne and study... haveing nede and non othyr exhibicion', who were to be salaried at eight marks a year for *two* years at Cambridge, where they were to pray daily for the souls of those named; they, with the other five priests 'hyred and in my salary', were to gather at her tomb to commemorate her year day. Also to remember her year day during the two year period were the monks of St Benet's at Holm and Bromholm, the canons of Langley, all the houses of friars in Norfolk, the nuns of Carrow, Thetford, Bungay, Flixton, Marham, Blackborough, Shouldham, Crabhouse, Redlingfield, and Bruisyard: the two houses of Benedictines and the Premonstratensians of Langley were each to have £1, every convent of friars and nuns 10s.

Plenty of prayers; plenty of remembrance too, much of it for her father and mother, most of it for her mother. Elizabeth also remembered the churches she knew: Winterton; the chapel at East Somerton, of which the Clere family had long had the advowson; Ormesby, both St Margaret and St Michael (£10 towards the making of the steeple at the former and a special gift of two quarters of malt for the latter); Stratton Strawless;

---

[54] This confirms that Elizabeth's mother was Margaret Rees, daughter and heir of William Rees, as Blomefield has it: II, pp. 611–12. For William Rees, see *The History of Parliament. The House of Commons 1386–1421*, IV, pp. 187–89.

Keswick; Tharston (whose steeple got only £1); the neighbouring
churches of Tasburgh and the two Forncetts; and Freethorp. Tacolneston
was honoured with 'an hool vestement of Reed with Flowers of gold
embrowded', while every church 'withinne Flegge' was to have 3s 4d. As
an afterthought, some folios later, the church of Wood Rising was
bequeathed the large sum of 66s 8d.[55]

After churches came charity. It *was* charity: the prayers of those
grateful for Elizabeth's generosity are not mentioned. First, came 'every
pore tennant howsholder in Ormesby... as holdyth hoolly of me'; each
was to have four bushels of malt, or for lack of malt four bushels of
barley, or failing both 1s. For every tenant who held 'party of me and part
of othyr lordshippes' there was to be two bushels or 6d. The corn, or if it
was the shillings and sixpences, was to 'be led hom to their howses', and
delivery was to be made within thirty days of Elizabeth's burial. 'And
thus thurgh al my lordshippes', every quarter, until 200 marks had been
spent. Secondly, it was impecunious students, 'v chyldryn at Cantebrygge
wele entyrd in gramer or they come ther and dysposed to be preestes', to
study there until they were twenty-four years of age on scholarships of
five marks a year, 'and they to be of my kynne or of my tennantes chylder
if eny suche be and if none suche be thenne of Norffolk and Suffolk'.
Thirdly, there were 'vj pore maydenys', each to have 66s 8d towards her
marriage. Fourth and last came the users of the highways on her Norfolk
estates; repairs on the roads were to begin immediately after Elizabeth's
death until 100 marks had been disbursed.

Elizabeth's lively charitableness may also be discerned in the Ormesby
accounts: she did not leave remembrance of those less fortunate than
herself until the point of death. Pairs of shoes for kitchen boys and gowns
(one even with a be-ribboned hood) for a retired maid, mother of one of
the kitchen boys, gifts of grain or malt to the four convents of friars at
Yarmouth and to the guilds of Ormesby, especially for their feasting and
at play-time, £2 towards the rebuilding of the Franciscan church at
Yarmouth in 1470–1, pennies for the lepers at the gates of Yarmouth, and
fines in the manor court pardoned: these are examples of her charity when
she was staying at Ormesby.[56] One wonders who were the beneficiaries
when she was at Norwich.

[55] Wood Rising was an important estate of Sir Richard Southwell, who with Sir Ralph
Shelton was one of Elizabeth's two executors. To Katherine Southwell, Sir Richard's wife,
Elizabeth left 'a flatte gylt pece covered, pounced with byrdes and lylyes'.

[56] PRO, SC6/941/1, 10, 13; 942/1, 3, 4, 5, 8, 10.

So much then for prayers and public works. Both have an impressive range, and display an attention to detail which looks convincingly like Elizabeth's. What is missing also makes an impression; neither self-regard nor self-aggrandizement are evident. The sums of money are invariably generous; given Elizabeth's station in life they might almost be reckoned lavish. Elizabeth showed herself no less considerate where the members, perhaps especially the women members, of her family were concerned. Robert had four daughters. One of them, Elizabeth and no doubt the eldest, was her grandmother's god-daughter; she had been married to John, the son and heir of Sir Edmund Bedingfield of Oxburgh, Norfolk. John, about whom nothing else is known, must have died before the marriage was consummated, for, says Elizabeth, if her granddaughter will marry again and 'if she wole be rewled in hyr mariage by my sone Robert hyr fadyr', she is to have the 500 marks 'that I and my sone Robert must and owe to have of Sir Edmund Bedyngfeld knyght for suche mony as he had of me for the mariage of John his sone and heyr to my seyd god doughtyr'. Elizabeth Bedingfield was also to have 'a lytel Shyppe chest at Norwych with the Stuffe therin and my vyolet gowne furred with mynkes'.[57] Audrey and Dorothy, Robert's two unmarried daughters, were each to have a silver cup, Audrey's with 'an Egle streynyng an hare', Dorothy's with 'a byrde enamelled in the knoppe'. More importantly, they were to have £200 apiece towards their marriages, so long as they married with their father's consent. Because Anne, the fourth daughter, was a Poor Clare at Denny in Cambridgeshire, if either Audrey or Dorothy died before she was married then Denny was to have 40 marks 'toward the makyng of a newe halle ther', which it ought to have had, both Audrey and Dorothy dying before they could be married (Anne lived for at least another thirty-five years, as she features in her father's will of 1529). Although Anne Clere at Denny got no immediate bequest, other nuns did. Elizabeth Clere at Bungay got 40s, while the £5 that house of Benedictine nuns owed Elizabeth she forgave.[58] To three daughters of her friend William White, all nuns, Mary at Carrow, Alice at Denny, and the unnamed third at Barking, she left 20s apiece. Elizabeth also arranged for Robert to pay Mary and Alice annual pensions out of the property of their

[57] Elizabeth did marry again: her second husband was Sir Robert Peyton of Isleham, Cambridgeshire.

[58] Elizabeth Clere was a daughter of Edmund Clere of Stokesby; he left her £5 in his will of 1484, bequeathing twice that amount to another daughter, Alice, a Poor Clare at Bruisyard: NRO, NCC, Reg. Wolman, fol. 15.

father at Moulton, which she had purchased, Mary 26s 8d, Alice 20s; from the same source Robert was also required to pay an annual pension of 20s to Anne Clere at Denny and one of the same sum to Elizabeth's servant Margery Harneys. We will return to servants in a moment.

To Robert himself, because he was his mother's only surviving son and at last was about to come into both his father's and her property, she did not need to be especially generous. Besides, and characteristically, Elizabeth and Robert had already made an arrangement about jewels, plate, and 'othyr moveable goodes' on 17 May 1477; nonetheless, she also gave him all her 'brasse, pewtyr and laton and othyr Stuffe of Beddyng and nappry' at Norwich (except 'a coffre called Standard that I have ther' and most of what was in it), all her 'Stuffe of howseholde' at Tacolneston (except 'a doseyn spones of the beste'), a 'gret cuppe gylte with armes of Cleres and Uvedales', and a 'flat pece chased oncovered', both of which were at Norwich. Finally, Robert, the supervisor of the will, was given £40 'to his husbondry'.

Besides Clere grandchildren Elizabeth also had Shelton ones; they were the children of Sir Ralph Shelton and her daughter Margaret. To Margaret herself she left her rosary beads of gold and a 'sparver' [bed-canopy] of red silk, which Elizabeth asked Margaret to bequeath at her death to her daughter, Alice Heveningham, and her best gown 'furred with marteyns'. Alice herself was left 'a carpett and an owche [brooch] with a cheyne and the perle at the ende'.[59] There were three Shelton boys: John, the son and heir, got 'a gret Salte of sylver'; Ralph, the second son, got £10 and 'a gilte Goblet covered and a strawbery in the knoppe'; and Richard had £10 and 'a standyng pece of sylver with a coveryng and a Roos on the covyr and a wrethe abowte the cuppe'. Elizabeth may have favoured Ralph; he was to have the remainder of Claydon and Tharston after Sir Robert Clere's male heirs.

Where grandsons are concerned there is a surprising omission: William Clere, Robert's eldest son. The only mention Elizabeth Clere makes of William is in connection with Claydon and Tharston. When the two years during which their revenues were being used to support those who were praying for Elizabeth were up, Robert was to have the two estates. Not until William was thirty and only then if he was 'of good sadde and vertuous disposicion and Rewle lykly so to contynue' were the feoffees, by Elizabeth's instruction, to make a settlement of the two estates on

---

[59] Alice's husband, according to Blomefield III, p. 62, was John Heveningham of Ketteringham, Norfolk, who died in 1530.

Robert and his male heirs. This looks like 'a smack in the eye', unless William was having a riotous and misspent youth. Unlike Sir John Clere, his as yet unborn half-brother, however, William did not live long enough to have a riotous and misspent adulthood.[60] There was time enough for him to marry Elizabeth Paston in 1498, but William died in 1501 still, it seems, short of thirty.

Another missing person from Elizabeth's will is Robert Clere's wife, Anne Hopton.[61] We might have expected to find her there, were it not for the fact, surprising or otherwise, that Elizabeth concentrates upon her immediate family, that is Robert, Margaret, and their children. Sir Ralph Shelton does not get left anything either. Elizabeth might have done much, or enough for Anne and Ralph in her lifetime, or she might have thought not being Cleres they did not warrant her remembering them, even with what we might want to call a token bequest. Her concentration on close family members is the more marked in that only one friend, Katherine Southwell, is bequeathed anything; friends are lacking in this will, perhaps because like Margaret and Agnes Paston they had been out-lived. Servants Elizabeth does not forget. One of them was certainly also a friend, Margery Harneys getting an annuity as well as a bequest of £6 13s 4d. Two other servants, Mary Lyncolne and John Thurstan, received £2 each, while John, 'my chylde of my chaumbre' was to have 66s 8d 'if he wole be a prentyse to eny crafte and ellse to be delyverd hym by the discrecion of myn executours as they may and shal see that he wole be of good and vertuous condicion and of disposicion to lyve trewly'. Harry Fox was to have 20s and John Boteller was to get £10 to be paid when the executors 'shal see and thynke he hath nede to at dyverse tymes to lyve bye'. The impression has to be of Victorian values in late fifteenth-century England: Elizabeth was generous but her generosity was for those who demonstrated that they deserved it.

The testament was witnessed by Sir Ralph Shelton, Robert Clere, John and William Barly, and Richard Southwell, and the will by them, Robert Stevenson and Margery Harneys. Elizabeth probably died on 1 March 1493.[62] Like her friends Agnes and Margaret Paston, she did not choose

---

[60] For Sir John Clere, see *The History of Parliament. The House of Commons 1509–1558*, ed. by S. T. Bindoff (London: Secker and Warburg for the History of Parliament Trust, 1982), p. 651: the biography is by Roger Virgoe.

[61] According to her brass at Ormesby, Anne died on 23 January 1505, viz. 1506 I take it: Blomefield V, pp. 1576–77.

[62] *CIPM Henry VII*, I, p. 392.

to be buried beside a husband. The body of the long-dead Robert Clere reposed in St Margaret's church, Ormesby; Elizabeth Clere was buried in a tomb at the chantry she had established in Norwich cathedral.[63] Her will was proved quickly, on 6 March 1493. Unfortunately, nearly £500 in cash, silver spoons, and a dish worth £10, belonging to Elizabeth and deposited in Norwich priory for safe-keeping by the executors, were stolen in September 1495, so perhaps not everyone got what she wanted them to have.[64] On the other hand no jewels were taken. That 'devys' of Elizabeth Clere's which Margaret Paston had borrowed to adorn her neck one grand day in Norwich over forty years before: was it those golden beads given to Margaret Shelton, inherited, one hopes, by Alice Heveningham, or that 'owche with a cheyne and the perle at the ende' which Elizabeth left directly to Alice, or some other piece long since lost, pawned, or given away?

It would not be inappropriate to end where we began, with Elizabeth Clere's jewellery, jewellery lent out of friendship, and lent by way of friendship with Margaret Paston. There is, nonetheless, one letter of Elizabeth's we have not dealt with.[65] It is to Margaret Paston and in its fashion it testifies just as strongly to the close association of Elizabeth with the Pastons. In the body of the letter, which dates from shortly after the death of John Paston I, Elizabeth asked Margaret to return documents concerning various of her properties which John had had from her; as William Paston I, she says, 'was of councell bothe with my moder [Margaret Uvedale] and my moderlawe [Elizabeth Braunch-Clere-Rothenhale]', she also thinks there might be material relating to what she calls 'my liflode', and she names the estates which compose it. For, she continues, 'ye have right weell and conciensly delyvered certeyn persones the evidences longyng to hem and I truste veryly ye wil the same to me'. The final few lines of the letter are among the most revealing in the Paston collection, indicating as they do how different was the fifteenth century from the twentieth, but I am concluding with them because they are also an indication of the integrity of Elizabeth's friendship with Margaret:

---

[63] Blomefield II, p. 512. Her late husband, Robert Clere, had wished to be buried at Ormesby and he was; his brass there recorded the date of his death as 2 August 1446 (Blomefield V, pp. 1576–77), the day before his nuncupative will was drawn up.

[64] Roger Virgoe's indispensable notes, this time in his file on Richard Southwell and on PRO, KB 27/952, Trinity 14 Henry VII, Plea Roll 36.

[65] Davis II, no. 724.

Cosyn, ther cam a man fro Norwiche to me and fonde be the weye certeyn rolles and toke hem me... [they] belong to you and not to me; wherfore I sende hem you be the bryngger of this bille.

It may seem a small thing that Elizabeth Clere did: no more than lending Margaret Paston a necklace for a day. Nevertheless, integrity, sincerity, honesty are composed of a multitude of small actions, the opposite of the grandiose gesture offered occasionally. It is such integrity that Felicity Riddy has invariably displayed; in honouring Elizabeth, therefore, I have sought also to honour Felicity.

III. Household Matters:
Family, Society, Place, and Space

In Bed with Joan of Kent:
The King's Mother and the Peasants' Revolt

W. M. ORMROD

INTRODUCTION: TEXTS AND EVENTS

In their accounts of the attack on the Tower of London on 14 June 1381, two of the most important chroniclers of the Peasants' Revolt, Jean Froissart and Thomas Walsingham, refer to a dramatic confrontation between the rebels and Joan of Kent, Princess of Wales and mother of the young Richard II. Here is Froissart's version of the event:

> On the Friday in the morning, the people, being at St Katherine's near to the Tower [of London], began to apparel themselves and to cry and shout... And then the king sent to them that they should withdraw to a fair, plain place called Mile End, and there the king would grant them what they desired... Then the people began to depart... [But] as soon as the Tower gate had opened and the king had gone forth... Wat Tyler, Jack Straw and John Ball and more than four hundred entered into the Tower and broke up chamber after chamber, and at last they found the archbishop of Canterbury, Simon [Sudbury], a valiant and wise man, chancellor of England... These gluttons took him and struck off his head; and they also beheaded the lord [grand prior] of Saint John [of Jerusalem—that is, Sir John Hales, the treasurer—] and a Franciscan friar in the service of the duke of Lancaster... and a serjeant at arms called John Leg; and these four heads were set on four long spears and were set on high on London Bridge, as though they had been traitors to the king and to the realm. *Also these*

I am grateful to Gloria Betcher, Joel Burden, Joanna Chamberlayne, Sylvia Federico, John Carmi Parsons, and Jocelyn Wogan-Browne for comments on earlier drafts.

gluttons entered into the chamber of the princess [of Wales] and broke her
bed, whereupon she was so afraid that she swooned; and her valets and
servants took her in their arms and carried her to a postern on the waterside
and put her in a barge, and from there, in secret, took her to a house called
the Queen's Wardrobe; and there she stayed all day and all night, like a
woman half dead, until she was comforted by her son...[1]

Walsingham's version differs in detail, but clearly relates to the same
episode:

Who could ever have believed that such rustics—and most inferior ones at
that—would dare (not in crowds but individually) to enter the chamber of
the king and of his mother with their filthy sticks, and, undeterred by any of
the soldiers, to stroke and lay their uncouth and sordid hands on the beards
of several most noble knights... The rebels suggested that the soldiers
might swear to help seek the traitors of the kingdom, although they
themselves could not avoid the obvious marks of treachery in that they had
raised flags and pennants and had not hesitated to make armed entry...
After the rebels had done all these things and had gained access singly
and in groups to the chambers in the Tower, they arrogantly lay and sat
on the king's bed while joking; and several asked the king's mother to kiss
them. But (marvellous to relate) the many knights and squires dared not
resist any of these unseemly deeds, nor raise their hands in opposition, nor
keep the rebels quiet by means of secret words. *The rebels, who had*
formerly belonged to the most lowly condition of serf, went in and out like
lords; and swineherds set themselves above soldiers, although not knights
but rustics...[2]

These two highly charged accounts have failed to generate very much
scholarly attention, for the simple reason that they cannot easily be

---

[1] Jean Froissart, *Oeuvres*, ed. by J. B. M. C. Kervyn de Lettenhove, 25 vols (Brussels:
Victor Devaux, 1870–77), IX, 404. Translation freely adapted from Berners's version of
Froissart as printed in R. B. Dobson, *The Peasants' Revolt of 1381*, 2nd edn (London:
Macmillan, 1983), p. 191 (my italics). The original of the italicized section reads: 'Encore
entrèrent cil glouton en la cambre de la princesse et despécièrent tout son lit, dont elle fu si
eshidée que elle s'en pasma.'

[2] Thomas Walsingham, *Historia Anglicana*, ed. by H. T. Riley, 2 vols, Rolls Series, 28
(London: Longman and others, 1863–64), I, 459, as translated by Dobson, pp. 171–72 (my
italics). The original of the italicized section reads: 'Et cum omnia facerent, et, ut diximus,
plerique soli in cameras concessissent, et sedendo, jacendo, jocando, super lectum regis
insolescerent; et insuper, matrem regis ad oscula invitarent quidam... Intrabant et exibant
ut domini, qui quondam fuerant vilissimae conditionis servi; et praeferebant se militibus
non tam militum, sed rusticorum, subulci.'

accommodated into a definitive historical narrative of the events of 1381.[3] One of the other chroniclers, Henry Knighton, agrees with Froissart and Walsingham that Joan was present in the Tower on 14 June, but fails to mention a meeting between the rebels and the princess.[4] Meanwhile, the London Letter Book H and the *Anonimalle* chronicle flatly contradict such accounts by claiming that Joan accompanied the king to the meeting with the rebel leaders at Mile End, which (by general consensus, but in fact contrary to Froissart's chronology) took place at the very time that the Tower was being stormed.[5] The other relevant chroniclers—including the well-informed Monk of Westminster—provide no mention of Joan at all, and the public records yield no corroborative evidence either for the episode at the Tower or even for the princess's presence in London at the time of the rising. It is hardly surprising, then, that historians have tended to set aside the question of Joan of Kent's involvement in the Peasants' Revolt as at best 'a matter of debate'.[6]

The present study does not attempt to succeed where others have failed by constructing a detailed itinerary of Joan of Kent during the summer of 1381. Instead, it takes what is so often seen merely as a problem in the evidence and uses it as an opportunity to discuss some possible inter-pretations of the meeting between the princess and the rebels. The question of whether or not the encounter actually took place thereby becomes rather less important than its treatment and function within the contemporary and near-contemporary narratives of the rising.[7] Such an

---

[3] For the principal such attempts, see G. Kriehn, 'Studies in the Sources of the Social Revolt in 1381', *American Historical Review*, 7 (1901), 254–85, 458–84; B. Wilkinson, 'The Peasants' Revolt of 1381', *Speculum*, 15 (1940), 12–35; H. M. Hansen, 'The Peasants' Revolt of 1381 and the Chronicles', *Journal of Medieval History*, 6 (1980), 393–415.

[4] *Knighton's Chronicle*, ed. by G. H. Martin (Oxford: Clarendon Press, 1995), pp. 210–13; Dobson, p. 182.

[5] Dobson, pp. 161, 209. Kriehn, p. 278, and Dobson, p. 209, n. 1, accept this version of the princess's itinerary. Wilkinson, pp. 20–24, and, most recently, N. Saul, *Richard II* (London: Yale University Press, 1997), p. 68, attempt to reconcile these with Froissart, Walsingham, and Knighton by suggesting that Joan set out with the king to Mile End but turned back. However, Hansen, pp. 395–415, in demonstrating that the *Anonimalle* chronicle tends merely to perpetuate errors evident in the London Letter Book H, raises questions as to whether these latter accounts should be privileged. See also *The Anonimalle Chronicle 1333 to 1381*, ed. by V. H. Galbraith (Manchester: Manchester University Press, 1927), p. 195, n. to p. 144.

[6] Dobson, p. 191, n. 1.

[7] For a similar exercise, see D. Pearsall, 'Interpretative Models for the Peasants' Revolt', in *Hermeneutics and Medieval Culture*, ed. by P. J. Gallacher and H. Dimico (Albany:

approach also helps to create a broader agenda for the study of the Peasants' Revolt by highlighting important issues of gender, transgression, and power in the England of Richard II.

SPATIAL POLITICS: CHAMBERS AND BEDS

Not surprisingly, both Froissart and Walsingham infuse their reports of the meeting between the princess and the rebels with images of violation. Two particular spatial elements—the chamber and the bed—allow us to appreciate some of the deeper cultural reverberations of such imagery. The rebels are made to breach the convention, observed both in the king's household and in all larger domestic establishments, that drew very precise distinctions between those persons who were restricted to the public space of the hall (*aula*) and those who were allowed access to the personal apartments of the lord and his family (the *camera*). The issue was particularly significant at a time when kings (like other lords) were increasingly eschewing the life of the hall and conducting more and more of their governmental activities in the principal or 'great' chamber.[8] The chamber, in short, was much more than merely the royal sleeping quarters; the rebels' invasion of that space in 1381, like their attacks on the royal treasuries and archives both at the Tower and at Westminster,[9] signified their successful infiltration into some of the very nerve centres of the fourteenth-century English state.

More particularly, it is the political imagery attaching to the bed that provides this episode with its special character. In the later Middle Ages, beds—and more specifically canopied beds—were, in Penelope Eames's words, 'inseparably associated with prestige, honour, power, wealth and privilege'.[10] For Froissart and Walsingham, and for their audiences, the bed was therefore not merely an allusion to the intimate nature of the

---

State University of New York Press, 1989), pp. 63–70. For the place of this 'new historicist' approach in traditional historical methodology, see R. J. Evans, *In Defence of History* (London: Granta Books, 1997), esp. pp. 75–128.

[8] C. Given-Wilson, *The Royal Household and the King's Affinity. Service, Politics and Finance in England 1360–1413* (New Haven: Yale University Press, 1986), p. 29.

[9] W. M. Ormrod, 'The Peasants' Revolt and the Government of England', *Journal of British Studies*, 29 (1990), 1–30 (pp. 2–10).

[10] P. Eames, 'Furniture in England, France and the Netherlands from the Twelfth to the Fifteenth Century', *Furniture History*, 13 (1977), 1–303 (p. 86).

confrontation but also a means of emphasizing the direct political challenge posed to a person of high status. In this respect, the chroniclers' related accounts of the attack on John of Gaunt's London residence, the Savoy, are particularly revealing. These not only stress the fact that the rebels broke into the private apartments but also itemize the goods and furnishings they destroyed: in the words of the *Anonimalle* chronicle, 'They took all the torches they could find, and lit them, and burnt all the cloths, coverlets and beds, as well as all the very valuable testers, of which one, decorated with heraldic shields, was said to be worth a thousand marks.'[11] This explicit reference to the use of heraldry as a prominent feature of decoration on beds and bed-hangings provides an additional explanation as to why the rebels of 1381 should have identified such items as appropriate targets for destruction. Froissart's image of the broken bed therefore becomes a paradigm of the general attack on all tangible symbols of authority during the Peasants' Revolt.[12]

That said, some of the differences of detail—especially the fact that Froissart chooses to locate the episode in and around the princess's bed while Walsingham places the rebels on the king's bed—may help us to identify the more precise political messages intended by the chroniclers. Because of its similarity to a canopied throne, the king's state bed was an item of furniture closely associated with the iconography of sovereignty. In later medieval France in particular, the royal bed was an integral element in the elaborate court ceremonial that preceded the coronation, and gave its name to the occasion on which the king dispensed his prerogative powers in the Parlement of Paris (the so-called *lit de justice*).[13] Although the iconographical tradition was less strong in England, it is known that Henry III's bed was taken to symbolize the permanent presence of the English monarch in the Painted Chamber at Westminster Palace in the thirteenth century; and Edward III chose to

---

[11] Adapted from Dobson, p. 157; for other accounts, see Dobson, pp. 169–70, 183–84, 200, 206, 209. This episode (unlike that at the Tower) is corroborated by the public records: Dobson, pp. 148–49, 213, 220, 225–56, 321; A. J. Prescott, 'Judicial Records of the Rising of 1381' (unpublished doctoral thesis, University of London, 1984), p. 292. During his dispute with the Londoners in 1377, Gaunt's arms had been publicly displayed reversed (denoting treason): *Anonimalle Chronicle*, pp. 104–5.

[12] Froissart, IX, 404.

[13] R. A. Jackson, *'Vive le Roi': A History of the French Coronation from Charles V to Charles X* (Chapel Hill: University of North Carolina Press, 1984), p. 28; E. A. R. Brown and R. C. Famiglietti, *The Lit de Justice: Semantics, Ceremonial and the Parlement of Paris, 1300–1600* (Sigmaringen: Jan Thorbecke, 1994), pp. 21–22.

advertise his claim to the French throne in another state bed held at
Westminster which he bequeathed to his grandson in 1377.[14] Since the
Tower of London had very largely ceased to act as a royal residence by
1381, the very presence of state beds in the fortress might be taken as
having a symbolic significance.[15] It may also be the case, therefore, that
Walsingham's decision to locate the meeting with the princess on and
around the *king's* bed served to reinforce his emphasis on the *treasonous*
nature of the rebels' activities, to which we shall return.

SEXUAL POLITICS: REPUTATION, RAPE, AND ROYALTY

The beds of royal women were, by contrast, much more closely
associated with conjugal relations and childbearing: although queens
exercised their political authority by hearing petitions in their
bedchambers, such occasions seem to have been limited to the ceremonial
conventions following a royal birth (in the course of which the queen's
bed also provided the starting-point for the procession to her churching).[16]
The more intimate and explicitly sexual connotations arising from Joan's
presence in the bedchamber were evidently not lost on either Walsingham
or Froissart: the former's use of phallic imagery in his description of the
rebels' 'filthy sticks' has been noted in the critical literature;[17] while
Froissart's emphasis on how the rebels broke—literally 'dismembered'
(*despécièrent*)—the princess's bed could be read as a particularly striking
metaphor of physical violence. Over-familiarity between rustics and
royals was, of course, one of the chroniclers' abiding themes: it was the
offence thus caused to the king that ultimately led to the assassination of
Wat Tyler at Smithfield.[18] The element of lewdness and prurience evident

---

[14] P. Binski, *The Painted Chamber at Westminster*, Society of Antiquaries of London
Occasional Papers: New Series, IX (London: Society of Antiquaries, 1986), pp. 35–36; J.
Nichols, *A Collection of all the Wills... of the Kings and Queens of England* (London:
Society of Antiquaries, 1780), p. 61.

[15] R. Storey, 'The Tower of London and the *Garderobae armorum*', *Royal Armouries
Yearbook*, 3 (1998), 176–83, notes (p. 179) the clearing of the queen's chamber of
armaments when Anne of Bohemia took up residence in the Tower in 1382.

[16] J. C. Parsons, 'Ritual and Symbol in the English Medieval Queenship to 1500',
Cosmos, 7 (1992), 60–77 (pp. 65–67).

[17] P. Strohm, *Hochon's Arrow* (Princeton: Princeton University Press, 1992), p. 48.

[18] Dobson, pp. 177–78, 195–96, 203, 207.

in their treatment of the story of Princess Joan may in fact suggest that the chroniclers were in this case adapting an altogether cruder story that had its origins in popular rather than polite accounts of the rising,[19] and which (because of her contemporary reputation as a sexual libertine)[20] may originally have identified Princess Joan as deserving of such victimization. On the other hand, it is an obvious point that any sexual innuendo remaining in the written account would have been intended not as a slur on the princess but as a means of stressing the particularly heinous nature of the offence committed by the rebels in the Tower.

Such a line of thinking inevitably also raises questions about the possible legal definition of that offence. Although the judicial records generated in the aftermath of the Peasants' Revolt yield interesting parallel cases of threats, insults and assaults committed upon women,[21] they include few cases of rape:[22] indeed, the general absence of such charges is often taken as proof of the high level of discipline among the rebel bands in the south-east of England.[23] In the princess's case, however, special circumstances may have applied. The statute of treasons

---

[19] For the integration of other 'popular' material into the chroniclers' accounts of 1381, see S. Justice, *Writing and Rebellion: England in 1381* (Berkeley: University of California Press, 1994), pp. 193–254. The striking similarities between Froissart's and Walsingham's accounts of the episode (Hansen, p. 410) could also suggest a common source. For the survival of a popular mythology of the revolt, see I. M. W. Harvey, 'Was There Popular Politics in Fifteenth-Century England?', in *The McFarlane Legacy: Studies in Late Medieval Politics and Society*, ed. by R. H. Britnell and A. J. Pollard (Stroud: Sutton, 1995), pp. 155–74 (pp. 167–68).

[20] M. Galway, 'Joan of Kent and the Order of the Garter', *University of Birmingham Historical Journal*, 1 (1947), 13–50; R. Barber, *Edward, Prince of Wales and Aquitaine* (London: Penguin Books, 1978), pp. 173–74; Strohm, p. 175; J. Chamberlayne, 'Joan of Kent's Tale: Adultery and Rape in the Age of Chivalry', *Medieval Life*, 5 (1996), 7–9.

[21] See, e.g., W. E. Flaherty, 'The Great Rebellion in Kent of 1381 Illustrated from the Public Records', *Archaeologia Cantiana*, 3 (1860), 65–96 (pp. 77, 82–83, 85); W. M. Palmer, 'Records of the Villein Insurrection in Cambridgeshire', *East Anglian*, 6 (1895–6), 81–84, 97–102, 135–39, 167–72, 209–12, 234–37 (pp. 97–98, 99, 101, 169–70); A. Réville, *Le soulèvement des travailleurs d'Angleterre en 1381* (Paris: Picard, 1898), pp. 202, 207–08, 215, 220.

[22] For one example, see Palmer, 'Records', pp. 137–38. The subject is explored in more detail by S. Federico, 'Transgression, Order, and Revenge: Women's Participation in the Rising of 1381' (unpublished paper delivered at the 32nd International Congress on Medieval Studies, University of Western Michigan, 1997).

[23] See, most recently, E. B. Fryde, *Peasants and Landlords in Later Medieval England* (Stroud: Sutton, 1996), p. 46.

of 1352 had specifically declared the rape of the king's consort, his eldest daughter, or the wife of his eldest son to be high treason.[24] Although, as the *mother* of the king, Joan of Kent did not strictly fall within this privileged category of royal women (a point to which we will need to return), it seems plausible that Walsingham at least constructed his story of the encounter between the rebels and the princess in potentially sexual terms as a means of articulating the treasonous status of the crimes committed by those who stormed the Tower on 14 June.[25] Within his account of the same episode, indeed, Walsingham makes a more explicit reference to the statute of 1352 by defining the unfurling of banners (and thus the raising of war against the king) as an act of treason. Froissart too sets up an explicit opposition between the rebels' claim that Sudbury, Hales and their other victims were 'traitors to the king and to the realm' and their unwarranted behaviour in terrorizing the king's mother within her apartments. If this is the case, then the variations in the location and potential gendering of the raid on the Tower, interesting as they are in demonstrating different emphases in the treatment of the story, do not ultimately prevent us from concluding that both chroniclers sought to represent the episode as a dramatic fulfilment of the rebels' crimes against the state.

THE POLITICS OF CLOSURE: KINGSHIP AND CHIVALRY

They were also well aware that the encounter was a gross offence against chivalry. Both Walsingham's description of ribaldry in the king's bed and Froissart's emotive account of the destruction of the princess's bed could be read as deliberate reversals of the more usual conventions of contemporary courtly literature. These conventions, observed in such near-contemporary texts as *Sir Gawain and the Green Knight* and *Troilus and Criseyde*, often made the bedroom the domain of the lady: even if her authority depended on male complicity and was constructed only within the context of a love-game, it tended to accord her an assertive role in any assignations that took place there.[26] It was this reversal of normative

---

[24] *Rotuli parliamentorum*, 6 vols (London: House of Lords, 1783), II, 239; *Statutes of the Realm*, 10 vols (London: Record Commission, 1810–28), I, 320.

[25] For the use of a similar strategy in indictments arising from the revolt, see Prescott, p. 22.

[26] J. Mann, 'Sir Gawain and the Romance Hero', in *Heroes and Heroines in Medieval English Literature*, ed. by L. Carruthers (Woodbridge: Boydell and Brewer, 1994), pp.

gender roles that also allowed chivalric culture to countenance the playing out of games—in this case often of a rumbustious nature—in and around *men's* beds: Edward I and Edward II are both known to have observed the custom, again echoed in *Gawain*, of allowing themselves to be caught in bed and ransomed by the ladies of the court.[27] It was clearly a very different matter, however, when the invasion of the chamber was carried out by low-status men and the focus of their attack was a high-status woman. Whereas a popular account of the meeting in the Tower might have celebrated its social anomalies as a form of carnival,[28] no polite audience could surely have contemplated reading the chroniclers' treatment of the episode as anything other than a deeply offensive challenge to a distinctively feminine form of authority.

If they did indeed appropriate a piece of popular story-telling, then, it is evident that the chroniclers—particularly Froissart—sought to re-invest it with courtly values by using Joan of Kent's predicament to highlight the urgent need—not only of the princess, but of the realm as a whole—for a chivalric champion. Froissart had already established this theme through his (unique) account of the threats made to Princess Joan by the rebels of Kent during her journey from Canterbury to London in the early stages of the rising.[29] The same theme is found in a related episode from 1381, reported in Knighton and elsewhere, recounting the tribulations of another member of the royal family, Constance of Castile, duchess of

---

105–17; *Troilus and Criseyde*, Book III, ll. 736–1190, in *The Riverside Chaucer*, ed. by L. D. Benson, 3rd edn (Oxford: Oxford University Press, 1987), pp. 523–29. Compare Malory's treatment of the issue when Launcelot upbraids Mellyagaunte for entering Guinevere's chamber ('ye ded nat youre parte nor knyghtly, to touche a quenys bed whyle hit was drawyn and she lyyng therein'): Sir Thomas Malory, *Works*, ed. by E. Vinaver, 2nd edn (London: Oxford University Press, 1997), p. 658, ll. 34–6.

[27] R. Hutton, *The Rise and Fall of Merry England* (Oxford: Oxford University Press, 1996), pp. 59–60, places this practice in a courtly context; P. Chaplais, *Piers Gaveston: Edward III's Adoptive Brother* (Oxford: Clarendon Press, 1994), pp. 8–9, and J. C. Parsons, *Eleanor of Castile: Queen and Society in Thirteenth-Century England* (Basingstoke: Macmillan, 1994), p. 50, relate it to popular Hocktide observations.

[28] For the application of such an approach to other features of the revolt, see Strohm, pp. 33–56; Justice, pp. 153–55.

[29] Dobson, p. 139. Joan might have been visiting Canterbury for the feasts of Pentecost and Trinity (which fell on 2 and 9 June in 1381) and for the anniversary of the Black Prince (8 June). For context, see C. Wilson, 'The Medieval Monuments', in *A History of Canterbury Cathedral*, ed. by P. Collinson, N. Ramsay and M. Sparks (Oxford: Oxford University Press, 1995), pp. 451–510 (p. 458 and n. 32, p. 495 and n. 192).

Lancaster: bereft of her good lord, John of Gaunt, who was conducting business on the Scottish march, the duchess fled from Leicester to Pontefract, only to be refused entry to her husband's castle by unworthy servants preoccupied with concern for their own safety.[30] Back at the Tower, Walsingham similarly emphasizes the inadequacy and coward-liness of the members of the royal household left behind with the king's mother. It is in Froissart, however, that the story of Joan's apparent abandonment by her entourage is properly resolved through the young king's arrival at La Riole after the Mile End meeting[31] and, more particularly, by his return there following the second encounter with the rebels and the slaughter of Wat Tyler at Smithfield:

> ... the king and his lords and all his company... entered into London with great joy. And the first journey that the king made, he went to the lady princess his mother, who was in a castle in La Riole called the Queen's Wardrobe, and there she had tarried two days and two nights right sore abashed, as she had good reason. *And when she saw the king her son, she greatly rejoiced and said, 'Ah, fair son, what pain and great sorrow I have suffered for you this day.' Then the king answered and said, 'Certainly, madam, I know it well; but now rejoice yourself and thank God, for now it is time. I have this day recovered my inheritance and the realm of England, which I had nearly lost.'*[32]

Here, then, in the chivalric chronicle *par excellence*, a dramatic *dénouement* is created for the purpose of representing the Christ-like boy king as the self-proclaimed saviour of his kingdom.[33] It is interesting to notice how this final scene in Froissart's account of the London rising

---

[30] *Knighton's Chronicle*, pp. 230–31. The treatment in *Anonimalle Chronicle*, pp. 141–42, is somewhat different.

[31] Froissart, IX, 406; Dobson, p. 193.

[32] Froissart, IX, 416; translation adapted from Dobson, p. 198 (my italics). The original of the italicized section reads: 'Quant elle vei le roy son fil, si fu toute resjoïe: "Ha! biaux fils, com jou ay huy eu en coer grant paine et grant angoisse pour vous!" Dont respondy li rois, et dist: "Certes, madame, je le say bien. Or bien vous resjoïssés, car il est heure, et loés Dieu; car je ay huy recouvré mon hiretage et le roiaulme d'Engletière que je avoice perdu."' The issue of whether the princess did indeed take refuge at La Riole is a subject that demands fuller treatment elsewhere.

[33] For Froissart's representation of Richard in 1381, see J. W. Sherborne, 'Charles VI and Richard II', in *Froissart: Historian*, ed. by J. J. N. Palmer (Woodbridge: Boydell Press, 1981), pp. 50–63 (pp. 53–54). For Richard's self-image in this regard, see J. L. Gillespie, 'Richard II: Chivalry and Kingship', in *The Age of Richard II*, ed. by J. L. Gillespie (Stroud: Sutton, 1997), pp. 115–38.

parallels those in the Chandos Herald's *Life of the Black Prince*, where Richard II's father is twice depicted returning from youthful military exploits to be presented before his own mother, Queen Philippa.[34] For Froissart (who knew the Herald's text well),[35] Joan of Kent becomes not merely a symbol of vulnerability but a royal patroness who validates her son's deeds: the hero is identified not simply by his decisive actions against the rebels but by his willingness to submit himself to his lady, herself in some respects the conscious representative of the Virgin Mary. In its deliberate attempts to establish Richard II's credibility as a worthy successor to Edward III and the Black Prince, Froissart's account of the king's visits to the princess of Wales therefore provide a particularly potent resolution to the story of the Peasants' Revolt in chivalric—and in some respects positively Messianic—terms.

THE POLITICS OF CLOSURE: QUEENSHIP AND INTERCESSION

The discussion thus far has deliberately sought not to draw distinctions between the reality of events in 1381 and the manner in which they were shaped by the imaginations of the chroniclers. However, while Froissart subsequently found a neat ending to his story in the re-assertion of chivalric values and the symbolic restoration of royal authority, those members of political society who had lived through the events of the Peasants' Revolt knew perfectly well that the resolution of the crisis was at once more difficult, more protracted, and more pragmatic. Although they embarked enthusiastically on a programme of severe repression during the summer of 1381, both crown and polity seem gradually to have realized that this was not a lasting solution and sought instead to resolve the crisis through conciliation.[36] In the parliament of November– December 1381 Richard II's government accordingly issued an amnesty: with certain named exceptions, all those indicted for involvement in the revolt were allowed to purchase general pardons from the chancery.[37] Because the chroniclers tended to assume that the revolt ended with an

---

[34] *Life of the Black Prince by the Herald of Sir John Chandos*, ed. by M. K. Pope and E. C. Lodge (Oxford: Clarendon Press, 1910), ll. 461–71, 1469–78.

[35] J. J. N. Palmer, 'Book I (1325–78) and its Sources', in *Froissart: Historian*, ed. by Palmer, pp. 7–24.

[36] For the development of this policy, see Prescott, p. 353.

[37] Dobson, pp. 331–33.

exercise of force, they gave little attention to the amnesty and found it unnecessary to explain the change of policy that it represented. The political community, by contrast, was obviously anxious to demonstrate that it had neither surrendered to the demands of the former rebels nor recognized the legitimacy of the revolt. A new, transformative element therefore had to be introduced into the equation in order to explain and validate such a sudden change of public policy. The fact that only the public records found it necessary to identify such a transformative element—in the person of the new queen, Anne of Bohemia—sets up an interesting distinction between the roles allotted to royal women in the immediate political discourses of 1381 and the later re-workings of the revolt at the hands of the chroniclers.

Both political and literary constructions of conciliation in the Middle Ages recognized that a king's decision to set aside the masculine tendency towards vengeance and to accept the feminine quality of mercy ought to be initiated (and was therefore legitimized) by the intervention of the queen.[38] Since the parliament of 1381 itself coincided with the journey of Anne of Bohemia to England for her marriage to Richard II, it is hardly surprising that the general pardon issued in this assembly and proclaimed in the shires declared the amnesty to have been granted 'at the special request of the noble lady, Lady Anne, daughter of the noble Prince Charles, lately emperor of Rome, and soon to arrive, if God pleases, as queen of England'.[39] Before she had ever set foot on English soil, then, Anne of Bohemia was being publicly portrayed as the conscience of king and people, the harbinger of peace, and the guarantor of domestic harmony.

It is naturally interesting to speculate as to whether, had it not been for this convenient coincidence, the role of mediator might have been fulfilled by Joan of Kent herself. Certainly, the princess had an established record as peace-maker. She had already attempted to dispel the violent conflict between John of Gaunt and the Londoners in 1377,

[38] J. C. Parsons, 'The Queen's Intercession in Thirteenth-Century England', in *Power of the Weak: Studies on Medieval Women*, ed. by J. Carpenter and S.-B. MacLean (Urbana: University of Illinois Press, 1995), pp. 147–77; J. C. Parsons, 'The Intercessionary Patronage of Queens Margaret and Isabella of France', in *Thirteenth Century England VI*, ed. by M. Prestwich, R. H. Britnell and R. Frame (Woodbridge: Boydell and Brewer, 1997), pp. 144–56; Strohm, pp. 95–119; Carolyn P. Collette, 'Joan of Kent and Noble Women's Roles in Chaucer's World', *The Chaucer Review*, 33 (1999), 350–62.

[39] Dobson, p. 332. For the proclamation, see *Calendar of Close Rolls, Richard II*, 6 vols (London: HMSO, 1914–27), II, 104–05.

and to intervene (probably again on Gaunt's behalf) in the proceedings taken by the bishops against Wyclif in 1378. Later, in 1385, she was also to promote a personal reconciliation between Richard II and Gaunt, and (less successfully) to plead for an end to a bitter feud between two of her own offspring, the king and his half-brother John Holand.[40] Since her son's accession she had also, in a more general sense, acted regularly as an intermediary for those seeking access to the royal grace for the granting of pardons—a role that would have been seen as particularly fitting for the successful resolution of the Peasants' Revolt.[41]

Three factors, however, appear to militate against the notion that Joan could have been credibly portrayed as a conciliator in the highly-charged political situation of 1381. The first is the suggestion, outlined above, that the story of Joan of Kent's treatment at the hands of the rebels in the Tower of London may already have been in circulation before its inclusion in the chronicles. If that is the case, then the lords and commons in the parliament of 1381 would surely have found it highly implausible, as well as inappropriate, to have the princess represented as intercessor for her erstwhile tormentors. Secondly, and regardless of the origins of the episode at the Tower, there is the fact that Joan of Kent had effectively declared her public support for the policy of repression that preceded the general pardon by securing a royal commission to investigate offences committed on her own estates during the time of the revolt.[42] This suggests that the princess may have shared the reluctance of certain other great landholders to accept the amnesty:[43] certainly (and unlike her daughter-in-law) she made no use of her influence at court to seek special pardons for former insurgents until her solitary and belated intervention on behalf of Thomas Sampson, the prominent Suffolk rebel, in 1383.[44] Finally, there is Joan of Kent's anomalous position as the

---

[40] Saul, pp. 12, 21, 120.

[41] *Calendar of Patent Rolls, Richard II*, 6 vols (London: HMSO, 1895–1909), I, 35, 267, 282, 293, 295, 324, 335, 342, 349, 376, 392, 440, 546; II, 20. It is interesting that such brokering was also conducted by the princess's ladies: *CPR, Richard II*, I, 483, 506, 529.

[42] *CPR, Richard II*, II, 78–79.

[43] For which see J. A. Tuck, 'Nobles, Commons and the Great Revolt of 1381', in *The English Rising of 1381*, ed. by R. H. Hilton and T. H. Aston (Cambridge: Cambridge University Press, 1984), pp. 194–212; Fryde, pp. 242–55.

[44] *CPR, Richard II*, II, 226. For Sampson (whose own three beds were itemized in the inventory of his goods taken after the revolt), see E. Powell, *The Rising in East Anglia in 1381* (Cambridge: Cambridge University Press, 1896), pp. 143–45; R. Hilton, *Bond Men*

mother of a king without the title and authority of a queen. Insofar as the responsibility to supplicate for the royal mercy was enshrined in and bestowed through the rite of coronation,[45] Joan of Kent's status as mediator can only ever have had real credibility so long as there was no queen consort.[46] (Her two recorded interventions after the marriage of her son, both of them in 1385, concerned quarrels within the king's family and were notably less public and political than those associated either with Queen Philippa or with Anne of Bohemia.)[47]

All of this suggests that the personal experience of the king's mother during the rebellion, and the inevitable diminution of her status following her son's marriage, would have made it impossible for political society in the winter of 1381–82 to construct her as the agent of reconciliation between the establishment and the former rebels. Anne of Bohemia, by contrast, had neither suffered at the hands of the rebels nor been implicated in the suppression of the revolt; as a new arrival to the kingdom she not only embodied the public person of the queen consort lacking since the death of Queen Philippa in 1369 but also represented a veritable *dea ex machina* whose pleas for mercy could be accepted as a genuine and spontaneous outpouring of feminine compassion.

In the present context, the particular interest of this point lies in the variation that emerges from the political and the historical discourses. Once the crown's change of attitude to the former rebels had been explicitly justified by the intervention of the new queen, it was simply

---

Made Free (London: Methuen, 1977), p. 180. For Anne's role in seeking pardons for the rebels of 1381, see *CPR, Richard II*, II, 103, 159, 203, 206, 211, 215, 223, 297, 399.

[45] J. C. Parsons, 'The Pregnant Queen as Counsellor and the Medieval Construction of Motherhood', in *Medieval Mothering*, ed. by J. C. Parsons and B. Wheeler (New York: Garland Press, 1996), pp. 39–61; J. Chamberlayne, 'Fertility Rite or Authority Ritual: The Queen's Coronation in England, 1445–1487' (forthcoming).

[46] See also, in another context, Parsons, 'Intercessionary Patronage', pp. 149–50.

[47] For which see Strohm, pp. 95–119. Strohm in fact tends to treat Joan of Kent as a queen and in another place actually refers to her as such (p. 48). Galway, pp. 29, 34, argues (without citations) that Joan was accorded the title of queen in her own lifetime; this may have something to do with the fact that the Black Prince was sometimes referred to as Edward IV (Barber, pp. 242–43). There is no evidence, however, that Joan sought after the death of her husband and the accession of her son to exercise the rights of the queen consort; nor did she use the title and privileges of 'king's mother' later associated with Lady Margaret Beaufort: M. K. Jones and M. G. Underwood, *The King's Mother: Lady Margaret Beaufort, Countess of Richmond and Derby* (Cambridge: Cambridge University Press, 1992), p. 292.

accepted as a *fait accompli*: this, coupled with an ambivalence over the advantages of a marriage alliance with Bohemia, explains why the chroniclers, writing from hindsight, either forgot or ignored the role given to the queen in the amnesty of 1381 and had so little to say in general about Anne's arrival, coronation, and marriage early in 1382.[48] On the other hand, the very fact that the young queen had been publicly represented as the bringer of peace also meant that two of the chroniclers at least were subsequently free to depict the other key female member of the royal family, the king's mother, as victim rather than champion of the rebels—and in the process, as has been suggested here, to integrate an otherwise somewhat problematic account of the rebels' activities at the Tower of London into their dramatic renditions of the Peasants' Revolt.

CONCLUSION

A series of contrasts therefore appears to emerge in the representations of royal women during and after the Peasants' Revolt: contrasts between narrative strategies and political discourses, between princesses and queens, between victims and conciliators. It is almost as though the account of Princess Joan's meeting with the rebels—a story which, as has been suggested here, may already have had currency before its integration into the chronicles—was itself partly responsible for shaping the princess's subsequent reputation and career. Lacking the title of queen herself, and quickly superseded as royal mediator by her new daughter-in-law, the king's mother retreated rapidly into political obscurity.[49] This process of self-effacement is strikingly exemplified in Joan's decision to be buried, not at the royal mausoleum of Westminster or at the Black Prince's burial place of Canterbury,[50] but in the church of the friars minor at Stamford (Lincolnshire), 'in my chapel ... near the monument ... of my

---

[48] Saul, pp. 90, 455.

[49] Joan made a small number of successful appeals for royal pardons in 1383–84 (*CPR, Richard II*, II, 226, 229, 268, 319, 332, 441, 448); but after 1382 she was clearly outshone in this respect by Queen Anne (*CPR, Richard II*, II, 103, 114, 159, 203, 206, 211, 215, 223, 236, 243, 297, 399, 411, 433, 440, 448).

[50] The fact that Joan and the Black Prince had founded twin chantries at Canterbury suggests that her earlier intention was to be buried there: K. P. Wentersdorf, 'The Clandestine Marriages of the Fair Maid of Kent', *Journal of Medieval History*, 5 (1979), 203–31 (pp. 218, 227); Wilson, p. 494.

deceased [first] husband, the earl of Kent'.[51] That Joan thus effectively
demoted herself from princess to countess presumably says something not
simply about her religious sensibilities and family affections but also
about her retreating political identity during the last phase of her life.[52]
Moreover, it is a nice coincidence, if nothing more, that the Franciscan
church in Stamford already contained the tomb of Joan's royal cousin,
Blanche, Lady Wake, whose scandalous treatment by the bishop of Ely in
the 1350s had famously provoked Edward III to take personal
responsibility for the case and act, in effect, as Blanche's chivalric
champion.[53] Since courtly society had also apparently chosen to depict
Joan of Kent in 1381 as a defenceless widow seeking assistance from a
knightly hero within her family, it may not be too mischievous to suggest
that the story of the princess's meeting with the rebels, and the political
messages with which it became invested, actually took on a reality of
their own that helped to shape the image of Richard II's mother for the
remainder of her earthly life and, in some senses, beyond.

---

[51] Nichols, p. 78.

[52] It must also be acknowledged, of course, that royal women did not always choose to be
buried with kings, and that the appeal of the Franciscans proved very powerful: see J. C.
Parsons, '"Never was a body buried in England with such solemnity and honour": The
Burials and Posthumous Commemorations of English Queens to 1500', in *Queens and
Queenship in Medieval Europe*, ed. by A. Duggan, (Woodbridge: Boydell and Brewer,
1997), pp. 317–37 (pp. 330–31).

[53] G. E. Cokayne, *The Complete Peerage*, new edn, 13 vols (London: St Catherine Press,
1910–59), XII², 304, n. (f); Royal Commission on Historical Monuments, England, *An
Inventory of Historical Monuments: The Town of Stamford* (London: HMSO, 1977), p. 88,
no 189; J. Aberth, *Criminal Churchmen in the Age of Edward III. The Case of Bishop
Thomas de Lisle* (University Park: Pennsylvania State University Press, 1996), pp. 117–
42. Blanche was the sister of Henry of Grosmont, duke of Lancaster (and thus aunt of yet
another courtly heroine, Blanche, wife of John of Gaunt); her husband, Thomas, Lord
Wake, was also uncle to Joan of Kent. Close connections are also suggested by the fact
that Joan had been granted Blanche Wake's dower lands after the latter's death in 1380:
CPR, Richard II, II, 536.

Heroic Subjects: Women and the Alliterative *Morte Arthure*

ARLYN DIAMOND

Now I have told you the whole story of the prince's life; forgive me if I have passed over matters lightly, but a book as big as the romances of king Arthur, Alexander or Charlemagne could have been written about it, simply to record his deeds, prowess, largesse and wisdom, and to tell how he was always wise, loyal, catholic, and eager for the common good. He died nobly, acknowledging God as his Creator, and saying to his household: 'Lords, look at me, for God's sake; you see that we are not lords here. Everyone must go this way, and no-one can turn aside. I beg you in all humility to pray for me.'

> Chandos Herald, *Life of the Black Prince*[1]

Such deeds of arms were done there that Roland and Oliver and Ogier le Danois, who was so courteous, might have met their match. Men of worth, bold and insolent, could be seen there. The noble and gentle prince was there too, and made a fine beginning as a knight. He made a raid across the Cotentin, burning everything and laying waste, from La Hogue, Barfleur, Carentan, Saint Lô, Bayeux and as far as Caen.

> Chandos Herald, *Life of the Black Prince*

I wish to thank Jocelyn Wogan-Browne and Carolyn Collette for all their help with this article.

[1] Ed. and trans. by Richard Barber, in *The Life and Campaigns of the Black Prince* (Woodbridge: Boydell Press, 1979), pp. 138, 87. Some critics think the Life is a possible source for the poem: see *Morte Arthure*, ed. by John Finlayson, York Medieval Texts (Evanston: Northwestern University Press, 1967), p. 32. Larry D. Benson, 'The Date of the *Alliterative Morte Arthure*', in *Medieval Studies in Honor of Lillian Herlands Hornstein*, ed. by Jess Bessinger Jr. and Robert Raymo (New York: New York University Press, 1976), p. 19.

Many of us in literature began our work on medieval women by looking at 'images of women in…', hoping that would tell us something about real medieval women, or what medieval authors thought about real women, or at least allow us to talk about somebody female besides the Wife of Bath. In the years since, Felicity Riddy and others have shown us the rewards of going beyond static representations of female figures, the importance of placing texts back into their scrupulously researched contexts, moving from the particulars of the manuscript as a material object to contemporary literary theory and back again, so that we understand far more about the culture and the lives that produced and received the works we study. To look at images now seems naïve. To look at images of women in the *Alliterative Morte Arthure* seems perverse, given how rarely they appear and how little they seem to signify in Arthur's heroic rise and fall and yet, as I hope to show, their apparently insignificant presence within the narrative embeds its heroic action in a civic domain the perspective of which is never directly articulated or fully realized but nevertheless, present. Critical discussion of the poem has been dominated by questions of Arthur's personal morality—is he too proud, too violent—or by discussions of the morality of war itself.[2] My focus is different, seeking to understand better the poet's social imagination through the female figures who seem so peripheral to the lives of his exemplary heroes and yet perform a crucial ideological and poetic role. [3]

The romance itself, the story of Arthur's Roman wars and tragic death, is heroic, masculine, and fully and powerfully realized. Its 4300 alliterative long lines evoke a landscape of bold and violent actions, of deep bonds between peers, of the pleasures of victory. Almost all of it takes place in the knight's world of council chamber, camp, and

---

[2]   A significant portion of modern criticism on the poem concerns itself with these questions. William Matthews, *The Tragedy of Arthur* (Berkeley: University of California Press, 1960) generated a critique of Arthur as tyrant which strongly influences later work, including the essays in *The Alliterative Morte Arthure: A Reassessment of the Poem* , ed. by Karl Heinz Göller (Cambridge: D. S. Brewer, 1981). See Michael Foley, 'The Alliterative *Morte Arthure*: An Annotated Bibliography, 1950–1975', *Chaucer Review*, 14 (1980), 166–87.

[3]   Two recent articles, which constitute a striking intervention in the poem's critical history, concern themselves with the construction of Arthur's masculinity: Jeff Westover, 'Arthur's End: The King's Emasculation in the Alliterative *Morte Arthure*', *Chaucer Review*, 32 (1998), 310 –24; Anne Clark Bartlett, 'Cracking the Penile Code: Reading Gender and Conquest in the Alliterative *Morte Arthure*', *Arthuriana*, 8 (1998), 56–75.

battlefield. The action begins when ambassadors from the Roman emperor, Lucius, appear demanding tribute. Arthur, having already conquered most of Europe, asserts his own ancestral rights to the title of emperor. His men, bored with peace and fearing the loss of their chivalric fame, enthusiastically cry, 'Now wakenes the war! Worshipped be Crist!' (l. 257).[4] The rest of the poem recounts a series of victories over the king's enemies in France and Italy. His triumphant progress to Rome and then the Holy Land is halted only when he learns that his regent Mordred has betrayed him, marrying Guenevere and seizing the British throne. Arthur and his men return home immediately and ultimately defeat the traitor, but at the cost of their own lives. This epic Arthur is not as familiar to us as the impotent ruler we know from French romance, or even from Malory, who used the *Alliterative Morte Arthure* as his main source for Book V of his own work.[5] The alliterative poet's version is based on a chronicle tradition which identifies Arthur with the history of Great Britain, and makes him the epitome of a great ruler.[6]

In a poem which defines kingship in terms of reputation, conquest, and the *comitatus*, it is not surprising that there are only four consequential females in the poem.[7] They are Guenevere; the Duchess of Brittany (who has been murdered by a giant); the latter's foster-mother; and the Duchess of Lorraine. The first three are the poet's means of invoking what is otherwise practically invisible in his story, the society for which Arthur as king is responsible—people's daily lives, the relationships and buildings and routines and activities which constitute ordinary social existence. I believe that the fourth, the Duchess of Lorraine, because of this metonymic function, becomes the poet's way of confronting the terrible, and for him, inescapable paradox of heroic narrative—that saviours are

---

[4] All citations will be from *King Arthur's Death*, ed. by Larry D. Benson (Exeter: University of Exeter, 1986), the most easily available edition. (I have not reproduced his accent marks.) The fullest edition is *Morte Arthure: A Critical Edition*, ed. by Mary Hamel (New York: Garland, 1984). Glosses are mine.

[5] Elizabeth Archibald, 'Beginnings: *The Tale of King Arthur* and *King Arthur and the Emperor Lucius*', in *A Companion To Malory*, ed. by Elizabeth Archibald and A. S. G. Edwards (Cambridge: D. S. Brewer, 1996), pp. 145–51.

[6] Robert H. Fletcher, *The Arthurian Material in the Chronicles*, 2nd edn (New York: Burt Franklin, 1966). The affair between Lancelot and Guenevere is not part of this tradition, and Lancelot is a very minor knight in the poem.

[7] Arthur has a dream (ll. 3223–3445) in which Fortuna appears, but she is a figure outside the social realm which interests me here.

necessarily destroyers. As she kneels before Arthur at the gates of her ruined city, Metz, the Duchess for a moment forces us to consider the cost of royal honour, a cost which romance usually protects us from. Like the Chandos Herald cited above, the alliterative poet is deeply invested in knighthood as ideal and practice, and as a consequence is unable to resolve the dilemma inherent in Arthur's role, or explicate the meaning of his tragedy, except by a return to traditional medieval morality. So, in the passages devoted to Arthur's dream of Fortune, we learn once more that the greatest men are subject to the inexorable spin of Fortune's wheel, and that, as Arthur's 'philosophers' explain, he has sinned in shedding blood and must pay (ll. 3218–3455). Then, they tell him, his life 'shall in romaunce be redde with real [royal] knightes' (l. 3440), renown and repentance co-existing in the same uneasy but familiar apposition in the poem as in the biography of the Black Prince.

I want to argue that attention to the treatment of female figures in this work suggests a more complex, if incomplete, understanding of the medieval yearning for hero-kings, despite what people knew of armed conflict. The philosophers who explicate Arthur's dreams know exactly what they signify. Unlike those learned men, I cannot read the appearances of these women to find within the text a conscious solution to the dilemma of war, since I believe as females they embody its contradictions, but offer us no overt *moralitas* or comforting *sententia*. In the discussion that follows I quote extensively, because the meanings I want to address exist on the level of language, in the juxtaposition of ideas, in subtle choices of diction, imagery, and syntax, and thus disappear when paraphrased or summarized.

Women in the poem are always encountered in public, in passages which slip back and forth between particular women and the king's more general concerns. Arthur's farewell to Guenevere occurs after he has already disposed of her, so to speak. She forms one item in a long list of obligations handed over to Mordred, no less and no more an object of the king's concern than his lands, his game, his laws:

> I make thee keeper, Sir Knight, of kingrikes many,
> Warden worshipful, to weld all my landes
> That I have wonnen of war in this world rich.
> I will that Waynor, my wife, in worship be holden,
> That her want no wele ne welth that her likes;
> Look my kidd casteles be clenlich arrayed,
> There sho maye sujourn herselve with seemlich bernes;
> Fond my forestes be frithed, of frendship for ever,

> That none warray my wild but Waynor herselven,
> And that in the sesoun when grees is assigned,
> That sho take her solace in certain times.
> Chaunceller and chamberlain change as thee likes,
> Auditours and officers, ordain them thyselven,
> Both jurees and judges, and justices of landes;
> Look thou justify them well that injury workes. (ll. 649–63)[8]

Arthur's speech slips without any break from the queen's 'solace' to chancellors and chamberlains, and it is difficult to know if he is still thinking of her, or of the populace at large. When we actually see him with Guenevere, the scene is suffused with a relatively detached sentimentality. He is shown empathizing with her grief but expresses none of his own, no pain at leaving her.

> Now he takes his leve and lenges no longer,
> At lordes, at lege-men that leves hym behinden;
> And senn that worthiliche wye went unto chamber
> For to comfort the queen, that in care lenges.
> Waynor waikly weepand him kisses,
> Talkes to him tenderly with teres ynow;
> 'I may werye the wye that this war moved,
> That warnes me worship of my wedde lorde.
> All my liking of life out of land wendes,
> And I in langour am left, leve ye, forever.
> Why ne might I, dere love, die in your armes,
> Ere I this destainy of dole sholde drie by mine one?'
> 'Greve thee not, Gaynour, for Goddes love of heven,
> Ne grouch not my ganging; it shall to good turn!
> Thy wandrethes and thy weeping woundes mine herte.
> I may not wite of this wo for all this world rich.' (ll. 693–708)[9]

---

[8] I make you regent, sir knight, of many kingdoms, honoured guardian, to rule all the lands I have won by war in this great world. I desire my wife, Guenevere, to be honoured, so that she lacks no possessions or luxury which might please her. See that my noble castles be properly maintained, where she may reside with suitable lords. See that my forests are preserved, for the sake of my lasting friendship. Let none hunt but Guenevere, but only in the appropriate season, when the game is sufficiently fat, so that she takes her pleasures in fixed times. Chancellors and chamberlains replace as you will; name your own auditors and officers, juries and judges, justices of the peace. See that you do justice to those who do harm.

[9] Now he takes his leave of the lords and vassals who remain behind and stays no longer. Afterwards that worthy man went into the chamber to comfort the queen, who lingers in sorrow. Guenevere, softly weeping, kisses him, speaks to him tenderly with plenteous

Like his forests, his castles, his auditors and his judges, Guenevere is part of the social infrastructure Arthur is leaving behind, but must not abandon. The careful planning, the organization of resources, the practical details so noteworthy in this passage are elsewhere in the poem characteristic of Arthur's military operations. What I want to emphasize here is not Guenevere's status as possession, however valued, or his obvious limitations as a husband, but the way in which she forms part of the continuous and difficult world of king-as-administrator. As Arthur reminds Mordred,

> Thou has clenly the cure that to my crown longes
> Of all my wordles wele and my wife eek. (ll. 673–74)[10]

There is no opposition of public-private, male-female in this poem, only the juxtaposition of two kinds of public realms: one masculine and martial, represented by knights, the other heterosexual and quotidian, represented by the noble women who are part and figure of the world which knighthood in chivalric theory sustains and protects. The other roles which romance grants to ladies, to be the object of the knight's endeavours, as the companions and arbiters of his elegant festivities and the reward of his prowess as courtly mistress or rich heiress, are absent in this narrative. Women are here a source of more-or-less anxious care, always grieving victims, never a source of pleasure.

This identification of women with a network of royal responsibilities—people, buildings, offices, systems—becomes even clearer in the next section I want to examine, Arthur's defeat of the giant at St Michael's Mount. When Arthur learns that a fiend 'that tormentes thy pople [people]' (l. 842), has abducted, raped, and murdered the Duchess of Brittany, he goes off to defeat a figure who is evil incarnate, the dark mirror or opposite of everything a good king is meant to represent. The encounter, notable for its epic excesses, wealth of detail, and mordant humour, proves the king's moral right to the throne. Arthur protects

---

tears: 'I may curse the man who started this war, and who denies me the honour of my husband. All my pleasure in life departs from this land, and I in misery am left, believe me, forever. Why might I not, dear love, die in your arms, before I suffer alone this sorrowful fate?' 'Grieve not, Guenevere, for God's love, nor grumble at my leaving—it shall turn out well. Your distress and your weeping wound my heart. I cannot bear to experience this woe, for all this noble world.'

[10] You have completely the responsibility which belongs to my crown, of all my worldly possessions, and my wife, too.

women; the giant rapes and murders them. Arthur weeps for the innocent; the giant eats small children. Arthur is a member of a loving community, generous to his adherents; the giant is an isolated figure whose only relationships are greedy and violent. The epic tone, the use of an idyllic landscape to introduce the episode, the single combat, mark a return to an unproblematic heroic past, carefully framed, symbolically crucial but in structural terms a digression from the poem's main action, which is the war against Lucius.[11]

But if this is, as has been claimed, a notably phallic contest,[12] it is also the one place in the poem where there is a developed and authoritative female voice. Much of what we know about the giant is narrated by a grieving widow, 'wringand her handes, / And gretand [weeping] on a grave grisly teres' (ll. 950–51). She warns the incognito king, who claims that he has been sent as a messenger for 'mendement [redress] of the pople' (l. 989), that were he 'wighter [more valiant] than Wade, or Wawain either' (l. 964), he could not defeat such a monster.

> For bothe landes and lythes full little by he settes;
> Of rentes ne of red gold reckes he never,
> For he will lenge out of law, as himself thinkes,
> Withouten license of lede, as lorde in his owen. (ll. 994–97)[13]

Fifteen kings have sent him their beards as tribute, 'for saught of the pople' [for the sake of reconciliation] (l. 1007), and until he gets Arthur's, 'hurdes he here to outraye his pople' [he dwells here to harass his—i.e. Arthur's—people] (l. 1010). What follows is a spectacular demonstration to her and to all those he is supposed to protect that he is a king who can live up to the reputation his knights have earned him.

The giant's victims are both specific—the poor duchess slit to the navel (l. 979), the three wretched maidens turning the spits on which Christian infants cook (l. 1029)—, and the more generalized 'people'. When Arthur first learns of the abduction he grieves for the lady, but he also cries out in pity 'of the pople' (l. 888). This association of a particular female body, needing protection, with an abstract concept of

---

[11] John Finlayson, 'Rhetorical "Descriptio" of Place in the Alliterative *Morte Arthure*', *Modern Philology*, 61 (1963), 1–11.

[12] Bartlett, 'Cracking the Penile Code', pp. 59–68.

[13] Full little he cares for territories and estates. He never thinks of revenues or gold, for he will dwell outside the law, as he pleases, without anyone's permission, like a lord in his own lands.

the king's subjects recurs in the poem as a natural relationship in the poet's mind. There are almost forty uses of '*pople*' in the poem, three-quarters of them meaning 'subjects of the king'. These subjects, frequently modified by a possessive, are almost always spoken of as objects of royal pity, and/or of violence. Their victimization, like the Duchess's, demands Arthur's response. In this episode alone there are ten uses of '*pople*'. When Arthur encounters the cannibalistic monster in person, the poet tells us that 'because of his pople, / His herte bleedes for bale [anguish]' (ll. 1053–54). His role as protector of all his subjects, not just of the noblewoman who occasions the encounter, is formally acknowledged by a grateful crowd, praising him as 'governour under Gode', who has 'in thy realtee [royalty] revenged thy pople' (ll. 1198–1207). Arthur's final acts are to distribute the giant's treasure 'to my dere pople', and to found a convent in memory of the duchess. Like the preservation of castles and forests linked syntactically to Guenevere, the building of a convent in memory of the duchess associates the figures of royal ladies with permanency and stability. By the alchemy of lordship, Arthur's guardianship of the private, vulnerable female somehow transforms her body into a monument to royal responsibility for all his people.

These scenes and associations I have been tracing are quite clearly the poet's own elaborations on the material he inherits, enriching but not yet complicating our response to Arthur's campaigns. The Roman challenge and the eager reaction it evokes from the ambitious warriors of Arthur's court, Arthur's praise of his knights and the battle with the giant form part of Geoffrey of Monmouth's foundational text, and are retained in his Anglo-Norman and Middle English translators, Wace and Layamon, but the alliterative poet reworks the giant episode to highlight Arthur's heroism.[14] He also emphasizes the theme of Arthur as nurturer versus the giant as (literally) devourer, for example transforming the latter's diet from mere beasts to baptized infants 'chopped in a chargeur of chalk-white silver,/ with pickle and powder of precious spices' (ll. 1026–27). Arthur's protective function as king, more broadly dispersed in the sources, becomes more focussed, as does the symbolic link between particular noblewomen and a more abstract 'people' the text has earlier established.

---

[14] On the poem's use of these texts see J. L. N. O'Laughlin, 'The English Alliterative Romances', in *Arthurian Literature in the Middle Ages*, ed. by Roger S. Loomis (Oxford: Clarendon Press, 1959), pp. 523–24.

However, in the poem's account of the Siege of Metz, this association between Arthur's conquests and the comfort and safety of noblewomen/ subjects becomes enormously problematic. Having defeated the Roman troops, Arthur and his army march on Lorraine, whose Duke is called a 'renk rebel' [a man rebellious] to the Round Table (l. 2402). Metz is the Duke's chief city, the object of a fierce assault described in great detail, detail which heretofore has only been lavished on accounts of battles between knights. Generally, when critics discuss this part of the poem they attend less to the actual siege than to what is really a digression. Once his siege weaponry is in place before the city walls, Arthur sends Gawain and some young knights off on a foraging expedition which is described at length (ll. 2482–3010), before the narrative returns to the actual conquest of Metz. In this interlude Gawain, roaming 'wonders to seek' (l. 2514), is delighted to encounter a pagan prince at a ford. They battle to the point of death, exchange vows of friendship and are healed of their fatal wounds by a magical potion. Then the incredibly outnumbered foragers defeat the Duke of Lorraine and his forces. This is clearly an episode from a *roman d'aventure*, in which the good always triumph despite the odds, plots are freed from the constraints of probability, and the brotherhood and prowess of knighthood, not national interest, matters most. When Gawain encourages his knights by saying they will be 'loved with ladies' (l. 2866) we know that momentarily at least we are in a different poem. The sylvan beauty of the landscape which introduces this episode underscores the difference between the kind of romance-world in which no permanent harm is ever done, and the world of the main campaign, in which actions have real consequences. As the battle with the giant, introduced by similar scenery, is deliberately epic, and unrealistic, this is deliberately escapist, and unrealistic.

The poet's sources for this expansive and nostalgic return to traditional romance, the Foray of Gadres episode of Alexander legend, and the Fierebras episode of Charlemagne legend, are almost always, and misleadingly, referred to as the sources of the siege of Metz itself.[15] However, neither episode accounts for the poem's description of what happens within the actual city . The siege of Metz is part of the alliterative *Morte's* celebrated 'realism', the mode which suggests that the overarching narrative of Arthur's march on Rome is immersed in a known

---

[15] Hamel's very useful survey of sources (pp. 34–58) demonstrates the consistency of this confusion.

and knowable world.[16] Metz is a new site, physically and ideologically, for Arthurian romance, and therefore worth further consideration. Both the detailed account of the siege and the terser account of its outcome—Arthur's encounter with the Duchess and the defeated inhabitants of Metz—are unfamiliar and thought-provokingly different in their tone and associations from what has come before in the poem.

The metonymic equivalences I have tried to establish—women, subjects, protection, systems—implode in the siege's conclusion. They have not been replaced by the familiar trope of women as invaded bodies, the metaphorical double of the sacked castle. Women are still protected, but the structures they inhabit both literally and figuratively are destroyed in the relentless necessities of war. The description of the battered city seems to be a unique realization in late-medieval narrative of what war against civilians looks like.[17] Metz is literally turned inside out, as the narrative exposes the plaster walls, chimneys, inns, chapels, and hospitals which are the signs of wealth and civic and domestic order.

> The king then to assaut he sembles his knightes
> ...
> Then boldly they busk and bendes engines
> Paises in pillotes and proves their castes.
> Minsteres and masondewes they mall to the erthe,
> Churches and chapels chalk-white blaunched,
> Stone steeples full stiff in the street ligges,
> Chambers with chimnees and many chef inns
> Paised and pelled down plastered walles. (ll. 3032–42)[18]

The move from Arthur's role as master of the technology of war to his role as guardian of women and children appears nearly seamless. This passage immediately continues:

---

[16] Lee Patterson, 'The Romance of History and the Alliterative *Morte Arthure*', *Negotiating the Past* (Madison: University of Wisconsin Press, 1987), p. 212. This article is a very sophisticated historicization of the poem.

[17] For comparison, see the alliterative 'Siege of Jerusalem' and the alliterative 'Gest Historiale of the Destruction of Troy', both works the poet probably knew, and the sieges in Chaucer's 'Knight's Tale' and *Troilus and Criseyde*.

[18] The king then gathers his knights for the attack. Then boldly they draw down the beam of the catapults, load in shot and try their aim. Monasteries and hospitals they beat down to the ground. Churches and chapels, white-washed chalk-white, sturdy stone steeples, lie in the street, rooms with chimneys and many fine homes. They battered and beat down plastered walls.

The pine of the pople was pitee for to here!
Then the duchess her dight with damesels rich,
The countess of Crasine with hir clere maidens,
Kneeles down in the kirnelles there the kyng hoved,
On a covered horse, comlyly arrayed,
They knew him by countenaunce and cried full loud:
'King crowned of kind, take keep to these wordes!
We beseek you, sir, as soveraign and lord,
That ye save us today, for sake of your Crist;
Send us some succour and saughte with the pople,
Ere the citee be sodenly with assaut wonnen!'
He veres his vesere with a vout noble,
With visage virtuous, this valiant berne;
Meles to her mildly with full meek wordes:
'Shall none misdo you, madame, that to me longes;
I give you charter of pees, and your chef maidens,
The childer and the chaste men, the chevalrous knightes;
The duke is in daunger; dredes it but little!
He shall be deemed full well, dout you nought elles.' (ll. 3043–61)[19]

There are distinct echoes of Arthur's speeches to Mordred and to
Guenevere cited above, (p. 296) as he establishes order and makes sure
the Duchess and her children are provided for:

He devised and delt to diverse lordes
A dower for the duchess and her dere childer;
Wrought wardenes by wit to weld all the landes
That he had wonnen of war through his wise knightes.(ll. 3072–75)[20]

---

[19] The pain of the people was pitiful to hear. Then the duchess went with her noble ladies,
with the Countess of Quercy (?) and her noble maidens. They kneel down in the
battlements, where the king stood, on a caparisoned horse, splendidly arrayed. They knew
him by his appearance, and cried loudly, 'King crowned by right, take heed to these words.
We beseech you, sir, as sovereign and lord, that you save us today for the sake of your
Christ. Grant us some protection and make peace with the people, before the city is at once
won by assault.' He opens his visor, with a noble expression, with a virtuous countenance,
this valiant man, speaks to her mildly, with truly meek words: 'None shall ill-use you,
madam, who belongs to me. I give you and your noble maidens a formal pledge of peace,
and the children, the clergy and chivalrous knights. The duke is in my power, but do not
fear. He shall be judged full well, doubt it not.'

[20] He allotted and distributed to different lords a dowry for the duchess and her beloved
children. By good sense he made governors to rule all the lands that he had won by war
through his skilled knights.

Thus, what he seizes by war—the city of Metz—he appropriates morally by his concern for the Duchess who surrenders it. Once more his right to rule is yoked to his care for noble women.

There is really no precedent in the poem, or in its sources, for this remarkable combination of images of destruction and of benevolence.[21] Ruined buildings are juxtaposed to the figure of a kind, virtuous conqueror; reality confronts legend. As Lee Patterson has said, 'the effects of war on society as a whole are rendered with a dispassionate attention that is all the more moving for its self-restraint'.[22] The poet makes some attempts to ameliorate the brutality of the siege, partly with the piling up of adjectives like 'mild' and 'meek', and partly by eliminating guns from Arthur's weaponry, although by the end of the fourteenth century they would normally have been used.[23] Nonetheless, the collocation of women, buildings, and Arthur collapses here. The conqueror and the protector can no longer be reconciled through the displacement of violence onto an acceptable target, whether giants or pagan warriors. Metz is officially the Duke's city, but affectively and poetically it belongs to the Duchess. She and Metz occupy the same physical and rhetorical space, whereas the Duke is encountered only on the field.

The Siege of Metz has been seen by a number of critics as marking a turning point in the poem, when Arthur turns from hero to villain.[24] Rather than entering into an argument about whether or not this poem is 'anti-war' or to what extent Arthur exhibits the sin of pride, I would like to focus more on what Metz as a specific locale might signify, a subject which has received remarkably little critical attention. Since the attack on Metz is the poet's invention, it is worth considering why this particular city, which would not have been familiar to English audiences from Arthurian tradition or the campaigns of the Hundred Years War, is singled out. Larry Benson accounts for Metz's presence by its position on the pilgrimage route to Rome known as the 'German way,' but clearly for the poet Metz is more than an arbitrary stop on Arthur's route.[25] I suspect,

---

[21] Malcolm Hebron, *The Medieval Siege* (Oxford: Clarendon Press, 1997), p 61. Hebron believes the poet draws on both contemporary experience and literary texts to describe the siege, but finds no precedents for the particular images used.

[22] Page 212.

[23] Hebron, pp. 60–61.

[24] See, for example, Matthews, Hamel, Göller.

[25] 'The Date of the Alliterative Morte Arthure', pp. 21–22. Adam Usk, whom Benson cites as an example of someone using a similar route, does not pass through Metz at all.

but cannot yet prove, that the English poet knew the so-called Lorraine cycle, a series of twelfth- and thirteenth-century *chansons de geste* which recount a seemingly endless series of wars between the Dukes of Lorraine, whose chief city is Metz, and the lords of Bordeaux.[26] One reason for believing that these poems, rather than the real Metz, are his inspiration, is his description of it as 'citee of that seinour [the Duke of Lorraine] that soveraign is holden' (l. 2419). In fact, in the fourteenth century, Metz was a major trading centre, with a peculiarly independent status as a free city under the Emperor.[27] Its citizens, and especially the ruling oligarchy, fiercely resisted any ducal claims. By good fortune, we have a fourteenth-century verse chronicle from Metz, recounting the extraordinary virtues and prowess of its citizens, and telling how in 1324 it successfully defended itself against an alliance composed of Jean of Luxembourg, King of Bohemia, Baldwin, archbishop of Treves, Edward I, count of Bar, and Ferry IV, Duke of Lorraine.[28] The chronicle begins by describing the city:

> Touttes flours sormonte la rose;
> Chescuns sceit bien c'est veriteit;
> Pour ceu vous ai dist ceste chose
> Qu'ensi fait Mets toutes citeis,
> Car en lie maint prosperiteit,
> Franchise, avoir et gens pitouse,
> Cortoisie et humiliteit. (ll. 8–14)

(Everyone knows this truth, that the rose surpasses all flowers; I remind you of this, that in the same way Metz surpasses all cities. In her reside prosperity, franchise, wealth, charity, courtesy, and humility.)

Metz's wealth, its prestige in trade and manufacture, its ancient history are all evoked when the English poet tells us it is 'in Lorraine alosed

---

The Chronicle of Adam Usk, ed. and trans. by Chris Given-Wilson (Oxford: Clarendon Press, 1997), pp. 152–53. George Parks, in *The English Traveler to Italy* (Rome: Edizioni de Storia, n.d.), v. I, barely mentions late-medieval Metz, which seems to have been a very minor stop for pilgrims.

[26] Catherine Jones, in *The Noble Merchant: Problems of Genre and Lineage in Hervis De Mes*, Studies in the Romance Languages (Chapel Hill: University of North Carolina, 1993), briefly summarizes the cycle, pp. 13–17.

[27] Alain Girardot, 'La Republique Messine,' in *Histoire de Metz*, ed. by François-Yves Le Moigne (Toulouse: Privat, 1986), 145–146.

[28] *La Guerre de Metz en 1324: poème du XIVe siècle*, ed. by F. Bonnardot and E. de Bouteiller (Paris: Firmin-Didot, 1875).

[praised] as London is here' (l. 2418). When he says this, he momentarily steps out of the Arthurian past, where Lorraine was never important, and into the late fourteenth-century world he and his audience know. The common locus of action in the romance is the court, the field, or the wilderness. When this poet imagines Metz, he imagines, briefly, something new. He speaks not of its fortifications but what exists within its walls: human activity, productivity, natural, religious, and social order. The white chimneys and plastered walls are references to a world which is opposed to heroism, because, unlike knights, ordinary people require peace in order to prosper. The restoration of the Duchess's dowry will not rebuild the shops and houses which belong to the citizens. By broadening the social context, by depicting a new landscape, not the spring landscape looking back to an idealized literary past, but a city with all its activity and variety, the poet makes us recognize the social, as opposed to the moral or individual, price of heroic conquests. In Metz, the link between women, stability, Arthurian rule, and material permanence is broken.

Although unusual for Northern Europe in its independent status, Metz is typical of many fourteenth-century cities, which under the impetus of the Hundred Years War, quickly became adept at self-defence, devoting a significant part of their resources to fortifications and armed response.[29] The Metz chronicler proudly lists all the city's preparations for resisting enemies: raising money and troops, digging massive ditches, reinforcing walls etc. He would sympathize with the citizens who shoot at Arthur from their walls (ll. 2425–26). I am not going so far as to claim here that the Middle English poet shares the viewpoint of the French chronicler who constantly praises citizens of all ranks, or that he is interested in giving shape and depth to an alternative world, that of the bourgeoisie and other urban citizens. Indeed, by conflating the Metz of his time with the Metz of an epic literary past, he is able to contain the challenge to feudal hierarchy offered by a city which is self-reliant, neither needing nor desiring lords to protect it. Any explicit critiques the poem offers are framed in conservative terms—fortune and sin. Rather than pursuing the values the city represents as a counter-voice to heroic chivalry, the poem returns to its familiar perspective, linking women and 'the people' as objects of royal responsibility. In the final assault Metz is rendered as innocent and as passive as the Duchess. She is in many ways a familiar

---

[29] Michael Wolfe, 'Siege Warfare and the *Bonnes Villes* of France', in *The Medieval City Under Siege*, ed. by Ivy A. Corfis and Michael Wolfe (Woodbridge: Boydell Press, 1995), pp. 59–60.

figure, the supplicant queen so popular in medieval literature and chronicle.[30] Her dramatization of her weakness before a sympathetic audience is a test of the powerful male's capacity for pity, his acquiescence a sign of his power.[31] However, if the spectacle of the Duchess on her knees before Arthur calls attention to his magnanimity, the descriptive language forces our attention back to the setting, the ruined city which he has created.

The trope of the vulnerable woman is both enabling and crippling for the poet of the *Morte Arthure*. It allows him to think about the world outside the scope of his inherited material, to allude to it by drawing on his (and our) culture's ingrained belief that females need guardianship, and are valuable precisely because that need inspires virtue in the powerful. Always dependent and never independent, she can never offer, on behalf of the world she ostensibly represents, a new perspective on heroism and hierarchy as a model of rule. Through her we can count the cost of war, and deplore the violence which is so much a part of human history. However, she can never help us critique the structures and ideas which make war so much a part of social arrangements. The rebellious lovers of courtly romance unmask the costs of feudal marriage, suggesting alternatives in the process. Because the vulnerable female in the alliterative poet's thought and text never rises above the role she plays as the object of chivalric anxiety, she can never force an examination of the costs of the virtues she inspires. Certainly the passive females here are neither historically nor textually determined. Romances, chronicles, and chansons de geste are full of strong-willed and articulate women, ready to give advice. When the Black Prince writes to his wife, Joan of Kent, 'My dearest and truest sweetheart and beloved companion, as to news, you will want to know that we were encamped in the fields near Navarrete...',[32] he assumes that she can take an intelligent interest in his activities. The Arthur who is the hero of this romance could never write such a letter to Guenevere. Exchanges between women and men presuppose a world of interdependence which in this poem exists only

---

[30] Paul Strohm, 'Queens As Intercessors,' *Hochon's Arrow* (Princeton: Princeton University Press, 1992), pp. 95–119.

[31] Felicity Riddy, 'Engendering Pity in the *Franklin's Tale*,' in *Feminist Readings in Middle English Literature*, ed. by Ruth Evans and Lesley Johnson (London: Routledge, 1994), pp.54–71. She notes how 'pity as a social virtue sanctifies hierarchy ...it is a masculinist strategy' (p. 57).

[32] Barber, p. 83.

between peers—the knights of the Round Table. The poem's women are part of the king's own affinity—wife, wife's cousin, royal ward—but no more autonomous than the poor widow beloved of homilists. Women, like the undifferentiated 'people' over whom the king rules, can offer nothing but their need for a strong protector. Strength and weakness intertwine to fix a hierarchy which can be destroyed (as treachery destroys the Arthurian dream) but never undone. When Arthur loses his knights at the end, he becomes like a woman, a grieving widow, weeping over Gawain's body, unable to imagine a life lived on other terms.

> I may werye and weep and wring mine handes,
> For my wit and my worship away is forever!
> Of all lordshippes I take leve to mine end! (ll. 4286–88)[33]

In our own world, like the poet, or like the reader who, at the end of the manuscript, denying its account of Arthur's death, wrote 'Here lies Arthur, king once and king to be',[34] we too seem to crave heroes to save us, even while we watch on the evening news the weeping women such heroes are doomed to create.

---

[33] I may curse and weep and wring my hands, for my reason and honour are gone forever. I take leave of all honours at my death.

[34] Benson, *King Arthur's Death*, p. 238.

Houses and Households in Late Medieval England: An Archaeological Perspective

JANE GRENVILLE

We may think we can understand the operation of the medieval household from documentary sources alone, and it is true that court depositions, wills, inventories, tales of domestic circumstance, books of etiquette and didactic poems all have much to say about the workings of the medieval *familia*. However, my principal contention in this paper is that until we begin to comprehend the material framing of social practice, we cannot really speak of 'women's place' in the household (or, for that matter, anyone else's).

I do not wish to dwell on a discussion of the definition of the term 'household' in a medieval urban context. It is a subject that has received much consideration, both in print and in informal discussion.[1] David Herlihy asserts that the late medieval 'household is a co-residential group with parents and children—the primary biological descent group—at its core'.[2] I take a broader view: cross-culturally the related terms 'household', 'family', 'housegroup' all usually denote the smallest unit of social reproduction in spite of the fact that they may have very different

---

[1] See for example Peter Laslett and Richard Wall, *Household and Family in Past Time*, (Cambridge: Cambridge University Press, 1972); Jean-Louis Flandrin, *Families in Former Times*, translated from the French by Richard Southern (Cambridge: Cambridge University Press, 1976); David Herlihy, *Medieval Households* (Cambridge, MA: Harvard University Press, 1985); Barbara Hanawalt, *The Ties that Bound* (Oxford: Oxford University Press, 1986); P. J. P. Goldberg, *Women, Work and Life Cycle in a Medieval Economy* (Oxford: Clarendon Press, 1992), and the forthcoming volumes from the York Urban Households Research Group series.

[2] Herlihy, p. 132.

meanings in terms of consanguinity (members of a household are not
necessarily related, whereas those of a family generally are, through
blood or affinity). This essay, however, concerns households in terms of
space and social practice. Having outlined a theoretical approach to the
role of space in social practice and a methodology for its study, I will
illustrate the potential of that methodology in understanding social space
in medieval York. The results presented here represent some of the first
applications of this type of analysis to the urban domestic buildings of
medieval England: work in progress under the aegis of the Medieval
Urban Household Research Group, based at the Centre for Medieval
Studies at the University of York promises further insights in the future.

I. FINDING A THEORETICAL BASELINE AND DEVELOPING A METHODOLOGY

Archaeologists have always been interested in the configuration of space.
The relative positions of finds and of excavated features have been carefully recorded since scientific excavation began and as standing buildings
were drawn into the archaeological repertoire, a similar rigour was
applied. Theoretical positions have changed. Early work sought to
classify material into typologies. A desire to understand behaviour in the
past led to work within the positivist school of 'New Archaeology' in the
1960s and '70s, which saw finds distributions as essentially illustrative of
economic systems and social relationships—material culture was
recognized as a *passive* reflection of social action. More recently, the role
of spatial relationships in the regulation of social action has attracted the
attention of the social sciences more generally and archaeology, within
the broad church of 'post-processual' archaeology, has taken its cue from
sociologists, geographers, architects, and anthropologists to consider the
active role of material culture and its spatial relationships in the
construction of social identity and social behaviour.[3]

---

[3] Not only my professional formation as an archaeologist but personal experience has
forced me to confront the immediacy of the agency of the material setting in social action.
During a recent trip to Japan, I was taken by my hostess for a bathe at a hot springs spa.
Although I had read in travel guides that there is a very specific etiquette in such
situations, my response followed my own, culturally specific, reading of the surroundings:
faced with what looked to me like a small swimming pool, I leapt in. The look of
anguished horror on my minder's face made me realize instantly what I had done—you
should never get into a Japanese bath or hot springs pool without soaping and showering

Methodologically, even in these more dynamic conceptualizations of space, the identification of specific aspects of the material record with exclusive gender patterns is difficult. Straightforward equations between material culture and social status are notoriously unreliable: one-to-one attributions of 'female space' or 'male space' are simplistic and open to challenge, on both theoretical and methodological grounds. The social use of space is more nuanced and subtle than a simple male/female dichotomy allows. Roberta Gilchrist's ground-breaking studies of gendered space wisely focus on the higher status arena of castles where we might expect the separation of the relatively few women in residence (the Earl of Northumberland's household in the fifteenth century contained one hundred and sixty six men and nine women), and on nunneries, culturally encoded as distinctively female spaces (initially constructed as such by *male* interests and certainly inclusive of domains and activities gendered masculine, such as the eucharistic rites of priests and the spiritual direction of confessors).[4] In the busy, crowded context of the medieval town, female and male routines surely coincided physically daily, hourly and minute by minute. While questions of where men or women carried out separate social activities are interesting and important, so too are those of how they interacted in the household, and how gender-specific or mixed activities can be related to the social construction of the household. In looking for exclusively female space, we may be ignoring by far the greater part of women's lives.

How is the archaeologist, whose principal (but by no means sole) category of evidence is material culture, to make a culture-specific identification of social space and hence of the role of buildings and their contents in the construction, reproduction, and subversion of social structure? The problem is not a new one: the relationship between social units and the space that they occupied has frequently been examined in

---

very thoroughly first. The clear water of the pool is for soaking and rinsing clean bodies, and emphatically not for washing dirty ones. The heinous nature of my action was comparable to defecating in an English swimming pool. My embarrassment was made more acute by the fact that, as in one of those lurid recurring nightmares of adolescence, I was actually stark naked. (If it is easy to make such a mistake in one's own life, how much easier to overlook the material conditions of a relatively well-documented past period and to miss a number of important cues and interrelations.)

[4]   Roberta Gilchrist, 'Medieval Bodies in the Material World: Gender, Stigma and the Body', in *Framing Medieval Bodies,* ed. by Sarah Kay and Miri Rubin (Manchester: Manchester University Press, 1994), pp. 43–61.

prehistoric and ethnographic contexts.[5] Archaeologists have addressed the problem with varying levels of success.[6] Throughout this essay, the term 'social space' will be used to indicate this relationship between space and behaviour. 'Material culture' refers to the things that people put into their buildings and to the physical structure of the buildings themselves.

II. METHODOLOGICAL TOOLS FOR INVESTIGATING MEDIEVAL HOUSEHOLDS

Three bodies of work provide particularly helpful tools here: a sociologist's account of the relationship between individual action and social structure, and two new archaeological categories of investigation. Anthony Giddens has proposed a powerful model of the reflexive nature of the relationship between individual action and social structure in his 'theory of structuration'.[7] He argues that actions take place within the preconditions set by social structures, which he defines as 'rule-resource sets, involved in the institutional articulation of social systems'. The results (intended and unintended) of those actions in turn have an impact

---

[5]   See for example J. Carsten and S. Hugh-Jones, *About the House: Lévi-Strauss and Beyond* (Cambridge: Cambridge University Press, 1995); Linda Donley-Reid 'A Structuring Structure: The Swahili House', in *Domestic Architecture and the Use of Space*, ed. by Susan Kent (Cambridge: Cambridge University Press, 1990), pp. 114–26; Donald Sanders, 'Behavioural Conventions and Archaeology: Methods for the Analysis of Ancient Architecture', in *Domestic Architecture and the Use of Space*, pp. 43–72; Ruth E. Tringham 'Households with Faces: The Challenge of Gender in Prehistoric Architectural Remains', in *Engendering Archaeology: Women and Prehistory*, ed. by Joan M. Gero and Margaret W. Conkey (Oxford: Blackwell, 1991), pp. 93–131.

[6]   There are three notable volumes of collected papers containing case studies, mainly dealing with excavated remains, and some zanier than others: *The Social Archaeology of Houses*, ed. by Ross Samson (Edinburgh: Edinburgh University Press, 1990); *Architecture and Order: Approaches to Social Space*, ed. by Michael Parker Pearson and Colin Richards (London: Routledge, 1994); *Meaningful Architecture: Social Interpretations of Buildings*, ed. by Martin Locock (Aldershot: Avebury, 1994).

[7]   Anthony Giddens, *New Rules of Sociological Method: a Positive Critique of Interpretative Sociologies* (London: Hutchinson, 1976); *Central Problems in Social Theory: Action, Structure and Contradiction in Social Analysis* (London: Macmillan, 1979); *The Constitution of Society: Outline of the Theory of Structuration* (Cambridge: Polity Press, 1984); J. B. Thompson, 'The Theory of Structuration', in *Social Theory of Modern Societies: Anthony Giddens and his Critics*, ed. by David Held and J. B. Thompson (Cambridge: Cambridge University Press, 1989).

on social structure, reinforcing it, weakening it, or deliberately challenging it. (A social gaffe, for instance, reinforces accepted etiquette in that the offender is unlikely to repeat the mistake). Structures are thus reproduced or modified by actions, and actions are defined and delimited by structures, even in situations where those structures are being challenged. 'Structuration' is the *process* of this loop. It is not, in itself, anything to do with physical structures, although one often hears it erroneously used in that sense in informal discussion. The implications for the issue of space were articulated by Giddens in his 1979 recension of the theory of structuration:

> Most forms of social theory have failed to take seriously enough *not only the temporality of social conduct but also its spatial attributes*. At first sight, nothing seems more banal and uninstructive than to assert that social activity occurs in time and space. But neither time nor space have been incorporated into the centre of social theory; rather, they are ordinarily treated more as 'environments' in which social action is enacted.[8]

In *The Constitution of Society* Giddens further argues for the importance of space, in the form of specific 'locales' as an active component, complete with physical cues, in social encounters. Familiarity with the locale induces 'ontological security', by which he means a solidly-based knowledge of 'how to go about' one's daily business (we have all experienced the ontological insecurity of an unfamiliar place).[9] Giddens suggests that 'locales' may be distinguished from simple 'places' by their zoning, both physical and temporal. As an example he takes the subdivisions of the contemporary house, with its various function-specific rooms such as bedrooms and bathrooms, noting that their use changes depending upon the time of day.[10]

Archaeologists have eagerly used Giddens's theory in seeking to identify within the physical remains of the past (both structures and artefacts) those elements of meaning which might lead us to a clearer understanding of the societies that created them as dynamic rather than static. There remain problems in the application of the theory of

---

[8]   *Central Problems*, p. 202, original italics.

[9]   If one considers how much more frightening a new school is to a small child than a new office to an adult worker, then one begins to understand the importance of structuration in fostering feelings of competence and confidence in social actors—adults have had longer to learn the rules, but every situation brings its own familiarities and fears.

[10]   *Constitution*, p. 119.

structuration in that a 'place' may seem identifiable to the stranger, but its
significance as a 'locale' may be quite other than that which one expects.
It can be difficult to recognize the significance of locales in their function
at a given time in the past while they continue to exist today as physical
places but with mutated meanings. (There are, for instance, obvious
problems of contemporary cultural overlay when it comes to interpreting
medieval buildings in which one works or shops daily and reconstructing
the meanings they held for their original users). Nevertheless,
archaeologists are continuing to explore the structuring of material
conditions in which medieval people lived and the kinds of power
relations which material culture was used to reproduce, and much
attention has been paid to the identification of locales and their associated
social meanings in the archaeological record.[11]

My own approach in the York Household Project develops from
Giddens's fundamental insight on the interactive nature of social action
and social structuring of space. I use a combination of detailed
stratigraphic analysis of buildings (by which I mean the use of close
observation of the relative chronology of elements within the structure)
with the study of buildings as the locale for the interplay of social
relations. This methodology has been successfully applied to other
categories of building within medieval York to illuminate the dynamics of
social networks at the levels of neighbourhood, parish, guild, and city
networks,[12] and is currently being developed for households.

---

[11] In medieval archaeology we are fortunate to have two trail-blazing full-length studies,
one on nunneries (Roberta Gilchrist, *Gender and Material Culture: The Archaeology of
Religious Women* (London: Routledge, 1994)) and the other on late medieval domestic
halls (Matthew Johnson, *Housing Culture: Traditional Architecture in an English Landscape* (London: University College London Press, 1993)) both dealing in an extensive
fashion with large groups of buildings. More recently, Katherine Giles has moved the
study forward significantly with her very detailed consideration of the precise relationship
between locale and social action in a highly specific context, that of three urban guildhalls.
Her work goes a long way to answering some of the methodological problems raised in
this paper, and I am indebted to her for many fruitful conversations on the matter: see
Katherine Giles, 'The Familiar Fraternity: Guildhalls and Social Identity in Late Medieval
and Early Modern York', in *The Familiar Past? Archaeologies of Late-Historical Britain*,
ed. by Sarah Tarlow and Susie West (London: Routledge, 1999); Katherine Giles,
'Guildhalls and Social Identity in York, c. 1350–1630' (unpublished doctoral thesis,
University of York, 1999).

[12] See, for instance Katherine Giles 'The Familiar Fraternity'; also Alex Woodcock
'Social and Symbolic Space in the Late Medieval Parish Church: an Archaeology of All
Saints North Street, York' (unpublished master's thesis, University of York, 1996).

In order to understand the recursive nature of social action and social structure, however, we must observe not only the original construction and the more major incidents of alteration but also minor adjustments to internal space and the use of particular construction techniques as visual cues to social actors. Here the ideas of Amos Rapoport are particularly useful for providing clear categories of evidence to consider.[13] He identifies three kinds of element within buildings: fixed features, semi-fixed features and moveable objects. By fixed features, he means the structural elements of a building—its walls, floors, ceilings, and roofs. Semi-fixed fixtures include furnishings, decorations, and moveable partitions. Non-fixed features are the people, their behaviour, and activities. Within the physical structure of the building we may make observations at two of Rapoport's three levels—those of fixed and semi-fixed features. As I will argue below à propos the timber frame of 7 Shambles, choices made in the construction of fixed features (such as roof type and patterns of wall-bracing, for instance), carry more than simply functional meaning. Semi-fixed features, such as temporary partitions, which may be identified in evidence as ephemeral as a line of empty nail-holes, have often been overlooked in past studies, but can raise many important issues.[14] Detailed recording can lead to an understanding of when, within the relative chronology of the house, a given partition was inserted and when it was removed. When seeking an understanding of the structure of the household, such information becomes critical: the question becomes not only *when* but *why* such changes were made. Are we observing changes in household size, family dynamics, commercial operations, or a combination of these and other factors? The detailed stratigraphic observation of the structure feeds back into the theoretical research agenda.

For me, Rapoport's categories have provided a strikingly useful, simple and elegant framework within which to work, for they constantly remind me to consider carefully the relationships between the fixed and semi-

---

[13] Amos Rapoport, 'Systems of Activities and Systems of Settings', in *Domestic Architecture and the Use of Space*, ed. by Susan Kent (Cambridge: Cambridge University Press, 1990), pp. 9–20 (p. 9).

[14] Royal Commission on Historical Monuments (England) (RCHME), *An Inventory of the Historical Monuments in the City of York Volume 111: South-West of the Ouse* (London: HMSO, 1972); *An Inventory of the Historical Monuments in the City of York Volume IV: Outside the City Walls East of the Ouse* (London: HMSO, 1975); *Volume V: The Central Area* (London: HMSO, 1981).

fixed features (which make up most of the evidence from which I work) and the people who used them, who are the real subject of my study. Rapoport does not offer any quick solutions, but he does provide some caveats. One must beware of the temptation to assume that there is a direct relationship between architecture and behaviour. He notes that it is unsafe to assume that architecture 'encloses behaviour and does so tightly' and hence that 'inferences from architecture to activities ... become much more difficult'.[15] This is because the same space can change its nature by the re-organisation of semi-fixed features and the various activities of its occupants. In commenting on the relevance of this to the study of past societies, he notes that 'the inevitable absence of people makes inference from environment to activities much more difficult. *It also makes analysis of semi-fixed cues critical*'.[16] Further, he insists that single settings are not adequate units of analysis and that a single action can only be understood in the context of a series of activities or as part of daily, weekly, or seasonal behaviour patterns. It follows that single houses, or even groups of houses, are not sufficient units of analysis, but that the spaces in between must also be understood— neighbourhood and urban space become central in an understanding of the function of the urban house. Tucked away in his argument, but of crucial importance for the York project, is the comment that: 'the distinction commonly made between 'function' and 'meaning' is incorrect; meaning is not only part of function but *it is often the most important function*'.[17]

The third of my methodological tools is a way of looking at buildings developed at the Bartlett School of Architecture by Bill Hillier and Julienne Hanson.[18] Access analysis at its simplest is a method of mapping movements through buildings. It is an exercise to allow the comparison of one building with another by identifying the elements and relations which make up the character of its social space. By defining relationships through an understanding of the relationship between spaces, rather than the specific size and status properties of individual rooms, a configura-

---

[15] Rapoport, p. 11.

[16] Rapoport, p. 13, original italics.

[17] Rapoport, p. 12, original italics.

[18] Bill Hillier and Julienne Hanson, *The Social Logic of Space* (Cambridge: Cambridge University Press, 1984); Julienne Hanson, *Decoding Homes and Houses* (Cambridge: Cambridge University Press, 1998).

tional analysis is possible. Put simply, the resulting illustration shows not the plan of the building, but a series of circles, representing rooms, and lines representing access between them (for example, see the access analysis demonstrated in fig. 2 below). Since access in European buildings is normally through doorways, effectively the method is allowing an objective analysis of the degree of control and privacy indicated by the relative position of a room within a house. Thus a room which is immediately reached from the street might be seen as one that is essentially a public space (such as a shop) or a room given over to hospitality (a medieval hall) or a servants' area (a kitchen). It is unlikely to be understood as a private apartment, to which access is limited to selected members of the household. Such spaces might occur more 'deeply' within the access diagram. It is easy to see how such an analytical device privileges the understanding of insider-outsider relationships and underplays the importance of semi-fixed and moveable features in the understanding of the meanings attached to a space. Nevertheless, as a means of sensitizing the investigator to the less immediately apparent implications of the disposition of rooms within a building, it remains a useful tool. As will be seen in the examples, it is therefore important that it is used in conjunction with other observations.

III. IMPLEMENTING THE METHODOLOGY—TWO MEDIEVAL TOWNHOUSES IN YORK

The later medieval townhouses of York constitute a remarkably well-preserved group, despite the depredations of continuous commercial use over five or six hundred years. Their potential for analysis along the methodological lines discussed above will be briefly illustrated here from two examples, though it must be stressed that these are preliminary results and a great deal of work remains to be done in developing and applying the combination of stratigraphical analysis and attention to locale.[19]

My first example of this kind of recording is work at Bowes Morrell House (111 Walmgate), a fifteenth-century house close to Walmgate Bar, one of the main city gates (fig. 1). The building has been examined both by the Royal Commission on the Historical Monuments of England

---

[19] I am grateful to my former students for permission to discuss the results of their fieldwork here.

Figure 1. General view of Bowes Morrell House. Photo courtesy of the author.

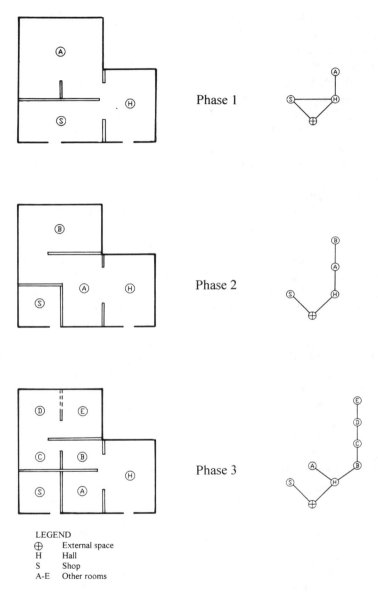

LEGEND
⊕   External space
H   Hall
S   Shop
A-E   Other rooms

Figure 2. Access analysis diagram of Bowes Morrell House.

(RCHME) and within my project by Nicolette Froud.[20] Originally built around 1400, the house was L-shaped, containing a hall parallel to the street frontage in its shorter wing, with a shop unit beside it to the front of a larger wing also running back from the street at right angles. Both Froud and the RCHME note that the shop unit was originally accessible from the hall (figure 2, Phase I, shows this, both as a true plan and as an access diagram), but only Froud goes on to document its sealing off, not only from the open hall, but from the main range of which, structurally, it forms a part (see Phase 2 of figure 2, where the horizontal access line between the shop and the hall is removed in the access diagram). Furthermore, within the right-angled range, detailed recording of ephemeral features such as nail holes and paint traces demonstrates increasing subdivision between the fifteenth and the seventeenth centuries (Phase 3 of figure 2 shows how this process produced a much 'deeper' access pattern, with five stages instead of the two illustrated in the Phase 1 access diagram). The open hall itself was subdivided by an inserted floor in the post-medieval period. I would argue that what we see here are the material mechanisms by which social (and possibly gender) relations within the household are being structured. Access analysis reveals an increasingly complicated situation through the later medieval period. Space to the rear of the building is progressively subdivided and commercial activities, formerly central to the daily life of the household, are clearly and consciously removed, visually and in terms of access, from the rest of the space.

If power structures are not merely reflected but actively structured in material settings, then we are able to observe here changing attitudes towards commerce, changing economic circumstance and a concomitant change in attitudes towards family relations, hospitality towards non-family members and the oversight of domestic labour. As social space is altered, so too is social experience. Archaeology is thus demonstrating here the material mechanisms by which household dynamics *changed* and a diachronic picture is built up. Such an interpretation of material conditions as an *active* agent in the construction of social relations rather than simply a mirror of them, raises further questions concerning the nature of the change: whether changing economic circumstances led to the subletting of the shop unit as an independent business, or whether changing social attitudes demanded the separation of domestic and

---

[20] Nicolette N. Z. Froud, 'Bowes Morrell House, 111 Walmgate; An Archaeological Case Study on Aspects of Private and Public Use of Space in a Timber-Framed Town House' (unpublished master's thesis, University of York, 1995). RCHME Vol. 5 (see note 14), p. 241.

commercial space. Can we look at other types of building, such as parish churches or guildhalls, or open spaces such as market places and streets to explore this theme? How far can we find these concerns reflected in the work of colleagues in other disciplines? We may well be observing an increasing tendency to accommodate servants separately towards the end of the fifteenth century,[21] but the archaeology suggests that we could look more closely at the material record for an understanding, rather than a simple description, of such processes, and the comparison of a series of observations in different houses or different types of building may lead us to revise our understanding of the documentary record. Is Bowes Morrell House typical of its period? Or are we looking at more specific localized issues such as the economic and social conditions in the Walmgate area of the medieval city? By offering a chronological indicator and the opportunity to make topographical comparisons, archaeology is providing the opportunity to understand social change through the mechanism of its material context.

To find such comparisons, we can look at my second example, the fifteenth-century house at 7 The Shambles, York where Rosemary Hayden has shown that we may be able to infer some social meanings embedded in fixed features (fig. 3).[22] Here a careful observation of former internal subdivisions and the recording of the structure of the external walls suggests that circulation around the building was cued by the orientation of the braces (triangular strengthening timbers between the main posts and beams) in the side walls (fig. 4). On the ground and uppermost floor, the braces faced to the south-west, but on the middle floor they pointed north-east. This corresponded with the lines of access through the house, which were deliberately set to run along alternate sides of the building. The very construction of the house is here used to reinforce the sense of ontological security in its inhabitants, to signal appropriate behaviour, and the same phenomenon can be observed in the carpenters' treatment of the roof. Access analysis (fig. 5) reveals a simple use of space, compared to the intricacies of Bowes Morrell House. The only major subdivision occurs at the top of the house, where the attic storey was subdivided and there was no access between the front and the back rooms, which were approached via separate staircases or ladders. These rooms were differentiated structurally by the use of different types

---

[21] P. J. P. Goldberg, personal communication.

[22] Rosemary Hayden, 'Living and Trading Conditions in the Shambles, 1300 to 1600' (unpublished master's thesis, University of York, 1995).

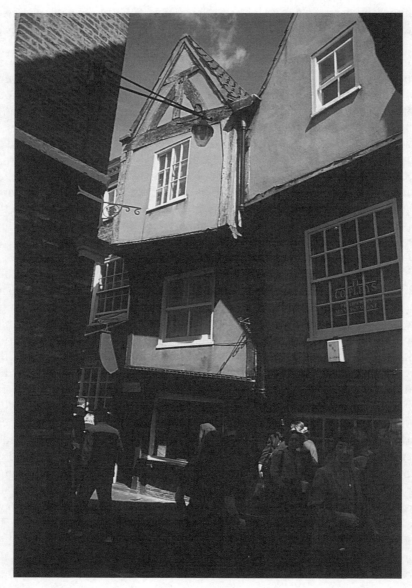

Figure 3. General view of 7 Shambles. Photo courtesy of the author.

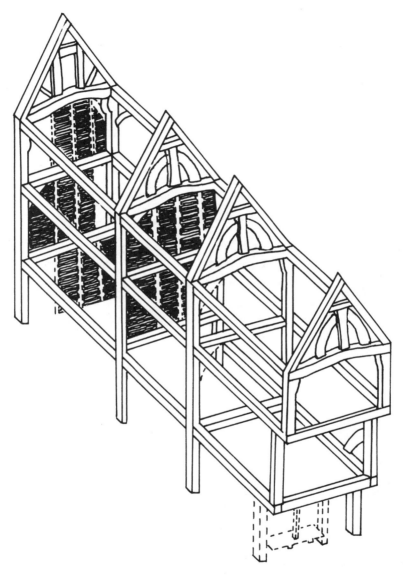

Figure 4. The timber frame at 7 Shambles.

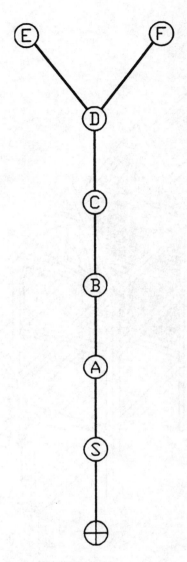

Figure 5. Access analysis of 7 Shambles.

of roof truss. These can be seen in figure 4: the construction at the front is clearly different and in carpenters' parlance is known as a crown post roof, while that to the rear is a queen post roof. Often these types are regarded as being of different dates (with crown posts earlier) but the detailed observation of the building sequence here shows clearly that these were contemporary. Both would have been visible inside within the rooms they spanned, and the crown post on the front gable is visible externally to this day (and continues to be admired by passing tourists). Both types of roof function equally efficiently, so what seems clear here is that their meaning differed. Crown posts, a construction type associated most strongly with the rich and politically powerful south-east of the country, indicate the high status of the front room, whilst queen posts (previously thought to indicate a later construction technique) denote a servants' room. Furthermore, the oft-held view that a relatively inaccessible room must be one where privacy was a principal requirement is gainsaid by the upper front room whose importance was reinforced by the visibility from the street of the crown post gable. In this respect, 7 The Shambles reflects the constructional syntax of Bowes Morrell House. It seems that the positioning and signalling of the 'inner sanctum' of the household reflects not so much a desire for privacy on the part of the owner, as a wish to be *seen* to be exclusive.

If we relate this evidence to the social practice of those inhabiting the building (the Shambles was dominated by butchers in the fifteenth and sixteenth centuries)[23] then interesting issues arise. Heather Swanson has noted that although the butchers were amongst the wealthiest and most successful citizens of medieval York, they were nonetheless discriminated against in terms of access to civic office.[24] Katherine Giles suggests that this may have been a deliberate policy and that the butchers actively chose to distance themselves from civic government.[25] How far are the butchers attempting to signal their membership of civic society or to establish their independence from it? Compared to Bowes Morrell House, the shop area of 7 Shambles remains relatively open visually, and accessible physically, from the rear of the building. Side passages provide access for beasts to the slaughter yards behind the houses, but the use of

---

[23] P. J. P. Goldberg, *Women, Work and Life Cycle in a Medieval Economy: Women in York and Yorkshire c. 1300–1520* (Oxford: Clarendon Press, 1992), p. 66.

[24] H. C. Swanson, *Medieval Artisans: an Urban Class in Late Medieval England* (Oxford: Oxford University Press, 1989).

[25] Pers. comm.

bracing patterns to signal routes around the house, at ground-floor level as well as above, suggest that use of internal spaces for access was common. There is no differentiation of space within the building until one reaches the top floor, where separate accommodation for masters and servants is clearly indicated. This house, by the later fifteenth century, then, is very differently articulated from Bowes Morrell House. Instead of a series of private spaces, we see here areas of common access with clear cues to enable not only the family, but the entire household and possibly also outsiders, to move appropriately around the building. While attempts have been made to infer a sense of social exclusion among the butchers from documentary records, the material construction of their household relations indicates a more nuanced support for the hypothesis. If just two studies can produce such revealing differences, and raise such interesting new questions, then the potential offered by a more extensive study is very great indeed.

In so far as the identification of specifically *female* activity within the household is concerned (that is, within household spaces as conceived in the dynamic and interactive terms outlined above, rather than in essentialized notions of female space), it is within the moveable and semi-fixed features of Rapoport's schema that evidence may begin to emerge. Within this category one might include furnishings, fittings, and household goods, which, unlike room partitions, might be routinely moved about in order to adapt social space to different activities at different times of the day, month, or year. In excavation, archaeologists routinely expect to find items of domestic equipment on house sites. Analyses of their distributions may allow conclusions to be drawn concerning specialist work areas, kitchens, animal accommodation and so forth, but since most domestic artefacts are thrown away or lost, rather than simply left for the archaeologist to find in the position in which they were used, distributions from excavation are far more likely to represent patterns of discard rather than patterns of use.

Thus the authors of the Museum of London's catalogue of medieval household finds are pessimistic regarding their fascinating and extensive material because of its provenance in the dumps along the Thames foreshore: 'the ideal of retrieving assemblages that accurately reflect individual households has not yet been realised in London and may prove too elusive ever to be achieved'.[26] This, however, seems to me to be an

---

[26] Geoff Egan, *Medieval Finds from Excavations in London 6: The Medieval Household, Daily Living c. 1150–c. 1450* (London: Stationery Office, 1998), p. 5.

unduly negative view of the potential for increasing our understanding of household dynamics through a study of its portable furnishings and everyday objects. No single discipline in isolation can lay claim to the potential to provide an understanding of the construction of the household as a social entity, but as with the consideration of the standing buildings themselves, I would argue that what is really required is a detailed interdisciplinary survey of household items from survivals, artistic representations, and documentary and literary references.[27] The purpose of such an investigation is not the accumulation of empirical evidence for the materiality of the medieval household for its own sake, but rather as the raw material for an analysis of the structuration processes of medieval society, and particularly to further our understanding of the role of the locale in that process. Thus a methodologically refined analysis of household finds, even from dumps, may lead us to helpful conclusions. David Gaimster of the British Museum has recently attempted just such an exercise, using national distribution patterns from excavation coupled with the evidence of sacred art (and particularly representations of the Annunciation) to suggest that fifteenth- and sixteenth-century majolica and stonewares may have held particular significance in the context of household piety.[28] Such observations accord closely with Amos Rapoport's contention that 'the fixed-feature elements can be taken as invariant yet, by changing the arrangement of furniture, profound changes ... are expressed and different activities take place.... The semi-fixed features change more easily and co-vary with activities, both guiding and reflecting them'.[29] The potential for detailed work in this area is very great indeed.

---

[27] John P. Allen, *Medieval and Post-medieval Finds from Exeter, 1971–1980* (Exeter: Exeter City Council, 1984); Martin Biddle, *Object and Economy from Medieval Winchester*, 2 vols (Oxford: Clarendon Press, 1990); Sue Margeson, *Norwich Households: The Medieval and Post-Medieval Finds from Norwich Survey Excavations, 1971–1978* (Norwich: Norwich Survey et al., 1993).

[28] David Gaimster, 'Distant Voices, Still-lifes: Late Medieval Religious Panel Painting as a Context for Archaeological Ceramics', in *Medieval Europe: Brugge 1997, Volume 10: Method and Theory in Historical Archaeology*, ed. by G. De Boe and F Verhaeghe, IAP Rapporten (Zellik: Instituut voor het Archeologisch Patrimonium, 1997), pp. 37–46.

[29] Rapoport, p. 13.

IV. CONCLUSION

An understanding of the recursive role of material culture in social practice is critical. Giddens's structuration theory acts as a useful 'sensitizing device' and the methodological tools provided by the notion of fixed, semi-fixed, and moveable features and the use of access analysis help us conceptualize and investigate past social spaces. In interpreting the specific uses of social space, an explicitly contextual view must be taken and it is here that interdisciplinary studies become not a luxury, but an absolute necessity. I have here suggested some ways in which archaeological recording and observation may be refined to deliver more telling analyses of buildings and their multiple uses, not by seeking to make simple attributions of gender or function to certain areas, but by applying particular theoretical constructs to the analysis of the evidence and contextualizing the conclusions within the framework provided by interdisciplinary projects. By refining and challenging one another's assumptions and results, we may be able to provide a more subtle picture of the medieval household. But there is plenty more work to be done before we can begin to answer the presently unanswerable question recently asked of me by a doctoral student in the Centre for Medieval Studies: 'What kind of houses *did* single women live in?'

Unnatural Mothers and Monstrous Children in *The King of Tars* and *Sir Gowther*

JANE GILBERT

It hardly needs to be said that the Middle Ages was not politically correct where physical and mental difference or handicap was concerned. A great variety of personal characteristics might be considered as 'monstrous', because not conforming to the divinely ordered scheme.[1] In this essay, I shall examine two different sorts of monstrous birth which occur in Middle English popular romances: the physical monster found in the late thirteenth-century *The King of Tars* (hereafter *KT*), and the moral monster of the late fourteenth-century *Sir Gowther* (hereafter *SG*).[2] My argument

---

I should like to express my gratitude to Arlyn Diamond, Malcolm Gilbert, Sarah Kay, and J. P. Murphy for their many helpful comments on earlier drafts of this essay.

[1] For general studies of medieval teratology, see Claude Kappler, *Monstres, démons et merveilles à la fin du Moyen Age* (Paris: Payot, 1980), and David Williams, *Deformed Discourse: The Function of the Monster in Mediaeval Thought and Literature* (Exeter: University of Exeter Press, 1996).

[2] Quotations are from *The King of Tars*, ed. by Judith Perryman (Heidelberg: Winter, 1980), and from *Sir Gowther* in *Six Middle English Romances*, ed. by Maldwyn Mills (London: Dent, 1973). Both editions are based on the Auchinleck Manuscript; *The Auchinleck Manuscript: National Library of Scotland, Advocates' MS 19.2.1*, ed. by Derek Pearsall and I. C. Cunningham (London: Scolar Press, 1977), has a facsimile and full discussion. For the other surviving manuscripts, see Gisela Guddat-Figge, *Catalogue of Manuscripts Containing Middle English Romances* (Munich: Fink, 1976), pp. 211–13 (*SG*: London, British Library, MS Royal 17 B.xliii); 145–51 (*KT*: London, British Library, MS Additional 22283 [Simeon Manuscript]); 269–79 (*KT*: Oxford, Bodleian Library, MS English Poetry A.1 [Vernon Manuscript]). Discussion of thematic differences between the surviving manuscripts of *KT* can be found in Perryman, pp. 58–69; of *SG* in Andrea Hopkins, *The Sinful Knights: A Study of Middle English Penitential Romance* (Oxford: Clarendon Press, 1990), pp. 223–25.

will be constructed around two sorts of theory equally concerned with
problems of order: medieval physiology and Lacanian psychoanalysis. It
is common practice today to ground an interpretation of a medieval literary text either in detailed historical contextualization or in rigorous
modern conceptualization. Integrating these two approaches, however,
deepens both, for it allows the historical specificities both of the texts
under discussion and of the discussion itself to emerge more sharply.
Felicity Riddy's own work shows the insights that can result from such a
methodology; I hope to follow her example here.

My particular focus is on how the child's monstrosity relates to its
parents. We are accustomed to the idea that monstrous births in medieval
literature may represent some failing on the part of one or both parents.[3]
Given our perception of the Middle Ages as a generally misogynistic
period, we are more ready to believe that it is the mother's (metaphorical)
monstrosity which is represented in the child; and historical and literary
work supports this idea in many instances. The mother's individual sin or
essential female nature often appear to be the cause of her child's de-
formities.[4] If we are really to understand the complex cultural currents
involved here, however, we must situate the mother's role in a broader
context. I wish to show how the 'monstrous birth' topos works, in both

---

[3]   This sin might be sexual: John Boswell, *The Kindness of Strangers: The Abandonment
of Children in Western Europe from Late Antiquity to the Renaissance* (London: Penguin,
1988), pp. 338–39. It was also common for a child's monstrosity to be ascribed to sins
other than sexual on the parents' part, or to a variety of quite other causes: see Kappler,
Monstres, pp. 223–31.

[4]   On maternal sexual sin, see Clarissa W. Atkinson, *The Oldest Vocation: Christian
Motherhood in the Middle Ages* (Ithaca and London: Cornell University Press, 1991), pp.
91–94; Doris Desclais Berkvam, *Enfance et maternité dans la littérature française des
XIIe et XIIIe siècles* (Paris: Champion, 1981), pp. 14–17. One reason given for the
Church's prohibition of sexual relations while a woman was menstruating or lactating was
that any foetus conceived then would be damaged (often monstrous), since menstrual
blood was perceived as poisonous. See William F. MacLehose, 'Nurturing Danger: High
Medieval Medicine and Problem(s) of the Child', in *Medieval Mothering*, ed. by John
Carmi Parsons and Bonnie Wheeler (New York and London: Garland, 1996), pp. 3–24;
Ottavia Niccoli, '"Menstruum quasi Monstruum": Monstrous Births and Menstrual Taboo
in the Sixteenth Century', in *Sex and Gender in Historical Perspective: Selections from
'Quaderni Storici'*, ed. by Edward Muir and Guido Ruggiero, trans. by Margaret A.
Gallucci with Mary M. Gallucci and Carole C. Gallucci (Baltimore: Johns Hopkins Uni-
versity Press, 1990), pp. 1–25. Kappler discusses the female who is monstrous because
sexual: *Monstres*, pp. 263–79. Marie-Hélène Huet discusses a Renaissance view of mon-
sters as representing the dangerous power of the female imagination: *The Monstrous
Imagination* (Cambridge, MA: Harvard University Press, 1993).

KT and *SG*, as a focus for anxieties about the masculine, and specifically about paternity. Moreover, I want to relate the personal situations and narratives of the characters to the social constructions within the texts, and to the politics of the texts themselves. Herein lie the particular advantages of Lacan's work: his analytical focus is not on the insufficiencies of the mother but on those of the father, while he emphasizes the political dimension of both paternity and maternity.

Paternity is a complex issue in both the romances with which I am concerned. Fatherhood is disputed between various candidates, or even denied completely. In *SG*, paternity is attributed to a demon, while in *KT*, paternity is initially withheld, the child left fatherless. It is clear that, in each text, what we today would call the 'biological father' is not considered to fulfil the criteria required for recognition as a 'father' in the fully legitimated and legitimating sense. By charting the process by which a father can be recognized as such, both romances pose the question 'what does it mean to be a father?' This, according to Lacan, is the great question of Freudian psychoanalysis.[5] Lacan himself insists that paternity is above all, and in all its forms, a cultural construct. In this connection, he attacks Ernest Jones:

> Concerning, in effect, the state of beliefs in some Australian tribe, [Jones] refused to admit that any collectivity of men could fail to recognize the fact of experience that, with certain enigmatic exceptions, no woman gives birth to a child without having undergone coitus, or [could] even be ignorant of the lapse of time between the two events. [The problem with Jones's position is that] the credit that seems to me to be accorded quite legitimately to the human capacities to observe the real is precisely that which has not the slightest importance in the matter.
>
> For, *if the symbolic context requires it*, paternity will nonetheless be attributed to the fact that the woman met a spirit at some fountain or some rock in which he is supposed to live.
>
> It is certainly this that demonstrates that *the attribution of procreation to the father can only be the effect of a pure signifier, of a recognition, not of a real father, but of what religion has taught us to refer to as the Name-of-the-Father.*[6]

---

[5] '[T]oute l'interrogation freudienne se résume à ceci – *Qu'est-ce que c'est qu'être un père?*', Jacques Lacan, *Le Séminaire, Livre IV: La relation d'objet, 1956–57*, ed. by Jacques-Alain Miller (Paris: Seuil, 1994), p. 204.

[6] Lacan, 'On a question preliminary to any possible treatment of psychosis', in *Écrits: A Selection*, trans. by Alan Sheridan (New York: Norton, 1977), pp. 179–225 (p. 199, my italics).

For a father to be so recognized, a whole range of cultural and institutional forces must be mobilized and criteria met. According to Lacan, human paternity exists as a kind of signifier, whose signified is what he calls the symbolic Father. Being purely abstract, a position rather than a figure, the symbolic Father should not be thought of as a personification of paternity, but functions as the 'alibi éternel' on which all actual fathers depend.[7] Although individual men may exercise the paternal function and thus represent the symbolic Father up to a point, none can ever fully occupy the position. Any human father is necessarily inadequate to the role, yet the whole notion of human paternity relies on the supposition of there existing someone, somewhere, who can fully assume that role.[8]

Unlike paternity, which (being thus artificial, man-made) clearly falls within the area of culture, maternity is commonly thought of as a fact of nature.[9] *Pater semper incertus est, mater certissima*.[10] Such a distinction is borne out in *KT* and *SG*. Each text manifests anxiety about the proper behaviour and role of the mother, but these are secondary concerns. Where we are uncertain who should even be considered the father (or fathers) of each monstrous child, there is no question about the identity of the mother. Both poems root their portrayal of maternity in biological motherhood, and this identification of mothering with the maternal body plays down the cultural aspect in favour of what are presumably put forward as timeless and universal physiological processes. However, the

---

[7] *Séminaire IV*, p. 210.

[8] *Séminaire IV*, p. 205. This 'someone' must, however, remain unidentified, for the symbolic Father is strictly unrepresentable. The claim by any named individual to exercise the paternal function fully and adequately can only be made within the order which Lacan calls the imaginary: *Séminaire IV*, pp. 210, 276. Whereas the symbolic order is an abstract, mathematical structure, the imaginary is the domain of images, identifications, and phenomena. For a helpful account of the three orders (real, imaginary, and symbolic), see Malcolm Bowie, *Lacan* (London: Fontana, 1991), pp. 88–121.

[9] The idea that femaleness is associated with nature and maleness with culture has a long history within the west and other cultures, and was for a time thought to be universal. *Nature, Culture and Gender*, ed. by Carol MacCormack and Marilyn Strathern (Cambridge: Cambridge University Press, 1980), contains useful examinations and critiques of these notions.

[10] The ancient Latin tag is quoted by Freud, 'Family Romances', in *The Standard Edition of the Complete Psychological Works of Sigmund Freud*, trans. by James Strachey, 24 vols (London: Hogarth, 1953–74), 9 (1959), pp. 235–41 (p. 239). The tag is connected to the nature/culture divide by Sarah Kay, 'Motherhood. The Case of the Epic Family Romance', in *Shifts and Transpositions in Medieval Narrative (A Festschrift for Elspeth Kennedy)*, ed. by Karen Pratt (Cambridge: D. S. Brewer, 1994), pp. 23–36 (p. 24).

texts represent these processes differently, relying on contesting theories of maternal biology; and thus history is reintroduced.[11] The physiological theory chosen relates to the political siting of mothers and fathers within the particular text.[12] In this sense, maternity is always 'unnatural': however rooted in a fantasy of naturalness, it is as much a cultural phenomenon as paternity, its construction similarly variable in different symbolic contexts. It is the symbolic contexts governing the representation both of paternity and of maternity that I am concerned to investigate in *KT* and *SG*.

THE KING OF TARS

The monstrous child in *KT* is the offspring of a forced marriage between a Saracen Sultan and a Christian Princess, daughter of the eponymous King of Tars. Although the Princess pretends to convert, 'Ihesu forghat sche nought' (l. 507). When the child of this mixed-faith marriage is born, it is a shapeless lump of inanimate flesh:

> [L]im no hadde it non.
> Bot as a rond of flesche yschore   [hewn off]
> In chaumber it lay hem bifore
>   Withouten blod & bon.
> For sorwe the leuedi wald dye   [lady]
> For it hadde noither nose no eye,
>   Bot lay ded as the ston. (ll. 579–85)

The question of who is responsible for this monstrosity is debated. Father blames mother, mother father. The Sultan prays to his 'goddes' to transform the lump, but in vain. Only when baptized does it become a human child (ll. 775–83).

Historical physiology throws light on the aetiology of this monstrous birth. The poet is drawing on Aristotelian conception theory, in which, as

---

[11] Apart from the works cited in nn. 3 and 4, recent studies of medieval motherhood include: *A History of Women in the West, II: Silences of the Middle Ages*, ed. by Christiane Klapisch-Zuber (Cambridge, MA: Harvard University Press, 1992); and Barbara Newman, *From Virile Woman to WomanChrist: Studies in Medieval Religion and Literature* (Philadelphia: University of Pennsylvania Press, 1995).

[12] These theories are therefore not 'mentalities', in the sense of unconscious substrata of thought, but represent the author's choice—conscious or not—from among a number of conflicting accounts.

is well known, the mother's contribution is only the basic *matter*: the material, fleshly substance from which the child will be made.[13] (*Mater*, as we are often reminded, was thought in the Middle Ages to be derived etymologically from *materia*.[14]) The father, through his seed, supplies the 'life or spirit or form', the vital principle which transforms the matter into a human child and animates it.[15] As the Princess knows, it is this second element that the lump lacks:

> Yif it were cristned aright
> It schuld haue fourme to se bi sight
>   With lim & liif to wake. (ll. 760–62)

Fourme here has its technical sense. Shapeless, lifeless chunk of flesh, the lump-child is a fictional approximation to Aristotelian matter, the result of a conception in which the paternal role has failed. The particular monstrosity of the lump in *KT* results from the fact that it is solely and exclusively its mother's child.

This does not imply, however, that the monstrosity is its mother's fault. On the contrary: the poem shows that it is the father who is to blame for the child's condition. Aristotle's view of the father as giver of the form that shapes matter is paralleled by Lacan's description of the paternal function as the imposition of order on the chaos of nature. For Lacan, this is above all a matter of rendering humans distinct from animals, a task which centres in the regulation of sexuality: 'the primordial Law is [...] that which in regulating marriage ties superimposes the kingdom of culture on that of a nature abandoned to the law of mating'.[16] The paternal function thus appears in the essentially human activity of the creation and enforcement of kin groups and marriage rules. Two integral parts of this process are the incest taboo and the inscription of a lineage descending

---

[13] A brief and clear description of the male and female roles in Aristotelian, Hippocratic, and Galenic theories of conception is given by Atkinson, *Oldest Vocation*, pp. 46–51. Joan Cadden, *Meanings of Sex Difference in the Middle Ages: Medicine, Science and Culture* (Cambridge: Cambridge University Press, 1993), has a much more detailed account of the theories in their classical (pp. 13–39) and medieval (pp. 117–30) forms, as well as a description of their transmission to the medieval West (pp. 39–53). Of the authorities Cadden cites, the closest to *KT* is Albertus Magnus (pp. 121, 126–30).

[14] Isidore of Seville, *Etymolgiae*, IX, v, 6: 'Mater dicitur, quod exinde efficiatur aliquid; mater enim quasi materia, nam causa pater est' (*PL* 82 (1850), p. 354).

[15] Caroline Walker Bynum, *Fragmentation and Redemption: Essays on Gender and the Human Body in Medieval Religion* (New York: Zone, 1992), p. 100.

[16] 'Function and Field of Speech and Language', *Écrits*, pp. 30–113 (p. 66).

through the father, that parent who can only be recognized symbolically. It is this line of patrilineal descent that the Sultan fails to impose when he is unable to father his child. As the Princess tells him after the transformation of the lump into a child, this is not a question of biology:

> The soudan seyd, 'Leman min,   [My love]
> Ywis ich am glad afin   [certainly]
>   Of this child that y se.'
> 'Ya, sir, bi seyn Martin,
> Yif the haluendel wer thin   [half]
>   Wel glad might thou be.'
> 'O dame,' he seyd, 'hou is that?
> Is it nought min that y bighat?'
>   'No sir,' than seyd sche,
> 'Bot thou were cristned so it is   [unless]
> Thou no hast no part theron, ywis,
>   Noither of the child ne of me.' (ll. 805–16)

The paternity lacking to the Sultan represents not so much biological fatherhood (he 'begot' the child) as the right to be named as the child's father. In Lacanian terms, the problem lies with the attribution of procreation. An individual father can only accede to the capacities and rights of paternity insofar as he is a channel for the Name-of-the-Father, linked as a sign to the symbolic Father. The Sultan, clearly, is not. And without symbolic paternity, human beings cannot reproduce, in the sense that they cannot pass on the cultural qualities that distinguish a fully human existence from the merely fleshly one of animals.

Form is given to the lump when baptism installs the Christian God as its Father. It therefore appears that it is his paganism which has prevented the Sultan from occupying the paternal position. *KT* thus identifies the Christian God as the sole and all-powerful guarantor of paternity. Procreation cannot be attributed to the man who does not acknowledge this God as the 'eternal alibi' of fatherhood. Lacan's insistence that the position of the symbolic Father cannot be completely filled without losing the symbolic status which is its essence, however, highlights the political agenda served by this identification in *KT*. The lump represents not some naïve popular belief that certain historical peoples could not literally procreate, but the ideological contention that non-Christians are incapable of exercising the paternal function.[17] Paganism is represented here as the

---

[17] The Sultan's inability to impose the symbolic boundary separating humans from animals is confirmed by the numerous comparisons of him and other Saracens to wild beasts (e.g. ll. 93, 98, 105).

realm of the natural, the maternal, and the animal, all of which, however necessary as a basis for humanity, will never themselves become human without the input of father and culture.

The transformation of the lump is thus in many ways a less important miracle than that of the Sultan. The patrilineage which Lacan claims to be a defining characteristic of encultured humanity is not established with the baptism of the son, but must wait until the father takes the plunge. As he does so, his skin colour turns from black to white: a powerful and deeply racist image for his entry into the realm of paternity, here identified with the earthly Christian regime.[18] The Sultan's insertion into the Christian lineage is confirmed as he gains not only a son but also a father: the King of Tars, his father-in-law, with whom he promptly embarks on a crusade against his own people, and whose name and honour he is perhaps to inherit (as Gowther too inherits from his wife's father).[19] Such an ending would be appropriate to what we have seen of the text: the name borne by both men and by the text itself, and which indicates a patrilineage stretching off into past and future, would be a fictional approximation to the Name-of-the-Father.

Where then does the text leave the Princess—she whose fundamental exclusion from the cultural domain is graphically illustrated by her monstrously formless child? Although Aristotelian physiology might appear to privilege form over matter, and therefore father over mother, in a simple and absolute way, KT shows how complex the gender politics involved in practical deployments of this theory can be. From the thirteenth century onwards (as is well known), medieval theology and piety concentrated increasingly on Christ's humanity rather than on his divini-

---

[18] Among the six analogues of KT cited by Perryman (pp. 42–49), only one other represents the monstrous child as a formless lump. Two others have a completely hairy child. Three portray the creature as a compound: half-human and half-animal, half-hairy and half-smooth, or half-beautiful and half-ugly. Behind such a hybrid lies, not the Aristotelian theory of reproduction found in KT, but the Hippocratic and Galenic traditions, in which both parents contribute seeds which fuse to form the child. While we should be wary of assuming that this would necessarily result in a very different deployment of gender from that found in KT, it does appear that the authors of these analogues subordinated gender difference to racial difference, whereas KT's author combined them in a mutually supportive matrix.

[19] A leaf missing from the Auchinleck manuscript means that we lack the end of KT. Perryman (p. 9) calculates that a maximum of 169 lines have been lost, but notes that Pearsall estimates forty to sixty. MS V has a ten-line closing stanza after the point where MS A breaks off.

ty. Christ's humanity itself became sacred; and this humanity depended centrally on his physical, material existence, his being flesh and blood. And this flesh and blood was considered to derive from his only human parent. A double revaluation thus took place. The flesh acquired a value different from that which it was often accorded in earlier Christianity: no longer the home of sin and decay, it became the stuff of Christ's Incarnation. The Virgin Mary also gained a new importance, both as a human and as a mother. Her maternity, if not her womanhood, revered as the source of Christ's sacred humanity, she was lauded as a necessary—though not sufficient—condition of the salvation Christ offers.[20] This attitude to the Virgin colours the treatment of the Princess in *KT*. The text's exemplar of humility and Christian fortitude, the Princess plays a crucial mediating role as the material and moral means by which Christ is introduced into the Sultan's pagan world. Not herself the catalyst in the Sultan's conversion, she is at every point instrumental in engineering that conversion. She it is who bears the lump-child, she who calls on the Christian priest who will insert both son and father into the paternal order.[21] Essentially alien to the paternal realm though she is, she serves that realm with true submission, and thereby gains value within it. The role of the 'natural' woman, it appears, is to support the paternal order: her nature can and must advance his culture.

SIR GOWTHER

Gowther is literally and figuratively a devil-child. Begotten on his mother by a demon who has taken the shape of the Duke her husband, Gowther in his youth commits a series of brutal and sacrilegious crimes. He then converts, and carries out a penance which finally leads him to sainthood. Just as in *KT*, the child's monstrosity in *SG* is intimately related to the symbolic contexts of parenthood; the contexts themselves are, however, rather different.

---

[20] In this account I am following Bynum, *Fragmentation*. For a succinct account of the associations between the feminine and the flesh, see pp. 98–101. In the MS A version of *KT*, the lump is referred to repeatedly as *flesche* (ll. 607, 622, 639, 662, 752, 772) until its transformation, when it becomes a *child* (l. 781 and onwards). This distinction is not found in MSS VS.

[21] Her mediating role is thus to some extent analogous to that of the priest. On the Virgin Mary as priest, see Bynum, *Fragmentation*, pp. 100–01.

The text describes Gowther's abominable behaviour as determined by his paternity:

> Erly and late, lowde and styll,
> He wold wyrke is fadur wyll
>   Wher he stod or sete. (ll. 172–74)   [wherever]

Presumably, this refers to the will of the demon; certainly, the Duke is appalled by Gowther's behaviour. In my view, however, the demonic father is here above all a negative representation of the human father: the demon's strength is drawn from the Duke's weakness. At the physical level, the Duke's failure to engender a child creates a reproductive gap for the incubus to fill.[22] As in *KT*, biological deficiency images cultural inadequacy. Having discussed the inscription of lineage in relation to *KT*, I want to focus here on that other element central to the paternal function: the incest taboo. Gowther begins his career of infamy by sucking nine wet-nurses to death, before tearing at his mother's breast:

> He snaffulld to hit soo,   [worried at]
> He rofe tho hed fro tho brest. (ll. 126–27)   [tore]

These attacks have generally been viewed as Gowther's rejection of feminine nurture, but they may be more accurately read as a continuous, insatiable demand placed upon that nurture.[23] Unconstrained breast-feeding is

---

[22] Even at the most literal level, Gowther's paternity is irremediably blurred. A recent reading of *SG* points out that the prologue (found only in MS B) appears to refer to the theories of Aquinas, according to which a demon cannot engender a human child because it has no human substance. The semen which an incubus deposits in a mortal woman was earlier collected by it from a mortal man, whom it seduced in the shape of a succubus. Gowther might therefore be any man's son—even the Duke's! See Hopkins, *Sinful Knights*, pp. 165–68. This does not mean that *SG* does not clearly identify the demon as a father to Gowther, said to be Merlin's half-brother on the father's side (ll. 94–96). Gowther's mother also tells him he is the fiend's son (for discussion, see pp. 341–343). In an interestingly feminocentric interpretation, Margaret Robson argues that although the Duke blames his wife for their childlessness, the speed with which she conceives with a different partner suggests that it is the Duke who is infertile: 'Animal Magic: Moral Regeneration in *Sir Gowther*', *Yearbook of English Studies*, 22 (1992), 140–53 (p. 141).

[23] For instance, Robson, 'Animal Magic', p. 143; Jeffrey Jerome Cohen, 'Gowther among the Dogs: Becoming Inhuman c. 1400', in *Becoming Male in the Middle Ages*, ed. by Jeffrey Jerome Cohen and Bonnie Wheeler (New York: Garland, 1997), pp. 219–44 (pp. 224–25). Cohen's sophisticated Deleuzian interpretation sees Gowther's monstrosity as that of any pre-oedipal child before the installation of the Name-of-the-Father.

here equivalent to a foreclosure against the incest taboo.[24] In his ferocious attacks on the breast, Gowther is rejecting not maternity, but the paternal authority that would forbid him absolute access to the maternal body. The Duke remains spectacularly incapable of imposing any limitations on the behaviour of the adult Gowther, who takes the paternal realm as his parti- cular enemy. Raping and pillaging to his heart's content, he concentrates his efforts on churchmen and on chaste women: those who, by their dedi- cation to God or to the Christian paterfamilias, have a special relation to the Name-of-the-Father. In the face of this delinquency, the Duke loses heart and dies 'for sorro' (l. 151) at his son's crimes. If the symbolic Father is the locus of the interdiction on which culture as such is based (Lacan plays constantly on the homophony in French between *nom* and *non*, such that the Name-of-the-Father is also the No-of-the-Father), then the Duke is evidently inadequate to that role.

It would be wrong, however, to interpret the Duke's inadequacy as personal, for it is also his society's. Again and again we see how symbolic structures fail to imprint themselves on Gowther. His baptism does not transform the monster into a good Christian child, as it does in *KT*. Similarly ineffective is knighthood:

> He was so wekyd in all kyn wyse
> Tho dyke hym myght not chastyse,
> > Bot made hym knyght that tyde,
> With cold brade bronde:
> Ther was non in that londe
> > That dynt of hym durst byde. (ll.145–50)   [blow... endure]

Robert le diable, the thirteenth-century French text of which *SG* is an adaptation, explains the theory behind this action: knighthood may work a secular miracle, transforming the boy's evil character.[25] In *SG*, however,

---

[24] See *Séminaire IV*, p. 183, where Lacan describes the child's sating itself at the real object that is the breast as a foreclosure against the frustration that is an inherent feature of the symbolic order.

[25] *Robert le diable*, ed. by E. Löseth, SATF (Paris: Didot, 1903); MS A, ll. 235–44. The clearer explanation is found in MS B, which Löseth prints at the bottom of the page (p. 16). For comparison of this text with *SG*, see Hopkins, *Sinful Knights*, pp. 145–58, and Dorothy S. McCoy, 'From Celibacy to Sexuality: An Examination of Some Medieval and Early Renaissance Versions of the Story of Robert the Devil', in *Human Sexuality in the Middle Ages and the Renaissance*, ed. by Douglas Radcliffe-Umstead (Pittsburgh: Pittsburgh University Press, 1978), pp. 29–39. Robert's character is no more improved by knighthood than Gowther's. The only case of successful transformation known to me

knighthood not only has no positive effects, it even seems to make
Gowther worse: the sword of his dubbing is conflated with that with
which he attacks his countrymen. It appears, then, that the established
means of enculturation practised by both Church and secular society are
incapable of bringing the child into the symbolic order. Paternity in this
text is essentially interrupted, flawed; whether individual or social, its
relation to the Name-of-the-Father is an imperfect one.[26]

As far as the father goes, then, Gowther's monstrosity both resembles
and diverges from that of the lump in *KT*: both are images of their father's
failure to perform the paternal function, although the religious and social
contexts of that failure are different. The mother's position, by contrast,
varies substantially between the two poems; as does the construction of
maternity itself. Unlike in *KT*, where the focus was on conception, *SG*
foregrounds nutrition. As described above, breast-feeding figures in
Gowther's first, infant outrage. Later on, Gowther's people lament his
existence by saying: 'Evyll heyle [...] that ever modur him fed' (ll. 161–
62). The use of wet-nurses in the narrative suggests that 'fed' here
probably includes foetal nourishment in the womb, of which breast-
feeding was thought to be the continuation: the maternal blood that
nourished the foetus was after the birth transmuted into milk. The
nourishment in question was not a purely physiological process. Both the
blood and the milk that the child ingested were thought to carry in them
qualities of character from the person feeding to the child fed. Hence the
great concern in this period for the social and moral status of wet-nurses.
Text after text, both medical and literary, insists that the nurse should be a
woman of rank and of good moral standing, as well as healthy and a good
milk supplier.[27] A major distinction between *KT*'s and *SG*'s visions of
maternity therefore emerges. Whereas the former sees maternity as mere
provision of a universal, undifferentiated substance on which the paternal
form will impose all its humanizing characteristics, the latter represents it
as a cultural mechanism for transmitting social qualities and values from
one generation to the next.[28] Maternity in *SG* is not opposed to paternity

---

occurs to Gilles de Chin, in the romance of that name: see Berkvam, *Enfance et Maternité*,
pp. 81–84.

[26] The devil-spawn Gowther is not the only 'monstrous' child in the text. The Princess,
child of the impeccable Emperor and his irreproachable wife, is dumb. It is this that first
draws her to Gowther, equally silent during his penance.

[27] For medieval ideas about breast-feeding, see Atkinson, *Oldest Vocation*, pp. 57–62.

[28] In Aristotelian theory, the mother could strictly speaking pass nothing on to her child.
The pragmatic recognition of a child's physical resemblance to its mother thus posed

as nature is to culture. Culture is still coded as paternal, but in *SG* the mother plays her supporting role from within the cultural domain, instead of outside it as in *KT*.

According to the theory of motherhood as nourishment, both Gowther's mother and his wet-nurses (said to be 'full gud knyghttys wyffys', l. 109 and 'ladys feyr and fre', l. 117), ought to transmit to him their own nobility of character. Yet it appears that they cannot. The positive cultural qualities carried by both milk and blood fail to 'take' in Gowther. Gowther's monstrosity thus reflects, not his mother's nature, but the failure of her culture. Like the earthly father, the mother cannot be a means of enculturation in this text because enculturation by human means alone is impossible; and this impossibility is the meaning of Gowther's monstrosity.

Gowther's rampaging assault on the Name-of-the-Father comes to an end only when he finally discovers his paternity. An old Earl suggests that such an evil creature cannot be of Christian stock, but must be a devil's son. Gowther turns to his mother to learn his father's identity, threatening to kill her if she lies. Nevertheless, her first answer is an untruth: his father, she says, was 'My lord […], that dyed last' (l. 223). When Gowther declares his disbelief, she gives in:

> 'Son, sython Y schall tho sothe say:
> In owre orchard apon a day,
>   A fende gat the thare;
> As lyke my lorde as he myght be,
> Underneyth a cheston tre.'
>   Then weppyd thei bothe full sare.
> 'Go schryfe the, modur, and do tho best,
> For Y wyll to Rome or that Y rest,   [before]
> To lerne anodur lare.'   [rule of living]
> This thoght come on hym sodenly:
> 'Lorde, mercy,' con he cry
>   To God that Maré bare. (ll. 226–37)

The Duchess's revelation prompts a transformation scene equivalent to that of the lump in *KT*. Although Gowther accepts his demonic paternity at the biological, animal level, at the symbolic, human level he repudiates it (going to learn 'anodur lare'). When he recognizes his own sinfulness

---

serious problems (for an overview of medieval discussions of family resemblance in the context of conception theory, see Cadden, *Meanings*, pp. 117–30).

and acknowledges divine authority, he bows to the Name-of-the-Father for the first time in his life, and enters the symbolic order.

Why should the discovery that the Duke was not his father have such a dramatic effect on Gowther? An explanation can be sought in Freudian and Lacanian theory. According to Freud, human civilization originated with an act of patricide. The first humans lived in a semi-animal state, in which a tyrannical father-figure monopolized sexual and other resources. Although the dominant male was eventually killed by his rebellious son-figures, this act brought no liberation. Guilt and the need for social order necessitated the reinvention of the father as a mythical locus of authority, to which the children then submitted voluntarily.[29] In line with this Freudian scenario, Lacan insists that the installation of the father as symbolic authority and the establishment of the moral Law require a recognition of the father's death, and even the acceptance of responsibility for that death:

> The necessity of [Freud's] reflexion led him to link the appearance of the signifier of the Father, as author of the Law, with death, even to the murder of the Father—thus showing that if this murder is the fruitful moment of debt through which the subject binds himself for life to the Law, the symbolic Father is, in so far as he signifies this Law, the dead Father.[30]

If we follow Lacan, only a father who is radically absent—for instance, being dead—can fill the position of the symbolic Father without its collapsing into the domain of the imaginary. In the Duke's case, death alone was apparently not enough to ensure absence. The Duke becomes truly absent to Gowther only when the Duchess reveals that he was never the boy's father. After this revelation, the Duke's death finally becomes psychologically operative for Gowther. That death and his own responsibility for it now contribute to Gowther's entry into the symbolic order. The son can recognize the symbolic Father only in this doubly absent man—a man never his biological father and one driven to his death by Gowther's own actions. The conversion is effected: Gowther embraces the value-system of his human father, and thus voluntarily claims kin with him. The irrelevance (or even absence) of consanguinity in this lineage, as in that which links the Sultan and the King of Tars, highlights its arti-

---

[29] *Totem and Taboo*, in *The Standard Edition*, Vol. 13 (see n. 10), pp. 1–161. Lacan insists that this account is to be read not as an attempt at history, but as a myth (*Séminaire IV*, pp. 210–11).

[30] 'On a question', p. 199.

ficial, cultural status. However, whereas living men like those in *KT* are denied the position of symbolic Father in the strict Lacanian sense, the Duke is dead and gone; Gowther's adoption of him therefore allows the Duke finally to stand for the symbolic Father, signifier of the Law to which Gowther subjects himself.

This appearance in *SG* of the Lacanian symbolic, based on absence, frustration, and guilt, is not, however, sustained. Like *KT*, *SG* makes the ideological move of identifying the Christian God as the supreme Father: Gowther, like the lump, is transformed as he becomes Christian. The father becomes present and omnipotent, and thus paternity's realm is again shifted from the symbolic to the imaginary. There are, nevertheless, significant differences between the two poems here. In *SG*, the paternal realm is not identified with temporal Christendom, as it is in *KT*, but with God alone. Gowther's conversion cannot be brought about by institutional or authoritarian means, but results from a personal revelation. He enters into subjection freely.[31] In *SG*, temporal patriarchy exists in divorce from the divine Father.[32] Given this ideological perspective, it could be said that Gowther's early monstrosity—which, I have argued, expresses the failure of human culture and paternity—is that of all earthly society, in its separation from the Father who is its guarantor. Although only this extraordinary child appears to be monstrous, all humans are equally so unless (like Gowther) they come to personal—not institutional—realization of God. Gowther, the 'varré corsent parfett' (l.

---

[31] '"Subjection" signifies the process of becoming subordinated by power as well as the process of becoming a subject. [...] [T]he subject is initiated through a primary submission to power': Judith Butler, *The Psychic Life of Power: Theories in Subjection* (Stanford: Stanford University Press, 1997), p. 2.

[32] In this reading, Gowther's refusal to obey the Pope when the latter tells him to lay down his falchion indicates not Gowther's mistake, but the Pope's. Even the established Church is included here in the temporal order. This interpretation also supplies an explanation for the poem's ambivalence towards Gowther's mother. On the one hand, she transgresses against the temporal paternal order by praying for a child 'on what maner scho no rogth' (l. 63), by committing adultery (consciously or not) with the demon, and by passing the child thus conceived off as her husband's. On the other hand, she repeatedly submits herself to the will of God (contrast the mother in *Robert le diable*; Hopkins, *Sinful Knights*, p. 147), and the parodic annunciation she invents to cover up her demonic conception manifests a desire to imitate the Virgin Mary. These acts suggest her adherence to the divine paternal realm. Since this order is incompatible with and superior to the earthly, her sins against temporal patriarchy have a positive as well as a negative value. Thus, if her actions are responsible for Gowther's monstrosity, they also prefigure his ultimate move towards God.

721) who specializes in curing deformity, in restoring order to the monstrous, is to lead the way to Christ.[33]

However different in many ways the monstrous children of *KT* and *SG* are, juxtaposing them within the analytical framework I have used brings out important similarities between them. In each text, the monstrous child is not simply a misogynistic projection, but represents a complex negotiation of gender roles and symbolic contexts. Each poem uncovers the mechanisms by which (within the terms of that particular work) paternity can be attributed: in other words, the relationship between the Name-of-the-Father and human subjects, both male and female. Although initially they focus on the human father's inadequacy to the role of symbolic Father, both romances ultimately make an ideological move which identifies the Father with the Christian God (viewed in contradistinction to paganism in *KT*, to the temporal in *SG*), a move that involves a shift out of the aegis of the symbolic and into that of the imaginary. They thus transcend their anxieties about paternity: God as Father answers all, in Him all Christian fathers and mothers are redeemed. To my mind, however, this transcendence is less interesting than the inquiry into earthly parenthood and the exposure of its inadequacies: the monstrous child is, in a sense, the truer expression of the human.

---

[33] MS B of the poem refers to Gowther as 'seynt Gotlake' and, as is commonly remarked, ends with the words 'explicit vita sancti'.

Clothing Paternal Incest in *The Clerk's Tale*, *Émaré* and the *Life of St Dympna*

ANNE SAVAGE

A common element unites the three texts read here, Chaucer's *Clerk's Tale*, the anonymous fourteenth-century romance *Émaré*, and the late medieval *Life of St Dympna* based on Capgrave's fifteenth-century version of Peter of Cambrai's thirteenth-century life.[1] In each, a father constructs the circumstances in which he could marry his daughter. In *The Clerk's Tale* Griselda, believing her daughter to have been killed when a baby on her husband's orders, is called upon to prepare nuptial quarters for his second marriage to their daughter; the given motive is that her husband Walter is testing her vow to be obedient to him. (It is frequently assumed of *The Clerk's Tale* that Walter being aware of the identity of his daughter, wouldn't *really* marry her—would he?). Émaré's mother dies at her daughter's birth and the baby is sent away from court to be fostered; when Émaré is brought back as a young girl, her father falls in love with her and demands to marry her. She refuses and is cast out to sea. In the life of Dympna, a virgin Christian flees a pagan father-king: like Émaré's father, the king wants to marry her because her mother has died, and only she is worthy to succeed her mother. The king finds Dympna at her refuge in Gheel, confronts her with marriage again, and decapitates her when she refuses.

---

[1] For texts see *The Riverside Chaucer*, ed. by Larry D. Benson (Boston: Houghton Mifflin, 1987); *Émaré* in *Middle English Metrical Romances*, ed. by W. H. French and C. B. Hale (New York: Prentice Hall, 1930; repr. New York: Russell and Russell, 1964), pp. 421–55; *The Life of Holy Dympna*, in *The Lives of Women Saints of our Contrie of Englond*, ed. by C. Horstmann, EETS, os 86 (Millwood, NY: Kraus, 1987; orig. publ. London: Trübner, 1896), pp. 43–49. For the transmission of Dympna's story, see Horstmann, Introduction, pp. vi–xi.

Despite generic differences, all thus have in common the issue of their relation to an actual, but largely invisible social phenomenon, and a particularly painful issue of gender relations: father-daughter incest. As narratives concerned in different ways with the disposition of lineal and sexual capital and the social practices of marriage and celibacy, there is considerable overlap between them. These similarities suggest that saints' lives can illuminate the workings of romance, the genre in which readings of medieval English narratives as incest-texts have largely been focussed.

All three narratives point to the issue of father-daughter incest, and all drop it as though it were a non-issue. Readers and audiences are insulated from the social fact of paternal incest by narrative stratagem: in each case it is set up as an important feature of the narrative line, then dispensed with in the particular circumstances. Yet the narratives, by their structures and conclusions, silently invite further consideration of the contradictions thus offered. Readings of Émaré's and Griselda's stories have taken up this invitation: Anne Laskaya, for instance, in her study of 'the rhetoric of incest', has argued that a basic principle of such stories is the 'strategy of muting and evading women's suffering'.[2] Margaret Robson's challenging paper re-ascribes some agency to the heroines of incest tales by viewing them in Freudian terms as a test cases in thinking about feminine desire for the father.[3] I will here argue that such interpretations are beside the (carefully-constructed and yet vanishing) narrative point of these stories, as well as being inherently unlike the social facts of father-daughter incest. Even if little girls commonly want to marry someone like their father, they do not pursue sex and marriage with him while pretending that this is his idea; usually it *is* his idea. In any case, the powers and the responsibility for the realization of incestuous desire lie with the father: the question of social responsibility is not laid aside by the argument that the stories represent female desire. In the romance and the exemplary tale considered here, and in the passion of St Dympna, alternate stripping and veiling of the issue reveals the mass of contradictory understandings of and responses to father-daughter incest (which extends to any male family

---

[2] 'The Rhetoric of Incest in the Middle English *Émaré*', in *Violence Against Women in Medieval Texts*, ed. by Anna Roberts (Gainesville: University Press of Florida, 1998), pp. 97–114.

[3] Margaret Robson, 'Cloaking Desire: Re-reading *Emaré*', in *Romance Reading on the Book: Essays on Medieval Narrative Presented to Maldwyn Mills*, ed. by Jennifer Fellows, Rosalind Field, Gillian Rogers and Judith Weiss (Cardiff: University of Wales Press, 1996), 64–76.

member in authority, including spiritual advisors). All three narratives illustrate *social* responses to paternal incest, reinforcing fundamental contradictions which involve knowing and not knowing about it, representing and not representing it, and speaking or being silent about it.

This ambivalence has continuities with modern socio-institutional responses, and is also present in other medieval sources to which we might turn for historical contextualizations for these narratives. Here too, representation of incest is approached very closely, but is redirected away before actual representation. Thus a dark area is mapped out in obverse: we can trace its precise outline and determine its dimensions. As Felicity Riddy showed à propos courtesy books, the obvious and even self-declared purposes and motives of a text can be seen to point at an opposing state of affairs, quite different sources and reasons for its existence; our 'looking behind' texts contributes to our knowledge of where they stood for their own audiences and readers, as well as ourselves.[4]

There has been much recent discussion of the pronouncements and the silences of the pastoral handbooks, and their principal source of authority, canon law. Kathryn Gravdal, for instance, has argued that the father's absence from medieval legal discourses about sexual abuse within the nuclear family suggests that paternal incest was seen as a less serious sin.[5] Megan McLaughlin, rebutting this argument, points out that the silence of written law codes on father-daughter incest is not the same as its erasure in the practices and judgements of the secular courts.[6]

Both these opposing arguments point to the way paternal incest was acknowledged as a real possibility, but not often addressed directly in medieval society. Pastoral manuals are forthright in their descriptions of sexual sin, but sexual activity between parents and children is simply left out. Vociferously stern about incest, pastoral handbooks discuss it almost exclusively in terms of marital relations within closer kinship terms than the church allows. When referred to, incest is thus in a much less threatening form than in the immediate family, with the back turned *almost*, but not quite, on its more fearful forms. The *Fasciculus morum*,

---

[4] '"Mother Knows Best": Reading Social Change in a Courtesy Text', *Speculum*, 71 (1996), 66–86.

[5] Kathryn Gravdal, 'Confessing Incests: Legal Erasures and Literary Celebrations in Medieval France', *Comparative Literature Studies*, 32 (1995), 280–95 (pp. 280–91).

[6] Megan McLaughlin, '"Abominable Mingling": Father-Daughter Incest and the Law', *Medieval Feminist Newsletter*, 24 (1997), 26–30.

for instance, treats incest as a subset of lechery and focusses on the behaviour of priests, the men for whom any sexual sin involving another person is 'incestuous'. The concern here is with the apostasy of the cleric and dishonour to the institution.[7] (Not incest, but sodomy is said to be too horrendous to be described).[8] Paternal incest is implicitly 'covered' through other categories, such as 'VII. viii *Stuprum*' [violating a virgin] and general prohibitions, such as 'thou shalt not commit adultery, that is, you shall not take any woman without permission from God and the Church'.[9] Perhaps incest is 'covered' by the excusal of women who were forced to have sex: '[i]f they were forced to do it, I say that such a deed has brought them great merit and is no stain on their virginity'.[10] But this is in any case a minor note: the general discussion of lechery is heavily weighted with comments on the sinful nature of women.

Robert Mannyng's vernacular manual, *Handlyng Synne*, deals with incest as a branch of lechery, too, but is a little more explicit: 'men take kyn in felawrede,/ and wyth hem doth flesshëly dede' (including in this women with whom one's male kin have had sex).[11] Its most explicit incest tale, however, does not deal with incest committed by fathers within the immediate biological family group. In the section on the seventh sacrament, baptism, the story is told of a man who takes his goddaughter home to celebrate the Easter of her baptism and who instead 'lay by hys god-dohtyr that yche [very] nyht' (l. 9732). Knowing his sin, he fears the social peril of staying away from church—by which people will know he is in a state of sin—more than the peril of his soul. Although he fears some terrible retribution, over the course of a week nothing happens, so

---

[7] *Fasciculus Morum: A Fourteenth-Century Preacher's Handbook*, ed. and trans. by Siegfried Wenzel (University Park: Pennsylvania State University Press, 1989); see the chapter on lechery, pp. 648–733. 'Et nota: sub hac specie continetur luxuria clericorum et religiosum, quorum peccatum magis considerandum est' ('Notice that this branch comprises lechery among clerics and religious. Their sin is more grievous than that of other people.'), pp. 683–84.

[8] 'Quam horrore accepto transeo, aliiquis relinquens exponendam' ('I pass it over in horror and leave others to describe it'), *ibid.*, pp. 686–87.

[9] 'Non mechaberis,' hoc est, nullam mulierum [accipies] sine licentia Dei et Ecclesie', *ibid.*, p. 670.

[10] '...[s]cilicet quod ad hoc vi fuerunt coacte, dico quod illud fit maximi meriti nec aliquid contra virginitatem', *ibid.*, pp. 672–73.

[11] 'men take their kin in intercourse and do the carnal deed with them': *Robert of Brunne's "Handlyng Synne" AD 1303*, ed. by F. J. Furnivall, EETS, OS 119, 123 (London: Kegan Paul, Trench, Trübner, 1901), ll. 7369–70.

"he wendë [thought] God had hyt forgete [forgotten about it]' (l. 9755). On the seventh day, he dies, and after his death his grave emits a stinking fire, which destroys his body entirely. The circumstances of the crime are described very plainly, and the godfather is shown as drinking enough to overcome any inhibitions he has. Although the story concerns a god-daughter, the girl's place could be taken by any young female relative, and perhaps the story 'stands' in some way for the crime closer to home. It is not, however, treated as the victim's story in any way—a feature which the romance narratives and Dympna's *Life* do not share, and which I will examine below.

As already noted, the most persistent practical ecclesiastical concern with incest has to do with marital unions between relatives by blood or marriage, not sexual violation within the family.[12] Where marital 'incest' is dealt with in canon law, it is done with extreme seriousness. Georges Duby comments on this kind of incest:

> An incestuous marriage was regarded as null and void. It was not a marriage at all; it did not exist. It was as if the two fleshes had never become one, as if the blood relationship had prevented such a fusion. Incest belonged to a sector of morality apart from all others.[13]

But Duby's conclusions on incest concern public morality, not what went on in private, and they starkly outline that dark area by illuminating the institutionalized 'looking away' phenomenon which I am speaking of here. Child sexual abuse is placed in a sector of morality *so much further* apart from all others that it is hard to see, discuss, or otherwise deal with directly. An explicit literary expression of the problem of the unmentionable is in the introduction to Chaucer's *Man of Law's Tale*, where the teller publicly excludes several incestuous stories from his repertoire as being 'wikke', 'cursed', 'horrible', 'unkynde abhominacions' (ll. 77–88), though he notes that 'Chaucer' has dealt with them. As Elizabeth Archibald notes, 'it is generally agreed that the Man of Law's remark should be taken as an ironic example of the way that prudes will describe

---

[12] James A. Brundage notes: 'Scholars have speculated that the new incest laws were designed to benefit the church financially ... [by increasing] the likelihood that the Church would inherit property from wealthy persons, who, under the new rules, would be less able to use intrafamilial marriage alliances to keep control of familial estates within their kinship group' (*Law, Sex and Christian Society in Medieval Europe* (Chicago: University of Chicago Press, 1987), p. 88 and nn. 40, 41).

[13] Georges Duby, *The Knight, the Lady and the Priest*, trans. by Barbara Bray (New York: Pantheon Books, 1983), pp. 69–70.

explicitly the very topics which they are in the process of condemning as too outrageous to discuss'.[14] And since he is a prude constructed by Chaucer himself, the relationship between knowing about incest and censoring speech about it is here rooted in paradox. From the distant to the recent past, even when child sexual abuse has been proven, ecclesiastical and legal systems have conspired in the stratagem of silence to help society insulate itself, first, from the fact of child sexual abuse by those in authority in religious and educational institutions, and by fathers and other men in positions of trust; and, second, from institutionalized complicity in its continuance. It seems that this was also a feature of medieval society.

The burden of legal proof posed difficulties for children, and even for mothers or older siblings with knowledge of the abuse.[15] Young children would be unlikely to have any sense of their 'rights' in such matters, while both girls and boys at the age of twelve were held responsible for their own actions under criminal law.[16] Again, as now, feelings of guilt about being the object of paternal sex, whether resulting from a girl's own fear of disbelief, blame, and paternal violence, or whether induced by paternal accusation, might well interfere with initiating a legal process; likewise, maternal or sibling fear and shame. The fear of counter-charges of promiscuity would also be a powerful deterrent even in the case of a girl who wished to bring a charge of rape against any man—her father included. Nassyngton's fourteenth-century *Speculum Vitae* associates fornication of all kinds with women's lust and greed, so that they will consent to incestuous sex like any other:

> and forsake nan of alle of kyn
> that has wille with tham to syn
> Fader, ne sone, ne cosyn, ne brodere,
> this synne ys mare greif than the todere.[17]

---

[14] *Apollonius of Tyre: Medieval and Renaissance Themes and Variations* (Cambridge: D. S. Brewer, 1991), pp. 260–261.

[15] See James A. Brundage, 'Playing by the Rules', in *Desire and Discipline: Sex and Sexuality in the Premodern West*, ed. by Jacqueline Murray and Konrad Eisenbichler (Toronto: University of Toronto Press, 1996), pp. 26–28.

[16] Barbara Hanawalt, *Growing Up in Medieval London* (Oxford: Oxford University Press, 1993) p. 112.

[17] 'And forsake no one among their kinsmen who wish to commit sin with them—not father, son, cousin, or brother. This sin is a greater wrong than the others': see John W. Smeltz, '*Speculum Vitae*: An Edition of British Museum Manuscript Royal 17.C.viii',

'Actual cases of incest, however, were rarely reported'.[18] Against the forces of institutional silence, which fail to address this particular situation explicitly, against the burden of perceived female responsibility for men's sexual sin, and against the suspicion, sometimes hatred of women expressed by ecclesiastical legislators of social attitudes, a girl would have found little in the way of support.

Turning back to the three narratives reveals some continuities. Griselda's obedience in preparing for her husband's second marriage to a twelve-year-old likewise points to the social pressures which enforce maternal helplessness, as well as those forces which veil the idea that Walter might really have this course of action in mind. Apart from the fact that we have read *The Clerk's Tale*, or its Petrarchan original, before, there is nothing in the narrative to assure us that he does not. He commands 'the court of Rome, in subtil wyse/ Enformed of his wyl' (ll. 737–38) to counterfeit the necessary bulls to release him from his marriage to Griselda; this is not, like Émaré's father, *specifically* to wed his own daughter—and yet the stage is set for this.[19] Nobody knows the girl is his daughter except Walter, and the manservant who took her to Bologna, who has not been in evidence in the story since he took away Walter's son, seven years before. It seems less likely that Walter carries out a plan to convince Griselda he will marry again than that he actually *changes his mind* when moved by Griselda's fair welcome of his new bride, and by her admonition that he not 'prikke with no tormentynge/ This tendre mayden, as ye han doon mo' (ll. 1038–39), since the girl has not been raised in poverty, and could probably not endure the hardships 'a

(unpublished doctoral dissertation, Duquesne University, 1977), p. 441 (quoted by Ruth Mazzo Karras, 'Sex, Money and Prostitution in Medieval English Culture', in *Desire and Discipline*, ed. by Murray and Eisenbichler, pp. 201–16 (p. 211, n. 34 and p. 209).

[18] Hanawalt, *Growing Up*, p. 122; see note 49. In the Consistory Court, the four cases were of 'spiritual kin'—that is, godparents. None ended in conviction.

[19] Walter's arrangements with the court of Rome are baffling, but nonetheless firm, about his powers over this matter. The first says that 'the court of Rome' is at his command 'swiche bulles to devyse/ As to his crueel purpos may suffyse' (ll. 739–40). The second stanza uses the word '*countrefete* the popes bulles... as by the popes dispensacion', ll. 743–46). Is there somewhere at the court of Rome an office dealing with rulers' wishes to test their wives, which can be commanded to fabricate papal dispensation to marry again? It may be interpreted here that these powers have been informed that Walter does not really mean to get rid of Griselda permanently, and he does not really plan to marry another. On the other hand, it may be read as giving him the power to do whatever he wishes *in order to test Griselda*.

povre fostred creature' (l. 1043) like herself has done. Unlike Petrarch's lord, Chaucer's Walter does not feel any deep remorse until this moment, until seeing how 'sad [serious] and constant' (l. 1047) Griselda is, he finally declares "'This is ynogh'" (l. 1051). The Clerk and no doubt most readers share the belief that this is far, far too much to impose on a real woman. However, the Clerk mitigates the 'too much' by rejecting the tale's chaff-like literal sense; the story becomes, at least in the Clerk's unworldly allegorical interpretation, what the soul might need to bear under the burden of adversity God sometimes lays on us. The apparent direction of the narrative at that crucial point is blatantly—perhaps deliberately—ignored.

Again, the ease with which Émaré's father obtains a papal dispensation to marry her both points to social complicity and protests it: he sends counsellors to Rome, who

> ...wente to the courte of Rome,
> And browht the Popus bullus sone,
>> To wedde hys dowhter dere (ll. 238–40).

It is hinted that the counsellors are reluctant—'They durste [dared] not breke hys commandement' (l. 236)—but the way the poet declares their reluctance implies also that no one protested. Yet Émaré protests very explicitly:

> 'Nay, syr, God of heuen hyt forbede
> that euer do so we shulde!
>
> Yyf hyt so betydde that ye me wedde
> And we shulde play togedur in bedde,
>> Bothe we were forlorne!
> The worde shulde sprynge fer and wyde;
> In all the worlde on euery syde
>> the worde shulde be borne.
> Ye ben a lorde of gret pryce;
> Lorde, lette neuur suche sorow aryce;
>> Take God you beforne!
> That my fadur shulde wedde me,

> God forbede that I hyt so se,
>> That wered the crowne of thhorne!' (ll. 251–64)[20]

One particular aspect of marriage ritual highlights both the implications of incest for the audience and the continuities with the saint's life: all three heroines, along with Griselda's daughter, are dressed for marriage by a gift of clothing from their suitors/husbands.

> The husband's gifts not only responded to a demand for reciprocity [with respect to the dowry]: they were also indispensable symbolic agents in the integration of the wife into another household and lineage. They were signs that relations had been initiated between the husband's group, redefined to include his wife, and the wife's family of birth... Moreover, ethnological literature has often shown that the dressing of the bride is a rite of passage, more precisely, a rite of integration.[21]

Following Émaré in her journeys, constantly covering the body her father lusted for and wished to 'play with in bed', is the bejewelled cloak emblazoned with four pairs of faithful lovers which her father places on her, just before she declares her refusal of him. She is wearing it when Sir Kador finds her in the boat in which her father sets her adrift: 'a glysteryng thyng' (l. 350); she wears it at the feast he later holds for her, where her future husband sees and falls in love with her, and likewise when his mother sees and conceives a hatred for her; she wears it when cast adrift again with her new-born son because of her mother-in-law's wicked plot; when washed up in Rome, and, seven years later, when re-united with her husband. When people see her, they see it. It has a noble origin, made by the heathen Emir's daughter ('the Amerayle dowhter of hethennes', l. 109), with three pairs of romance lovers, and herself and her beloved, in the corners. It has been taken in battle by a visitor to Émaré's father's court, the King of Sicily, and put on her by her father as a dress. Its splendour bestows on Émaré a visible transcendence: 'She semed non erthely wommon' (l. 245; 'non erdly thyng' l. 396; 'none erdyly wyght [earthly creature]', l. 701). This strange sign has in common

---

[20] "'No, sir, God of heaven forbid that we should ever do such a thing! If it were to happen that you wed me and we were to have intercourse with each other in bed, we would both be lost! The word would leap far and wide: everywhere throughout the world it would be known. You are a lord of high rank: Lord, never allow so sorrowful a thing to happen; take God as your guide! That my father should wed me—God who bore the crown of thorns forbid that I should ever see such a thing!'"

[21] Christiane Klapisch-Zuber, *Women, Family and Ritual in Renaissance Italy*, trans. by Lydia G. Cochrane (Chicago: University of Chicago Press, 1987), p. 224.

with Griselda's rare—even unbelievable—patience, and even more with the allegorical sense the Clerk bestows on it, the divorce from worldliness, from the stains and ugliness of sin. Like Dympna's marriage to her heavenly bridegroom, made possible by her beheading, Émaré's cloak and Griselda's allegorical dress clothe the worldly appearance of incestuous desire in the story, sending the heroines off, unstained, to a better life—however it may seem otherwise to earthly eyes.

And yet, in terms of real clothing for the ritual of marriage, Griselda's clothing and Émaré's cloak have a familiar social role: all have been bestowed by a father-husband for the purpose of claiming her publicly as his own. Variations on this practice were pan-European in the fourteenth and fifteenth centuries; and while the modern-day wedding dress and nuptial wardrobe are not routinely provided by the groom, they still serve the purpose of marking publicly the movement away from the father, who 'gives away' his daughter, to the husband who receives her. This is no less the case with hagiographic heroines. In her heavenly espousal, Dympna's virgin body will be re-clothed in light, and crowned with a special crown, an *aureola*. That she passes from an earthly father to a heavenly bridegroom does not affect the social point: indeed as with all virgin martyrs, Dympna's real father is her heavenly one. Thus the roles of father and husband in the virgin martyr's life are taken by different persons of the Holy Trinity. In the romance hagiography of the virgin martyr, escape from the secular institutions of marital exchange relies on a long tradition of Christological prestidigitation with the persons of the Trinity in relation to the Virgin: she is the daughter of the Father, the mother of the Son, and yet both are the same God. This is only possible through Christian paradox: no carnal sex is involved, though the result is incarnation. This incest is reversed in valence because it is offered as a unique contradiction of all that incest usually involves.

Romance and hagiographic versions of bridal rituals thus overlap. The 'vesting of the bride' in fourteenth and fifteenth-century Italy shared a common term with the dressing of the new nun, *vestizione*.[22] In the English anchoritic literature which has provided some of the virgin martyr narratives best known today, all virgins are dressed by their heavenly bridegroom in radiance, while being crowned as eternal virgins. The anchoress herself does not go to her wedding in her habit, but naked, for her virgin body to be reclothed by her bridegroom in heaven, while virgin martyrs are all, in the tradition of extreme reversals common to anchoritic

---

[22] Klapisch-Zuber, p. 230, n. 64.

thinking, stripped naked rather than clothed by their male suitors/per-
secutors.[23] The basic forms and rituals of contemporary marriage
exchange are preserved: the bride willingly gives her body to her husband, and he dresses it accordingly. Likewise, in the figure of Griselda,

> taken virgin, poor and naked (in Pesellino's iconography... she does not
> even have a shift to throw on to receive the ring), richly adorned for the
> wedding ceremonies in the presence of her baron husband's vassals, then
> sent back by him *en chemise* to the hut in which she was born—
> Boccaccio's contemporaries would have recognized acts and behaviours
> rooted in nuptial practices of their times.[24]

Klapisch-Zuber gives full details of the economy of exchange in terms of
wedding clothing; here it suffices to note that if the father is both the
giver and taker of his own daughter, while clothing her for her marriage
to himself, there is no exchange at all: none of the heroines bring a dowry
with them, though all are marked for possession by their nuptial clothing.
This economic side of the representations of incest is not to be
underestimated in these three stories, since marriage, however
romanticized in medieval literary happy endings, remained largely an
economic institution. It was most women's only security: Griselda's
poverty and Émaré's destitution are central at critical points in the
narrative, pointing to the equal plight of the girl who says yes and the girl
who says no when she is in her father's or husband's control. (Poverty in
the religious life, as represented in a figure such as Dympna, is part of the
hagiographic genre's goal of secular reversal; it is an investment in the
future).

St Dympna's father is a pagan, so we might conclude that, throughout
the period from Peter of Cambrai's thirteenth-century version through to
Capgrave's, his behaviour has a ready explanation in the religious
training and cultural bias of the writers of Dympna's life. Yet the secular
world is so often 'paganized' for medieval audiences as a contrast to the

---

[23] *Ancrene Wisse* describes the anchoritic habit as a professional uniform only, of little
importance: see *Anchoritic Spirituality: Ancrene Wisse and Related Works*, trans. with
notes by Anne Savage and Nicholas Watson (Mahwah, NJ: Paulist Press, 1991), p. 50,
while the bridal gown—which is never taken off, it seems—is described, along with the
aureola worn by virgins in heaven, on p. 233. For the whole Middle English text, see *The
English Text of the* Ancrene Riwle. Ancrene Wisse. *MS. Corpus Christi College
Cambridge 402*, ed. by J. R. R. Tolkien, EETS 249 (London: Oxford University Press,
1962).

[24] Klapisch-Zuber, pp. 228–29, and see n. 58.

religious life that Dympna's father may be as uncomfortably close to home as those simple parallels, the world, the flesh, and the devil. These intimate enemies are seen in household terms in anchoritic virginity literature:

> 'Forget your people and your father's house.' 'Your people' are what David calls the gathering within you of fleshly thoughts, which incite you and draw you on to marriage and a husband's kisses. These are Babylon's people, the devil's army, who are intent on leading Syon's daughter into the world's slavery.[25]

Not only fathers, but suitors of virgin martyrs are also normally pagans: in the extreme view constructed for the anchoritic virgin and her virgin martyr heroine, all sexual men are pagans, idol-worshippers.

Dympna, like other virgin martyrs, has left all that behind her, and has no intention of returning:

> ...the diuell desiring to reduce the virgin to profane Idolatrie againe, so inflamed the kings hart with incestuous loue, that presentlie he [her father] began to wooe her with flattering and faire promises, offering her all glorie, riches and honour, if she would be his wife.[26]

Like Émaré, she replies

> that she would neuer consent to that impietie: adding that by no law nor righte, the daughter might defile her fathers beadd [command], nor by such shamefull wickednes staine and infame [make infamuous] all her stocke and posteritie for euer. (pp. 43–44)

Her father then, like the rich and powerful antagonists of the anchoritic virgin martyrs and the fathers of romance, threatens to compel her. When he catches up with Dympna at last in Gheel, he offers, like St Katherine's persecutor Maxentius, to make her into a pagan goddess, erecting a beautiful statue of her in a temple.[27] After killing her priest (who has just warned her 'neuer to yield to the king in that villanie, leste she incurred the eternall kings displeasure', p. 46), her father turns to moral blackmail:

> 'O my daughter why sufferest thou thy father to be so plunged in sorrowes? Why doost thou not pittie him? Why despisest thou him that loueth thee: harken vnto me and thou shalt want nothing...' (p. 46)

---

[25] *Holy Maidenhood*, in Savage and Watson, *Anchoritic Spirituality*, p. 225.

[26] *The Life of Holie Dympna*, p. 43 (henceforth referenced by page number in the text).

[27] *St Katherine*, in *Anchoritic Spirituality*, p. 275.

While it is on the one hand a matter of course that he plead like a disappointed lover, he has no right to place himself in this category; the deliberate blurring of kinds of love is meant to confuse his daughter, and, combined with the threat of violence, might well have been compelling to any girl of less resilience than a well-informed virgin martyr. (That apparently unnecessary warning by her priest, that she not give in, gains some conviction here). Again, like other virgin martyrs, Dympna faces and overcomes the interchangeably pagan/sexual threats to her chastity through death: her beheading after the attempt to possess her by her father, a pagan of secular power, allows the narrative line a disruption, glossed by transcendence when Dympna goes to her heavenly bridegroom.

The force of a narrative line set up and then prevented naturally leaves audiences contemplating the void where that line of narrative led. It seems to me that this and other features of *The Clerk's Tale*, *Émaré*, and the *Life of St Dympna* both ask this contemplation of their audiences and decently cover its content. These narratives avert the terrible fact of paternal sexual assault, but nevertheless introduce it; they require the possibility of 'the unspeakable' for quite different reasons, and yet all evoke it through the construction of an innocent female victim (or victims) suffering through a father's sin, rather than through the misogynist commonplaces we have seen which characterize official writing about incest in the category of lechery or other sins. In *Émaré*, her father's incestuous plans set the action, so that she becomes Égaré (Lost) through her refusal, and remains lost to him until the end of the story, in which Émaré's wicked, letter-replacing mother-in-law has been killed, but her father, who also cast her out to sea, is reconciled without penalty. In the story of Griselda, Walter's plans for a second marriage to his own daughter, and their redirection, end Griselda's tests of obedience, restore her royal marital status, and culminate in the Clerk of Oxenford's allegorical interpretation of her wifely and maternal suffering. Dympna's suffering, though a direct result of her father's frustrated lust for her, is smoothly subsumed into the genre of the virgin martyr passion: the fact of her pagan antagonist's being her father, as with the other virgin martyrs, tends to fade from view in the universal threat of sex.

In spite of the strong narrative profile of the paternal attempt at or possibility of incest—it gets Émaré's narrative underway, is instrumental in the resolution of Griselda's plight, and is the whole reason for Dympna's flight and execution—nothing points to it directly as being of importance *for what it is*. It seems simply a narrative device for initiating, motivating, or ending some other actions, which are the ones we are to pay attention to. It seems *not* to be a narrative possibility which is averted in the first case by Émaré's refusal to marry her father in spite of the Church's approval, in the second case by Walter's unprecedented surge of remorse, and in the third by Dympna's final refusal and beheading. In each case it is set up as a likely or possible result of the narrative line; it seems strange that it should be trivialized or forgotten in any way.

'Averting the eyes' is a typical social response to the sexual abuse of daughters by fathers, and yet it follows that there must be something to avert the eyes from before this deliberate inattention can occur. The three stories draw attention, *if we permit it,* to this behavioural complex: first, the notion that paternal incest is a real phenomenon with a disastrous effect on the daughter and family; and, second, the refusal to acknowledge that it can really occur, or the insistence that it is really something else—a test of the woman's character only, or a momentary slip caused by madness, or a purely pagan habit. All three narratives, however bold in their introduction and use of the unspeakable, draw back from any suggestion of its performance. All three also make their heroines young, but not children under the law, and all offer happy endings (Dympna's beheading generically signifies her union with her eternal beloved in heaven, and is thus as much a romance closure as the other two narratives).

Do these stories exalt the female victim? That is, do they have sympathy with women, rather than misogyny, at their heart? Yes, but in *Émaré* and *The Clerk's Tale*, stereotypically negative images of women counterbalance the daughters' perfection in the form of Émaré's wicked mother-in-law and the 'real' wives addressed at the end of the Clerk's story. These evoke quite clearly the Wife of Bath, through the characterization of wives as fierce, husband-bullying, camel-like or tiger-like creatures capable of violence to their menfolk (ll. 1195–1206). Men here, moreover, are counselled not to test their wives as Walter did *because they will not succeed* (ll. 1180–82). 'Official' attitudes to women are maintained, even or perhaps especially with respect to Dympna: women are either very very good, or very very bad, and for the most part, authors collude with Chaucer's Clerk's sentiment:

> It were ful hard to fynde now-a-dayes
> In al a toun Grisildis thre or two (*The Clerk's Tale*, ll. 1164–65).

So it appears that none of these stories is meant to take up a social cause, or even to evoke the possibility of *contemporary fathers'* similar behaviour. Thus, in spite of there being none of the particular kind of misogyny which implicitly or explicitly leaves the women responsible for their fathers' sin (as in the Freudian view summed up in Margaret Robson's paper), we seem to be left with the *status quo* of the pastoral manuals, mitigated by the circumstances of the stories: '[i]f they were forced to do it, I say that such a deed has brought them great merit and is no stain on their virginity'.[28]

And yet this is not the whole story. All three narratives have a dimension of social satire which is relevant to the dropped issue of paternal incest. Why else does the composer of *Émaré* point so explicitly at the ready compliance of the Church in Émaré's father's plans? Émaré makes the decision to stand against him with the conviction and eloquence of a virgin martyr (see p. 352 above). Satire of religious institutions and their representatives is a familiar dimension of writing associated with the religious life. Christina of Markyate's unpleasant experiences at the hands of Ranulf, the bishop of Durham, function likewise as satire, when he makes an attempt on her virginity, and, in failure, 'appoints' Burhred as her fiancé in what eventually becomes a conspiracy with her parents to destroy her vow of chastity. In this monastic biography, laymen and bishops can be represented as sexual predators as Christina's spiritual and blood family plot to force her into a secular economy of exchange in which even her mother colludes.[29] The anchoritic guide, *Ancrene Wisse*, offers us the figure of the overdressed young priest who comes to ogle white-skinned holy virgins;[30] Margery Kempe has much to say to Archbishop Arundel about the poor example his people offer to the world.[31]

Even a tale with a happy married ending participates in this kind of criticism when its heroines—virgin, or, like Griselda and Émaré, holy enough to acquire a kind of virtual virginity—are persecuted with the collusion of the Church. Conversely, in Dympna's *Life*, the Church is on her side against a pagan, that is, secular, world. Dympna's father and his advisors belong to this secular world, which even goes against its own

---

[28]   See n. 10 above.

[29]   *The Life of Christina of Markyate*, ed. and trans. by C. H. Talbot (Oxford: Clarendon Press, 1959), pp. 42–45, 50–55, 73–75.

[30]   See *Ancrene Wisse*, in *Anchoritic Spirituality*, p. 68.

[31]   *The Book of Margery Kempe*, ed. by Sanford Brown Meech and Hope Emily Allen, EETS 212 (London: Oxford University Press, 1940 for 1939), p. 36. For discussion of Margery as a social satirist, see Lynn Staley, *Margery Kempe's Dissenting Fictions* (University Park: Pennsylvania State University Press, 1994).

laws to satisfy the lust of a man in authority. The anchoritic examples of the heroic virgin set the stage for later romantic and hagiographical models of the extreme woman who does not cede her moral ground either to threatening men or inner weakness. Griselda's plight and the Clerk's and Chaucer's discomfort with the resolution of *The Clerk's Tale* point bewilderingly to both feminine and masculine confusion about male authority: on the one hand, Walter is a cruel and weak husband; on the other, he can be authoritatively allegorized *out of all recognition* as God the Father. That this itself is uncomfortable leaves the story and its literary reading mired in the literal awfulness of the narrative line, both before Walter changes his mind, and after he terminates Griselda's woes. No one could realistically say that no permanent damage would be done in real life—which is where the audience is always left ultimately when a story is over.

Griselda's compliance is schematic: she undertakes to obey Walter 'in will as well as word' from the beginning; would she have done so had she known Walter's new wife to be their daughter? Why keep this fact available only to the audience and Walter's conscience, except to leave open the possibility that he could have married his daughter, and no one but himself and the audience would have known? That is, Walter *could have got away with* it.[32] Is there the nagging necessity to avert the eyes from the notion that some fathers do? I cannot answer this question, except to say that I find *The Clerk's Tale* uncomfortable in more ways than I can account for. The fictional Clerk is also very uneasy about the match of the literal to the allegorical, and he insists that no man should test his wife's patience in the same way: Griselda, he claims, 'really is' an exemplary wife (ll. 1142–47).[33] Yet he equally insists that 'real wives' should never, never be bullied like this, while Chaucer's *Envoy* to the Tale insists that wives should rather resort to violence before their husbands can even *think* of stepping out of line (ll. 1195–1206). The redirection of the narrative declares it *necessary* that Griselda be kept in ignorance of the truth of the incestuous possibility until it has been erased by Walter's

---

[32] The legalistic argument—that the bulls were counterfeit—seems manufactured and farfetched in the circumstances. A 'Court of Rome' which would fabricate the kind of dispensation Walter 'commands' (see n. 19 above) is not to be trusted to come to the rescue of Griselda's marriage.

[33] The Host appears to disregard without comment the allegorical interpretation, wishing that his wife had heard the story (ll. 1214–15). The implication is that he wishes he had a Griselda for a wife, and then he could get away with whatever he wanted.

staging of a resolution, assisted further by the Clerk's intellectual diversion. The story could not be what it is at all with a Griselda who would not bend to Walter's will in *everything*.

The decent clothing covering the possibility of paternal incest in these stories can, if we wish, be removed. Medieval audiences, like ourselves, are invited by their composers to ignore the distracting change of narrative direction. A sanctified allegorical interpretation; a glistening, concealing golden cloak; pagan clothing; all have something underneath; we know what it is, and are glad, perhaps, that we are not *required* to look at it.

The Earliest Heretical Englishwomen

PETER BILLER

The earliest heretical Englishwomen are usually thought of as later medieval Lollards, but in fact there are two earlier figures, about whom very little is known. One was a Cathar in mid-twelfth century England, and the other a Cathar or Cathar adherent in late thirteenth century Languedoc. In the following I look mainly at the second of these, addressing what can be known about her, the further conjectures about her that are plausible, and the theological culture of northern European heretical women.[1]

Two Dominican inquisitors, Pons of Parnac and Renous de Plassac, were hearing witnesses in Toulouse during the mid-1270s,[2] and, in the volume which preserves the record of these sessions, thirty-five folios contain the interrogation over several days in 1274 of a man called Raymond Frugon, who lived in Roquevidal, about thirty-two kilometres east of Toulouse.[3] Part of Raymond's deposition deals with one Aimeri of Toulouse, and it goes like this.

---

[1]   The first is discussed in my 'William of Newburgh and the Cathar Mission to England', in *Life and Thought in the Northern Church: Essays in Honour of Claire Cross*, ed. by Diane Wood, Studies in Church History, Subsidia, 12, (Woodbridge: Boydell Press, 1999), pp. 11–30.

[2]   The records survive in a copy made in the late seventeenth century by scribes working under a French Royal counsellor, Jean de Doat (Charles Molinier, *L'Inquisition dans le midi de France au XIIIe et au XIVe siècle: Étude sur les sources de son histoire* (Paris: no publisher, printed at L'imprimerie de P. Privat, Toulouse, 1890), p. 34; Yves Dossat, *Les crises de l'inquisition Toulousaine au XIIIe siècle (1233–1273)* (Bordeaux: Imprimerie Bière, 1959), p. 39, no 8).

[3]   Paris, Bibliothèque Nationale, MS Collection Doat 25, fols 90^r-125^r.

Item, he says that Aimeri of Toulouse came once to his house, together with the aforesaid Pons Fogacier of Toulouse, and William [the] Smith of Lavaur. He saw all of these entering the lower part of the house to go to these heretics [= Cathar perfects], and they stayed a long time with them. However he [Raymond] did not otherwise see him [Aimeri] together with the aforesaid heretics. [Asked] about the date, [he said it was] a year before last winter.

Item, on another occasion the same Aymeri—very well dressed—went through Roquevidal with some English woman. And after a few days the same Aymeri, stripped of almost everything, returned to his [Raymond's] house. He told what had happened. He was travelling to Lombardy with the aforesaid woman [the English woman] and some other woman. While they were asleep in some house, the two women were taken from him, and also all the money and the clothes they were carrying. He [Aimeri] had almost been captured as well, but he managed to run and get away. [Asked] about the date, [he said] the same as before.[4]

There is just this one, solitary, momentary and mysterious appearance of an Englishwoman, *mulier anglica*, among the several thousand pages, printed and unprinted, containing such records of interrogations and sentences, which are the surviving traces of inquisition into Cathar heretics in Languedoc between the 1230s and the 1320s. There are many women from Languedoc among these records, ordinary women who were not implicated; some other women who shared in the beliefs of the Cathars and supported them, called 'believers', *credentes*; and some who became Cathars themselves, 'Good Women', *Bonae mulieres*, or, in the

---

[4] MS Doat 25, fols 104ᵛ-5ʳ: 'Item, dixit quod Aimericus de Tholosa venit semel ad domum ipsius testis unacum Poncius Fogacerii de Tholosa et Guillelmi fabri de Vauro praedictis, qui omnes ipso teste vidente intraverunt in sotulum ad ipsos haereticos, et fuerunt ibi diu cum eis. Ipse testis tamen non vidit eum cum praedictis haereticis aliter. De tempore, in hyeme proximo praeterita fuit annus. Item, idem Aymericus ['totus spoliatus': crossed through] optime indutus transivit alias per Rocavidal cum quadam muliere Anglica, et post paucos dies idem Aymericus totus spoliatus fere rediit ad domum ipsius testis, narrans quod, dum iret in Lombardiam cum praedicta muliere et quaedam aliae [mistake for: 'quadam alia'], fuerunt sibi ablatae in itinere dum iacerent in quadam domo ambae mulieres, et pecunia tota, et vestes quas portabant, et fere ipse fuerat captus, sed evaserat per forsam de corer. De tempore, quod supra.' The depositions of about 5000 people interrogated about heresy in the Toulousain in 1245–46 contain instances of men called 'Anglicus', for example W[illelmus] Anglicus of Montesquieu, and Thomas Anglicus of Gaja-la-Selve, Toulouse, Bibliothèque Municipale, MS 609, fols 102ʳ and 195ᵛ. William the Englishman had seen Cathars, but denied belief or other involvement with them, while Thomas the Englishman denied any contact or involvement.

more frequent language of the depositions, 'heretics', *hereticae*, and to later historians, 'perfects', *perfectae*.[5] There are hundreds of these in the depositions, and much circumstantial detail is recorded about them. Although there is much to be said about the way these records 'constructed' reality, most of the time the solidity of *a* past reality of which they are traces is manifest. This past reality included women in families of Cathar sympathizers playing a large role in supporting and maintaining Cathar perfects, and in transmitting Cathar teachings, within their families and among their relatives and friends. Some of them themselves became Good Women, sometimes just for a year or two around adolescence, sometimes later, when they were widows or left their husbands to do this, and they then remained as perfects for many years or for the rest of their lives. In Languedoc before 1209, in relatively peaceful and open conditions for the Cathars, many of these lived a communal life in houses, following a routine of prayer and fasting, in some ways like nuns or beguines. Both before and after 1209 there were also *perfectae* travelling in pairs, one with her 'companion', *socia*, in a form of life which has parallels with that of the (male) mendicants. Although modern historians have interpreted these Cathar women in many different ways,[6] they agree about their basic pattern of life and they use broadly the same technique of describing them by parading the abundant and rich detail of the Languedoc depositions.

Side by side, then, we have this well-known and rather substantial picture of the Cathar *perfectae* of Languedoc and the solitary appearance of the *mulier anglica*. They point to what is ignored, something which, even if it is not ignored, can never be well known: Cathar women in northern Europe. There is a triple problem here. First, Catharism in northern Europe is a barely known phenomenon. Secondly, in the scanty evidence which survives, such as brief chronicle entries about executions, the male gender of the word used—*heretici*, or *Publicani*—sometimes prevents women's appearing in the only surviving record. Thus a letter from the Archbishop of Sens, written about 1221, says that 'certain *men* of La Charité-sur-Loire' ('quidam homines de Caritate') have fallen into

---

[5]   See Richard Abels and Ellen Harrison, 'The Participation of Women in Languedocian Catharism', *Medieval Studies,* 41 (1979), 215–51, and Anne Brenon, *Les femmes cathares* (Paris: Perrin, 1992).

[6]   Peter Biller, 'Cathars and Material Women', in *This Body of Death. Medieval Theology and the Natural Body*, ed. by Peter Biller and A. J. Minnis, York Studies in Medieval Theology, 1 (York: York Medieval Press, 1997), pp. 61–107 (pp. 64–81).

heresy. Men only? No, for later on in the letter the archbishop instructs
the bishop of Auxerre to 'impose solemn and public satisfaction,
according to ... the condition, *sex*, age and knowledge of the delinquent
person', and we know from elsewhere of the strength of the women who
were Cathars in La Charité:[7] the evidence is quoted later in this paper.[8]

The third problem concerns modern awareness of Cathars. By the late
twelfth century 'Albigensian' (from Albi) was becoming one of the most
popular terms to denote them, just as Languedoc and Italy had become the
promised lands of heresy. Allied to the wonderful survivals of evidence
from the inquisition of Languedoc, this has produced the modern image
of Catharism as a southern European matter. But it had not always been
so, and indeed it is the north-west which seems to have been the earliest
area of Cathar implantation and Cathar strength. The most convincing
account of the implantation of Catharism in western Europe is that put
forward in 1994 by Bernard Hamilton.[9] Combined with early studies of
heresy and its repression in northern France by Émile Chénon and
Charles Homer Haskins and the more recent general history by Jean
Duvernoy,[10] Hamilton's work provides us with this. Men from northern
France, *Francia*, set up the first Latin dualist Church in Constantinople
around 1100, and returned thence to *Francia*, setting up the first western
European Cathar bishopric there. Catharism spread strongly in north-
western Europe, into the Rhineland, parts of Flanders, and north-western
France, and the diocese of Auxerre in particular. Northern Cathars were
dealt hammer-blows in persecutions in the 1160s, around 1180, and
finally in the 1230s.

The evidence is scant. There is some evidence of wealth, strong adherence in the upper echelons of northern French and Flemish towns, and

---

[7] André Wilmart, 'Une lettre sur les cathares du Nivernais (V. 1221)', *Revue
Bénédictine*, 47 (1935), 72–74 (p. 74): 'satisfactionem sollempnem et publicam imponatis
... pro conditione et sexu, pro etate et scientia delinquentis persone'.

[8] See below, p. 368.

[9] Bernard Hamilton, 'Wisdom from the East: the Reception by the Cathars of Eastern
Dualist Texts', in *Heresy and Literacy, 1000–1500*, ed. by Peter Biller and Anne Hudson
(Cambridge: Cambridge University Press, 1994), pp. 38–60.

[10] Émile Chénon, 'L'Hérésie à La Charité-sur-Loire et les débuts de l'inquisition
monastique dans la France du Nord au XIIIe siècle', *Nouvelle Revue Historique de Droit
Français et Étranger*, 41 (1917), 299–345; Charles Homer Haskins, 'Robert le Bougre
and the Beginnings of Inquisition in Northern Europe', in his *Studies in Medieval Culture*
(Oxford: Clarendon Press, 1929), pp. 193–244; Jean Duvernoy, *L'Histoire des cathares*
(Toulouse: Éditions Privat, 1979), pp. 107–50.

participation of Cathar perfects in the higher learning of northern schools.[11] Where the ecclesial organization of Cathars in the south is known in such detail that scholars can even draw up lists of Cathar deaneries, there is very little in the north. However, occasionally there is a detail which parallels details from the south. For example, there is a particular northern French Cathar *bishop*, who took part in a Council in Languedoc;[12] the description in a German source of a ritual performance, the administration of the Cathar *consolamentum*, with the imposition of a book;[13] and the words 'perfects'[14] and 'Good Man' and 'Good Woman'.[15] And even where there is a distinctive northern usage, calling the perfects 'consolaters' (*consolatores*),[16] its obvious derivation and meaning— providers of the *consolamentum*—reassuringly refers to the same 'sacramental' system. These examples confirm what common sense would suggest, that we should envisage northern Catharism as essentially similar to southern European Catharism in its ecclesial structure and liturgy. That is to say, it will have had an all-male hierarchy of bishops; perfects who led a 'religious' life, in houses; and followers and supporters, the *credentes*. Their liturgy, translated into Latin probably in Constantinople, may well have been only in Latin.[17] How we should envisage Catharism fitting into the very different society and culture of north-western Europe is, however, a different matter.

What of women? From the very earliest *possible* references to Cathars in the twelfth century—Soissons around 1114—we see women occasion-

---

[11] Peter Biller, 'The Northern Cathars and Higher Learning', in *The Medieval Church: Universities, Heresy and the Religious Life. Essays in Honour of Gordon Leff*, ed. by Peter Biller and Barrie Dobson, Studies in Church History, Subsidia, 11 (Woodbridge: Boydell Press, 1999), pp. 25–53.

[12] Duvernoy, *Histoire*, p. 147; on the council, see Bernard Hamilton, 'The Cathar Council of Saint-Félix Reconsidered', *Archivum Fratrum Praedicatorum*, 48 (1978), 23–53.

[13] Hamilton, 'Wisdom from the East', p. 46. The *consolamentum* was the central Cathar rite, whose reception made a believer into a member of the Cathar Church, a *perfect*; part of the rite was imposition on the recipient's head of a book containing a Gospel or the New Testament.

[14] Eckbert of Schönau, *Sermo 5 contra haereticos*, Migne, PL 195. 31.

[15] Évrard de Béthune, *Liber antihaeresis*, IV, ed. by J. Gretser and cited here from the reprint in Marguerin de La Bigne, *Bibliotheca patrum et veterum auctorum ecclesiasticorum*, 4, part 1 (Paris: Compagnie du Grand Navire, 1624), col. 1098.

[16] Chénon, 'Hérésie à La Charité-sur-Loire', 320 and n. 1, quoting a letter of Innocent III: 'quosdam haeresiarchas, quos *consolatores* appellant'.

[17] On the languages of the liturgy, see Hamilton, 'Wisdom from the East', pp. 48–49.

ally in the sources, implicated in heresy, individual, usually unnamed and with virtually no detail. At Soissons a mature woman, *matrona*, believed for a year;[18] at Cologne a young (or single) woman, *virgo*, is among those executed.[19] The one generalizing text we have, a letter written by Eversin of Steinfeld to St Bernard of Clairvaux reporting on Cathars found in the Rhineland, briefly but clearly indicates that there are women among both the perfects—Eversin calls them *electi*—and among the *credentes*.[20]

Northern European Cathars included *perfectae*, but it is not easy to say much about them. Eversin of Steinfeld makes it clear that Cathar women could be of any former marital status, widows, virgins, or wives. He described them as *feminae continentes*, chaste women; earlier he had given a part description of the ministering of the *consolamentum* to arrive at the status of a perfect. Fragmentarily, then, the northern evidence constructs the dots and dashes of a monochrome sketch which is essentially the same as the detailed and coloured southern picture. The Cathars of La Charité included *burgenses* of both sexes, so northern female Cathars came at least in part from this high urban estate.[21] A letter of Innocent III (1202) refers to some of these women of La Charité, repentant former Cathars; whether *perfectae* or *credentes* we do not know. 'Certain women of La Charité' ('Mulieres ... quasdam de Charitate') had presented themselves, appealing against their excommunication.[22] Putting to one side a complex legal situation, analyzed by Chénon, we should note these women acting in common, as they will also have acted before they repented. It is the nearest we get to a hint of the

---

[18] Guibert de Nogent, *Autobiographie*, III. xvii, ed. by Edmond-René Labande, Les classiques de l'histoire de France au Moyen Age (Paris: Belles Lettres, 1981), pp. 434–35. In English translation in *Heresies of the High Middle Ages*, ed. by Walter L. Wakefield and Austin Patterson Evans, Records of Civilisation Sources and Studies 81 (New York and London: Columbia University Press, 1969), p. 104.

[19] Caesar of Heisterbach, *Dialogus Miraculorum*, V. xix, ed. by Joseph Strange, 2 vols (Cologne, Bonn, and Brussels: J. M. Heberle (H. Lempertz & Co.), 1851), i. 299. See also *Corpus documentorum inquisitionis haereticae pravitatis Neerlandicae*, ed. by Paul Fredericq, 5 vols (Ghent and 's Gravenhage: J. Vuylsteke and Martinus Nijhoff, 1889–1902), i. 48, no. 48, where those accused in Arras in 1183 were of all estates: 'nobiles, ignobiles, clerici, milites, rustici, virgines, vidue, et uxorate'.

[20] Eversin's letter is printed in older editions of St Bernard's letters (for example, Migne, PL 182. 676–80), and is translated in Wakefield and Evans, *Heresies of the High Middle Ages*, pp. 127–32, with detailed notes on pp. 680–82.

[21] Chénon, 'Hérésie à La Charité-sur-Loire', p. 312 n. 4.

[22] Quoted by Chénon, 'Hérésie à La Charité-sur-Loire', p. 311 n. 1.

element of community we would expect to see among women linked by adherence to Cathars. It is *perhaps* a hint that Cathar *perfectae,* living communally as they did in Languedoc, had held up for women in La Charité a more formal model of the idea of community. I am assuming that the 'certain women of La Charité' were repentant *credentes*, but of course they may have been repentant *perfectae.* Before leaving this topic it is worth noting that Eversin of Steinfeld wrote of the *feminae continentes* among the Cathars as being not only among the *perfectae* but also among the *credentes.*

A famous story set in Rheims in the late 1170s was recounted by Gervase of Tilbury to the Cistercian chronicler Ralph of Coggeshall. It presents Gervase attempting to chat up a girl he wanted to get off with: my language is intended to shock the reader into further reflection. She refused, and Gervase discovered through what she said that she was a heretic.[23] The story has much to say about two women's theological knowledge. Gervase knew the girl was heretical because of the theological content of her reply. She had been instructed by an older woman who was brought before the archbishop and his clerics. The old woman was able to debate with them questions and citations of Holy Scripture, coming up with subtle interpretations of all the authorities that were put to her. While the old woman escaped by magic, the young girl persisted in her belief and was burnt to death. I am putting to one side a difficulty in the story, magic, and the question of how readers were intended to react—and how in fact they reacted—to this singularly nasty story.[24] My concern, rather, is the specific impression of learning which is given by these two women: one a beginner in theology but already thinking theologically and prepared to be a martyr, and the other a woman of many years, much theological learning, and considerable ability in interpreting authoritative texts during theological debate. The story may

---

[23] Ralph of Coggeshall, *Chronicon Anglicanum*, ed. by Joseph Stevenson, Rolls Series, 66 (London, Oxford, Cambridge, Edinburgh, and Dublin: Longman, Trübner, Parker, MacMillan, A. & C. Black, A. Thom, 1875), pp. 121–25; in English translation in Wakefield and Evans, *Heresies of the High Middle Ages*, pp. 251–53.

[24] On the background to this see John W. Baldwin, *Masters, Princes and Merchants: The Social Views of Peter the Chanter and His Circle*, 2 vols (Princeton: Princeton University Press), i. 321–22. In his *Verbum abbreviatum* Peter the Chanter said that some worthy women who rejected the lecherous advances of priests were being accused of being Cathars; PL 205. 230 and 205. 547, cited by Baldwin, *Masters, Princes and Merchants*, ii. 215 n. 53. The clear implication is blackmail—threat of denunciation unless the women gave in.

be coloured by two commonplaces about heretics, one the cleverness of
the heresiarch or heretical teacher and the simplicity of adherents whom
they deceive and teach, and the other the *mulierculae* (pejoratively
understood as 'silly little women') who are led astray by heretics.[25] I say
'coloured', in order to suggest that here *topoi* are coloured lenses through
which reality is being glimpsed, distorting the younger woman into a girl
with a relatively shallow theological grip, and using the shadow of magic
to cast suspicion on the older woman's real and deep theological
knowledge.

This story accords well with the one northern Cathar *perfecta* about
whom we know quite a lot. The locale is near Mont-Aimé in Champagne,
and in the 1230s, before the great trial of Cathars which took place at
Mont-Aimé in 1239, at the conclusion of which about 180 Cathars were
executed.[26] The source of our knowledge of the *perfecta* is a Dominican,
Stephen of Bourbon, whose manual for preachers includes many stories,
each illustrating a point about faith or morals, 'in order', wrote Stephen in
the preface, 'to make [it] more quickly understood, more easily known,
and more strongly remembered'.[27] This treatise inserts its material into
the seven gifts of the Holy Spirit, and the first topic dealt with under the
third gift, knowledge, is penitence. Penitence should be faithful, and the
penitence of those without true faith cannot please God. Illustrating this is
a story about a Cathar woman, to whose judges Stephen had talked.

For once there is a name: Aubrée or Alberte (Alberea).[28] Stephen says
nothing about her estate in the world, and we can do no more than recall
that most of our information about Catharism in northern France points to
noble and high urban milieux. Aubrée was a married woman before becoming a *perfecta*. There was family affiliation: her son Theobald became
a *perfectus*. At the time she becomes known she was a *vetula*, old woman,
but writers' frequent pejorative use of *vetula* means we cannot rely on it
much to denote old age precisely, and we do not know how long Aubrée
had been a *perfecta*.

---

[25] See my 'Heresy and Literacy: Earlier History of the Theme', in *Heresy and Literacy*,
ed. by Biller and Hudson, pp. 1–18 (p. 3).

[26] Duvernoy, *Histoire*, pp. 126–28.

[27] The story is in Stephen of Bourbon, *Tractatus de variis materiis praedicabilibus*, III.i,
ed. by Albert Lecoy de la Marche, *Anecdotes historiques, légendes et apologues tirés du
recueil inédit d'Étienne de Bourbon, Dominicain du XIIIe siècle*, Société de l'histoire de
France, Ouvrages in-octavo, 185 (Paris: Librairie Renouard, H. Loones, successeur, 1877),
p. 4: 'ut cicius ... caperetur, facilius cognosceretur, forcius in memoria retineretur'.

[28] Stephen, *Tractatus*, pp. 149–50 no 170.

Aubrée's abstinence as a *perfecta* was known. 'On account of her error she did not eat meat, nor eggs, nor cheese, and she abstained from many things on account of her sect's teaching' ('propter errorem suam non comedebat carnes, non ova, non caseum, et a multis secundum secte sue doctrinam abstinebat'). This can be compared to the promise taken by two Languedocian women, when receiving the *consolamentum* and becoming *perfectae* at Villemur some time before 1209. 'She the witness [Arnaude] and the said Peirona the witness's sister promised that henceforth they would not eat meat, eggs, cheese, or anything fatty, except oil and fish ('ipsa testis et dicta peirona soror ipsius testis promiserunt ... quod Vlterius non comederent carnes, nec oua, nec Caseum, nec aliquam uncturam, nisi de oleo et piscibus').[29] Both the similarity in the details of diet and Stephen's insistence on the diet being in accord with the sect's teaching makes it clear that a Cathar perfect's *abstinentia* was at issue here, and this detail is reassuring to anyone worried about identifying Aubrée as a Cathar *perfecta*.[30] Aubrée followed the abstinences of a Cathar *perfecta* and she was regarded by local people as a very holy woman, *sanctissima*, and for Stephen and his readers the point was the paradox, that without right faith all of this was useless, however impressive. Aubrée was burnt to death, as was also her son.

What stands out in Stephen's account of Aubrée are the theological statements she made at her trial. She had been taking communion, but only fictitiously, in order to avoid detection. Cathar rejection of the material world and material bodies as the evil creations of the ruler of this world rendered pointless any faith in or devotion towards Christ's *body*. She seems to have been questioned about the theological value of such

---

[29] Paris, Bibliothèque Nationale, MS Collection Doat 23, fol. 4ᵛ. Evocative pages are devoted to these two *perfectae* in Brenon, *Femmes cathares*, pp. 13–19. On the diet of Cathar religious and its theological underpinning in abhorrence of eating food produced by coition and—or—because Cathar belief in transmigration suggested that warm-blooded animals might contain human souls, see Jean Duvernoy, *La religion des Cathares* (Toulouse: Éditions Privat, 1976), pp. 172–74, and Bernard Hamilton, 'The Cathar Idea of Spiritual Perfection', in *The Medieval Church: Universities, Heresy and the Religious Life. Essays in Honour of Gordon Leff*, ed. by Peter Biller and Barrie Dobson, Studies in Church History, Subsidia, 11 (Woodbridge: Boydell Press, 1999), pp. 5–23 (pp. 21–22).

[30] There is no space to pursue here the theme of the similarity of Cathar perfects' diet (however distinctive its theological basis) and the diet of some Catholic religious. This is one similarity among many in the forms of life of Catholic and heretical religious, which was Herbert Grundmann's theme in his *Religiöse Bewegungen im Mittelalter* (1st edn, Berlin: Verlag Dr Emil Eberling, 1935; 2nd edn, Hildesheim: Georg Olms Verlagsbuchhandlung, 1961).

acts—consecration of bread and wine and their reception—and her answer was rendered thus by Stephen. She declared that 'these works were from the devil, and [that they were] infected and [that they were] infecting souls' ('omnia opera ista esse dyaboli et infecta et inficiencia animas'). There are several screens between us and Aubrée's answers. What she said to her judges will have been longer, and probably in several parts: a statement of the evil principle's creation of the material world, a statement about the status of created matter, and a statement about created matter's effects on the soul. These statements were remembered by her judges and reported to Stephen, and Stephen remembered them, selecting them for his representation of Aubrée. Both judges and Stephen seem to have been impressed by this aspect of Aubrée, her theological articulacy as well as her asceticism and sanctity, while at the same time what she actually said was distilled and abbreviated. Brief the report may be, but it still reflects Aubrée's grasp of fundamental Cathar theology and her ease with theological vocabulary and theological propositions.

Surveying some of these fragments about northern Cathar women, I suggest that [a] we should bear in mind the essential similarity of the ecclesial pattern of Catharism in the north and the south, [b] but that we should reflect on the great differences between the milieux in which Catharism was embedded. One contrast concerns the marriage-pattern. In parts, at least, of north-western Europe, girls married in their twenties, after working and earning, and many men and women remained un-married, living singly, while in much of southern Europe girls married in their early to mid-teens and most got married. Eversin of Steinfeld's description of Cathars having a distinct *group of chaste* women among the *credentes* as well as the *perfectae* stands in some contrast to Languedocian Catharism. Although we have little material for further speculation, it is worth reflecting on the fundamental contrasts of the two milieux, and the singularity of Northern European Catharism having chaste Cathar non-'religious' women. Another contrast is cultural. Throughout Latin Christendom women were largely excluded from literacy, more so than laymen, but there are regional nuances. This exclusion was more extreme in Languedoc, whereas a minority of northern women were not so excluded,[31] and a handful were among the most learned people of the

---

[31] Peter Biller, 'Women and Texts in Languedocian Catharism', in *Women, the Book and the Godly. Selected Proceedings of the St Hilda's Conference, 1993*, ed. by Lesley Smith and Jane H. M. Taylor (Woodbridge: D.S. Brewer, 1995), pp. 171–82 (p. 182).

twelfth century. Again, the traces of high theological culture among *northern* Cathar women should be set against this pattern.

What of England? The north-west European map of the Cathars leads us not to be surprised at their appearance in England.[32] We know for certain of one Cathar mission into England in the early 1160s, a Cathar was executed in England in 1210 and Cathars came into England in 1211. Less clear in their significance are warnings or action about heresy in the province of York in the first half of the 1190s and 1236, and in the diocese of Salisbury in the late 1230s or the 1240s. Much of the geography here is pointed, with on the one hand the origin of the 1160s mission in Germany, and on the other hand the involvement of port-towns, towns which were accustomed to the inflow of people from Germany and the Low Countries: London, where the execution of 1210 took place, and York, where there was suspicion about a heretic in 1236.

In the case of the 1160s mission, we know that the thirty or more Cathars who came in were both men and women.[33] They lived in England for some time. The first identifiable English heretical woman is described by the Yorkshire chronicler who is the most detailed source, William of Newburgh, as 'gathered' by the Cathars 'into their assembly' ('suo coetui aggregarunt'). Given that in Cathar theology the only members of the *ecclesia* were those who had received the *consolamentum*, this means that she became a *perfecta*. The woman 'they had seduced in England left them through fear of punishment'.

If she merits attention as the first known heretical Englishwoman, and a Cathar perfect at that, what of later ones? We can only speculate. One theme for speculation is women being among any later Cathar intrusions into England; the male gender of the *quidam* who entered England in 1210 or 1211 is grammatical in the first instance, and could cover for

---

[32] For the following, see Duvernoy, *Histoire des Cathares*, pp. 149–50, and Biller, 'William of Newburgh'.

[33] The mission is described by William of Newburgh, in a passage whose best edition is in *Councils & Synods with other Documents Relating to the English Church, I, A.D. 871–1204*, ed. by Dorothy Whitelock, Martin Brett and Christopher N. L. Brooke, 2 parts (Oxford: Clarendon Press, 1981), ii. 923–25 (see introduction and notes on pp. 920–21), and which is available in translation in Wakefield and Evans, *Heresies of the High Middle Ages*, pp. 245–47. The mission is studied by Hans-Eberhard Hilpert, 'Die Insel der Gläubigen? Über die verspätete Ankunft der Inquisition im *regnum Angliae*', in *Die Anfänge der Inquisition im Mittelalter*, ed. by Peter Segl, Bayreuther historische Kolloquien, 7 (Cologne, Weimar, and Vienna: Böhlau, 1993), pp. 253–68, and Biller, 'William of Newburgh'.

Cathars of both sexes.[34] Another theme for speculation is the south: the trading link with Bordeaux may have brought English women as well as men into south-western France, and thence towards Toulouse.

Let us return to the deposition of Raymond Frugon which was quoted earlier, and his description of the English woman who passed through Roquevidal. From where did this *mulier anglica* hail? And why was she seen by Raymond of Roquevidal? The man who gave evidence about her, Raymond, was about as deeply steeped in Catharism as a mere *credens* could be. A believer in Catharism since around 1249, he had abjured in front of an inquisitor (around 1258), but he had resumed his Cathar faith, and when appearing again in front of inquisitors in 1274 he was able to give a fairly systematic account of Cathar doctrines—something only rarely found in depositions by *credentes*. He mentioned many in his family—his mother, wife, brother, sister-in-law, brother's father-in-law—and without exception they were all Cathar *credentes*. In the early 1270s Catharism was a clandestine affair. Only a few perfects were still active in Languedoc—by this time most were away in Lombardy—and those who were carrying out their functions of preaching and administering the *consolamentum* were doing so only with great difficulty. Raymond's home in Roquevidal was one of their safe-houses.[35] Over the two years before Raymond's interrogation, two Cathar perfects, Guillaume Prunel and Bernard of Tilhol, had made Raymond's house their headquarters, staying in its lower part for a week or a fortnight at a time, receiving visits and gifts, and preaching. Raymond was part of the system of supply, fetching for them food, money, clothing, and other material necessities; fish and *focaccia* were on the menu, and pepper was available. And Raymond was instrumental in the perfects' secret operations, for example twice arranging for them to go to the bedsides of dying women to administer the *consolamentum*.

And then there was Lombardy. Raymond's home was a clearing-house of information about Lombardy. There is a woman from Roquevidal, says Raymond, now living in Toulouse, and her daughter Jordana was a

---

[34] Ralph of Coggeshall, *Chronicon Anglicanum*, ed. by Reinhold Pauli, in *Ex scriptoribus rerum Anglicarum saec. XII et XIII*, ed. by Felix Liebermann and Reinhold Pauli, Monumenta Germaniae Historica, Scriptores, 27 (Hannover and Leipzig: Hahn, 1885), p. 357: 'Albigenses heretici in Angliam veniunt, et quidam intercepti comburiuntur'. This does not appear in the Rolls Series edition.

[35] On Roquevidal in this period, see Élie Griffe, *Le Languedoc cathare et l'inquisition (1229–1329)* (Paris: Letouzey & Ané, 1980), pp. 136–37.

'vested' *perfecta* in Lombardy.[36] Lombardy is where the perfects are, and the references to Lombardy are almost invariably to people going to Lombardy to the perfects: preparing to go, raising money to travel, sending on money in advance, going, and having mishaps on the way. The motive is sometimes not spelled out, but when it is made explicit either someone is described as fleeing to Lombardy because they are a heresy suspect, or they are said to be going to Lombardy to become a perfect.[37]

The English woman was certainly going to Lombardy to the perfects. Accompanied by a man from Toulouse who had much to do with the perfects of Roquevidal, and going on a dangerous journey which ended in disaster, this much is clear, but her precise purpose in going is not spelled out, nor her status as *perfecta* or *credens*. The majority of pairs of women described travelling in the depositions consisted of a *perfecta*, usually named, and her female companion, also a *perfecta* but referred to as her *socia*, who is often unnamed. Given that the English woman was travelling with another woman, unnamed, she may well have been a *perfecta*. We would not expect perfects to be consulted about the journey of a *credens* to Lombardy. If Aimeri's earlier visit to the village and long consultation with two male perfects was connected with the project for him to guide the English woman and her companion to Lombardy, then the affair was of considerable importance. Such would be certainly the safe-conduct of two *perfectae*, wanted by inquisitors, from Languedoc into Lombardy. That Aimeri was *optime indutus* when accompanying the *mulier anglica*, on this occasion so well-dressed that it occasioned remark and was remembered, argues for the appropriateness of such high style for a man accompanying a woman of high status. But whether she was of high estate in the world or the high status of a *perfecta*—or both—we cannot be sure.

As we have seen, the first identifiable English heretical woman was reported by William of Newburgh. Describing her as a *muliercula*, a little or silly woman, William was mechanically applying to her a word which he borrowed from Scripture, which told him that heretics 'creep into

---

[36] MS Doat 25, f. 122ʳ⁻ᵛ: 'Item credit firmiter quod Terrena ... et stat nunc in Tholosa ... est credens et amica haereticorum. ... Item, est de genere multum infecto de haeresi, et quia habebat filiam suam Jordanam, quae <est> haeretica vestita in Lombardia'.

[37] MS Doat 25, fol. 91ᵛ: 'Raymundus textor de sancto Felice ... venit ad dictam domum petens instanter haereticos, et volens eos multum videre, quia iam congregaverat peccuniam suam cum qua volebat ire in Lombardiam ad haereticandum'; fol. 124ʳ: 'Raymundum de Siren, qui postmodum fugit in Lombardiam et se fecit haereticum'.

houses and lead captive *mulierculae*' (II Timothy 3. 6). The second identifiable English heretical woman is glimpsed in the record of Raymond's interrogation, passing through Roquevidal on her way to Lombardy, and then being captured while asleep, presumably by inquisitors or their agents, while her Cathar guide legged it to safety. The first heretical English woman to survive in the sources is at the same time veiled for ever from us by the orthodoxy and lack of sympathy which led the Yorkshire chronicler to dismiss her with a pejorative noun from Scripture. The second one momentarily appears in the light through inquisitors' questions and Raymond's memory, and then recedes into the darkness, disappearing for ever from view.[38]

They came first. Their voices are lost now, but not quite their memory, nor their proud primacy in the history of dissenting and rebellious English women.

---

[38] Various women bearing the name 'Anglesia' and 'Englesia' appear in the Languedocian sources as Cathar perfects or believers, for example, in MSS Doat 21, fol. 150[r], Doat 23, fols 92[v] and 100[r–v], and Doat 26, fol. 74[r]; Toulouse, Bibliothèque Municipale 609, fols 83[r] and 90[r]. See Anne Brenon, *Le petit livre aventureux des prénoms occitans au temps du catharisme* (Portet-sur-Garonne: Éditions Loubatières, 1992), p. 60, under 'Anglica, Englèsa', where Brenon states that 'ce prénom géographique assez courant signifiait *Anglaise*'. Worth consulting on women's names in this area and period is John Hine Mundy, *Men and Women at Toulouse in the Age of the Cathars*, Studies and Texts, 101 (Toronto: Pontifical Institute of Mediaeval Studies, 1990), pp. 39–40 and n. 104. Mundy points out that some exotic place-names (for example, Babilonia, India) were given to women, not to signify origin but simply for colour. This could explain one *perfecta* who was called *Irlanda* (MS Doat 26, fol. 60[r]). However, the form of the English cases—*Anglesia* rather than *Anglia*—poses a difficulty. In the other cases what is applied to a woman is the name of the country itself, not the name of being a woman of that country: 'India', not 'Indian woman'. See note 4 above for two men called *Anglicus*. I am grateful to Professor John Mundy for responding to my queries on this matter, and to Dr Caterina Bruschi for checking and extending my list of references to *Anglesia*, and also for the suggestion that this enquiry might be irrelevant as far as England is concerned: *Anglesia* could be based on Angles, a place near Alassazeiras. If it could be demonstrated, however, that *Anglesia* meant *Englishwoman*, the bearing of this name by some Languedocian Cathar women would be worth further thought.

'A peler of Holy Cherch':
Margery Kempe and the Bishops

SARAH REES JONES

> Derworthy dowtyr, lofe thow me wyth al thin hert, for I love the wyth al
> myn hert and wyth al the mygth of my Godhed, for thow wer a chosen
> sowle wythowt begynnyng in my syghte and a peler of Holy Cherch. My
> mercyful eyne arn evyr upon the. It wer unpossibyl to the [for you] to
> suffyr the scornys and despytes that thow schalt have ne were only my
> grace supportyng the.[1]

So Christ comforts Margery after the first occasion in the book when she
is accused of being a Lollard. The image of Margery as a 'pillar of Holy
Church' is not a universally accepted one. While many readers have emphasized Margery's essential orthodoxy, for others it is her challenge to
male ecclesiastical and secular authority which is the essential characteristic of her *Book*.[2] Intriguingly, Margery's relationship with ecclesiastical authority remains ambiguous. For Lynn Staley, Kempe 'negotiates a

---

[1]   *The Book of Margery Kempe*, ed. by Lynn Staley, TEAMS Middle English Texts
Series, (Kalamazoo: Medieval Institute Publications, Western Michigan University, 1996),
ll. 669–73.

[2]   Anthony Goodman, 'The Piety of John Brunham's Daughter of Lynn', in *Medieval
Women: Essays Dedicated and Presented to Professor Rosalind M. T. Hill,* ed. by Derek
Baker (Oxford: Blackwell, 1978), pp. 347–58; Clarissa Atkinson, *Mystic and Pilgrim: The
Book and the World of Margery Kempe,* (Ithaca: Cornell University Press, 1983); David
Aers, *Community, Gender and Individual Identity: English Writing 1360–1430* (London:
Routledge, 1988), pp. 108–16; Anne Hudson, *The Premature Reformation: Wycliffite
Texts and Lollard History* (Oxford: Clarendon Press, 1988), pp. 435–36; Sarah Beckwith,
'Problems of Authority in Late Medieval English Mysticism: Language, Agency and
Authority in the *Book* of Margery Kempe', *Exemplaria*, 4 (1992), 171–99.

space somewhere between institutional faith and outright heresy.'[3] To date discussion of this ambiguity has focussed on the degree to which Margery's desire for an active life of devotion could be accommodated within the church. But what does the *Book* say about the role of the clergy in the church? This paper focusses on the narrative function of the male authority figures, the bishops, in order to raise new questions about the purpose and audience of the book.

Although *The Book of Margery Kempe* is still often popularly referred to as an 'autobiography', academic commentators have long distanced themselves from such a literal reading of the life it describes.[4] Instead, as a 'spiritual' life, the story of Margery Kempe was influenced by traditions of hagiography and mystical writing.[5] This in turn raises the complex question of authorship. Who were the male scribes whom the narrator in the text claims were charged with the writing of successive versions of the book, and what role did either they or Kempe play in the composition of the text?[6] The fictional nature of the book has been most forcefully argued by Staley. She concludes that we must distinguish between Kempe, the skilled author of the book, and Margery, the fictional character constructed by Kempe to explore a world tormented by 'the disparity between social myths and social realities'.[7] Yet Staley still

---

[3]   Lynn Staley, *Margery Kempe's Dissenting Fictions* (University Park: Pennsylvania State University Press, 1994), p.10.

[4]   B. A. Windeatt, *The Book of Margery Kempe,* (London and Harmondsworth: Penguin, 1985), pp. 9, 22–27.

[5]   Hope Emily Allen, 'Prefatory Note', in *The Book of Margery Kempe*, ed. by S. B. Meech, EETS, os 212, (1940), pp. liii–lxii; H. P. Weissman, 'Margery Kempe in Jerusalem: *Hysterica Compassio* in the Late Middle Ages, in *Acts of Interpretation: The Text in its Contexts 700–1600*, ed. by Mary J. Carruthers & Elizabeth D. Kirk (Norman, OK: Pilgrim Books, 1982), pp. 204–15; Thomas J. Heffernan, *Sacred Biography, Saints and their Biographers in the Middle Ages* (New York: Oxford University Press, 1988), 184–89; Janette Dillon, 'Holy Women and their Confessors or Confessors and their Holy Women? Margery Kempe and the Continental Tradition', in *Prophets Abroad, the Reception of Continental Holy Women in Late-Medieval England*, ed. by Rosalynn Voaden (Woodbridge: D. S. Brewer, 1998), 116–17 & nn. 3, 5.

[6]   John C. Hirsch, 'Author and Scribe in the Book of Margery Kempe', *Medium Aevum*, 44 (1975), 145–50; Beckwith, 'Problems of Authority' *passim*; R. C. Ross, 'Oral Life, Written Text: The Genesis of the Book of Margery Kempe', *YES*, 22 (1992): 226–37; K. Lochrie, *Margery Kempe and Translations of the Flesh*, (Philadelphia: University of Pennsylvania Press, 1991), pp. 97–134; Dillon, 'Holy Women', 137–38 & n. 72.

[7]   Staley, 'Introduction', in Staley, *The Book of Margery Kempe*, p. 8.

asserts that Kempe is an essentially female voice. Her femaleness imparts an innate radicalism to her analysis of contemporary authority.[8] Yet, if we are sceptical of Margery, the central character of the book, should we not also be sceptical of Kempe the author?

Famously, there is no evidence outside the text that Margery Kempe, either author or subject, ever existed.[9] Biographical details of some of her family have been supplied by modern readers,[10] and we can further reinforce her credibility by locating her in the flourishing world of the later-medieval bourgeois woman.[11] All too easily she seems to allow us to escape the impersonal generalizations of social history, through the rediscovery of individual experience.[12] But we should not allow this historical verisimilitude to sanction a belief in Kempe any more than it can sanction the events described in the book.

The idea that *The Book of Margery Kempe* is a work of fiction designed to either entertain or instruct its audience can still shock and alarm. Even Staley's comparatively modest assertion, that Margery is a fictive creation of the author Kempe, has provoked a vigorous re-assertion of the essential reality of Margery.[13] Yet it remains a curious and striking paradox that scholars who wish to embrace the veracity of either Margery or Kempe continue to reduce the demonstrably historical figures in the book to secondary authorial devices. On several occasions, Margery is confronted by, or seeks the approval of, senior clergy: Philip Repingdon (bishop of Lincoln, 1404–1419), Thomas Arundel (archbishop

---

[8] *Ibid.,* p. 9; Staley, *Dissenting Fictions,* pp. 83–126.

[9] A Margery Kempe joined the fraternity of the Trinity in Lynn in 1438, but nothing, other than assumption, links this character to the eponymous subject of the book. Atkinson, *Mystic and Pilgrim,* pp. 18, 76; Staley, *Dissenting Fictions*, pp. 50, 60, n., 75.

[10] Windeatt, *Book of Margery Kempe,* pp. 10–15; Goodman, 'The Piety of John Brunham's Daughter', pp. 351–52.

[11] Sheila Delany, 'Sexual Economics, Chaucer's Wife of Bath and the *Book of Margery Kempe*', *Minnesota Review,* N. S. 5 (1975), 104–13; Atkinson, *Mystic and Pilgrim,* pp. 67–101.

[12] By contrast the text itself seems designed to obscure Kempe's historical identity, (ll. 130–31, 198–99). For the revival of the historical vignette see Caroline M. Barron, 'Introduction: The Widow's World', in *Medieval London Widows 1300–1500,* ed. by Caroline M. Barron & Anne F. Sutton (London: Hambledon Press, 1994), p. xv.

[13] M. J. Wright, 'What They Said to Margery Kempe: Narrative Reliability in her Book', *Neophilologus,* 79 (1995), 497–508; Janet Wilson, 'Communities of Dissent: The Secular and Ecclesiastical Communities of Margery Kempe's Book', in *Medieval Women in their Communities,* ed. by Dianne Watt (Cardiff: University of Wales Press, 1997), pp. 156, 176–77.

of Canterbury, 1396–97, 1399–1414), Thomas Peverel (bishop of Worcester, 1407–19), Henry Bowet (archbishop of York, 1407–23), and Henry Chichele (archbishop of Canterbury, 1414–43). How do these historical characters, including such notable champions of the new orthodoxy of Lancastrian England, serve the purpose of the book? Episcopal approval of Margery has been interpreted, by some, as a means of emphasizing the orthodoxy of a potentially unorthodox figure, by others as the ultimate symbol of the male authority against which she must struggle to perfect her own sense of her vocation.[14] Both these interpretations concur in maintaining the experience of Margery as the central truth of the work, and both confer on the bishops nothing more than an auxiliary role in the quest for Margery Kempe's individuality.

What would happen if we sought to retrieve the bishops from the literary sidelines and reconsidered the purpose of these historical characters in the text? The very title, *The Book of Margery Kempe*, directs our attention to the singular character of Margery, but this is, of course, a modern invention and the only medieval manuscript of the text is much more circumspect. On the first page is the rubric 'Liber Montis Gracie. This boke is of Mountgrace', but otherwise there is simply the opening sentence:

> Here begynnyth a schort tretys and a comfortabyl for synful wrecchys, wherin thei may have gret solas and comfort to hem and undyrstondyn the hy and unspecabyl mercy of ower sovereyn Savyowr Cryst Jhesu, whos name be worscheped and magnyfyed wythowten ende, that now in ower days to us unworthy deyneth to exercysen hys nobeley and hys good-nesse.(ll. 1–5)

As part of the intended audience of sinful wretches the reader is then treated to the exemplary, if deeply troubled, life of another sinful creature seeking the way of Christ. Surely the subject of the book is not just Margery, but the Church, that is the many communities of lay and clerical sinners through which Christ (in this case accompanied by Margery) seeks to reveal his love. If the Church is placed at the centre, rather than the periphery of the book, then the position of the historical leaders of the Church becomes a much more meaningful one.

---

[14] Goodman, 'The Piety of John of Brunham's Daughter', pp. 348–49, 354–56; Atkinson, *Mystic and Pilgrim*, pp. 119–20; Aers, *Community, Gender and Individual Identity*, pp. 108–16; Hudson, *Premature Reformation*, p. 435; M. Glasscoe, *English Medieval Mystics: Games of Faith*, (Harlow: Longmans, 1993), p. 274; Staley, *Dissenting Fictions*, pp. 5–8, 108, 120–1.

Placing the Church, and in particular the clergy, at the centre of *The Book of Margery Kempe* is not just a wilful act of imagination, especially since the book itself can be located within a well-established tradition of clerical criticism. Many scholars have built on the initial work of Hope Emily Allen in exploring how the *Book* is modelled upon the continental tradition of lives of holy women.[15] These lives, including one of the earliest, Jacques de Vitry's life of Marie d'Oignies, were typically composed by a male confessor and intended as works of instruction for the clergy in their missionary work among the urban laity.[16] Their purpose was partly to chastise the clergy and to inspire them in their pastoral work through the example of particular devotion among the laity, and especially among women.[17] As Janette Dillon has shown, Margery Kempe was not alone among holy women in being portrayed as being able to detect the sins of the clergy, especially the sin of unchastity.[18] According to Dillon Margery's life only exceeds the conventions of confessors' lives of holy women in one significant respect, namely her willingness to disobey her confessor: '*The Book of Margery Kempe* embraces disobedience more frequently and openly than any other female revelations' (p. 134). Instead the *Book* emphasizes Margery's obedience to Christ, whose authority is demonstrated to be superior to, and more direct than, that of her confessor.[19] Here then we have a tradition of writing by men and for men, but using the example of women as a correctional impetus.

Dillon's conclusions are important for they show both how *The Book of Margery Kempe* can be located within a tradition of clerical chastisement embodied in confessors' lives of holy women, but also how

---

[15]   Allen, 'Prefatory Note', pp. liii–lvii; Dillon, 'Holy Women', pp. 116–17 & nn. 3, 5.

[16]   Heffernan, *Sacred Biography,* pp. 255–58; Staley, *Dissenting Fictions,* pp. 33, 44–47; Giles Constable, *Three Studies in Medieval Religious and Social Thought: The Interpretation of Mary and Martha; The Ideal of the Imitation of Christ; The Orders of Society* (Cambridge: Cambridge University Press, 1995).

[17]   Ernest W. McDonnell, *The Beguines and the Beghards in Medieval Culture* (New York: Octagon Books, 1969), pp. 25, 30–36; Brenda M. Bolton, '*Mulieres Sanctae*', in *Sanctity and Secularity: the Church and the World,* ed. by Derek Baker, Studies in Church History, 10 (1973), pp. 83–84; B. Z. Kedar, *Crusade and Mission: European Approaches Toward the Muslims* (Princeton: Princeton University Press, 1984), p. 117; Brenda M. Bolton, 'Daughters of Rome: All One in Christ Jesus', in *Women in the Church,* ed. by William J. Sheils & Diana Wood, Studies in Church History, 27 (1990), pp. 102–03.

[18]   Dillon, 'Holy Women', pp.129–32.

[19]   *Ibid.* , p.140.

The Book developed that tradition into a critique of confession itself. This is significant within the historical context of clerical reform proposed by Archbishop Arundel and others in the years around 1400. For the increased emphasis on direct personal experience of Christ, and the promotion of the Eucharist, which is so evident in *The Book*, reflects a similar change of emphasis in manuals, such as the *Speculum Christiani*, written for the instruction of the clergy by associates of Arundel in Cambridge and the northern province.[20] According to Jonathan Hughes this shift in emphasis was only partly a reaction to Lollard attacks on the sacraments, for it also embodied an increasing emphasis on the 'sacrosanctity of the inner spiritual life' as the programme of evangelization succeeded in advancing lay literacy and religious understanding.[21] Indeed Jeremy Catto has argued that ecclesiastical approval of independent lay spirituality was a particular feature of the English Church under Henry V, in which personal devotion was linked to public worship through the development of liturgy and the patronage of new religious orders such as the Carthusians and the Brigittines in Sheen, Syon, and at Mount Grace.[22] The lay person's direct relationship with Christ, far from being a denial of priestly authority, could be used to strengthen clerical authority if focussed on the symbolic union of the Eucharist.

Not only therefore can we locate *The Book of Margery Kempe* within the general tradition of clerical chastisement through the medium of lives of holy women, but we can further identify its reformation of that tradition within the particular context of clerical reform embraced by Arundel's associates and successors, including members of the Carthusian house at Mount Grace. Although there is no evidence to show that *The Book* was composed at Mount Grace, such a provenance for its earliest known copy might provoke the question, do we have here a book written by clergy, for the instruction of clergy, at a particular moment in the reform of the church?

---

[20] Jonathan Hughes, 'The Administration of Confession in the Diocese of York in the Fourteenth Century', in *Studies in Clergy and Ministry in Medieval England*, ed. by David M. Smith, Borthwick Studies in History 1 (York: University of York, 1991), pp. 160–62. Cf. Staley, *Dissenting Fictions*, p. 146.

[21] Hughes, 'Administration of Confession', pp. 157–59; cf. Miri Rubin, *Corpus Christi. The Eucharist in Late Medieval Culture* (Cambridge: Cambridge University Press, 1991), pp. 330–31; Robert N. Swanson, *Church and Society in Late Medieval England*, (Oxford: Blackwell, 1989), p. 276.

[22] J. Catto, 'Religious Change under Henry V', in *Henry V: the Practice of Kingship*, ed. by G. L. Harriss (Oxford, Oxford University Press, 1985), pp. 109–11.

The holy life of Margery Kempe, and her criticism of many of the clergy she meets, fits well therefore within the intertwined ecclesiastical traditions of clerical reform and instruction on the one hand, and lay evangelization on the other. Her dependence (and implicitly that of the Church) on a Eucharistic union with Christ, rather than the advice of her confessor, is one timely feature of the book. But another equally important contemporary theme is the role of the bishops in smoothing Margery's path to sanctity in the book, just as Arundel, Chichele, and their associates guided the reform of the clergy in the Church.

EPISCOPAL AUTHORITY IN THE STRUCTURING OF THE TEXT

If the text is viewed as a work of hagiography, then the ordering of the muddled chronology of the narrative takes on new meaning.[23] The purpose of hagiography was not just to idealize the individual saint, but provide testimony of the continuing life of Christ in the Church. How is Christ's love for the clergy revealed in the ordering of *The Book*?

At critical moments in the narrative it is episcopal authority which licenses Margery's quest for spiritual authority, and episcopal intervention divides the text into five parts.

1. Margery's conversion (Book 1, chapters 1–16)

The story of Margery's conversion revolves around her confrontation and rejection of first worldly and then spiritual pride (Book 1, chapters 1–5). Only then is Margery rewarded with her first vision of the life of Christ, of his nativity, and she begins to develop a wider reputation, travelling with her husband on pilgrimage to York, Bridlington, and Canterbury. She is portrayed as afraid of preaching to nobody, but when she starts lecturing the monks of Canterbury she is accused of being a Lollard and threatened with execution (Book 1, chapter 13). Faced with the prospect of martyrdom Margery is reassured by Christ, who tells her to adopt the dress of a holy woman. At this critical juncture in the text Margery turns,

---

[23] Hirsch, 'Author and Scribe', pp. 148–49; Glasscoe, *English Medieval Mystics*, pp. 287–311. The following account of the structure of the text was developed independently from that of Glasscoe, although both share some common points in the organization of chapters into sections.

as was proper, to episcopal authority.[24] She visits Philip Repingdon, the bishop of Lincoln, and seeks confirmation from him of her vow of chastity, symbolized by the adoption of white clothing and a ring, but, although sympathetic, he sends her instead to his superior, Thomas Arundel Archbishop of Canterbury in Lambeth Palace, and also suggests that she should seek full confirmation of her vows only after completing a pilgrimage to Jerusalem.[25] In both encounters the bishops use the example of Margery to correct and chastise the clerical members of their households, for their failure to accept her witness and for their tendency to blasphemy (ll. 792–95, 841–44). Acceptance by first bishop and then archbishop thus completes the story of Margery's conversion. But the acceptance is still provisional and can only be fulfilled through visiting the sites of the source of all episcopal authority: Jerusalem and Rome.

2. The justification of Margery's faith and witness (Book 1, chapters 17–25)

So far the book has built up a picture of Margery developing from extremely unpromising origins into a woman on the verge of acceptance as a licensed vowess. The narrative is then broken by a series of 'flashbacks' to her earlier life, in which the reader is given a number of contexts for the particular nature of her piety. It is in this section of the work that she is located within recent traditions of mysticism, and she is shown to have been inspired by the examples of other holy women from Mary Magdalen, to more contemporary figures such as Bridget of Sweden, or Julian of Norwich. This section is particularly concerned to justify Margery's gift of tears, which the text frequently emphasizes are unacceptable to so many of her critics, clerical and lay. The mystics, the Church fathers, St Paul and Christ himself are all cited as authorities (ll. 899, 961–82, 1061–64, 1164–67). Thus her piety is established as orthodox, albeit by locating it within a very recent, even avant-garde, tradition which many found hard to accept.

---

[24] Virginia Davis, 'The Rule of St Paul, the First Hermit, in Late Medieval England', in *Monks, Hermits, and the Ascetic Tradition*, ed. by William J. Sheils, Studies in Church History 22 (Oxford: Blackwell, 1985), pp. 203–14; Mary C. Erler, 'Three Fifteenth-Century Vowesses', in Barron & Sutton, *Medieval London Widows*, pp. 165–67.

[25] Just as the identity of Margery is obscured by the scribe, so the bishops are referred to by their titles rather than their names, so emphasizing their official status.

It is here too that Margery's powers of prophecy, and her ability to reveal sin, are fully developed and justified. The section culminates with the priestly scribe explaining the grounds of his own final conviction, following Margery's revelation of a false cleric and a false book-seller (chapter 24), and ends with the use of her prophetic power to affirm episcopal authority. In the dispute over a petition for the full parochial status of a chapel, the bishop of Norwich offered a compromise 'with certeyn condycyons' to the petitioners. The petitioners were, however, thwarted, as Margery prophesied, because 'thei obeyd not ne lyked not the menys whech wer proferyed hem' (ll. 1371, 1376). The case was lost, and the 'parysch cherch stod stylle in her worshep and hyr degre', because of the upstarts' disobedience to the bishop, as revealed by Margery's 'sothfast and sekyr' (ll. 1379–81).

By establishing a range of authorities for Margery's spirituality the book has confirmed the legitimacy of the bishops' provisional acceptance of her in chapters 15 and 16. More importantly this section demonstrates that the episcopacy can accommodate, indeed even promote, new forms of devotion which challenge the credulity of their lesser clergy, but in fact are justified by the founding fathers of the Church and the grace of Christ himself.

3. The consecration and fulfilment of Margery's vocation (Book 1, chapters 26–44)

In chapter 26 the narrative resumes with Margery's pilgrimage to Jerusalem, in obedience to the bishop of Lincoln. As the narrative leaves England, her form of devotion is almost immediately affirmed by a papal legate (chapter 27), and her vocation is confirmed in intensely dramatic visions of the Passion in Jerusalem (chapter 28). While kneeling at the tomb of the Virgin Mary she is again reassured by Christ that her devotions lie within the authority of his 'Holy Cherch' (ll. 1679–88). However it is only after returning to Rome (the fount of all episcopal authority) that she finally adopts the white clothing while staying in the hospital of St Thomas of Canterbury (chapter 31),[26] and achieves a

---

[26] For the importance of Rome in the church life of Lancastrian England see, John A. F. Thomson, '"The Well of Grace", Englishmen and Rome in the Fifteenth Century', in *The Church, Politics and Patronage in the Fifteenth Century*, ed. by R. Barrie Dobson (Stroud: Sutton, 1984), pp. 99–114.

symbolic union with Christ in the church of the Apostles and in the presence of the Trinity, who also confirm the orthodoxy of the gift of the fire of Christ's love (chapter 35). Returning to Lynn, she publicly demonstrates her newly confirmed vocation by receiving communion, dressed in white, on Trinity Sunday. The theme of controversy and conflict with both laity and lesser clergy continues throughout. Nevertheless the major narrative demonstrates that Margery's provisional acceptance by the English episcopacy has been fulfilled in the apostolic see in Rome, and celebrated on that feast of orthodoxy, Trinity Sunday, at home.

4. Margery's trials and the proving of her true faith (Book 1, chapters 45–55)

Margery's public status within the English national church has still not been established. Her major trials then begin. 'Bishop's men', too fashionably dressed, summon her to meet Thomas Peverel, the bishop of Worcester. He, however, contradicts his men by flatly denying the need for concern (chapter 45). Following a pilgrimage to Santiago (which is barely described), Margery is arrested by the mayor of Leicester and tried before the abbot and dean of Leicester (chapters 46–48). They are also convinced, but her local immunity is ensured only by a second visit to the bishop of Lincoln (chapter 49).[27] On a visit to York she is tried again by the archbishop, Henry Bowet, first in Cawood, and secondly, after her re-arrest by servants of the Duke of Bedford, in Beverley (chapters 50–54). Although she has convinced a range of senior clergy on no fewer than four occasions, Margery returns to London. Only when she has received a letter of confirmation from the head of the whole English Church, Archbishop Chichele of Canterbury, is she able to return home to Lynn.[28]

The account of Margery's travels and trials embrace the length and breadth of England, from London to York, and from Lynn (and Norwich) to Bristol, emphasizing not only her national appeal, but the national presence of the authorizing force of the higher clergy.[29]

---

[27] The diocese of Lincoln was the largest and most populous in England, extending from the Humber to the Thames (Swanson, *Church and Society*, pp. 1–3).

[28] The text emphasizes the superiority of Canterbury to York (ll. 3218–21).

[29] Cf. Staley, *Dissenting Fictions*, p. 129. However, towns did not just represent mercantile wealth, but as centres of royal government were also symbols of the extent of

5. Margery's life of teaching. Passing on the word to others. (Book 1, chapters 56–89; Book 2)

Her conversion and public status fully established, at least within the text, the narrative moves on to describe her settled life of witness to Christ's Passion within her parish. The mystical qualities of her piety are reiterated (chapters 58, 62), and the parochial framework of her life is emphasized (chapters 57, 61, 63, 67–71, 73-76, 78, 81–82). A continuing veneration for the saints, and especially the Trinity is emphasized (chapters 64–66, 86, 89). An epilogue in Book 2 tells of one last journey to the Continent which culminates with pilgrimages to Wilsnak and Aachen (centres of the cult of the Holy Blood and the Virgin Mary), and then to Syon Abbey outside London before a final return home to Lynn. These final scenes in the centres of the new orthodoxy of the Lancastrian Church provide a fitting finale not just for Margery,[30] but for the sanctification of the Lancastrian episcopacy's ecclesiastical project.[31]

There is thus a clear spiritual structure to the text of learning, instruction, confirmation and consecration, trial and resolution in the Church. Throughout this spiritual journey it is the episcopacy who authorize Margery's vision and license her for the next stage in her vocational career. Their authority is further symbolized in the imagery of the Holy Trinity, the central role of the Eucharist, and in the choice of locations (Canterbury, London, York, Rome, Syon) of some of the decisive moments in Margery's transformation. But is their function simply to establish Margery's orthodoxy, or is there a wider message for the church here?

EPISCOPAL AUTHORITY AND CRITICISM OF THE CLERGY

Margery's relations with the bishops she meets are positive and characterized by the achievement of concord. Both Repingdon and Bowet are portrayed as needing to be convinced, but they are convinced, and the

---

both nation and state (see, e.g., Lorraine Attreed, 'The Politics of Welcome: Ceremonies and Constitutional Development in Later Medieval English Towns', in *City and Spectacle in Medieval Europe*, ed. by Barbara A. Hanawalt & Kathryn L. Reyerson (Minneapolis: University of Minnesota Press, 1994), pp. 224–25).

[30] Rubin, *Corpus Christi*, pp. 314–15; Staley, *Dissenting Fictions,* pp. 168–69.

[31] Catto, 'Religious Change', pp. 109–11.

orthodox, even somewhat clerical, nature of the defences used to
convince them have often been commented upon.[32] Nowhere are the
bishops' morals criticized as are those of their junior colleagues in the
Church. By contrast, many of the lesser clergy Margery encounters are
alienated by her behaviour and, in turn, these clergy are the subject of
considerable criticism. Indeed the very wide range of different kinds of
clergy who are paraded in turn before the reader suggests a kind of social
satire. A monk is accused of lechery (chapter 12), the clerical advisors of
the bishops are accused of blasphemy, vanity, pride, and anger (chapters
16, 45, 52), a friar is implicated with gluttony (Book 2, chapter 7), while
others are accused of slander and disobedience, and one young man is
shown to have lost his priestly position through committing assault and
murder (chapter 24). The accusations are reminiscent of conventional
ecclesiastical criticism of clerical standards, arising out of the bishops'
normal jurisdiction over their clergy. For these 'sins' are precisely the
kinds of offences which would come before the episcopacy in the
diocesan courts, as they exercised their fundamental responsibility for the
pastoral care of the clergy.[33]

Margery's accusations were thus part of an established clerical critique
of the clergy, but the *Book* develops this critique further by linking
Margery's ability to reveal clerical sin, to her ability to enhance the
ecclesiastical careers of those priests who are convinced by her. For
example, early in her travels Margery dines in a monastery and converts
one of the monks, who had at first despised her. He asks her 'I pray the
telle me whethyr I schal be savyd or nowt and in what synnes I have most
dysplesyd God, for I wyl not levyn the but thow con telle me my synne'
(ll. 591–93). At mass Margery seeks Christ's advice and he tells her 'sey
in the name of Jhesu that he hath synned in letthery, in dyspeyr, and in
worldly goodys kepying'(ll. 597–98). The monk accepts this counsel and
is rewarded with virtue and high office: 'Another tyme when the creatur
cam agayn to the same place, the fornseyd monke had forsakyn hys offyce
at hir cownsel, and was turnyd fro hys synne, and was mad suppriowr of
the place, a wel governyd man and wel dysposyd, thankyd be God, and
made this creatur gret cher and hyly blyssed God that evyr he saw hir'(ll.
615–19). Later in the book a young priest is rewarded with a benefice
after he has accepted Margery's instruction (chapter 58).

---

[32] Aers, *Community*, pp. 113–14; Lochrie, *Translations of the Flesh*, esp. pp 107–13;
Glasscoe, *English Medieval Mystics*, p. 301; Staley, *Dissenting Fictions*, pp. 6–7, 119–21.

[33] Swanson, *Church and Society*, pp.163–66.

In this manner the author is able to chastise a full range of clergy from the humble clerk to the high-handed intellectual advisors of the archiepiscopal courts. The clergy are castigated for conventional moral weaknesses, but more serious is the criticism of the weakness of their pastoral care for the laity. Margery is represented as a challenging subject, whose beliefs and behaviour defy conservative clerical ideas of 'correct' devotion. She is constantly depicted as a rather unlikely candidate for the role of a holy woman. The text does not hesitate to portray her weaknesses and crudities, even as it portrays her transcendence of them. While conflict between Margery and the lesser clergy is surely one of the key themes of the text, 'resolution' of this conflict is provided by the bishops' acceptance of Margery through which they 'correct' and 'instruct' their clergy. Thus the text asserts the authority of the episcopacy over their clergy, warning the clergy of the potential dangers to which they are exposing the church through their moral laxity and inability to adapt to the needs of a demanding laity.

> 'Thu brekyst the comawndmentys of God ... thu devowryst and destroist the flowerys and blomys of vertuows levyng to thyn endles dampnacyon and many mannys hyndryng lesse than thu have grace of repentawns and amendyng.' Than the Erchebisshop likyd wel the tale and comendyd it, seying it was a good tale (ll. 3004–09.)

EPISCOPAL AUTHORITY AND SECULAR AUTHORITY

One last threat to the authority of the episcopacy is represented in the form of the authority of the state. In Lancastrian England archiepiscopal and royal authority were intertwined, and that relationship was a cause of conflict as well as a source of strength for the higher clergy.[34] Since 1401 the state had taken a formal and active involvement in the defence of the faith, and in 1414 instructions had been sent to bailiffs, mayors, and sheriffs to seek out heretics.[35] In the *Book* a hierarchy of such secular officials is presented to the reader (from the town officials of Leicester to the king's own brother and vice-regent, the Duke of Bedford). Like the

---

[34] Margaret Aston, '"Caim's Castles": Poverty, Politics and Disendowment', in Dobson, *Church, Politics and Patronage,* pp. 45–81; R. L. Storey, 'Episcopal King-Makers in the Fifteenth Century', *ibid.,* pp. 82–98; Catto, 'Religious Change', p. 97.

[35] Swanson, *Church and Society,* pp. 338–47.

lesser clergy, each in turn fails the test presented by the character of
Margery. Once again it is the senior clergy in Leicester, the bishop of
Lincoln, and the Archbishop of York who resolve the conflicts and
thereby assert their own higher spiritual authority. This new challenge to
episcopal authority, from secular officials, (as for the first time matters of
faith became allied with matters of political allegiance), was thus resisted.
The innate mystery of the spiritual life of the Church was reasserted.

                              CONCLUSION

Read in this way, the *Book* is in an affirmation of the authority of the
episcopacy over the national Church in England, in a world of new challenges to that authority from secular officials, from the laity and, above
all, from the weaknesses, divisions, and conservatism of their lesser
clergy. The manner in which the bishops are deployed in the *Book of
Margery Kempe* permits the author both to portray the episcopacy as
triumphing over potential heretics, through their frequent assertion of
Margery's orthodoxy, and to assert episcopal willingness to accept and
acclaim new forms of devotion. It is therefore fitting that the finale of the
book is set in the Carthusian house at Sheen (or perhaps with the
Brigittines at Syon),[36] those Lancastrian centres of strict observance
which embraced both the vernacular, and the active devotions of the laity.
It is equally fitting that the only known copy of the *Book* was kept at the
Carthusian House of Mount Grace.
    Located within a tradition of clerical chastisement the *Book* is not
about Margery, but about the Church, about relationships between clergy
and laity, and in particular about the authority of the archbishops and
bishops in the ancient, but newly reformed, Church of England. Many of
the new works associated with that reforming vigour were not intended
for circulation beyond the clergy. Jonathan Hughes has argued that
vernacular texts such as the *Speculum Christiani* were intended for, and
circulated among the clergy.[37] Rosemary Lees has even more forcefully
argued that other texts which were associated with Syon and the
Carthusians, were deliberately restricted in their circulation and probably

---

[36] Although the text says Sheen (l. 611) the author would seem to mean Syon (Staley, *The
Book of Margery Kempe*, p. 228 n.).

[37] Hughes, 'Administration of Confession', pp. 103–04.

intended primarily for the members of those orders.[38] Adapting an established genre of holy lives, and drawing on other materials associated with the new learning,[39] the compilers of *The Book of Margery Kempe* used it to illustrate a series of threats to the authority of the clergy that needed to be recognized and accommodated in their pastoral work. It was, perhaps, a book written by clergy, for clergy, and about clergy.[40] But only one copy of the Book survives. Was this an experiment which backfired? Did the story of Margery, however retold, still seem too seditious? Was it only ever intended for a very limited circulation? Did it quickly seem irrelevant as conditions in the Church changed?

If the *Book* really was written by men, for men, and about men, where does that leave the female voice of Margery? Liberated, would be one answer to that question. At least liberated from the constraints imposed on femaleness in the past. The parochial, domestic nature of Margery's religion, the feminine appropriateness of her hysteria, and her empowerment through embracing chastity could all be shown not to be what a woman wanted, but what men wanted women to be. Do we really want another virgin martyr? Are these 'feminine' values only to be associated with women and never with men?

Modern readers often *want* Margery to be 'real' and for the book to be her voice. We now believe more in Margery than we do in the clergy or the Church. In the early fifteenth century it is possible that the authors of this book believed in both. Margery, or at least people like Margery, were an important part of the Church, but ultimately it was that Church and the authority of its consecrated leaders in Christ, which was the real truth and the real concern of *The Book*.

---

[38] Rosemary A. Lees, *The Negative Language of the Dionysian School of Mystical Theology: An Approach to the Cloud of Unknowing,* Analecta Cartusiana 107 (Salzburg: Institut für Anglistik und Amerikanistik, 1983), vol. 2, pp. 422–79. I am grateful to Carol Meale for this reference.

[39] Gail McMurray Gibson, *The Theater of Devotion: East Anglian Drama and Society in the Late Middle Ages* (Chicago: University of Chicago Press, 1989), pp. 49–53, 97–98; Lochrie, *Translations of the Flesh*, pp. 76–88.

[40] For a recent argument that the British readers of Hildegard of Bingen were primarily male and clerical see Kathryn Kerby-Fulton, 'Hildegard and the Male Reader: a Study in Insular Reception', in Voaden, *Prophets Abroad*, pp. 1–18.

Outdoing the Daughters of Syon?: Edith of Wilton and the Representation of Female Community in Fifteenth-Century England

JOCELYN WOGAN-BROWNE

The very notion of a holy female enclave can imply a group enclosed from time, history, generation, and transmission. Yet what is abjected at one level is often returned at another, and a female community may powerfully represent both for itself and for the outside world a symbolic treasury of virtue by which the purity and continuity of a lineage, proprietorship, or regime are underwritten. This is notably the case in the late medieval proliferation of rewritings of early British princess and abbess saints, whether in 'nationalizing' legendaries or the representation of particular saints and their monastic or other client communities.[1] Indebted, like much else in this field, to Felicity Riddy's refocussing of attention on the social and textual communities of late medieval women, the present essay examines the early fifteenth-century English Life of Edith of Wilton to argue for politicized and unhomogenizing readings of female communities and their texts, whether in their internal or external relations.[2]

I am indebted to Ann Hutchison for generously-shared scholarship on Syon and to her and to Arlyn Diamond for helpful editing.

[1] Much further study (of for instance the increased numbers of British abbesses in late manuscripts of the *South English Legendary* and of the British legendaries organized by alphabetical rather than calendrical order following Tynemouth's *Nova Legenda Anglie*) is needed. For a preliminary survey of abbess saints, see Jocelyn Wogan-Browne, 'Queens, Virgins, and Mothers', in *Women and Sovereignty*, ed. by Louise Fradenburg (Edinburgh: Edinburgh University Press, 1992), pp. 14–35.

[2] Felicity Riddy, '"Women talking of the things of God": A Late Medieval Female Sub-Culture', in *Women and Literature in Britain 1150–1500*, ed. by Carol M. Meale (Cambridge: Cambridge University Press, 1993, repr. 1996), pp. 104–27.

The participation of women in Lancastrian literature's politics and anxieties is, perhaps, less easily traced than that of men, and, indeed, most late medieval lives re-using Anglo-Saxon royal women saints are of figures from monasteries that had long been refounded, in tenth-century or later 'reforms', as male houses.[3] Edith's Life, however, is the biography of a female saint in an ancient and continuously female community. Edith (d. AD 984) was the patron saint of the royal Benedictine nunnery of Wilton in the diocese of Salisbury. An illegitimate daughter of Edgar (king of Wessex AD 959–75 and closely associated with Anglo-Saxon Benedictine reform), Edith was placed in Wilton from infancy, together with her mother, Edgar's ex-concubine Wultrud. In the late eleventh century, Goscelin, author of the Latin *vita* that is one of the major sources for Edith's English life, also wrote a treatise for Eve, an ex-nun of Wilton, in which he glitteringly envisions Wilton as England's Syon, an ark of spiritual and social prestige.[4] By the early fifteenth century the role of England's Syon had been given to Henry V's new Brigittine foundation of that name in Middlesex (begun 1415), but Wilton remained a prosperous abbey, with young women entering it in significant numbers throughout the fifteenth century and with the high number of thirty-three nuns in residence at the Dissolution.[5] Wilton had three chantries and a small college of secular priests attached to it, as well as rights to appoint to a number of parish churches and prebends in the diocese. The anonymous Middle English Life of Edith is almost certainly by a cleric associated with the abbey.[6]

---

[3]   Of the nine native foundress-abbesses cited in the fifteenth-century poem known as 'Why I Can't Be a Nun' (*Six Ecclesiastical Satires*, ed. by James M. Dean (Kalamazoo: Medieval Institute Publications, Western Michigan University, 1991), pp. 227–46 (p. 242/ll. 378–88), for example, only Edith's community was still a female house.

[4]   *The Liber confortatorius of Goscelin of St Bertin*, ed. by C. H. Talbot, *Analecta Monastica*, 3rd ser., ed. by M. M. Lebreton, J. Leclercq, C. H. Talbot (Rome: Pontifical Institute of St Anselm, 1955), Bk IV, pp. 113–15. On the Goscelin *vita* see A. Wilmart, 'La Légende de ste Édith en prose et vers par le moine Goscelin', *AB* 56 (1938), 5–101, 265–307. An abridged Life is extant in the *Nova Legenda Anglie* (ed. by C. Horstmann (Oxford: Clarendon Press, 1901), I, pp. 311–15).

[5]   *The Victoria County History of England, Wiltshire* vol. III, ed. by R. B. Pugh and Elizabeth Critall (London: Oxford University Press for the Institute for Historical Research, 1956), p. 239.

[6]   A list of 1394 names nine chaplains as saying mass at Wilton abbey: see *The Register of John Waltham, Bishop of Salisbury 1388–95* ed. by T. C. B. Timmins, Canterbury and York Society (Woodbridge: Boydell and Brewer, 1994), no. 972A. Waltham, himself a

Although her Life is a narrative of some 5000 lines, Edith is possibly the most static female saint in the British pantheon. She is nursed in Wilton, brought up in Wilton, according to her *vitae*, Latin and vernacular, she refused all advancement in order to stay at home in Wilton with her mother Wultrud. She dies at Wilton at the age of twenty-three and her relics and miracles continue there in her long post-mortem career. This stasis is however not without several kinds of meaning. Horstmann (the most recent editor, in 1881, of Edith's vernacular Life) thought that the narrative's purpose was practical: to instruct the Wilton nuns so that they would know more about the founders for whom it was their vocation to pray.[7] Certainly, the narrative promises that it will

> ... yow telle by goddys grace
> For whom ye ben yholde to preyye fore
> And who were first funders of that place (ll. 314–16)

(...tell you, by the grace of God, for whom you are obliged to pray and who were the first founders of [Wilton]).

Moreover royal male patrons and founders play a large role both in the narrative of the Life and in its manuscript presentation, where they are signalled by marginal *notae* and where the English narrative is followed by a Latin list of the house's founders.[8] This list makes no mention of

---

Yorkshire man, brought Northerners into the diocese (which would fit with the mixture of NW and SW forms in the language of the scribe of *Edith*, see n. 8 below). One chaplain of Wilton, Elisha Pese (probably the Ellis Pusee of Waltham's register), was given a licence on 29 May 1411 to hear the confessions of Alice Hallum, kinswoman of Robert Hallum, bishop of Salisbury from 1407–17: see *Registrum Roberti Hallum, Diocesis Saresbiriensis 1407–17*, ed. by Joyce M. Horn, Canterbury and York Society 72 (York: Canterbury and York Society, 1982), p. 147, no. 992.

[7] *S. Editha sive Chronicon Vilodunense im Wiltshire Dialekt*, ed. by C. Horstmann (Heilbronn: Henninger, 1883), p. v: further quotations referenced in the text by line number (runic letters silently transliterated and Horstmann's capitalization and punctuation sometimes altered). A new edition of the life by John Ayto was announced in 1977 (see further n. 12 below).

[8] London, British Library MS Cotton Faustina B. iii, fols 263^{r-v}, in the same contemporary if not identical hand as the main text. *Edith* (fols 199^r–263^r (modern pencil foliation)) is extant only here and is accompanied by an incomplete life of Etheldreda of Ely (fols 265^r–279^v) in the same metre (and same hand), a coupling which suggests a wider agenda than the representation of Wilton to itself. (Etheldreda became the patron saint of the Augustinian priory of Canonsleigh, Devonshire, following its refoundation in 1284 as a female house by Maud de Clare, Countess of Gloucester.) A lacuna (covering Edgar's pursuit of Wultrud and Edith's birth in Wilton) between what are now fol. 210^r

Henry V's death in 1422 or of his son, Henry VI (born 1421), and the
Life is usually dated to *c.* 1420. Such a dating supports Horstmann's
argument for the Life's function, since its initial production cannot then
be linked with the most obvious early fifteenth-century occasion for it, the
indulgence issued in 1425 by the Bishop of Salisbury (John Chandler,
bishop 1417–1426, formerly a Wilton chaplain) for visitors to Edith's
shrine on her feast day (16th September).[9]

But Horstmann's account leaves the production and reception of the
Edith Life neatly circular, an enclosed and enclosing life for consumption
in a gynaceum. Although I do not want to dispute a Wilton provenance,
nor the Wilton community as an audience for the Life, I do want to argue
that, both as an image *of* Wilton and as reading *for* Wilton, what
Horstmann saw as a devotional house-history for women is much less
innocently and mono-valently pious than his account suggests. For, as
much as a text informing the Wilton nuns of their history, or representing
the Wilton community to its local patrons and its shrine to pilgrims from
further afield, the *Edith* Life writes Wilton into a Henrician monasticism,
in which the authority of this ancient Wessex nunnery and its virgin
patron saint are inflected with Lancastrian concerns. Henry V's personal
patronage focussed on the newer, more austere orders, and his Brigittine
and Carthusian foundations were in the South East of the country,
specifically around the ex-Ricardian site of the palace of Sheen.[10] Yet

---

and fol. 211[r] is the result, as far as can be determined, of the loss of a whole quire (6
bifolia), even though, exceptionally, there is no catchword now extant on fol. 210[v]. (I am
grateful to Mrs Patricia Basing, Curator at the Department of Manuscripts, British Library,
for help over the quiring of this manuscript, fols 265–71 of which have been made into a
quire of 8 in error during modern re-binding.) The manuscript was copied by someone
whose English included northernisms (see Michael Benskin, 'In Reply to Dr Burton',
Leeds Studies in English, 22 (1991), 246–51), and the text composed in or near Wilton.
Though plain, workaday and without ruling, the manuscript is a practised piece of work,
copied, perhaps rather rapidly, by someone familiar with Latin and vernacular books and
their conventions. A chaplain of Wilton remains a likely candidate for the scribe of the two
lives as also for their authorship (though the nature of the occasional scribal errors, as of
the text's language, suggests they were not the same person).

[9]   Sar. reg. Chandler fol. 44, quoted in VCH *Wilts* II, p. 239, n. 87 (see now *The Register
of John Chandler, Dean of Salisbury 1404–17*, ed. by T. C. B. Timmins, Wiltshire Record
Society 39 (Devizes: Wiltshire Record Society, 1984). Subsequent use of the life for such
purposes is of course not ruled out, regardless of when it was composed.

[10] Joel Rosenthal, 'Kings, Continuity and Ecclesiastical Benefaction in 15th Century
England', in *People, Politics and Community in the late Middle Ages*, ed. by Joel T.
Rosenthal and Colin Richmond (New York: St Martin's Press, 1984 and Stroud: Sutton,

Syon of Middlesex seems not to have been alone in its capacity or desire to express royal ecclesiastical policy. Chaplains and clergy in the Salisbury diocese were geographically removed from London (and France, where Henry spent much of his brief reign), but linked to the crown through, among other ties, Robert Hallum's role in Henry's imperial and papal policies. Hallum, Bishop of Salisbury 1407–17, was not only Henry's chief negotiator at the Council of Constance, but the centre of an intelligent and efficient group of reforming conservative orthodox clerics in the Salisbury diocese. If a Wilton chaplain indeed composed the Life, he can hardly have escaped awareness of Henry's ecclesiastical concerns: there need be nothing provincial consequent on the regional origins of a text and community such as *Edith*.[11] John Ayto's demonstration that the manuscript of *Edith* was marked up for printing suggests too, that, like Syon, Wilton was interested in ways of disseminating images of itself, images, I shall argue, of Wilton as an ideal aristocratic holy household and as a community with particularly valuable sacralizing powers for the Lancastrian dynasty.[12]

In the first place, the language of Edith's Life is worth consideration. Late Middle English is not an inevitable language for a nunnery's house history, but expresses a choice of register. Among aristocratic women of this period, French texts are nearly as readily to be found as English (Wilton itself had had a translation of the Benedictine rule into French prescribed for it in an episcopal visitation of 1379).[13] The 1394 will of

1987), pp. 161–75 (p. 163). Henry himself was probably born on Edith's feast day, but there is no evidence for his personal cult of Edith, and neither she nor Wilton is mentioned in his will (see Christopher Allmand, *Henry V* (New Haven: Yale University Press, 1992: new edn, 1997), p. 7; Patrick and Felicity Strong, 'The Last Will and Codicil of Henry V', *EHR* 96 (1981), 80–102, p. 93).

[11] Allmand discusses Hallum's role in the Council of Constance, pp. 238–39: see also Catto, 'Religious Change...'. Hallum's successor, John Chandler (Bishop of Salisbury 1417–26), for instance, had been a Wilton chaplain, and a canon and archdeacon of Salisbury. He knew Joan of Kent (Richard II's mother); was treasurer of Princess Blanche's household for Henry IV, took the princess to Cologne for her marriage and was treasurer to Queen Joan whom he escorted from Brittany (see Timmins, *Register of John Chandler*, p. xiii).

[12] John Ayto, 'Marginalia in the Manuscript of the *Life of St Edith*: New Light on Early Printing', *The Library* 5th ser., 32 (1977), 27–36: I thank Alexandra Barratt for this reference.

[13] For the decree see VCH, *Wilts* II, p. 238, n. 83. About a hundred French texts can be counted in David Bell's catalogue of provenanced nunnery manuscripts (*What Nuns Read:*

Joan Formage, abbess of Wilton's neighbouring princess-minster, Shaftesbury, exemplifies both the networks of professional and personal relations among the Wiltshire nunneries and the documentary as well as literary use of French. Formage willed 'a l'abbesse de Wylton, un paire des anes [asses] et un anel d'or oue un paire de rubie fiche en icelle [a ring of gold with a pair of rubies set in it]': her third best mantle was to go to 'dame Johan Wytfeld, noneyne de Wylton'.[14] In this milieu, a Wilton chaplain, in part dependent on abbess patronage, might well have tried to make his mark in French.[15]

No more than the choice of English was *Edith*'s particular stylistic register inevitable. The Life's long-line quatrains are characterized by Horstmann as 'extraordinarily primitive... chronicle-like, naive...', but also 'not without a certain historical richness' (*S. Editha*, p. vii). What might have been expected at this period, especially where a royal nunnery is concerned, is an ornate neo-Chaucerian style, as with Bokenham's highly rhetorical *Legendys of Hooly Wummen* of 1443–47, or Lydgate's *Troy Book* (commissioned in 1412 by Prince, later King, Henry) and other major Lancastrian rewritings of fourteenth-century courtly tradition. The four-stressed, unspectacularly-rhymed loose long-line of the *Edith* quatrains, however, does precisely signify 'historicity', especially among texts from the South West. In the early fifteenth century, before Lydgatian and Central-East Anglian writing was consolidated as *the* Lancastrian style, this might well have seemed authoritative for the writing of English history.[16] The language and verse-form of Edith's Life

---

Books and Libraries in Medieval English Nunneries, Cistercian Studies Series 158, Kalamazoo: Cistercian Publications, 1995). For a French house-history of this period, see Mary Bateson, 'The Register of Crabhouse Nunnery', *Norfolk Archaeology*, 2 (1892), 1–71, item 2. English kings themselves at this date conducted much of their business in French and their cultural propaganda in English (Allmand, *Henry V*, pp. 420–25).

[14] See *The Register of John Waltham*, no. 121, pp. 31–32 (p. 32).

[15] The surnames of the Wilton chaplains (Blokkesworth, Dressoure, Gilberd, Menziter, Marchaunt, Pusee, Pynkaunt, Shupton, Smith) in Waltham's list (see n. 6 above) suggest that many were meritocrats, needing patronage from the diocese, the abbess, or the king.

[16] An especially pertinent South West Midlands text is *The Metrical Chronicle of Robert of Gloucester* (ed. by W. A. Wright, R. S. 2 vols (London: Eyre and Spottiswoode for HMSO, 1887): on the *Chronicle*'s borrowing from hagiography see Beatrice D. Brown, 'Robert of Gloucester's *Chronicle* and the *Life of St Kenelm*', *MLN*, 41 (1926), 13–23. For texts from Wiltshire, see *A Linguistic Atlas of Late Medieval English*, ed. by Angus McIntosh, M. L. Samuels, Michael Benskin et al. (Aberdeen: Aberdeen University Press, 1986), vol. 1 , pp. 248–49; for examples of South West and Southern texts see *The Idea of*

are neither *faute de mieux*, nor testimony to an absence of Latinity among Wilton's nuns, or to English monoglottism in the convent's community. Rather they are choices appropriate to the Life's portrayal of the English kings and the English history which figure so largely in it. That the Life comes with a manuscript apparatus of Latin authority (marginal notes of sources, and a following list of *auctores* as well as the previously-mentioned founders' list) is arguably a feature of *English* literary style in the later Middle Ages and familiar in the manuscripts of many writers from Mannyng to Gower, Lydgate, and others.

From the first to the last of its thirty royal founders, the Latin list in the manuscript of *Edith* insists on patrilineal continuity and authority, with 'filius' or, on occasion, 'frater' succeeding each other up to Henry V no less firmly than the agnatic filiation of the Trinity itself. The miniature holy female kinship of Edith and her mother Wultrud here sacralizes a long male lineage preluding the Lancastrians. Within the Life's narrative, Edith's father, Edgar, is the major figure, but Edith and her miracles are also firmly associated with every English king up to Henry II. Egbert, the initial royal founder of Wilton, unites four of the seven Anglo-Saxon kingdoms together (l. 32) and changes the name of 'Bretayne' to 'Englond' (ll. 43–44). Saxons are to be called Englishmen and not [H]Engist's men, Britons are Welshmen and no longer Cadwallader's men—'And thus Englonde toke first his [its] name/In the gode kyng Egbertys tyme/Ryht as we clepe yet the same [the very name that we still use]', (ll. 106–08)—and Egbert and his male descendants now continue re-founding and increasing the endowment of Wilton.[17] This careful establishment of the co-dependence of royalty and monasticism in an England united at least by nomenclature is a prelude to the life of 'Alured the gode kynge' (l. 373) and his re-foundation of Wilton (ll. 370–661).

The history culminates in Edith's father, Edgar, crowned by Dunstan with the consent of 'alle Englond' because he was 'a vertuose thynge' (ll. 780–81). Edgar himself is portrayed as resolutely 'monfulle... in his gouernyng' (l. 828, also l. 834). This insistently masculine representation

---

the Vernacular: An Anthology of Middle English Literary Theory 1280–1520, ed. by Jocelyn Wogan-Browne, Nicholas Watson, Andrew Taylor, and Ruth Evans (University Park: Pennsylvania State University Press, 1999), esp. Parts 2.8 (Bishop Fox's letter to Southern nunneries) and 2.9 (the Amesbury *Letter*), and p. 383.

[17] On Hengist as founder of English see also Gower, *Confessio Amantis*, Latin Prologue (in the later prologue for Henry IV, ll. 3–4: ed. and trans. in *The Idea of the Vernacular* pp. 174–75).

of rule is complemented not by a queen consort, but by the Life's account
of holiness and national value in a female community. Not only is governance constructed as highly 'monfulle' under Edgar, but his vision of his
pregnant greyhound, whose whelps bark within her belly at their mother
and the king, is explicated as presaging a monstrous birth of heresy (ll.
918–25) and looks remarkably like a rationale for Henry's efficient
extirpation of Lollards.[18] Edgar's role as a figure of the Benedictine tenth-
century reform is consonant with Henry V's own policy. Henry's concern
with Benedictine monasticism and monialism was, like Edgar's before
him, reformist, part of his policy of order, control, and the eradication of
dissent in a newly tightened relation of church and state.[19]

The Life's many reminders of Edith's claim to represent holy
nationhood for England also seem significant against this background of
Henry V's church policy. Wilton's national resonance is underlined by
Edith's determination to stay at home. She does not want abbesshood at
Winchester, Barking, or Wilton, and she refuses the thrones of England
and France in favour of devotional building within Wilton:

> ... myche more thought he had a chapelle to make
> In worshyppe of seynt Denys and of his day
> Then to bene quene of Englonde and Fraunce yfere (ll. 1751–53).

> (...she was much more concerned to have a chapel made in St Denys's
> honour than to be queen of England and France together).

Here, as in Edith's association with St Denys throughout the narrative, the
Life (within a few years of Agincourt), annexes the principal national cult
of France to Britain while reinforcing the English claim to both. Edith's
devotion to the saint also promotes Wilton as a sacred site of national
identity to rival St Denys in Paris, and, in an English account of an
English saint, adds chronological depth to English claims to the French
crown.[20]

---

[18] Wilton's own diocese of Salisbury saw heresy trials up to the late fifteenth century
(Andrew D. Brown, *Popular Piety in Late Medieval England: The Diocese of Salisbury
1250–1550*, Oxford: Clarendon Press, 1995, p. 217): M. Henry Crumpe (d. after 1401),
one of the authorities named in the *Edith* manuscript, was accused of Lollardy (see
Richard Sharpe, *Latin Writers of Great Britain* (Turnhout: Brepols, 1997), p. 167.

[19] See Jeremy Catto, 'Religious Change under Henry V', in *Henry V: The Practice of
Kingship*, ed. by G. L. Harriss (Oxford: Oxford University Press, 1985), pp. 97–115.

[20] Late Middle English Lives of St Denys are included in the *South English Legendary*,
the 1438 *Gilte Legende* and Caxton's *Golden Legend* (see Charlotte D'Evelyn and Anna J.
Mill, 'Saints' Legends', *Manual of the Writings in Middle English*, ed. by Albert E.

As an ancient royal nunnery, Wilton itself is a relic of regnal and spiritual power (in the principal medieval sense of relic, i.e. *pignus*, 'a
pledge'), and relics are an important concern of Edith and Wultrud in the
Life.[21] They spend the enormous sum of 'two thowsonde shyllyngus' (l.
1396) and use their influence with Benno (Edith's tutor and a canon at
Trier in the Rheinland), to obtain part of Trier abbey's 'preciose tresere'
(l. 1391) of a nail from the crucifixion.[22] This acquisition is ascribed to
their piety. Personal devotion to, and ownership of, relics was certainly a
routine aspect of aristocratic women's religious lives, as also of their
patronage.[23] But Trier was the German seat of the late-medieval Holy
Roman Empire and home to very celebrated relics indeed.[24] Edith and
Wultrud are acquiring contact relics imprinted with imperial dynastic
power as well as with the Passion.

After her death, Edith herself becomes Wilton's leading relic and her
shrine-cloth bleeds threateningly when illegitimately handled (ll. 2622–
29). Miracles of protection and vengeance are presented as Edith's
particular *forte*. She punishes shrine violators with blindness, for instance
(ll. 3559–635), and threatens the sceptical King Cnut (ll. 3387–94). Once
the famous dancers of Kolbeck are trapped in the perpetual ring-dance

---

Hartung (New Haven: Connecticut Academy of Arts and Sciences, 1970), vol. 2, pp. 578–
79). There are two fifteenth-century French verse texts on St Denys (*The Octosyllabic Vie
de Saint Denis*, ed. by James H. Baltzell (Genève: Droz, 1953), p. 10), and a prose
fifteenth-century Life, for which see Charles J. Liebman, *Étude sur la vie en prose de saint
Denis* (Genève and New York: W. F. Humphrey, 1942).

[21] On the significances of relics see Virginia Reinburg, 'Remembering the Saints', in
Memory in the Middle Ages, ed. by Nancy Netzner and Virginia Reinburg (Chestnut Hill,
MA: Boston College Museum of Art, 1995), pp. 17–33.

[22] See also *Edith*, ll. 3215–39 (Wultrud's ring of profession as relic), ll. 2975–3042
(Wultrud and Edith's acquisition of St Iwi's relics for Wilton).

[23] See, for example, the will of Marie, Countess of St Pol (d. 1377), who lived principally
in England and left relics to most of the many religious houses with which she had
contacts (Hilary Jenkinson, 'Mary de Sancto Paulo, Foundress of Pembroke College,
Cambridge', *Archaeologia*, 66 (1914–15), 401–46: text of the [French] will, pp. 432–35).

[24] The value of the nail-relic is stressed: it is 'muche derre [more expensively] boght' than
the Jews 'bouht god of Judas' (l. 1404). In a fifteenth-century chronicle, St Louis of
France is reported as saying that he would rather lose his realm's best city than lose his
nail-relic (quoted in Liebman, *Étude sur la vie en prose de saint Denis*, p. xxi, n. 2). The
relic had its own narrative ('Histoire de la perte et récupération du saint clou en 1233', in
P. Aubry, 'Comment fut perdu et retrouvé le saint clou de l'abbaye de Saint-Denys', *Revue
Mabillon*, 2 (1906), 185–92, 286–300 and 3 (1907), 43–50, 147–82).

monastic and national purity.[25] Edith's vengeance miracles resonate beyond the customary function of asserting and defending a particular monastic community's prerogatives to suggest Wilton's status as a national engine of intercession and the maintenance of order.[26]

Like vengeance, penance can re-pattern the relations of past and present. Penitential asceticism and devout intercession were important functions of nunneries and positioned female communities as agents of social and spiritual exchange.[27] The figure of Edith as virgin patroness of Wilton in the Life is closely and importantly linked with that of her concubine abbess-mother. This is the very aspect of Edith's *vita* one might have expected to see minimized for its capacity symbolically to blemish the saint's integrity, but the mother-daughter configuration is insisted on and amplified. This may be partly because Wultrud, like other holy ex-concubines such as the Magdalen (or biological mothers such as Margery Kempe), achieves the status of holy woman and of honorary virginity through penance and asceticism.[28] She has a subordinate but efficacious saintly career of visions and cures founded on the status gained by her 'long marterdom' (l. 2174) of suffering and concern for her daughter. At Edith's death, Wultrud appoints poor people and chantry chaplains to pray and sing masses for her (ll. 2117–18, 2329–32), and she remains anxious until Edith's miracles of healing and cure signal that her daughter is in heaven. Good women's work of service to their biological and spiritual families is never done, and Wultrud, claims the narrative, is not lazy like many other women who weep at their children's death but subsequently forget to go on doing anything about it (ll. 2165–68). This may well have served as an example of good conduct and as a reminder to

---

[25] See Willis Jonson, 'The Myth of Jewish Male Menses', *JMH*, 24 (1998), 273–95.

[26] In its insistence on the signifying and transformative powers of relic and miracle, the Life has analogies with the concerns Paul Strohm sees as characteristic of 'Lancastrian legitimative self transformation' ('Counterfeiters, Lollards, Lancastrian Unease', *New Medieval Literatures*, 1 (1997), 31–58).

[27] See Barbara Newman, 'On the Threshold of the Dead: Purgatory, Hell, and Religious Women', in her *From Virile Woman to WomanChrist* (Philadelphia: University of Pennsylvania Press, 1995), pp. 108–37; Christine Carpenter, 'The Religion of the Gentry of Fifteenth-Century England', in *England in the Fifteenth Century*, ed. by Daniel Williams (Woodbridge: Boydell Press, 1987), pp. 53–74.

[28] At the revelation of the miraculous freshness and sweetness of Edith's exhumed body, Wultrud is described as singing the Te Deum 'wt other *maydenus*' (italics mine, l. 2580).

the families of the diocese of the continuing importance of the nunnery's intercessions,[29] but it also underlines the importance of the mother-daughter configuration in the Life.

For all Edith's superior virgin status, the mother-daughter relation is complementary. As Wultrud is a figure of honorary virginity conferred by penance, so Edith (most unusually for a female virgin saint), moves between unblemished virgin integrity and the marked body more familiar from purgatorial vision.[30] At Edith's translation in the middle of the poem, her body is 'as hole lygyung as euer aliue ye hit seye' (l. 2474), and there is particular stress on the freshness of the thumb she had used in making the sign of the cross. But her body is also *not* whole. As Edith herself points out in a visionary appearance, the organs of perception ('felyng and seyght', l. 2477) which she used 'childlyche' [childishly] when young are rotted, as are the 'organys' of her 'nother lemys' [lower limbs] which have been taken away not for her own remissness, but 'more for my fader gulte' (l. 2491). Imperfect because indelibly informed by a specific history of transgression and punishment, the purgatorial body often appears, in the later Middle Ages, in mother-daughter confrontations.[31] Here that relationship is the matrix within which Edith's body bears—and sacralizes—a history of imperfection. Illegitimate but royal, intact but blemished, Edith's body can assert Edgar as flawed in his

---

[29] Thus, for instance, the 1386 will of Nicholas Bonham (who had been Knight of the Shire, Steward of the Borough of Wilton, and Justice of the Peace) left gifts to the abbess of Wilton and to his own daughter who was a nun there, and 12d to each nun of the abbey to pray for his soul and that of his parents and benefactors (G. J. Kidston, 'Some Early Wills of the Bonham Family', *Wiltshire Archaeological and Natural History Magazine*, 48 (1938), 273–91: for other such wills see Brown, *Popular Piety*, p. 31, n. 26). Nearly a century later the obits of Bonham daughters were still being entered in the calendar of a psalter used at Wilton as nuns to be themselves prayed for (Oxford, Bodleian Library, MS Rawlinson G.23, fol. 7ʳ [K]atr[i]ne Bonham (May, 1498); fol. 7ᵛ, Jehaine Bonman (June, 1462).

[30] For visions from late medieval Winchester and Salisbury see Robert Easting, *Visions of the Other World in Middle English*, Annotated Bibliographies of Old and Middle English Literature III (Cambridge: D. S. Brewer, 1997): for a nun's vision (from, probably, Winchester in 1422), see *A Revelation of Purgatory by an Unknown Fifteenth-Century Woman Visionary*, ed. by Marta Powell Harley, Studies in Women and Religions 18 (New York: Edwin Mellen, 1985).

[31] See e.g. Gwenevere and her mother's ghost (discussed by Helen Phillips, 'The Ghost's Baptism in *The Awyntyrs off Arthure*', *Medium Aevum*, 58 (1989), 49–58), and St Birgitta's monitory mother from hell (*The Liber Celestis of St Bridget of Sweden*, ed. by Roger Ellis, EETS 291 (Oxford: Oxford University Press, 1987), Bk VI, ch. 52, p. 441).

own person, but whole and sacred in his sovereignty. In the context of the Lancastrian regime, produced with dubious legitimacy from Henry IV's acquisition of the English throne, Edith and her mother become a peculiarly resonant configuration. Paul Strohm has argued that Henry IV's burial of Richard II in remote Langley Abbey had occasioned a Lancastrian disjunction between the king's perishable and his sacral bodies: this required healing by Henry V's 1413 Westminster reburial of Richard (in effect, Strohm argues, the election of a dynastically-legitimate symbolic father).[32] The virgin saint Edith, reappearing to her concubine mother and her royal community in the most sacred and authoritative of revenant modes, the vision of a saint, enables dynastic recuperation via a holy female symbolic.

English royalty has often known when to do penance, from Henry II on his knees for Becket at Rocamadour to Elizabeth II bowing her head at her daughter-in-law's funeral cortège. Such symbolic concession wards off stronger challenges, and Henry V himself gave a masterly processional display of penitential humility on return from Agincourt. The Life's emphasis on Wultrud and Edith as a miniature holy female kinship re-patterning past and present through the powers of retribution and penance is far from incompatible with a bid for the representation of Wilton in the terms of Henrician churchmanship. It also suggests that the punitively marked bodies of women in purgatorial vision encode transformative power and not just endemic victimhood as one of the cultural characteristics of women.

The community embodied in Edith's Life is far less enclosed and static than either Horstmann's argument or the Life's own assertion of stable and enduring sacred power implies, and political and rhetorical claims inflect the representation of life within Wilton much as they do its relations with the outside world.[33] No aspect of *Edith* is a straightforward transcription of life in late medieval female communities. In living under her mother's governance, for instance, Edith not only asserts that the

---

[32] 'The Trouble with Richard: The Reburial of Richard II and Lancastrian Symbolic Strategy', *Speculum*, 71 (1996), 87–111 (pp. 89, 104).

[33] King Atwolf, one of the Life's early founders, goes to Wilton because 'Wyltone was a gode toune tho' (l. 178): Wilton had a gild and presumably a market from at least the twelfth century (see R. H. Britnell, *The Commercialization of English Society: 1000–1500* (Cambridge: Cambridge University Press, 1993; 2nd edn Manchester: Manchester University Press, 1996), p. 27), and a hospital opposite the nunnery gates (Roberta Gilchrist, *Gender and Material Culture: The Archaeology of Religious Women* (London: Routledge, 1994), p. 74).

virtue of the English crown and the royalty of the nunnery continue in Wilton, but exemplifies the dynamic deployment of humility as a solvent for issues of rank and class in nunneries (as elsewhere in courtly life).[34] Like other late medieval royal virgins, Edith is constantly 'besy.../ To serue hure sustren wt alle mekenes / As was Martha or Mary' (ll. 1053–55).[35] This invocation of Martha and Mary collapses a traditional distinction to make both the active and the contemplative life forms of service, thus legitimating a wide range of pursuits and providing an attractive image of life in Wilton. Preferring the 'matte [mat] of the Angoras [anchoress] ... yclosyd in stone' (ll.1234–35), Edith rejects the English throne for the choir-nun's reading and contemplative opportunities:

> Hurre was leuer to here mayteynesse and masse
> And vpon hure boke to rede and spelle
> Nen to be duchas, quene, or cowntasse (ll. 1582–84).

(She preferred to hear matins and mass and to study and recite from her book than to be duchess, queen, or countess).

But her portrait (though, and indeed *because*, it values the liturgical and devotional reading embraced by lay and professed women in their psalters and books of hours) is of a vigorous, educated, noblewoman patroness, such as an aristocratic choir-nun might well be. (The Life generally assumes that in a prestigious nunnery institutional life was routinely a version of upper-class household and family living—including over-generous hospitality, 'to gret excesse of householde' (l. 4740), as practised by one abbess).[36] With assistance from her tutor the monk Benno, Edith both paints the image of the passion on the walls of her new

---

[34] Marilyn Oliva, 'Aristocracy or Meritocracy: Office Holding Patterns in Late Medieval English Nunneries', in *Women in the Church*, ed. by W. J. Sheils and Diana Wood, SCH 27 (Oxford: Blackwell, 1990), pp. 197–208. Joan Beauchamp, the king's kinswoman (d. 1416), was abbess of Wilton in 1415, but some names in the surviving Wilton calendars suggest a much wider class-range in the families who contributed nuns to the house.

[35] So for instance, Bradshaw's St Radegund, princess-abbess of Poitiers and patron of the nunnery that became Jesus College, Cambridge, is said to clean her nuns' shoes and to do latrine duty (*The Life of St Radegund* ed. by F. Brittain (Cambridge: Bowes and Bowes, 1923), p. 26).

[36] The *topos* of nuns' improvidence is reiterated in bishops' registers: in Wilton visitations of 1370 and 1400, problems were noted which have been interpreted as showing incompetence, but the 1423 visitation by Archbishop Chichele pronounced all well with both the spiritualities and the temporalities (Critall, *VCH*, p. 239).

chapel for St Denys (l. 1781–88, also l. 1170) and always bears the image ('purtatur', l. 1785) of the Passion in her heart (in the approved manner recommended for women in religion by Nicholas Love).[37] And in addition to architectural patronage and embroidery she can write and 'purtrey' (l. 1158), harp, sing, 'carff welle ymagus and peyntede bothe' (ll. 1169–70), though she loves best 'to rede and syng vpon here boke' (l. 1180).

The Life's account of Edith may be designed to represent Wilton as a learned community comparable with Syon or other Benedictine nunneries such as Barking (or it may be that Syon's own Brigittine practice owes something to indigenous communities and expectations).[38] The ladies of Wilton (almost invariably called 'ladyes', much more rarely 'mynchyns' [nuns], in the Life) are represented in terms often common with the life of Syon: they are always, for instance, shown going to their 'chambers' (ll. 1270, 4952), as did Syon nuns for private reading.[39]

This portrait may also express clerical expectations or hopes regarding the patronage of a wealthy and high-ranking community. Among its many recognitions of aristocratic nuns' power and rank is the Life's readiness to set limits to the deference of Edith and her companions to their spiritual and ecclesiastical directors—at least when clergy of other affiliations than Wilton are concerned. Thus Edith defeats bishop Æthelwold of Winchester over questions of dress, arguing that under 'clothing of royal pomp' (l. 1208) there may be 'an abundance of good qualities' ('vrtwys werkus gret pleynte'): the Holy Ghost as gladly dwells under a mantle furred with beaver as a rough goat's fell.[40] Her Life's promotion of her contemplative abilities does not exclude Edith's being, as many late medieval nuns wished to be, a woman wearing some personalized version of clothing, and hence marking rank and

---

[37] For Love's use of internalized passion meditation, see Wogan-Browne, Watson et al., *The Idea of the Vernacular*, 3.10, (pp. 252–55).

[38] For Wilton's books, see David Bell, *What Nuns Read*: for its book list, see *English Benedictine Libraries: the Shorter Catalogues* ed. by R. Sharpe, J. Carley, R. Thomson, and A. G. Watson, Corpus of British Medieval Library Catalogues 4 (London: British Library, 1996), Wilton B III, pp. 645–46.

[39] Ann M. Hutchison, pers. comm., and 'What the Nuns Read: Literary Evidence from the English Bridgettine House Syon Abbey', *Mediaeval Studies*, 57 (1995), 205–22.

[40] See ll. 1213–16 and Susan J. Millinger, 'Humility and Power: Anglo-Saxon Nuns in Anglo-Norman Hagiography', in *Distant Echoes: Medieval Religious Women I*, ed. by John A. Nichols and Lillian T. Shank (Kalamazoo: Cistercian Publications, 1984), pp. 115–29.

individuality. (So too, Joan Formage valued both personal and professional ties: in her will she wanted her wimples, veils, sleeves, and 'rochettes' [smocks] to go to the poor nuns of her house and especially to 'those who are of our blood and those whom we have made nuns').[41] In this context of great ladies modifying institutional culture to their family values and styles, Edith's refusal to leave her mother can be read as a persistent valuation of 'fleschly' kinship in spite of clerical and institutional demands for control of women's affective ties within and outside the cloister.[42]

Successful resistance to churchmen is most notable in the Life's concerns with relics. No sooner does the prestigious Trier nail-relic purchased by Edith and her mother arrive at Wilton than Bishop Æthelwold descends from Winchester to request a piece of it. Unwilling to refuse him, Wultrud and Edith reluctantly allow a priest to begin filing off a portion of the relic, which then bleeds copiously. All spend the night in sorrow and penitence and the relic is found completely whole once again in the morning. Æthelwold retreats, perceiving that Wultrud and Edith have greater rights (of devotion and expenditure); that God loved these ladies 'ryht entierly' (l. 1494); and that, although they had not liked to say so to him,

> Thus holy wymmennus wylle nas not therto
> That he ony thyng of that preciose releke shulle haue (ll. 1481–82).

(It was not the wish of these holy women that he should have any part of that precious relic).

In this represented resistance to praelatical partition and fragmentation of nunnery resources, bleeding is a tactical weapon and not just a sign of the affectivity so dominant in our accounts of the meaning of feminized blood-shedding. Like the defence of her own shrine offered by Edith's body, this is no self-containing representation but a deployment of symbolic currencies in which the holy female enclave has powerful and multiple concerns. Clerical mediation of a community's symbolic capital

---

[41] 'Et nomement as eux qui sount de nostre saunk et as eux qui soient queuz nous avoms faitz noneynes', in the will quoted above, n. 14.

[42] Actual maternity was officially decried in favour of symbolic spiritual maternity; as Felice Lifshitz points out, an *abbatissa* is etymologically a female father ('Is Mother Superior? Towards a History of Feminine *Amtscharisma*', in *Medieval Mothering*, ed. by Bonnie Wheeler and John Carmi Parsons (New York: Garland, 1996), pp. 117–38. Representations of nuns with their biological mothers are relatively rare.

to the outside world testifies as much to a shared political agenda on the part of Wilton's great ladies and their staff as to male hegemony over women monastics.

Re-imagining such groups and re-reading their reading and their household documents, as Felicity Riddy's work has challenged us to do, is still difficult, not least because of the strength of our own longings for predecessors in acceptable images, for diachronic community.[43] The ladies (actual and aspirant) of Henrician Wilton may well have formed a group with unpleasant political and class assumptions. But their Life of Edith (of which only a much-truncated account has been given here) counters any perception of late medieval female community or its texts as undifferentiatedly pious, let alone subsumable to the pieties of our own desire for predecessors.

---

[43] See Nicholas Watson, 'Desire for the Past', *SAC*, 21 (1999), 59–98.

List of Contributors and Editors

Priscilla Bawcutt is an Honorary Professor in the Department of English Language and Literature, University of Liverpool.

Peter Biller is in the History Department and the Centre for Medieval Studies, University of York.

Julia Boffey is in the School of English and Drama, Queen Mary and Westfield College, University of London.

Carolyn P. Collette is in the English Department, Mount Holyoke College, Massachusetts.

Patricia Cullum is in the Department of History, Politics, and Modern Languages, University of Huddersfield.

Arlyn Diamond is in the English Department, University of Massachusetts, Amherst.

Jane Gilbert is in the French Department, University College, University of London.

Jeremy Goldberg is in the History Department and the Centre for Medieval Studies, University of York.

Douglas Gray is a Fellow of Lady Margaret Hall, University of Oxford

Jane Grenville is in the Department of Archaeology and the Centre for Medieval Studies, University of York.

Ann Hutchison is in the Pontifical Institute for Mediaeval Studies, University of Toronto.

Eric J. Johnson is a postgraduate at the Centre for Medieval Studies, University of York.

Lesley Johnson was formerly in the School of English, University of Leeds, and now works in Germany.

Katherine J. Lewis is in the Department of History, Politics, and Modern Languages, University of Huddersfield.

Ceridwen Lloyd-Morgan is a member of the Department of Manuscripts and Records, National Library of Wales, Aberystwyth.

Sally Mapstone is a Fellow of St Hilda's College, University of Oxford.

Carol M. Meale formerly taught in the Department of English and the Centre for Medieval Studies and is now Senior Research Fellow of the University of Bristol.

Noël James Menuge was formerly a postgraduate at the Centre for Medieval Studies, University of York.

Alastair Minnis is in the English Department and the Centre for Medieval Studies, University of York.

W. M. Ormrod is in the History Department and the Centre for Medieval Studies, University of York.

Helen Phillips is in the Department of English, University of Liverpool.

Kim M. Phillips is in the History Department, University of Auckland.

Sarah Rees Jones is in the History Department and the Centre for Medieval Studies, University of York.

Colin Richmond is in the History Department, University of Keele.

Anne Savage is in the English Department, McMaster University.

Rosalynn Voaden is in the English Department, Arizona State University.

Nicholas Watson is in the English Department, University of Western Ontario.

Jocelyn Wogan-Browne is in the English Department and the Centre for Medieval Studies, Fordham University.

Index

Aachen: 47, 387
Aarts, Florent G. A. M.: 172
Abels, Richard: 365
Aberdeen: 18
Aberdour: 34
Aberth, J.: 292
Abingdon Apocalypse: 25
Abingdon Priory: 25
Ada, Countess of Northumberland: 22, 27
Adam de Helay: 115, 116, 125–28
Adam de Hopton: 115–17, 120, 122, 124, 125, 127, 128
Adam Fullarton: 25
Adam of St Victor: 85
Aers, David: 92, 183, 199, 206, 211, 212, 214, 216, 377, 380, 388
Æthelwold, Bishop of Winchester: 407, 408
Agatha, St: 71
Agincourt: 400, 405
Agnes Barbour: 80
Agnes Blackburn: 225
Agnes Lond': 221
Agnes Paston: 253–55, 257, 260, 262, 271
Agneta Goze, *alias* Lippard: 103. *See also* Anni Goch
Aimeri of Toulouse: 363, 364, 375
Albert the Great: 95
Albertano of Brescia: 158

Aldgate: 45
Alexander Hume: 26
Alexander Montgomerie: 28
Alexander the Great: 293, 301
Algermissen, Konrad: 87
Alice Blackburn: 221, 223–25, 232, 234
Alice Bolton: 221
Alice Bolton, nee Blackburn: 221, 223, 232, 236
Alice Clere at Bruisyard: 269
Alice Cook: 80
Alice de Denby: 115
Alice Hallum: 395
Alice Heveningham: 270, 272
Alice Perrers: 171
Alice White at Denny: 269, 270
Alison Sandilands: 25
Alison Strynger: 223
All Saints, North Street, York: 222, 224, 230
Allen, Hope Emily: 43, 50, 52–54, 82, 222, 359, 378, 381
Allen, John P.: 327
Allmand, Christopher: 397, 398
Alston, R. C.: 20
Anderson, David: 145
Anderson, W. J.: 24
Andrew Lundy's Primer: *See* manuscripts: Blairs College, National Library of Scotland, Dep. 221/5

Andrew, St: 24
Angharad James: 112
Ann Griffiths: 112
Anna Goze: 103. *See also* Anni Goch
Anna of Hungary: 21
Anne Bourgchier: 265
Anne Clere at Denny: 269, 270
Anne Clere, nee Hopton: 256, 262, 264, 271
Anne Knevet: 187, 188, 197
Anne Mortimer, Lady March: 72
Anne Mowbray: 266
Anne Neville: 237
Anne of Bohemia: 97, 282, 288, 290, 291
Anne Paston: 264
Anne, Queen: 29
Anne, St: 58, 219, 222, 228–35
Anni Goch: 102–107
Anselm: 178
Anthony Babyngton: 237
Anthony, St: 230, 233
Antioch: 80
Antonelli, Roberto: 132
apRoberts, Robert P.: 199, 212
Arabella Stuart: 29, 30
Archibald Whitelaw: 131
Archibald, Earl of Moray: 32, 33
Archibald, Elizabeth: 295, 349
Aristotle: 202, 203, 209, 212
Arkinholme: 32
Arnaude: 371
Arthur, King: 293–308
Assisi, Basilica of St Francis: 58
Aston, Margaret: 171, 175, 389
Atkinson, Clarissa W.: 330, 334, 340, 377, 379, 380
Attreed, Lorraine: 387
Atwolf, King: 405
Aubrée: 370, 371
Aubry, P.: 401
Auchinleck Manuscript: *See* manuscripts: Edinburgh: National Library of Scotland: Advocates MS 19.2.1
Audrey Clere: 269

Augustine, St: 75, 174
Austria-Tyrol, Duke of: 19
Auxerre: 366
Auxerre, Bishop of: 366
Averroes: 202, 203
Avis Mone: 66
Avril, F.: 29
Aylsham: 262
Ayto, John: 395, 397
Backhouse, Janet: 21, 25
Baehrens, Æ.: 131
Bainbridge, Virgina R.: 71
Bala: 108
Baldwin, Archbishop of Treves: 305
Baldwin, John W.: 369
Baltzell, James H.: 401
Barasch, Moshe: 187
Barber, R.: 283, 290, 293, 307
Barking: 269, 400, 407
Barney, Stephen A.: 132
Barr, Helen: 51
Barratt, Alexandra: 58
Barron, Caroline M.: 379, 384
Barrow, G. W. S.: 27
Bartlett, Anne Clark: 294, 299
Basing, Patricia: 396
Bäumer, Remigius: 89
Bawcutt, Priscilla: 17, 23, 28, 30, 32
Beadle, Richard: 38, 53, 54, 56, 63, 175, 187
Beatrix, Prioress: 22
Beattie, William: 41
Beckwith, Sarah: 51, 59, 377, 378
Becon, Thomas: 25
Bedford, Duke of: 386, 389
Bell, David: 397, 407
Bell, Susan Gloag: 18, 221, 225, 232
Bennett, H. S.: 198
Bennett, Josephine Walters: 41
Benno: 401, 406
Benoît de Saint-Maure: 132, 134, 138–41, 143, 144, 200
Benskin, Michael: 396, 398
Benson, Larry D.: 94, 132, 162, 166, 285, 293, 295, 304, 308, 345
Benson, Robert G.: 186

Berkvam, Doris Desclais: 330, 340
Bernard of Clairvaux, St: 174, 182, 239, 246, 368
Bernard of Tilhol: 374
Bessinger Jr., Jess: 293
Betcher, Gloria: 277
Bettenson, Henry: 75
Beverley: 63, 386
Beverley Minster: 57
Bezzola, Reto R.: 140
Biddle, Martin: 327
Biller, Peter: 363, 365–67, 370–73
Binski, P.: 282
Bishop's Lynn: 52
Blackborough: 267
Blackburn (Lancs.): 223
Blackburn family: 220–22, 224, 230, 232–35
Blackburnshire: 223, 224
Blackie, E. M.: 47
Blades, William: 240
Blaise, St: 218, 224, 233
Blake, N. F.: 42
Blamires, Alcuin: 101
Blanchard, Joel: 154
Blanche Wake, Lady: 292
Blanche, Princess: 397
Blanche, wife of John of Gaunt: 292
Bloch, R. Howard: 216
Blokkesworth, Chaplain: 398
Blomefield, Francis: 260, 262, 264, 266, 267, 270, 271, 272
Blume, Clemens: 87, 95
Blunt, J. H.: 88
Boccaccio, Giovanni: 30, 101, 134, 143–146, 200–02, 211, 214, 355
Boffey, Julia: 33, 45, 72
Bokenham: See Osbern Bokenham
Bolton Hours: See manuscripts: York:Minster Library: MS Additional 2
Bolton, Brenda M.: 381
Bonaventure, St: 203, 204, 206, 207
Bonnardot, F.: 305
Bordeaux: 305, 374
Borgnet, August: 95

Boswell, John: 330
Botsford, Clarissa: 152
Bower, Walter: 22
Bowes Morrell House: 317–19, 321, 325, 326
Bowie, Malcolm: 332
Boyd, Beverley: 86
Braddy, Haldeen: 151
Bradley, E. T.: 29
Bradshaw,: 406
Bray, Jennifer R.: 57
Breadalbane, Earl of: 25
Bremmer, Jan: 186, 196
Brenon, Anne: 365, 371, 376
Bretons: 262
Brett, Martin: 373
Brian Sandford: 232
Brian Stapleton of Happisburgh (Hawesborough): 257
Bridget of Sweden, St: 59, 63, 65, 219, 222, 234–36, 384, 404
Bridlington: 52, 383
Bristol: 61, 386
Britain: 400
Britnell, R. H.: 263, 405
Brittany: 397
Brittany, Duke of: 19
Bromholm: 266, 267
Bromwich, Rachel: 104
Brooke, Christopher N. L.: 373
Brown, Andrew D.: 400, 404
Brown, Beatrice D.: 398
Brown, Carleton: 35, 83, 85–87, 98
Brown, E. A. R.: 281
Bruges: 246
Bruisyard: 267
Brundage, James A.: 117, 123, 125, 349, 350
Brunet, J.-C.: 40
Bruschi, Caterina: 376
Buchanan, P. H.: 21
Bühler, Curt F.: 237, 238, 239, 241, 242, 245, 247
Bungay: 265, 267, 269
Burden, Joel: 277

Burgh St Mary: 262
Burnley, David: 214, 215
Burnley, J. D.: 158
Butler, Judith: 343
Byles, A. T. P.: 238
Bynum, Caroline Walker: 92, 334, 337
Cadden, Joan: 334, 341
Cadwaladr y Prydydd: 108, 110–12
Caer-gai: 108, 109
Caesar of Heisterbach: 368
Caister: 259
Calin, William: 151
Cambridge: 267, 382
Cambridge, Earl of: 234
Cambridgeshire: 269
Campbell, Mary B.: 37
Campbell, P. G. C.: 238–
Canonsleigh, Devonshire: 395
Canterbury: 285, 291, 383, 385–87
Capgrave, John: 345–61
Carley, J.: 407
Carpenter, Christine: 173, 403
Carrow: 267, 269
Carsten, J.: 312
Cartwright, Jane: 107
Casagrande, Dominico: 84
Casson, L. F.: 187
Castle Bolton: 234
Catherine of Aragon: 22
Catherine of Siena, St: 22
Catherine Ruthven, Lady of Glenorchy:
    27
Catto, Jeremy: 382, 387, 389, 397, 400
Cawood: 386
Caxton: See William Caxton
Cazelles, Brigitte: 74
Chamberlayne, Joanna: 277, 283, 290
Champagne: 370
Chance, Jane: 145
Chandler, B.: 22
Chandos Herald: 287, 293, 296
Chaplais, P.: 285
Charlemagne: 293, 301
Charles V: 152–54
Charles VI: 153, 154
Charles, Earl of Lennox: 29

Charles, Prince: 288
Chaucer, Geoffrey: 33, 44, 94–98, 132,
    139, 142–47, 151–68, 199–216,
    242, 243, 248, 302, 345–61
Cheetham, Francis: 59
Cheney, C. R.: 53
Chénon, Émile: 366–68
Cherry Hinton (Cambs.): 235
Chesney, Kathleen: 43, 248
Chotzen, Theodore M.: 101, 108
Christian de Lindsay: 27, 28
Christian of Montmirail, Lady of
    Coucy: 27
Christina of Markyate: 359
Christine de Pizan: 73, 81, 82, 101,
    152, 153, 159, 209–12, 215, 237–
    49
Christopher, St: 233
Cicero: 247
Clarissa de Denby: 115
Clark, Linda: 252
Clay, J. W.: 80
Claydon: 266, 267, 270
Clément Marot: 28
Cleminson, Ralph: 30
Clere family: 255, 256, 260, 264, 270,
    271
Cockburn family: 34
Cockburn, H. A.: 25
Cockburn, Sir Robert: 25
Cohen, Elizabeth S.: 117
Cohen, Jeffrey Jerome: 338
Cokayne, George: 234, 235, 292
Collette, Carolyn P.: 288, 293
Collins, Francis: 224
Cologne: 36, 47, 368, 397
Connolly, Thomas: 162
Constable, Giles: 180
Constance de Skelmanthorpe: 115, 116
Constance of Castile, Duchess of
    Lancaster: 286
Constans, Léopold: 134, 139
Constantinople: 36, 367
Cookes: 262
Coopland, G. W.: 154
Copland: 47

Cornell, Henrik: 59
Cowan, I. B.: 18, 22
Crabhouse: 267
Craig, Barbara M.: 166
Craigie, J.: 29
Craigie, W. A.: 28
Crampton, Georgia Ronan: 94
Cranmer, Thomas, Archbishop of
    Canterbury: 25, 97
Crawford and Balcarres, Earl of: 27
Crawford, Anne: 251
Craymer, Suzanne: 59
Critall, Elizabeth: 394, 406
Cromwell, Oliver: 109
Cunningham, I. C.: 72, 131, 329
Cuthbert, St: 224, 232, 233
Cutler, John L.: 35
D'Evelyn, Charlotte: 400
Dafydd ap Gwilym: 101
Dafydd Llwyd o Fathafarn: 109
Danzig: 47
Dares: 134, 139, 140
Darnaway Castle in Morayshire: 32
David Aubert: 43
David II of Scotland: 25
David Lindsay, Sir: 20, 26, 34
David, Alfred: 94
Davidson, Clifford: 49, 53
Davies, Sioned: 110
Davis, J. Conway: 248
Davis, Norman: 80, 246, 251, 253–55,
    257–65, 272
Davis, Virgina: 384
de Bouteiller, E.: 305
de Pizan: See Christine de Pizan
Dean, James M.: 236, 394
Deansley, Margaret: 57
Deguileville: See Guillaume de
    Deguileville
Delany, Sheila: 379
Denise Clere, nee Witchingham: 256,
    260
Denny: 269
Denys, St: 400, 401, 407
Derbyshire: 187
Dervorguilla Balliol, Lady: 23, 27

Deschamps: 154
Devonshire: 395
Diamond, Arlyn: 185, 189, 329, 393
Dickman, Susan: 50
Dictys Cretensis: 139, 140
Diehl, Patrick S.: 87
Diekstra, F. N. M.: 172
Diller, Hans-Jürgen: 61
Dillon, Janette: 50, 378, 381
Dilworth, Mark: 23
Dinshaw, Carolyn: 200
Dobson, Barrie: 224
Dobson, R. B.: 53, 278, 279, 281, 282,
    285–88
Dominic, St: 219
Donaldson, E. Talbot: 138, 139
Donaldson, G.: 19
Donnelly, Mark: 69
Dorothy Clere: 269
Dorothy, St: 44
Dorrell, Margaret: 53
Dossat, Yves: 363
Douglas family: 32, 33
Dressoure, Chaplain: 398
Dreves, Guido M.: 83, 87, 91, 93, 95
Duby, Georges: 349
Duff, E. Gordon: 41
Duffy, Eamon: 39, 63, 79
Dunbar: See William Dunbar
Duncan Campbell, seventh Laird of
    Glenorchy, Sir: 27
Dunstan: 399
Durkan, John: 18, 20, 24, 34
Dutka, Joanna: 52
Dutton, Anne: 221
Duvernoy, Jean: 366, 367, 370, 371,
    373
Dyer, Christopher: 174
Eames, Penelope: 280
Easson, D. E.: 22
East Anglia: 247
East Somerton: 262, 263, 267
Easting, Robert: 404
Easton, Martha: 71
Eberly, Susan: 59
Eckbert of Schönau: 367

Edgar, King of Wessex: 394, 395, 399,
    400, 404
Edinburgh: 22, 25
Edith of Wilton: 393–409
Edmund Bedingfield of Oxburgh, Sir:
    265, 269
Edmund Clere of Caister: 256, 262
Edmund Clere of Horninghall: 259
Edmund Clere of Ormesby: 252, 261
Edmund Clere of Stokesby: 252, 256,
    259, 261, 262, 269
Edmund de la Pole: 230
Edmund of Stokesby: 252
Edmund Paston: 264
Edmund Rede of Boarstall, Sir: 45, 46
Edmund, St: 233
Edward Aetheling: 23
Edward I: 285
Edward I, Count of Bar: 305
Edward II: 25, 285
Edward III: 171, 281, 287, 292
Edward IV: 246, 290
Edward Stanley, Lord Monteagle: 80
Edward the Black Prince: 222, 287,
    290, 291, 293, 296, 307
Edward, St: 98
Edwards, A. S. G.: 33, 42, 72, 73
Edwards, Robert R.: 190
Egan, Geoff: 326
Egbert: 399
Eisenhut, W.: 139
Elcho: 34
Eleanor (d. 1480): 19
Eleanor, daughter of James I, Duchess
    of Austria-Tyrol: 30
Elen Engan: 114. See also Ellen Hughes
Elisabet Coton: 187, 197
Elisabet Frauncys: 187, 197
Elisha Pese, or Ellis Pusee: 395. See
    also Chaplain Pusee
Elizabeth Auchinleck: 22
Elizabeth Bedingfield, nee Clere: 269
Elizabeth Braunch: 256, 260, 272
Elizabeth Clere at Bungay: 269
Elizabeth Clere, nee Uvedale: 251–73
Elizabeth Danielstoun: 24

Elizabeth de Denby: 115
Elizabeth Dunbar: 32, 33
Elizabeth I: 29
Elizabeth II: 405
Elizabeth Melville, Lady Comrie: 26
Elizabeth Paston: 253, 264, 271
Elizabeth Uvedale: See Elizabeth Clere,
    nee Uvedale
Elizabeth Wauton: 122
Elizabeth, daughter of Margaret
    Hepburn: 33
Elizabeth, Duchess of Norfolk: 264
Elizabeth, Lady FitzHugh: 235
Elizabeth, mother of John the Baptist,
    St: 32, 58
Ellen Hughes, also Elen Engan: 112
Ellis, Roger: 59, 65, 404
Elsbeth von Katzenellenbogen, Herrin
    von Erlbach: 45
Ely, Bishop of: 292
Elyanor Guldeford: 187, 197
Emden, Alfred: 220
England: 20, 22, 24, 27, 34, 69, 169,
    225, 227, 239, 241, 247, 248, 280,
    281, 283, 288, 363, 373, 380, 385,
    386, 389, 390, 399, 400, 401
Enguerrand de Guines: 27
Erasmus, St: 44
Erler, Mary C.: 65, 172, 210, 384
Esmé Stewart of Aubigny: 26
Esther Inglis: 19, 25
Etheldreda of Ely: 395
Eupham Melvill: 26
Evans, Austin Patterson: 368, 369, 373
Evans, R. J.: 280
Evans, Ruth: 178, 399
Eversin of Steinfeld: 368, 372
Évrard de Béthune: 367
Famiglietti, R. C.: 281
Farmer, David Hugh: 57
Farmer, Sharon: 160
Federico, Sylvia: 277, 283
Fellows, Jennifer: 187, 188
Fenster, T. S.: 210
Ferdinand, King of the Romans: 21
Ferguson, F. S.: 35

Ferry IV, Duke of Lorraine: 305
Findern Manuscript: *See* manuscripts: Cambridge: University Library MS Ff. 1. 6
Finlayson, John: 293, 299
FitzHugh family: 234
Flaherty, W. E.: 283
Flanders: 366
Flandrin, Jean-Louis: 309
Fletcher, Alan J.: 170, 171
Fletcher, Robert H.: 295
Flixton: 265, 267
Foley, Michael: 294
Forncett: 268
Foss Bridge: 230
Foster, Frances: 54
Fox, Denton: 132
Foxe, John: 25, 26
Fradenburg, L. O.: 21
France: 24, 26, 34, 239, 241, 248, 281, 366, 397, 400, 401
Fredericq, Paul: 368
Freethorp: 262, 268
French, W. H.: 345
Frere, W. H.: 96
Freud, Sigmund: 332, 342
Fries, Maureen: 199
Frijhoff, Willem: 196
Froud, Nicolette N. Z.: 320
Fryde, E. B.: 283, 289
Furnivall, F. J.: 78, 348
Furnivall, Frederick J.: 190
Fyler, John M.: 37
Gaimster, David: 327
Galbraith, V. H.: 279
Galloway, David: 52
Galway, M.: 283, 290
Gameson, Richard: 23
Gardner, Arthur: 57
Gaunt, Simon: 70, 76
Gavin Douglas: 22, 27
Gee, Eric: 223
Geoffrey of Monmouth: 300
George Gordon, Master of Huntly: 32
Germany: 36, 373
Gervase of Tilbury: 369

Gibson, Gail McMurray: 49, 55, 59, 63, 64, 391
Giddens, Anthony: 312–14, 328
Gilberd, Chaplain: 398
Gilbert Hay, Sir: 27
Gilbert, Malcolm: 329
Gilchrist, Roberta: 186, 311, 314, 405
Giles, Katherine: 314, 325
Gillespie, J. L.: 286
Gilson, J.: 45
Giotto: 58
Girardot, Alain: 305
Girvan, R.: 18
Given-Wilson, C.: 280
Glasscoe, M.: 380, 383, 388
Goldberg, Jeremy: 217, 221, 227
Goldberg, P. J. P.: 118, 309, 321, 325
Göller, Karl Heinz: 294, 304
Goodich, Michael: 225
Goodman, Anthony: 52, 377, 379, 380
Goold, G. P.: 133–35, 138
Gordon, R. K.: 200
Goscelin of Canterbyury: 394
Gower: *See* John Gower
Granger, William: 89
Gravdal, Kathryn: 69, 70, 76, 118, 119, 347
Gray, Douglas: 38, 84, 95, 241, 243, 247
Gray, M. M.: 33
Great Moulton: 262
Green, Richard Firth: 171, 184
Greene, R. L.: 20, 39
Gregory: 174
Grew, Frances: 171
Griffe, Élie: 374
Griffin, N. E.: 200
Grigson, Geoffrey: 36
Grundmann, Herbert: 371
Guibert de Nogent: 368
Guido delle Colonne: 144, 200, 211, 213
Guillaume de Deguileville: 92, 94, 95, 96
Guillaume Prunel: 374
Gwerful Mechain: 102–09, 114

Habicht, Werner: 186
Haddington: 22
Hale, C. B.: 345
Hall, G. D. G.: 117
Hamel, Mary: 295, 301, 304
Hamilton, Bernard: 36, 366, 367, 371
Hanawalt, Barbara: 117, 190, 309, 350, 351
Hanna, Ralph, III: 46, 49, 170
Hansen, E. T.: 211, 215
Hansen, H. M.: 279, 283
Hansen, Inez: 140
Hansford, Margaret: 80
Hanson, Julienne: 316
Harding, Wendy: 65
Hardman, Phillipa: 72
Harley, Marta Powel: 404
Harries, Leslie: 102, 107
Harris, Kate: 187
Harris, Sylvia: 36
Harrison, Ellen: 365
Harry Fox: 271
Harthan, John: 25
Hartung, Albert E.: 39
Harvey, Barbara F.: 153
Harvey, I. M. W.: 283
Haskins, Charles Homer: 366
Hatcher, Elizabeth R.: 199
Hatcher, Jane: 224
Havely, N. R.: 98, 142, 143, 145, 201
Haycock, Marged: 102, 103, 105, 107
Hayden, Rosemary: 321
Hebron, Malcolm: 304
Hector Boece: 20
Hector, L. C.: 153
Heffernan, Thomas J.: 378, 381
Heinrich Steinhöwel: 30
Helen Maitland: 28
Helena, St: 36
Hellinga, Lotte: 198
Helmholz, Richard: 117, 119, 120, 121, 123, 125
Hengist: 399
Henisch, B. A.: 23, 30
Henry Balnaves: 25
Henry Bowet, Archbishop of York: 380,

386, 387, 390
Henry Chichele, Archbishop of Canterbury: 380, 383, 386, 406
Henry Crumpe, M.: 400
Henry de Bracton: 117, 128
Henry FitzHugh: 235
Henry II: 399, 405
Henry III: 281
Henry IV: 235, 397, 405
Henry Johnston: 223
Henry Knighton: 279, 285
Henry of Grosmont, Duke of Lancaster: 292
Henry V: 382, 394, 396–400, 405
Henry VI: 396
Henry VII: 21
Henry, Lord FitzHugh of Ravensworth: 235
Henry, Lord Scrope of Masham: 235
Henry, Lord Sinclair: 33
Henryson, Robert: See Robert Henryson
Hereford: 103
Hereford, diocese, Consistory Court: 103
Herlihy, David: 309
Hermann the German: 202, 203
Hewitt, G.: 25
Hexter, Ralph H.: 140, 141, 144
Hicks, Eric: 157
Higgins, Iain Macleod: 37
Hildegard of Bingen: 391
Hillier, Bill: 316
Hillyard, B.: 18
Hilpert, Hans-Eberhard: 373
Hilton: 57, 180
Hilton, R.: 289
Hirsch, John C.: 60, 378, 383
Hoccleve: See Thomas Hoccleve
Hodnett, Edward: 41, 42
Hofmann, Hans: 36
Holbrook, Sue Ellen: 60
Hollis, A. S.: 136
Holy Island: 263
Homer: 133
Hooper, John: 25
Hopkins, Andrea: 329, 338, 339, 343

Horn, Joyce M.: 395
Hornby: 80
Horstmann, C.: 72, 345, 394–96, 398, 405
Howard, Donald: 163
Howells, Nerys: 102
Howlett, Caroline: 69, 82
Hucking Church, Kent: 80
Hudson, Anne: 175, 366, 370, 377, 380
Huet, Marie-Hélène: 330
Hughes, Jonathan: 228, 234, 235, 382, 390
Hull: 61, 80
Humber: 386
Humphrey Stafford, Duke of Buckingham: 237, 246
Huneycutt, L. L.: 23
Hussey, Arthur: 80
Hutchison, Ann M.: 393, 407
Hutton, R.: 285
Huw Cadwaladr: 108
Ieuan Dyfi: 102–05, 107, 109, 111
Innes, Cosmo: 27
Innocent III: 368
Isabel Blackburn: 225, 232
Isabel Bolton: 225
Isabel, daughter of Charles VI: 153
Isabella, Duchess of Brittany: 19, 23, 29
Isidore of Seville: 203, 334
Isobel Melvill: 34
Italy: 248, 366
Iwi, St: 401
Jack Straw: 277
Jackson, R. A.: 281
Jackson, W. A.: 35
Jacobson, Howard: 134, 135
Jacobus de Voragine: 89
Jacques de Vitry: 381
James Compostella, St: 61
James I: 19, 30. See also James VI (of Scotland)
James II: 32
James III: 131
James IV: 19–21, 131
James Melvill: 26, 34
James Ryman: 39

James Stirling of Keir, Sir: 24
James V: 19, 20, 23
James VI: 19, 26, 29
James, Earl of Morton: 25
James, M. R.: 25, 40
James, Mervyn: 61
James, St: 233
Jane Carew: 251, 252
Jane Chisholm: 24
Jane Fychan: 108. See also Jane Vaughan
Jane Keir, Lady: 24
Jane Vaughan: 108–114
Jean de Berry: 238, 246
Jean de Doat: 363
Jean de Meung: 101
Jean Fleming, Lady: 31
Jean Froissart: 277, 279–87
Jean Hubert: 29
Jean Le Feron: 31
Jean Molinet: 248
Jean of Luxembourg, King of Bohemia: 305
Jean Trepperel: 40
Jean, daughter of Margaret Hepburn: 33
Jehanne de Chastillon: 155
Jenkins, Dafydd: 108
Jenkinson, Hilary: 401
Jerome, St: 23
Jerusalem: 59, 384, 385
Jesus College, Cambridge: 406
Jewel, John, Bishop of Salisbury: 25
Joan Beauchamp, Abbess of Wilton: 406
Joan Beaufort: 19
Joan Blackburn: 221, 222
Joan de Denby: 115
Joan Formage, Abbess of Shaftesbury: 398, 408
Joan of Kent, Princess of Wales: 277–92, 307, 397
Joan, daughter of Edward II: 25
Johannes de Caulibus: 182
John Alcock, Bishop: 42
John Audelay: 39
John Ball: 169, 277

John Balliol: 27
John Barly: 271
John Bedingfield: 269
John Blackburn: 223, 224
John Bolton: 221, 225, 236
John Boteller: 271
John Bradford: 25
John Brunham: 52
John Chandler, Bishop of Salisbury: 396, 397
John Clere of Ormesby: 252, 256, 260, 261
John Clere, Sir: 271
John Cockburn of Ormiston: 25
John Cok: 263
John de Denby: 115
John de Richmonde: 224
John de Rotherfield: 116, 117, 123, 125–27
John Erskine, seventh Earl of Mar: 26
John Fastolf, Sir: 237, 246–48
John Gower: 46, 248, 399
John Hales, Sir: 277, 284
John Heveningham of Ketteringham: 270
John Heydon: 257
John Holand: 289
John Hopton of Blythburgh: 264
John Kemp, Archbishop and Chancellor: 257
John Kendall: 263
John Knox: 25, 34
John Lacy: 218, 220
John Leg: 277
John Lippard of Norton: 103, 104
John Maitland of Thirlestane, Sir: 31
John Mandeville, Sir: 41
John Marion: 97
John Neville, Lord Latimer of Danby Castle: 234
John of Beverley, St: 218, 224
John of Bridlington, St: 57, 224
John of Gaunt: 184, 224, 281, 286, 288
John of Hildesheim: 36, 37, 40
John Orre, Friar: 220
John Paston I: 80, 251–55, 257, 259, 260, 272

John Paston II: 246, 254, 255
John Paston III: 254, 262, 264
John Pecham, Archbishop of Canterbury: 179
John Rothenhale, Sir: 261
John Shelton: 270
John Shirley: 46
John Siferwas: 220
John the Baptist, St: 230
John Thurstan: 271
John Thwaites: 187
John Tiptoft, Earl of Worcester: 247
John Waltham, Bishop of Salisbury: 394, 398
John Wyndham: 254
John, Lord Scrope of Upsal: 80
Johnson, Matthew: 314
Johnston, Alexandra F.: 53, 62
Johnston, Dafydd: 109
Jolliffe, P. G.: 45
Jones, Catherine: 305
Jones, Martin: 185
Jones, Michael K.: 20, 290
Jonson, Willis: 403
Jordana: 374
Julian of Norwich: 66, 384
Jung, Marc-René: 139
Justice, Steven: 175, 184, 283, 285
Kahrl, Stanley J.: 56
Kappeler, Susanne: 74, 78, 81
Kappler, Claude: 329, 330
Karras, Ruth Mazzo: 351
Katherine of Alexandria, St: 71, 230, 356
Katherine of Vadstena, St: 236
Katherine Southwell: 268, 271
Kay, Sarah: 329, 332
Kedar, B. Z.: 381
Keen, Maurice: 153
Keiser, George: 175
Kellner, Leon: 188
Kelly, H. A.: 214
Kempe, Margery: *See* Margery Kempe
Kent: 187, 285
Ker, Neil: 23, 24, 228
Kermode, Jenny: 232

Kern, Annette: 39
Kervyn de Lettenhove, J. B. M. C.: 278
Keswick: 262, 268
Kidston, G. J.: 404
King, Katherine Callen: 134
King, Pamela: 225
Kingsford, C. L.: 186
Kinsley, James: 83
Kirschbaum, Ewald: 93
Kriehn, G.: 279
Kroll, Wilhelm: 140
Krueger, Roberta L.: 71
Krynen, Jacques: 154
Kuhn, Sherman: 193
Kurath, Hans: 193
La Charité-sur-Loire: 365, 366, 368
La Riole: 286
Labande, Edmond-René: 368
Lacan, Jacques: 331, 332, 334–36, 339, 342
Lambert, Mark: 199
Lambeth Palace: 384
Lancaster: 380, 385, 389, 390, 394, 398
Langland: 169, 175, 184
Langley: 267
Langley Abbey: 405
Languedoc: 363–67, 372, 375
Larrington, Carolyne: 49, 50, 63
Laskaya, Anne: 346
Laslett, Peter: 309
Lattimore, Richmond: 133
Laurent de Premierfait: 247
Laurentin, René: 84
Lawlor, John: 203
Lawson, Alexander: 26
Layamon: 300
Lecoy de la Marche, Albert: 370
Lees, Rosemary A.: 390, 391
Leicester: 286, 386, 389, 390
Leicester, Abbot and Dean of: 386
Leicester, mayor of: 386
Lennox, Duke of: 26
Leo VI, King of Armenia: 153
Leominster, Deanery of: 103
Leonard, St: 224, 233
Leroquais, V.: 20

Letts, Malcolm: 41, 186
Lewis, C. S.: 199, 200, 202, 204, 208, 209, 214
Lewis, Henry: 104
Lewis, Katherine J.: 73, 119
Lewis, R. E.: 42, 193
Liddy, Lisa: 115
Liebermann, Felix: 374
Liebman, Charles J.: 401
Lifshitz, Felice: 408
Lincoln: 386
Lincoln Cathedral: 57
Lincolnshire: 291
Lindsay, Lord: 27
Linz, Daniel: 70
Llanuwchllyn: 108
Lloyd, John Edward: 108
Lloyd-Morgan, Ceridwen: 102, 112
Lochrie, Karma: 50, 378, 388, 391
Locock, Martin: 312
Lodge, E. C.: 287
Lombardy: 374, 375, 376
London: 45, 234, 247, 255, 264, 277, 281, 285, 286, 306, 326, 373, 386, 387, 397
Long Stratton: 265
Lorraine: 305
Loserth, J.: 183
Löseth, E.: 339
Louis of France, St: 401
Louis XI: 19
Louis, Cameron: 40
Love: See Nicholas Love
Low Countries: 39, 366, 373
Lucca: 225, 227
Lumiansky, R. M.: 38, 134, 144
Lyall, R. J.: 19, 27, 131
Lydgate, John: 27, 40, 69, 72, 101, 144, 248, 398, 399
Lyle, William: 27
Lynch, Kathryn L.: 37
Lynch, Michael: 18, 25
Lynn: 61, 222, 379, 386, 387
MacCormack, Carol: 332
MacCracken, Henry Noble: 39, 46, 69, 72

MacDonald, A. A.: 18, 20
Machaut: 151
Machiavelli: 29
MacLehose, William F.: 330
Macmahon, K. A.: 57
Maddern, Philippa C.: 119
Maidment, James: 22
Maitland family: 28, 34
Maitland Quarto: 28
Maitland, Sir Richard: 22
Major, J. Russell: 196
Malamuth, Neil: 70
Malcolm III: 23
Malory: *See* Thomas Malory, Sir
Manly, J. M.: 44
Mann, Jill: 43, 212, 284
Mann, N.: 31
Mantova: 248
manuscripts
  Aberystwyth
    National Library of Wales
      MS 17520: 218
      MS Brogyntyn I.3: 109
      MS Cwrtmawr 128: 110
      MS Cwrtmawr 204: 112
      MS Cwrtmawr 204B: 110, 111
      MS Peniarth 125: 109
      MS Peniarth 239: 112
      MS Peniarth 239B: 112
  Alnwick
    MS 498: 21
  Bangor
    University of Wales
      MS Bangor 421: 109
  Basle
    University Library
      MS 58: 45
  Berlin
    Staatsbibliothek Preussischer
      Kulturbesitz
        cod. theol. lat. 565: 37
  Boston
    Public Library
      MS f. Med. 94: 27
  Boulogne-sur-Mer
    Bibliothèque Municipale

      MS 93: 218, 219, 230
Brandenburg, MS I, 1. 176: 37. *See*
  manuscripts: Berlin:
  Staatsbibliothek Preussischer
  Kulturbesitz: cod. theol. lat. 565
Cambridge
  Fitzwilliam Museum
    MS 62: 23
  Magdalene College
    Pepys Library, MS 1408: 28
    Pepys Library, MS 2006: 41
  St John's College
    MS 129: 218, 224
  Trinity College
    MS O.3.10: 218, 219
    MS O.5.2: 187
    MS R.5.43: 41
    MS R.15.21: 219
  University Library
    MS Additional MS 43: 40
    MS Ee. 4. 32: 36, 41
    MS Ff. 1. 6 (the 'Findern
      Manuscript'): 187
    MS Ff. 3. 11: 187
    MS Kk. 1. 3: 40
Cambridge, MA
  Harvard
    MS Eng. 530: 41
Edinburgh
  National Library of Scotland
    Advocates MS 18.4.8: 131
    Advocates MS 19.2.1
      (Auchinleck Manuscript):
      72, 329
    Bdg.S.53: 24
    Blairs College, Dep. 221/1: 24
    Blairs College, H.14.10: 24
    Fort Augustus Abbey, Acc.
      11218/7: 23
    MS 10,000: 22
    MS 16,499: 22
    MS 21,000: 24
  University Library, De.3.70: 28
  University Library, De.10.1: 31
  University Library, MS 150: 22
Lincoln

Cathedral
  MS 91: 39, 42
London
  British Library
    MS Additional 15005: 112
    MS Additional 22283 (Simeon
      Manuscript): 329
    MS Additional 25693: 21
    MS Additional 30897: 170,
      175
    MS Additional 36983: 44
    MS Additional 42555: 25
    MS Additional 54782
      (Hastings Hours): 220
    MS Cotton Faustina B.iii: 395
    MS Cotton Vespasian D.viii:
      56
    MS Cotton Vespasian E.xvi:
      45
    MS Egerton 826: 170, 174,
      175
    MS Harley 838: 237
    MS Harley 1704: 41, 43
    MS Harley 2250: 88
    MS Harley 5642: 29
    MS Royal 2 A.xvii: 218
    MS Royal 14 E.ii: 246
    MS Royal 17 B.xliii: 329
    MS Royal 18 A.x: 36, 45
    MS Stowe 951: 46
    MS Yates Thompson 13: 25,
      219
  Lambeth Palace
    MS 72: 40
    MS 491: 37
Longleat
  MS 253: 238, 241, 246, 247
New York
  Pierpont Morgan Library
    MS M. 105: 224
Oxford
  Bodleian Library
    MS Arch. Selden. B. 24: 33
    MS Ashmole 59: 46
    MS Ashmole 61: 72, 78, 79,
      80, 81

MS Bodley 416: 170, 177
MS Bodley 581: 219
MS Douce 301: 40
MS Douce 365: 43
MS Eng. poet. a.1 (Vernon
  Manuscript): 43, 329
MS Fairfax 5: 23
MS Lat. liturg. f.2: 218, 230
MS Lat. liturg. f.5: 23
MS Laud misc. 210: 42, 169,
  170, 175, 177, 179
MS Laud misc. 658: 40, 41
MS Laud misc. 749: 40
MS Rawlinson G.23: 404
Keble College
  MS 47: 222
St John's College
  MS 94: 218, 220
Paris
  Bibliothèque Nationale
    MS Collection Doat 21: 376
    MS Collection Doat 23: 376
    MS Collection Doat 25: 363,
      364, 371, 375
    MS Collection Doat 26: 376
    MS fr. 1175: 155
    MS lat. 1369: 23
    MS lat. 1390: 20
    MS lat. N. A. 588: 23
Rennes
  Bibliothèque Municipale
    MS 22: 218
Stonyhurst College
  MS B. 23: 41
Toulouse
  Bibliothèque Municipale
    MS 609: 364, 376
Vienna
  Austrian National Library
    MS lat. 1897: 21
York
  Borthwick Institute of Historical
    Research
    Archbishops Register 12
      (1383): 116
    CP E 62 (1348): 115

Minster Library
   MS Additional 2 (Bolton
      Hours): 217, 226, 229
   MS Additional 67: 218
Manzalaoui, M. A.: 46
Mapstone, Sally: 23, 25
Marchaunt, Chaplain: 398
Margaret (d. 1445): 19, 21
Margaret Bate: 80
Margaret Beaufort, Lady: 20, 34, 188,
   290
Margaret Blackburn, nee Ormeshead:
   217–36
Margaret Hansford: 80
Margaret Hepburn: 33
Margaret of Anjou, Queen: 251
Margaret of Antioch, St: 69–82
Margaret of Burgundy: 43
Margaret of Scotland, Queen: 23
Margaret of Scotland, St: 24
Margaret Ottryngton: 220
Margaret Paston, nee Mautby: 80, 251,
   252, 254, 255, 259, 260, 262, 264,
   265, 271–73
Margaret Shelton, nee Clere: 256, 261,
   263, 265, 270, 271
Margaret Tudor: 19, 20–22, 20, 29
Margaret Uvedale, nee Rees: 256, 265,
   267, 272
Margaret, St: 233
Margareta Moningtown: 45
Marged ferch Ifan: 110
Margery Baxter: 66
Margery Harneys: 270, 271
Margery Kempe: 42, 47, 49–67, 359,
   377–91, 403
Margeson, Sue: 327
Margolis, Nadia: 151
Marham: 267
Marie d'Oignies: 63, 381
Marie Maitland: 28
Marie, Countess of Mar: 26, 31
Marie, Countess of St Pol: 401
Marion Scott: 24
Marion, daughter of the second Lord
   Lyle: 27

Marione Crafurde: 23
Marjorie Roger: 25
Marshall, John: 56
Marshall, P. K.: 131, 140
Marshall, R.: 28
Martin, G. H.: 279
Martin, St: 224, 230
Mary Cleophas: 229, 230
Mary Gray: 24
Mary Lyncolne: 271
Mary of Burgundy: 18
Mary of Guise: 19, 21, 23, 31
Mary Queen of Scots: 18–21
Mary Salome: 229, 230
Mary White at Carrow: 269, 270
Mary, daughter of Henry VII: 21
Matthews, William: 294, 304
Maud de Clare, Countess of Gloucester:
   395
Maud Stranslea: 45
Maud, Countess of Cambridge: 234
Mautby: 260
Mautby family: 260
McCarthy, Adrian James: 170, 171, 174
McCoy, Dorothy S.: 339
McDonnell, Ernest W.: 381
McFarlane, K. B.: 248
McGregor, Margaret: 80
McIntosh, Mary: 70
McLaughlin, Megan: 347
McMunn, Meradith: 27
McNiven, Peter: 218, 233, 234
McRee, Benjamin R.: 61
McRoberts, D.: 19–25
Meale, Carol M.: 19, 33, 35, 72, 73,
   187–89, 197, 235, 391
Meech, Sanford Brown: 50, 52, 53, 82,
   222, 359
Meek, Mary E.: 200
Meikle, H. W.: 29
Meister, Ferdinand: 133
Menuge, Noël James: 119
Menziter, Chaplain: 398
Meredith, Peter: 50, 56, 66
Merionethshire: 105, 108
Mernissi, Fatima: 185, 186

Metz: 301, 304, 305, 306
Michael, St: 44, 225, 232, 233
Micklegate: 220, 221, 224
Middlesex: 394, 397
Middleton, Anne: 155
Midlands: 169, 170, 171
Mieszkowski, Gretchen: 142, 200
Milan: 36
Miles, Margaret M.: 73
Mill, Anna J.: 400
Miller, Jacques-Alain: 331
Millett, Bella: 69
Millinger, Susan J.: 407
Mills, David: 38
Mills, Maldwyn: 187, 188, 329
Mills, Robert: 69, 70
Minnis, A. J.: 96, 202, 203, 211, 213
Mirk: 38, 42
Molinier, Charles: 363
Mombello, Gianni: 237
Mone, F. J.: 87, 95
Monro, Cecil: 252
Mont-Aimé: 370
Montgomerie Manuscript: *See*
    manuscripts: Edinburgh University
    Library, De.3.70
Montgomeryshire: 105
Moon, Helen M.: 170
Morgan, Nigel: 22, 218
Morse, Charlotte C.: 96
Moulton: 270
Mount Grace: 382, 390
Muir, W.: 33
Mundy, John Hine: 376
Murphy, J. P.: 329
Murray, A. T.: 133
Muscatine, Charles: 151
Navarrete: 307
Neergaard, Margrethe de: 171
Nelson, Alan H.: 52
Newcastle under Lyme: 218, 220
Newcastle-upon-Tyne: 254
Newman, Barbara: 333, 403
Newton: 260
Newton, Peter: 218
Nicholas Blackburn: 220, 222–25, 230,

234, 236
Nicholas Blackburn junior: 224
Nicholas Bonham: 404
Nicholas Carew, Sir: 251
Nicholas Love: 38, 54–56, 59, 60, 407
Nicholas Trevet: 203
Nicholas Waterford: 220, 228
Nicholas Wattre, Friar: 220
Nicholas, J. G.: 248
Nichols, J.: 282, 292
Nichols, N. H.: 81
Nicholson, R.: 19
Ninian, St: 218
Nolan, Barbara: 140, 141, 144, 201,
    213
Noonan, J. T.: 124
Norfolk: 40, 66, 187, 251, 252, 257,
    259–63, 265, 266–70
North Street, York: 221
Northumberland: 234
Northumberland, Duke of: 21
Northumberland, Earl of: 311
Norton, Parish of: 103
Norwich: 52, 59, 251, 254, 257, 262,
    266–68, 270, 272, 273, 384–86
Norwich cathedral: 266, 272
Norwich, Bishop of: 385
Offord, M. Y.: 188
Ogden, M. S.: 39
Olibrius: 75–78, 81
Oliva, Marilyn: 406
Oman, Charles: 95
Orkneys: 30
Orme, Nicholas: 117, 172, 186
Ormesby: 258–68, 271, 272
Ormrod, W. M.: 280
Osbern Bokenham: 72, 77, 79, 81, 398
Ovid: 132–47, 201
Owen, A. E. B.: 187
Owen, Morfydd: 108
Paccagnini, G.: 248
Page, William: 220
Palmer, J. J. N.: 286, 287
Palmer, W. M.: 283
Pantzer, Katherine: 35
Paris: 400

Parks, George: 305
Parsons, John Carmi: 277, 282, 285, 288, 290, 292
Pas de Calais: 27
Paston: 261
Pastons: 254, 255, 264
Patrick Cockburn of Clerkington: 24
Patterson, Lee: 145, 215, 302, 304
Paues, Anna: 183
Pauli, Reinhold: 374
Pearsall, Derek: 43, 72, 188, 279, 329, 336
Pearson, Michael Parker: 312
Peirona: 371
Pembroke, Countess of: 31
Penketh, S.: 18
Perry, G. G.: 42
Perryman, Judith: 329, 336
Perthshire: 25
Peter Houston: 27
Peter Lombard: 204
Peter Mancroft, St: 59
Peter of Cambrai: 345–61
Peter of Milan, otherwise Peter Martyr: 219
Peter the Chanter: 369
Petit, Aimé: 139, 140
Petrarch: 29, 31, 351, 352
Petroff, Elizabeth: 151
Petronius: 202
Pfaff, Richard: 234
Philip Braunch: 260
Philip Repingdon, Bishop of Lincoln: 379, 384–87, 390
Philip Sidney, Sir: 31
Philippa, Princess: 235
Philippa, Queen: 290
Philippe de Mézières: 151–68
Phillips, Helen: 94, 95, 98
Phillips, Kim M.: 119, 125, 186
Picherit, Jean-Louis G.: 152
Pierre de Craon: 155
Piper, A. J.: 175
Pisanello: 248
Pitcairn, R.: 26
Poirion, Daniel: 155

Pollard, A. W.: 35
Pons Fogacier of Toulouse: 364
Pons of Parnac: 363
Pontefract: 286
Poole, R. L.: 183
Pope, M. K.: 287
Powell, E.: 289
Prescott, A. J.: 281, 284, 287
Pugh, R. B.: 394
Pujmanová, Olga: 38
Purves, J.: 29
Pusee, Chaplain: 398. *See* also Elisha Pese
Pynkaunt, Chaplain: 398
Queen Philippa: 287
Quilligan, Maureen: 74
Quixley: 46
Raby, F. J. E.: 95
Radegund, Abbess of Poitiers, St: 406
Radnor: 103
Radnorshire: 103, 105
Raine, J.: 80, 234
Rainthorp Hall: 260
Ralph of Coggeshall: 369, 374
Ralph Shelton esquire of Shelton: 265, 270
Ralph Shelton, Sir: 256, 262, 268, 270, 271
Ranulf, Bishop of Durham: 359
Rapoport, Amos: 315, 316, 326, 327
Rastall, Richard: 50, 58
Rawcliffe, Carole: 252
Raymo, Robert: 293
Raymond Frugon: 363, 374, 376
Reames, Sherry: 151, 160, 161
Redgrave, G. R.: 35
Redlingfield: 267
Rees Jones, Sarah: 233
Reinburg, Virginia: 401
Renfrewshire: 27
Renous de Plassac: 363
Revell, Peter: 45
Reynaud, N.: 29
Reynthorp: 262
Rheims: 369
Rhineland: 366

Rhys Goch Eryri: 104
Richard de Helay: 116
Richard Duke of York: 39
Richard Holland: 32, 33
Richard II: 98, 277, 280, 286–89, 292, 397, 405
Richard Maitland of Lethington, Sir: 28
Richard of St Laurent: 96
Richard Plantagenet: 234
Richard Rolle: 57, 178, 228, 234
Richard Russell: 230
Richard Scrope, Archbishop of York: 217–20, 225, 230, 232–35
Richard Scrope, Archbishop of York, Archbishop of York: 232, 235
Richard Shelton: 270
Richard Southwell, Sir: 262, 268, 271, 272
Richard Thwaite: 197
Richard Wells of Scratby: 259
Richard, Duke of York: 266
Richards, Clive: 312
Richards, W. Leslie: 109
Richmond: 223, 224, 233, 235
Richmond castle: 235
Richmond, Colin: 254, 265
Richmondshire: 233, 234, 235
Rickert, Edith: 44
Ricoeur, Paul: 86
Riddy, Felicity: 28, 32, 33, 35, 67, 84, 115, 142, 152, 169, 189, 197, 198, 223, 228, 273, 294, 307, 330, 347, 393, 409
Ridley, Jasper: 25, 34
Rigg, A. G.: 95
Riley, H. T.: 278
Rivers, Earl: 240
Rivers, Earl Jeffrey: 74
Robbins, Rossell Hope: 35, 187
Robert Bolton: 221
Robert Bruce: 32
Robert Clere of Ormesby: 251, 252, 254, 256, 260, 261, 263, 266, 267, 272
Robert Clere of Ormesby, Sir: 255, 256, 261–64, 269–71

Robert Clere of Stokesby: 252, 256
Robert Hallum, Bishop of Salisbury: 395, 397
Robert Henryson: 131, 132, 143, 147
Robert Holcot: 202
Robert Langton: 47
Robert Lyle: 27
Robert Mannyng: 348, 399
Robert Peyton of Isleham, Sir: 269
Robert Reynes of Acle: 40
Robert Stevenson, parson of Tacolneston: 266, 267, 271
Robert Thornton: 39, 42
Robert Wyer: 237
Roberts, Anna: 346
Roberts, Brynley F.: 104, 110
Roberts, Thomas: 104, 110
Robertson, D. W.: 208, 209
Robinson, J. W.: 53
Robinson, P.: 20
Robson, Margaret: 338, 346, 359
Rocamadour: 405
Roger Hayles: 266
Rogers, Charles: 25
Rogers, William E.: 94, 96
Rolle, Richard: See Richard Rolle
Rome: 64, 236, 384–87
Roodenburg, Herman: 187, 196
Roquevidal: 363, 374–76
Rosenthal, Joel: 396
Roskell, J. S.: 252
Ross, Anthony: 18, 24
Ross, Robert C.: 60, 378
Rowland Vaughan of Caer-gai: 108, 109
Rubin, Miri: 382, 387
Ruggieri, R. M.: 248
Russell, Diana E. H.: 70
Russell, J.: 24
Rusteyns: 260, 262
Salih, Sarah: 69, 73, 77
Salisbury: 373, 394, 397, 400, 404
Salter, Elizabeth: 77
Salter, H. E.: 45
Samson, Ross: 312
Sanders, Donald: 312

Sanderson, M. B.: 24
Santiago: 386
Sappho: 28
Sargent, Michael G.: 54–56, 182
Saul, Nigel: 174, 279, 289, 291
Savage, Anne: 355, 356
Scase, Wendy: 231, 232
Schaer, Frank: 37
Scheffczyk, Leo: 89
Schibanoff, Susan: 37
Schmitt, Jean-Claude: 186, 191
Scotland: 17–34, 131
Scott, A. B.: 202, 203
Scott, Kathleen L.: 41, 194, 218, 219,
    221, 222, 228
Scott, Margaret: 219
Scrope family of Masham: 234
Segal, Lynne: 70
Seneca: 203
Senis besyde Edinburgh: 23
Sens, Archbishop of: 365
Serjeantson, Mary S.: 72, 81
Seton, Lady: 22
Severs, J. Burke: 39
Seymour, M. C.: 41
Shaftesbury: 398
Shakespeare, William: 143, 216
Shambles, The: 315, 321–25
Sharman, Julian: 18
Sharpe, Charles K.: 26
Sharpe, Richard: 400, 407
Shaw, Patrick: 224
Sheehan, M. M.: 123, 125
Sheen: 382, 390, 396
Sheingorn, Pamela: 62
Shelton: 265
Sherborne, J. W.: 286
Sheridan, Alan: 331
Shouldham: 267
Shrewsbury, Earl of: 29
Shupton, Chaplain: 398
Silvana Vecchio: 152
Simeon Manuscript: *See* manuscripts:
    London: British Library: MS
    Additional 22283
Simmons, Thomas F.: 96

Simon Sudbury, Archbishop of
    Canterbury: 277, 284
Simpson, James: 249
Sire de Coucy: 27
Sitha, St: 220–36
Skeeters, Martha C.: 61
Sleidan: 27
Smeltz, John W.: 350
Smith, Chaplain: 398
Smith, Lesley: 221
Smith, Llinos Beverley: 102–04
Smith, Lucy Toulmin: 71, 72
Smith, Richard: 227
Smith, Sidonie: 118
Smithfield: 282, 286
Soissons: 367
Southern, Richard: 309
Spector, Stephen: 58, 66
St Benet's at Holm: 266, 267
St John Parish at Ouse Bridge End: 221
St Mary in the Fields, Chapel of the
    College of: 267
St Mary, College of: 267
St Mary's, York: 81
Staley, Lynn: 50, 65, 82, 183, 359, 377–
    82, 386–90
Stamford: 292
Stapleton family of Bedale: 234
Stell, G.: 23
Stephen of Bourbon: 370, 371
Stephen Scrope: 237–39, 241, 246–48,
    253
Stevenson, Joseph: 369
Stewardson family: 257–59
Stewart, A. M.: 30, 31
Stewart, Marion: 32
Stewarts, Lords of Lorne: 24
Stonyhurst manuscript: *See*
    manuscripts: Stonyhurst College:
    MS B. 23
Storey, R.: 282
Storey, R. L.: 389
Strachey, James: 332
Strange, Joseph: 368
Strathern, Marilyn: 332
Stratton Strawless: 262, 267

Strohm, Paul: 98, 117, 118, 122, 282, 283, 285, 288, 290, 307, 403, 405
Strong, Felicity: 397
Strong, Patrick: 397
Stürzinger, J. J.: 92, 94, 95
Suffolk: 261, 262, 264, 266, 268, 289
Sutcliffe, Sebastian: 222, 225, 234
Sutton, Anne F.: 39
Swanson, Heather C.: 325
Swanson, R. N.: 85, 382, 386, 388, 389
Sweden: 236
Sweden, King of: 235
Sweeney, Del: 174
Sweetheart Abbey: 23
Syon Abbey: 219, 235, 382, 387, 390, 394, 397, 407
Tacolneston: 260, 262, 265, 267, 268, 270
Takamiya, Toshiyuki: 57
Talbot, C. H.: 359, 394
Tanner, Laura E.: 74
Tasburgh: 268
Tate, Robert Brian: 47
Taylor, Andrew: 178, 399
Taylor, Jane: 221
Taymouth Castle: 25
Thames: 326, 386
Tharston: 260, 262, 265–70
Theobald: 370
Thetford: 267
Thomas Anglicus of Gaja-la-Selve: 364
Thomas Aquinas, St: 200, 204–07, 338
Thomas Arundel, Archbishop of Canterbury: 55, 359, 380, 382–84
Thomas Becket, St, Archbishop of Canterbury: 405
Thomas Blakburn: 224
Thomas Brews, Sir: 265
Thomas Burgh: 72
Thomas Burneby: 252
Thomas Dennis: 257
Thomas Green: 258, 259
Thomas Hoccleve: 40, 210
Thomas Malory, Sir: 295
Thomas Marke, Archdeacon of Norfolk: 265

Thomas of Acon, St: 234
Thomas Peverel, Bishop of Worcester: 380, 386
Thomas Rotherham, Archbishop of York: 80
Thomas Rychers of Somerton: 262
Thomas Sampson: 289
Thomas Scauceby: 221
Thomas the Englishman: 364
Thomas Uvedale: 256, 267
Thomas Vautrollier: 25
Thomas Walsingham: 277–86
Thomas Warde of Westminster: 257
Thomas Wimbledon: 41
Thomas, Lord Scales: 259
Thomas, Lord Wake: 292
Thomasin Hopton: 265
Thompson, J. B.: 312
Thompson, John J.: 72
Thomson, John A. F.: 385
Thomson, R.: 407
Thurston, Carol: 74
Timmins, T. C. B.: 394, 396, 397
Toft Green: 220
Toulousain: 364
Toulouse: 363, 374, 375
Tower of London: 277–91
Toynbee, M. R.: 23, 29
Trier: 401, 408
Tringham, Ruth E.: 312
Tristram, E. W.: 71
Tuck, J. A.: 289
Turville-Petre, Thorlac: 47, 96, 225
Tuve, Rosemond: 239, 240, 245
Twycross, Meg: 50, 66
Tyndale, William: 25
Tynemouth: 393
Underwood, M. G.: 290
Unterkircher, Franz: 21
Usk, Adam: 304
Uvedale family: 256, 259, 260, 270
Vadstena: 235
Vaux Hall: 262
Verducci, Florence: 136, 137
Vernon Manuscript: See manuscripts: Oxford: Bodleian Library: MS Eng.

poet. a.1
Villemur: 371
Vinaver, Eugene: 285
Virgoe, Norma: 259, 266
Virgoe, Roger: 254, 262, 263, 266, 271, 272
Voaden, Rosalynn: 185
Wace: 300
Wakefield, Walter L.: 368, 369, 373
Walker, Sue Sheridan: 117
Wall, Richard: 309
Walmgate: 317, 321
Walter Balle: 267
Walter del Brome: 115
Walter Hilton: 228, 234
Walter Map: 101
Ward, H. L. D.: 46
Warner, G.: 45
Warner, G. F.: 19
Warner, Marina: 69, 89
Waryn Herman: 258
Wasson, John: 52
Wat Tyler: 277, 282, 286
Watson, A. G.: 407
Watson, Nicholas: 57, 172, 178, 355, 356, 399, 407, 409
Webster, M.: 172
Wedgwood, J. C.: 252
Weissman, H. P.: 378
Wenham, Peter: 224, 233
Wentersdorf, K. P.: 291
Wenzel, Siegfried: 348
Wessex: 396
Westlake, H. F.: 63, 71, 72
Westminster: 279, 280, 282, 291, 405
Westminster Abbey: 98
Westminster Palace: 281
Westminster, Monk of: 279
Westover, Jeff: 294
Wetherbee, Winthrop: 145
Wheatley, Henry B.: 187
Whitehead, Christiania: 43
Whitelock, Dorothy: 373
Wickham, Glynne: 38
Wilkins, E. H.: 134
Wilkinson, B.: 279

Willard, Charity Cannon: 157
Willelmus Anglicus of Montesquieu: 364
William Alexander: 31
William Barly: 271
William Bondes: 261
William Bosevill: 117, 124, 125, 128
William Calthorpe, Sir: 264
William Caxton: 40, 47, 188, 197, 198, 238, 240, 247
William Chisholm, Bishop of Dunblane: 24
William Clere: 260, 261, 264, 265, 270, 271
William Clifford: 234
William de Hopton: 115, 116, 120, 122–28
William de Lindsay, Lord of Lamberton: 27
William de Thorpe: 220
William Drummond of Hawthornden: 18
William Dunbar: 17–18, 20, 31, 33, 83
William Elphinstone: 18
William Flete: 179
William Fowler: 29, 31
William Gunwarby, Bishop of Dunkeld: 80
William Hopton, Sir: 262, 264
William Jenny: 257
William Lychfield: 44
William of Aragon: 211
William of Nassington: 46
William of Newburgh: 363, 373, 375, 376
William of York, St: 218
William Paston I: 254, 261, 272
William Paston II: 255
William Paston III: 255
William Paston IV: 264
William Rees: 267
William Revetour: 225
William Seymour: 29
William Stewardson I: 257–59
William Stewardson II: 257, 258
William Stewart: 20

William the Englishman: 364
William White: 257, 262, 269
William Witchingham of Witchingham, Sir: 260
William Worcester: 254
William Worcestre: 247, 248
William, Archbishop of York, St: 57, 218, 233
William, smith of Lavaur: 364
Williams, Anne: 74
Williams, David: 329
Williams, Franklin B.: 30
Williams, Glanmor: 104, 108
Williams, Ifor: 104, 108
Williamson, Joan B.: 153, 155, 156, 160
Wilmart, André: 366, 394
Wilsnak: 387
Wilson, C.: 285, 291
Wilson, Janet: 379
Wilton: 393–409
Wiltshire: 398
Wimsatt, James I.: 151
Winchester: 400, 404
Windeatt, Barry A.: 139, 140, 145, 146, 186, 200, 378, 379
Winstead, Karen A.: 70, 72, 73
Winterton: 262, 263, 267
Wissowa, Georg: 133

Wogan-Browne, Jocelyn: 178, 277, 293, 399, 407
Wolfe, Michael: 306
Wolpers, Theodor: 84
Wood Rising: 268
Wood, Diane: 363
Woodcock, Alex: 314
Woodforde, Christopher: 59
Woolf, Rosemary: 84, 85, 87, 99
Wright, Joseph: 173
Wright, M. J.: 379
Wright, W. Aldis: 188, 398
Wultrud: 394, 395, 399, 401, 403–05, 408
Wyclif, John: 169, 171, 174, 175, 183, 184, 289
Wymondham: 260, 262
Wynkyn de Worde: 40–42, 46
Yarmouth: 266, 268
Yeo, Elspeth D.: 17, 24, 26
York: 51, 52–57, 63, 81, 82, 116, 217–36, 309–28, 373, 383, 386, 387
York Minster: 222, 233
Yorkshire: 115, 218, 376, 395
Young, Karl: 62
Ziegler, Vickie: 190
Zita: See Sitha, St
Zupitza, Julius: 195

Tabula Gratulatoria

Peter V. Addyman
Judith Aldridge
Flora Alexander
Rosamund Allen
Richard Almond
Malcolm Andrew
Elizabeth Archibald
John H. Arnold
Virginia R. Bainbridge
Anthony Bale
Alexandra Barratt
Caroline M. Barron
Priscilla Bawcutt
Cordelia Beattie
Peter Biller
Alcuin Blamires
Julia Boffey
Kari Elisabeth Børresen
Joel Burden
James P. Carley
Charlotte Carpenter
Michael Clanchy
Helen Cooper
Carolyn Collette
Peter Coss
Claire Cross
David J.F. Crouch
Patricia Cullum
Sioned Davies
Isabel Davis
Enrica de Domínquez
Vincent DiMarco
Arlyn Diamond
Barrie Dobson
A.I. Doyle
Fiona Dunlop

Richard Eales
Mary Erler
Ruth Evans
Ken Farnhill
Rosalind Field
Simon Forde
Mary Garrison
Simon Gaunt
Jane Gilbert
Jeremy Goldberg
Douglas Gray
Jane Grenville
C.A. Grisé
Linda Tollerton Hall
Antonina Harbus
Philippa Hardman
Paul Hardwick
Louise Harrison
Nick Havely
Judith Herrin
Terry Hoad
Karen Hodder
Matthew Holford
Mari Hughes-Edwards
Chris Humphrey
Ann M. Hutchison
Ronnie Jack
Jacqueline Jenkins
Eric Johnson
Lesley Johnson
Elspeth Kennedy
Katherine Kerby-Fulton
Annette Kern-Stähler
Ann Kettle
Pamela King
Erik Kooper

Maryanne Kowaleski
Carolyne Larrington
Joanna L. Laynesmith
Hermione Lee
Katherine Lewis
Amanda Lillie
Ceridwen Lloyd-Morgan
Lara S. McClure
Alasdair A. MacDonald
Sally Mapstone
Carol Meale
Noël James Menuge
Paule Mertens-Fonck
Alastair Minnis
Philip Morgan
Anneke Mulder-Bakker
Saara Nevanlinna
Debbie O'Brien
Bernard O'Donoghue
Mark Ormrod
Caroline Palmer
Derek Pearsall
Stephen Penn
Helen Phillips
Kim M. Phillips
Ad Putter
Sarah Rees Jones
Jane Rendall
Colin Richmond
John Riddy

Margaret Robson
Gillian Rudd
Sarah Salih
Corinne Saunders
Anne Savage
Wendy Scase
Julie Ann Smith
Fiona Somerset
A.C. Spearing
Sheila Sweetinburgh
Toshiyuki Takamiya
Craig Taylor
John J. Thompson
Matthew Townend
Christian Turner
Elizabeth M. Tyler
Elizabeth Urquhart
Johan Verstockt
Rosalynn Voaden
David Wallace
Nicholas Watson
Carole Weinberg
Sharon Wells
Abigail Wheatley
Louise Wheatley
Sarah Rhiannon Williams
Jocelyn Wogan-Browne
Jenny Wormald
Sibylle Zipperer